PARAGON
ISSUES IN
PHILOSOPHY

PARAGON ISSUES IN PHILOSOPHY

African Philosophy: The Essential Readings
Critical Theory and Philosophy
Critical Theory: The Essential Readings
Existence and Consolation: Reinventing...African Philosophy
Foundations of Cognitive Science: The Essential Readings
Foundations of Philosophy of Science: Recent Developments
Global Ethics: Seminal Essays
Global Justice: Seminal Essays
Life, Liberty, and the Pursuit of Happiness, Version 4.0
Living Philosophy
Meaning and Truth: Essential Readings in Modern Semantics
Philosophy and Cognitive Science
Philosophy and Feminist Criticism
Philosophy of Science
Philosophy of Human Rights
Philosophy of Sex and Love: An Introduction
Philosophy of Sport
Philosophy of Technology: An Introduction
Philosophy of the United States
Postmodern Rationality, Social Criticism, and Religion
Problems in Personal Identity
Self-Interest and Beyond
Social and Political Philosophy
The US Supreme Court and Medical Ethics
Woman and the History of Philosophy
World Religions in a Postmodern Age

THE PARAGON ISSUES IN PHILOSOPHY SERIES

At colleges and universities, interest in the traditional areas of philosophy remains strong. Many new currents flow within them, too, but until recently many of these went largely unnoticed in undergraduate philosophy courses. The Paragon Issues in Philosophy Series responds to both perennial and newly influential concerns by bringing together a team of able philosophers to address the fundamental issues in philosophy today and to outline the state of contemporary discussion about them.

More than twenty-five volumes have been published; they are organized into three major categories. The first covers the standard topics—metaphysics, theory of knowledge, ethics, and political philosophy—stressing innovative developments in those disciplines. The second focuses on more specialized but still perennial concerns in the philosophies of science, religion, history, sport, and other areas. The third category explores work that relates philosophy to specialized fields such as feminist criticism, medicine, economics, technology, and literature.

The level of writing is aimed at undergraduate students who have little previous experience studying philosophy. The books provide brief but accurate introductions that appraise the state of the art in their fields and show how the history of thought about their topics has developed. Each volume is complete in itself but also complements others in the series.

Traumatic change characterizes recent decades. All of our pivotal issues involve philosophical questions. We remain grateful to the late Professor Frederick Sontag for helping to design this series. It has now secured a place among philosophy departments throughout the English-speaking world. As we continue to locate and update new texts for this series, we hope that it will help to encourage the understanding needed to chart a future that will be as complicated and problematic as it is promising.

John K. Roth
Claremont McKenna College

Gordon L. Anderson
Paragon House

THE PHILOSOPHY OF HUMAN RIGHTS

PATRICK HAYDEN

THE PHILOSOPHY OF HUMAN RIGHTS

First Edition 2001

Published in the United States by
Paragon House
3600 Labore Road
St. Paul, MN 55110

Library of Congress Cataloging-in-Publication Data

Hayden, Patrick, 1965-
The philosophy of human rights / Patrick Hayden.
p. cm. -- (Paragon issues in philosophy)
Includes bibliographical references and index.
ISBN 1-55778-790-5
1. Human rights--Philosophy. 2. Civil rights--Philosophy. I. Title. II. Series.

JC571 .11358 2001
323'.01--dc21

00-057137

Manufactured in the United States of America

10 9 8

For current information about all releases from Paragon House,
visit the web site at www.ParagonHouse.com

For Katherine

CONTENTS

PREFACE

Human rights and philosophy compose a fascinating and complex relationship. This is because human rights—the rights that one has simply by virtue of being human—are both justifiable moral claims and contested political realities. How those claims and realities are to fit together, however, elicits a great number of responses that have a wide and varied history. This book aims to shed some light on those responses as well as on the many questions that prompt them: Are there such things as human rights? What is the nature and source of human rights? What human rights are there and how do we justify them? Are human rights universal or are they culturally relative? How should we deal with genocide and ethnic cleansing? Do human rights belong to groups or only to individuals? How do we understand the rights of women, gays, and lesbians as human rights issues? Should we link human rights with the preservation of the natural environment? These are some of the questions that animate philosophical discussions of human rights, and which are examined in the following readings.

I have designed this book as a text for undergraduate and graduate courses in social and political philosophy, moral theory and applied ethics, and international politics. Because the issues discussed in this book are matters of conceptual analysis as well as problems of social, political, and legal policy, I have placed the historical development of human rights into both theoretical and practical contexts. I did so motivated by the thought that an attempt to survey the philosophy of human rights should engage not only in the analysis of fundamental, abstract, and sophisticated questions, but also in the examination of the particular, concrete, and often-tragic problems of our times. A book on the philosophy of human rights should, I think, sharpen our theoretical and ethical understanding, and compel us to rethink and revise our assumptions on critical issues that feature prominently in the debates and events surrounding human rights in the world today.

With this in mind, the writings collected in this book fall into two broad categories. Some are excerpts from classic and modern works that address the philosophical dimensions of human rights, while others are current theoretical and applied discussions of practical problems confronting the implementation of human rights in contemporary society. In making my selection of writings, then, I have had three considerations in mind.

First, I have sought to present texts that are not confined to those appearing recently in academic journals, but to include relevant passages from important writings over the entire period—stretching back more than two thousand years—during which the subject of the rights, liberties, and duties of persons have been addressed by serious thinkers. These earlier texts are particularly important to include in a collection of this kind since they provide the foundational ideas that have shaped the past and present discussion of human rights issues and struggles.

Secondly, as I mentioned above, I have attempted to integrate selections that are not confined to theoretical analyses of the topic of human rights. The authors included therefore represent a broad spectrum of scholars and practitioners, embracing the work of political scientists, social theorists, and specialists in international relations and law in addition to well-known philosophers. Because human rights issues transcend the conceptual and involve many pressing demands in world politics and social justice, I have been concerned to include the thoughts of those working on such issues. Their views on the subject are thus of special significance since they seek to utilize theory in the practical domain. In addition, I have included a substantial selection of international human rights documents, for the purpose of providing the requisite political and legal contexts for the ideas presented here. In some cases the documents have been edited to delete certain provisions, in order to focus on the most relevant clauses. I have done so in the hope that, by examining these declarations and covenants in conjunction with the excerpts of the philosophical literature, the reader will deepen her understanding of why and how the contending philosophical arguments have been applied in the human rights field.

Finally, I have aspired to make the selections fairly broadly based, in terms of both geography and perspective. Many collections on human rights have tended to be confined entirely to Western writers. I have therefore sought to maintain a wider perspective, including readings that address human rights from Western and non-Western points of view through the writings of ancient, modern, and contemporary philosophers from diverse cultures and intellectual traditions. Nevertheless, it is the case that the vast majority of philosophical works devoted to the development and analysis of the idea of human rights have been produced by Anglo-European thinkers, and many of these by thinkers identified with the analytic tradition. Consequently, the selection of writings in this volume reflects this present balance.

This work is divided into two main parts, each of which is then divided further into smaller sections. Part One centers around the arguments systematically developed by moral and political philosophers concerning the nature, source, and scope of human rights. Classical, modern, Western, and non-Western theories are presented in a fairly comprehensive survey of the main contending points of view. In this Part the material is arranged chronologically. Part Two deals explicitly with contemporary international controversies such as the universalism and relativism debate; genocide and its recent manifestation as "ethnic cleansing"; the rights of women, gays, lesbians, and ethnic minorities; and the right to environment. While there are surely more issues that can be covered, I have chosen these topics to highlight some of the principal human rights issues that are now, and will be for the foreseeable future, at the center of world political and moral concerns.

There are twelve sections and fifty-three readings in all, inclusive of the human rights documents. Short introductions to Parts One and Two provide conceptual maps of the terrain to be covered. Each reading is also briefly introduced to focus attention on the insights and issues that arise in the selection. Discussion questions at the end of each selection are intended to help students develop their understanding of, and own positions on, the arguments raised in the readings. Also included at the end of each section are suggestions for further reading on the topics contained in that section. As a whole, then, *The Philosophy of Human Rights* balances the examination of philosophical problems with contemporary issues, both in content and in organization.

I wish to thank the friends and colleagues who inspired me with intelligent discussion and debate on questions of human rights as I prepared this book, particularly Tom Lansford, Dennis Kalob, Wayne Lesperance, James Walsh, and Paul Voice, as well as John K. Roth for his suggestions and support. The staff at Paragon House has been most accommodating and enthusiastic about this project, especially Laureen Enright, who has been very patient and helpful with my questions. I am also grateful to the staff at the Danforth Library of New England College for their valuable assistance in tracking down references and texts; Katherine Van Weelden and Ellen Ashton saved me from frustration on a number of occasions. Brendan Fitzherbert, my research assistant, capably aided me in completing some of the more time-consuming tasks of this project. Finally, a very special thanks goes to my wife, Katherine, whose love, support, and encouragement sustained me throughout this project.

PART ONE

Introduction to Part One:

HISTORY AND THEORIES OF HUMAN RIGHTS

While the concept of human rights has a long history, in order to fully understand and appreciate the contemporary debate about human rights it is necessary to examine closely the landmark writings of European modernity which have so fundamentally shaped that debate. The religious, scientific, and political revolutions of the sixteenth and seventeenth centuries initiated a momentous shift in thinking about the nature of human beings and the character of a just social order. From these cultural transformations emerged increasingly sophisticated philosophies that inspired public opinion and processes of dramatic social change during the seventeenth, eighteenth and nineteenth centuries, most notably the American and French Revolutions. These events resulted in the development of democratic governments founded on the rights of man rather than the divine right of kings.

Philosophically, there are several concepts that have significantly shaped the character of the modern age and, as a result, our present thinking about human rights. Perhaps the most central of these is the idea of reason. Indeed, the early modern period is often referred to as the "Age of Reason" and the "Enlightenment." An important ethical tradition that influenced the modern emphasis on reason is that of natural law.

Natural law doctrine is grounded in ancient Greek philosophy, Judeo-Christian scripture, and Roman moral and legal thought. Representatives of the natural law tradition include Greek philosophers such as Plato and Aristotle, Stoics of the Hellenistic and Roman periods such as the statesman Cicero, and Medieval Christian philosophers such as Thomas Aquinas. In its basic form, natural law theory holds that there are immutable "higher laws" of nature (both human nature and the universe in general), which often are thought to exist as part of the law of God. These laws constitute moral norms or prescriptions about right conduct. Through their use of reason, a common faculty endowed to all human beings, humans are able to access and act in accordance with the universal values of natural laws, thereby bringing about the moral and political order required for the common good. Natural law thinkers thus hold that human beings share a common ability to distinguish right from wrong and that humans can deduce rules of moral conduct consonant with the universal nature of right and wrong. While the early natural law thinkers did not have at least any clearly defined notion of human rights, they did lay the groundwork for thinking about the essence of being human as a moral good, often formulated around the concept of justice.

Beginning in the seventeenth century, the theory of natural law became secularized. The Dutch legal philosopher and diplomat Hugo Grotius, for example, advanced the argument that natural law can be regarded as independent of God. According to Grotius, natural law is a dictate of "right reason" in conformity with the rational and sociable nature of humanity. Right reason includes the power of judging what is right, which is defined by Grotius as one of the moral qualities or powers essential to human nature. Grotius described these powers as "rights," an interpretation that was to have a profound affect on later philosophers. In this way Grotius helped initiate modern thinking about human rights by associating rationality with the idea that each person possesses rights simply by being human.

The idea of reason, and of its proper use in thinking about correct human conduct, becomes primary for the modern philosophers who developed the insights of the natural law theorists into a second significant concept, that of natural rights. Natural rights theory—the chief exponents of which are included in the following selections—proposes that some essential feature common to all persons, such as rationality, grounds certain inherent rights in human nature. Typical of the natural rights attributed to humans by the theorists of the early modern period, such as Thomas Hobbes and especially John Locke, are those to life, liberty, property, and happiness. A core idea of natural rights theorists, then, is that there are some basic or fundamental rights that we have simply because we are human beings. Because all persons everywhere share that which makes us human, the rights that belong to us naturally are also universal.

While early natural rights theorists identified only a limited number of general rights, what is most notable about the doctrine is that those rights are understood to exist prior to and independently of any given political society. As such, natural rights are inalienable, that is, they can be neither taken away nor conferred by society. Politically, this notion coincided with the novel idea that the purpose of government is to protect the natural rights of its subjects, such that political authority is legitimate only insofar as it respects those rights. Clearly, the ethical and political views of the natural rights tradition motivated, to varying degrees, the beliefs and actions of those at the fore of the revolutionary democratic struggles in France and America, struggles fueled by "self-evident" truths regarding the rights inherent to the nature of each individual.

In arguing that all humans possess certain natural rights that cannot be taken away from them, natural rights philosophers helped to specify two more related ideas, namely, equality and freedom, that have since played a prominent role in the elaboration of the concept of human rights. While equality can have several different meanings, in a fundamental sense the concept of natural rights implies that all humans are in some way equal because they possess the same basic rights. Early political expressions of the moral claim to human equality are found in the American Declaration of Independence, which asserts that "all men are created equal," and in the French Declaration of the Rights of Man and of the Citizen, which states that "All men are by nature free and equal in respect of their rights."

While the precise character and conditions of this equality vary from one theorist to another, it seems at minimum to require that all persons be treated in a similar fashion out of respect for their rights. For natural rights theory, a conception of what human beings are like "by nature" leads to a conception of how they ought to be treated. For this reason, natural rights are often thought of as moral rights, that is, as general moral claims or entitlements that exist independent of formal recognition in a legal system; they are rights that all humans *ought* to have recognized. Critics have pointed out of course that even as such assertions of human equality have been made numerous individuals, such as women and assorted ethnic and religious groups, in fact have been treated unequally. Nevertheless, it is also true that the language of equal (moral) rights has been effectively employed by individuals and groups in order to justify eliminating whatever arbitrary inequalities they suffer under.

Freedom, or liberty, is a strong complement to the idea that all people are equally entitled to fundamental rights. Generally speaking, freedom connotes an ability to act on our own choices, and suggests an absence of constraint on our actions. Freedom is relevant to a theory of natural rights because those rights cannot be realized if our conduct is so constrained or obstructed that we are unable to act in order to pursue their fulfillment. The freedom to choose one's own way of life, for example, is basic to most if not all philosophers in the natural rights tradition. Liberty is often subtly distinguished from freedom by being defined as the specific use of freedom for some good, desirable purpose or end. Thus, natural rights are in many cases designated as particular liberties, such as freedom of speech, freedom of assembly, freedom to own and exchange property, and freedom of religion. The underlying perception is that absolute freedom is not compatible with the respect and protection of the rights of all; some minimal constraints are needed to give equal consideration to each person's rights. The German philosopher Immanuel Kant presents an influential moral and political theory that combines the concepts of reason, equality, and freedom into the idea that human beings are "ends in themselves." Because we are rational people, able to choose our own ends, we should not be treated merely as means but respected as autonomous persons. Ultimately, Kant declares that civil society should protect each person's equal right to freedom, which is to be exercised under the influence of rationality and, therefore, in agreement with the duties of justice and morality.

However, while thinkers such as Hobbes, Locke, and Kant formulate various theories in support of universal rights, others such as Jeremy Bentham and Karl Marx express doubts or serious criticisms about the possibility of such rights. Others still, such as Jean-Jacques Rousseau and John Stuart Mill, support many of the concerns addressed by natural rights theory yet provide differing explanations for how it is that rights function in society. Furthermore, Mary Wollstonecraft was one of the earliest feminists to expose the hypocrisy of the idea of the rights of "man," and to demand equal rights for women as well. But despite these disagreements, all of the philosophers included in Sections One and Two have contributed enormously to our current understanding of human rights and their overall connection to political life in general.

The ideas briefly surveyed so far provide the basic philosophical foundation for subsequent attempts to articulate systematic accounts of the nature, justification, and scope of human rights per se. These contemporary arguments are considered in Sections Three and Four. The arguments among moral and political philosophers of the twentieth century, at least in the Anglo-American tradition, have expanded on the ideas of early modern thinkers in the search for increasingly sophisticated justifications of human rights that move beyond the moral reasoning provided by natural law theory, namely, the Jeffersonian idea that truths concerning human rights are "self-evident." If there are such things as human rights, we should be able to offer good reasons that explain what these rights are and why they ought to be effectively respected and guaranteed. This is an especially pressing issue given the pluralism of moral, political, and religious views that exist in the contemporary world. H. L. A. Hart is an important transitional figure here, since he argues for a minimal right of liberty compatible with natural rights doctrine, although only this right is logically presupposed when other civil and political rights are appealed to.

The other authors included in these sections advance a wide variety of fascinating and eclectic responses to the justificatory questions of what are the sources, scope, and content of human rights. Philosophers such as Joel Feinberg, Thomas Pogge, and Martha Nussbaum view human rights as important components of social justice, that is, they seek to define human rights as moral claims or entitlements to social goods such as liberty, income, wealth, opportunity, education, and health care. From these views, human rights are essentially inviolable kinds of entitlement that are required to attain basic security, well-being, self-respect and dignity for all persons. These goods, and other interests such as liberty, can be regarded as morally relevant principles or grounds for justifying human rights. Nussbaum argues, for instance, that such requirements and entitlements support our functional capabilities to flourish in important human ways. While this may be true, Maurice Cranston suggests that it will be more difficult than we think to decide *which* rights are to be included among the human rights to which all persons are entitled, particularly when it comes to categories of economic, social, and cultural rights. Thus while human rights can be justified, precisely what content these rights can be said to have—that is, *which* specific rights are universal human rights—is a question open to much debate.

The preference for justificatory argument has been challenged by other philosophers, however, most notably those associated with the contemporary Continental European and "postmodern" schools of thought. Following up on the powerful criticisms made by Friedrich Nietzsche of Enlightenment humanism's universal moral claims, the American philosopher Richard Rorty contends that the doctrine of human rights cannot be justified by any supposedly secure theoretical foundation. Rejecting what he considers to be dogmatic metaphysical ideals about human nature and humanity in general, Rorty argues that support for human rights can be based only upon the contingent values and beliefs of the Western human rights culture which pragmatically attempts to manipulate our sentiments in response to oppression. Continental thinkers such as Jacques Derrida similarly reject assumptions regarding the notion of a knowable human essence. However, Derrida locates a ground for human rights in the interpersonal relationship of self and other. The freedom and difference of the other, and of the self as other we might say, constitutes a basis for constructing human rights claims to respect and dignity.

Of course Western philosophers are not the only thinkers who have examined the kinds of intellectual and practical concerns that have come to characterize the modern discourse on human rights. The selections in Section Five move beyond the discussion of morality, rights, and political society in the Western philosophical tradition to provide a glimpse of how thinkers in other cultures have approached such topics. While Western philosophers have tended to emphasize individual rights grounded in features such as rationality and the ability to choose freely for our own purposes, many non-Western philosophical traditions give primary emphasis to the inseparability of individuals and communities. In the thinking of Confucius, for example, society is viewed as an organic whole upon which individuals are dependent. In a just or virtuous state there can be no such thing as individual rights claims against the government; rather, individuals have a duty to contribute to the unity and harmony of the state.

Similar views about the importance of unified community and the obligation of all people to the good of the community are found in many African, as well as Islamic, social and political ideas. Often, as in Islamic theology, everyone in the community (or *Ummah*) is obligated to cultivate its well-being in light of the law and will of Allah, which serves to prescribe proper human conduct. Of course, as the Sudanese legal scholar Abdullahi Ahmed An-Na'im explains in his analysis of the Islamic law *shari'a* and human rights, various and sometimes conflicting interpretations of traditional principles of Islamic theology have been formulated.

In addition, other non-Western schools of thought support the good of individuals when bad rulers or governments may harm that good. Mo Tzu, an ancient Chinese philosopher born after the death of Confucius, argued that justice should be administered impartially so that the needs and interests of all can be cared for equally within a system of humane governance. Still others, including the Buddha (Siddharta Gautama), encouraged a sense of compassion and love for other human beings that might be seen as a welcome contrast to the "cold logic" of reason preferred by many Western thinkers. The value of compassion as a moral feeling that can, and should, move us to help end the suffering of others is a theme powerfully articulated as well by the Fourteenth Dalai Lama in his appeal to the necessity of universal human rights.

The readings that follow in Part One are concerned with all of the concepts and issues briefly described above, as well as many others not touched upon. Through these readings the idea of human rights begins not only to take shape, but also to assume rich and complex expressions, definitions, and assessments. Along with the numerous philosophical explorations of the idea of human rights, some of the greatest human achievements have been the social, political, and legal struggles to put that idea into practice, particularly within the structure of national and international law. In Section Six, several results of those struggles are included in the form of historically significant and foundational documents that bear witness to the birth of human rights in positive law and public policy. From the English Bill of Rights of 1689 to the radical declarations of the American and French revolutions, human rights begin to move from a nascent moral ideal to a prominent social and political reality. It is not until after World War II, however, and the horrors of genocide and rampant discrimination witnessed around the globe, that human rights came fully into their own as a primary international concern. Following the formation of the United Nations in 1945, the UN General Assembly adopted the Universal Declaration of Human Rights (UDHR) on December 10, 1948. The Universal Declaration has become the cornerstone of efforts to promote and implement international human rights. Finally, a number of regional human rights treaties and charters have been created in recent years which supplement the principles outlined in the UDHR. Some of these incorporate provisions that are said to reflect and safeguard non-Western customs and traditions. In conjunction with the philosophical readings contained in Part One, then, these documents provide a solid base upon which to build a thoughtful understanding of the idea of human rights.

Section 1:
CLASSICAL PERSPECTIVES

1. PLATO

Plato (427-347 B.C.), born in Athens, is regarded as one of the greatest thinkers who ever lived. Raised during the period of the Peloponnesian War, Plato became a friend and student of Socrates, whose trial and death occurred in 399 B.C. Plato established his philosophical school, the Academy, in Athens following Socrates' death and taught there for the remainder of his life. Plato's influence on intellectual history has been immense. His writings, in the form of dialogues that usually feature Socrates as the principal narrator, cover metaphysics, epistemology, psychology, ethics, and politics. The following selection is from Plato's masterpiece, the *Republic,* in which Plato maintains that justice is a good to be chosen for its own sake and that it is a fundamental virtue of an ideal, well-ordered society. In this dialogue, the character of Socrates is asked to define justice, which he does by explaining how it would appear first in a just state and then in a just individual. Justice in a state consists of its various classes performing their proper functions, and justice in the soul exists when each of its parts performs its proper function as well. While Plato does not appeal to the idea of human rights, he does formulate a powerful argument for the type of human rational capacities that he thinks must be realized in accordance with the nature of the good, if a just community is to be achieved.

Text—The Republic

Reprinted from The Dialogues of Plato, *translated by Benjamin Jowett. London: Macmillan, 1892.*

BOOK II

With these words I was thinking that I had made an end of the discussion; but the end, in truth, proved to be only a beginning. For Glaucon, who is always the most pugnacious of men, was dissatisfied at Thrasymachus' retirement; he wanted to have the battle out. So he said to me: Socrates, do you really wish to persuade us, or only to seem to have persuaded us, that to be just is always better than to be unjust?

I should wish really to persuade you, I replied, if I could.

Then you certainly have not succeeded. Let me ask you now:— How would you arrange goods—are there not some which we welcome for their own sakes, and independently of their consequences, as, for example, harmless pleasures and enjoyments, which delight us at the time, although nothing follows from them?

I agree in thinking that there is such a class, I replied.

Is there not also a second class of goods, such as knowledge, sight, health, which are desirable not only in themselves, but also for their results?

Certainly, I said.

And would you not recognize a third class, such as gymnastic, and the care of the sick, and the physician's art; also the various ways of money-making—these do us good but we regard them as disagreeable; and no one would choose them for their own sakes, but only for the sake of some reward or result which flows from them?

There is, I said, this third class also. But why do you ask?

Because I want to know in which of the three classes you would place justice?

In the highest class, I replied, among those goods which he who would be happy desires both for their own sake and for the sake of their results.

Then the many are of another mind; they think that justice is to be reckoned in the troublesome class, among goods which are to be pursued for the sake of rewards and of reputation, but in themselves are disagreeable and rather to be avoided.

I know, I said, that this is their manner of thinking, and that this was the thesis which Thrasymachus was maintaining just now, when he censured justice and praised injustice. But I am too stupid to be convinced by him.

I wish, he said, that you would hear me as well as him, and then I shall see whether you and I agree. For Thrasymachus seems to me, like a snake, to have been charmed by your voice sooner than he ought to have been; but to my mind the nature of justice and injustice have not yet been made clear. Setting aside their rewards and results, I want to know what they are in themselves, and how they inwardly work in the soul. If you please, then, I will revive the argument of Thrasymachus. And first I will speak of the nature and origin of justice according to the common view of them....

They say that to do injustice is, by nature, good; to suffer injustice, evil; but that the evil is greater than the good. And so when men have both done and suffered injustice and have had experience of both, not being able to avoid the one and obtain the other, they think that they had better agree among themselves to have neither; hence there arise laws and mutual covenants; and that which is ordained by law is termed by them lawful and just. This they affirm to be the origin and nature of justice:—it is a mean or compromise, between the best of all, which is to do injustice and not be punished, and the worst of all, which is to suffer injustice without the power of retaliation; and justice, being at a middle point between the two, is tolerated not as a good, but as the lesser evil, and honoured by reason of the inability of men to do injustice. For no man who is worthy to be called a man would ever submit to such an agreement if he were able to resist; he would be mad if he did. Such is the received account, Socrates, of the nature and origin of justice....

On what principle, then, shall we any longer choose justice rather than the worst injustice?...

I told them what I really thought, that the enquiry would be of a serious nature, and would require very good eyes.... Justice, which is the subject of our enquiry, is, as you know, sometimes spoken of as the virtue of an individual, and sometimes as the virtue of a state.

True, he replied.

And is not a state larger than an individual?

It is.

Then, in the larger of quantity, justice is likely to be larger and more easily discernible. I propose therefore that we enquire into the nature of justice and injustice, first as they appear in the state, and secondly in the individual, proceeding from the greater to the lesser and comparing them.

That, he said, is an excellent proposal.

And if we imagine the state in process of creation, we shall see the justice and injustice of the state in process of creation also....

BOOK IV

But where, amid all this, is justice? son of Ariston, tell me where. Now that our city has been made habitable, light a candle and search...and let us see where in it we can discover justice and where injustice....

Well, then, I hope to make the discovery in this way: I mean to begin with the assumption that our state, if rightly ordered, is perfect.

That is most certain.

And it being perfect, is therefore wise, and valiant and temperate and just....

First among the virtues found in the state, wisdom comes into view...and is there any knowledge in our recently-founded state among any of the citizens which advises, not about any particular thing in the state, but about the whole, and considers how a state can best deal with itself and with other states?

There certainly is.

And what is this knowledge, and among whom is it found? I asked.

It is the knowledge of the guardians, he replied, and is found among those whom we were just now describing as perfect guardians....

Will not the guardians be the smallest of all the classes who receive a name from the profession of some kind of knowledge?

Much the smallest.

And so by reason of the smallest part or class, and of the knowledge which resides in this presiding and ruling part of itself, the whole state, being thus constituted according to nature, will be wise; and this, which has the only knowledge worthy to be called wisdom, has been ordained by nature to be of all classes the least.

Most true....

Again, I said, there is no difficulty in seeing the nature of courage, and in what part that quality resides which gives the name of courageous to the state.

How do you mean?

Why, I said, everyone who calls my state courageous or cowardly, will be thinking of the part which fights and goes out to war on the state's behalf.

No one, he replied, would ever think of any other.

The rest of the citizens may be courageous or may be cowardly, but their courage or cowardice will not, as I conceive, have the effect of making the city either the one or the other.... Then now, I said, you will understand what our object was in selecting our soldiers....

Now, can we find justice without troubling ourselves about temperance?

I do not know how that can be accomplished, he said, nor do I desire that justice should be brought to light and temperance lost sight of; and therefore I wish that you would do me the favour of considering temperance first....

Temperance, I replied, is the ordering or controlling of certain pleasures and desires.... The meaning is, I believe, that in the human soul there is a better and also a worse principle; and when the better has the worse under control, then a man is said to be master of himself; and this is a term of praise; but when, owing to evil education or association, the better principle, which is the smaller, is overwhelmed by the greater mass of the worse—in this case he is blamed and is called the slave of self and unprincipled.

Yes, there is reason in that.

And now, I said, look at our newly-created state, and there you will find one of these two conditions realized; for the state, as you will acknowledge, may be justly called master of itself, if the words "temperance" and "self-mastery" truly express the rule of the better part over the worse.

Yes, he said, I see that what you say is true....

And if there be any state in which rulers and subjects will be agreed as to the question who are to rule, then again it will be our state?

Undoubtedly.

And the citizens being thus agreed among themselves, in which class will temperance be found—in the rulers or in the subjects?

In both, as I should imagine, he said....

And so, I said, we may consider three out of the four virtues to have been discovered in our state. The last of those qualities which make a state virtuous must be justice, if only we knew what that was....

You remember the original principle which we were always laying down at the foundation of the state, that one man should practice one thing only, the thing to which his nature was best adapted;—now justice is this principle or a part of it.

Yes, we often said that one man should do one thing only.

Further, we affirmed that justice was doing one's own business, and not being a busybody; we said so again and again, and many others have said the same to us.

Yes, we said so.

Then to do one's own business in a certain way may be assumed to be justice...on this view also justice will be admitted to be the having and doing what is a man's own, and belongs to him....

I proceeded to ask: When two things, a greater and less, are called by the same name, are they like or unlike in so far as they are called the same?

Like, he replied.

The just man then, if we regard the idea of justice only, will be like the just state? He will.

And a state was thought by us to be just when the three classes in the state severally did their own business; and also thought to be temperate and valiant and wise by reason of certain other affections and qualities of these same classes?

True, he said.

And so of the individual: We may assume that he has the same three principles in his own soul which are found in the state; and he may be rightly described in the same terms, because he is affected in the same manner?

Certainly, he said....

And so, after much tossing, we have reached land, and are fairly agreed that the same principles which exist in the state exist also in the individual, and that they are three in number.

Exactly.

Must we not then infer that the individual is wise in the same way, and in virtue of the same quality which makes the state wise?

Certainly.

Also that the same quality which constitutes courage in the state constitutes courage in the individual, and that both the state and the individual bear the same relation to all the other virtues?

Assuredly.

And the individual will be acknowledged by us to be just in the same way in which the state is just?

That follows, of course.

We cannot but remember that the justice of the state consisted in each of the three classes doing the work of its own class?

We are not very likely to have forgotten, he said.

We must recollect that the individual in whom the several qualities of his nature do their own work will be just, and will do his own work?

Yes, he said, we must remember that too.

And ought not the rational principle, which is wise and has the care of the whole soul, rule, and the passionate or spirited principle to be the subject and ally?

Certainly.

And, as we were saying, the united influence of music and gymnastic will bring them into accord, nerving and sustaining the reason with noble words and lessons, and moderating and soothing and civilizing the wildness of passion by harmony and rhythm.

Quite true, he said.

And these two, thus nurtured and educated, and having learned truly to know their own functions, will rule over the concupiscent, which in each of us is the largest part of the soul and by nature most insatiable of gain; over this they will keep guard, lest, waxing great and strong with the fullness of bodily pleasures, as they are termed, the concupiscent soul, no longer confined to her own sphere, should attempt to enslave and rule those who are not her natural-born subjects, and overturn the whole life of man.

Very true, he said.

Both together will they not be the best defenders of the whole soul and the whole body against attacks from without—the one counseling, and the other fighting under his leader and courageously executing his commands and counsels?

True.

And he is to be deemed courageous whose spirit retains in pleasure and in pain the commands of reason about what he ought or ought not to fear?

Right, he replied.

And him we call wise who has in him that little part which rules, and which proclaims these commands—that part too being supposed to have a knowledge of what is for the interest of each of the three parts and of the whole?

Assuredly.

And would you not say that he is temperate who has these same elements in friendly harmony, in whom the one ruling principle of reason, and the two subject ones of spirit and desire, are equally agreed that reason ought to rule, and do not rebel?

Certainly, he said, that is the true account of temperance, whether in the state or individual.

And surely, I said, we have explained again and again how and by virtue of what quality a man will be just.

That is very certain.

And is justice dimmer in the individual, and is her form different, or is she the same which we found her to be in the state?

There is no difference in my opinion, he said....

Justice [in the individual is] concerned...not with the outward man, but with the inward, which is the true self and concernment of man. For the just man does not permit the several elements within him to interfere with one another, or any of them to do the work of others; he sets in order his own inner life, and is his own master and his own law, and at peace with himself. And when he has bound together the three principles within him, which may be compared to the higher, lower, and middle notes of the scale, and the intermediate intervals—when he has bound all these together, and is no longer many, but has become one entirely temperate and perfectly adjusted nature, then he proceeds to act, if he has to act (whether in a matter of property, or in the treatment of the body, or in some affair of politics or private business) always thinking and calling that which preserves and cooperates with this harmonious condition, just and good action; and the knowledge which presides over it, wisdom. And that which at any time impairs this condition, he will call unjust action; and the opinion which presides over it, ignorance.

You have said the exact truth, Socrates.

Very good. And if we were to affirm that we had discovered the just man and the just state, and the nature of justice in each of them, would we be telling a falsehood?

Most certainly not.

May we say so, then?

Let us say so.

And now, I said, injustice has to be considered.

Clearly.

Must not injustice be a strife which arises among the three principles—a meddlesomeness, and interference, and rising up of a part of the soul against the whole, an assertion of unlawful authority, which is made by a rebellious subject against a true prince, of whom he is the natural vassal? What is all this confusion and delusion but injustice and intemperance and cowardice and ignorance, and every form of vice?

Exactly so.

And if the nature of justice and injustice be known, then the meaning of acting unjustly and being unjust, or, again, of acting justly, will also be perfectly clear?

What do you mean? he said.

Why, I said, they are like disease and health, being in the

soul just what disease and health are in the body.

How so? he said.

Why, I said, that which is healthy causes health, and that which is unhealthy causes disease.

Yes.

And just actions cause justice, and unjust actions cause injustice.

That is certain.

And the creation of health is the institution of a natural order and government of one by another in the parts of the body; and the creation of disease is the production of a state of things at variance with this natural order.

True.

And is not the creation of justice the institution of a natural order and government of one by another in the parts of the soul, and the creation of injustice the production of a state of things at variance with the natural order?

Exactly so, he said.

Then virtue is the health and beauty and well-being of the soul, and vice the disease and weakness and deformity of the same?

True.

And do not good practices lead to virtue, and evil practices to vice?

Assuredly.

Still our old question of the comparative advantage of justice and injustice has not been answered: Which is the more profitable, to be just and act justly and practice virtue, whether seen or unseen of gods and men, or to be unjust and act unjustly, if only unpunished and unreformed?

In my judgment, Socrates, the question has now become ridiculous. We know that when the bodily constitution is gone, life is no longer endurable, though pampered with all kinds of meats and drinks, and having all wealth and all power. And shall we be told that when the very essence of the vital principle is undermined and corrupted, life is still worth having to a man, if only he be allowed to do whatever he likes with the single exception that he is not to acquire justice and virtue, or to escape from injustice and vice—assuming them both to be such as we have described?

Yes, I said, the question is, as you say, ridiculous.

Questions for Reflection

1. Thrasymachus and Glaucon present the "common view" that it is better to be unjust and prosperous than to be just and modest. Do you agree that people would not be just if they could get away with being unjust?

2. Socrates asserts that justice in the state is "doing one's own business" as well as "having and doing what is a man's own." Do you think this is an adequate conception of justice?

3. Socrates argues that it is good to be just because the harmony of the just person's soul represents a kind of "moral health." Do you find this a convincing argument? Why or why not?

2. ARISTOTLE

Aristotle (384-322 B.C.) was born in Stagira in Macedonia. His father was physician to Amnytas II, king of Macedonia. As a youth, Aristotle came to Athens and entered Plato's Academy, where he remained for the next twenty years. Following Plato's death, Aristotle returned to Macedonia and became tutor to the young Alexander the Great. Later, Aristotle went back to Athens and established his own school, the Lyceum. Like Plato, Aristotle covered a wide variety of subjects in his writings, including logic, mathematics, physics, rhetoric, ethics, and politics. In our reading from the *Politics,* Aristotle considers the political state as a form of natural association in relation to the nature of human beings as political animals. Because humans are by nature political animals, according to Aristotle, they attain their highest good, i.e., justice, only in a true and not perverted state.

Text—Politics

Reprinted from The Politics of Aristotle, *translated by Benjamin Jowett. Clarendon Press, 1885.*

BOOK I, 1

Every state is a community of some kind, and every community is established with a view to some good; for mankind always acts in order to obtain that which they think good. But if all communities aim at some good, the state or political community, which is the highest of all and which embraces all the rest, aims at good in a greater degree than any other, and at the highest good.

Some people think that the qualifications of a statesman, king, householder, and master are the same, and that they differ not in kind but only in the number of their subjects. For example, the ruler over a few is called a master; over more, the manager of a household; over a still larger number, a statesman or king—as if there were no difference between a great household and a small state. The distinction which is made between the king and the statesman is as follows: When the government is personal, the ruler is a king; when, according to the rules of the political science, the citizens rule and are ruled in turn, then he is called a statesman.

But all this is a mistake; for governments differ in kind, as will be evident to anyone who considers the matter according to the method which has hitherto guided us. As in other departments of science, so in politics, the compound should always be resolved into the simple elements or least parts of the whole. We must therefore look at the elements of which the state is composed, in order that we may see in what the different kinds of rule differ from one another, and whether any scientific result can be attained about each one of them.

BOOK I, 2

He who thus considers things in their first growth and origin, whether a state or anything else, will obtain the clearest view of them. In the first place there must be a union of those who cannot exist without each other—namely, of male and female—that the race may continue (and this is a union which is formed, not of deliberate purpose, but because, in common with other animals and with plants, mankind have a natural desire to leave behind them an image of themselves), and of natural ruler and subject, that both may be preserved.... Out of these two relationships between man and woman, master and slave, the first thing to arise is the family.... The family is the association established by nature for the supply of men's everyday wants, and the members of it are called by Charondas "companions of the cupboard," and by Epimenides the Cretan "companions of the manger." But when several families are united, and the association aims at something more than the supply of daily needs, the first society to be formed is the village. And the most natural form of the village appears to be that of a colony from the family, composed of the children and grandchildren....

When several villages are united in a single complete community, large enough to be nearly or quite self-sufficing, the state comes into existence, originating in the bare needs of life and continuing in existence for the sake of a good life. And therefore, if the earlier forms of society are natural, so is the state, for it is the end of them, and the nature of a thing is its end. For what each thing is when fully developed, we call its nature, whether we are speaking of a man, a horse, or a family. Besides, the final cause and end of a thing is the best, and to be self-sufficing is the end and the best.

Hence it is evident that the state is a creation of nature, and that man is by nature a political animal. And he who by nature and not by mere accident is without a state, is either a bad man or above humanity.... Now, that man is more of a political animal than bees or any other gregarious animal is evident. Nature, as we often say, makes nothing in vain, and man is the only animal whom she has endowed with the gift of speech. And whereas mere voice is but an indication of pleasure or pain, and is therefore found in other animals (for their nature attains to the perception of pleasure and pain and the intimation of them to one another, and no further), the power of speech is intended to set forth the expedient and inexpedient, and therefore likewise the just and the unjust. And it is a characteristic of man that he alone has any sense of good and evil, of just and unjust, and the like, and the association of living beings who have this sense makes a family and a state.

Further, the state is by nature clearly prior to the family and to the individual, since the whole is of necessity prior to the part. For example, if the whole body be destroyed, there will be no foot or hand, except in an equivocal sense, as we might speak of a stone hand; for when destroyed the hand will be no better than that. But things are defined by their working and power; and we ought not to say that they are the same when they no longer have their proper quality, but only that they have the same name. The proof that the state is a creation of nature and prior to the individual is that the individual, when isolated, is not self-sufficing; and therefore he is like a part in relation to the whole. But he who is unable to live in society, or who has no need because he is sufficient for himself, must be either a beast or a god; he is no part of a state.

A social instinct is implanted in all men by nature, and yet he who first founded the state was the greatest of benefactors. For man, when perfected, is the best of animals, but when separated from law and justice, he is the worst of all—since armed injustice is the more dangerous, and he is equipped at birth with arms, meant to be used by intelligence and virtue, which he may use for the worst ends. Therefore, if he have not virtue, he is the most unholy and the most savage of animals, and the most full of lust and gluttony. But justice is the bond of men in states; for the administration of justice, which is the determination of what is just, is the principle of order in political society.

BOOK III, 6

We have next to consider whether there is only one form of government or many, and if many, what they are, and how many, and what are the differences between them.

A constitution is the arrangement of magistracies in a state, especially of the highest of all. The government is everywhere sovereign in the state, and the government is in fact the constitution. For example, in democracies the people are supreme, but in oligarchies, the few; and therefore we say that these two forms of government also are different. And so in other cases.

First, let us consider what is the purpose of a state, and how many forms of government there are by which human society is regulated. We have already said, in the first part of this treatise, when discussing household management and the rule of a master, that man is by nature a political animal. And therefore, men, even when they do not require one another's help, desire to live together. They are also brought together by their common interests in proportion as they [each achieve a] measure of well-being. This is certainly the chief end, both of individuals and of states. And also for the sake of mere life (in which there is possibly some noble element so long as the evils of existence do not greatly overbalance the good) mankind meet together and maintain the political community. And we all see that men cling to life even at the cost of enduring great misfortune, seeming to find in life a natural sweetness and happiness.

There is no difficulty in distinguishing the various kinds of authority; they have been often defined already in discussions outside the school. The rule of a master, although the slave by nature and the master by nature have in reality the same interests, is nevertheless exercised primarily with a view to the interest of the master, but accidentally considers the slave, since, if the slave perishes, the rule of the master perishes with him. On the other hand, the government of a wife and children and of a household, which we have called household management, is exercised in the first instance for the good of the governed or for the common good of both parties, but essentially for the good of the governed, as we see to be the case in medicine, gymnastic, and the arts in general, which are only accidentally concerned with the good of the artists themselves. For there is no reason why the trainer may not sometimes practice gymnastics, and the helmsman is always one of the crew. The trainer or the helmsman considers the good of those committed to his care. But when he is one of the persons taken care of, he accidentally participates in the advantage, for the helmsman is also a sailor, and the trainer becomes one of those in training. And so in politics: when the state is framed upon the principle of equality and likeness, the citizens think that they ought to hold office by turns. Formerly, as is natural, everyone would take his turn of service; and then again, somebody else would look after his interest, just as he, while in office, had looked after theirs. But nowadays, for the sake of the advantage which is to be gained from the public revenues and from office, men want to be always in office. One might imagine that the rulers, being sickly, were only kept in health while they continued in office; in that case we may be sure that they would be hunting after places. The conclusion is evident: that governments which have a regard to the common interest are constituted in accordance with strict principles of justice, and are therefore true forms; but those which regard only the interest of the rulers are all defective and perverted forms, for they are despotic, whereas a state is a community of freemen.

BOOK III, 7

Having determined these points, we have next to consider how many forms of government there are, and what they are; and in the first place what are the true forms, for when they are determined the perversions of them will at once be apparent. The words "constitution" and "government" have the same meaning, and the government, which is the supreme authority in states, must be in the hands of one, or of a few, or of the many. The true forms of government, therefore, are those in which the one, or the few, or the many, govern with a view to the common interest; but governments which rule with a view to the private interest, whether of the one or of the few, or of the many, are perversions. For the members of a state, if they are truly citizens, ought to participate in its advantages. Of forms of government in which one rules, we call that which regards the common interests, *kingship* or *royalty*; that in which more than one, but not many, rule, *aristocracy*—and it is so called either because the rulers are the best men, or because they have at heart the best interests of the state and of the citizens. But when the citizens at large administer the state for the common interest, the government is called by the generic name: a *constitution*. And there is a reason for this use of language. One man or a few may excel in virtue, but as the number increases it becomes more difficult for them to attain perfection in every kind of virtue—though they may in military virtue, for this is found in the masses. Hence in a constitutional government the fighting-men have the supreme power, and those who possess arms are the citizens.

Of the above-mentioned forms, the perversions are as follows: of royalty, tyranny; of aristocracy, oligarchy; of constitutional government, democracy. For tyranny is a kind of monarchy which has in view the interest of the monarch only; oligarchy has in view the interest of the wealthy; democracy, of the needy: none of them the common good of all....

BOOK III, 13

In all sciences and arts the end is a good, and the greatest good and in the highest degree a good in the most authoritative of all—this is the political science of which the good is justice, in other words, the common interest. All men think justice to be a sort of equality; and to a certain extent they agree in the philosophical distinctions which have been laid down by us about Ethics. For they admit that justice is a thing and has a relation to persons, and that equals ought to have equality. But there still remains a question: equality or inequality of what? Here is a difficulty which calls for political speculation. For very likely some persons will say that offices of state ought to be unequally distributed according to superior excellence, in whatever respect, of the citizen, although there is no other difference between him and the rest of the community; for that those who differ in any one respect have different rights and claims. But, surely, if this is true, the complexion or height of a man, or any other advantage, will be a reason for his obtaining a greater share of political rights. The error here lies upon the surface, and may be illustrated from the other arts and sciences. When a number of flute players are equal in their art, there is no reason why those of them who are better born should have better flutes given to them; for they will not play any better on the flute, and the superior instrument should be reserved for him who is the superior artist....

Now what is just or right is to be interpreted in the sense of "what is equal"; and that which is right in the sense of being equal is to be considered with reference to the advantage of the state, and the common good of the citizens. And a citizen is one who shares in governing and being governed. He differs under different forms of government, but in the best state he is one who is able and willing to be governed and to govern with a view to the life of virtue....

BOOK IV, 11

We have now to inquire what is the best constitution for most states, and the best life for most men, neither assuming a standard of virtue which is above ordinary persons, nor an education which is exceptionally favored by nature and circumstances, nor yet an ideal state which is an aspiration only, but having regard to the life in which the majority are able to share, and to the form of government which states in general can attain. As to those aristocracies, as they are called, of which we were just now speaking, they either lie beyond the possibilities of the greater number of states, or they approximate to the so-called constitutional government, and therefore need no separate discussion. And in fact the conclusion at which we arrive respecting all these forms rests upon the same grounds. For if what was said in the Ethics is true, that the happy life is the life according to virtue lived without impediment, and that virtue is a mean, then the life which is in a mean, and in a mean attainable by every one, must be the best. And the same the same principles of virtue and vice are characteristic of cities and of constitutions; for the constitution is in a figure the life of the city.

Now in all states there are three elements: one class is very rich, another very poor, and a third in a mean. It is admitted that moderation and the mean are best, and therefore it will clearly be best to possess the gifts of fortune in moderation; for in that condition of life men are most ready to follow rational principle. But he who greatly excels in beauty, strength, birth, or wealth, or on the other hand who is very poor, or very weak, or very much disgraced, finds it difficult to follow rational principle. Of these two the one sort grow into violent and great criminals, the others into rogues and petty rascals. And two sorts of offenses correspond to them, the one committed from violence, the other from roguery. Again, the middle class is least likely to shrink from rule, or to be over-ambitious for it; both of which are injuries to the state. Again, those who have too much of the goods of fortune, strength, wealth, friends, and the like, are neither willing nor able to submit to authority. The evil begins at home; for when they are boys, by reason of the luxury in which they are brought up, they never learn, even at school, the habit of obedience. On the other hand, the very poor, who are in the opposite extreme, are too degraded. So that the one class cannot obey, and can only rule despotically; the other knows not how to command and must be ruled like slaves. Thus arises a city, not of freemen, but of masters and slaves, the one despising, the other envying; and nothing can be more fatal to friendship and good fellowship in states than this: for good fellowship springs from friendship; when men are at enmity with one another, they would rather not even share the same path. But a city ought to be composed, as far as possible, of equals and similars; and these are generally the middle classes. Wherefore the city which is composed of middle-class citizens is necessarily best constituted in respect of the elements of which we say the fabric of the state naturally consists. And this is the class of citizens which is most secure in a state, for they do not, like the poor, covet their neighbors' goods; nor do others covet theirs, as the poor covet the goods of the rich; and as they neither plot against others, nor are themselves plotted against, they pass through life safely. Wisely then did Phocylides pray—"Many things are best in the mean; I desire to be of a middle condition in my city."

Thus it is manifest that the best political community is formed by citizens of the middle class, and that those states are likely to be well-administered in which the middle class is large, and stronger if possible than both the other classes, or at any rate than either singly; for the addition of the middle class turns the scale, and prevents either of the extremes from being dominant. Great then is the good fortune of a state in which the citizens have a moderate and sufficient property; for where some possess much, and the others nothing, there may arise an extreme democracy, or a pure oligarchy; or a tyranny may grow out of either extreme—either out of the most rampant democracy, or out of an oligarchy; but it is not so likely to arise out of the middle constitutions and those akin to them.

Questions for Reflection

1. Aristotle contends that because human beings are "political animals" the state arises by nature. Do you agree that the state is "natural"? Do you agree that the state is prior to the individual?

2. In Aristotle's view, justice can be considered a kind of equality which requires equal treatment for equals and unequal treatment for unequals. Do you agree or not with Aristotle? Why?

3. According to Aristotle justice is a "mean" between two extremes. Given this definition, how is justice to be achieved in a political state? What are the capabilities and deficiencies of various forms of government with respect to Aristotle's doctrine?

3. CICERO

The Roman lawyer, statesman, and essayist Cicero (106-43 B.C.) was a prominent proponent of the Stoic philosophy. Stoicism originated in Athens around 300 B.C. through the teachings of the Greek philosopher Zeno. The Stoics believed that the end of all action is a life in agreement with nature, which is ordered according to a rational plan. Thus, an ethically good life is one in which human rationality is made to conform to the rational order of nature. From this theoretical framework emerges the idea of the law of nature, that is, a universal moral law that corresponds to the rational capacities of all human beings. Cicero contributed greatly to the theory of natural law, arguing that individuals have an obligation to respect their fellow human beings and that the laws of all political communities are legitimate only insofar as they conform to the higher law of nature.

Text—On the Laws

Reprinted from On the Nature of the Gods: On Divination, On Fate, On the Republic, On the Laws, and On Standing for the Consulship. *Translated by C. D. Yonge. London: George Bell, 1907.*

BOOK ONE

Marcus: Can you imagine any other field of debate that provides as much scope for considering the topics of man's natural endowments, the capacity of the human mind to realize those noble projects we were created to initiate and perfect, the relationships of men to one another as individuals, and the natural groupings of men into communities. In trying to explain these phenomena we may discover the first principles of law and justice.

Atticus: You believe, then, that the fundamentals of justice should be deduced not from a praetor's proclamation, as many now assert, nor from the Twelve Tables of the Law, as our forefathers maintained, but from the innermost depths of philosophy?

Marcus: Well, Pomponius Atticus, in this discussion we are

not trying to answer the questions of how to protect our clients in a lawsuit, or what advice to give our consultants. That may be an important matter, as indeed it is. Many a famous man of the past has thought it was, and one lawyer of great prestige and knowledge still does. In our discussion, however, we shall embrace the whole realm of universal law, in such a way as to leave the so-called civil law to its proper narrow sphere. For first we must discover the nature of justice itself, and that is to be sought in the nature of man....

Marcus: Do grant me this, then, Pomponius Atticus—for I know my brother Quintus' opinion—that the whole universe is governed by the energy of the immortal gods, by their special nature, their rational faculties, their power, their intelligence, their will, or whatever other word may be chosen to express more clearly what I want to say. If you do not agree, we must begin the argument at this point.

Atticus: I grant whatever you ask. For the chirping birds and rippling streams make it unlikely that any of my fellow scholars will hear me.

Marcus: You are right to be cautious, for even good men sometimes lose their tempers; and they would be highly indignant if they heard you betraying the first principle of noble Epicurus, "God takes no care either of himself or of anyone else."

Atticus: Go on, I beg you; I am waiting to see where my concession will take us.

Marcus: I shall not keep you waiting any longer. This is the logical deduction: that the animal called man, who is prudent, intelligent, complex, and keen, capable of remembering, of reasoning, and of planning, has been created in his magnificent state by the supreme God. He alone out of so many kinds and species of animals is able to reason and reflect, while all other creatures are incapable of it. What faculty more godlike than reason can be found, whether in man or anywhere, in heaven or earth? When this gift is mature and perfected, it may rightly be called wisdom. Inasmuch as there is no attribute superior to reason, and it is present in both God and man, it must be the essential basis for communion between man and God.

Since reason then is common to them both, the sense of right is also common to them. As the latter is, in reality, law, we should think of men and gods as linked together by law. Furthermore, those who are partners in law are necessarily also partners in justice, and those who share the same law and the same justice must be considered members of the same commonwealth. If, in addition, they obey the same supreme power and authority, their association is even more close. Now they do all obey the celestial order, the divine mind, the all-powerful God. Therefore, the whole universe should be regarded as one commonwealth of men and gods.

In commonwealths a certain order, which we shall discuss in its proper place, distinguishes ranks on the basis of family lineage. But the order of nature is much more glorious and splendid, since, according to it, men are the direct descendants and kindred of the gods. For whenever we consider the nature of the universe, we always, of course, say that once in the order of the endless progressions and revolutions of the heavenly bodies a period arrived suitable for the creation of the human race. The species spread far and wide over the earth, and was blessed by the divine gift of a soul. His other weak and frail qualities man acquired from his mortal nature, but his mind came from God. Hence we may claim we are kin, relatives or offspring of the celestial deities.

And out of many species of creatures, there is none but man that possesses any notion of God, whereas among men there is no nation either so effete or so savage as not to know that it must believe in a god, even if it does not know what sort of god he should be. From this fact we conclude that God is acknowledged by man, who almost remembers and knows his true origin. Moreover, the same moral excellence is characteristic of man and of God, and not of any other species. This excellence is simply Nature developed and brought to her fullest realization. In such ways does man resemble God. What affinity could be closer or more plain? . . .

Marcus: The topics I have been discussing are indeed momentous. But of all the ideas propounded by learned scholars none is more important to understand clearly than this, that man was born for justice, and that justice was established not by the judgment of men but by Nature. This truth will become even more manifest if we study the kinship of man to his fellow man. For no one object is so like another as we men are like one another. If corrupt customs and fickle prejudices had not diverted weak minds from their proper lines of development, there would be no closer likeness between the various sides of one man's character than between men themselves everywhere. Hence whatever definition we give a single man applies to all men.

So the statement that there are no differences dividing the human species is sound; for one definition would not include all men if there were a difference. Certainly the power to reason, in which alone we surpass the beasts, and by means of which we can infer, argue, refute, converse, and bring an enterprise to completion, is common to all men. We have an equal chance to learn, although the kind and degree of our knowledge may differ. In all of us, the senses perceive the same objects and are affected in the same manner. The fundamental principles of knowledge impressed on the mind, of which I have already spoken, are impressed alike on the minds of all. The faculty of speech, also, which is the interpreter of the mind, expresses everywhere the same ideas, although it may differ in the actual words used.

Thus too, there is no member of any nation who cannot attain true virtue, if he takes Nature as his guide. And human beings are conspicuously like each other not only in their goodness, but also in their shortcomings. For all men are attracted by pleasure, which has a certain resemblance to natural good, although it may lead to disgrace. Its charm and sweetness make it delightful, and so through a mental error we grasp it as beneficial. In our ignorance too we all shun death as if it were a violation of Nature's law, and cling to life, since it keeps us in the environment into which we were born. We all consider pain the greatest of evils, not only for the actual discomfort it gives us, but also because it implies the approach of death. Because too there is a resemblance between nobility and honor, men who are honored we consider happy, and obscure persons wretched. Troubles, joys, desires, and fears pervade all our minds in the same way.

People differ in their beliefs, but is it not merely that those who worship the cat and the dog as gods labor under a different superstition from that which flourishes in other lands? What nation, however, does not hold in high esteem courtesy, kindness, gratitude, and appreciation? What nation does not shun or detest the proud, the malicious, the cruel, and the ungrateful? We may thus conclude that, since the whole human race is so unified in itself, the same system of right living makes all men better. If you approve these remarks, I shall go on to others, but if any doubts occur to you, we would better clear them up first.

Atticus: We agree to everything, if I may answer for the two of us.

Marcus: It follows then that Nature created all mankind to share and enjoy the same sense of right, and I wish it understood throughout our discussion that the right of which I may speak is derived from Nature. However, the corruption caused by our bad habits is so powerful that it puts out the fires of virtue kindled by Nature, and contrary vices spring up and grow strong. But if wise men, prompted by Nature, would agree with the poets that whatever touches humanity concerns them too, then everyone would cultivate justice. For all to whom Nature gave the power of reasoning have received from her also the ability to reason correctly. Thus has arisen law, which is right reason as expressed in commands and prohibitions; and from law has come justice. Therefore, since Nature gave us all the ability to reason, she gave us also justice. Socrates was right in denouncing the man who first separated his personal advantage from justice; he used to complain that this separation had been the source of all evil.

Hence we may go on to assert that when one wise man feels that warm emotion which is everywhere pervasive for another equally virtuous person, there follows the inevitable result, which some find unbelievable; he loves the other man no less than he loves himself. For what difference can there be between them, when all their interests are the same? But if one makes the slightest room for his own private interest, it is the end of even nominal friendship. We all know that as soon as one wants something for himself more than for the other, there is no friendship.

I have said all this in preparation for the rest of the discussion, that you may more clearly perceive that Nature is the source of justice. After a few more words on the subject, I shall proceed to take up the civil law, the starting point of our whole conversation.

Quintus: You will need very few more arguments. For I am convinced from what you have said to Atticus that Nature is the source of justice.

Atticus: How could I think anything else, now that you have so firmly established all your points? First, that we men are bountifully equipped by the gifts of the gods; second, that all mankind follows the same plan of life; finally, that all are bound together by a natural sense of good will, and by a common law. Now that we have acknowledged that all these points are, as I believe them to be, correct, we cannot consistently separate Nature from law and justice....

Marcus: If punishment or fear or suffering is all that keeps men from a wicked and evil life, and not the baseness of the conduct itself, then no one is really unjust, and the greatest sinners should be called unwise rather than wicked. Likewise, those of us who practice virtue do it not for herself alone but for motives of advantage and profit, and are shrewd and not good. For what will the man who dreads nothing but a witness or a judge do in the dark? What will he do if in the desert he finds someone weak and alone, whom he may rob of a big sum of gold? A man who is naturally just and good will speak to him, help him, and escort him on his way. But you can see what will be done by that other man, who never does anything for a fellow creature and measures everything by his own advantage. If he says he would not take the weaker man's life or steal his gold, the reason for his denial can never be that he regards the act as intrinsically base, but that he is afraid he might be caught and suffer the consequences. Of such an attitude not only wise men, but even simple folk would be ashamed.

It is, however, quite absurd to call just every article in the decrees and laws of nations. What if those laws were enacted by tyrants? Suppose the Thirty Tyrants at Athens had set up laws which pleased all the Athenians; merely for such a reason could those laws be considered just? No more just, I believe, than our law, instituted during the interregnum, that a dictator could with impunity put to death any citizen he chose without a hearing.

The essential justice that binds human society together and is maintained by one law is right reason, expressed in commands and prohibitions. Whoever disregards this law, whether written or unwritten, is unjust. But if justice is defined as mere compliance with the written laws and decrees of nations, and if too, as the same school affirms, all actions are to be measured by their utility, a man who thinks to gain advantage thereby will disregard the laws, if he can. It follows that the only real justice is that based on Nature, and that any law enacted merely for utility's sake can be abrogated by some other utility.

If Nature does not endorse our law, all virtue will be thrown to the winds. For what except Nature can inspire us to generosity, patriotism, piety, charity, or gratitude? All such virtues spring from our natural inclination to love one another. This is the basic principle of justice, and without it we should feel neither good will toward our fellow men, nor reverence for the gods. For the latter, I think, is not the result of fear, but of the kinship of man to God. But if laws are to be made by popular demand, official decrees, or judicial decisions, then it might become right to rob, commit adultery, or bear false witness, wherever such acts were approved by the votes and decisions of the multitude. If the ideas and desires of foolish men can subvert Nature by a simple vote, can they not compel us to treat evil and harmful actions henceforth as good and helpful? If a law can make justice the fruit of wrongdoing, cannot the same law make good come from evil? It is only Nature's precepts that teach us to distinguish between a good law and a bad.

But with Nature's help we can draw distinctions between right and wrong, and between honorable and shameful actions. Our own common sense gives us the first principles of understanding, and impresses them on our minds, so that we connect honorable qualities with virtue and all that is disgraceful with vice. It is folly to suppose that such judgments are matters of our own opinion and not natural instincts. Not by opinion, but by Nature do we judge the excellence of a tree or a horse. This being so, whatever is either honorable or shameful we must judge with the help of Nature. If virtue in general were but a matter of our opinion, the same opinion would recognize particular virtues. Yet no one can judge by a man's external appearance, instead of by his conduct, whether he is wise and prudent. The basis of his reputation is our correct reasoning, which is certainly a faculty of Nature. The same thing is true of all honorable qualities. We judge truth and falsehood, the logical and the illogical, on their intrinsic merits, not by external standards, and so do we recognize the consistent plan of life, which is virtue, and the inconstancy, which is vice.

Can we not judge the character of young men in the same manner? Is there any way but the natural one to estimate their qualities, and the virtues and vices which arise from those qualities? And must we not measure by Nature's standards all their other honorable or shameful traits? Whatever is praiseworthy must have some intrinsic good to be praised! Goodness is not just a matter of opinion—what idea is more absurd than that? Since then we distinguish good from evil by its nature, and since these qualities are fundamental in Nature, surely by a similar logic we may discriminate and judge between what is honorable and what is base according to Nature....

The natural conclusion of this whole discussion should be evident from what I have just said. It is that both righteousness and honor should be pursued for their intrinsic worth. All good men indeed love justice and righteousness for their own sake, and no good man would make the mistake of loving something that did not deserve it. So we must seek out and cultivate the right for its own sake, and justice also. This being true, we must practice all other virtues too for their own sake.

Questions for Reflection

1. According to Cicero, there is an unchangeable and universal law of nature, manifest as right reason or conscience, innate to every human being. How does this law of nature function in relation to justice? What are its implications for morality in general?
2. How can the law of nature support the idea that all humans should have the same rights and duties?
3. Compare Cicero's Stoicism with Aristotle's philosophy. How different are the two philosophies in what they say about justice, law, and equality? Do you prefer Cicero's or Aristotle's theory?

4. ST. THOMAS AQUINAS

Thomas Aquinas (c. 1225-1274), born in Roccasecca, Italy, was perhaps the greatest of the medieval scholastic philosophers. Scholasticism was a school of philosophy that attempted to reconcile Christian faith, the doctrines of the Catholic Church, and rational thought. In his most important work, the *Summa Theologica*, Aquinas produced a systematic introduction to theology, including the definition and classification of kinds of law. Aquinas defines law in general as a rule of human action determined by reason, directed towards the common good shared by all humans. Aquinas distinguishes four forms of law—eternal law, natural law, divine law, and human law—that are essentially related and inform the basic moral task of human beings: to do good and avoid evil. For Aquinas, this task is the first precept of natural law.

Text—Summa Theologica

Reprinted from Summa Theologica, *translated by the English Dominican Fathers. New York: Benziger Brothers, 1915.*

QUESTION 90: OF THE ESSENCE OF LAW

First Article: Whether law is something pertaining to reason?

I answer that, Law is a rule and measure of acts, whereby man is induced to act or is restrained from acting: for *lex* (law) is derived from *ligare* (to bind), because it binds one to act. Now the rule and measure of human acts is the reason, which is the first principle of human acts.... Reason has its power of moving from the will...for it is due to the fact that one wills the end, that the reason issues its commands as regards things ordained to the end. But in order that the volition of what is commanded may have the nature of law, it needs to be in accord with some rule of reason. And in this sense is to be understood the saying that the will of the sovereign has the force of law; otherwise the sovereign's will would savor of lawlessness rather than of law.

Second Article: Whether the law is always directed to the common good?

I answer that, as stated above, the law belongs to that which is a principle of human acts, because it is their rule and measure. Now as reason is a principle of human acts, so in reason itself there is something which is the principle in respect of all the rest: wherefore to this principle chiefly and mainly law must needs be referred.—Now the first principle in practical matters, which are the object of the practical reason, is the last end: and the last end of human life is bliss or happiness, as stated above. Consequently the law must needs regard principally the relationship to happiness. Moreover, since every part is ordained to the whole, as imperfect to perfect; and since one man is a part of the perfect community, the law must needs regard properly the relationship to universal happiness. Wherefore the Philosopher [Aristotle], in the above definition of legal matters mentions both happiness and the body politic, for he says that we call those legal matters *just*, "which are adapted to produce and preserve happiness and its parts for the body politic," since the state is a perfect community, as he says in *Politics* I, 1.... Therefore every law is ordained to the common good....

QUESTION 91: OF THE VARIOUS KINDS OF LAW

First Article: Whether there is an eternal law?

I answer that...a law is nothing else but a dictate of practical reason emanating from the ruler who governs a perfect community. Now it is evident, granted that the world is ruled by Divine Providence, as was stated in the First Part, that the whole community of the universe is governed by Divine Reason. Wherefore the very Idea of the government of things in God the Ruler of the universe, has the nature of a law. And since the Divine Reason's conception of things is not subject to time but is eternal, according to Proverbs viii. 23, therefore it is that this kind of law must be called eternal.

Second Article: Whether there is a natural law?

I answer that, as stated above, law, being a rule and measure, can be in a person in two ways: in one way, as in him that rules and measures; in another way, as in that which is ruled and measured, since a thing is ruled and measured, in so far as it partakes of the rule or measure. Wherefore, since all things subject to Divine providence are ruled and measured by the eternal law…it is evident that all things partake somewhat of the eternal law, in so far as, namely, from its being imprinted on them, they derive their respective inclinations to their proper acts and ends. Now among all others, the rational creature is subject to Divine providence in the most excellent way, in so far as it partakes of a share of providence, by being provident both for itself and for others. Wherefore it has a share of the Eternal Reason, whereby it has a natural inclination to its proper act and end: and this participation of the eternal law in the rational creature is called the natural law. Hence the Psalmist after saying: "Offer up the sacrifice of justice," as though someone asked what the works of justice are, adds: "Many say, Who showeth us good things?" in answer to which question he says: "The light of Thy countenance, O Lord, is signed upon us": thus implying that the light of natural reason, whereby we discern what is good and what is evil, which is the function of the natural law, is nothing else than an imprint on us of the Divine light. It is therefore evident that the natural law is nothing else than the rational creature's participation of the eternal law….

QUESTION 92: OF THE EFFECTS OF LAW

First Article: Whether an effect of law is to make men good?

I answer that, as stated above, a law is nothing else than a dictate of reason in the ruler by whom his subjects are governed. Now the virtue of any subordinate thing consists in its being well subordinated to that by which it is regulated: thus we see that the virtue of the irascible and concupiscible faculties consists in their being obedient to reason; and accordingly "the virtue of every subject consists in his being well subjected to his ruler," as the Philosopher says. But every law aims at being obeyed by those who are subject to it. Consequently it is evident that the proper effect of law is to lead its subjects to their proper virtue: and since virtue is "that which makes its subject good," it follows that the proper effect of law is to make those to whom it is given, good, either simply or in some particular respect....

Since then every man is a part of the state, it is impossible that a man be good, unless he be well proportionate to the common good: nor can the whole be well consistent unless its parts be proportionate to it. Consequently the common good of the state cannot flourish, unless the citizens be virtuous, at least those whose business it is to govern. But it is enough for the good of the community, that the other citizens be so far virtuous that they obey the commands of their rulers. Hence the Philosopher says that "the virtue of a sovereign is the same as that of a good man, but the virtue of any common citizen is not the same as that of a good man."

A tyrannical law, through not being according to reason, is not a law, absolutely speaking, but rather a perversion of law....

QUESTION 95: OF HUMAN LAW

Second Article: Whether every human law is derived from the natural law?

I answer that, as Augustine says, "that which is not just seems to be no law at all"; wherefore the force of a law depends on the extent of its justice. Now in human affairs a thing is said to be just, from being right, according to the rule of reason. But the first rule of reason is the law of nature, as is clear from what has been stated above. Consequently every human law has just so much of the nature of law, as it is derived from the law of nature. But if in any point it deflects from the law of nature, it is no longer a law but a perversion of law....

QUESTION 96: THE POWER OF HUMAN LAW

Fourth Article: Does Human Law Bind a Man in Conscience?

I answer that...laws framed by men are either just or unjust. If they be just, they have the power of binding the conscience from the eternal law whence they are derived.... Now laws are said to be just on three counts; from their end, when they are ordered for the common good, from their authority, when what is enacted does not exceed the lawgiver's power, and from their form, when for the good of the whole they place burdens in equitable proportion on subjects.... On the other hand, laws may be unjust in two ways: first, by being contrary to human good...as when an authority imposes on his subjects burdensome laws, conducive, not to the common good, but rather to his own cupidity or vainglory.... Such are acts of violence rather than laws.... Therefore, such laws do not bind in conscience.... Secondly, laws may be unjust through being opposed to the divine good...such are the laws of tyrants.... Laws of this kind must in no way be observed...and in such cases a man is not obliged to obey, if without scandal or greater damage he can resist.

QUESTIONS FOR REFLECTION

1. According to Aquinas, why is an appeal to principles of the good or justice necessarily embedded in the natural law? How does natural law relate to human law?
2. How is it that a human law can fail to have the character of law per se? What are the implications of Aquinas' view in terms of evaluating human practices and institutions?
3. Do you agree with the distinction Aquinas draws between just laws and "perverse" laws? Develop examples of each type of law.

5. HUGO GROTIUS

The Dutch lawyer, diplomat, and legal philosopher Hugo Grotius (1583-1645) is considered the father of modern international law. Melding the traditions of medieval scholasticism and Greek and Roman natural law theory, Grotius regarded the foundation of international law to be a universal law of nature. As a dictate of human reason, which is similar in all peoples, natural law provides a moral standard common to all human beings. According to Grotius, the core doctrine of natural law is the right to self-preservation possessed equally by all individuals. As a result, the customary law of each state must be constrained by the basic law of nature and thus the rights of peoples and individuals to self-preservation. In this way Grotius makes a significant contribution to the modern notions of international rights and duties.

Text—The Rights of War and Peace (1625)

Reprinted from The Rights of War and Peace. *Translated by A. C. Campbell. New York and London: M. W. Dunne, 1901.*

BOOK I, CHAPTER I

III. As the Rights of War is the title, by which this treatise is distinguished, the first inquiry, as it has been already observed, is, whether any war be just, and, in the next place, what constitutes the justice of that war. For, in this place, right signifies nothing more than what is just, and that, more in a negative than a positive sense; so that RIGHT is that, which is not unjust. Now any thing is unjust, which is repugnant to the nature of society, established among rational creatures. Thus for instance, to deprive another of what belongs to him, merely for one's own advantage, is repugnant to the law of nature, as Cicero observes in the fifth Chapter of his third book of offices; and, by way of proof, he says that, if the practice were general, all society and intercourse among men must be overturned. Florentinus, the Lawyer, maintains that is impious for one man to form designs against another, as nature has established a degree of kindred amongst us. On this subject, Seneca remarks that, as all the members of the human body agree among themselves, because the preservation of each conduces to the welfare of the whole, so men should forbear from mutual injuries, as they were born for society, which cannot subsist unless all the parts of it are defended by mutual forbearance and good will. But as there is one kind of social tie founded upon an equality, for instance, among brothers, citizens, friends, allies, and another on pre-eminence, as Aristotle styles it, subsisting between parents and children, masters and servants, sovereigns and subjects, God and men. So justice takes place either amongst equals, or between the governing and the governed parties, notwithstanding their difference of rank. The former of these, if I am not mistaken, may be called the right of equality, and the latter the right of superiority.

IV. There is another signification of the word RIGHT, different from this, but yet arising from it, which relates directly to the person. In which sense, RIGHT is a moral quality annexed to the person, justly entitling him to possess some particular privilege, or to perform some particular act. This right is annexed to the person, although it sometimes follows the things, as the services of lands, which are called REAL RIGHTS, in opposition to those merely PERSONAL. Not because these rights are not annexed to persons, but the distinction is made, because they belong to the persons only who possess some particular things. This moral quality, when perfect is called a FACULTY; when imperfect, an APTITUDE. The former answers to the ACT, and the latter to the POWER, when we speak of natural things.

V. Civilians call a faculty that Right, which every man has to his own; but we shall hereafter, taking it in its strict and proper sense, call it a right. This right comprehends the power, that we have over ourselves, which is called liberty, and the power, that we have over others, as that of a father over his children, and of a master over his slaves. It likewise comprehends property, which is either complete or imperfect; of the latter kind is the use or possession of any thing without the property, or power of alienating it, or pledges detained by the creditors till payment be made. There is a third signification which implies the power of demanding what is due, to which the obligation upon the party indebted, to discharge what is owing, corresponds....

IX. There is also a third signification of the word Right, which has the same meaning as Law, taken in its most extensive sense, to denote a rule of moral action, obliging us to do what is proper. We say OBLIGING us. For the best counsels or precepts, if they lay us under no obligation to obey them, cannot come under the denomination of law or right. Now as to permission, it is no act of the law, but only the silence of the law; it however prohibits any one from impeding another in doing what the law permits. But we have said, the law obliges us to do what is proper, not simply what is just; because, under this notion, right belongs to the substance not only of justice, as we have explained it, but of all other virtues. Yet from giving the name of a RIGHT to that, which is PROPER, a more general acceptation of the word justice has been derived. The best division of right, in this general meaning, is to be found in Aristotle, who, defining one kind to be natural, and the other voluntary, calls it a LAWFUL RIGHT in the strictest sense of the word law; and some times an instituted right. The same difference is found among the Hebrews, who, by way of distinction, in speaking, call that natural right, PRECEPTS, and the voluntary right, STATUTES.

X. Natural right is the dictate of right reason, shewing the moral turpitude, or moral necessity, of any act from its agreement or disagreement with a rational nature, and consequently that such an act is either forbidden or commanded by God, the author of nature. The actions, upon which such a dictate is given, are either binding or unlawful in themselves, and therefore necessarily understood to be commanded or forbidden by God. This mark distinguishes natural right, not only from human law, but from the law, which God himself has been pleased to reveal, called, by some, the voluntary divine right, which does not command or forbid things in themselves either binding or unlawful, but makes them unlawful by its prohibition, and binding by its command. But, to understand natural right, we must observe that some things are said to belong to that right, not properly, but, as the schoolmen say, by way of accommodation. These are not repugnant to natural right, as we have already observed that those things are called JUST, in which there is no injustice. Some times also, by a wrong use of the word, those things which reason shews to be proper, or better than things of an opposite kind, although not binding, are said to belong to natural right.

We must farther remark, that natural right relates not only to those things that exist independent of the human will, but to many things, which necessarily follow the exercise of that will. Thus property, as now in use, was at first a creature of the human will. But, after it was established, one man was prohibited by the law of nature from seizing the property of another against his will....

Now the Law of Nature is so unalterable, that it cannot be changed even by God himself. For although the power of God is infinite, yet there are some things, to which it does not extend. Because the things so expressed would have no true meaning, but imply a contradiction. Thus two and two must make four, nor is it possible to be otherwise; nor, again, can what is really evil not be evil. And this is Aristotle's meaning, when he says, that some things are no sooner named, than we discover their evil nature. For as the substance of things in their nature and existence depends upon nothing but themselves; so there are qualities inseparably connected with their being and essence. Of this kind is the evil of certain actions, compared with the nature of a reasonable being.... There are also some things allowed by the law of nature, not absolutely, but according to a certain state of affairs. Thus, by the law of nature, before property was introduced, every one had a right to the use of whatever he found unoccupied; and, before laws were enacted, to avenge his personal injuries by force....

XII. The existence of the Law of Nature is proved by two kinds of argument, *a priori*, and *a posteriori*, the former a more abstruse, and the latter a more popular method of proof. We are said to reason *a priori*, when we show the agreement or disagreement of any thing with a reasonable and social nature; but *a posteriori*, when without absolute proof, but only upon probability, any thing is inferred to accord with the law of nature, because it is received as such among all, or at least the more civilized nations. For a general effect can only arise from a general cause. Now scarce any other cause can be assigned for so general an opinion, but the common sense, as it is called, of mankind. There is a sentence of Hesiod that has been much praised, that opinions which have prevailed amongst many nations, must have some foundation. Heraclitus, establishing common reason as the best criterion of truth, says, those things are certain which generally appear so. Among other authorities, we may quote Aristotle, who says it is a strong proof in our favour, when all appear to agree with what we say, and Cicero maintains that the consent of all nations in any case is to be admitted for the law of nature. Seneca is of the same opinion, any thing, says he, appearing the same to all men is a proof of its truth. Quintilian says, we hold those things to be true, in which all men agree. We have called them the more civilized nations, and not without reason. For, as Porphyry well observes, some nations are so strange that no fair judgment of human nature can be formed from them, for it would be erroneous. Andronicus, the Rhodian says, that with men of a right and sound understanding, natural justice is unchangeable. Nor does it alter the case, though men of disordered and perverted minds think otherwise. For he who should deny that honey is sweet, because it appears not so to men of a distempered taste, would be wrong. Plutarch too agrees entirely with what has been said, as appears from a passage in his life of Pompey, affirming that man neither was, nor is, by nature, a wild unsociable creature. But it is the corruption of his nature which makes him so: yet by acquiring new habits, by changing his place, and way of living, he may be reclaimed to his original gentleness. Aristotle, taking a description of man from his peculiar qualities, makes him an animal of a gentle nature, and in another part of his works, he observes, that in considering the nature of man, we are to take our likeness from nature in its pure, and not in its corrupt state.

XIII. It has been already remarked, that there is another kind of right, which is the voluntary right, deriving its origin from the will, and is either human or divine.

XIV. We will begin with the human as more generally known. Now this is either a civil right, or a right more or less extensive than the civil right. The civil right is that which is derived from the civil power. The civil power is the sovereign power of the state. A state is a perfect body of free men, united together in order to enjoy common rights and advantages. The less extensive right, and not derived from the civil power itself, although subject to it, is various, comprehending the authority of parents over children, masters over servants, and the like. But the law of nations is a more extensive right, deriving its authority from the consent of all, or at least of many nations.

It was proper to add MANY, because scarce any right can be found common to all nations, except the law of nature, which itself too is generally called the law of nations. Nay, frequently in one part of the world, that is held for the law of nations, which is not so in another. Now this law of nations is proved in the same manner as the unwritten civil law, and that is by the continual experience and testimony of the Sages of the Law. For this law, as Dio Chrysostom well observes, is the discoveries made by experience and time. And in this we derive great advantage from the writings of eminent historians.

XV. The very meaning of the words divine voluntary right, shows that it springs from the divine will, by which it is distinguished from natural law, which, it has already been observed, is called divine also. This law admits of what Anaxarchus said, as Plutarch relates in the life of Alexander, though without sufficient accuracy, that God does not will a thing, because it is just, but that it is just, or binding, because God wills it. Now this law was given either to mankind in general, or to one particular people. We find three periods, at which it was given by God to the human race, the first of which was immediately after the creation of man, the second upon the restoration of mankind after the flood, and the third upon that more glorious restoration through Jesus Christ. These three laws undoubtedly bind all men, as soon as they come to a sufficient knowledge of them....

Questions for Reflection

1. Grotius argues that the core of the universal morality grounded in the law of nature is the recognition of rational self-preservation. How does this argument support the claim that each person has a "right" to self-preservation?

2. How does Grotius explain the difference between "natural" right and "voluntary" right?

3. Grotius conceives of rights as moral *powers* (of acting, of judging, and so forth). Given this notion of rights conceived in terms of power, is there any distinction to be made between "might" and "right"? Why, or why not?

Further Readings for Section 1

Bull, Hedley, Benedict Kingsbury, and Adam Roberts, eds. *Hugo Grotius and International Relations*. Oxford: Clarendon Press, 1990.

Donnelly, Jack. "Natural Law and Right in Aquinas' Political Thought." *Western Political Quarterly* 33 (1980): 520-35.

Finnis, John. *Natural Law and Natural Rights*. Oxford: Oxford University Press, 1982.

Hunt, H.A.K. *The Humanism of Cicero*. Melbourne: Melbourne University Press, 1954.

Irwin, T. H. *Plato's Ethics*. Oxford: Oxford University Press, 1995.

Kraut, Richard. *Socrates and the State*. Princeton: Princeton University Press, 1984.

Lisska, Anthony. *Aquinas' Theory of Natural Law*. Oxford: Oxford University Press, 1996.

Miller, Fred. *Nature, Justice, and Rights in Aristotle's Politics*. Oxford: Oxford University Press.

Nussbaum, Martha C. *The Fragility of Goodness*. Cambridge: Cambridge University Press, 1986.

Schofield, Malcolm. *The Stoic Idea of the City*. Cambridge: Cambridge University Press, 1991.

Section 2:
MODERN PERSPECTIVES

6. THOMAS HOBBES

The English philosopher Thomas Hobbes (1588–1679) is probably the writer most responsible for inaugurating modern social and political philosophy. The son of the Vicar of Westport, Hobbes was educated at Oxford University where he studied mathematics and scholastic philosophy. Following his graduation from Oxford he became tutor for the family of William Cavendish, Earl of Devonshire. In 1640, Hobbes began to formulate his philosophical system inspired by the materialist view of the world presented in Galileo's mechanistic theories of physical nature. However, the civil war in England interrupted Hobbes's work on the three treatises he planned to write, dealing respectively with the natural world, human nature, and political society. Hobbes pursued his inquiry on politics over the next several years, though, and in 1651 his masterpiece in political philosophy, *Leviathan*, was published.

In the *Leviathan*, Hobbes begins with an account of human nature and argues that all of our actions are performed for self-interested reasons, primarily to obtain satisfaction and avoid harm, a view that is now referred to as psychological egoism. He also describes an amoral, pre-political stage of human social development, a "state of nature," where people live independently under conditions of suspicion, insecurity, and conflict. All humans are basically equal in terms of their desires and abilities, yet our natural egoism combined with competition for limited resources leads to a state of perpetual war of all against all, in which life is "solitary, poor, nasty, brutish, and short."

Hobbes argues that several motives, including fear of death and the desire to have the material goods needed for a condition of welfare, cause people to create a political society by means of a "social contract." The basis of the social contract is natural law, which Hobbes identifies through a lengthy list of specific laws of nature that serve as rational precepts for the maintenance of social order, flowing from self-interested prudence. For Hobbes, the source of natural law consists in the fundamental natural right to life of each person, "the liberty each man hath, to use his own power, as he will himself, for the preservation of his own nature." In order to escape the state of nature and create a government, however, all persons must agree to mutually transfer their right of absolute liberty (as absence of constraint) to a political sovereign—the state or Leviathan—which is then empowered to enforce security by punishing those who violate the agreement to obey the laws of society. Although Hobbes conceives of the sovereign as the supreme authority, it is important to note that the power of the sovereign is derived not from the divine right of kings but from the natural right of the people through the event of the social contract. In this way Hobbes initiates an important tradition of ethical and political theory known as *contractarianism* that is modified and extended by Locke, Rousseau and Kant.

We begin our examination with Hobbes's description of the state of nature in Part I of the *Leviathan*, followed by his discussion of the origin of the state or commonwealth.

Text—Leviathan (1651)

Reprinted from The English Works of Thomas Hobbes, *edited by Sir William Molesworth. London: John Bohn, 1839.*

CHAPTER 13: OF THE NATURAL CONDITION OF MANKIND AS CONCERNING THEIR FELICITY AND MISERY

Nature hath made men so equal, in the faculties of the body and mind, as that though there be found one man sometimes manifestly stronger in body, or of quicker mind than another, yet when all is reckoned together, the difference between man and man is not so considerable, as that one man can thereupon claim to himself any benefit to which another may not pretend, as well he. For as to the strength of body, the weakest has strength enough to kill the strongest, either by secret machination, or by confederacy with others that are in the same danger with himself.

And as to the faculties of the mind, setting aside the arts, grounded upon words, and especially that skill of proceeding upon general and infallible rules, called science; which very few have, and but in few things; as being not a native faculty, born with us; nor attained, as prudence, while we look after somewhat else, I find yet a greater equality amongst men than that of strength. For prudence is but experience; which equal time equally bestows on all men, in those things they equally apply themselves unto. That which may perhaps make such equality incredible is but a vain conceit of one's own wisdom, which almost all men think they have in a greater degree than the vulgar; that is, than all men but themselves, and a few others, whom by fame or for concurring with themselves, they approve. For such is the nature of men, that howsoever they may acknowledge many others to be more witty, or more eloquent, or more learned, yet they will hardly believe there be many so wise as themselves; for they see their own wit at hand, and other men's at a distance. But this proveth rather that men are in that point equal, than unequal. For there is not ordinarily a greater sign of the equal distribution of anything, than that every man is contented with his share.

From this equality of ability ariseth equality of hope in the attaining of our ends. And therefore if any two men desire the same thing, which nevertheless they cannot both enjoy, they become enemies; and in the way to their end, which is principally their own conservation, and sometimes their delectation only, endeavor to destroy or subdue one another. And from hence it comes to pass that where an invader hath no more to fear than another man's single power; if one plant, sow, build, or possess a convenient seat, others may probably be expected to come prepared with forces united, to dispossess and deprive him, not only of the fruit of his labor, but also of his life or liberty. And the invader again is in the like danger of another.

And from this diffidence of one another, there is no way for any man to secure himself so reasonable as anticipation; that is, by force, or wiles, to master the persons of all men he can, so long, till he see no other power great enough to endanger him: and this is no more than his own conservation requireth, and is generally allowed....

Again, men have no pleasure, but on the contrary a great deal of grief, in keeping company, where there is no power able to overawe them all. For every man looketh that his companion should value him, at the same rate he sets upon himself: and upon all signs of contempt, or undervaluing, naturally endeavors, as far as he dares (which amongst them that have no common power to keep them in quiet, is far enough to make them destroy each other), to extort a greater value from his condemners, by damage; and from others, by the example.

So that in the nature of man we find three principal causes of quarrel. First, competition; secondly, diffidence; thirdly, glory.

The first maketh men invade for gain; the second, for safety; and the third, for reputation. The first use violence, to make themselves masters of other men's persons, wives, children, and cattle; the second, to defend them; the third, for trifles, as a word, a smile, a different opinion and any other sign of undervalue, either direct in their persons, or by reflection in their kindred, their friends, their nation, their profession, or their name.

Hereby it is manifest that during the time men live without a common power to keep them all in awe, they are in that condition which is called war; and such a war, as is of every man against every man.... Whatsoever therefore is consequent to a time of war, where every man is enemy to every man, the same is consequent to the time wherein men live without other security than what their own strength and their own invention shall furnish them withal. In such condition there is no place for industry, because the fruit thereof is uncertain, and consequently no culture of the earth; no navigation, nor use of the commodities that may be imported by sea; no commodious building; no instruments of moving and removing such things as require much force; no knowledge of the face of the earth; no account of time; no arts; no letters; no society; and, which is worst of all, continual fear and danger of violent death; and the life of man, solitary, poor, nasty, brutish, and short....

To this war of every man, against every man, this also is consequent: that nothing can be unjust. The notions of right and wrong, justice and injustice, have there no place. Where there is no common power, there is no law; where no law, no injustice. Force and fraud are in war the two cardinal virtues. Justice and injustice are none of the faculties neither of the body nor mind. If they were, they might be in a man that were alone in the world, as well as his senses, and passions. They are qualities that relate to men in society, not in solitude. It is consequent also to the same condition, that there be no propriety, no dominion, no "mine" and "thine" distinct; but only that to be every man's that he can get; and for so long as he can keep it. And thus much for the ill condition which man by mere nature is actually placed in; though with a possibility to come out of it, consisting partly in the passions, partly in his reason.

The passions that incline men to peace are fear of death; desire of such things as are necessary to commodious living; and a hope by their industry to obtain them. And reason suggesteth convenient articles of peace, upon which men may be drawn to agreement. These articles are they which otherwise are called the laws of nature: whereof I shall speak more particularly in the two following chapters.

CHAPTER 14: OF THE FIRST AND SECOND NATURAL LAWS, AND OF CONTRACTS

The RIGHT OF NATURE, which writers commonly call *jus naturale*, is the liberty each man hath to use his own power as he will himself, for the preservation of his own nature; that is to say, of his own life; and consequently, of doing anything which in his own judgment and reason he shall conceive to be the aptest means thereunto.

By LIBERTY, is understood, according to the proper signification of the word, the absence of external impediments: which impediments may oft take away part of a man's power to do what he would; but cannot hinder him from using the power left him, according as his judgment and reason shall dictate to him.

A LAW OF NATURE, *lex naturalis*, is a precept or general rule, found out by reason, by which a man is forbidden to do that which is destructive of his life, or taketh away the means of preserving the same; and to omit that by which he thinketh it may be best preserved. For though they that speak of this subject, use to confound *jus* and *lex*, *right* and *law*, yet they ought to be distinguished; because RIGHT consisteth in liberty to do or to forbear; whereas LAW determineth and bindeth to one of them; so that law and right differ as much as obligation and liberty, which in one and the same matter are inconsistent.

And because the condition of man, as hath been declared in the precedent chapter, is a condition of war of every one against every one, in which case every one is governed by his own reason, and there is nothing he can make use of that may not be a help unto him in preserving his life against his enemies, it followeth that in such a condition every man has a right to everything, even to one another's body. And therefore, as long as this natural right of every man to everything endureth, there can be no security to any man, how strong or wise soever he be, of living out the time which nature ordinarily alloweth men to live. And consequently it is a precept, or general rule of reason, *that every man ought to endeavor peace, as far as he has hope of obtaining it; and when he cannot obtain it, that he may seek and use all helps and advantages of war.* The first branch of which rule containeth the first and fundamental law of nature; which is, *to seek peace, and follow it.* The second, the sum of the right of nature: which is, *by all means we can, to defend ourselves.*

From this fundamental law of nature, by which men are commanded to endeavor peace, is derived this second law: *that a man be willing, when others are so too, as far-forth as for peace and defense of himself he shall think it necessary, to lay down this right to all things, and be contented with so much liberty against other men as he would allow other men against himself.* For as long as everyman holdeth this right of doing anything he liketh, so long are all men in the condition of war. But if other men will not lay down their right, as well as he, then there is no reason for any one to divest himself of his: for that were to expose himself to prey, which no man is bound to, rather than to dispose himself to peace. This is that law of the Gospel: *whatsoever you require that others should do to you, that do ye to them.* And that law of all men, *What you do not want done to you, do not do unto others.*

To lay down a man's right to anything is to divest himself of the liberty of hindering another of the benefit of his own right to the same. For he that renounceth or passeth away his right, giveth not to any other man a right which he had not before, because there is nothing to which every man had not right by nature, but only standeth out of his way, that he may enjoy his own original right, without hindrance from him; not without hindrance from another. So that the effect which redoundeth to one man, by another man's defect of right, is but so much diminution of impediments to the use of his own right original.

Right is laid aside either by simply renouncing it or by transferring it to another. By simply RENOUNCING, when he cares not to whom the benefit thereof redoundeth. By TRANSFERRING, when he intendeth the benefit thereof to some certain person or persons....

Whensoever a man transferreth his right, or renounceth it, it is either in consideration of some right reciprocally transferred to himself, or for some other good he hopeth for thereby. For it is a voluntary act: and of the voluntary acts of every man, the object is some good to himself. And therefore there be some rights which no man can be understood by any words, or other signs, to have abandoned or transferred. As first a man cannot lay down the right of resisting them that assault him by force to take away his life; because he cannot be understood to aim thereby at any good to himself. The same may be said of wounds, and chains, and imprisonment; both because there is no benefit consequent to such patience, as there is to the patience of suffering another to be wounded or imprisoned, as also because a man cannot tell, when he seeth men proceed against him by violence, whether they intend his death or not. And lastly the motive and end for which this renouncing and transferring of right is introduced, is nothing else but the security of a man's person, in his life and in the means of so preserving life, as not to be weary of it. And therefore if a man by words, or other signs, seem to despoil himself of the end for which those signs were intended, he is not to be understood as if he meant it, or that it was his will, but that he was ignorant of how such words and actions were to be interpreted.

The mutual transferring of right is that which men call CONTRACT....

A covenant not to defend myself from force, by force, is always void. For, as I have shown before, no man can transfer or lay down his right to save himself from death, wounds, and imprisonment, the avoiding whereof is the only end of laying down any right; and therefore the promise of not resisting force, in no covenant transferreth any right, nor is obliging. For though a man may covenant thus, *unless I do so, or so, kill me*, he cannot covenant thus, *unless I do so, or so, I will not resist you when you come to kill me*. For man by nature chooseth the lesser evil, which is danger of death in resisting, rather than the greater, which is certain and present death in not resisting....

CHAPTER 15: OF OTHER LAWS OF NATURE

From that law of nature, by which we are obliged to transfer to another such rights, as being retained, hinder the peace of mankind, there followeth a third; which is this, *that men perform their covenants made*; without which, covenants are in vain, and but empty words; and the right of all men to all things remaining, we are still in the condition of war.

And in this law of nature consisteth the fountain and original of JUSTICE. For where no covenant hath preceded, there hath no right been transferred, and every man has right to everything; and consequently, no action can be unjust. But when a covenant is made, then to break it is unjust: and the definition of INJUSTICE is no other than *the not performance of covenant*. And whatsoever is not unjust is *just*.

But because covenants of mutual trust, where there is a fear of not performance on either part, as hath been said in the former chapter, are invalid, though the original of justice be the making of covenants, yet injustice actually there can be none, till the cause of such fear be taken away; which while men are in the natural condition of war cannot be done. Therefore before the names of just and unjust can have place, there must be some coercive power to compel men equally to the performance of their covenants, by the terror of some punishment, greater than the benefit they expect by the breach of their covenant; and to make good that propriety, which by mutual contract men acquire, in recompense of the universal right they abandon: and such power there is none before the erection of a commonwealth. And this is also to be gathered out of the ordinary definition of justice in the schools: for they say that *justice is the constant will of giving to every man his own*. And therefore where there is no *own*, that is no propriety, there is no injustice; and where there is no coercive power erected, that is, where there is no commonwealth, there is no propriety, all men having right to all things: therefore where there is no commonwealth, there nothing is unjust. So that the nature of justice consisteth in keeping of valid covenants; but the validity of covenants begins not but with the constitution of a civil power, sufficient to compel men to keep them; and then it is also that propriety begins....

And though this may seem too subtle a deduction of the laws of nature, to be taken notice of by all men; whereof the most part are too busy in getting food, and the rest too negligent to understand; yet to leave all men inexcusable, they have been contracted into one easy sum, intelligible, even to the meanest capacity; and that is, *Do not that to another, which thou wouldest not have done to thyself*; which sheweth him, that he has no more to do in learning the laws of nature, but, when weighing the actions of other men with his own, they seem too heavy, to put them into the other part of the balance, and his own into their place, that his own passions, and self-love, may add nothing to the weight; and then there is none of these laws of nature that will not appear unto him very reasonable....

The laws of nature are immutable and eternal; for injustice, ingratitude, arrogance, pride, iniquity, acception of persons, and the rest, can never be made lawful. For it can never be that war shall preserve life, and peace destroy it....

CHAPTER 17: OF THE CAUSES, GENERATION, AND DEFINITION OF A COMMONWEALTH

The final cause, end, or design of men, who naturally love liberty, and dominion over others, in the introduction of that restraint upon themselves, in which we see them live in commonwealths, is the foresight of their own preservation, and of a more contented life thereby; that is to say, of getting themselves out from that miserable condition of war, which is necessarily consequent, as hath been shown, to the natural passions of men, when there is no visible power to keep them in awe, and tie them by fear of punishment to the performance of their covenants, and observation of those laws of nature set down in the fourteenth and fifteenth chapters.

For the laws of nature, as *justice*, *equity*, *modesty*, *mercy*, and, in sum, *doing to others as we would be done to*, of themselves, without the terror of some power to cause them to be observed, are contrary to our natural passions, that carry us to partiality, pride, revenge, and the like. And covenants, without the sword, are but words, and of no strength to secure a man at all. Therefore notwithstanding the laws of nature, which every one hath then kept, when he has the will to keep them, when he can do it safely, if there be no power erected, or not great enough for our security, every man will and may lawfully rely on his own strength and art, for caution against all other men. And in all places where men have lived by small families, to rob and spoil one another has been a trade, and so far from being reputed against the law of nature, that the greater spoils they gained, the greater was their honor; and men observed no other laws therein, but the laws of honor; that is, to abstain from cruelty, leaving to men their lives, and instruments of husbandry. And as small families did then, so now do cities and kingdoms, which are but greater families, for their own security, enlarge their dominions, upon all pretenses of danger, and fear of invasion, or assistance that may be given to invaders, and endeavor as much as they can to subdue or weaken their neighbors, by open force and secret arts, for want of other caution, justly; and are remembered for it in after ages with honor....

The only way to erect such a common power as may be able to defend them from the invasion of foreigners and the injuries of one another, and thereby to secure them in such sort as that by their own industry, and by the fruits of the earth, they may nourish themselves and live contentedly, is to confer all their power and strength upon one man, or upon one assembly of men, that may reduce all their wills, by plurality of voices, unto one will:

which is as much as to say, to appoint one man, or assembly of men, to bear their person; and every one to own and acknowledge himself to be author of whatsoever he that so beareth their person shall act, or cause to be acted, in those things which concern the common peace and safety; and therein to submit their wills, every one to his will, and their judgments to his judgment. This is more than consent, or concord; it is a real unity of them all in one and the same person, made by covenant of every man with every man, in such manner as if every man should say to every man, *I authorize and give up my right of governing myself, to this man or to this assembly of men, on this condition, that thou give up thy right to him and authorize all his actions in like manner.* This done, the multitude so united in one person is called a COMMONWEALTH, in Latin CIVITAS. This is the generation of that great LEVIATHAN, or rather, to speak more reverently, of that *mortal god*, to which we owe under the *immortal God*, our peace and defense. For by this authority, given him by every particular man in the commonwealth, he hath the use of so much power and strength conferred on him, that by terror thereof, he is enabled to perform the wills of them all, to peace at home, and mutual aid against their enemies abroad. And in him consisteth the essence of the commonwealth; which, to define it, is *one person, of whose acts a great multitude, by mutual covenants one with another, have made themselves every one the author, to the end he may use the strength and means of them all, as he shall think expedient, for their peace and common defense.*

And he that carrieth this person is called SOVEREIGN, and said to have sovereign power; and every one besides, his SUBJECT....

CHAPTER 21: OF THE LIBERTY OF SUBJECTS

LIBERTY, or FREEDOM, signifieth, properly, the absence of opposition; by opposition, I mean external impediments of motion; and may be applied no less to irrational and inanimate creatures than to rational. For whatsoever is so tied, or environed, as it cannot move but within a certain space, which space is determined by the opposition of some external body, we say it hath not liberty to go further. And so of all living creatures whilst they are imprisoned, or restrained, with walls or chains; and of the water whilst it is kept in by banks or vessels, that otherwise would spread itself into a larger space, we use to say, they are not at liberty to move in such manner as without those external impediments they would. But when the impediment of motion is in the constitution of the thing itself, we use not to say, it wants the liberty, but the power to move; as when a stone lieth still, or a man is fastened to his bed by sickness.

And according to this proper and generally received meaning of the word, a freeman is he, that in those things, which by his strength and wit he is able to do, is not hindered to do what he has a will to. But when the words *free*, and *liberty*, are applied to anything but bodies, they are abused; for that which is not subject to motion, is not subject to impediment; and therefore, when it is said for example, *the way is free*, no liberty of the way is signified, but of those that walk in it without stop. And when we say *a gift is free*, there is not meant any liberty of the gift, but of the giver, that was not bound by any law or covenant to give it. So when we speak freely, it is not the liberty of voice, or pronunciation, but of the man, whom no law hath obliged to speak otherwise than he did. Lastly, from the use of the word *free-will*, no liberty can be inferred of the will, desire, or inclination, but the liberty of the man; which consisteth in this, that he finds no stop in doing what he has the will, desire, or inclination to do.

Fear and liberty are consistent; as when a man throweth his goods into the sea for fear the ship should sink, he doth it nevertheless very willingly, and may refuse to do it if he will: it is therefore the action of one that was free; so a man sometimes pays his debt, only for fear of imprisonment, which because nobody hindered him from detaining, was the action of a man at liberty. And generally all actions which men do in commonwealths, for fear of the law, are actions which the doers had liberty to omit.

Liberty and necessity are consistent, as in the water that hath not only liberty, but a necessity of descending by the channel; so likewise in the actions which men voluntarily do: which, because they proceed from their will, proceed from liberty; and yet, because every act of man's will, and every desire and inclination proceedeth from some cause, and that from another cause, in a continual chain, whose first link is in the hand of God the first of all causes, proceed from necessity. So that to him that could see the connection of those causes, the necessity of all men's voluntary actions would appear manifest. And therefore God, that seeth and disposeth all things, seeth also that the liberty of man in doing what he will, is accompanied with the necessity of doing that which God will, and no more nor less. For though men may do many things which God does not command, nor is therefore author of them; yet they can have no passion nor appetite to anything, of which appetite God's will is not the cause. And did not His will assure the necessity of man's will, and consequently of all that on man's will dependeth, the liberty of men would be a contradiction and impediment to the omnipotence and liberty of God. And this shall suffice, as to the matter in hand, of that natural liberty, which only is properly called liberty.

But as men, for the attaining of peace, and conservation of themselves thereby, have made an artificial man, which we call a commonwealth; so also have they made artificial chains, called *civil laws*, which they themselves, by mutual covenants, have fastened at one end to the lips of that man, or assembly, to whom they have given the sovereign power; and at the other end to their own ears. These bonds, in their own nature but weak, may nevertheless be made to hold, by the danger, though not by the difficulty of breaking them.

In relation to these bonds only it is that I am to speak now of the liberty of subjects. For seeing there is no commonwealth in the world wherein there be rules enough set down for the regulating of all the actions and words of men, as being a thing impossible; it followeth necessarily, that in all kinds of actions by the laws pretermitted, men have the liberty of doing what their own reasons shall suggest, for the most profitable to themselves. For if we take liberty in the proper sense for corporal liberty, that is to say, freedom from chains and prison, it were very absurd for men to clamor as they do for the liberty they so manifestly enjoy.

Again, if we take liberty for an exemption from laws, it is no less absurd for men to demand as they do that liberty by which all other men may be masters of their lives. And yet, as absurd as it is, this is it they demand; not knowing that the laws are of no power to protect them, without a sword in the hands of a man, or men, to cause those laws to be put in execution. The liberty of a subject lieth therefore only in those things which in regulating their actions, the sovereign hath pretermitted: such as is the liberty to buy and sell, and otherwise contract with one another; to choose their own abode, their own diet, their own trade of life, and institute their children as they themselves think fit; and the like.

QUESTIONS FOR REFLECTION

1. How does Hobbes characterize human equality?
2. Why does Hobbes contend that there is no justice or injustice in the state of nature? Do you find convincing Hobbes's claim that justice exists after the creation of the state? Why or why not?
3. Why does Hobbes claim that there are some rights which no person can transfer? What practical consequences, according to Hobbes, follow from this conclusion? What is your view?

7. JOHN LOCKE

John Locke (1632–1704), the English philosopher and political theorist, was educated at Westminster School in London and then Oxford University, where he received his bachelor's degree in 1656 and his master's degree in 1657. Beginning in 1675 Locke spent several years living in France and later in Holland, returning to England after the Revolution of 1689 when William and Mary assumed the English throne.

Locke's two greatest philosophical works were published in 1690—his treatise on metaphysics and epistemology, *An Essay Concerning Human Understanding*, and his political analysis, *Two Treatises of Government*. The *First Treatise* is intended primarily as a critique of the doctrine of divine right (i.e., the theory of government that holds that a sovereign receives the right to rule directly from God and not from the people) defended by the royalist Sir Robert Filmer. The *Second Treatise* advances Locke's positive theory concerning the origin, extent, and end of civil government. Locke, like Hobbes, begins his account with a description of the pre-political state of nature, but in Locke's view the state of nature is not "nasty" and "brutish" as Hobbes believed. Instead, Locke contends that the actions of people are controlled by natural law, defined as the manifestation of human reason, which restricts the egoism of pure self-interest and promotes more sociable forms of conduct.

In the state of nature, according to Locke, all persons are obligated to preserve their lives, their liberty and their possessions—Locke's three basic natural rights to life, liberty, and property—and, moreover, to assist others in doing the same. Inevitably, however, the difficulties of enacting the natural law given the disorder found in the state of nature engenders a desire to form a government. Through the mechanism of the social contract, a government is created when everyone agrees to transfer their rights to execute the law of nature to a political authority.

An important difference between Hobbes and Locke emerges at this point. For Locke, the voluntary transfer of natural right to the sovereign is partial rather than absolute, as it is for Hobbes. People consent to obey the government only insofar as it effectively protects and guarantees their individual rights, thereby enhancing their freedom; if it fails to do so, or actively violates their rights, the people are released from all ties of obedience and may rightfully overthrow that government. Locke therefore increases the natural rights recognized in social contract theory and uses those rights to establish the supremacy of the people and to limit the authority of the government. From this perspective, Locke supplies many of the ingredients for the political theory of liberalism.

Text—The Second Treatise of Government (1690)

Reprinted from Two Treatises of Government, *Book II. London: A. Millar, 1764.*

CHAPTER 2: OF THE STATE OF NATURE

4. To understand political power aright, and derive it from its original, we must consider what estate all men are naturally in, and that is, a state of perfect freedom to order their actions, and dispose of their possessions and persons as they think fit, within the bounds of the law of Nature, without asking leave or depending upon the will of any other man.

A state also of equality, wherein all the power and jurisdiction is reciprocal, no one having more than another, there being nothing more evident than that creatures of the same species and rank, promiscuously born to all the same advantages of Nature, and the use of the same faculties, should also be equal one amongst another, without subordination or subjection, unless the lord and master of them all should, by any manifest declaration of his will, set one above another, and confer on him, by an evident and clear appointment, an undoubted right to dominion and sovereignty....

6. But though this be a state of liberty, yet it is not a state of license; though man in that state have an uncontrollable liberty to dispose of his person or possessions, yet he has not liberty to destroy himself, or so much as any creature in his possession, but where some nobler use than its bare preservation calls for it. The state of Nature has a law of Nature to govern it, which obliges every one, and reason, which is that law, teaches all mankind who will but consult it, that being all equal and independent, no

one ought to harm another in his life, health, liberty or possessions; for men being all the workmanship of one omnipotent and infinitely wise Maker; all the servants of one sovereign Master, sent into the world by His order and about His business; they are His property, whose workmanship they are made to last during His, not one another's pleasure. And, being furnished with like faculties, sharing all in one community of Nature, there cannot be supposed any such subordination among us that may authorize us to destroy one another, as if we were made for one another's uses, as the inferior ranks of creatures are for ours. Every one as he is bound to preserve himself, and not to quit his station willfully, so by the like reason, when his own preservation comes not in competition, ought he as much as he can to preserve the rest of mankind, and not unless it be to do justice on an offender, take away or impair the life, or what tends to the preservation of the life, the liberty, health, limb, or goods of another.

7. And that all men may be restrained from invading others' rights, and from doing hurt to one another, and the law of Nature be observed, which willeth the peace and preservation of all mankind, the execution of the law of Nature is in that state put into every man's hands, whereby every one has a right to punish the transgressors of that law to such a degree as may hinder its violation. For the law of Nature would, as all other laws that concern men in this world, be in vain if there were nobody that in the state of Nature had a power to execute that law, and thereby preserve the innocent and restrain offenders; and if any one in the state of Nature may punish another for any evil he has done, every one may do so. For in that state of perfect equality, where naturally there is no superiority or jurisdiction of one over another, what any may do in prosecution of that law, every one must needs have a right to do.

CHAPTER 4: OF SLAVERY

21. The natural liberty of man is to be free from any superior power on earth, and not to be under the will or legislative authority of man, but to have only the law of Nature for his rule. The liberty of man in society is to be under no other legislative power

but that established by consent in the commonwealth, nor under the dominion of any will, or the restraint of any law, but what that legislative shall enact according to the trust put in it. Freedom, then, is not what Sir Robert Filmer tells us: "A liberty for every one to do what he lists, to live as he pleases, and not to be tied by any laws"; but freedom of men under government is to have a standing rule to live by, common to every one of that society, and made by the legislative power erected in it....

CHAPTER 5: OF PROPERTY

... 27. Though the earth and all inferior creatures be common to all men, yet every man has a "property" in his own "person." This nobody has any right to but himself. The "labour" of his body and the "work" of his hands, we may say, are properly his. Whatsoever, then, he removes out of the state that Nature hath provided and left it in, he hath mixed his labour with it, and joined to it something that is his own, and thereby makes it his property. It being by him removed from the common state Nature placed it in, it hath by this labour something annexed to it that excludes the common right of other men. For this "labour" being the unquestionable property of the labourer, no man but he can have a right to what that is once joined to, at least where there is enough, and as good left in common for others....

CHAPTER 7: OF POLITICAL OR CIVIL SOCIETY

... 87. Man being born, as has been proved, with a title to perfect freedom and an uncontrolled enjoyment of all the rights and privileges of the law of Nature, equally with any other man, or number of men in the world, hath by nature a power not only to preserve his property—that is, his life, liberty, and estate, against the injuries and attempts of other men, but to judge of and punish the breaches of that law in others, as he is persuaded the offense deserves, even with death itself, in crimes where the heinousness of the fact, in his opinion, requires it. But because no political society can be, nor subsist, without having in itself the power to preserve the property, and in order thereunto punish the offenses of all those of that society, there, and there only, is political society where every one of the members hath quitted this natural power, resigned it up into the hands of the community in all cases that exclude him not from appealing for protection to the law established by it. And thus all private judgment of every particular member being excluded, the community comes to be umpire, and by understanding indifferent rules and men authorized by the community for their execution, decides all the differences that may happen between any members of that society concerning any matter of right, and punishes those offenses which any member hath committed against the society with such penalties as the law has established; whereby it is easy to discern who are, and are not, in political society together. Those who are united into one body, and have a common established law and judicature to appeal to, with authority to decide controversies between them and punish offenders, are in civil society one with another; but those who have no such common appeal, I mean on earth, are still in the state of Nature, each being where there is no other, judge for himself and executioner; which is, as I have before showed it, the perfect state of Nature....

CHAPTER 8: OF THE BEGINNING OF POLITICAL SOCIETIES

95. Men being, as has been said, by nature all free, equal, and independent, no one can be put out of this estate and subjected to the political power of another without his own consent, which is done by agreeing with other men, to join and unite into a community for their comfortable, safe, and peaceable living, one amongst another, in a secure enjoyment of their properties, and a greater security against any that are not of it. This any number of men may do, because it injures not the freedom of the rest; they are left, as they were, in the liberty of the state of Nature. When any number of men have so consented to make one community or government, they are thereby presently incorporated, and make one body politic, wherein the majority have a right to act and

conclude the rest.

96. For, when any number of men have, by the consent of every individual, made a community, they have thereby made that community one body, with a power to act as one body, which is only by the will and determination of the majority... and so everyone is bound by that consent to be concluded by the majority....

99. Whosoever, therefore, out of a state of Nature unite into a community, must be understood to give up all the power necessary to the ends for which they unite into society to the majority of the community, unless they expressly agreed in any number greater than the majority. And this is done by barely agreeing to unite into one political society, which is all the compact that is, or needs be, between the individuals that enter into or make up a commonwealth. And thus, that which begins and actually constitutes any political society is nothing but the consent of any number of freemen capable of majority, to unite and incorporate into such a society. And this is that, and that only, which did or could give beginning to any lawful government in the world....

CHAPTER 9: ON THE ENDS OF POLITICAL SOCIETY AND GOVERNMENT

123. If man in the state of Nature be so free as has been said, if he be absolute lord of his own person and possessions, equal to the greatest and subject to nobody, why will he part with his freedom, this empire, and subject himself to the dominion and control of any other power? To which it is obvious to answer, that though in the state of Nature he hath such a right, yet the enjoyment of it is very uncertain and constantly exposed to the invasion of others; for all being kings as much as he, every man his equal, and the greater part no strict observers of equity and justice, the enjoyment of the property he has in this state is very unsafe, very insecure. This makes him willing to quit this condition which, however free, is full of fears and continual dangers; and it is not without reason that he seeks out and is willing to join in society with others who are already united, or have a mind to unite for the mutual preservation of their lives, liberties and

estates, which I call by the general name—property.

124. The great and chief end, therefore, of men uniting into commonwealths, and putting themselves under government, is the preservation of their property; to which in the state of Nature there are many things wanting.

Firstly, there wants an established, settled, known law, received and allowed by common consent to be the standard of right and wrong, and the common measure to decide all controversies between them. For though the law of Nature be plain and intelligible to all rational creatures, yet men, being biased by their interest, as well as ignorant for want of study of it, are not apt to allow of it as a law binding to them in the application of it to their particular cases.

125. Secondly, in the state of Nature there wants a known and indifferent judge, with authority to determine all differences according to the established law. For every one in that state being both judge and executioner of the law of Nature, men being partial to themselves, passion and revenge is very apt to carry them too far, and with too much heat in their own cases, as well as negligence and unconcernedness, make them too remiss in other men's.

126. Thirdly, in the state of Nature there often wants power to back and support the sentence when right, and to give it due execution. They who by any injustice offended will seldom fail where they are able by force to make good their injustice. Such resistance many times makes the punishment dangerous, and frequently destructive to those who attempt it.

127. Thus mankind, notwithstanding all the privileges of the state of Nature, being but in an ill condition while they remain in it are quickly driven into society. Hence it comes to pass, that we seldom find any number of men live any time together in this state. The inconveniencies that they are therein exposed to by the irregular and uncertain exercise of the power every man has of punishing the transgressions of others, make them take sanctuary under the established laws of government, and therein seek the preservation of their property. It is this makes them so willingly give up every one his single power of punishing to be exer-

cised by such alone as shall be appointed to it amongst them, and by such rules as the community, or those authorized by them to that purpose, shall agree on. And in this we have the original right and rise of both the legislative and executive power as well as of the governments and societies themselves.

128. For in the state of Nature, to omit the liberty he has of innocent delights, a man has two powers. The first is to do whatsoever he thinks fit for the preservation of himself and others within the permission of the law of Nature; by which law, common to them all, he and all the rest of mankind are one community, make up one society distinct from all other creatures, and were it not for the corruption and viciousness of degenerate men, there would be no need of any other, no necessity that men should separate from this great and natural community, and associate into lesser combinations. The other power a man has in the state of Nature is the power to punish the crimes committed against that law. Both these he gives up when he joins in a private, if I may so call it, or particular political society, and incorporates into any commonwealth separate from the rest of mankind.

129. The first power—viz., of doing whatsoever he thought fit for the preservation of himself and the rest of mankind, he gives up to be regulated by laws made by the society, so far forth as the preservation of himself and the rest of that society shall require; which laws of the society in many things confine the liberty he had by the law of Nature.

130. Secondly, the power of punishing he wholly gives up, and engages his natural force, which he might before employ in the execution of the law of Nature, by his own single authority, as he thought fit, to assist the executive power of the society as the law thereof shall require. For being now in a new state, wherein he is to enjoy many conveniencies from the labor, assistance, and society of others in the same community, as well as protection from its whole strength, he is to part also with as much of his natural liberty, in providing for himself, as the good, prosperity, and safety of the society shall require, which is not only necessary but just, since the other members of the society do the like.

131. But though men when they enter into society give up the equality, liberty, and executive power they had in the state of

Nature in the hands of the society, to be so far disposed of by the legislative as the good of the society shall require, yet it being only with an intention in every one the better to preserve himself, his liberty and property (for no rational creature can be supposed to change his condition with an intention to be worse), the power of the society or legislative constituted by them can never be supposed to extend farther than the common good, but is obliged to secure every one's property by providing against those three defects above mentioned that made the state of Nature so unsafe and uneasy. And so, whoever has the legislative or supreme power of any commonwealth is bound to govern by established standing laws, promulgated and known to the people, and not by extemporary decrees, by indifferent and upright judges, who are to decide controversies by those laws; and to employ the force of the community at home only in the execution of such laws or abroad to prevent or redress foreign injuries and secure the community from inroads and invasion. And all this to be directed to no other end but the peace, safety, and public good of the people.

QUESTIONS FOR REFLECTION

1. Locke's emphasis on natural rights focuses on those to life, liberty, and property. What relationship do those rights have to each other? Do you think those rights are sufficient for establishing and maintaining civil society?

2. Why does Locke maintain that people must surrender their natural right to punish wrongdoers when they form a political community?

3. Locke contends that people do not surrender their natural rights when they establish a political society and government; rather, they entrust the government with the task of securing and protecting their rights. What benefits do you think follow from accepting the premise that certain rights held by individuals are unalienable? What difficulties might arise from Locke's position?

8. JEAN-JACQUES ROUSSEAU

Born in Geneva, Jean-Jacques Rousseau (1712–1778) established himself as one of the greatest intellectuals of the Enlightenment while living a complex and sometimes difficult life. An orphan at the age of ten, Rousseau ran away from the home of his aunt when he was sixteen. Rousseau later lived in Paris and then served as secretary to the French ambassador to Venice. In 1750, Rousseau entered an essay contest sponsored by the Academy of Dijon and won first prize for his essay *Discourse on the Arts and Sciences*, in which he argues that modern civilization corrupts rather than improves human morals. Entering another contest of the Academy of Dijon in 1754, Rousseau published a second major essay, the *Discourse on the Origin of Inequality*. Here Rousseau argues that the natural goodness and compassion of human beings have been deformed by modern culture, in particular by social and political institutions devised around inequalities in wealth and power. In 1762 Rousseau published both his book on education, *Emile*, and his primary political treatise, *The Social Contract*.

In *The Social Contract* Rousseau attempts to explain why it is that we accept the authority of society. Following both Hobbes and Locke, Rousseau draws upon the idea of the social contract in order to demonstrate how society can be formed without involuntary domination. In the state of nature, Rousseau maintains, individuals are naturally free. The aim of forming a political community, which is accomplished by individuals joining together into a contract, is to enable people to perfect their natural virtues and exercise their basic right to individual freedom, through the law and security provided by an artificial civil society. The terms of the voluntary agreement establish the manner and scope of exercising political authority. While sovereign authority does exist under the contract and must be obeyed, because authority is based on the freely given consent of the people it recognizes the equality and autonomy that all persons rightly deserve—thereby removing the illegitimate "chains" of political oppression.

Rousseau's theory offers an inspiring vision of an egalitarian social life in which all persons are free since everyone is subjected only to a rule of law that is self-imposed through the "general will" of the community. By means of the social contract, individuals exchange their particular natural freedom for a civil liberty defined by the good of the entire society. In this way Rousseau presents a theory of the state that places more emphasis on the collective dimension of human existence than the individualism found in the theories of Hobbes and Locke. Rousseau's ideals of a direct democracy that reflects the general will of all the citizenry influenced the French revolutionary government.

Text—The Social Contract (1762)

Reprinted from The Social Contract, *translated by Henry J. Tozer, third edition. London: Swan Sonnenschein & Co., 1902.*

BOOK I

Chapter 1: Subject of the First Book

Man is born free, and everywhere he is in chains. Many a one believes himself the master of others, and yet he is a greater slave than they. How has this change come about? I do not know. What can render it legitimate? I believe that I can settle this question.

If I considered only force and the results that proceed from it, I should say that so long as a people is compelled to obey and does obey, it does well; but that, so soon as it can shake off the yoke and does shake it off, it does better; for, if men recover their freedom by virtue of the same right by which it was taken away, either they are justified in resuming it, or there was no justification for depriving them of it. But the social order is a sacred right which serves as a foundation for all others. This right, however, does not come from nature. It is therefore based on conventions....

Chapter 4: Slavery

Since no man has any natural authority over his fellow-men, and since force is not the source of right, conventions remain as the basis of all lawful authority among men.

If an individual, says Grotius, can alienate his liberty and become the slave of a master, why should not a whole people be able to alienate theirs, and become subject to a king? In this there are many equivocal terms requiring explanation; but let us confine ourselves to the word *alienate*. To alienate is to give or sell. Now, a man who becomes another's slave does not give himself; he sells himself at the very least for his subsistence. But why does a nation sell itself? So far from a king supplying his subjects with their subsistence, he draws his from them; and, according to Rabelais, a king does not live on a little. Do subjects, then, give up their persons on condition that their property also shall be taken? I do not see what is left for them to keep.

It will be said that the despot secures to his subjects civil peace. Be it so; but what do they gain by that, if the wars which his ambition brings upon them, together with his insatiable greed and the vexations of his administration, harass them more than their own dissensions would? What do they gain by it if this tranquillity is itself one of their miseries? Men live tranquilly also in dungeons; is that enough to make them contented there? The Greeks confined in the cave of the Cyclops lived peacefully until their turn came to be devoured.

To say that a man gives himself for nothing is to say what is absurd and inconceivable; such an act is illegitimate and invalid, for the simple reason that he who performs it is not in his right mind. To say the same thing of the whole nation is to suppose a nation of fools; and madness does not confer rights.

Even if each person could alienate himself, he could not alienate his children; they are born free men; their liberty belongs to them, and no one has a right to dispose of it except themselves. Before they have come to years of discretion, the father can, in their name, stipulate conditions for their preservation and welfare, but not surrender them irrevocably and unconditionally; for such a gift is contrary to the ends of nature, and exceeds the rights of paternity. In order, then, that an arbitrary government might be legitimate, it would be necessary that the people in each generation should have the option of accepting or rejecting it; but in that case such a government would no longer be arbitrary.

To renounce one's liberty is to renounce one's quality as a man, the rights and also the duties of humanity. For him who renounces everything there is no possible compensation. Such a renunciation is incompatible with man's nature, for to take away all freedom from his will is to take away all morality from his actions. In short, a convention which stipulates absolute authority on the one side and unlimited obedience on the other is vain and contradictory. Is it not clear that we are under no obligations whatsoever towards a man from whom we have a right to demand everything? And does not this single condition, without equivalent, without exchange, involve the nullity of the act? For what right would my slave have against me, since all that he has belongs to me? His rights being mine, this right of me against myself is a meaningless phrase....

Thus, in whatever way we regard things, the right of slavery is invalid, not only because it is illegitimate, but because it is absurd and meaningless. These terms, *slavery* and *right*, are contradictory and mutually exclusive. Whether addressed by a man to a man, or by a man to a nation, such a speech as this will always be equally foolish: "I make an agreement with you wholly at your expense and wholly for my benefit, and I shall observe it as long as I please, while you shall also observe it as long as I please."

Chapter 8: The Civil State

The passage from the state of nature to the civil state produces in man a very remarkable change, by substituting in his conduct justice for instinct, and by giving his actions the moral quality that they previously lacked. It is only when the voice of duty succeeds physical impulse, and law succeeds appetite, that man, who till then had regarded only himself, sees that he is obliged to act on other principles, and to consult his reason before listening to his inclinations. Although, in this state, he is deprived of many advantages that he derives from nature, he acquires equally great ones in return; his faculties are exercised and developed; his ideas are expanded; his feelings are ennobled; his whole soul is exalted to such a degree that, if the abuses of this new condition did not often degrade him below that from which he has emerged, he ought to bless without ceasing the happy moment that released him from it for ever, and transformed him from a stupid and ignorant animal into an intelligent being and a man.

Let us reduce this whole balance to terms easy to compare. What man loses by the social contract is his natural liberty and an unlimited right to anything which tempts him and which he is able to attain: what he gains is civil liberty and property in all that he possesses. In order that we may not be mistaken about these compensations, we must clearly distinguish natural liberty, which is limited only by the powers of the individual, from civil liberty, which is limited by the general will; and possession, which is nothing but the result of force or the right of first occupancy, from property, which can be based only on a positive title.

Besides the preceding, we might add to the acquisitions of the civil state moral freedom, which alone renders man truly master of himself; for the impulse of mere appetite is slavery, while obedience to a self-prescribed law is liberty. But I have already said too much on this head, and the philosophical meaning of the term liberty does not belong to my present subject....

BOOK II

Chapter 4: The Limits of the Sovereign Power

If the state or city is nothing but a moral person, the life of which consists in the union of its members, and if the most important of its cares is that of self-preservation, it needs a universal and compulsive force to move and dispose of every part in the manner most expedient for the whole. As nature gives every man an absolute power over all his limbs, the social pact gives the body politic an absolute power over all its members; and it is this same power which, when directed by the general will, bears, as I said, the name of sovereignty.

But besides the public person, we have to consider the private persons who compose it, and whose life and liberty are naturally independent of it. The question, then, is to distinguish clearly between the respective rights of the citizens and of the sovereign, as well as between the duties which the former have to fulfill in their capacity as subjects and the natural rights which they ought to enjoy in their character as men.

It is admitted that whatever part of his power, property, and liberty each one alienates by the social compact is only that part of the whole of which the use is important to the community; but we must also admit that the sovereign alone is judge of what is important.

All the services that a citizen can render to the state he owes to it as soon as the sovereign demands them; but the sovereign, on its part, cannot impose on its subjects any burden which is useless to the community; it cannot even wish to do so, for, by the law of reason, just as by the law of nature, nothing is done without a cause.

The engagements which bind us to the social body are obligatory only because they are mutual; and their nature is such that in fulfilling them we cannot work for others without also working for ourselves. Why is the general will always right, and why do all invariably desire the prosperity of each, unless it is because there is no one but appropriates to himself this word each and thinks of himself in voting on behalf of all? This proves that equality of rights and the notion of justice that it produces are derived from the preference which each gives to himself and consequently from man's nature; that the general will, to be truly such, should be so in its object as well as in its essence; that it ought to proceed from all in order to be applicable to all; and that it loses its natural rectitude when it tends to some individual and determinate object, because in that case, judging of what is unknown to us, we have no true principle of equity to guide us.

Indeed, so soon as a particular fact or right is in question with regard to a point which has not been regulated by an anterior general convention, the matter becomes contentious; it is a process in which the private persons interested are one of the parties and the public the other, but in which I perceive neither the law which must be followed, nor the judge who should decide. It would be ridiculous in such a case to wish to refer the matter for an express decision of the general will, which can be nothing but the decision of one of the parties, and which, consequently, is for the other party only a will that is foreign, partial, and inclined on such an occasion to injustice as well as liable to error. Therefore, just as a particular will cannot represent the general will, the general will in turn changes its nature when it has a particular end, and cannot, as general, decide about either a person or a fact. When the people of Athens, for instance, elected or deposed their chiefs, decreed honors to one, imposed penalties on another, and by multitudes of particular decrees exercised indiscriminately all the functions of government, the people no longer had any general will properly so called; they no longer acted as a sovereign power, but as magistrates. This will appear contrary to common ideas, but I must be allowed time to expound my own.

From this we must understand that what generalizes the will is not so much the number of voices as the common interest which unites them; for, under this system, each necessarily submits to the conditions which he imposes on others—an admirable union of interest and justice, which gives to the deliberations of the community a spirit of equity that seems to disappear in the discussion of any private affair, for want of a common interest to unite and identify the ruling principle of the judge with that of the party.

By whatever path we return to our principle we always arrive at the same conclusion, viz. that the social compact establishes among the citizens such an equality that they all pledge themselves under the same conditions and ought all to enjoy the same rights. Thus, by the nature of the compact, every act of sovereignty, that is, every authentic act of the general will, binds or favors equally all the citizens; so that the sovereign knows only the body of the nation, and distinguishes none of those that compose it. What, then, is an act of sovereignty properly so called? It is not an agreement between a superior and an inferior, but an agreement of the body with each of its members; a lawful agreement, because it has the social contract as its foundation; equitable, because it is common to all; useful, because it can have no other object than the general welfare; and stable, because it has the public force and the supreme power as a guarantee. So long as the subjects submit only to such conventions, they obey no one, but simply their own will; and to ask how far the respective rights of the sovereign and citizens extend is to ask up to what point the latter can make engagements among themselves, each with all and all with each.

Thus we see that the sovereign power, wholly absolute, wholly sacred, and wholly inviolable as it is, does not, and cannot, pass the limits of general conventions, and that every man can fully dispose of what is left to him of his property and liberty by these conventions; so that the sovereign never has a right to burden one subject more than another, because then the matter becomes particular and his power is no longer competent.

These distinctions once admitted, so untrue is it that in the social contract there is on the part of individuals any real renunciation, that their situation, as a result of this contract, is in reality preferable to what it was before, and that, instead of an alienation, they have only made an advantageous exchange of an uncertain and precarious mode of existence for a better and more assured one, of natural independence for liberty, of the power to injure others for their own safety, and of their strength, which others might overcome, for a right which the special union renders inviolable.

Questions for Reflection

1. Rousseau insists that slavery and rights are contradictory and mutually exclusive. Why does he say that? Do you agree or disagree?

2. What sorts of arguments does Rousseau make to show the connection between the rights of individuals and their obligations to others?

3. Rousseau, much like Locke, argues that the primary benefit of the social contract is the enhancement of liberty, while Hobbes contends that the primary benefit is social stability. Which conclusion do you agree with? Is the type of freedom advocated by Rousseau the same as that endorsed by Locke or Hobbes? If not, how do they differ?

9. EDMUND BURKE

Born in Ireland, the philosopher and statesman Edmund Burke (1729-1797) earned degrees in classics and law before becoming a member of the House of Commons in 1765. Burke's political ideas are considered both practical and conservative. His most famous work, *Reflections on the Revolution in France*, was published in 1790 following the French Revolution of the previous year. In this book, Burke denounces the claims to absolute liberty and universal rights voiced by the revolutionaries as abstract and dangerous principles, and argues instead that "real" rights must always be restricted and subordinated to the need for social order and stable government. For Burke, liberty also has to be restrained so that the wisdom of established custom can support prudent social and political institutions.

Text—Reflections on the Revolution in France (1790)

Reprinted from Reflections on the Revolution in France. *London: J. Dodsley, 1790.*

The True Principle of Social Stability

(a) Leveling is a False Principle of Equality

Believe me, Sir, those who attempt to level, never equalize. In all societies, consisting of various descriptions of citizens, some description must be uppermost. The levelers, therefore, only change and pervert the natural order of things; they load the edifice of society by setting up in the air what the solidity of the structure requires to be on the ground. The association of tailors and carpenters, of which the republic (of Paris, for instance) is composed, cannot be equal to the situation into which by the worst of usurpations—an usurpation on the prerogatives of nature—you attempt to force on them.

The Chancellor of France, at the opening of the states, said, in a tone of oratorical flourish, that all occupations were honorable. If he meant only that no honest employment was disgraceful, he would not have gone beyond the truth. But in asserting that anything is honorable, we imply some distinction in its favor. The occupation of a hairdresser or a working tallow-chandler cannot be a matter of honor to any person—to say nothing of a number of other more servile employments. Such descriptions of men ought not to suffer oppression from the state; but the state suffers oppression if such as they, either individually or collectively, are permitted to rule. In this you think you are combating prejudice, but you are at war with nature....

The Consequences for France of Having Abandoned These True Principles

It is said that twenty-four millions ought to prevail over two hundred thousand. True; if the constitution of a kingdom be a problem of arithmetic. This sort of discourse does well enough with the lamppost for its second; to men who *may* reason calmly, it is ridiculous. The will of the many and their interest must very often differ, and great will be the difference when they make an evil choice. A government of five hundred country attorneys and obscure curates is not good for twenty-four millions of men, though it were chosen by forty-eight millions, nor is it the better for being guided by a dozen of persons of quality who have betrayed their trust in order to obtain that power. At present, you seem in everything to have strayed out of the high road of nature....

The True Principles of Government

(a) The Erroneous Concept of the Rights of Men

It is no wonder, therefore, that with these ideas of everything in their constitution and government at home, either in church or state, as illegitimate and usurped, or at best as a vain mockery, they look abroad with an eager and passionate enthusiasm. Whilst they are possessed by these notions, it is vain to talk to them of the practice of their ancestors, the fundamental laws of their country, the fixed form of a constitution whose merits are confirmed by the solid test of long experience and an increasing public strength and national prosperity. They despise experience as the wisdom of unlettered men; and as for the rest, they have wrought underground a mine that will blow up, at one grand explosion, all examples of antiquity, all precedents, charters, and acts of parliament. They have "the rights of men." Against these there can be no prescription, against these no agreement is binding; these admit no temperament and no compromise; anything withheld from their full demand is so much of fraud and injustice. Against these their rights of men let no government look for security in the length of its continuance, or in the justice and lenity of its administration. The objections of these speculatists, if its forms do not quadrate with their theories, are as valid against such an old and beneficent government as against the most violent tyranny or the greenest usurpation. They are always at issue with governments, not on a question of abuse, but a question of competency and a question of title. I have nothing to say to the clumsy subtlety of their political metaphysics. Let them be their amusement in the schools.... But let them not break prison to burst like a Levanter, to sweep the earth with their hurricane and to break up the fountains of the great deep to overwhelm us.

(b) The True Concept of the Rights of Men

Far am I from denying in theory, full as far is my heart from withholding in practice (if I were of power to give or to withhold) the *real* rights of men. In denying their false claims of right, I do not mean to injure those which are real, and are such as their pretended rights would totally destroy. If civil society be made for the advantage of man, all the advantages for which it is made become his right. It is an institution of beneficence; and law itself is only beneficence acting by a rule. Men have a right to live by that rule; they have a right to do justice, as between their fellows, whether their fellows are in public function or in ordinary occupation. They have a right to the fruits of their industry and to the means of making their industry fruitful. They have a right to the acquisitions of their parents, to the nourishment and improvement of their offspring, to instruction in life, and to consolation in death. Whatever each man can separately do, without trespassing upon others, he has a right to do for himself; and he has a right to a fair portion of all which society, with all its combinations of skill and force, can do in his favor. In this partnership all men have equal rights, but not to equal things. He that has but five shillings in the partnership has as good a right to it as he that has five hundred pounds has to his larger proportion. But he has not a right to an equal dividend in the product of the joint stock; and as to the share of power, authority, and direction which each individual ought to have in the management of the state, that I must deny to be amongst the direct original rights of man in civil society, for I have in my contemplation the civil social man, and no other. It is a thing to be settled by convention.

If civil society be the offspring of convention, that convention must be its law. That convention must limit and modify all the descriptions of constitution which are formed under it. Every sort of legislative, judicial, or executory power are its creatures. They can have no being in any other state of things; and how can any man claim under the conventions of civil society rights which do not so much as suppose its existence—rights which are absolutely repugnant to it? One of the first motives to civil society, and which becomes one of its fundamental rules, is that no man should be judge in his own cause. By this each person has at once divested himself of the first fundamental right of uncovenanted man, that is, to judge for himself and to assert his own cause. He abdicates all right to be his own governor. He inclusively, in a great measure, abandons the right of self-defense, the first law of nature. Men cannot enjoy the rights of an uncivil and of a civil state together. That he may obtain justice, he gives up his right of determining what it is in points the most essential to him. That he may secure some liberty, he makes a surrender in trust of the whole of it.

(c) The True Nature of Government

Government is not made in virtue of natural rights, which may and do exist in total independence of it, and exist in much greater clearness and in a much greater degree of abstract perfection; but their abstract perfection is their practical defect. By having a right to everything they want everything. Government is a contrivance of human wisdom to provide for human *wants*. Men have a right that these wants should be provided for by this wisdom. Among these wants is to be reckoned the want, out of civil society, of a sufficient restraint upon their passions. Society requires not only that the passions of individuals should be subjected, but that even in the mass and body, as well as in the individuals, the inclinations of men should frequently be thwarted, their will controlled, and their passions brought into subjection. This can only be done *by a power out of themselves*, and not, in the exercise of its function, subject to that will and to those passions which it is its office to bridle and subdue. In this sense the restraints on men, as well as their liberties, are to be reckoned among their rights. But as the liberties and the restrictions vary with times and circumstances and admit to infinite modifications, they cannot be settled upon any abstract rule; and nothing is so foolish as to discuss them upon that principle.

The moment you abate anything from the full rights of men, each to govern himself, and suffer any artificial, positive limitation upon those rights, from that moment the whole organization of government becomes a consideration of convenience. This it is which makes the constitution of a state and the due distribution of its powers a matter of the most delicate and complicated skill. It requires a deep knowledge of human nature and human necessities, and of the things which facilitate or obstruct the various ends which are to be pursued by the mechanism of civil institutions. The state is to have recruits to its strength, and remedies to its distempers. What is the use of discussing a man's abstract right to food or medicine? The question is upon the method of procuring and administering them. In that deliberation I shall always advise to call in the aid of the farmer and the physician rather than the professor of metaphysics.

The science of constructing a commonwealth, or renovating it, or reforming it, is, like every other experimental science, not to be taught *a priori*. Nor is it a short experience that can instruct us in that practical science, because the real effects of moral causes are not always immediate; but that which in the first instance is prejudicial may be excellent in its remoter operation, and its excellence may arise even from the ill effects it produces in the beginning. The reverse also happens: and very plausible schemes, with very pleasing commencements, have often shameful and lamentable conclusions. In states there are often some obscure and almost latent causes, things which appear at first view of little moment, on which a very great part of its prosperity or adversity may most essentially depend. The science of government being therefore so practical in itself and intended for such practical purposes—a matter which requires experience, and even more experience than any person can gain in his whole life, however sagacious and observing he may be—it is with infinite caution that any man ought to venture upon pulling down an edifice which has answered in any tolerable degree for ages the common purposes of society, or on building it up again without having models and patterns of approved utility before his eyes.

(d) The Principle of the Law of Nature not Applicable to a Complex Society

These metaphysic rights entering into common life, like rays of light which pierce into a dense medium, are by the laws of nature refracted from their straight line. Indeed, in the gross and complicated mass of human passions and concerns the primitive rights of men undergo such a variety of refractions and reflections that it becomes absurd to talk of them as if they continued in the simplicity of their original direction. The nature of man is intricate; the objects of society are of the greatest possible complexity; and, therefore, no simple disposition or direction of power can be suitable either to man's nature or to the quality of his affairs. When I hear the simplicity of contrivance aimed at and boasted of in any new political constitutions, I am at no loss to decide that the artificers are grossly ignorant of their trade or totally negligent of their duty. The simple governments are fundamentally defective, to say no worse of them. If you were to contemplate society in but one point of view, all these simple modes of polity are infinitely captivating. In effect each would answer its single end much more perfectly than the more complex is able to attain all its complex purposes. But it is better that the whole should be imperfectly and anomalously answered than that, while some parts are provided for with great exactness, others might be totally neglected or perhaps materially injured by the overcare of a favorite member.

The pretended rights of these theorists are all extremes; and in proportion as they are metaphysically true, they are morally and politically false. The rights of men are in a sort of middle, incapable of definition, but not impossible to be discerned. The rights of men in governments are their advantages; and these are often in balances between differences of good, in compromises sometimes between good and evil, and sometimes between evil and evil. Political reason is a computing principle: adding, subtracting, multiplying, and dividing, morally and not metaphysically, or mathematically, true moral denominations.

By these theorists the right of the people is almost always sophistically confounded with their power. The body of the community, whenever it can come to act, can meet with no effectual resistance; but till power and right are the same, the whole body of them has no right inconsistent with virtue, and the first of all virtues, prudence. Men have no right to what is not reasonable and to what is not for their benefit.

QUESTIONS FOR REFLECTION

1. What does Burke mean when he states that government is founded on human "wants" rather than on human or natural "rights"?

2. Why does Burke claim that "the restraints on men, as well as their liberties, are to be reckoned among their rights"? Do you agree with this claim?

3. How does Burke distinguish between "real" and "pretended" rights? What real rights does Burke think people have?

10. THOMAS PAINE

Thomas Paine (1737-1808) was one of the most famous social and political thinkers of the late eighteenth century. Born in England, he immigrated to America in 1774 where he quickly became a vocal advocate of the separation of the American colonies from England. A supporter of the idea of popular and limited government, Paine published *The Rights of Man* in 1791 as a response to Burke's critique of the French Revolution. Paine argues strongly against tyranny and proposes that only a democratic government founded on the natural "rights of man" is able to secure peace and justice. Paine's stirring defense of liberty greatly inspired the struggle of the colonists and served as a foundation for later political claims to the moral status of rights.

Text—The Rights of Man (1792)

Reprinted from The Writings of Thomas Paine, *Vol. 2, edited by Moncure Daniel Conway. New York: Knickerbocker Press, 1894.*

I have now to follow Mr. Burke through a pathless wilderness of rhapsodies, and a sort of descant upon governments, in which he asserts whatever he pleases, on the presumption of its being believed, without offering either evidence or reasons for so doing.

Before anything can be reasoned upon to a conclusion, certain facts, principles, or data, to reason from, must be established, admitted, or denied. Mr. Burke with his usual outrage, abused the *Declaration of the Rights of Man*, published by the National Assembly of France, as the basis on which the constitution of France is built. This he calls "paltry and blurred sheets of paper about the rights of man." Does Mr. Burke mean to deny that no *man* has any rights? If he does, then he must mean that there are no such things as rights anywhere, and that he has none himself; for who is there in the world but man? But if Mr. Burke means to admit that man has rights, the question then will be: What are those rights, and how man came by them originally?

The error of those who reason by precedents drawn from antiquity, respecting the rights of man, is that they do not go far enough into antiquity. They do not go the whole way. They stop in some of the intermediate stages of an hundred or a thousand years, and produce what was then done, as a rule for the present day. This is no authority at all. If we travel still farther into antiquity, we shall find a direct contrary opinion and practice prevailing; and if antiquity is to be authority, a thousand such authorities may be produced, successively contradicting each other; but if we proceed on, we shall at last come out right; we shall come to the time when man came from the hand of his Maker. What was he then? Man. Man was his high and only title, and a higher cannot be given him. But of titles I shall speak hereafter.

We are now got at the origin of man, and at the origin of his rights. As to the manner in which the world has been governed from that day to this, it is no farther any concern of ours than to make a proper use of the errors or the improvements which the history of it presents. Those who lived a hundred or a thousand years ago, were then moderns, as we are now. They had *their* ancients, and those ancients had others, and we also shall be ancients in our turn. If the mere name of antiquity is to govern in the affairs of life, the people who are to live an hundred or a thousand years hence, may as well take us for a precedent, as we make a precedent of those who lived an hundred or a thousand years ago. The fact is, that portions of antiquity, by proving everything, establish nothing. It is authority against authority all the way, till we come to the divine origin of the rights of man at the creation. Here our enquiries find a resting-place, and our reason finds a home. If a dispute about the rights of man had arisen at the distance of an hundred years from the creation, it is to this source of authority they must have referred, and it is to this same source of authority that we must now refer.

Though I mean not to touch upon any sectarian principle of religion, yet it may be worth observing, that the genealogy of Christ is traced to Adam. Why then not trace the rights of man to the creation of man? I will answer the question. Because there have been upstart governments, thrusting themselves between, and presumptuously working to *un-make* man.

If any generation of men ever possessed the right of dictating the mode by which the world should be governed for ever, it was the first generation that existed; and if that generation did it not, no succeeding generation can show any authority for doing it, nor can set any up. The illuminating and divine principle of the equal rights of man (for it has its origin from the Maker of man) relates, not only to the living individuals, but to generations of men succeeding each other. Every generation is equal in rights to generations which preceded it, by the same rule that every individual is born equal in rights with his contemporary.

Every history of the creation, and every traditionary account, whether from the lettered or unlettered world, however they may vary in their opinion or belief of certain particulars, all agree in establishing one point, *the unity of man*; by which I mean that men are all of *one degree*, and consequently that all men are born equal, and with equal natural right, in the same manner as if posterity had been continued by *creation* instead of *generation*, the latter being the only mode by which the former is carried forward; and consequently every child born into the world must be considered as deriving its existence from God. The world is as new to him as it was to the first man that existed, and his natural right in it is of the same kind.

The Mosaic account of the creation, whether taken as divine authority or merely historical, is full to this point, *the unity or equality of man*. The expression admits of no controversy. "And God said, Let us make man in our own image. In the image of God created he him; male and female created he them." The distinction of sexes is pointed out, but no other distinction is even implied. If this be not divine authority, it is at least historical authority, and shows that the equality of man, so far from being a modern doctrine, is the oldest upon record.

It is also to be observed that all the religions known in the world are founded, so far as they relate to man, *on the unity of man*, as being all of one degree. Whether in heaven or in hell, or in whatever state man may be supposed to exist hereafter, the good and the bad are the only distinctions. Nay, even the laws of governments are obliged to slide into this principle, by making degrees to consist in crimes and not in persons.

It is one of the greatest of all truths, and of the highest advantage to cultivate. By considering man in this light, and by instructing him to consider himself in this light, it places him in a close connection with all his duties, whether to his Creator or to the creation, of which he is a part; and it is only when he forgets his origin, or, to use a more fashionable phrase, his *birth* and *family*, that he becomes dissolute. It is not among the least of the evils of the present existing governments in all parts of Europe that man, considered as man, is thrown back to a vast distance from his Maker, and the artificial chasm filled up with a succession of barriers, or sort of turnpike gates, through which he has to pass. I will quote Mr. Burke's catalogue of barriers that he has set up between man and his Maker. Putting himself in the character of a herald, he says: "We fear God—we look with awe to kings—with affection to Parliaments—with duty to magistrates—with reverence to priests, and with respect to nobility." Mr. Burke has forgotten to put in "chivalry." He has also forgotten to put in Peter.

The duty of man is not a wilderness of turnpike gates, through which he is to pass by tickets from one to the other. It is plain and simple, and consists but of two points. His duty to God, which every man must feel; and with respect to his neighbor, to do as he would be done by. If those to whom power is delegated do well, they will be respected: if not, they will be despised; and with regard to those to whom no power is delegated, but who assume it, the rational world can know nothing of them.

Hitherto we have spoken only (and that but in part) of the natural rights of man. We have now to consider the civil rights of man, and to show how the one originates from the other. Man did not enter into society to become *worse* than he was before, nor to have fewer rights than he had before, but to have those rights better secured. His natural rights are the foundation of all his civil rights. But in order to pursue this distinction with more precision, it will be necessary to mark the different qualities of natural and civil rights.

A few words will explain this. Natural rights are those which appertain to man in right of his existence. Of this kind are all the intellectual rights, or rights of the mind, and also all those rights of acting as an individual for his own comfort and happiness, which are not injurious to the natural rights of others. Civil rights are those which appertain to man in right of his being a member of society. Every civil right has for its foundation some natural right pre-existing in the individual, but to the enjoyment of which his individual power is not, ill all cases, sufficiently competent. Of this kind are all those which relate to security and protection.

From this short review it will be easy to distinguish between that class of natural rights which man retains after entering into society and those which he throws into the common stock as a member of society.

The natural rights which he retains are all those in which the *power* to execute is as perfect in the individual as the right itself. Among this class, as is before mentioned, are all the intellectual rights, or rights of the mind; consequently religion is one of those rights. The natural rights which are not retained, are all those in which, though the right is perfect in the individual, the power to execute them is defective. They answer not his purpose. A man, by natural right, has a right to judge in his own cause; and so far as the right of the mind is concerned, he never surrenders it. But what availeth it him to judge, if he has not power to redress? He therefore deposits this right in the common stock of society, and takes the arm of society, of which he is a part, in preference and in addition to his own. Society *grants* him nothing. Every man is a proprietor in society, and draws on the capital as a matter of right.

From these premises two or three certain conclusions will follow:

First, That every civil right grows out of a natural right; or, in other words, is a natural right exchanged.

Secondly, That civil power properly considered as such is made up of the aggregate of that class of the natural rights of man, which becomes defective in the individual in point of power, and answers not his purpose, but when collected to a focus becomes competent to the purpose of every one.

Thirdly, That the power produced from the aggregate of natural rights, imperfect in power in the individual, cannot be applied to invade the natural rights which are retained in the individual, and in which the power to execute is as perfect as the right itself.

Questions for Reflection

1. According to Paine, what is the origin of the rights of man? How does Paine criticize Burke on this issue?
2. How, for Paine, do governments "un-make man"? What other alternative role for governments does he describe?
3. What is Paine's conception of the relationship between natural and civil rights? In what ways is Paine's conception similar to Hobbes's, Locke's, and Rousseau's accounts?

11. MARY WOLLSTONECRAFT

The English theorist Mary Wollstonecraft (1759-1797) was a major figure in the Enlightenment project of radical social and political reform. Her principal work, *A Vindication of the Rights of Woman*, was published in 1792. In this book Wollstonecraft vigorously argues that all persons, men and women alike, possess the power of reason. Because reason is the source of the dignity and moral worth of human beings, she contends, the equal possession of reason requires the equal moral worth of women and men. Consequently, it is a violation of the dignity and worth of women to deny them social and political equality and the same rights as men. Wollstonecraft's work thus represents a significant attempt to move the discourse of natural rights, which had traditionally overlooked the historical inequality and marginalization of women, toward becoming a discourse of *human* rights.

Text—A Vindication of the Rights of Woman (1792)

Reprinted from A Vindication of the Rights of Woman. *London: Walter Scott, 1891.*

INTRODUCTION

After considering the historic page, and viewing the living world with anxious solicitude, the most melancholy emotions of sorrowful indignation have depressed my spirits, and I have sighed when obliged to confess, that either nature has made a great difference between man and man, or that the civilization which has hitherto taken place in the world has been very partial. I have turned over various books written on the subject of education, and patiently observed the conduct of parents and the management of schools; but what has been the result?—a profound conviction that the neglected education of my fellow-creatures is the grand source of the misery I deplore; and that women, in particular, are rendered weak and wretched by a variety of concurring causes, originating from one hasty conclusion. The conduct and manners of women, in fact, evidently prove that their minds are not in a healthy state; for, like the flowers which are planted in too rich a soil, strength and usefulness are sacrificed to beauty; and the flaunting leaves, after having pleased a fastidious eye, fade, disregarded on the stalk, long before the season when they ought to have arrived at maturity.—One cause of this barren blooming I attribute to a false system of education, gathered from the books written on this subject by men who, considering females rather as women than human creatures, have been more anxious to make them alluring mistresses than wives; and the understanding of the sex has been so bubbled by this specious homage, that the civilized women of the present century, with a few exceptions, are only anxious to inspire love, when they ought to cherish a nobler ambition, and by their abilities and virtues exact respect.

In a treatise, therefore, on female rights and manners, the works which have been particularly written for their improvement must not be overlooked; especially when it is asserted, in direct terms, that the minds of women are enfeebled by false refinement; that the books of instruction, written by men of genius, have had the same tendency as more frivolous productions; and that, in the true style of Mahometanism, they are only considered as females, and not as a part of the human species, when improvable reason is allowed to be the dignified distinction which raises men above the brute creation, and puts a natural scepter in a feeble hand.

Yet, because I am a woman, I would not lead my readers to suppose that I mean violently to agitate the contested question respecting the equality or inferiority of the sex; but as the subject lies in my way, and I cannot pass it over without subjecting the main tendency of my reasoning to misconstruction, I shall stop a moment to deliver, in a few words, my opinion.—In the government of the physical world it is observable that the female, in general, is inferior to the male. The male pursues, the female yields—this is the law of nature; and it does not appear to be suspended or abrogated in favor of woman. This physical superiority cannot be denied—and it is a noble prerogative! But not content with this natural pre-eminence, men endeavor to sink us still lower, merely to render us alluring objects for a moment; and women, intoxicated by the adoration which men, under the influence of their senses, pay them, do not seek to obtain a durable interest in their hearts, or to become the friends of the fellow creatures who find amusement in their society.

I am aware of an obvious inference:—from every quarter have I heard exclamations against masculine women; but where are they to be found? If by this appellation men mean to inveigh against their ardor in hunting, shooting, and gaming, I shall most cordially join in the cry; but if it be against the imitation of manly virtues, or, more properly speaking, the attainment of those talents and virtues, the exercise of which ennobles the human character, and which raises females in the scale of animal being, when they are comprehensively termed mankind;—all those who view them with a philosophical eye must, I should think, wish with me, that they may every day grow more and more masculine....

CHAPTER 1: THE RIGHTS AND INVOLVED DUTIES OF MANKIND CONSIDERED

In the present state of society it appears necessary to go back to first principles in search of the most simple truths, and to dispute with some prevailing prejudice every inch of ground. To clear my way, I must be allowed to ask some plain questions, and the answers will probably appear as unequivocal as the axioms on which reasoning is built; though, when entangled with various motives of action, they are formally contradicted, either by the words or conduct of men.

In what does man's pre-eminence over the brute creation consist? The answer is as clear as that a half is less than the whole; in Reason.

What acquirement exalts one being above another? Virtue; we spontaneously reply.

For what purpose were the passions implanted? That man by struggling with them might attain a degree of knowledge denied to the brutes; whispers Experience.

Consequently the perfection of our nature and capability of happiness, must be estimated by the degree of reason, virtue, and knowledge, that distinguish the individual, and direct the laws which bind society: and that from the exercise of reason, knowledge and virtue naturally flow, is equally undeniable, if mankind be viewed collectively.

The rights and duties of man thus simplified, it seems almost impertinent to attempt to illustrate truths that appear so incontrovertible; yet such deeply rooted prejudices have clouded reason, and such spurious qualities have assumed the name of virtues, that it is necessary to pursue the course of reason as it has been perplexed and involved in error....

CHAPTER 2: THE PREVAILING OPINION OF A SEXUAL CHARACTER DISCUSSED

... But avoiding, as I have hitherto done, any direct comparison of the two sexes collectively, or frankly acknowledging the inferiority of woman, according to the present appearance of things, I shall only insist that men have increased that inferiority till women are almost sunk below the standard of rational creatures. Let their faculties have room to unfold, and their virtues to gain strength, and then determine where the whole sex must stand in the intellectual scale. Yet let it be remembered, that for a small number of distinguished women I do not ask a place.

It is difficult for us purblind mortals to say to what height human discoveries and improvements may arrive when the gloom of despotism subsides, which makes us stumble at every step; but, when morality shall be settled on a more solid basis, then, without being gifted with a prophetic spirit, I will venture to predict that woman will be either the friend or slave of man. We shall not, as at present, doubt whether she is a moral agent, or the link which unites man with brutes. But, should it then appear, that like the brutes they were principally created for the use of man, he will let them patiently bite the bridle, and not mock them with empty praise; or, should their rationality be proved, he will not impede their improvement merely to gratify his sensual appetites. He will not, with all the graces of rhetoric, advise them to submit implicitly their understanding to the guidance of man. He will not, when he treats of the education of women, assert that they ought never to have the free use of reason, nor would he recommend cunning and dissimulation to beings who are acquiring, in like manner as himself, the virtues of humanity.

Surely there can be but one rule of right, if morality has an eternal foundation, and whoever sacrifices virtue, strictly so called, to present convenience, or whose duty it is to act in such a manner, lives only for the passing day, and cannot be an accountable creature....

For that [women] are bound by the adamantine chain of destiny is most certain, if it be proved that they are never to exercise their own reason, never to be independent, never to rise above opinion, or to feel the dignity of a rational will that only bows to God, and often forgets that the universe contains any being but itself and the model of perfection to which its ardent gaze is turned, to adore attributes that, softened into virtues, may be imitated in kind, though the degree overwhelms the enraptured mind.

If, I say, for I would not impress by declamation when Reason offers her sober light, if they are really capable of acting like rational creatures, let them not be treated like slaves; or, like the brutes who are dependent on the reason of man, when they associate with him; but cultivate their minds, give them the salutary, sublime curb of principle, and let them attain conscious dignity by feeling themselves only dependent on God. Teach them, in common with man, to submit to necessity, instead of giving, to render them more pleasing, a sex to morals.

Further, should experience prove that they cannot attain the same degree of strength of mind, perseverance, and fortitude, let their virtues be the same in kind, though they may vainly struggle for the same degree; and the superiority of man will be equally clear, if not clearer; and truth, as it is a simple principle, which admits of no modification, would be common to both. Nay, the order of society as it is at present regulated would not be inverted, for woman would then only have the rank that reason assigned her, and arts could not be practiced to bring the balance even, much less to turn it.

These may be termed Utopian dreams.—Thanks to that Being who impressed them on my soul, and gave me sufficient strength of mind to dare to exert my own reason, till, becoming dependent only on him for the support of my virtue, I view, with indignation, the mistaken notions that enslave my sex.

I love man as my fellow; but his scepter, real, or usurped, extends not to me, unless the reason of an individual demands my homage; and even then the submission is to reason, and not to man. In fact, the conduct of an accountable being must be regulated by the operations of its own reason; or on what foundation rests the throne of God?

It appears to me necessary to dwell on these obvious truths, because females have been insulated, as it were; and, while they have been stripped of the virtues that should clothe humanity, they have been decked with artificial graces that enable them to exercise a short-lived tyranny. Love, in their bosoms, taking place of every nobler passion, their sole ambition is to be fair, to raise emotion instead of inspiring respect; and this ignoble desire, like the servility in absolute monarchies, destroys all strength of character. Liberty is the mother of virtue, and if women are, by their very constitution, slaves, and not allowed to breathe the sharp invigorating air of freedom, they must ever languish like exotics, and be reckoned beautiful flaws in nature;—let it also be remembered, that they are the only flaw.

As to the argument respecting the subjection in which the sex has ever been held, it retorts on man. The many have always been enthralled by the few; and monsters, who scarcely have shown any discernment of human excellence, have tyrannized over thousands of their fellow creatures. Why have men of superior endowments submitted to such degradation? For, is it not universally acknowledged that kings, viewed collectively, have ever been inferior, in abilities and virtue, to the same number of men taken from the common mass of mankind—yet, have they not, and are they not still treated with a degree of reverence that is an insult to reason; China is not the only country where a living man has been made a God. Men have submitted to superior strength to enjoy with impunity the pleasure of the moment—women have only done the same, and therefore till it is proved that the courtier, who servilely resigns the birthright of a man, is not a moral agent, it cannot be demonstrated that woman is essentially inferior to man because she has always been subjugated.

Brutal force has hitherto governed the world, and that the science of politics is in its infancy, is evident from philosophers scrupling to give the knowledge most useful to man that determinate distinction.

I shall not pursue this argument any further than to establish an obvious inference, that as sound politics diffuse liberty, mankind, including woman, will become more wise and virtuous.

CHAPTER 12: ON NATIONAL EDUCATION

... In short, in whatever light I view the subject, reason and experience convince me that the only method of leading women to fulfill their peculiar duties, is to free them from all restraint by allowing them to participate the inherent rights of mankind.

Make them free, and they will quickly become wise and virtuous, as men become more so; for the improvement must be mutual, or the injustice which one half of the human race are obliged to submit to, retorting on their oppressors, the virtue of man will be worm-eaten by the insect whom he keeps under his feet....

A man has been termed a microcosm, and every family might also be called a state. States, it is true, have mostly been governed by arts that disgrace the character of man; and the want of a just constitution, and equal laws, have so perplexed the notions of the worldly wise, that they more than question the reasonableness of contending for the rights of humanity. Thus morality, polluted in the national reservoir, sends off streams of vice to corrupt the constituent parts of the body politic; but should more noble, or rather, more just principles regulate the laws, which ought to be the government of society, and not those who execute them, duty might become the rule of private conduct.

QUESTIONS FOR REFLECTION

1. Why, according to Wollstonecraft, have women been held to a different standard of virtue than men?
2. In Wollstonecraft's view, why is sexual difference not a morally relevant difference? How does this view relate to her claim for equal rights?
3. What are the consequences of Wollstonecraft's argument for the theory of natural rights? For the character and role of government?

12. IMMANUEL KANT

Immanuel Kant (1724–1804) was born, lived, and died in Königsberg, eastern Prussia. Kant studied science, history and philosophy at the University of Königsberg from 1740–1747 and, after working as a private tutor for several years, served as a *Privatdozent* (a lecturer paid by the students who attended his lectures) at the University until 1770. That same year Kant was appointed Professor of Logic and Metaphysics by the University, where he taught until 1796. While Kant published several works as a young scholar, his most important writings appeared in his middle and later years. In 1781 he published the *Critique of Pure Reason*, which had a major impact on epistemology and metaphysics during his lifetime as well as throughout the modern period. Kant's subsequent publications attempt to work out the implications of his critical analysis of human reason for the areas of aesthetics, morality, and politics.

In the *Groundwork for the Metaphysics of Morals* (1785), Kant presented his basic moral theory, arguing that the only thing that is unconditionally good is a good will. According to Kant, a person who acts with a good will acts on the basis of neither the desires that influence the action nor the consequences that result from it, but instead on the recognition that the action is obligatory or necessary. This means the person acts in accord with what Kant calls the categorical imperative, which can be formulated as "Act only on that maxim which you can at the same time will that it should be a universal law," that is, a law that everyone should obey. Kant's categorical imperative represents a form of *deontological* ethical theory (from the Greek *deon*, meaning "duty"), which is the view that defines right action in terms of obligations and duties, rather than the consequences or results of an action. This is in contrast to *teleological* ethical theories (from the Greek *telos*, meaning "end" or "goal"), which hold that the best consequences or results determine the rightness of an action. Kant believed that an action willed from the categorical imperative is done with a necessary view to treating all persons, including ourselves, as ends in themselves and not merely as means to other ends. Only in this way is it possible to respect the intrinsic freedom, equality, autonomy, and dignity of human beings.

In several later essays, Kant sought to clarify the relationship of his moral theory to political practice. The selection that follows is from "On the Common Saying: This May be True in Theory, But it does not Apply in Practice," published in 1793. Here Kant discusses how a civil state is justified on the basis of a social contract that expresses the conception of humanity as an end in itself. In a just civil government the rights of humanity are secured, establishing a reciprocal obligation on the part of each citizen to respect the rights of everyone else. Thus some limitations on freedom do exist, through the rule of law and the state's right to punish, but these limitations are legitimate since they actually increase freedom by prohibiting (and redressing) the types of wrongs characteristic of the lawless state of nature. For Kant, then, the value of legitimate government is that it guarantees our natural right to freedom and provides us a foundation from which to acquire other rights.

Text—The Principles of Political Right (1793)

Reprinted from Kant's Principles of Politics, *translated by W. Hastie. Edinburgh: T. & T. Clark, 1891.*

The establishment of a *civil constitution* in society is one of the most important facts in human history. In the principle on which it is founded this institution differs from all the other forms of social union among mankind. Viewed as a compact...by which numbers of men are united into one society, the formation of a civil constitution has much in common with all other forms of social union in respect of the mode in which it is carried out in practice. But while all such compacts are established for the purpose of promoting in common some chosen end, the civil union is essentially distinguished from all other by the principle on which it is based. In all social contracts we find a union of a number of persons for the purpose of carrying out some one end which they all have in common. But a union of a multitude of men, viewed as an end in itself that every person *ought to carry out*, and which consequently is a primary and unconditional duty amid all the external relations of men who cannot help exercising a mutual influence on one another,—is at once peculiar and unique of its kind. Such a union is only to be found in a society which, by being formed into a civil state, constitutes a commonwealth. Now the end which in such external relations is itself a duty and even the highest formal condition—the *conditio sine qua non*—of all other external duties, is the realization of the rights of men under public compulsory laws, by which every individual can have what is his own assigned to him and secured against the encroachments or assaults of others.

The idea of an external law generally arises wholly out of the idea of human freedom, or liberty, in the external relations of men to one another. As such, it has nothing specially to do with the realization of happiness as a purpose which all men naturally have, or with prescribing the means of attaining it; so that therefore such a prescription in any statute must not be confounded with the motive behind the law itself. Law in general may be defined as the limitation of the freedom of any individual to the extent of its agreement with the freedom of all other individuals, in so far as this is possible by a universal law. Public law, again, is the sum of the external laws which make such a complete agreement of freedom in society possible. Now as all limitation of freedom by external acts of the will of another is a mode of coercion or compulsion, it follows that the civil constitution is a relation of free men who live under coercive laws, without otherwise prejudicing their liberty in the whole of their connection with others....

The civil state, then, regarded merely as a social state that is regulated by righteous laws, is founded upon the following rational principles:

1. The *liberty* of every member of the society as a *man*;

2. The *equality* of every member of the society with every other, as a *subject*;

3. The *independence* of every member of the commonwealth, as a *citizen*.

These principles are not so much laws given by the State when it is established as they are fundamental conditions according to which alone the institution of a State is possible, in conformity with the purely rational principles of external human right generally.

1. The *liberty* of every member of the State as a man is the first principle in the constitution of a rational commonwealth. I would express this principle in the following form: "No one has a

right to compel me to be happy in the peculiar way in which he may think of the well-being of other men; but every one is entitled to seek his own happiness in the way that seems to him best, if it does not infringe the liberty of others in striving after a similar end for themselves when their liberty is capable of consisting with the right of liberty in all others according to possible universal laws." A government founded upon the principle of benevolence toward the people—after the analogy of a father to his children, and therefore called a paternal government—would be one in which the subject would be regarded as children or minors unable to distinguish what is beneficial or injurious to them. These subjects would be thus compelled to act in a merely passive way; and they would be trained to expect all that ought to make them happy, solely from the judgment of the sovereign and just as he might will it, merely out of his goodness. Such a government would be the greatest conceivable despotism; for it would present a constitution that would abolish all liberty in the subjects and leave them no rights. It is not a paternal government, but only a patriotic government that is adapted for men who are capable of rights, and at the same time fitted to give scope to the good-will of the ruler. By "patriotic" is meant that condition of mind in which every one in the State—the head of it not excepted—regards the commonwealth as the maternal bosom, and the country as the paternal soil out of and on which he himself has sprung into being, and which he also must leave to others as a dear inheritance. Thus, and thus only, can he hold himself entitled to protect the rights of his fatherland by laws of the common will, but not to subject it to an unconditional purpose of his own at pleasure.

This right of liberty thus belongs to him as a man, while he is a member of the commonwealth; or, in point of fact, so far as he is a being capable of rights generally.

2. The *equality* of every member of the State as a subject is the second principle in the constitution of a rational commonwealth. The formula of this principle may be put thus: "Every member of the commonwealth has rights against every other that may be enforced by compulsory laws, from which only the sovereign or supreme ruler of the State is excepted, because he is

regarded not as a mere member of the commonwealth, but as its creator or maintainer; and he alone has the right to compel without being himself subject to compulsory law." All, however, who live under laws in a State are its subjects; and, consequently, they are subjected to the compulsory law, like all other members of the commonwealth, one only whether an individual sovereign or a collective body, constituting the supreme head of the State and as such being accepted as the medium through which alone all rightful coercion or compulsion can be exercised. For, should the head of the State also be subject to compulsion, there would no longer be a supreme head, and the series of members subordinate and superordinate would go on upward *ad infinitum*. Again, were there in the State two such powers as persons exempt from legal compulsion, neither of them would be subject to compulsory laws, and as such the one could do no wrong to the other; which is impossible.

This thoroughgoing equality of the individual men in a State as its subjects is, however, quite compatible with the greatest inequality in the extent and degrees of their possessions, whether consisting in corporeal or spiritual superiority over others, or in the external gifts of fortune, or in rights generally—of which there may be many—in relation to others. Thus the prosperity of the one may greatly depend on the will of another, as in the case of the poor in relation to the rich. One may even have of necessity to obey and another to command, as in the relations of children to parents and of wife to husband. Again, one may have to work and another to pay, as in the case of a day laborer; and so on. But in relation to the involved law of right, which as the expression of the universal will of the State can be only one, and which regards the form of the right, and not the matter or object to which the right refers: in all cases, the persons as subjects are to be regarded as *all equal* to one another. For no one has a right to compel or coerce any one whomsoever in the State, otherwise than by the public law and through the sovereign or ruler executing it; and any one may resist another thus far, and through the same medium. On the other hand, no one can lose this right, as a title to proceed by legal compulsion against others, except by his own fault or a criminal act. Nor can any one divest himself of it voluntarily, or by a compact, so as to bring it about by a supposed act of right, that he should have no rights but only duties toward others; for in so doing he would be depriving himself of the right of making a compact, and consequently the act would annul itself.

Out of this idea of the equality of men as subjects in the commonwealth, there arises the following formula: "Every member of the State should have it made possible for him to attain to any position or rank that may belong to any subject to which his talent, his industry or his fortune may be capable of raising him; and his fellow subjects are not entitled to stand in the way by any hereditary prerogative, forming the exclusive privilege of a certain class, in order to keep him and his posterity forever below them."

For all law consists merely in restriction on the liberty of another to the condition that is consistent with my liberty according to a universal law; and national law in a commonwealth is only the product of actual legislation conformable to this principle and conjoined with power, in virtue of which all who belong to a nation as its subjects find themselves in a condition constituted and regulated by law (*status juridicus*). And, as such, this condition is in fact a condition of equality inasmuch as it is determined by the action and reaction of free wills limiting one another, according to the universal law of freedom; and it thus constitutes the civil state of human society. Hence the inborn right of all individuals in this sphere (that is, considered as being prior to their having actually entered upon juridical action) to bring compulsion to bear upon any others is entirely identical and equal throughout, on the assumption that they are always to remain within the bounds of unanimity and concord in the mutual use of their liberty. Now birth is not an act on the part of him who is born, and consequently it does not entail upon him any inequality in the state of law, nor any subjection under laws of compulsion other than what is common to him with all others as a subject of the one supreme legislative power; and, therefore, there can be no inborn privilege by way of law in any member of the commonwealth as a subject before another fellow subject. Nor, consequently, has any one a right to transmit the privilege or prerogative of the rank which he holds in the commonwealth to his posterity so that they should be, as it were, qualified by birth for the rank of nobility; nor should they be prevented from attaining by their own merit to the higher stages in the gradations of social rank....

3. The *independence* of a member of the commonwealth as a citizen, or fellow legislator, is the third principle or condition of law in the State. In the matter of the legislation itself, all are to be regarded as free and equal under the already-existing public laws; but they are not to be all regarded as equal in relation to the right to give or enact these laws. Those who are not capable of this right are, notwithstanding, subjected to the observance of the laws as members of the commonwealth, and thereby they participate in the protection which is in accordance therewith; they are, however, not to be regarded as citizens but as protected fellow subjects. All right, in fact, depends on laws. A public law, however, which determines for all what is to be legally allowed or not allowed in their regard is the act of a public will, from which all law proceeds and which therefore itself can do no wrong to any one. For this, however, there is no other will competent than that of the whole people, as it is only when all determine about all that each one in consequence determines about himself. For it is only to himself that one can do no wrong. But if it be another will that is in question, then the mere will of any one different from it could determine nothing for it which might not be wrong; and consequently the law of such a will would require another law to limit its legislation. And thus no particular will can be legislative for a commonwealth. Properly speaking, in order to make out this, the ideas of the external liberty, equality and *unity* of the will of *all* are to be taken into account; and for the last of these independence is the condition, since the exercising of a vote is required when the former two ideas are taken along with it. The fundamental law thus indicated, which can only arise out of the universal united will of the people, is what is called the *original contract*....

We have next to consider what follows by way of corollary from the principles thus enunciated. We have before us the idea of an original contract as the only condition upon which a civil, and therefore wholly legal, constitution can be founded among men, and as the only basis upon which a State can be established. But this fundamental condition—whether called an original contract or a social compact—may be viewed as the coalition of all the private and particular wills of a people into one common and public will, having a purely juridical legislation as its end. But it is not necessary to presuppose this contract or compact to have been actually a *fact*; nor indeed is it possible as a fact. We have not to deal with it as if it had first to be proved from history that a people into whose rights and obligations we have entered as their descendants did actually on a certain occasion execute such a contract, and that a certain evidence or instrument of an oral or written kind regarding it must have been transmitted so as to constitute an obligation that shall be binding in any existing civil constitution. In short, this idea is merely an *idea* of reason; but it has undoubtedly a practical reality. For it ought to bind every legislator by the condition that he shall enact such laws as might have arisen from the united will of a whole people; and it will likewise be binding upon every subject, in so far as he will be a citizen, so that he shall regard the law as if he had consented to it of his own will. This is the test of the rightfulness of every public law. If the law be of such a nature that it is *impossible* that the whole people could give their assent to it, it is not a just law. An instance of this kind would be a law enacting that a certain class of subject should have all the privileges of hereditary rank by mere birth. But if it be *possible* that a people consent to a law, it is a duty to regard it as just, even supposing that the people were at the moment in such a position or mood that if it were referred to them their consent to it would probably be refused.

This limitation, however, manifestly applies only to the judgment of the legislator and not to that of the subject. If then, under a certain actual state of the law, a people should conclude that the continuance of that law would probably take away their happiness, what would they have to do? Would it not be a duty to resist the law? The answer can only be that the people should do nothing but obey. For the question here does not turn upon the happiness which the subject may expect from some special institution or mode of administering the commonwealth, but the primary concern is purely that of the right which has thus to be secured to every individual. This is the supreme principle from which all the maxims relating to the commonwealth must proceed; and it cannot be limited by anything else. In regard to the interest of happiness, no principle that could be universally applicable can be laid down for the guidance of legislation; for not only the circumstances of the time but the very contradictory and ever-changing opinions which men have of what will constitute happiness make it impossible to lay down fixed principles regarding it; and so the idea of happiness, taken by itself, is not available as a principle of legislation. No one can prescribe for another as to what he shall find happiness in.... Along with this, the individual is left undisturbed in his right to seek his happiness in whatever way may seem to him best, if only he does not infringe the universal liberty secured through the law by violating the rights of other fellow subjects....

There is, then, a general principle whereby the people may assert their rights negatively, so has as merely to judge that a certain thing is to be regarded as not ordained by the supreme legislation in accordance with their best will. This principle may be expressed in the following proposition: What a people could not ordain over itself ought not to be ordained by the legislator over the people.

QUESTIONS FOR REFLECTION

1. How does Kant describe the right of equality? How far does equality extend in the civil state?

2. What do you think Kant means when he says, "What a people could not ordain over itself ought not to be ordained by the legislator over the people"?

3. According to Kant, the principle of happiness cannot provide the justification needed to establish a legitimate government. Why does Kant claim this? Do you agree or not? Why?

13. JEREMY BENTHAM

Jeremy Bentham (1748–1832) is considered the founder of the British utilitarian tradition. Born in London, Bentham was, like Locke, educated at Westminster School and Oxford University. A student of law, Bentham became a leading advocate of liberal legal and political reform in England. His theory of *utilitarianism* is based on the so-called "principle of utility." As declared by Bentham in *A Fragment on Government*, published in 1776, this principle means that "it is the greatest happiness of the greatest number that is the measure of right and wrong."

For Bentham, the basis of moral value is to be found in the two primary motives for human behavior: the avoidance of pain and the obtainment of pleasure. He claims that human beings act in order to maximize their self-interest, that is, producing pleasure or happiness and avoiding pain. Thus, utilitarian moral theory asserts that actions are to be evaluated by their consequences: right actions promote happiness and prevent harm, wrong actions cause pain and impede the procurement of pleasure. Bentham's political theory argues, in contrast to Kant's, that systems of government and legislation ought to be rationally revised in order to develop laws, policies, and institutions that are most useful for promoting the general happiness, that is, the happiness of as many individuals as possible.

Bentham believed that his utilitarian ethic was eminently practical, based on empirically observable phenomena. He criticized social contract and natural law theories as nothing more than "fictions" that offer unhistorical abstractions from the publicly accessible facts of social reality. In Bentham's view, there is no such thing as the "natural" liberty advocated by philosophers such as Locke, because people have always lived in society. Furthermore, he contends that laws are to be regarded only as the commands of state authority and not of nature or God.

In the following selection, Bentham analyzes the French Declaration of the Rights of Man and of the Citizen in order to condemn the idea of natural rights. In Bentham's opinion, rights are only the products of existing law and therefore cannot precede government. Furthermore, because natural rights are claimed to be moral rights independent of any government, such rights present a threat to the general happiness and order of society since they imply that allegedly unjust laws and governments may be disobeyed.

It is clear, then, that Bentham is strongly opposed to the idea of natural rights. Nevertheless, his criticisms have forced theorists of natural, moral, and human rights to refine their arguments and elaborate their claims more extensively. In that way, Bentham's work is useful for our own present purposes.

Text—Anarchical Fallacies: A Critical Examination of the Declaration of Rights

Reprinted from The Works of Jeremy Bentham, *Volume Two. Edited by John Bowring. Edinburgh: 1838-1843.*

PRELIMINARY OBSERVATIONS

The Declaration of Rights—I mean the paper published under that name by the French National Assembly in 1791—assumes for its subject-matter a field of disquisition as unbounded in point of extent as it is important in its nature. But the more ample the extent given to any proposition or string of propositions, the more difficult it is to keep the import of it confined without deviation, within the bounds of truth and reason. If in the smallest corners of the field it ranges over, it fail of coinciding with the line of rigid rectitude, no sooner is the aberration pointed out, than (inasmuch as there is no medium between truth and falsehood) its pretensions to the appellation of a truism are gone, and whoever looks upon it must recognise it to be false and erroneous,—and if, as here, political conduct be the theme, so far as the error extends and fails of being detected, pernicious....

Here, then, is the radical and all-pervading error—the attempting to give to a work on such a subject the sanction of government; especially of such a government—a government composed of members so numerous, so unequal in talent, as well as discordant in inclinations and affections....

The revolution, which threw the government into the hands of the penners and adopters of this declaration, having been the effect of insurrection, the grand object evidently is to justify the cause. But by justifying it, they invite it: in justifying past insurrection, they plant and cultivate a propensity to perpetual insurrection in time future; they sow the seeds of anarchy broad-cast: in justifying the demolition of existing authorities, they undermine all future ones, their own consequently in the number....

The more *abstract*—that is, the more *extensive* the proposition is, the more liable is it to involve a fallacy. Of fallacies, one of the most natural modifications is that which is called *begging the question*—the abuse of making the abstract proposition resorted to for proof, a lever for introducing, in the company of other propositions that are nothing to the purpose, the very proposition which is admitted to stand in need of proof.

Is the provision in question fit in point of expediency to be passed into a law for the government of the French nation? That, *mutatis mutandis*, would have been the question put in England: that was the proper question to have been put in relation to each provision it was proposed should enter into the composition of the body of French laws.

Instead of that, as often as the utility of a provision appeared (by reason of the wideness of its extent, for instance) of a doubtful nature, the way taken to clear the doubt was to assert it to be a provision fit to be made law for all men—for all Frenchmen—and for all Englishmen, for example, into the bargain. This medium of proof was the more alluring, inasmuch as to the advantage of removing opposition, was added the pleasure, the sort of titillation so exquisite to the nerve of vanity in a French heart—the satisfaction, to use a homely, but not the less apposite proverb, of teaching grandmothers to suck eggs. Hark! ye citizens of the other side of the water! Can you tell us what rights you have belonging to you? No, that you can't. It's *we* that understand rights: not our own only, but yours into the bargain; while you, poor simple souls! know nothing about the matter....

Such is the morality of this celebrated manifesto.... The logic of it is of a piece with its morality:—a perpetual vein of nonsense, flowing from a perpetual abuse of words,—words having a variety of meanings, where words with single meaning were equally at hand.... In a play or novel, an improper word is but a word: and impropriety, whether noticed or not, is attended with no consequences. In a body of laws—especially laws given as constitutional and fundamental ones—an improper word may be a national calamity:—and civil war may be the consequence of it....

Article 1

Men [all men] are born and remain free and equal in respect of rights. Social distinctions cannot be founded, but upon common utility.

In this article are contained, grammatically speaking, two distinct sentences. The first is full of error, the other of ambiguity.

In the first are contained four distinguishable propositions, all of them false—all of them notoriously and undeniably false:— 1. That all men are born free. 2. That all men remain free. 3. That all men are born equal in rights. 4. That all men remain (i.e. remain forever, for the proposition is indefinite and unlimited) equal in rights.

All men are born free? All men remain free? No, not a single man: not a single man that ever was, or is, or will be. All men, on the contrary, are born in subjection, and the most absolute subjection—the subjection of a helpless child to the parents on whom he depends every moment for his existence. In this subjection every man is born—in this subjection he continues for years—for a great number of years—and the existence of the individual and of the species depends upon his so doing....

All men born free? Absurd and miserable nonsense! When the great complaint...is—that so many men are born slaves. Oh! but when we acknowledge them to be born slaves, we refer to the laws in being; which laws being void, as being contrary to those laws of nature which are the efficient causes of those rights of man that we are declaring, the men in question are free in one sense, though slaves in another;—slaves, and free, at the same time:—free in respect of the laws of nature—slaves in respect of the pretended human laws, which, though called laws, are no laws at all, as being contrary to the laws of nature....

All men are born equal in right. The rights of the heir of the most indigent family equal to the rights of the heir of the most wealthy? In what case is this true? I say nothing of hereditary *dignities* and *powers*. Inequalities such as these being proscribed under and by the French government in France, are consequently proscribed by that government under every other government, and consequently have no existence anywhere. For the total subjection of every other government to French government, is a fundamental principle in the law of universal independence—the French law. Yet neither was this true at the time of issuing this Declaration of Rights, nor was it meant to be so afterwards....

All men (i. e. all human creatures of both sexes) *remain equal in rights*. All men, meaning doubtless all human creatures. The apprentice, then, is equal in rights to his master; he has as much liberty with relation to the master, as the master has with relation to him; he has as much right to command and to punish him; be is as much owner and master of the master's house, as the master himself. The case is the same as between ward and guardian. So again as between wife and husband. The madman has as good a right to confine anybody else, as anybody else has to confine him. The idiot has as much right to govern everybody, as anybody can have to govern him. The physician and the nurse, when called in by the next friend of a sick man seized with a delirium, have no more right to prevent his throwing himself out of the window, than he has to throw them out of it. All this is plainly and incontestably included in this article of the Declaration of Rights: in the very words of it, and in the meaning—if it have any meaning....

Article 2

The end in view of every political association is the preservation of the natural and imprescriptible rights of man. These rights are liberty, property, security, and resistance to oppression.

Sentence 1. The end in view of every political association, is the preservation of the natural and imprescriptible rights of man. More confusion—more nonsense,—and the nonsense, as usual, dangerous nonsense. The words can scarcely be said to have a meaning: but if they have, or rather if they had a meaning, these would be the propositions either asserted or implied:—

1. That there are such things as rights anterior to the establishment of governments: for natural, as applied to rights, if it mean anything, is meant to stand in opposition to *legal*—to such rights as are acknowledged to owe their existence to government, and are consequently posterior in their date to the establishment of government.

2. That these rights *can not* be abrogated by government: for *can not* is implied in the form of the word imprescriptible, and the sense it wears when so applied, is the cutthroat sense above explained.

3. That the governments that exist derive their origin from formal associations, or what are now called *conventions*: associations entered into by a partnership contract, with all the members for partners,—entered into at a day prefixed, for a predetermined purpose, the formation of a new government where there was none before....

Such are the notions implied in this first part of the article. How stands the truth of things? That there are no such things as natural rights—no such things as rights anterior to the establishment of government—no such things as natural rights opposed to, in contradistinction to, legal: that the expression is merely figurative; that when used, in the moment you attempt to give it a literal meaning it leads to error, and to that sort of error that leads to mischief—to the extremity of mischief.

We know what it is for men to live without government—and living without government, to live without rights: we know what it is for men to live without government, for we see instances of such a way of life—we see it in many savage nations, or rather races of mankind...whose way of living is so well known to us: no habit of obedience, and thence no government—no government, and thence no laws—no laws, and thence no such things as rights—no security—no property....

In proportion to the want of happiness resulting from the want of rights, a reason exists for wishing that there were such things as rights. But reasons for wishing there were such thing as rights, are not rights;— a reason for wishing that a certain right were established, is not that right—want is not supply—hunger is not bread.

That which has no existence cannot be destroyed—that which cannot be destroyed cannot require anything to preserve it from destruction. *Natural rights* is simple nonsense: natural and imprescriptible rights, rhetorical nonsense,—nonsense upon stilts. But this rhetorical nonsense ends in the old strain of mischievous nonsense: for immediately a list of these pretended natural rights is given, and those are so expressed as to present to view legal rights. And of these rights, whatever they are, there is not, it seems, any one of which any government can, upon any occasion whatever, abrogate the smallest particle.

So much for terrorist language. What is the language of reason and plain sense upon this same subject? That in proportion as it is *right* or *proper*, i. e. advantageous to the society in question, that this or that right—a right to this or that effect—should be established and maintained, in that same proportion it is *wrong* that it should be abrogated: but that as there is no *right*, which ought not to be maintained so long as it is upon the whole advantageous to the society that it should be maintained, so there is no right which, when the abolition of it is advantageous to society, should not be abolished. To know whether it would be more for the advantage of society that this or that right should be maintained or abolished, the time at which the question about maintaining or abolishing is proposed, must be given, and the circumstances under which it is proposed to maintain or abolish it; the right itself must be specifically described, not jumbled with an indistinguishable heap of others, under any such vague general terms as property, liberty, and the like.

One thing, in the midst of all this confusion, is but too plain. They know not of what they are talking under the name of natural rights, and yet they would have them imprescriptible—proof against all the power of the laws—pregnant with occasions summoning the members of the community to rise ripe in resistance against the laws. What, then, was their object in declaring the existence of imprescriptible rights, and without specifying a single one by any such mark as it could be known by? This and no other—to excite and keep up a spirit of resistance to all laws—a spirit of insurrection against all governments—against the governments of all other nations instantly,—against the government of their own nation—against the government they themselves were pretending to establish—even that, as soon as their own reign should be at an end....

What I mean to attack is, not the subject or citizen of this or that country...but all anti-legal rights of man, all declarations of such rights. What I mean to attack is, not the execution of such a design in this or that instance, but the design itself.

It is not that they have failed in their execution of the design by using the same word promiscuously in two or three senses—contradictory and incompatible senses—but in undertaking to execute a design which could not be executed at all without this abuse of words. Let a man distinguish the senses...and he will find it impossible to make up any such declaration at all, without running into such nonsense as must stop the hand of the maddest of the mad....

Right, the substantive *right*, is the child of law: from *real* laws come *real* rights; but from *imaginary* laws, from laws of nature, fancied and invented by poets, rhetoricians, and dealers in moral and intellectual poisons, come *imaginary* rights.... And thus it is, that from *legal rights*, the offspring of law, and friends of peace, come *anti-legal rights*, the mortal enemies of law, the subverters of government, and the assassins of security.

QUESTIONS FOR REFLECTION

1. Should our actions, legislation, and public institutions be evaluated by their tendency to promote happiness? Is it possible to produce an account of happiness that is acceptable to everyone? Why or why not?
2. Does Bentham or Kant provide a more suitable understanding of liberty in relation to a system of law? Why?
3. Are natural rights imaginary "nonsense" as Bentham contends? Are they dangerous to society? How can we distinguish legal rights and moral rights?

14. KARL MARX

Karl Marx (1818–1883) was born in Trier, in what is now Germany. His father was a lawyer who converted to Protestantism in order to spare his family and business the restrictions on Jews that were sanctioned in Germany. In 1835, Marx enrolled to study law at the University of Bonn, transferring a year later to the University of Berlin where he studied law and philosophy. He received his doctorate in philosophy in 1841 for a thesis on ancient Greek atomism.

Unable to obtain a teaching position, Marx became a writer and editor for a liberal newspaper in Cologne, beginning a lifelong career as a journalist. Following the suppression of the newspaper by the government in 1843, Marx moved to Paris to edit a new journal. There he began a lifetime of collaboration with the political economist Friedrich Engels (1820–1895). Marx and Engels helped found the Communist League in 1848, publishing *The Communist Manifesto* that same year as a statement of the League's political doctrines. Due to his radical politics Marx was forced to emigrate, and he took up residence in London, where he lived for the rest of his life.

Marx's writings constitute a sustained critique of capitalism, particularly of the economic and social exploitation of the working class (proletariat) caused by a wage labor system that devalues the work of laborers in order to create profit for capitalists (bourgeoisie). According to Marx, capitalism produces oppressive social conditions marked by vast inequalities of wealth and power, which leads to the alienation of workers from the products of their labor, their coworkers and families, and eventually their own desires and interests. In order to build a political society based on genuine equality, Marx argued that capitalism must be abolished and replaced by communism. Under communism, collective ownership of the means of production will lead to the just and equitable distribution of goods based on need, eliminating the basis for class antagonisms and replacing competition with cooperation.

In the following selection, Marx responds to an analysis of Jewish emancipation by the theologian Bruno Bauer. In this early essay Marx argues that natural rights, or the rights of man, are "egoistic," concerned only with the personal interests of individuals rather than the interests of society as a whole. Consequently, natural rights, with their focus on negative liberty (freedom from interference), are an insufficient means for achieving positive human emancipation. Despite this criticism, Marx's comments contributed to the process of clarifying the importance of rights and expanding the list of rights well beyond those proposed by the early social contract theorists.

Text—On the Jewish Question (1844)

Published in the Deutsch-Französische Jahrbücher, *February 1844.*

The German Jews desire emancipation. What kind of emancipation do they desire? *Civic, political* emancipation....

At this point, the one-sided formulation of the Jewish question becomes evident.

It was by no means sufficient to investigate: Who is to emancipate? Who is to be emancipated? Criticism had to investigate a third point. It had to inquire: *What kind of emancipation* is in question? What conditions follow from the very nature of the emancipation that is demanded? Only the criticism of *political emancipation* itself would have been the conclusive criticism of the Jewish question and its real merging in the general question of the age....

We do not turn secular questions into theological ones; we turn theological questions into secular ones. History has long enough been merged in superstition, we now merge superstition in history. The question of the *relation of political emancipation to religion* becomes for us the question of the *relation of political emancipation to human emancipation*. We criticize the religious weakness of the political state by criticizing the political state in its *secular* form, apart from its weaknesses as regards religion. The contradiction between the state and a particular religion, for instance Judaism, is given by us a human form as the contradiction between the state and particular secular elements; the contradiction between the state and religion in general as the contradiction between the state and its presuppositions in general.

The *political* emancipation of the Jew, the Christian, and, in general, of religious man, is the *emancipation* of the state from

Judaism, from Christianity, from religion in general. In its own form, in the manner characteristic of its nature, the state as a state emancipates itself from religion by emancipating itself from the *state religion*—that is to say, by the state as a state not professing any religion, but, on the contrary, asserting itself as a state. The political emancipation from religion is not a religious emancipation that has been carried through to completion and is free from contradiction, because political emancipation is not a form of human emancipation which has been carried through to completion and is free from contradiction.

The limits of political emancipation are evident at once from the fact that the *state* can free itself from a restriction without man being *really* free from this restriction, that the state can be a *free state* without man being a *free man*....

Political emancipation is, of course, a big step forward. True, it is not the final form of human emancipation in general, but it is the final form of human emancipation *within* the hitherto existing world order. It goes without saying that we are speaking here of real, practical emancipation.

Man emancipates himself politically from religion by banishing it from the sphere of public law to that of private law. Religion is no longer the spirit of the state, in which man behaves—although in a limited way, in a particular form, and in a particular sphere—as a species-being, in community with other men. Religion has become the spirit of *civil society*, of the sphere of egoism.... It is no longer the essence of community, but the essence of difference. It has become the expression of man's *separation* from his *community*, from himself and from other men—as it was originally. It is only the abstract avowal of specific perversity, private whimsy, and arbitrariness. The endless fragmentation of religion in North America, for example, gives it even externally the form of a purely individual affair. It has been thrust among the multitude of private interests and ejected from the community as such. But one should be under no illusion about the limits of political emancipation. The division of the human being into a *public man* and a *private man*, the displacement of religion from the state into civil society, this is not a stage of political emancipation but its completion; this emancipation, therefore, neither abolished the *real* religiousness of man, nor strives to do so....

The members of the political state are religious owning to the dualism between individual life and species-life, between the life of civil society and political life. They are religious because men treat the political life of the state, an area beyond their real individuality, as if it were their true life. They are religious insofar as religion here is the spirit of civil society, expressing the separation and remoteness of man from man. Political democracy is Christian since in it man, not merely one man but everyman, ranks as sovereign, as the highest being, but it is man in his uncivilized, unsocial form, man in his fortuitous existence, man just as he is, man as he has been corrupted by the whole organization of our society, who has lost himself, been alienated, and handed over to the rule of inhuman conditions and elements—in short, man who is not yet a *real* species-being. That which is a creation of fantasy, a dream, a postulate of Christianity, i.e., the sovereignty of man—but man as an alien being different from the real man—becomes, in democracy, tangible reality, present existence, and secular principle....

Therefore, we do not say to the Jews, as Bauer does: You cannot be emancipated politically without emancipating yourselves radically from Judaism. On the contrary, we tell them: Because you can be emancipated politically without renouncing Judaism completely and incontrovertibly, *political emancipation* itself is not *human emancipation*. If you Jews want to be emancipated politically, without emancipating yourselves humanly, the half-hearted approach and contradiction is not in you alone, it is inherent in the *nature* and *category* of political emancipation. If you find yourself within the confines of this category, you share in a general confinement. Just as the state evangelizes when, although it is a state, it adopts a Christian attitude towards the Jews, so the Jew *acts politically* when, although a Jew, he demands civil rights.

But, if a man, although a Jew, can be emancipated politically and receive civic rights, can he lay claim to the so-called *rights of man* and receive them?… Let us examine, for a moment, the so-called rights of man—to be precise, the rights of man in their authentic form, in the form which they have among those who *discovered* them, the North Americans and the French! These rights of man are, in part, *political rights*, rights which can only be exercised in community with others. Their content is *participation* in the community, and specifically in the *political* community, in the life of the state. They come within the category of *political freedom*, the category of *civil rights*, which, as we have seen, in no way presuppose the incontrovertible and positive abolition of religion—nor, therefore, of Judaism. There remains to be examined the other part of the rights of man—the *rights of man*, insofar as these differ from the *rights of the citizen*.

Included among them is freedom of conscience, the right to practice any religion one chooses. The *privilege of faith* is expressly recognized either as a *right of man* or as the consequence of a right of man, that of liberty. *Declaration of the Rights of Man and of the Citizen*, 1791, Article 10: "No one is to be subjected to annoyance because of his opinions, even religious opinions." There is guaranteed, as one of the rights of man, "the freedom of every man to practice the *religion* of which he is an adherent."

The Declaration of the Rights of Man, etc., 1793, includes among the rights of man, Article 7: "The free exercise of religion." Indeed, in regard to man's right to express his thoughts and opinions, to hold meetings, and to exercise his religion, it is even stated: "The necessity of proclaiming these *rights* presupposes either the existence or the recent memory of despotism." Compare the Constitution of 1795, Section XIV, Article 354.

Constitution of Pennsylvania, Article 9, § 3: "All men have received from nature the imprescriptible *right* to worship the Almighty according to the dictates of their conscience, and no one can be legally compelled to follow, establish, or support against his will any religion or religious ministry. No human authority can, in any circumstances, intervene in a matter of conscience or control the forces of the soul."

Constitution of New Hampshire, Article 5 and 6: "Among these natural rights some are by nature inalienable since nothing can replace them. The rights of conscience are among them."

The incompatibility between religion and the rights of man is to such a degree absent from the concept of the rights of man that, on the contrary, a man's *right to be religious*, is expressly included among the rights of man. The privilege of faith is a *universal right of man*.

The *droits de l'homme*, the rights of man, are, as such, distinct from the *droits du citoyen*, the rights of the citizen. Who is this *man* as distinct from the *citizen*? None other than the *member of civil society*. Why is the member of civil society called "man," simply man; why are his rights called the "rights of man"? How is this fact to be explained? From the relationship between the political state and civil society, from the nature of political emancipation.

Above all, we note the fact that the so-called rights of man, as distinct from the rights of the citizen, are nothing but the rights of a member of civil society—i.e., the rights of egoistic man, of man separated from other men and from the community. Let us hear what the most radical Constitution, the Constitution of 1793, has to say: *Declaration of the Rights of Man and of the Citizen*, Article 2. "These rights, etc., (the natural and imprescriptible rights) are: *equality, liberty, security, property*."

What constitutes liberty?

Article 6. "Liberty is the power which man has to do everything that does not harm the rights of others," or, according to the *Declaration of the Rights of Man* of 1791: "Liberty consists in being able to do everything which does not harm others." Liberty, therefore, is the right to do everything that harms no one else. The limits within which anyone can act without harming someone else are defined by law, just as the boundary between two fields is determined by a boundary post. It is a question of the liberty of man as an isolated monad, withdrawn into himself.... But, the right of man to liberty is based not on the association of man with man, but on the separation of man from man. It is the right of this separation, the right of the *restricted* individual, withdrawn into himself.

The practical application of man's right to liberty is man's right to private property. What constitutes man's right to private property?

Article 16. (Constitution of 1793): "The right of *property* is that which every citizen has of enjoying and of disposing at his discretion of his goods and income, of the fruits of his labor and industry."

The right of man to private property is, therefore, the right to enjoy one's property and to dispose of it at one's discretion, without regard to other men, independently of society, the right of self-interest. This individual liberty and its application form the basis of civil society. It makes every man see in other men not the *realization* of his own freedom, but the *barrier* to it. But, above all, it proclaims the right of man "of enjoying and of disposing at his discretion of his goods and income, of the fruits of his labor and industry."

There remains the other rights of man: equality and security.

Equality, used here in its non-political sense, is nothing but the equality of the liberty described above—namely: each man is to the same extent regarded as such a self-sufficient monad. The Constitution of 1795 defines the concept of this equality, in accordance with this significance, as follows:

Article 5 (Constitution of 1795): "Equality consists in the law being the same for all, whether it protects or punishes."

And security?

Article 8 (Constitution of 1793): "Security consists in the protection afforded by society to each of its members for the preservation of his person, his rights, and his property."

Security is the highest social concept of civil society, the concept of police, expressing the fact that the whole of society exists only in order to guarantee to each of its members the preservation of his person, his rights, and his property. It is in this sense that Hegel calls civil society "the state of need and reason."

The concept of security does not raise civil society above its egoism. On the contrary, security is the *assurance* of egoism.

None of the so-called rights of man, therefore, go beyond egoistic man, beyond man as a member of civil society—that is, an individual withdrawn into himself, into the confines of his private interests and private caprice, and separated from the community. In the rights of man, he is far from being conceived as a species-being; on the contrary, species-life itself, society, appears as a framework external to the individuals, as a restriction of their original independence. The sole bond holding them together is natural necessity, need and private interest, the preservation of their property and their egoistic selves.

It is puzzling enough that a people which is just beginning to liberate itself, to tear down all the barriers between its various sections, and to establish a political community, that such a people solemnly proclaims (*Declaration* of 1791) the rights of egoistic man separated from his fellow men and from the community, and that indeed it repeats this proclamation at a moment when only the most heroic devotion can save the nation, and is therefore imperatively called for, at a moment when the sacrifice of all the interest of civil society must be the order of the day, and egoism must be punished as a crime. (*Declaration of the Rights of Man, etc.*, of 1793.) This fact becomes still more puzzling when we see that the political emancipators go so far as to reduce citizenship, and the *political community*, to a mere *means* for maintaining these so-called rights of man, that, therefore, the citizen is declared to be the servant of egotistic man, that the sphere in which man acts as a communal being is degraded to a level below the sphere in which he acts as a partial being, and that, finally, it is not man as citizen, but man as private individual who is considered to be the *essential* and *true* man.

"The aim of all political association is the preservation of the natural and imprescriptible rights of man." (*Declaration of the Rights, etc.*, of 1791, Article 2.) "Government is instituted in order to guarantee man the enjoyment of his natural and imprescriptible rights." (*Declaration, etc.*, of 1793, Article 1.) Hence, even in moments when its enthusiasm still has the freshness of youth and is intensified to an extreme degree by the force of circumstances, political life declares itself to be a mere *means*, whose purpose is the life is civil society. It is true that its revolutionary practice is in flagrant contradiction with its theory. Whereas, for example, security is declared one of the rights of man, violation of the privacy of correspondence is openly declared to be the order of the day. Whereas "unlimited freedom of the press" (Constitution of 1793, Article 122) is guaranteed as a consequence of the right of man to individual liberty, freedom of the press is totally destroyed, because "freedom of the press should not be permitted when it endangers public liberty." That is to say, therefore: The right of man to liberty ceases to be a right as soon as it comes into conflict with *political* life, whereas in theory political life is only the guarantee of human rights, the rights of the individual, and therefore must be abandoned as soon as it comes into contradiction with its *aim*, with these rights of man....

Feudal society was resolved into its basic element—*man*, but man as he really formed its basis—*egoistic* man.

This *man*, the member of civil society, is thus the basis, the precondition, of the *political* state. He is recognized as such by this state in the rights of man.

The liberty of egoistic man and the recognition of this liberty, however, is rather the recognition of the unrestrained movement of the spiritual and material elements which form the content of his life.

Hence, man was not freed from religion, he received religious freedom. He was not freed from property, he received freedom to own property. He was not freed from the egoism of business, he received freedom to engage in business.

The *establishment of the political state* and the dissolution of civil society into independent *individuals*—whose relation with one another on *law*, just as the relations of men in the system of estates and guilds depended on *privilege*—is accomplished by *one and the same act*. Man as a member of civil society—*non-political* man—inevitably appears, however, as the *natural* man. The "rights of man" appears as "natural rights," because conscious activity is concentrated on the political act. *Egoistic* man is the *passive result* of the dissolved society, a result that is simply found in existence, an object of immediate certainty, therefore a natural object. The *political revolution* dissolves civil life into its component parts, without *revolutionizing* these components themselves or subjecting them to criticism. It regards civil society, the world of needs, labor, private interests, civil law, as the *basis of its existence*, as a precondition not requiring further substantiation and therefore as its *natural basis*. Finally, man as a member of civil society is held to be man in his sensuous, individual, immediate existence, whereas *political* man is only abstract, artificial man, man as an allegorical, juridical person. The real man is recognized only in the shape of the *egoistic* individual, the *true* man is recognized only in the shape of the *abstract citizen*....

All emancipation is a *restoration* of the human world and relationships to *man himself*.

Political emancipation is the reduction of man, on the one hand, to a member of civil society, to an *egoistic, independent* individual, and, on the other hand, to a *citizen*, a juridical person.

Only when the real, individual man re-absorbs in himself the abstract citizen, and as an individual human being has become a *species-being* in his everyday life, in his particular work, and in his particular situation, only when man has recognized and organized his own powers as *social* powers, and, consequently, no longer separates social power from himself in the shape of *political* power, only then will human emancipation have been accomplished.

QUESTIONS FOR REFLECTION

1. Why does Marx believe that even if Jews obtain political equality with Christians they would still be living in a state of general enslavement?
2. How does Marx distinguish between political emancipation and human emancipation? In what ways do you agree or disagree with Marx's claims about religion?
3. What is the relationship between the "rights of man" and the "rights of citizens" according to Marx? How does he describe their differences? Do you think Marx's criticisms are correct? Why?

15. JOHN STUART MILL

John Stuart Mill (1806–1873), one of the most well-known philosophers of the nineteenth century, was born in London. He was educated at home by his father, James Mill, a distinguished economist and disciple of Jeremy Bentham. By the time Mill was 15 he had received a thorough education in Latin, Greek, history, logic, mathematics, and economics. At the age of 17, Mill began working as a clerk for the East India Company, eventually becoming a chief administrator during the course of his 35 year career. In 1865 Mill was elected to Parliament, where he continued to offer outspoken support for such social issues as women's suffrage, abolition of the death penalty, and Irish land reform. While never employed as a professional philosopher, Mill nonetheless published extensively as a prominent advocate of utilitarianism.

In our first selection, from his classic work *Utilitarianism* (1861), Mill defends utilitarianism as a teleological ethical theory because it maintains that what makes actions right or wrong are their consequences (see the Introductions to Kant and Bentham above). Mill contends that actions are right insofar as they tend to promote happiness or pleasure and wrong insofar as they produce unhappiness or pain. The most desirable actions are those that produce happiness for the greatest number of people. Discussing the relationship between utility and justice, Mill departs somewhat from Bentham and argues that moral rights ought to be defended because they help protect certain vulnerable aspects of human welfare and well-being (such as life and health). For Mill, moral rights function as rules that correspond with duties to avoid or prevent harmful behavior. Consequently, moral rights have social utility insofar as the protections they afford allow for the maximization of happiness.

In our second selection, from *On Liberty* (1859), Mill employs his utilitarian ethic in order to maintain the freedom of individuals to do whatever they like so long as they are not harming others. In Mill's view, his "liberty principle" promotes utility by protecting humanity's "permanent interests" in security and autonomy, interests which Mill believes are vital for obtaining happiness.

Text—Utilitarianism (1861)

Reprinted from Utilitarianism. *London: Longmans, Green, Reader & Dyer, 1871.*

Chapter 2: What Utilitarianism Is

....The creed which accepts as the foundation of morals "utility" or the "greatest happiness principle" holds that actions are right in proportion as they tend to promote happiness; wrong as they tend to produce the reverse of happiness. By happiness is intended pleasure and the absence of pain; by unhappiness, pain and the privation of pleasure. To give a clear view of the moral standard set up by the theory, much more requires to be said; in particular, what things it includes in the ideas of pain and pleasure, and to what extent this is left an open question. But these supplementary explanations do not affect the theory of life on which this theory of morality is grounded—namely, that pleasure and freedom from pain are the only things desirable as ends; and that all desirable things (which are as numerous in the utilitarian as in any other scheme) are desirable either for pleasure inherent in themselves or as means to the promotion of pleasure and the prevention of pain....

According to the greatest happiness principle, as above explained, the ultimate end, with reference to and for the sake of which all other things are desirable—whether we are considering our own good or that of other people—is an existence exempt as far as possible from pain, and as rich as possible in enjoyments, both in point of quantity and quality; the test of quality and the rule for measuring it against quantity being the preference felt by those who, in their opportunities of experience, to which must be added their habits of self-consciousness and self-observation, are best furnished with the means of comparison. This, being according to the utilitarian opinion the end of human action, is necessarily also the standard of morality, which may accordingly be defined "the rules and precepts for human conduct," by the observance of which an existence such as has been described might be, to the greatest extent possible, secured to all mankind; and not to them only, but, so far as the nature of things admits, to the whole sentient creation....

Chapter 5: On the Connection Between Justice and Utility

In all ages of speculation one of the strongest obstacles to the reception of the doctrine that utility or happiness is the criterion of right and wrong has been drawn from the idea of justice. The powerful sentiment and apparently clear perception which that word recalls with a rapidity and certainty resembling an instinct have seemed to the majority of thinkers to point to an inherent quality in things; to show that the just must have an existence in nature as something absolute, generically distinct from every variety of the expedient and, in idea, opposed to it, though (as is commonly acknowledged) never, in the long run, disjoined from it in fact....

To find the common attributes of a variety of objects, it is necessary to begin by surveying the objects themselves in the concrete. Let us therefore advert successively to the various modes of action and arrangements of human affairs which are classed, by universal or widely spread opinion, as just or as unjust. The things well known to excite the sentiments associated with those names are of a very multifarious character. I shall pass them rapidly in review, without studying any particular arrangement.

In the first place, it is mostly considered unjust to deprive anyone of his personal liberty, his property, or any other thing which belongs to him by law. Here, therefore, is one instance of the application of the terms just and unjust in a perfectly definite sense, namely, that it is just to respect, unjust to violate, the *legal rights* of anyone. But this judgment admits of several exceptions, arising from the other forms in which the notions of justice and injustice present themselves. For example, the person who suffers the deprivation may (as the phrase is) have *forfeited* the rights which he is so deprived of—a case to which we shall return presently. But also,

Secondly, the legal rights of which he is deprived, may be rights which *ought* not to have belonged to him; in other words, the law which confers on him these rights, may be a bad law. When it is so, or when (which is the same thing for our purpose) it is supposed to be so, opinions will differ as to the justice or injustice of infringing it. Some maintain that no law, however bad, ought to be disobeyed by an individual citizen; that his opposition to it, if shown at all, should only be shown in endeavoring to get it altered by competent authority. This opinion (which condemns many of the most illustrious benefactors of mankind, and would often protect pernicious institutions against the only weapons which, in the state of things existing at the time, have any chance of succeeding against them) is defended, by those who hold it, on grounds of expediency; principally on that of the importance, to the common interest of mankind, of maintaining inviolate the sentiment of submission to law. Other persons, again, hold the directly contrary opinion, that any law, judged to be bad, may blamelessly be disobeyed, even though it be not judged to be unjust, but only inexpedient; while others would confine the license of disobedience to the case of unjust laws: but again, some say that all laws which are inexpedient are unjust; since every law imposes some restriction on the natural liberty of mankind, which restriction is an injustice, unless legitimated by tending to their good. Among these diversions of opinion, it seems to be universally admitted that there may be unjust laws, and that law, consequently, is not the ultimate criterion of justice, but may give to one person a benefit, or impose on another an evil, which justice condemns. When, however, a law is thought to be unjust, it seems always to be regarded as being so in the same way in which a breach of law is unjust, namely, by infringing somebody's right; which, as it cannot in this case be a legal right, receives a different appellation, and is called a moral right. We may say, therefore, that a second case of injustice consists in taking or withholding from any person that to which he has a *moral right*.

Thirdly, it is universally considered just that each person should obtain that (whether good or evil) which he *deserves*, and unjust that he should obtain a good, or be made to undergo an evil, which he does not deserve. This is, perhaps, the dearest and most emphatic form in which the idea of justice is conceived by the general mind. As it involves the notion of desert, the question arises, what constitutes desert? Speaking in a general way, a person is understood to deserve good if he does right, evil if he does wrong; and in a more particular sense, to deserve good from those to whom he does or has done good, and evil from those to whom he does or has done evil. The precept of returning good for evil has never been regarded as a case of the fulfillment of justice, but as one in which the claims of justice are waived, in obedience to other considerations....

This, therefore, being the characteristic difference which marks off, not justice, but morality in general, from the remaining provinces of expediency and worthiness; the character is still to be sought which distinguishes justice from other branches of morality. Now it is known that ethical writers divide moral duties into two classes, denoted by the ill-chosen expressions, duties of perfect and of imperfect obligation; the latter being those in which, though the act is obligatory, the particular occasions of performing it are left to our choice, as in the case of charity or beneficence, which we are indeed bound to practice, but not toward any definite person, nor at any prescribed time. In the more precise language of philosophic jurists, duties of perfect obligation are those duties in virtue of which a correlative *right* resides in some person or persons; duties of imperfect obligation are those moral obligations which do not give birth to any right. I think it will be found that this distinction exactly coincides with that which exists between justice and the other obligation of morality. In our survey of the various popular acceptations of justice, the term appeared generally to involve the idea of a personal right—a claim on the part of one or more individuals, like that which the law gives when it confers a proprietary or other legal right. Whether the injustice consists in depriving a person of a possession, or in breaking faith with him, or in treating him worse than he deserves, or worse than other people who have no greater claims, in each case the supposition implies two things—a wrong done, and some assignable person who is wronged. Injustice may also be done by treating a person better than others; but the wrong in this case is to his competitors, who are also assignable persons. It seems to me that this feature in the case—a right in some person, correlative to the moral obligation—constitutes the specific difference between justice, and generosity or beneficence. Justice implies something which is not only right to do, and wrong not to do, but which some individual person can claim from us as his moral right. No one has a moral right to our generosity or beneficence, because we are not morally bound to practice those virtues towards any given individual. And it will be found with respect to this as to every correct definition, that the instances which seem to conflict with it are those which most confirm it. For if a moralist attempts, as some have done, to make out that mankind generally, though not any given individual, have a right to all the good we can do them, he at once, by that thesis, includes generosity and beneficence within the category of justice. He is obliged to say that our utmost exertions are *due* to our fellow creatures, thus assimilating them to a debt; or that nothing less can be a sufficient return for what society does for us, thus classing the case as one of gratitude; both of which are acknowledged cases of justice. Whenever there is a right, the case is one of justice, and not of the virtue of beneficence; and whoever does not place the distinction between justice and morality in general, where we have now placed it, will be found to make no distinction between them at all, but to merge all morality into justice....

To recapitulate: The idea of justice supposes two things—a rule of conduct and a sentiment which sanctions the rule. The first must be supposed common to all mankind and intended for their good. The other (the sentiment) is a desire that punishment may be suffered by those who infringe the rule. There is involved, in addition, the conception of some definite person who suffers by the infringement, whose rights (to use the expression appropriated to the case) are violated by it. And the sentiment of justice appears to me to be the animal desire to repel or retaliate a hurt or damage to oneself or to those with whom one sympathizes, widened so as to include all persons, by the human capacity of enlarged sympathy and the human conception of intelligent self-interest. From the latter elements the feeling derives its morality; from the former, its peculiar impressiveness and energy of self-assertion.

I have, throughout, treated the idea of a right residing in the injured person and violated by the injury, not as a separate element in the composition of the idea and sentiment, but as one of the forms in which the other two elements clothe themselves. These elements are a hurt to some assignable person or persons, on the one hand, and a demand for punishment, on the other. An examination of our own minds, I think, will show that these two things include all that we mean when we speak of violation of a right. When we call anything a person's right, we mean that he has a valid claim on society to protect him in the possession of it, either by the force of law or by that of education and opinion. If he has what we consider a sufficient claim, on whatever account, to have something guaranteed to him by society, we say that he has a right to it. If we desire to prove that anything does not belong to him by right, we think this done as soon as it is admitted that society ought not to take measure for securing it to him, but should leave him to chance or to his own exertions. Thus a person is said to have a right to what he can earn in fair professional competition, because society ought not to allow any other person to hinder him from endeavoring to earn in that manner as much as he can. But he has not a right to three hundred a year, though he may happen to be earning it; because society is not called on to provide that he shall earn that sum. On the contrary, if he owns ten thousand pounds three-per-cent stock, he *has* a right to three hundred a year because society has come under an obligation to provide him with an income of that amount.

To have a right, then, is, I conceive, to have something which society ought to defend me in the possession of. If the objector goes on to ask why it ought, I can give him no other reason than general utility. If that expression does not seem to convey a sufficient feeling of the strength of the obligation, nor to account for the peculiar energy of the feeling, it is because there goes to the composition of the sentiment, not a rational only but also an animal element—the thirst for retaliation; and this thirst derives its intensity, as well as its moral justification, from the extraordinarily important and impressive kind of utility which is concerned. The interest involved is that of security, to everyone's feelings the most vital of all interests. All other earthly benefits are needed by one person, not needed by another; and many of them can, if necessary, be cheerfully forgone or replaced by something else; but security no human being can possibly do without; on it we depend for all our immunity from evil and for the whole value of all and every good, beyond the passing moment, since nothing but the gratification of the instant could be of any worth to us if we could be deprived of everything the next instant by whoever was momentarily stronger than ourselves. Now this most indispensable of all necessaries, after physical nutriment, cannot be had unless the machinery for providing it is kept unintermittedly in active play. Our notion, therefore, of the claim we have on our fellow creatures to join in making safe for us the very groundwork of our existence gathers feelings around it so much more intense than those concerned in any of the more common cases of utility that the difference in degree (as is often the case in psychology) becomes a real difference in kind. The claim assumes that character of absoluteness, that apparent infinity and incommensurability with all other considerations which constitute the distinction between the feeling of right and wrong and that of ordinary expediency and inexpediency. The feelings concerned are so powerful, and we count so positively on finding a responsive feeling in others (all being alike interested) that *ought* and *should* grow into *must*, and recognized indispensability becomes a moral necessity, analogous to physical, and often not inferior to it in binding force.

Text—On Liberty (1859)

Reprinted from On Liberty. *London: Longmans, Green, Reader & Dyer, 1869.*

Chapter 1: Introductory

.... The object of this essay is to assert one very simple principle, as entitled to govern absolutely the dealings of society with the individual in the way of compulsion and control, whether the means used be physical force in the form of legal penalties or the moral coercion of public opinion. That principle is that the sole end for which mankind are warranted, individually or collectively, in interfering with the liberty of action of any of their number is self-protection. That the only purpose for which power can be rightfully exercised over any member of a civilized community, against his will, is to prevent harm to others. His own good, either physical or moral, is not a sufficient warrant. He cannot rightfully be compelled to do or forbear because it will be better for him to do so, because it will make him happier, because, in the opinion of others, to do so would be wise or even right. These are good reasons for remonstrating with him, or reasoning with him, or persuading him, or entreating him, but not for compelling him or visiting him with any evil in case he do otherwise. To justify that, the conduct from which it is desired to deter him must be calculated to produce evil to someone else. The only part of the conduct of anyone for which he is amenable to society is that which concerns others. In the part which merely concerns himself, his independence is, of right, absolute. Over himself, over his own body and mind, the individual is sovereign....

But there is a sphere of action in which society, as distinguished from the individual, has, if any, only an indirect interest; comprehending all that portion of a person's life and conduct which affects only himself, or if it also affects others, only with their free, voluntary, and undeceived consent and participation. When I say only himself, I mean directly, and in the first instance: for whatever affects himself, may affect others through himself; and the objection which may be grounded on this contingency, will receive consideration in the sequel. This, then, is the appropriate region of human liberty. It comprises, first, the inward domain of consciousness; demanding liberty of conscience, in the most comprehensive sense; liberty of thought and feeling; absolute freedom of opinion and sentiment on all subjects, practical or speculative, scientific, moral, or theological. The liberty of expressing and publishing opinions may seem to fall under a different principle, since it belongs to that part of the conduct of an individual which concerns other people; but, being almost of as much importance as the liberty of thought itself, and resting in great part on the same reasons, is practically inseparable from it. Secondly, the principle requires liberty of tastes and pursuits; of framing the plan of our life to suit our own character; of doing as we like, subject to such consequences as may follow, without impediment from our fellow-creatures, so long as what we do does not harm them, even though they should think our conduct foolish, perverse, or wrong. Thirdly, from this liberty of each individual, follows the liberty, within the same limits, of combination among individuals; freedom to unite, for any purpose not involving harm to others: the persons combining being supposed to be of full age, and not forced or deceived.

No society in which these liberties are not, on the whole, respected, is free, whatever may be its form of government; and none is completely free in which they do not exist absolute and unqualified. The only freedom which deserves the name, is that of pursuing our own good in our own way, so long as we do not attempt to deprive others of theirs, or impede their efforts to obtain it. Each is the proper guardian of his own health, whether bodily, or mental and spiritual. Mankind are greater gainers by suffering each other to live as seems good to themselves, than by compelling each to live as seems good to the rest.

Though this doctrine is anything but new, and, to some persons, may have the air of a truism, there is no doctrine which stands more directly opposed to the general tendency of existing opinion and practice. Society has expended fully as much effort in the attempt (according to its lights) to compel people to conform to its notions of personal, as of social excellence. The ancient commonwealths thought themselves entitled to practice, and the ancient philosophers countenanced, the regulation of every part of private conduct by public authority, on the ground that the State had a deep interest in the whole bodily and mental discipline of every one of its citizens; a mode of thinking which may have been admissible in small republics surrounded by powerful enemies, in constant peril of being subverted by foreign attack or internal commotion, and to which even a short interval of relaxed energy and self-command might so easily be fatal, that they could not afford to wait for the salutary permanent effects of freedom. In the modern world, the greater size of political communities, and above all, the separation between spiritual and temporal authority (which placed the direction of men's consciences in other hands than those which controlled their worldly affairs), prevented so great an interference by law in the details of private life; but the engines of moral repression have been wielded more strenuously against divergence from the reigning opinion in self-regarding, than even in social matters; religion, the most powerful of the elements which have entered into the formation of moral feeling, having almost always been governed either by the ambition of a hierarchy, seeking control over every department of human conduct, or by the spirit of Puritanism. And some of those modern reformers who have placed themselves in strongest opposition to the religions of the past, have been no way behind either churches or sects in their assertion of the right of spiritual domination....

Apart from the peculiar tenets of individual thinkers, there is also in the world at large an increasing inclination to stretch unduly the powers of society over the individual, both by the force of opinion and even by that of legislation: and as the tendency of all the changes taking place in the world is to strengthen society, and diminish the power of the individual, this encroachment is not one of the evils which tend spontaneously to disappear, but, on the contrary, to grow more and more formidable. The disposition of mankind, whether as rulers or as fellow-citizens, to impose their own opinions and inclinations as a rule of conduct on others, is so energetically supported by some of the best and by some of the worst feelings incident to human nature, that it is hardly ever kept under restraint by anything but want of power; and as the power is not declining, but growing, unless a strong barrier of moral conviction can be raised against the mischief, we must expect, in the present circumstances of the world, to see it increase.

QUESTIONS FOR REFLECTION

1. How does Mill justify the possession of moral rights? According to Mill, how do moral rights relate to justice?

2. Mill claims that the "tyranny of the majority" unjustifiably threatens the rights and liberty of individuals? Do you agree or not? Why?

3. Some critics have argued that utilitarianism fails to provide an adequate account of individual rights, since the rights of minorities may be denied if doing so makes the majority happy. Do you agree with this criticism? Why or why not? How do you think the theory of natural rights might avoid this potential problem?

FURTHER READINGS FOR SECTION 2

Avineri, Shlomo. *The Social and Political Thought of Karl Marx*. Cambridge: Cambridge University Press, 1968.

Beiner, Ronald. *Kant and Political Philosophy*. New Haven: Yale University Press, 1993.

Berlin, Isaiah. *Four Essays on Liberty*. Oxford: Oxford University Press, 1969.

Bobbio, Norberto. *The Age of Rights*. Translated by Allan Cameron. Cambridge: Polity Press, 1996.

Dunn, John. *The Political Thought of John Locke*. Cambridge: Cambridge University Press, 1969.

Gauthier, David. *The Logic of Leviathan: The Moral and Political Theory of Thomas Hobbes*. Oxford: Blackwell, 1978.

Gray, John. *Mill on Liberty: A Defence*. London: Routledge, 1983.

Haakonssen, Knud and Michael J. Lacey, eds. *A Culture of Rights: The Bill of Rights in Philosophy, Politics and Law*. Cambridge: Cambridge University Press, 1991.

Hamilton, Alexander, John Jay, and James Madison. *The Federalist Papers*. New York: Modern Library, 1937.

Hampton, Jean. *Hobbes and the Social Contract Tradition*. Cambridge: Cambridge University Press, 1986.

Kavka, Gregory. *Hobbesian Moral and Political Theory*. Princeton: Princeton University Press, 1986.

Korsgaard, Christine. *Creating the Kingdom of Ends*. Cambridge: Harvard University Press, 1996.

Lukes, Steven. *Marxism and Morality*. Oxford: Clarendon Press, 1985.
Lyons, David. *In the Interest of the Governed*. Oxford: Oxford University Press, 1991.
Macpherson, C. B. *The Political Theory of Possessive Individualism*. Oxford: Clarendon Press, 1962.
Raphael, D. D., ed. *Political Theory and the Rights of Man*. Bloomington and London: Indiana University Press, 1967.
Ryan, Alan. *J. S. Mill*. London: Routledge, 1974.
Shell, Susan Meld. *The Rights of Reason: A Study of Kant's Philosophy and Politics*. Toronto: University of Toronto Press, 1980.
Shklar, Judith. *Men and Citizens: A Study of Rousseau's Social Theory*. 2nd ed. Cambridge: Cambridge University Press, 1985.
Simmons, John. *The Lockean Theory of Rights*. Princeton: Princeton University Press, 1992.
——. *Moral Principles and Political Obligations*. Princeton: Princeton University Press, 1979.
Stephen, J. F. *Liberty, Equality, Fraternity*. Cambridge: Cambridge University Press, 1967.
Strauss, Leo. *Natural Right and History*. Chicago: University of Chicago Press, 1953.
Tuck, Richard. *Natural Rights Theories: Their Origin and Development*. Cambridge: Cambridge University Press, 1979.

Section 3:

CONTEMPORARY PERSPECTIVES

16. H. L. A. HART

H. L. A. Hart (1907-1992) was one of the major legal philosophers of the twentieth century and Professor of Jurisprudence in Oxford University from 1952 to 1968. Hart's theory is a form of legal positivism, derived from Bentham, which holds that law properly so-called consists of commands or rules posited by political authority. As a legal positivist, Hart argues that there is no conceptual overlap between law and morality of the kind asserted by natural law theorists. This is not to say, however, that moral considerations are necessarily excluded from the legal order. In his classic article reprinted below, Hart makes the conditional claim that *if* we can recognize the existence of at least one basic or natural right, it is the equal right to liberty, implied negatively as the basis for justifying interference in the freedom of others in order to protect the liberty of all persons.

Text—Are There Any Natural Rights?

From Philosophical Review *64 (1955). Copyright 1955, Cornell University. Reprinted by permission of the publisher.*

I shall advance the thesis that if there are any moral rights at all, it follows that there is at least one natural right, the equal right of all men to be free. By saying that there is this right, I mean that in the absence of certain special conditions which are consistent with the right being an equal right, any adult human being capable of choice (1) has the right to forbearance on the part of all others from the use of coercion or restraint against him save to hinder coercion or restraint and (2) is at liberty to do (i.e. is under no obligation to abstain from) any action which is not one coercing or restraining or designed to injure other persons.[1]

I have two reasons for describing the equal rights of all men to be free as a *natural* right; both of them were always emphasized by the classical theorists of natural rights. (1) This right is one which all men have if they are capable of choice: they have it *qua* men and not only if they are members of some society or stand in some special relation to each other. (2) This right is not created or conferred by men's voluntary action; other moral rights are. Of course, it is quite obvious that my thesis is not as ambitious as the traditional theories of natural rights; for although on my view all men are *equally* entitled to be free in the sense explained, no man has an absolute or unconditional right to do or not to do any particular thing or to be treated in any particular way; coercion or restraint of any action may be justified in special conditions consistently with the general principle. So my argument will not show that men have any right (save the equal right of all to be free) which is "absolute," "indefeasible," or "imprescriptible." This may for many reduce the importance of my contention, but I think that the principle that all men have an equal right to be free, meagre as it may seem, is probably all that the political philosophers of the liberal tradition need have claimed to support any programme of action even if they have claimed more. But my contention that there is this one natural right may appear unsatisfying in another respect; it is only the conditional assertion that *if* there are any moral rights then there must be this one natural right....

I

(A) Lawyers have for their own purposes carried the dissection of the notion of a legal right some distance, and some of their results[2] are of value in the elucidation of statements of the form "X has a right to..." outside legal contexts. There is of course no simple identification to be made between moral and legal rights, but there is an intimate connection between the two, and this itself is one feature which distinguishes a moral right from other fundamental moral concepts. It is not merely that as a matter of fact men speak of their moral rights mainly when advocating their incorporation in a legal system, but that the concept of a right belongs to that branch of morality which is specifically concerned to determine when one person's freedom may be limited by another's[3] and so to determine what actions may appropriately be made the subject of coercive legal rules. The words "*droit*," "*diritto*," and "*Recht*," used by continental jurists, have no simple English translation and seem to English jurists to hover uncertainly between law and morals, but they do in fact mark off an area of morality (the morality of law) which has special characteristics. It is occupied by the concepts of justice, fairness, rights, and obligation (if this last is not used as it is by many moral philosophers as an obscuring general label to cover every action that morally we ought to do or forbear from doing). The most important common characteristic of this group of moral concepts is that there is no incongruity, but a special congruity in the use of force or the threat of force to secure that what is just or fair or someone's right to have done shall in fact be done; for it is in just these circumstances that coercion of another human being is legitimate....

(B) I can best exhibit this feature of a moral right by reconsidering the question whether moral rights and "duties"[4] are correlative. The contention that they are means, presumably, that every statement of the form "X has a right to..." entails and is entailed by "Y has a duty (not) to...," and at this stage we must not assume that the values of the name-variables "X" and "Y" must be different persons. Now there is certainly one sense of "a right" (which I have already mentioned) such that it does not follow from X's having a right that X or someone else has any duty. Jurists have isolated rights in this sense and have referred to them as "liberties" just to distinguish them from rights in the centrally important sense of "right" which has "duty" as a correlative. The former sense of "right" is needed to describe those areas of social life where competition is at least morally unobjectionable. Two people walking along both see a ten-dollar bill in the road twenty yards away, and there is no clue as to the owner. Neither of the two are under a "duty" to allow the other to pick it up; each has in this sense a right to pick it up. Of course there may be many things which each has a "duty" not to do in the course of the race to the spot—neither may kill or wound the other—and corresponding to these "duties" there are rights to forbearances. The moral propriety of all economic competition implies this minimum sense of "a right" in which to say that "X has a right to" means merely that X is under no "duty" not to. Hobbes saw that the expression "a right" could have this sense but he was wrong if he thought that there is no sense in which it does follow from X's having a right that Y has a duty or at any rate an obligation.

(C) More important for our purpose is the question whether for all moral "duties" there are correlative moral rights, because those who have given an affirmative answer to this question have usually assumed without adequate scrutiny that to have a right is simply to be capable of benefiting by the performance of a "duty"; whereas in fact this is not a sufficient condition (and probably not a necessary condition) of having a right. Thus animals and babies who stand to benefit by our performance of our "duty" not to ill-treat them are said *therefore* to have rights to proper treatment. The full consequence of this reasoning is not usually followed out; most have shrunk from saying that we have rights against ourselves because we stand to benefit from our performance of our "duty" to keep ourselves alive or develop our talents. But the moral situation which arises from a promise (where the legal-sounding terminology of rights and obligations is most appropriate) illustrates most clearly that the notion of having a right and that of benefiting by the performance of a "duty" are not identical. X promises Y in return for some favour that he will look after Y's aged mother in his absence. Rights arise out of this transaction, but it is surely Y to whom the promise has been made and not his mother who *has* or *possesses* these rights. Certainly Y's mother is a person concerning whom X has an obligation and a person who will benefit by its performance, but the person *to whom* he has an obligation to look after her is Y. This is something *due to* or *owed* to Y, so it is Y, not his mother, whose right X will disregard and to whom X will have done *wrong* if he fails to keep his promise, though the mother may be physically injured. And it is Y who has a moral *claim* upon X; is *entitled* to have his mother looked after, and who can *waive* the claim and *release* Y from the obligation. Y is, in other words, morally in a position to determine by his choice how X shall act and in this way to limit X's freedom of choice; and it is this fact, not the fact that he stands to benefit, that makes it appropriate to say that he has a *right*. Of course often the person to whom a promise has been made will be the only person who stands to benefit by its performance, but this does not justify the identification of "having a right" with "benefiting by the performance of a duty." It is important for the whole logic of rights that, while the person who stands to benefit by the performance of a duty is discovered by considering what will happen if the duty is not performed, the person who has a right (to whom performance is *owed* or *due*) is discovered by examining the transaction or antecedent situation or relations of the parties out of which the "duty" arises....

(D) The essential connection between the notion of a right and the justified limitation of one person's freedom by another may be thrown into relief if we consider codes of behaviour which do not purport to confer rights but only to prescribe what shall be done. Most natural law thinkers down to Hooker conceived of natural law in this way: there were natural duties compliance with which would certainly benefit man—things to be done to achieve man's natural end—but not natural rights. And there are of course many types of codes of behaviour which only prescribe what is to be done, e.g. those regulating certain ceremonies. It would be absurd to regard these codes as conferring rights, but illuminating to contrast them with rules of games, which often create rights, though not, of course, moral rights.... Rights are typically conceived of as *possessed* or *owned by* or *belonging to* individuals, and these expressions reflect the conception of moral rules as not only prescribing conduct but as forming a kind of moral property of individuals to which they are as individuals entitled; only when rules are conceived in this way can we speak of *rights* and *wrongs* as well as right and wrong actions.

II

So far I have sought to establish that to have a right entails having a moral justification for limiting the freedom of another person and for determining how he should act; it is now important to see that the moral justification must be of a special kind if it is to constitute a right, and this will emerge most clearly from an examination of the circumstances in which rights are asserted with the typical expression "I have a right to...." It is I think the case that this form of words is used in two main types of situations: (A) when the claimant has some special justification for interference with another's freedom which other persons do not have ("*I* have a right to be paid what you promised for my services"); (B) when the claimant is concerned to resist or object to some interference by another person as having no justification ("*I* have a right to say what I think").

(A) *Special rights.* When rights arise out of special transactions between individuals or out of some special relationship in which they stand to each other, both the persons who have the right and those who have the corresponding obligation are limited to the parties to the special transaction or relationship. I call such rights special rights to distinguish them from those moral rights which are thought of as rights against (i.e. as imposing obligations upon) everyone, such as those that are asserted when some unjustified interference is made or threatened as in (B) above.

(i) The most obvious cases of special rights are those that arise from promises. By promising to do or not to do something, we voluntarily incur obligations and create or confer rights on those to whom we promise; we alter the existing moral independence of the parties' freedom of choice in relation to some action and create a new moral relationship between them, so that it becomes morally legitimate for the person to whom the promise is given to determine how the promisor shall act. The promisee has a temporary authority or sovereignty in relation to some specific matter over the other's will which we express by saying that the promisor is under an obligation to the promisee to do what he has promised.... The simplest case of promising illustrates two points characteristic of all special rights: (1) the right and obligation arise not because the promised action has itself any particular moral quality, but just because of the voluntary transaction between the parties; (2) the identity of the parties concerned is vital—only *this* person (the promisee) has the moral justification for determining how the promisor shall act. It is *his* right; only in relation to him is the promisor's freedom of choice diminished, so that if he chooses to release the promisor no one else can complain.

(ii) But a promise is not the only kind of transaction whereby rights are conferred. They may be *accorded* by a person consenting or authorizing another to interfere in matters which but for his consent or authorization he would be free to determine for himself. If I consent to your taking precautions for my health and happiness or authorize you to look after my interests, then you have a right which others have not, and I cannot complain of your interference if it is within the sphere of your authority. This is what is meant by a person surrendering his rights to another; and again the typical characteristics of a right are present in this situation: the person authorized has the right to interfere not because of its intrinsic character but because *these* persons have stood in *this* relationship. No one else (not similarly authorized) has any *right* to interfere in theory even if the person authorized does not exercise his right.

(iii) Special rights are not only those created by the deliberate choice of the party on whom the obligation falls, as they are when they are accorded or spring from promises, and not all obligations to other persons are deliberately incurred, though I think it is true of all special rights that they arise from previous voluntary actions. A third very important source of special rights and obligations which we recognize in many spheres of life is what may be termed mutuality of restrictions, and I think political obligation is intelligible only if we see what precisely this is and how it differs from other right-creating transactions (consent, promising) to which philosophers have assimilated it. In its bare schematic outline it is this: when a number of persons conduct any joint enterprise according to rules and thus restrict their liberty, those who have submitted to these restrictions when required have a right to a similar submission from those who have benefited by their submission. The rules may provide that officials should have authority to enforce obedience and make further rules, and this will create a structure of legal rights and duties, but the moral obligation to obey the rules in such circumstances is *due to* the co-operating members of the society, and they have the correlative moral right to obedience. In social situations of this sort (of which political society is the most complex example) the obligation to obey the rules is something distinct from whatever other moral reasons there may be for obedience in terms of good consequences (e.g. the prevention of suffering); the obligation is due to the co-operating members of the society as such and not because they are human beings on whom it would be wrong to inflict suffering....

The social-contract theorists rightly fastened on the fact that the obligation to obey the law is not merely a special case of benevolence (direct or indirect), but something which arises between members of a particular political society out of their mutual relationship. Their mistake was to identify *this* right-creating situation of mutual restrictions with the paradigm case of promising; there are of course important similarities, and these are just the points which all special rights have in common, viz. that they arise out of special relationships between human beings and not out of the character of the action to be done or its effects....

(B) *General rights*. In contrast with special rights, which constitute a justification peculiar to the holder of the right for interfering with another's freedom, are general rights, which are asserted defensively, when some unjustified interference is anticipated or threatened, in order to point out that the interference is unjustified. "I have the right to say what I think."[5] "I have the right to worship as I please." Such rights share two important characteristics with special rights. (1) To have them is to have moral justification for determining how another shall act, viz. that he shall not interfere.[6] (2) The moral justification does not arise from the character of the particular action to the performance of which the claimant has a right; what justifies the claim is simply—there being no special relation between him and those who are threatening to interfere to justify that interference—that this is a particular exemplification of the equal right to be free. But there are of course striking differences between such defensive general rights and special rights. (1) General rights do not arise out of any special relationship or transaction between men. (2) They are not rights which are peculiar to those who have them but are rights which all men capable of choice have in the absence of those special conditions which give rise to special rights. (3) General rights have as correlatives obligations not to interfere to which everyone else is subject and not merely the parties to some special relationship or transaction, though of course they will often be asserted when some particular persons threaten to interfere as a moral objection to the interference. To assert a general right is to claim in relation to some particular action the equal right of all men to be free in the absence of any of those special conditions which constitute a special right to limit another's freedom; to assert a special right is to assert in relation to some particular action a right constituted by such special conditions to limit another's freedom. The assertion of general rights directly invokes the principle that all men equally have the right to be free; the assertion of a special right (as I attempt to show in Section III) invokes it indirectly.

III

It is, I hope, clear that unless it is recognized that interference with another's freedom requires a moral justification the notion of a right could have no place in morals; for to assert a right is to assert that there is such a justification. The characteristic function in moral discourse of those sentences in which the meaning of the expression "a right" is to be found—"I have a right to...," "You have no right to...," "What right have you to...?"—is to bring to bear on interferences with another's freedom, or on claims to interfere, a type of moral evaluation or criticism specially appropriate to interference with freedom and characteristically different from the moral criticism of actions made with the use of expressions like "right," "wrong," "good," and "bad." And this is only one of many different types of moral ground for saying "You ought..." or "You ought not...." The use of the expression "What right have you to...?" shows this more clearly, perhaps, than the others; for we use it, just at the point where interference is actual or threatened, to call for the moral *title* of the person addressed to interfere; and we do this often without any suggestion at all that what he proposes to do is otherwise wrong and sometimes with the implication that the same interference on the part of another person would be unobjectionable....

We saw in Section II that the types of justification for interference involved in special rights was independent of the character of the action to the performance of which there was a right but depended upon certain previous transactions and relations between individuals (such as promises, consent, authorization, submission to mutual restrictions). Two questions here suggest themselves: (1) On what intelligible principle could these bare forms of promising, consenting, submission to mutual restrictions, be either necessary or sufficient, irrespective of their content, to justify interference with another's freedom? (2) What characteristics have these types of transaction or relationship in common? The answer to both these questions is I think this: if we justify interference on such grounds as we give when we claim a moral right, we are in fact indirectly invoking as our justification the principle that all men have an equal right to be free. For we are in fact saying in the case of promises and consents or authorizations that this claim to interfere with another's freedom is justified because he has, in exercise of his equal right to be free, freely chosen to create this claim; and in the case of mutual restrictions we are in fact saying that this claim to interfere with another's freedom is justified because it is fair; and it is fair because only so will there be an equal distribution of restrictions and so of freedom among this group of men. So in the case of special rights as well as of general rights recognition of them implies the recognition of the equal right of all men to be free.

Notes

1. Further explanation of the perplexing terminology of freedom is, I fear, necessary. *Coercion* includes, besides preventing a person from doing what he chooses, making his choice less eligible by threats; *restraint* includes any action designed to make the exercise of choice impossible and so includes killing or enslaving a person. But neither coercion nor restraint includes *competition*. In terms of the distinction between "having a right to" and "being at liberty to," used above and further discussed in sect. I, B, all men say have, consistently with the obligation to forbear from coercion, the *liberty* to satisfy if they can such at least of their desires as are not designed to coerce or injure others, even though in fact, owing to scarcity, one man's satisfaction causes another's frustration. In conditions of extreme scarcity this distinction between competition and coercion will not be worth drawing; natural rights are only of importance "where peace is possible" (Locke). Further, freedom (the absence of coercion) can be *valueless* to those victims of unrestricted competition too poor to make use of it; so it will be pedantic to point out to them that though starving they are free. This is the truth exaggerated by the Marxists whose *identification* of poverty with lack of freedom confuses two different evils.

2. As W. D. Lamont has seen: cf. his *Principles of Moral Judgement* (Oxford, 1946); for the jurists, cf. Hohfeld's *Fundamental Legal Conceptions* (New Haven, 1923).

3. Here and subsequently I use "interfere with another's freedom," "limit another's freedom," "determine how another shall act," to mean either the use of coercion or demanding that a person shall do or not do some action. The connection between these two types of "interference" is too complex for discussion here; I think it is enough for present purposes to point out that having a justification for demanding that a person shall or shall not do some action is a necessary though not a sufficient condition for justifying coercion.

4. I write "duties" here because one factor obscuring the nature of a right is the philosophical use of "duty" and "obligation" for all cases where there are moral reasons for saying an action ought to be done or not done. In fact "duty," "obligation," "right," and "good" come from different segments of morality, concern different types of conduct, and make different types of moral criticism or evaluation. Most important are the points (1) that obligations may be voluntarily incurred or created, (2) that they are *owed* to special persons (who have rights), (3) that they do not arise out of the character of the actions which are obligatory but out of the relationship of the parties. Language roughly though not consistently confines the use of "having an obligation" to such cases.

5. In speech the difference between general and special rights is often marked by stressing the pronoun where a special right is claimed or where the special right is denied. "You have no right to stop him reading that book" refers to the reader's general right. "*You* have no right to stop him reading that book" denies that the person addressed has a special right to interfere though others may have.

6. Strictly, in the assertion of a general right both the *right* to forbearance from coercion and the *liberty* to do the specified action are asserted, the first in the face of actual or threatened coercion, the second as an objection to an actual or anticipated demand that the action should not be done. The first has as its correlative an obligation upon everyone to forbear from coercion, the second the absence in any one of a justification for such a demand. Here, in Hohfeld's words, the correlative is not an obligation but a "no-right."

Questions for Reflection

1. How does Hart distinguish between "special" and "general" rights? Do you find any problems with Hart's description of general rights?
2. How convincing is Hart's claim that we have a justification for restricting another person's freedom?
3. Do you think that Hart is able to demonstrate the existence of a natural right to *freedom* rather than to, say, happiness or pleasure?

17. MAURICE CRANSTON

Maurice Cranston (1920-1993) was a distinguished political theorist and professor of political science at the London School of Economics. He was known especially for his award-winning biographies of Locke and Rousseau. In the following essay Cranston discusses different conceptions of human rights, in particular the distinction between civil and political rights and economic and social rights. The distinction between these two types of rights has been characterized in contemporary human rights debates as a differentiation between so-called *negative* rights (the civil and political rights of persons against the power of governments) and *positive* rights (the rights of persons to certain types of social and cultural opportunities and services and economic standards). The usefulness of this distinction has been challenged by many theorists. Cranston argues, however, that any rights which fail his proposed "test of practicability" should not be recognized as human rights.

Text—Human Rights, Real and Supposed

From Political Theory and the Rights of Man, *D. D. Raphael, ed. Bloomington: Indiana University Press, 1967. Reprinted by permission of Macmillan Press Ltd.*

It is said that when that remarkable American jurist Wesley Newcomb Hohfield tried to make the students at Yale Law School discriminate carefully between different uses of the term "right" in Anglo-American law, he earned himself considerable unpopularity; his pupils even got up a petition to have him removed from his Chair. If the analysis of positive rights is thus resisted by law students we should not be surprised if the analysis of human rights is ill-regarded by many politicians, publicists, and even political theorists. Some politicians, indeed, have a vested interest in keeping talk about human rights as meaningless as possible. For there are those who do not want to see human rights become positive rights by genuine enactments; hence the more nebulous, unrealistic, or absurd the concept of human rights is made out to be, the better such men are pleased.

I shall argue in this paper that a philosophically respectable concept of human rights has been muddled, obscured, and debilitated in recent years by an attempt to incorporate into it specific rights of a different logical category. The traditional human rights are political and civil rights such as the right to life, liberty, and a fair trial. What are now being put forward as universal human rights are social and economic rights, such as the right to unemployment insurance, old-age pensions, medical services, and holidays with pay. I have both a philosophical and a political objection to this. The philosophical objection is that the new theory of human rights does not make sense. The political objection is that the circulation of a confused notion of human rights hinders the effective protection of what are correctly seen as human rights.

One distinction which seems now well established in people's minds is that between human rights or the Rights of Man or natural rights (I take these expressions to mean the same thing) and positive rights, a distinction which corresponds to the distinction between natural law (or justice, or the moral law) and positive law.... The present century has seen a marked revival of consciousness of what is now generally known as human rights—a term which has the advantage over the older expression "natural rights" of not committing one too ostentatiously to any traditional doctrine of Natural Law. The reason for this revival is perhaps to be sought in history, first, in the great twentieth-century evils, Nazism, fascism, total war, and racialism, which have all presented a fierce challenge to human rights; and secondly, in an increased belief in, or demand for, equality among men. When the United Nations was set up by the victorious powers in the Second World War one of the first and most important tasks assigned to it was what Winston Churchill called "the enthronement of human rights:" The efforts that have been made at the United Nations to fulfill this promise have much to teach a political theorist.

At the inaugural meeting of the Economic and Social Council of the UN in May 1946, a Commission on Human Rights was appointed to submit to the General Assembly recommendations and reports regarding an "International Bill of Rights." English-speaking delegates on this Commission promptly put forward a draft "Bill of Rights" in the form of a draft convention or treaty which both named the specific rights to be recognized and provided for the setting up of international institutions to deal with any alleged breach of those rights. The English-speaking delegations not unnaturally interpreted the expression "Bill of Rights" as meaning an instrument of positive law, and therefore understood the duty of the Commission to be that of finding a formula for making human rights positive rights by making them enforceable. The Russian representative objected to these proposals. He said that it was premature to discuss any measure of a binding or judicial nature; the Soviet Union was willing to support a "Bill of Rights" only if it was understood as a manifesto or declaration of rights. Some years afterwards the United States followed the Russian example, and announced that it, too, would not commit itself to any legally binding convention for the international protection of human rights.

In the UN Commission on Human Rights a compromise was settled on. The Commission agreed first to produce a manifesto or declaration of human rights, and then afterwards begin to work out "something more legally binding" which it was decided to call a Covenant. The manifesto did not take long to produce. It was given the name of Universal Declaration of Human Rights and proclaimed by the General Assembly of the United Nations in December 1948....

One of the difficulties of translating the Universal Declaration of Human Rights into any kind of positive law is that the Declaration contains so much. It has no fewer than thirty articles. The first twenty spell out in detail the sort of rights that were named in the various classical statements of the Rights of Man: the rights to life, liberty, property, equality, justice, and the pursuit of happiness are articulated as, among other things, the right to freedom of movement; the right to own property alone as well as in association with others; the right to marry; the right to equality before the law and to a fair trial if accused of any crime; the right to privacy; the right to religious freedom; the right to free speech and peaceful assembly; the right to asylum. Among the institutions outlawed are slavery, torture, and arbitrary detention.

The Universal Declaration of 1948 did not, however, limit itself to this restatement of the familiar Rights of Man; it includes a further ten articles which name rights of a new and different kind.[1] Article 21 states that everyone has the right to take part in the government of his country, and further articles affirm the right to education; the right to work and to form trade unions; the right to equal pay for equal work; the right of everyone to a standard of living adequate to the health and well-being of himself and his family; the right to security in the event of unemployment, sickness, disability, widowhood, old age, or other lack of livelihood; the right to enjoy the arts and to share in scientific advancement and its benefits; and, what is even more novel, the right to rest, leisure, and "periodic holidays with pay."

The difference between these new rights and the traditional natural rights was not unnoticed by those responsible for drafting the Declaration. In the records of the Commission, the first twenty articles are called "political and civil rights" and the further rights "economic and social rights." These later rights appear to have been included under pressure from the Left; but there are many humanitarian people, apart from those on the Left, who (in my belief, unwisely) agree with their inclusion....[2]

One of the objections to regarding the "social and economic" rights as authentic human rights is that it would be totally impossible to translate them in the same way into positive rights by analogous political and legal action. There are other objections: but the time has now come to consider more carefully what is meant by a right, and then what kind of right a human right is. We have already noted the distinction between human rights and positive rights; I propose now to rearrange rights into two other categories; the one I shall call legal rights, the other moral rights.

(1) Legal rights may be distinguished as follows:

a. *General positive rights*: The rights that are enjoyed and fully assured to everyone living under a given jurisdiction or constitution.

b. *Traditional rights and liberties*: Burke said that the English people had risen against James II because he had taken away their traditional rights and liberties as Englishmen. The Vichy government took away many of the traditional rights and liberties of Frenchmen. This class of rights includes lost positive rights as well as existing positive rights.

c. *Nominal "legal" rights*: Even the least liberal nations tend to have "facade" constitutions[3] which "guarantee" freedom of speech, movement, assembly, and other such rights to their inhabitants. But where these nominal rights are not enforced, they cannot, of course, be classed as positive rights. We nevertheless see the demand in some such places for the nominal "legal" rights being made positive rights. One example is the demand of certain Polish intellectuals for that freedom of expression which their constitution assures them. An even more publicized example is the demand of the Negroes in the United States for the nominal legal right to vote, enter State schools, and so forth, to be translated into positive rights.

d. *Positive rights, liberties, privileges, and immunities of a limited class of persons*: Under this category we should have to include all rights which are attached to membership of a given category, e.g., the rights of clergymen, of peers, of doctors, of graduates of the University of Oxford, and of freemen of the City of London. The twentieth century has become impatient of privileges, and rights which were once enjoyed by a limited class of persons are often now claimed by all the inhabitants of a country. For example, the privileges of citizenship, the rights of ratepayers, as they were known in nineteenth-century England, are now enjoyed by all adult British subjects. A demand for the extension of rights within a political society is often confused with the demand for human rights. But the two are quite distinct.

e. *The positive rights, liberties, privileges, and immunities of a single person*: Here the examples are few, because the cases are few: the rights of the President of the United States, of the Chairman of the Senate; the rights of the King, or the Lord Chancellor, or the Archbishop of Canterbury, are examples. Since the decay of the doctrine of the Divine Right of Kings, this class of rights does not present much of a problem.

The foregoing classes cover the category of legal rights. Next in turn is the category of moral rights. In this case it will be convenient to reverse the order of generality.

(2) Moral Rights

a. *Moral rights of one person only*: We remember Bradley's famous phrase "my station and its duties": we can equally speak of "my station and its rights." I, and I alone, have a network of rights which arise from the fact that I have done certain deeds, paid certain monies, been elected to certain places, and so forth. Some of these rights are legal rights as well as moral rights. But in considering them as moral rights the question is not "Does the law uphold them?" but "Have I just claim to them?" Not all my moral rights may in fact be enjoyed. Often we become most conscious of our moral rights precisely when they are not upheld. I am inclined to say "I have a moral right to be told what is going on in my own house" when I realize I am not being told. So just as the crucial question with legal rights is "Are they secured and enjoyed?" the crucial question in a moral right is "Is there a just title?" Is there a sound moral claim? *Justification* is the central question.

b. *The moral rights of anyone in a particular situation*: This is the class of moral rights which belongs to everyone who comes into a certain specific category, e.g., that of a parent, or a tutor, or an *au pair* girl. So we can say of a person, if he is a member of this class, he is entitled to so and so. Claims to have such moral rights are pressed by proving that one does belong to the appropriate category.

c. *The moral rights of all people in all situations*: Because these rights are universal we should naturally expect them to be few in number; and we should expect them to be highly generalized in their formulation. It is easier to agree, for example, about the kind of deed which violates the right to life than it is to agree about any philosophical expression of the right to life. Moreover, it is inevitable that such a right as that to liberty will be somewhat differently understood in different societies, where the boundary between liberty and licence will be differently drawn. Again, our understanding of the right to property will differ according to the meaning we give to that richly ambiguous word.

The place which human rights occupy in my classification is readily understood. Human rights are a form of moral right, and they differ from other moral rights in being the rights of all people at all times and in all situations. This characteristic of human rights is recognized in the first paragraph of the preamble to the Universal Declaration of 1948, which says: "Whereas recognition of the inherent dignity and of the equal and inalienable rights of all members of the human family is the foundation of freedom, justice and peace in the world...."

Part of the difficulty of justifying human rights is their very universality. Moral rights of classes (2) (a) and (2) (b) above are justified by reference to the definite station or situation of the claimants. I claim a right to be told about the health of Nicholas Cranston by showing that I am his father. I do not think anyone else (except his mother) has the same right. But human rights do not depend in any way on the station or the situation of the individual. This is part of what is meant by saying they are "rights that pertain to a human being merely because he is a human being." If the validity of a moral right is commonly established by reference to the station or situation of the claimant, it is not altogether easy to see by what tests one could validate the rights which are *not* considered in relation to any definite situation.

Nevertheless there are some tests for the authenticity of a human right or universal moral right. Rights bear a clear relationship to duties. And the first test of both is that of practicability. It is not my duty to do what it is physically impossible for me to do. You cannot reasonably say it was my duty to have jumped into the Thames at Richmond to rescue a drowning child if I was nowhere near Richmond at the time the child was drowning. What is true of duties is equally true of rights. If it is impossible for a thing to be done, it is absurd to claim it as a right. At present it is utterly impossible, and will be for a long time yet, to provide "holidays with pay" for everybody in the world. For millions of people who live in those parts of Asia, Africa, and South America where industrialization has hardly begun, such claims are vain and idle.

The traditional "political and civil rights" can (as I have said) be readily secured by legislation; and generally they can be secured by fairly simple legislation. Since those rights are for the most part rights against government interference with a man's activities, a large part of the legislation needed has to do no more than restrain the government's own executive arm. This is no longer the case when we turn to "the right to work," "the right to social security," and so forth. For a government to provide social security it needs to do more than make laws; it has to have access to great capital wealth, and many governments in the world today are still poor. The government of India, for example, simply cannot command the resources that would guarantee each one of the 480 million inhabitants of India "a standard of living adequate for the health and well-being of himself and his family," let alone "holidays with pay."

Another test of a human right is that it shall be a genuinely universal moral right. This the so-called human right to holidays with pay plainly cannot pass. For it is a right that is necessarily limited to those persons who are *paid* in any case, that is to say, to the *employé* class. Since not everyone belongs to this class, the right cannot be a universal right, a right which, in the terminology of the Universal Declaration, "everyone" has. That the right to a holiday with pay is for many people a real moral right, I would not for one moment deny. But it is a right which falls into section (2) (b) of the classification of rights which I have set out above; that is, a right which can be claimed by members of a specific class of persons *because* they are members of that class.

A further test of a human right, or universal moral right, is the test of *paramount importance*. Here the distinction is less definite, but no less crucial. And here again there is a parallel between rights and duties. It is a paramount duty to relieve great distress, as it is not a paramount duty to give pleasure. It would have been my duty to rescue the drowning child at Richmond if I had been there at the time; but it is not, in the same sense, my duty to give Christmas presents to the children of my neighbours. This difference is obscured in the crude utilitarian philosophy which analyses moral goodness in terms of the greatest happiness of the greatest number: but common sense does not ignore it. Common sense knows that fire engines and ambulances are essential services, whereas fun fairs and holiday camps are not. Liberality and kindness are reckoned moral virtues; but they are not moral duties in the sense that the obligation to rescue a drowning child is a moral duty.

It is worth considering the circumstances in which ordinary people find themselves invoking the language of human rights. I suggest they are situations like these:

A black student in South Africa is awarded a scholarship to Oxford and then refused a passport by the South African government simply because he is black. We feel this is clear invasion of the human right to freedom of movement.

Jews are annihilated by the Nazi government, simply because they are Jews. We feel this is a manifest abuse (an atrocious abuse) of the human right to life.

In several countries men are held in prison indefinitely without trial. We feel this a gross invasion of the human right to liberty and to a fair trial on any criminal charge.

In considering cases of this kind, we are confronted by matters which belong to a totally different moral dimension from questions of social security and holidays with pay. A human right is something of which no one may be deprived without a grave affront to justice. There are certain deeds which should never be done, certain freedoms which should never be invaded, some things which are supremely sacred. If a Declaration of Human Rights is what it purports to be, a declaration of universal moral rights, it should be confined to this sphere of discourse. If rights of another class are introduced, the effect may even be to bring the whole concept of human rights into disrepute. "It would be a splendid thing," people might say, "for everyone to have holidays with pay, a splendid thing for everyone to have social security, a splendid thing to have equality before the law, and freedom of speech, and the right to life. One day, perhaps, this beautiful ideal may be realized...."

Thus the effect of a Universal Declaration which is overloaded with affirmations of so-called human rights which are not human rights at all is to push *all* talk of human rights out of the clear realm of the morally compelling into the twilight world of utopian aspiration. In the Universal Declaration of 1948 there indeed occurs the phrase a "common standard of achievement" which brands that Declaration as an attempt to translate rights into ideals. And however else one might choose to define moral rights, they are plainly *not* ideals or aspirations.

Rights have been variously defined by jurists and philosophers. Some have spoken of them in terms of "justifiable claims" or "moral titles"; others have analysed rights in terms of duty ("what we have an overwhelming duty to respect"); others again have preferred to speak of right conduct or obligation or of ought ("a man has a right whenever other men ought not to prevent his doing what he wants or refuse him some service he asks for or needs"). All these words—"right," "justice," "duty," "ought," "obligation"—are the key terms of what Kant called the "categorical imperative." What ought to be done, what is obligatory, what is right, what is duty, what is just, is not what it would be nice to see done one day; it is what is demanded by the basic norms of morality or justice.

An ideal is something one can aim at, but cannot by definition immediately realize. A right, on the contrary is something that can, and from the moral point of view *must*, be respected here and now. If this were not so, we should have to agree with Bentham; if the Rights of Man were ideals, to talk of them as rights at all would indeed be rhetorical nonsense. We can give sense to human rights only because we can reasonably claim that men have moral rights and that among the moral rights which each man has are some that he shares with all other men.

To deny that the "economic and social rights" are the universal moral rights of all men is not to deny that they may be the moral rights of some men. In the moral criticism of legal rights, it is certainly arguable that the privileges of some members of a certain community ought to be extended to other members (and perhaps all members) of that community. But this matter is correctly seen as a problem of *socialization* or *democratization*—that is, the extension of privileges and immunities—rather than as a problem about the universal rights of all men: and the case for any such specific claims to an extension of legal rights must be argued on other grounds.

Notes

1. C. J. Friedrich, in "Rights, Liberties, Freedoms: A Reappraisal," *American Political Science Review*, LVII, 4, (Dec. 1963), shows that some "social and economic rights" were known to the Age of Reason. He quotes the "right to work" being named by Turgot and Robespierre and gives references to eighteenth-century claims to the right to education.

2. E.g., Professor C. J. Friedrich (cf. previous note). Another champion of the view that social and economic rights should be interpreted as human rights is the late Pope, John XXIII. I have discussed his views in an article, "Pope John XXIII on Peace and the Rights of Man," *Political Quarterly*, Oct. 1963.

3. See G. Sartori, "Constitutionalism," *American Political Science Review*, Vol. LVI (Dec. 1962), pp. 853-65.

QUESTIONS FOR REFLECTION

1. Cranston takes issue with including economic, social, and cultural rights on a justifiable list of human rights. What are the tests he uses to propose which rights are justifiable? Do you find his argument convincing?

2. How would you go about offering a plausible justification *for* economic, social, and cultural rights to be included on a list of human rights?

3. Why does Cranston insist that human rights are not *ideals*?

18. JOEL FEINBERG

Joel Feinberg (1926-) is Professor Emeritus of Philosophy at the University of Arizona. He is the author of several books in moral, political and legal philosophy, including *Freedom and Fulfillment* (1992); *Harm to Others* (1987); and *Rights, Justice and the Bounds of Liberty* (1980). In the following selection, Feinberg analyzes rights in terms of what the jurist Wesley Hohfeld called "claim-rights." Human rights, Feinberg suggests, are moral claim-rights insofar as they entail rationally justified demands against others for the actual fulfillment of whatever the right is a right to. A world without such moral claims amounts to a "Nowheresville" that lacks an important basis for human dignity and self-respect.

Text—The Nature and Value of Rights

Joel Feinberg, "The Nature and Value of Rights." The Journal of Value Inquiry, *Vol. 4 (1970), pp. 243-57. Copyright 1970 by* The Journal of Value Inquiry. *Reprinted with kind permission from Kluwer Academic Publishers.*

1

I would like to begin by conducting a thought experiment. Try to imagine Nowheresville—a world very much like our own except that no one, or hardly any one (the qualification is not important), has *rights*. If this flaw makes Nowheresville too ugly to hold very long in contemplation, we can make it as pretty as we wish in other moral respects. We can, for example, make the human beings in it as attractive and virtuous as possible without taxing our conceptions of the limits of human nature. In particular, let the virtues of moral sensibility flourish. Fill this imagined world with as much benevolence, compassion, sympathy, and pity as it will conveniently hold without strain. Now we can imagine men helping one another from compassionate motives merely, quite as much or even more than they do in our actual world from a variety of more complicated motives.

This picture, pleasant as it is in some respects, would hardly have satisfied Immanuel Kant. Benevolently motivated actions do good, Kant admitted, and therefore are better, *ceteris paribus*, than malevolently motivated actions; but no action can have supreme kind of worth—what Kant called "moral worth"—unless its whole motivating power derives from the thought that it is *required by duty*. Accordingly, let us try to make Nowheresville more appealing to Kant by introducing the idea of duty into it, and letting the sense of duty be a sufficient motive for many beneficent and honorable actions. But doesn't this bring our original thought experiment to an abortive conclusion? If duties are permitted entry into Nowheresville, are not rights necessarily smuggled in along with them?

The question is well-asked, and requires here a brief digression so that we might consider the so-called "doctrine of the logical correlativity of rights and duties." This is the doctrine that (i) all duties entail other people's rights and (ii) all rights entail other people's duties. Only the first part of the doctrine, the alleged entailment from duties to rights, need concern us here. Is this part of the doctrine correct? It should not be surprising that my answer is: "In a sense yes and in a sense no." Etymologically, the word "duty" is associated with actions that are *due* someone else, the payments of debts *to* creditors, the keeping of agreements with promises, the payment of club dues, or legal fees, or tariff levies to appropriate authorities or their representatives. In this original sense of "duty," all duties are correlated with the rights of those *to* whom the duty is owed. On the other hand, there seem to be numerous classes of duties, both of a legal and non-legal kind, that are *not* logically correlated with the rights of other persons. This seems to be a consequence of the fact that the word "duty" has come to be used for any action understood to be *required*, whether by the rights of others, or by law, or by higher authority, or by conscience, or whatever. When the notion of requirement is in clear focus it is likely to seem the only element in the idea of duty that is essential, and the other component notion—that a duty is something *due* someone else—drops off.

Thus, in this widespread but derivative usage, "duty" tends to be used for any action we feel we *must* (for whatever reason) do. It comes, in short, to be a term of moral modality merely; and it is no wonder that the first thesis of the logical correlativity doctrine often fails.

Let us then introduce duties into Nowheresville, but only in the sense of actions that are, or believed to be, morally mandatory, but not in the older sense of actions that are due others and can be claimed by others as their right. Nowheresville now can have duties of the sort imposed by positive law. A legal duty is not something we are implored or advised to do merely; it is something the law, or an authority under the law, *requires* us to do whether we want to or not, under pain of penalty. When traffic lights turn red, however, there is no determinate person who can plausibly be said to claim our stopping as his due, so that the motorist owes it to *him* to stop, in the way a debtor owes it to his creditor to pay. In our own actual world, of course, we sometimes owe it to our *fellow motorists* to stop; but that kind of right-correlated duty does not exist in Nowheresville. There, motorists "owe" obedience to the Law, but they owe nothing to one another. When they collide, no matter who is at fault, no one is accountable to anyone else, and no one has any sound grievance or "right to complain."

When we leave legal contexts to consider moral obligations and other extra-legal duties, a greater variety of duties-without-correlative-rights present themselves. Duties of charity, for example, require us to contribute to one or another of a large number of eligible recipients, no one of whom can claim our contribution from us as his due. Charitable contributions are more like gratuitous services, favours, and gifts than like repayments of debts or reparations....

Now the digression is over and we can return to Nowheresville and summarize what we have put in it thus far. We now find spontaneous benevolence in somewhat larger degree than in our actual world, and also the acknowledged existence of duties of obedience, duties of charity, and duties imposed by exacting private consciences, and also, let us suppose, a degree of conscientiousness in respect to those duties somewhat in excess of what is to be found in our actual world. I doubt that Kant would be fully satisfied with Nowheresville even now that duty and respect for law and authority have been added to it; but I feel certain that he would regard their addition at least as an improvement. I will now introduce two further moral practices into Nowheresville that will make the world very little more appealing to Kant, but will make it appear more familiar to us. These are the practices connected with the notions of *personal desert* and what I call a *sovereign monopoly of rights*.

When a person is said to deserve something good from us what is meant in parts is that there would be a certain propriety in our giving that good thing to him in virtue of the kind of person he is, perhaps, or more likely, in virtue of some specific thing he has done. The propriety involved here is a much weaker kind than that which derives from our having promised him the good thing or from his having qualified for it by satisfying the well-advertised conditions of some public rule. In the latter case he could be said not merely to deserve the good thing but also to have a *right* to it, that is to be in a position to demand it as his due; and of course we will not have that sort of thing in Nowheresville. That weaker kind of propriety which is mere desert is simply a kind of *fittingness* between one party's character or action and another party's favorable response, much like that between humor and laughter, or good performance and applause....

In Nowheresville, nevertheless, we will have only the original weak kind of desert. Indeed, it will be impossible to keep this idea out if we allow such practices as teachers grading students, judges awarding prizes, and servants serving benevolent but class-conscious masters. Nowheresville is a reasonably good world in many ways, and its teachers, judges, and masters will generally try to give students, contestants, and servants the grades, prizes, and rewards they deserve. For this the recipients will be grateful; but they will never think to complain, or even feel aggrieved, when expected responses to desert fail. The masters, judges, and teachers don't *have* to do good things, after all, for *anyone*. One should be happy that they *ever* treat us well, and not grumble over their occasional lapses. Their hoped for responses, after all, are *gratuities*, and there is no wrong in the omission of what is merely gratuitous. Such is the response of persons who have no concept of *rights*, even persons who are proud of their own deserts.[1]

Surely, one might ask, rights have to come in somewhere, if we are to have even moderately complex forms of social organization. Without rules that confer rights and impose obligations, how can we have ownership of property, bargains and deals, promises and contracts, appointments and loans, marriages and partnerships? Very well, let us introduce all of these social and economic practices into Nowheresville, but *with one big twist*. With them I should like to introduce the curious notion of a "sovereign right-monopoly." You will recall that the subjects in Hobbes's *Leviathan* had no rights whatever against their sovereign. He could do as he liked with them, even gratuitously harm them, but this gave them no valid grievance against him. The sovereign, to be sure, had a certain duty to treat his subjects well, but this duty was owed not to the subjects directly, but to God, just as we might have a duty to a person to treat his property well, but of course no duty to the property itself but only to its owner. Thus, while the sovereign was quite capable of *harming* his subjects, he could commit no wrong against them that they could complain about, since they had no prior claims against his conduct. The only party *wronged* by the sovereign's mistreatment of his subjects was God, the supreme lawmaker. Thus, in repenting cruelty to his subjects, the sovereign might say to God, as David did after killing Uriah, "to Thee only have I sinned."

Even in the *Leviathan*, however, ordinary people had ordinary rights *against one another*. They played roles, occupied offices, made agreements, and signed contracts. In a genuine "sovereign right-monopoly," as I shall be using that phrase, they will do all those things too, and thus incur genuine obligations toward one another; but the obligations (here is the twist) will not be owed directly *to* promises, creditors, parents, and the like, but rather to God alone, or to the members of some elite, or to a single sovereign under God. Hence, the rights correlative to the obligations that derive from these transactions are all owned by some "outside" authority....

There will, of course, be delegated authorities in the imaginary world, empowered to give commands to their underlings and to punish them for their disobedience. But the commands are all given in the name of the right-monopoly who in turn are the only persons to whom obligations are owed. Hence, even intermediate superiors do not have claim-rights against their subordinates but only *legal* powers to create obligations in the subordinates to the monopolistic right-holders, and also the legal privilege to impose penalties in the name of that monopoly.

2

So much for the imaginary "world without rights." If some of the moral concepts and practices I have allowed into that world do not sit well with one another, no matter. Imagine Nowheresville with all of these practices if you can, or with any harmonious subset of them, if you prefer. The important thing is not what I've let into it, but what I have kept out. The remainder of this paper will be devoted to an analysis of what precisely a world is missing when it does not contain rights and why that absence is morally important.

The most conspicuous difference, I think, between the Nowheresvillians and ourselves has something to do with the activity of *claiming*. Nowheresvillians, even when they are discriminated against invidiously, or left without the things they need, or otherwise badly treated, do not think to leap to their feet and make righteous demands against one another though they may not hesitate to resort to force and trickery to get what they want. They have no notion of rights, so they do not have a notion of what is their due; hence they do not claim before they take. The conceptual linkage between personal rights and claiming has long been noticed by legal writers and is reflected in the standard usage in which "claim-rights" are distinguished from other mere liberties, immunities, and powers, also sometimes called "rights," with which they are easily confused. When a person has a legal claim-right to X, it must be the case (i) that he is at liberty in respect to X, i.e. that he has no duty to refrain from or relinquish X, and also (ii) that his liberty is the ground of other people's duties to grant him X or not to interfere with him in respect to X. Thus, in the sense of claim-rights, it is true by definition that rights logically entail other people's duties.... And yet this is not quite an accurate account of the matter, for it fails to do justice to the way claim-rights are somehow prior to, or more basic than, the duties with which they are necessarily correlated....

Many philosophical writers have simply identified rights with claims. The dictionaries tend to define "claims," in turn as "assertions of right," a dizzying piece of circularity that led one philosopher to complain—"We go in search of rights and are directed to claims, and then back again to rights in bureaucratic futility."[2] What then is the relation between a claim and a right?

As we shall see, a right is a kind of claim, and a claim is "an assertion of right," so that a formal definition of either notion in terms of the other will not get us very far. Thus if a "formal definition" of the usual philosophical sort is what we are after, the game is over before it has begun, and we can say that the concept of a right is a "simple, undefinable, unanalysable primitive." Here as elsewhere in philosophy this will have the effect of making the commonplace seem unnecessarily mysterious. We would be better advised, I think, not to attempt definition of either "right" or "claim," but rather to use the idea of a claim in informal elucidation of the idea of a right. This is made possible by the fact that *claiming* is an elaborate sort of rule-governed *activity*. A claim is that which is claimed, the object of the act of claiming.... If we concentrate on the whole activity of claiming, which is public, familiar, and open to our observation, rather than on its upshot alone, we may learn more about the generic nature of rights than we could ever hope to learn from a formal definition, even if one were possible. Moreover, certain facts about rights more easily, if not solely, expressible in the language of claims and claiming are essential to a full understanding not only of what rights are, but also why they are so vitally important.

Let us begin then by distinguishing between: (i) making claim to…, (ii) claiming that…, and (iii) having a claim. One sort of thing we may be doing when we claim is to *make claim to something*. This is "to petition or seek by virtue of supposed right; to demand as due." Sometimes this is done by an acknowledged rightholder when he serves notice that he now wants turned over to him that which has already been acknowledged to be his, something borrowed, say, or improperly taken from him….

Generally speaking, only the person who has a title or who has qualified for it, or someone speaking in his name, can make claim to something as a matter of right. It is an important fact about rights (or claims), then, that they can be claimed only by those who have them. Anyone can claim, of course, *that* this umbrella is yours, but only you or your representative can actually claim the umbrella. If Smith owes Jones five dollars, only Jones can claim the five dollars as his own, though any bystander can *claim that* it belongs to Jones. One important difference then between *making legal claim* to and *claiming that* is that the former is a legal performance with direct legal consequences whereas the latter is often a mere piece of descriptive commentary with no legal force. Legally speaking, *making claim to* can itself make things happen. This sense of "claiming," then, might well be called "the performative sense." The legal power to claim (performatively) one's right or the things to which one has a right seems to be essential to the very notion of a right. A right to which one could not make claim (i.e. not even for recognition) would be a very "imperfect" right indeed!

Claiming that one has a right (what we can call "propositional claiming" as opposed to "performative claiming") is another sort of thing one can do with language, but it is not the sort of doing that characteristically has legal consequences. To claim that one has rights is to make an assertion that one has them, and to make it in such a manner as to demand or insist that they be recognized…. What is essential to *claiming that* is the manner of assertion. One can assert without even caring very much whether anyone is listening, but part of the point of propositional claiming is to *make sure* people listen….

Even if there are conceivable circumstances in which one would admit rights diffidently, there is no doubt that their characteristic use and that for which they are distinctively well suited, is to be claimed, demanded, affirmed, insisted upon. They are especially sturdy objects to "stand upon," a most useful sort of moral furniture. Having rights, of course, makes claiming possible; but it is claiming that gives rights their special moral significance. This feature of rights is connected in a way with the customary rhetoric about what it is to be a human being. Having rights enables us to "stand up like men," to look others in the eye, and to feel in some fundamental way the equal of anyone. To think of oneself as the holder of rights is not to be unduly but properly proud, to have that minimal self-respect that is necessary to be worthy of the love and esteem of others. Indeed, respect for persons (this is an intriguing idea) may simply be respect for their rights, so that there cannot be the one without the other; and what is called "human dignity" may simply be the recognizable capacity to assert claims. To respect a person then, or to think of him as possessed of human dignity, simply *is* to think of him as a potential maker of claims. Not all of this can be packed into a definition of "rights"; but these are *facts* about the possession of rights that argue well their supreme moral importance. More than anything else I am going to say, these facts explain what is wrong with Nowheresville.

We come now to the third interesting employment of the claiming vocabulary, that involving not the verb "to claim" but the substantive "a claim." What is to *have a claim* and how is this related to rights? I would like to suggest that *having a claim consists in being in a position to claim, that is, to make claim to or claim that.* If this suggestion is correct it shows the primacy of the verbal over the nominative forms. It links claims to a kind of activity and obviates the temptation to think of claims as *things*, on the model of coins, pencils, and other material possessions which we can carry in our hip pockets....

Nearly all writers maintain that there is some intimate connection between having a claim and having a right. Some identify right and claim without qualification; some define "right" as justified or justifiable claim, others as recognized claim, still others as valid claim. My own preference is for the latter definition. Some writers, however, reject the identification of rights with valid claims on the ground that all claims as such are valid, so that the expression "valid claim" is redundant. These writers, therefore, would identify rights with claims *simpliciter*. But this is a very simple confusion. All claims, to be sure, are *put forward* as justified, whether they are justified in fact or not. A claim conceded even by its maker to have no validity is not a claim at all, but a mere demand. The highwayman, for example, *demands* his victim's money; but he hardly makes claim to it as rightfully his own.

But it does not follow from this sound point that it is redundant to qualify claims as justified (or as I prefer, valid) in the definition of a right; for it remains true that not all claims put forward as valid really are valid; and only the valid ones can be acknowledged as rights....

Another reason for not identifying rights with claims simply is that there is a well-established usage in international law that makes a theoretically interesting distinction between claims and rights. Statesmen are sometimes led to speak of "claims" when they are concerned with the natural needs of deprived human beings in conditions of scarcity. Young orphans *need* good upbringings, balanced diets, education, and technical training everywhere in the world; but unfortunately there are many places where these goods are in such short supply that it is impossible to provision all who need them. If we persist, nevertheless, in speaking of these needs as constituting rights and not merely claims, we are committed to the conception of a right which is an entitlement *to* some good, but not a valid claim *against* any particular individual; for in conditions of scarcity there may be no determinate individuals who can plausibly be said to have a duty to provide the missing goods to those in need. J. E. S. Fawcett therefore prefers to keep the distinction between claims and rights firmly in mind. "Claims," he writes, "are needs and demands in movement, and there is a continuous transformation, as a society advances [towards greater abundance] of economic and social claims into civil and political rights...and not all countries or all claims are by any means at the same stage in the process."[3] The manifesto writers on the other side who seem to identify needs, or at least basic needs, with what they call "human rights," are more properly described, I think, as urging upon the world community the moral principle that *all* basic human needs ought to be recognized as *claims* (in the customary *prima facie* sense) worthy of sympathy and serious consideration right now, even though, in many cases, they cannot yet plausibly be treated as *valid* claims, that is, as grounds of any other people's duties. This way of talking avoids the anomaly of ascribing to all human beings now, even those in pre-industrial societies, such "economic and social rights" as "periodic holidays with pay."

Still for all of that, I have a certain sympathy with the manifesto writers, and I am even willing to speak of a special "manifesto sense" of "right," in which a right need not be correlated with another's duty. Natural needs are real claims if only upon hypothetical future beings not yet in existence. I accept the moral principle that to have an unfulfilled need is to have a kind of claim against the world, even if against no one in particular. A natural need for some good as such, like a natural desert, is always a reason in support of a claim to that good. A person in need, then, is always "in a position" to make a claim, even when there is no one in the corresponding position to do anything about it. Such claims, based on need alone, are "permanent possibilities of rights," the natural seed from which rights grow. When manifesto writers speak of them as if already actual rights, they are easily forgiven, for this is but a powerful way of expressing the conviction that they ought to be recognized by states here and now as potential rights and consequently as determinants of *present* aspirations and guides to *present* policies. That usage, I think, is a valid exercise of rhetorical licence.

I prefer to characterize rights as valid claims rather than justified ones, because I suspect that justification is rather too broad a qualification. "Validity," as I understand it, is justification of a peculiar and narrow kind, namely justification within a system of rules. A man has a legal right when the official recognition of his claim (as valid) is called for by the governing rules. This definition, of course, hardly applies to moral rights, but that is not because the genus of which moral rights are a species is something other than *claims*. A man has a moral right when he has a claim the recognition of which is called for—not (necessarily) by legal rules—but by moral principles, or the principles of an enlightened conscience....

Whether we are speaking of claims or rights, however, we must notice that they seem to have two dimensions, as indicated by the prepositions "to" and "against," and it is quite natural to wonder whether either of these dimensions is somehow more fundamental or essential than the other. All rights seem to merge *entitlements to* do, have, omit, or be something with *claims against* others to act or refrain from acting in certain ways. In some statements of rights the entitlement is perfectly determinate (e.g. *to* play tennis) and the claim vague (e.g. *against* "some vague group of potential or possible obstructors"); but in other cases the object of the claim is clear and determinate (e.g. *against* one's parents), and the entitlement general and indeterminate (e.g. to be given a proper upbringing). If we mean by "entitlement" that *to* which one has a right and by "claim" something directed at those against whom the right holds...then we can say that all claim-rights necessarily involve both, though in individual cases the one element or the other may be in sharper focus.

In brief conclusion: To have a right is to have a claim against someone whose recognition as valid is called for by some set of governing rules or moral principles. To have a *claim* in turn, is to have a case meriting consideration, that is, to have reasons or grounds that put one in a position to engage in performative and propositional claiming. The activity of claiming, finally, as much as any other thing, makes for self-respect and respect for others, gives a sense to the notion of personal dignity, and distinguishes this otherwise morally flawed world from the even worse world of Nowheresville.

Notes

1. For a fuller discussion of the concept of personal desert see my "Justice and Personal Desert," *Nomos VI, Justice*, ed. C. J. Chapman (New York: Atherton Press, 1963), pp. 69-97.

2. H. B. Acton, "Symposium of 'Rights'," *Proceedings of the Aristotelian Society*, Supplementary Volume 24 (1950), pp. 107-108.

3. J. E. S. Fawcett, "The International Protection of Human Rights," in *Political Theory and the Rights of Man*, ed. D. D. Raphael (Bloomington: Indiana University Press, 1967), pp. 125 and 128.

Questions for Reflection

1. What is the distinction between moral claim-rights and legal claim rights? According to Feinberg's analysis, how do both rights fit together?

2. What does Feinberg mean when he states that to "respect a person then, or to think of him as possessed of human dignity, simply *is* to think of him as a potential maker of claims"? What kinds of things do you think people should be able to claim as rights?

3. On what basis does Feinberg argue that rights incorporate claims and entitlements? Do you agree or disagree with him?

19. THOMAS W. POGGE

Thomas W. Pogge (1953-) is Associate Professor of Philosophy at Columbia University and Member of the School of Social Science at the Institute for Advanced Study, Princeton University. He is the author of *Realizing Rawls* (1989) and numerous articles in social and political philosophy and ethics, with a special focus on issues of global justice. In this essay Pogge argues that human rights claims should be understood as asserting that each society ought to be organized so that all its members enjoy secure access to those rights. If a society does not organize itself in this way, then it violates a negative duty of justice, namely, the duty not to impose unjust social institutions on its members. This focus on duties is important because having secure access to the substance of any right requires others to perform a wide range of duties, including reforming or eliminating unjust social policies and institutions and ensuring the creation of just ones.

Text—How Should Human Rights Be Conceived?*

Originally published in Jahrbuch für Recht und Ethik *3 (1995), pp. 103-120. Revised version reprinted by permission of the author.*

Our current notion of human rights has evolved out of earlier notions of natural law and natural rights. We can begin to understand and analyze it by examining the continuities and discontinuities in this evolution. I will do this by focusing on the shifting constraints imposed, ideas suggested and possibilities opened and closed, by the three concepts rather than on the particular conceptions of them that have actually been worked out.[1]

All three concepts have in common that they were used to express a special class of moral concerns, namely ones that are among the most weighty of all as well as unrestricted and broadly sharable. These four common features of the three concepts constrain not the content of the select concerns, but their (potential) status and role. In regard to the first feature, it should be said that the natural-law and natural-rights idioms were also used to express the agent's liberty to pursue his own self-preservation and self-interest—as in Hobbes's famous assertion that "every man has a Right to every thing; even to one another's body."[2] Since the concept of human rights, which is at issue in this essay, has not been used in this vein, I will here leave such uses aside and focus on uses that present natural law, or the natural rights of others, as imposing moral constraints upon human conduct, practices and institutions.

Conceiving of moral concerns as weighty means thinking of them as ones that ought to play an important role in our reflection and discourse about, and ought to be reflected and respected in, our social institutions and conduct.

In conceiving of moral concerns as unrestricted, we believe that whether persons ought to respect them does not depend on their particular epoch, culture, religion, moral tradition or philosophy.[3] Unrestricted moral concerns need not make demands on everyone. The moral imperative that rulers are to govern in the interest of the governed, for example, may be unrestricted even while it makes demands only on those in power. But, not being spatially or temporally confined, unrestricted moral concerns are still, at least potentially, relevant to persons of all times and places and therefore should be understood and appreciated by all.

This suggests the fourth feature. In conceiving of moral concerns as broadly sharable, one thinks of them as capable of being understood and appreciated by persons from different epochs and cultures as well as by adherents of a variety of different religions, moral traditions and philosophies. They need not be (and perhaps no moral concerns could be) accessible in this way to all human persons, irrespective of when and where they live(d) and irrespective of their particular culture, religion, moral tradition and philosophy (or lack thereof). But they would not be broadly sharable, if they were not detached, or at least detachable, from any particular epoch, culture, religion, moral tradition and philosophy.[4] The notions of being unrestricted and being broadly sharable are related in that we tend to feel more confident about conceiving of a moral concern as unrestricted when this concern is not parochial to some particular epoch, culture, religion, moral tradition or philosophy.

So much for the continuities. To learn more about how the concept of human rights constrains content, about what moral concerns lend themselves to being expressed in terms of human rights, let us now look at the discontinuities in the historical evolution. Expressing moral constraints in the natural-rights rather than the natural-law idiom involves a significant narrowing of content possibilities by bringing in the idea that the relevant moral constraints are based on moral concern for certain subjects: rightholders. By violating a natural right, one wrongs the subject whose right it is. These subjects of natural rights are viewed as sources of moral claims and thereby recognized as having a certain moral standing and value. The natural-law idiom contains no such idea: It need not involve constraints on one's conduct toward other subjects at all and, even if it does, need not involve the idea that by violating such constraints one has wronged these subjects—one may rather have wronged God, for example, or have disturbed the harmonious order of the cosmos. In ruling out these (formerly prominent) alternative ideas, the shift from natural-law to natural-rights language constitutes a secularization which facilitates the presentation of a select set of moral concerns as broadly sharable in a world that has become much larger and more heterogeneous. This secularization centers around a specific view about the point of the moral constraints (duties, obligations) singled out as natural: The point of respecting them is the protection of others; one's concern to honor one's moral obligations is motivated by a deeper and prior moral concern for (the interests of) others.[5]

This specification of the point of moral constraints entails a narrowing of content possibilities. The natural-law idiom lends itself to expressing any moral concerns that might apply to human persons; but not all of these concerns can be expressed equally well in the language of natural rights. Three historically prominent categories of moral concerns that are endangered by the shift in terminology are religious duties, duties toward oneself and moral constraints upon our conduct toward animals. Ascribing rights to God seems awkward, because we do not think of Him as having vital interests that are vulnerable to human encroachment. Speaking of rights against oneself or of animal rights is problematic because of the connection between having rights and being entitled to claim (and to defend) one's rights as well as to protest (and sometimes to punish) the infringement of these rights.[6] We do not engage in such claiming, defending, protesting and punishing activities against ourselves; and animals seem unable to engage in them at all. In accepting this connection one need not endorse the stronger position, taken by Hart, that having a right presupposes the simultaneous ability to claim it.[7] One may instead, following Gewirth, find nothing odd in saying that a man who is now dead or in an irreversible coma has his rights violated when his will is overturned or when his body is kept alive against his express prior instructions. Here we can remember the man making claims before, and can imagine how he would have protested had he known about what is being done now. Similarly, one can say that maiming or killing an infant constitutes a violation of her rights, because we can once again imagine how she will protest the harms done to her, or would have done so in the future had she survived.[8] This contrasts with the case of non-human animals, which have no past or potential future ability to make claims: Here the language of rights can seem out of place.[9]

II

The language of human rights partakes in the specification that we have found to be involved in the shift from natural law to natural rights. Beyond that, it would seem to have a fourfold significance. First, it manifestly detaches the idea of moral rights from its historical antecedents in the medieval Christian tradition, thereby underscoring the secularization implicit in the first shift from the language of laws (commandments, duties) to that of rights. This serves the continued maintenance of broad sharability and makes fully explicit the connection between a special class of moral concerns and the status of certain beings, rightholders, as subjects of moral value.

In the same vein, the shift also indicates a reorientation of the sort for which Rawls has recently coined the phrase "political not metaphysical."[10] The adjective "human"—unlike "natural"—does not suggest an ontological status independent of any and all human efforts, decisions, (re)cognition. It does not rule out such a status either. Rather, it avoids these metaphysical and metaethical issues by implying nothing about them one way or the other. The potential appeal of the select moral concerns is thereby further broadened in that these concerns are made accessible also to those who reject all variants of moral realism—who believe, for instance, that the special moral status of all human beings rests on nothing more than our own profound moral commitment and determination that human beings ought to have this status.

Third, and most obvious, the shift strongly confirms that it is all and only human beings who give rise to the relevant moral concerns: All and only human persons have human rights and the special moral status associated therewith. The expression also suggests that human beings are equal in this regard. This view can be analyzed into two components. First: All human beings have exactly the same human rights. And second: The moral significance of human rights and human-rights violations does not vary with whose human rights are at stake; as far as human rights are concerned, all human beings matter equally.[11] Though the second component is only weakly suggested by the expression, it is, I believe, a fixed part of our current concept of human rights.

The fourth way in which the shift from natural to human rights has been significant is not suggested by the change in terminology, but seems to have contingently accompanied this change. One can approach the point through Article 17.2 of the Universal Declaration of Human Rights: "No one shall be arbitrarily deprived of his property." If a car is stolen, its owner has certainly been deprived of her property, and arbitrarily so. Still, we are unlikely to call this a violation of Article 17.2 or a human-rights violation. Why? Because it is only a car? I do not think so: The car may be its owner's most important asset; and the theft of food would not be considered a human-rights violation either, even if it were her entire reserve for the winter. An arbitrary confiscation of her car by the government, on the other hand, does strike us as a human-rights violation, even if she has several other cars left. This suggests that human-rights violations, to count as such, must be in some sense official, and that human rights thus protect persons only against violations from certain sources. Human rights can be violated by governments, certainly, and by government agencies and officials, by the general staff of an army at war and probably also by the leaders of a guerrilla movement or of a large corporation—but not by a petty criminal or by a violent husband. We can capture this idea by conceiving it to be implicit in the concept of human rights that human-rights postulates are addressed, in the first instance at least, to those who occupy positions of authority within a society (or other comparable social system).

We see here that the language of human rights involves a further narrowing of content possibilities—not on the side of the agent this time, but on the side of the recipient. Through the language of natural rights, one can demand (humanly possible) protection of persons against any threats to their well-being and agency; through the language of human rights, one demands protection only against certain ("official") threats. This narrowing is not, however, as severe as it may seem at first: As we shall see, the language of human rights involves a demand for protection not only against official violations but, more broadly, against official disrespect, and it addresses this demand not only to officials (those whose violations of a relevant right would count as human-rights violations), but also (at least) to those whose officials they are.

Before discussing these matters further in the next section, let me sum up my explication of the concept of human rights thus far. A commitment to human rights involves one in recognizing that human persons with a past or potential future ability to engage in moral conversation and practice have certain basic needs and that these needs give rise to weighty moral concerns.[12] The object of each of these basic human needs is the object of a human right.[13] Recognizing these basic needs as giving rise to human rights involves a commitment to oppose official disrespect for these needs on the part of one's own society (and other comparable social systems in which one is a participant).[14]

I will now try to clarify further the modern concept of human rights by explicating the notion of official disrespect embedded in it. This explication is normative to some extent. Those who use the concept are generally not entirely clear about what they mean by it. I want to be clearer here. And my account should then be tested not so much against what people actually say about human rights as against what they would or should affirm or deny upon reflection. Though my account is normative to this extent, its objective is still to reconstruct the meaning of a widely used expression. I am asking what we mean, or ought to mean, when we speak of a human right to X. I am not here asking the more significantly normative question which candidate human rights, if any, we ought to recognize. My examples from the Universal Declaration should be taken in this spirit. I am not presupposing that the human rights I discuss exist or ought to be recognized. I am merely asking what the assertion of a particular human right should reasonably be taken to mean.

III

The central instances of official disrespect are human-rights violations, and, in our world, the central instances of official agents are governments. Official disrespect for human rights is then paradigmatically exemplified by a government violating rights that are on the list of human rights. Governments may do so by creating or maintaining (unjust) laws that permit or require human-rights violations or they may do so "under the color of law," i.e. by perversely construing existing legislation as licensing human-rights-violating policies. Both these cases are amply illustrated by the Nazi period.

These paradigm cases of official disrespect bring out most clearly why, as is widely felt, there is something especially hideous, outrageous and intolerable about official disrespect, why official moral wrongs are worse than otherwise similar "private" moral wrongs, quite apart from the fact that they often harm more persons, or harm them more severely, than private wrongs. This feeling can be accounted for as follows: Official moral wrongs masquerade under the name of law and justice and they are generally committed quite openly for all to see: laid down in statutes and regulations, called for by orders and verdicts, and adorned with official seals, stamps and signatures. Such wrongs do not merely deprive their victims of the objects of their rights but attack those very rights themselves; they do not merely subvert what is right, but the very idea of right and justice. This conjecture explains, I think, why so many people feel more personally affronted by human-rights violations than by equivalent ordinary crimes, and also feel personally responsible in regard to them—why they see human rights as everyone's concern and feel implicated in, and experience shame on account of, what their government and its officials do in their name.

With these thoughts in mind, let us look at cases in the vicinity of the central ones. One obvious way of expanding beyond the paradigm is by broadening the definition of "government" so as to include not merely the highest officials in the three branches, but also the lower echelons of authority, including all the various functional and regional subunits of the three branches down to the smallest and lowest agencies and officials. Here it emerges that moral wrongs committed by an official fit the better under the label of "human-rights violation" the more closely they are related to his job and the more tolerated or encouraged they are throughout officialdom. A murder committed by a mailman, even if on duty, would hardly count as a human-rights violation, but torture administered by a policeman to a suspect would count, unless it is a truly isolated incident of conduct that is strongly discouraged within the police force and severely punished when discovered.

More interesting cases are the following: A government may,

for the time being, refrain from ordering or authorizing human-rights violations, and effectively prevent violations on the part of its various agencies and officials, but reserve for itself the legal power to order or authorize such violations at any time at its sole discretion. Conversely, a government may legally bind itself never to violate human rights and yet do nothing or very little to ensure that its various agencies and officers abide by this official prohibition. The government may also—while legally committing itself not to violate human rights and effectively enforcing this commitment against its own agencies and officials—fail to make such violations illegal for some or all of the persons and associations under its jurisdiction. Or it may pass or maintain the appropriate legislation but then do nothing or very little to enforce it. In view of this plurality of cases, how shall we explicate the idea of official disrespect for human rights?

To make these issues more concrete, let us focus on Article 19 of the Universal Declaration: "Everyone has the right to freedom of opinion and expression; this right includes freedom to hold opinions without interference and to seek, receive and impart information and ideas through any media and regardless of frontiers." We may suppose that we know precisely what the right here postulated is a right to: what sorts of conduct it protects in what particular contexts and circumstances. Let us also suppose that we know precisely what does and does not constitute interference with such protected conduct and hence a violation of the postulated right on the part of individual and collective agents. How do we get from this knowledge to a measure for official disrespect: to a way of assessing a society's human-rights record in regard to Article 19? The answer to this question, as we have seen, cannot be that we must simply count violations (weighted for severity, perhaps), as this would gloss over the important issue of the more or less official character of these violations.

Making the law alone the decisive yardstick for a society's human-rights record is implausible: Societies may be officially committed to Article 19, may even incorporate an appropriate right to freedom of expression into their constitutions, and their government officials may nevertheless violate this legal right frequently and with impunity—a possibility sadly illustrated by all too many showcase constitutions around the world. We can hardly celebrate such societies for their respect for human rights.

A more plausible proposal would have us focus on the extent to which the government, including its various agencies and officials, is actually interfering with protected conduct. We can infer that this idea has had some currency and appeal, I believe, from the upsurge in organized "private" violence we have seen in the 1980s: the proliferation of death squads in numerous authoritarian societies of Latin America and of "outraged citizens" in various Communist societies, for example. But currency is not plausibility; and we should certainly not settle for an understanding of "disrespect for human rights" that provides an incentive to governments to have their peaceful opponents killed by private government supporters rather than by the police. To make the proposal plausible, we must then go beyond the idea of "the government actually interfering." If protected conduct is interfered with with impunity by persons organized or encouraged by the government, then these interferences must be imputed to the government, must count as indicative of official disrespect.

This modification may not go far enough. Death squads and "outraged citizens" may engage in their bloody activities even without open or tacit government encouragement. Rich landowners may organize bands of thugs, for example, who prevent—through disruption, intimidation and violence—the expression of any political views that champion the interests of poor, landless peasants and migrant farm workers. Veterans of the revolution may organize in similar ways to suppress anti-communist propaganda. The government need not organize or encourage such activities—it merely stands idly by: fails to enact laws that proscribe such conduct or, if such laws are on the books, fails to enforce them effectively. (In such a scenario, government officials may even regret the activities and feel embarrassed by them. They nevertheless do not act because they fear that any measures to protect the rights of an unpopular group would diminish their own popularity. The parallel to foreigners' rights to physical security in Germany comes to mind.) We should consider such cases, as well, to exemplify official disrespect: Some persons are deprived of their freedom of expression and there is no official response, or at most a token response, to the deprivations.

Even this account is still not quite broad enough. An (almost) complete absence of interferences with protected conduct in some society may be due to the fact that people know only too well what sorts of opinions cannot be publicly expressed without serious risk of violent interference or punitive measures against oneself or one's family. They know what would happen to them if they spoke up, and they also know that their "protected" conduct would not be effectively protected in fact. Formerly defiant, they are now intimidated and demoralized. This change goes along with a dramatic decline in the frequency of actual interferences—yet surely we cannot say that the society's human-rights record has dramatically improved. This scenario, too, exemplifies official disrespect of the human right, even if this right is (in the unrealistic limiting case) never violated. It thereby presents in a most clearcut way the need to detach the notion of official disrespect from that of violations. What is relevant to a society's record in regard to, or to its degree of official disrespect for, a given human right is then (a) a proper subset of the occurring violations of this right (namely the "official" or "human-rights" violations) and (b) various facts about the government's and also the people's attitude (commitment and disposition) toward the right and all its occurring violations. Unofficial violations of a right that is on the list of human rights do not constitute human-rights violations; but official indifference toward such private violations does constitute official disrespect.

If official disrespect of this last kind is to be avoided, a society must ensure that persons are, and feel, secure in regard to the objects of their human rights. In considering what this entails, we will tend to look, once again, to the government first and foremost: to how the concern for these objects is incorporated into the law and constitution[15] and to the extent to which the government is disposed to suppress and punish (official and private) violations and makes this disposition known through word and deed.

But it makes sense to think more broadly here. What is needed to make the object of a right truly secure is a vigilant citizenry that is deeply committed to this right and disposed to fight for its political realization. (This does not mean that every last citizen must have this commitment and disposition—a minority may suffice, so long as it is clearly preponderant among those citizens who are actively engaged in the political life of their society.) A commitment by the citizenry is more reliable than one by the government, which, after all, may undergo a radical change in personnel from one day to the next. It tends to foster this commitment by the government—especially in democratic societies, which tend to produce the strongest incentives for government officials to be responsive to the people. And it also tends to preclude cases where impotence, not indifference, makes a government stand idly by when organized groups of its citizens violate the rights of others. Such cases, too, exemplify official disrespect when the people, who bear the ultimate responsibility for what happens on their society's territory, do not care enough about the objects of human rights to enable, encourage and (if need be) replace or reorganize their government so as to safeguard secure access to these objects for all.

While the government may then be the primary guardian of human rights and the prime measure of official disrespect, the people are their ultimate guardian on which their fulfillment crucially depends. It is said that peoples have the governments they deserve. This is true at least in one direction: It is rare for a people to have a much better government than it deserves for very long. And the sustained flourishing of respect for human rights depends then only in the first instance on a society's government: on its laws, constitution and political system as well as the attitudes of its politicians, judges and police. More deeply, it depends on the character of its people and thus also on its culture, education system and income distribution.

Let me reinforce these points in another context involving Article 5 of the Universal Declaration: "No one shall be subjected to torture or to cruel, inhuman or degrading treatment or punishment." In a good many countries, domestic servants, some indentured or virtual slaves, do not enjoy the object of this human right. In some of these societies, inhuman or degrading treatment of domestic servants by their employers is perfectly legal. In others, certain legal prohibitions are in place but ineffective: Most of the servants, often illiterate, are ignorant of their legal rights, convictions for mistreatment are extremely difficult if not impossible to obtain, punishments are negligible. Moreover, servants are also often forced to endure illegal conduct on account of economic necessity: They do not dare file complaints against their employers for fear of being fired. This fear is both justified and substantial, because they have only minimal financial reserves, there is a general oversupply of servants and/or they have reason to believe that their present employer would refuse to issue them the positive reference requisite to find new employment.

In this case, as well, the conditions described would seem to constitute a flaw in the societies' human-rights record. This flaw may be corrected through actively enforced legislation, but it may also be attacked, probably more effectively, through other measures, such as a literacy campaign, efforts to educate citizens about existing legislation and to create a culture of equal citizenship, the introduction or improvement of unemployment benefits, economic policies designed to expand educational and employment opportunities for the poor and so forth.

This conclusion may provoke the accusation that I have taken some of the "good" (civil) rights of the Universal Declaration and, by perverse reasoning, twisted them into their opposite: social and economic pseudo-rights. Yet another social democrat dressed in liberal's clothing. This accusation is not, I admit, far off the mark — though it must be shown, of course, where and how my argument goes wrong. I shall not worry about this accusation further, and proceed instead to a more straightforward explication of my understanding of the concept of human rights.

IV

On the face of it, the concept of rights—and hence more specifically the notion of human rights—suggests an interactional understanding, according to which each such right entails certain directly corresponding duties.[16] This picture leads into a familiar dispute about the character of these duties. On a minimalist account they must be purely negative (to refrain from violating the right in question); and some purported human rights—such as those postulated in Articles 22-29 of the Universal Declaration (rights to social security, work, rest and leisure, an adequate standard of living, education, culture, etc.)—must then be rejected as of the wrong form. On a maximalist account each human right entails both negative duties (to avoid) and positive duties (to protect and to help); and there is then nothing wrong with social, economic and cultural rights. According to the minimalist, human rights require only self-restraint; for the maximalist, by contrast, they require efforts to fulfill everyone's human rights anywhere on earth.[17]

I have been trying to transcend the terms of this debate in favor of an institutional understanding of human rights: By postulating a person P's right to X as a human right we are asserting that P's society ought to be (re)organized in such a way that P has secure access to X and, in particular, so that P is secure against being denied X or deprived of X officially: by the government or its agents or officials.[18] Avoidable insecurity of access (beyond certain reasonably attainable thresholds) constitutes official disrespect and tarnishes the society's human-rights record—significantly more so if it is due to official denial or deprivation, i.e. to human-rights violations.[19] Human rights are then moral claims upon the organization of one's society. However, since citizens are collectively responsible for their society's organization and its resulting human-rights record, human rights ultimately make demands upon (especially the more privileged) citizens. Persons are responsible for official disrespect for human rights within any social system in which they are influential participants.

In proposing this institutional understanding, I reject its interactional alternatives: I deny, for instance, that postulating that P has a human right to X is tantamount to the assertion that some or all individual and collective human agents have a moral duty—in addition to any legal duties they may have in their society—not to deny X to P or deprive her of X. In rejecting this alternative account, I am not denying that the postulate of a human right to X suggests or even implies this assertion. It is hard to see how one can, on the one hand, be committed to the claim that societies, for the sake of the persons living in them, ought to be organized so that these persons need not endure inhuman or degrading treatment and yet, on the other hand, not consider it morally wrong for persons to treat others in inhuman or degrading ways. A commitment to human rights will go along with interactional moral commitments; but this is no reason to identify the former with the latter.

On my understanding, too, human rights (conceptually) entail moral duties—but these are not corresponding duties in any simple way: The human right not to be subjected to cruel or degrading treatment gives me a duty to help ensure that those living in my society need not endure such treatment. Depending on context, this duty may, as we have seen, generate obligations to advocate and support programs to improve literacy and unemployment benefits when such programs are necessary to secure the object of this human right for a class of my compatriots (domestic servants).

Through reconceiving human rights in this way, the familiar dispute is transformed. For one thing, the institutional understanding makes available a plausible intermediate position between two interactional extremes: Responsibility for a person's human rights falls on all and only those who participate with this person in the same social system. It is their responsibility, collectively, to structure this system so that all its participants have secure access to the objects of their human rights. In our world, national societies are the paradigmatic example of relevant social systems, and the responsibility for the fulfillment of your human rights falls then upon your government and your fellow citizens.[20] The institutional understanding thus occupies an appealing middle ground: It goes beyond (minimalist interactional) libertarianism, which disconnects us from any deprivations that we do not directly bring about without falling into a (maximalist interactional) utilitarianism of rights, which holds each of us responsible for all deprivations whatever, regardless of the nature of our causal relation to them.[21]

But this is not all. The most remarkable feature of this institutional understanding is that it goes beyond minimalist libertarianism without denying its central tenet: that human rights entail only negative duties. The normative force of another's human right for you is that you must not participate in, and thereby help to uphold and to impose upon her, social institutions under which she does not have secure access to the object of her human right. You would be violating this duty, if you lived in a society in which such access is not secure (in which blacks are enslaved, women disenfranchised or servants mistreated, for example) and just went about your own business. Even if you owned no slaves and employed no servants yourself, you would still share responsibility: by contributing your labor to the society's economy, your taxes to its governments and so forth. You might honor your negative duty, perhaps, through becoming a hermit or an emigrant, but you could honor it more plausibly by working with others toward shielding the victims of injustice from the harms you help produce or, if this is possible, toward establishing secure access through institutional reform.[22]

V

If the libertarian constraint (rights entail only negative duties) is incorporated in this way, then it does not have the usual strong implications for what human rights there can be and also does not favor one side in the long-running dispute about whether the full list of human rights should contain only civil and political rights or should include social, economic and cultural rights as well.[23] Once we accept an institutional understanding of human rights, we can no longer reject social, economic and cultural rights on the ground that, insofar as they have any concrete moral significance at all, they impose limitless positive duties: require every person to become a soldier in the global struggle to secure the objects of these rights for human beings everywhere, irrespective of any and all relations between recruits and beneficiaries.[24] On my institutional understanding, human rights generate (only negative) moral duties through the following two claims:

1. A social order under which some or all participants avoidably lack secure access to the objects of some human rights—especially through official denial or deprivation—is to that extent unjust.

2. Persons share a collective responsibility for the justice of any social order in which they participate; they must not simply cooperate in imposing an unjust social order without attempting to reform it toward greater justice.[25]

A human right to the necessities of subsistence (as laid down, for example, in Article 25 of the Universal Declaration) becomes rather more plausible when construed along these lines. On the institutional (unlike the maximalist interactional) account, it involves no duty on everyone to help supply such necessities to those who would otherwise be without them. It rather involves a duty on citizens to ensure that the social order they collectively and coercively impose upon each of themselves is one under which each has secure access to these necessities, insofar as this is feasible. In its essentials, this moral position is one that, surprisingly perhaps, Charles Darwin has expressed rather well more than a century ago: "If the misery of our poor be caused not by laws of nature, but by our own institutions, great is our sin."[26]

Can we reject social, economic and cultural rights on the ground that, unlike the favored civil and political rights, they are in many actual social contexts fated to be mere manifesto rights? There is no clear canonical explication of the polemical expression "manifesto right," but perhaps we can clarify its meaning as follows: A postulated (legal or moral) right is a manifesto right if and only if

1) it is not now the case that all supposed rightholders have secure access to the object of the right; and

2a) it is left unspecified who is supposed to do what in order to bring it about that all supposed rightholders have secure access to the object of the right or

2b) the agents upon whom specific demands are made cannot reasonably meet these demands to the extent necessary to bring it about that all supposed rightholders have secure access to the object of the right.[27]

Since (1) is satisfied in the relevant cases, rebutting the manifesto charge requires that I deny both (2a) and (2b).

Let us begin with (2b). A society cannot reasonably guarantee to all of its members a happy love life or a trip to the moon. Rights to such benefits would therefore be mere manifesto rights. This defect can be avoided by relativizing the objects of the relevant rights to a society's possibilities: A society can work on removing restrictions and overcoming taboos and prejudices that make it harder for some of its members to enjoy a happy love life. The—now relativized—right not to be hampered in one's quest for a happy love life by nonessential restrictions or by avoidable taboos and prejudices is then not a manifesto right (which does not mean, of course, that it deserves inclusion on the list of human rights).

It can be demanded even from a very poor society that it make everyone's access to the necessities of subsistence as secure as possible. By understanding Article 25 as requiring this and nothing more—as not requiring that all must have enough to eat when enough food can simply not be produced—we rescue it from the charge that it, by virtue of satisfying (2b), postulates a mere manifesto right. And this understanding accords with common usage: A society's human-rights record is not blemished merely because it is, under prevailing conditions, unable to secure minimally adequate nutrition for all. The human right does not then entitle one to food that would have to be withheld from others who also need it to survive. Some may starve to death without any official disrespect of Article 25.

An analogous point holds true of civil rights: A poor society may not have the resources effectively to protect the physical security of all of its citizens. This does not show that Article 3 postulates a manifesto right. The human right there postulated does not entitle one to protection that would have to be withheld from others who need it just as much. So rights of both kinds are here on a par.

It may seem at first that the two kinds of rights fare quite differently with regard to (2a): The right postulated in Article 5 makes a very clear and specific demand on governments not to subject persons to cruel, inhuman or degrading treatment or punishment, while the right postulated in Article 25 seems merely to assert that it would be a good thing if (any society were so organized that) all had enough to eat. But this contrast is deceptive if it is true that even the most clearly civil of the human rights in the Universal Declaration—such as those postulated in the Articles 5, 17.2 and 19 we have looked at—require that interference with protected conduct, no matter by whom, must be effectively discouraged and suppressed. These civil rights require certain commitments and dispositions on the part of the citizenry, or so I have argued. Understanding them in this way does not turn them into manifesto rights: Each member of society, according to his or her means, is to help bring about and sustain a social and political order under which all have secure access to the objects of their civil rights. This demand, so abstractly put, is unspecific but, within any particular social context, will be quite specific: In a society in which domestic servants must often suffer inhuman and degrading treatment from their employers, citizens have a human-rights-based obligation to help institute appropriate legal protections as well as perhaps a literacy program and/or unemployment benefits. My understanding of the economic rights of Article 25 is closely parallel: Each member of society, according to his or her means, is to help bring about and sustain a social and economic order within which all have secure access to the necessities of subsistence. This unspecific demand may have quite specific implications in a given social context, e.g. in a society whose poorest members lack secure access to minimally adequate nutrition. Rights of both kinds are then on a par in this respect. And if situational specificity is what matters, then rights of both kinds escape clause (2a) and therefore cannot be assigned manifesto status.

I conclude that the institutional understanding of human rights makes sense. According to it, postulating a human right to X is tantamount to (a) recognizing that human beings have a basic need for X and (b) recognizing as a weighty moral reason the imperative that in one's society all should enjoy secure access to X, especially vis-à-vis threats of official violations.

Notes

*This essay first appeared in *Jahrbuch für Recht und Ethik* 3, 1995, 103-120. Work on it was supported by a 1993-94 Laurance S. Rockefeller Fellowship at the Princeton University Center for Human Values. I am greatly indebted to my colleagues there, and very specially to Amy Gutmann, for a most productive discussion of an earlier version. I also wish to thank my fellow-participants at the Law and Ethics Conference for their valuable comments and Eric Goldstein for extensive and very helpful written criticisms.

1. For more on the historical details, see esp. Richard Tuck, *Natural Rights Theories*, Cambridge, Cambridge University Press, 1979, and Richard Tuck, "The 'Modern' Theory of Natural Law" in Anthony Pagden, ed.: *The Languages of Political Theory in Early-Modern Europe*, Cambridge, Cambridge University Press, 1987.

2. Thomas Hobbes, *Leviathan*, ed. C. B. Macpherson, Harmondsworth, Penguin, 1981 [1651]), 190. As Tuck stresses in his later piece, such uses were exceedingly common in the period from Grotius to Kant.

3. One might make this condition somewhat more demanding: A moral concern is unrestricted only if how wrong given violations of it are does not depend on the violators' particular epoch, culture, religion, moral tradition or philosophy. Equal violations of it are equally wrong, irrespective of whether the violators are well-educated citizens of a developed 20th century society, say, or members of a far more primitive 13th century society. One must then add that, though equally wrong, they are not equally blameworthy; the perpetration of a massacre by typical German soldiers under Nazi rule is surely more blameworthy, more clearly beyond excuse, than that of an otherwise similar massacre by typical Mongol soldiers. I will not discuss these matters further here.

4. How expansively these five terms should be understood depends on the size and heterogeneity of the world we know. Today, a fairly expansive understanding is requisite: The time from the Renaissance to the French and American Revolutions can count as an epoch, but not the Thirty Years' War; Europe can count as a culture, but not Belgium; Christianity, and also atheism, can count as religions, but not Anglicanism; moral traditions might be utilitarianism, social contract theory, perfectionism and deontological ethics, but not the particular moral conceptions of Kant or Sidgwick; philosophies, finally, might include rationalism, empiricism, idealism, moral realism, intuitionism, but not particular variants of them. Without such an expansive understanding, sharability would not amount to very much in the present world: A moral concern could count as sharable in all five dimensions without being really broadly accessible.

That moral concerns are broadly sharable also means that understanding and appreciating them do not require mental faculties that a significant proportion of humankind does not have and cannot develop. Since sharability is a matter of degree, we can expect disagreement not only about whether particular moral concerns are accessible to particular persons (e.g. about whether human rights are accessible to the peoples of black Africa), but also about whether some given extent of accessibility is sufficient to render a particular moral concern broadly sharable.

5. J. L. Mackie uses the phrase "what gives point to" to single out this most important sense of priority. See his "Can There Be a Right-Based Moral Theory" in *Midwest Studies in Philosophy* 3, 1978, Postscript. This moral or foundational priority must be distinguished from conceptual or definitional priority, which may run the other way. As Mackie suggests, the concept of a duty may well be clearer than that of a right, and it may then make sense to define rights in terms of duties. Raz proposes a useful such definition: "'x has a right' if and only if x can have rights, and other things being equal, an aspect of x's well-being (his interest) is a sufficient reason for holding some other person(s) to be under a duty." See Joseph Raz, "On the Nature of Rights" in *Mind* 93, 1984, 194-214, at 194.

6. This connection is explicated and defended in Joel Feinberg: "The Nature and Value of Rights" in *The Journal of Value Inquiry* 4, 1970, 243-251.

7. For this position, together with its corollary that babies have no rights, see H. L. A. Hart: "Are There Any Natural Rights?" in *The Philosophical Review* 64, 1955, 175-191.

8. These and related points are made and defended more elaborately in Alan Gewirth, "The Basis and Content of Human Rights" in J. Roland Pennock and John W. Chapman, eds., *Nomos XXIII: Human Rights*, New York, New York University Press, 1981, 119-147.

9. For a more extensive discussion of the limitations of the rights idiom, see my "O'Neill on Rights and Duties" in *Grazer Philosophische Studien* 43, 1992, 233-247.

10. John Rawls, "Justice as Fairness: Political not Metaphysical" in *Philosophy and Public Affairs* 14, 1985, 223-252.

11. This second component is compatible with the view that the weight agents ought to give to the human rights of others varies with their relation to them—that agents have stronger moral reasons to secure human rights in their own country, for example, than abroad—so long as this is not seen as being due to a difference in the moral significance of these rights, impersonally considered. (I can believe that the flourishing of all children is equally important and also that I should show greater concern for the flourishing of my own children than for that of other children.)

12. The switch in idiom from "interests" to "needs" is meant merely to flag the idea that only the most important interests of human beings should be seen as giving rise to human rights. The switch is not supposed to prejudge any substantive questions about how human rights should be specified: Basic needs, just like interests, could still be conceived in a person-relative way (so that what a person's basic needs are depends in part on some of her personal characteristics such as gender or handicaps) or even in subjective terms (so that what a person's basic needs are depends in part on some of her goals, desires or preferences).

13. I intend the word "object" here in a broad sense so as not to prejudge any

substantive issues. The object of a right is whatever the right is a right to. Such objects might be freedoms-from, freedoms-to, as well as physical security or an adequate food supply.

14. I shall drop the bracketed addition from now on; but see note 20 below.

15. In the case of some human rights, (re)organizing a society so that all have secure access to its object will require that there be a legal right identical in content: It is hard to imagine a society under modern conditions whose members are secure in their property or have secure access to freedom of expression even while no legal right thereto exists. In other cases, an individual legal right of matching content may not be necessary. We can envision, for example, a society in which all have secure access to minimally adequate nutrition even without a legal right thereto. While a corresponding legal right may be necessary in some cases and unnecessary in others, such a legal right will in all cases be insufficient for maintaining secure access to the object of the human right to which it corresponds: A legal right may always be ineffective. (I assume that there is no human right whose sole object is that there be some legal right on the books.)

16. I have in mind here the general picture presented in W. N. Hohfeld, *Fundamental Legal Conceptions*, New Haven, Yale University Press, 1919. We find this picture used to explicate the notion of human rights in Carl Wellman, "A New Conception of Human Rights" in E. Kamenka and A. S. Tay, eds., *Human Rights*, New York, St. Martin's Press, 1968. See also Carl Wellman, *A Theory of Rights: Persons Under Laws, Institutions, and Morals*, Totowa, Rowman and Allanheld, 1985.

17. "A human right, then, will be a right whose beneficiaries are all humans and whose obligors are all humans in a position to effect the right"—David Luban, "Just War and Human Rights" in Charles Beitz, et al., eds., *International Ethics*, Princeton, Princeton University Press, 1985, 209. A comprehensive maximalist account is developed in Henry Shue, *Basic Rights*, Princeton, Princeton University Press, 1980/96. In a new afterword Shue cautions, however, that his position is less than fully maximalist. He holds that we are required to aid any persons whose rights have been violated—but not those whose rights are unfulfilled due to, say, natural causes (*ibid.* 159). I am not sure why this distinction should be morally significant.

18. By counting official denials and deprivations more heavily than otherwise equivalent private ones, I am abandoning a position I have defended in the past, the position namely that social institutions should be assessed from a broadly consequentialist prospective-participant perspective (such as Rawls's original position, for example). Prospective participants do not care whether the objects of their human rights are at risk on account of the government or on account of private agents. Hence they would, other things equal, allow the two kinds of risk an equal impact upon the moral assessment of social institutions. I now hold that the injustice of a society is significantly greater if, other things equal, insecure access to the objects of human rights is due to the risk of human-rights violations, i.e., the risk of being denied X or deprived of X officially. Even though a signifi-

cant risk of being executed for my expressed political beliefs is no worse for me than an otherwise equal risk of being killed by an assassin for the same reason, the former signifies a greater injustice in the relevant social order, a worse human-rights record on the part of the society in question. A fuller recantation of my earlier hypothetical-contract thinking is in "Three Problems with Contractarian-Consequentialist Ways of Assessing Social Institutions" in *Social Philosophy and Policy* 12, 1995, 241-66. Cp. also supra: the second paragraph of Section III.

19. Insisting on the relevance of insecure access is not new. The Universal Declaration itself proclaims (§28) that "everyone is entitled to a social and international order in which the rights and freedoms set forth in this Declaration can be fully realized." The Inter-American Court of Human Rights held Honduras responsible for crimes of "disappearing" persons (e.g., in *Velasquez*; July 29, 1988; series C, number 4), even without finding that government officials were involved in these crimes, which were nevertheless imputed to the government on the ground that it had failed to exercise due diligence to prevent and to respond to the crimes.

What is new about my understanding is that it links rights fulfillment with insecurity rather than violation: Even while P never ceases fully to enjoy X, her access to X may be insecure—as when persons relevantly like her (vocal government opponents, Jews) are beaten or threatened. On my understanding, P's human right to X is not fulfilled in this case (though it would be fulfilled in the converse case, where she does not enjoy X temporarily due to a crime, say, in a society that is very effective in preventing crimes of the relevant type). The other novelty is that I understand human rights as making claims not merely on the government but on the structure of the society and ultimately on all its members.

20. Still, the institutional understanding leaves room for the possibility that, even in peacetime, we share responsibility for human-rights fulfillment abroad. (Such responsibility is a given for the interactional maximalist and impossible for the interactional minimalist.) We have such responsibility if we are (privileged) participants in a transnational scheme of social institutions—including perhaps the territorial state with eminent domain over land and resources, the network of international law and diplomacy, international commodity markets, etc.—under which some persons are regularly, predictably and avoidably denied secure access to the objects of their human rights. I have myself tried to show that this empirical condition is satisfied in *Realizing Rawls*, Ithaca, Cornell University Press, 1989, Chapter 6; "Cosmopolitanism and Sovereignty" in *Ethics* 103, 1992, 48-75; and "An Egalitarian Law of Peoples" in *Philosophy and Public Affairs* 23, 1994, 195-224.

21. The expression "utilitarianism of rights" is from Robert Nozick, *Anarchy, State, and Utopia*, New York, Basic Books, 1974, 28. It fits rights-based consequentialist views that apply directly to agents—be they of the ideal or real, of the act, rule or motive variety. There are also other variants of consequentialism such as Bentham's utilitarianism, which applies to social institutions, and so there

could be a utilitarianism of rights of the institutional sort. One way in which such a position would differ from what I advocate here is clarified by note 18.

22. If we are, as I believe (see note 20), privileged participants in an international institutional order, then we may have a human-rights-based duty to work for its reform: toward a different global structure that would reduce or eliminate the incidence of wars and of severe poverty, both of which tend to produce human-rights violations and insecure access on a massive scale. See also my "Human Rights and Human Responsibilities" in Ciaran Cronin and Pablo De Greiff, eds.: *Transnational Politics and Deliberative Democracy*, Cambridge, MA: MIT Press, 2000.

23. This debate has occupied the United Nations since its founding, pitting the developed Western states first against the socialist states of the Soviet block and later against the newly independent states of the Third World.

24. In any case, the institutional understanding greatly reduces the practical importance of the dispute about what human rights there can be: As I have shown in the context of Article 5, establishing secure access to the objects of narrowly conceived civil rights may well involve us in creating and upholding social institutions that—through unemployment benefits and/or by fostering literacy, legal education and a culture of equal citizenship—would preclude extreme social and economic deprivation and dependency. Thus, even a narrow list of (exclusively civil and political) human rights might have many of the same practical implications as a broader one would have.

25. The degree of a person's responsibility for injustice must plausibly depend on the means at her disposal and perhaps also on how advantaged she is within the social order in question. The degree of a person's blameworthiness will depend on further factors as well, such as her education, experience and circumstances.

26. Quoted by Stephen Jay Gould in "The Moral State of Tahiti—and of Darwin" in *Natural History* 10/91, 12-19, at 19.

27. Compare, for example, Onora O'Neill, *Faces of Hunger*, London: Allen and Unwin, 1986, 101. It makes no sense, I think, to broaden this definition to include rights that cannot now be fulfilled because of the obduracy of the powers that be. Doing so would make all rights into manifesto rights in just those cases where it is most urgent to assert them. We don't want to say, I trust, that the rights of Jews violated by the Nazis in 1938-42 were mere manifesto rights.

Questions for Reflection

1. Pogge contends that, according to his institutional understanding of human rights, human rights entail only negative duties. How does he argue for this claim?

2. Explain what Pogge means when he states that human rights are "moral claims upon the organization of one's society." What is your evaluation of Pogge's position?

3. How does Pogge's institutional account of human rights address the concerns about social, economic and cultural rights raised by Cranston? With whom do you most agree (and why)?

20. MARTHA C. NUSSBAUM

Martha Nussbaum (1947-) is Ernst Freund Professor of Law and Ethics, The Law School, The Divinity School, and the Departments of Philosophy and of Classics, at the University of Chicago. Her work focuses on ancient Greek philosophy, contemporary moral and political philosophy, and the connections between philosophy and literature. Her many books include *The Fragility of Goodness* (1986); *Cultivating Humanity* (1997); *Sex and Social Justice* (1999); and *Women and Human Development: The Capabilities Approach* (2000). This selection presents Nussbaum's "capabilities approach" to human rights, in which she argues that human rights are claims to resources and opportunities that promote the fully human functioning of every individual. By asking how people are actually functioning, Nussbaum contends that a capabilities approach to human rights provides a strong basis for understanding what people require in order to become capable of performing the major areas of human functioning.

Text—Capabilities and Human Rights

From Fordham Law Review *66 (1997). Reprinted by permission of the publisher.*

Introduction

When governments and international agencies talk about people's basic political and economic entitlements, they regularly use the language of rights. When constitutions are written in the modern era, and their framers wish to identify a group of particularly urgent interests that deserve special protection, once again it is the language of rights that is regularly preferred.

The language of rights has a moral resonance that makes it hard to avoid in contemporary political discourse. But it is certainly not on account of its theoretical and conceptual clarity that it has been preferred. There are many different ways of thinking about what a right is, and many different definitions of "human rights."[1] For example, rights are often spoken of as entitlements that belong to all human beings simply because they are human, or as especially urgent interests of human beings *as human beings* that deserve protection regardless of where people are situated.[2] Within this tradition there are differences. The dominant tradition has typically grounded rights in the possession of rationality and language, thus implying that non-human animals do not have them, and that mentally impaired humans may not have them.[3] Some philosophers have maintained that sentience, instead, should be the basis of rights; thus, all animals would be rights-bearers.[4] In contrast to this entire group of natural-rights theorists, there are also thinkers who treat all rights as artifacts of state action.[5] The latter position would seem to imply that there are no human rights where there is no state to recognize them. Such an approach appears to the holders of the former view to do away with very point of rights language, which is to point to the fact that human beings are entitled to certain types of treatment *whether or not* the state in which they happen to live recognizes this fact.

There are many other complex unresolved theoretical questions about rights. One of them is the question whether the individual is the only bearer of rights, or whether rights belong, as well, to other entities, such as families, ethnic, religious, and linguistic groups, and nations. Another is whether rights are to be regarded as side-constraints on goal-seeking action, or as parts of a goal that is to be promoted.[6] Still another unresolved question is whether rights—thought of as justified entitlements—are correlated with duties. If A has a right to S, then it would appear there must be someone who has a duty to provide S to A. But it is not always clear who has these duties—especially when we think of rights in the international context. Again, it is also unclear whether all duties are correlated with rights. One might hold, for example, that we have a duty not to cause pain to animals without holding that animals have rights—if, for example, one accepted one of the classic accounts of the basis of rights that makes reference to the abilities of speech and reason as the foundation, and yet still believed that we have other strong reasons not to cause animals pain.

Finally, there are difficult theoretical questions about what rights are to be understood as rights *to*. When we speak of human rights, do we mean, primarily, a right to be treated in certain ways? A right to a certain level of achieved well-being? A right to certain resources with which one may pursue one's life plan? A right to certain opportunities and capacities with which one may, in turn, make choices regarding one's life plan? Political philosophers who debate the nature of equality standardly tackle a related question head on, asking whether the equality most relevant to political distribution should be understood, primarily, as equality of well-being, or equality of resources, or equality of opportunity, or equality of capabilities.[7] The language of rights to some extent cuts across this debate and obscures the issues that have been articulated.

Thus, one might conclude that the language of rights is not especially informative, despite its uplifting character, unless its users link their references to rights to a theory that answers at least some of these questions.[8] It is for this reason, among others, that a different language has begun to take hold in talk about people's basic entitlements. This is the language of capabilities and human functioning. Since 1993, the *Human Development Reports* of the United Nations Development Programme[9] ("UNDP") have assessed the quality of life in the nations of the world using the concept of people's capabilities, or their abilities to do and to be certain things deemed valuable.[10] Under the influence of economist/philosopher Amartya Sen, they have chosen that conceptual framework as basic to inter-country comparisons and to the articulation of goals for public policy.

Along with Sen, I have been one of the people who have pioneered what is now called the "capabilities approach," defending its importance in international debates about welfare and quality of life. My use of this language was originally independent, and reflected the fact that Aristotle used a notion of human capability (Greek *dunamis*) and functioning (Greek *energeia*) in order to articulate some of the goals of good political organization.[11] But the projects soon became fused: I increasingly articulated the Aristotelian idea of capability in terms pertinent to the contemporary debate,[12] while Sen increasingly emphasized the ancient roots of his idea.[13] In a variety of contexts, we argued that the capabilities approach was a valuable theoretical framework for public policy, especially in the international development context.[14] We commended it to both theoreticians and practitioners as offering certain advantages over approaches that focus on opulence—GNP per capita, or welfare—construed in terms of utility or desire-satisfaction, or even the distribution of basic resources.[15]

Both Sen and I stated from the start that the capabilities approach needs to be combined with a focus on rights. Sen wrote about rights as central goals of public policy throughout the period during which he developed the approach.[16] I stressed from the start that Aristotle's theory was grossly defective because it lacked a theory of basic human rights, especially rights to be free from government interference in certain areas of choice.[17] More recently, responding to communitarian critics of rights-based reasoning and to international discussions that denigrate rights in favor of material well-being, both Sen and I have even more strongly emphasized the importance of rights to our own capabilities approach. We stressed the various roles liberty plays within our respective theories and emphasized the closeness of our approach to liberal theories such as that of John Rawls.[18]

Moreover, rights play an increasingly large role inside the account of what the most important capabilities are. Unlike Sen, who prefers to allow the account of the basic capabilities to remain largely implicit in his statements, I have produced an explicit account of the most central capabilities that should be the goal of public policy. The list is continually being revised and adjusted, in accordance with my methodological commitment to cross-cultural deliberation and criticism. But another source of change has been an increasing determination to bring the list down to earth, so to speak, making the "thick vague conception of the good"[19] a little less vague, so that it can do real work guiding public policy. At this point, the aim is to come up with the type of specification of a basic capability that could figure in a constitution,[20] or perform, apart from that, the role of a constitutional guarantee.

In the process, I have increasingly used the language of rights, or the related language of liberty and freedom, in fleshing out the account of the basic capabilities. Thus, in "Human Capabilities," I speak of "legal guarantees of freedom of expression...and of freedom of religious exercise"[21] as aspects of the general capability to use one's mind and one's senses in a way directed by one's own practical reason. I also speak of "guarantees of non-interference with certain choices that are especially personal and definitive of selfhood," and of "the freedoms of assembly and political speech."[22] In a forthcoming paper, I actually use the language of rights itself in articulating the capability to seek employment outside the home, and several of the other important capabilities.[23] In part, this is a rhetorical choice, bringing the list of capabilities into relation with international human rights instruments that have a related content. But in part it also reflects a theoretical decision to emphasize the affiliations of the approach with liberal rights-based theories, in an era of widespread reaction against the Enlightenment and its heritage.[24]

But there are still some large questions to be answered. The relationship between the two concepts remains as yet underexplored. Does the capabilities view supplement a theory of rights, or is it intended to be a particular way of capturing what a theory of rights captures? Is there any tension between a focus on capabilities and a focus on rights? Are the two approaches competitors? On the other hand, is there any reason why a capabilities theorist should welcome the language of rights—that is, is there anything in the view itself that leads naturally in the direction of recognizing rights? Would a natural-law Catholic theorist who used an Aristotelian language of capability and functioning, but rejected liberal rights-based language, be making a conceptual error?[25] Does the capabilities view help us to answer any of the difficult questions that I sketched above, which have preoccupied theorists of rights? Does the capabilities view incline us to opt for any particular set of answers to the various questions about rights, or any particular conception of rights?

For example, is Sen justified in thinking that the capabilities view supports a conception of rights as goals, rather than as side-constraints?[26] Finally, is there any reason, other than a merely rhetorical one, why we should continue to use the language of rights in addition to the language of capabilities?

In short, the conceptual relationship needs further scrutiny[27].... I shall begin by describing the capabilities approach and the motivations for its introduction: what it was trying to do in political philosophy, how it commended itself by contrast to other standard ways of thinking about entitlements. Then I shall briefly clarify the connection between the capabilities approach and liberal theories of justice. Finally, I shall turn to my central topic, the relationship between rights and capabilities.

I. The Capabilities Approach: Motivation and Argument

Why, then, should there be a theory of human capabilities? What questions does it answer, and what is its practical point? Why should an international agency such as the UNDP use a measure of quality of life based on human capability and functioning, rather than other more traditional measures: for example, those based on opulence, utility, or a distribution of resources that satisfies some constraint, whether it be a social minimum, or the Rawlsian Difference Principle, or some more exacting egalitarian condition?

The account of human capabilities has been used as an answer to a number of distinct questions, such as: What is the living standard? What is the quality of life? What is the relevant type of equality that we should consider in political planning? It has also been closely linked to discussion of a theory of justice, because such a theory has a need for an account of what it is trying to achieve for people. I believe that the most illuminating way of thinking about the capabilities approach is that it is an account of the space within which we make comparisons between individuals and across nations as to how well they are doing. This idea is closely linked with the idea of a theory of justice, since one crucial aim of a theory of justice typically is to promote some desired state of people; and in "Aristotelian Social Democracy" I linked it very closely to an account of the proper goal of government, to bring all citizens up to a certain basic minimum level of capability. But up to a point, the approach is logically independent of a theory of justice, since a theory of justice may acknowledge many constraints with regard to how far it is entitled to promote people's well-being....

The capabilities idea is also closely linked to a concern with equality, in that Sen has always used it to argue that people are entitled to a certain level of rough material and social equality. But, strictly speaking, these two concerns of Sen's are logically independent. One might agree that capabilities are the relevant space within which to compare lives and nations, and yet hold that equality of capability is not the appropriate goal. Capabilities inform us as to what type of equality might be thought pertinent; they do not by themselves tell us whether we should value an equal distribution or some other distribution.

As a theory of the relevant space within which to make comparisons, the capabilities approach is best understood by contrasting it with its rivals in the international development arena. The most common method of measuring the quality of life in a nation and making cross-national comparisons used to be simply to enumerate GNP per capita.... In short, the crude approach does not even tell us who has the money, and thus typically gave high marks to nations such as South Africa, which contained enormous inequalities. Still less does it provide any information at all about elements of human life that might be thought very important in defining its quality, but that are not always well correlated with GNP per capita: educational opportunities, health care, life expectancy, infant mortality, the presence or absence of political liberties, the extent of racial or gender inequality.

Somewhat less crude is an economic approach that measures quality of life in terms of utility, understood as the satisfaction of preference or desire.[28] This approach at least has the advantage of concerning itself to some degree with distribution, in the sense that it does look at how resources are or are not going to work to make people's lives better. But it has severe shortcomings. First, there is the familiar problem that utilitarianism tends to think of the social total, or average, as an aggregate, neglecting the salience of the boundaries between individual lives.[29] As Rawls pointed out, this approach means that utilitarianism can tolerate a result in which the total is good enough, but where some individuals suffer extremely acute levels of deprivation, whether of resources or of liberty....[30]

A second problem with utilitarianism is its commitment to the commensurability of value, the concern to measure the good in terms of a single metric and thus to deny that there are irreducibly plural goods that figure in a human life.[31] Both Sen and I have pursued this question extensively, apart from our work on capabilities.[32] But it has also had importance in justifying the capabilities approach, since the quality of life seems to consist of a plurality of distinct features—features that cannot be simply reduced to quantities of one another. This recognition limits the nature of the tradeoffs it will be feasible to make.[33]

But a third feature of utilitarianism has been even more central the capability critique. As Sen has repeatedly pointed out, people's satisfactions are not very reliable indicators of their quality of life. Wealthy and privileged people get used to a high level of luxury, and feel pain when they do not have delicacies that one may think they do not really need. On the other hand, deprived people frequently adjust their sights to the low level they know they can aspire to, and thus actually experience satisfaction in connection with a very reduced living standard. Sen gave a graphic example: In 1944, the year after the Great Bengal Famine, the All-India Institute of Hygiene and Public Health did a survey.[34] Included in this survey were a large number of widows and widowers.[35] The position of widows in India is extremely bad, in all kinds of ways but notoriously in terms of health status.[36] But in the survey, only 2.5 percent of widows, as against 48.5 percent of widowers, reported that they were either ill or in indifferent health.[37] And when the question was just about "indifferent health," as opposed to illness—for which we might suppose there are more public and objective criteria—45.6 percent of widowers said their health was "indifferent," as opposed to zero percent of the widows.[38] The likely explanation for this discrepancy is that people who have regularly been malnourished, who have in addition been told that they are weak and made for suffering, and who, as widows, are told that they are virtually dead and have no rights, will be unlikely to recognize their fatigue and low energy as a sign of bodily disease; but not so for males, who are brought up to have high expectations for their own physical functioning. Sen concludes: "Quiet acceptance of deprivation and bad fate affects the scale of dissatisfaction generated, and the utilitarian calculus gives sanctity to that distortion."[39]

This phenomenon of "adaptive preferences"—preferences that adjust to the low level of functioning one can actually achieve—has by now been much studied in the economic literature,[40] and is generally recognized as a central problem, if one wants to use the utilitarian calculus for any kind of normative purpose in guiding public policy.[41] We are especially likely to encounter adaptive preferences when we are studying groups that have been persistent victims of discrimination, and who may as a result have internalized a conception of their own unequal worth. It is certain to be true when we are concerned with groups who have inadequate information about their situation, their options, and the surrounding society—as is frequently the case, for example, with women in developing countries. For these reasons, then, the utility-based approach seems inadequate as a basis for offering comparisons of quality of life.

Far more promising is an approach that looks at a group of basic resources and then asks about their distribution, asking, in particular, how well even the worst off citizens are doing with respect to the items on the list. Such is the approach of John Rawls, who, in *A Theory of Justice* and subsequent works, advanced a list of the "primary goods" intended to be items that all rational individuals, regardless of their more comprehensive plans of life, would desire as prerequisites for carrying out those plans.[42] These items would include liberties, opportunities, and powers, wealth and income, and the social basis of self-respect. More recently, Rawls has added freedom of movement and the free choice of occupation.[43] The idea is that we measure who is better off and less well off by using such a list of primary resources; that information is used, in turn, by the parties who are choosing principles of justice. Notice that this list is heterogeneous. Some of its items are capacities of persons such as liberties, opportunities, and powers, and the social basis of self-respect is a complex property of society's relation to persons, but income and wealth are pure resources. And income and wealth frequently play a central role in the measurement of who is better and worse off.[44] Rawls was at pains, moreover, to state that this list of "primary goods" is not a comprehensive theory of what is good or valuable in life.[45] For Rawls, the attraction of operating with a list of resources is that it enables the approach to steer clear of prescribing the basic values of human life, which individuals must be able to select for themselves, in accordance with their own more comprehensive religious or ethical conceptions.

Sen's basic argument against Rawls, for the past twenty years, has been that the space of resources is inadequate as a space within which to answer questions about who is better and who is worse off.[46] The inadequacy derives from the fact that individuals vary greatly in their need for resources and in their ability to convert resources into valuable functionings. Some of these differences are physical. Nutritional needs vary with age, occupation, and sex. A pregnant or lactating woman needs more nutrients than a non-pregnant woman. A child needs more protein than an adult. A person whose limbs work well needs few resources to be mobile, whereas a person with paralyzed limbs needs many more resources to achieve the same level of mobility. Many such variations escape our notice if we live in a prosperous nation that can afford to bring all individuals to a high level of physical attainment; in the developing world we must be highly alert to these variations in need. Some of the variations, again, are social, and have to do with traditional social hierarchies. If we wish to bring all citizens of a nation to the same level of educational attainment, we will need to devote more resources to those who encounter obstacles from traditional hierarchy or prejudice. Thus, women's literacy will prove more expensive than men's literacy in many parts of the world. This means that if we operate only with an index of resources, we will frequently reinforce inequalities that are highly relevant to well-being. An approach focusing on resources does not go deep enough to diagnose obstacles that can be present even when resources seem to be adequately spread around, causing individuals to fail to avail themselves of opportunities that they in some sense have, such as free public education, the right to vote, or the right to work.

For this reason, we argue that the most appropriate space for comparisons is the space of capabilities. Instead of asking "How satisfied is person A," or "How much in the way of resources does A command," we ask the question: "What is A actually able to do and to be?" In other words, about a variety of functions that would seem to be of central importance to a human life, we ask: Is the person capable of this, or not? This focus on capabilities, unlike the focus on GNP, or on aggregate utility, looks at people one by one, insisting on locating empowerment in *this* life and in *that* life, rather than in the nation as a whole. Unlike the utilitarian focus on satisfactions, it looks not at what people feel about what they do, but about what they are actually able to do.[47] Nor does it make any assumptions about the commensurability of the different pursuits. Indeed, this view denies that the most important functions are all commensurable in terms of a single metric and it treats the diverse functions as all important, and all irreducibly plural.[48] Finally, unlike the focus on resources, it is concerned with what is actually going on in the life in question: not how many resources are sitting around, but how they are actually going to work in enabling people to function in a fully human way.[49]

II. The Central Human Capabilities

Sen has focused on the general defense of the capability space, and has not offered any official account of what the most central human capabilities are, although in practice he has to some extent done so, by focusing on some areas of human life and not others in constructing the measures used in the *Human Development Reports*. Again, his recent book on India gives many concrete examples of the importance and the interrelationships of various concrete human capabilities.[50] I, by contrast, have focused on the task of producing such a working list, describing a methodology by which we might both generate and justify such a list[51] and defending the whole project of giving such a list against the objections of relativists and traditionalists.[52] The list is supposed to be a focus for political planning, and it is supposed to select those human capabilities that can be convincingly argued to be of central importance in any human life, whatever else the person pursues or chooses. The central capabilities are not just instrumental to further pursuits: They are held to have value in themselves, in making a life fully human. But they are held to have a particularly central importance in everything else we plan and choose. In that sense, central capabilities play a role similar to that played by primary goods in Rawls's more recent account: They support our powers of practical reason and choice, and have a special importance in making any choice of a way of life possible. They thus have a special claim to be supported for political purposes in societies that otherwise contain a great diversity of views about the good....

The list is an attempt to summarize the empirical findings of a broad and ongoing cross-cultural inquiry. As such, it is open-ended and humble; it can always be contested and remade. It does not claim to read facts of "human nature" off of biological observation, although it does of course take account of biology as a relatively constant element in human experience. Nor does it deny that the items on the list are to some extent differently constructed by different societies. Indeed; part of the idea of the list is that its members can be more concretely specified in accordance with local beliefs and circumstances. In that sense, the consensus it hopes to evoke has many of the features of the "overlapping consensus" described by Rawls.[53]

Here is the current version of the list, revised as a result of my recent visits to development projects in India:[54]

1. *Life.* Being able to live to the end of a human life of normal length; not dying prematurely, or before one's life is so reduced as to be not worth living.

2. *Bodily health.* Being able to have good health, including reproductive health; to be adequately nourished; to have adequate shelter.

3. *Bodily integrity.* Being able to move freely from place to place; to be secure against violent assault, including sexual assault and domestic violence; having opportunities for sexual satisfaction and for choice in matters of reproduction.

4. *Senses, imagination, and thought.* Being able to use the senses; being able to imagine, to think, and to reason—and to do these things in a "truly human" way, a way informed and cultivated by an adequate education, including, but by no means limited to, literacy and basic mathematical and scientific training. Being able to use imagination and thought in connection with experiencing and producing expressive works and events of one's own choice, religious, literary, musical, and so forth. Being able to use one's mind in ways protected by guarantees of freedom of expression with respect to both political and artistic speech and freedom of religious exercise. Being able to have pleasurable experiences and to avoid non-beneficial pain.

5. *Emotions.* Being able to have attachments to things and people outside ourselves; to love those who love and care for us, to grieve at their absence; in general, to love, to grieve, to experience longing, gratitude, and justified anger. Not having one's emotional development blighted by fear and anxiety. Supporting this capability means supporting forms of human association that can be shown to be crucial in their development.

6. *Practical Reason.* Being able to form a conception of the good and to engage in critical reflection about the planning of one's life. This entails protection for the liberty of conscience and religious observance.

7. *Affiliation.* (a) *Friendship.* Being able to live for and to others, to recognize and show concern for other human beings, to engage in various forms of social interaction; to be able to imagine the situation of another and to have compassion for that situation; to have the capability for both justice and friendship. Protecting this capability means, once again, protecting institutions that constitute such forms of affiliation, and also protecting the freedoms of assembly and political speech. (b) *Respect.* Having the social bases of self-respect and non-humiliation; being able to be treated as a dignified being whose worth is equal to that of

others. This entails provisions of non discrimination on the basis of race, sex, ethnicity, caste, religion, and national origin.

8. *Other species.* Being able to live with concern for and in relation to animals, plants, and the world of nature.

9. *Play.* Being able to laugh, to play, and to enjoy recreational activities.

10. *Control over one's environment.* (a) *Political.* Being able to participate effectively in political choices that govern one's life; having the right of political participation, protections of free speech and association. (b) *Material.* Being able to hold property (both land and movable goods); having the right to employment; having freedom from unwarranted search and seizure.

The list is, emphatically, a list of separate and indispensable components. We cannot satisfy the need for one of them by giving a larger amount of another. All are of central importance and all are distinct in quality. Practical reason and affiliation, I argue elsewhere, are of special importance because they both organize and suffuse all the other capabilities, making their pursuit truly human.[55] The individual importance of each component limits the trade-offs that it will be reasonable to make, and thus limits the applicability of quantitative cost-benefit analysis. At the same time, the items on the list are related to one another in many complex ways. One of the most effective ways of promoting women's control over their environment, and their effective right of political participation, is to promote women's literacy. Women who can seek employment outside the home have more resources in protecting their bodily integrity from assaults within it.

III. Capability of Goal

I have spoken of both functioning and capability. How are they related? Understanding this relationship is crucial in defining the relation of the "capabilities approach" to both liberalism and views of human rights. For if we were to take functioning itself as the goal of public policy, the liberal would rightly judge that we were precluding many choices that citizens may make in accordance with their own conceptions of the good, and perhaps violating their rights. A deeply religious person may prefer not to be well-nourished, but instead prefer to engage in strenuous fasting. Whether for religious or for other reasons, a person may prefer a celibate life to one containing sexual expression. A person may prefer to work with an intense dedication that precludes recreation and play. Am I declaring, by my very use of the list, that these are not fully human or flourishing lives? And am I instructing government to nudge or push people into functioning of the requisite sort, no matter what they prefer?

It is important that the answer to these questions is no. Capability, not functioning, is the political goal. Capability must be the goal because of the great importance the capabilities approach attaches to practical reason, as a good that both suffuses all the other functions, making them human rather than animal,[56] and figures itself as a central function on the list. It is perfectly true that functionings, not simply capabilities, are what render a life fully human: If there were no functioning of any kind in a life, we could hardly applaud it, no matter opportunities it contained. Nonetheless, for political purposes it is appropriate for us to strive for capabilities, and those alone. Citizens must be left free to determine their course after they have the capabilities. The person with plenty of food may always choose to fast, but there is a great difference between fasting and starving, and it is this difference that we wish to capture. Again, the person who has normal opportunities for sexual satisfaction can always choose a life of celibacy, and we say nothing against this. What I speak against, for example, is the practice of female genital mutilation, which deprives individuals of the opportunity to choose sexual functioning, and indeed, the opportunity to choose celibacy as well.[57] A person who has opportunities for play can always choose a workaholic life. Again, there is a great difference between that chosen life and a life constrained by insufficient maximum-hour protections and/or the "double day" that make women unable to play in many parts of the world.

I can make the issue clearer, and also prepare for discussion of the relationship between capabilities and rights, by pointing out that there are three different types of capabilities that figure in my analysis.[58] First, there are what I call *basic capabilities*: the innate equipment of individuals that is the necessary basis for developing the more advanced capability. Most infants have from birth the *basic capability* for practical reason and imagination, though they cannot exercise such functions without a lot more development and education. Second, there are *internal capabilities*: that is, states of the person herself that are, so far as the person herself is concerned, sufficient conditions for the exercise of the requisite functions. A woman who has not suffered genital mutilation has the *internal capability* for sexual pleasure; most adult human beings everywhere have the *internal capability* to use speech and thought in accordance with their own conscience. Finally, there are *combined capabilities*, which I define as internal capabilities *combined with* suitable external conditions for the exercise of the function. A woman who is not mutilated but secluded and forbidden to leave the house has internal but not combined capabilities for sexual expression—and work, and political participation. Citizens of repressive non-democratic regimes have the internal but not the combined capability to exercise thought and speech in accordance with their conscience. The aim of public policy is the production of *combined capabilities*. This idea means promoting the states of the person by providing the necessary education and care, as well as preparing the environment so that it is favorable for the exercise of practical reason and the other major functions.[59]

This explanation of the types of capability clarifies my position. I am not saying that public policy should rest content with *internal capabilities*, but remain indifferent to the struggles of individuals who have to try to exercise these capabilities in a hostile environment. In that sense, my approach is highly attentive to the goal of functioning, and instructs governments to keep functioning always in view. On the other hand, I am not pushing individuals into the function: once the stage is fully set, the choice is up to them....

The capability view justifies its elaborate list by pointing out that choice is not pure spontaneity, flourishing independently of material and social conditions. If one cares about people's powers to choose a conception of the good, then one must care about the rest of the form of life that supports those powers, including its material conditions....

The guiding thought behind this form of Aristotelianism is, at its heart, a profoundly liberal idea,[60] and one that lies at the heart of Rawls's project as well: the idea of the citizen as a free and dignified human being, a maker of choices.[61] Politics here has an urgent role to play, providing citizens with the tools that they need, both in order to choose at all and in order to have a realistic option of exercising the most valuable functions. The choice of whether and how to use the tools, however, is left up to the citizens, in the conviction that this choice is an essential aspect of respect for their freedom. They are seen not as passive recipients of social patterning, but as dignified free beings who shape their own lives.[62]

IV. Rights and Capabilities: Two Different Relationships?

How, then, are capabilities related to human rights? We can see, by this time, that there are two rather different relations that capabilities have to the human rights traditionally recognized by international human rights instruments. In what follows, I shall understand a human right to involve an especially urgent and morally justified claim that a person has, simply by virtue of being a human adult, and independently of membership in a particular nation, or class, or sex, or ethnic or religious or sexual group.

First, there are some areas in which the best way of thinking about rights is to see them as, what I have called, *combined capabilities* to function in various ways. The right to political participation, the right to religious free exercise, the freedom of speech, the freedom to seek employment outside the home, and the freedom from unwarranted search and seizure are all best thought of as human capacities to function in ways that we then go on to specify. The further specification will usually involve both an internal component and an external component: a citizen who is systematically deprived of information about religion does not really have religious liberty, even if the state imposes no barrier to religious choice. On the other hand, internal conditions are not enough: women who can think about work outside the home, but who are going to be systematically denied employment on account of sex, or beaten if they try to go outside, do not have the right to seek employment. In short, to secure a right to a citizen in these areas is to put them in a position of capability to go ahead with choosing that function if they should so desire.

Of course, there is another way in which we use the term "right" in which it could not be identified with a capability. We say that A has "a right to" seek employment outside the home, even when her circumstances obviously do not secure such a right to her. When we use the term "human right" this way, we are saying that just by virtue of being human, a person has a justified claim to have the capability secured to her: so a right in that sense would be prior to capability, and a ground for the securing of a capability. "Human rights" used in this sense lie very close to what I have called "basic capabilities," since typically human rights are thought to derive from some actual feature of human persons, some untrained power in them that demands or calls for support from the world. Rights theories differ about which basic capabilities of the person are relevant to rights, but the ones most commonly chosen are the power of reasoning, generally understood to be moral reasoning, and the power of moral choice.[63]

On the other hand, when we say, as we frequently do, that citizens in country C "have the right of free religious exercise," what we typically mean is that this urgent and justified claim is being answered, that the state responds to the claim that they have just by virtue of being human. It is in this sense that capabilities and rights should be seen to be equivalent: For I have said, combined capabilities are the *goals* of public planning.

Why is it a good idea to understand rights, so understood, in terms of capabilities? I think this approach is a good idea because we then understand that what is involved in securing a right to people is usually a lot more than simply putting it down on paper. We see this very clearly in India, for example, where the Constitution is full of guarantees of Fundamental Rights that are not backed up by effective state action. Thus, since ratification women have had rights of sex equality—but in real life they are unequal not only *de facto*, but also *de jure*. This inequality results from the fact that most of the religious legal systems that constitute the entire Indian system of civil law have unequal provisions for the sexes, very few of which have been declared unconstitutional.[64] So we should not say that women have equal rights, since they do not have the capabilities to function as equals. Again, women in many nations have a nominal right of political participation without really having this right in the sense of capability; for they are secluded and threatened with violence should they leave the home. This is not what it is to have a right. In short, thinking in terms of capability gives us a benchmark in thinking about what it is really to secure a right to someone.

There is another set of rights, largely those in the area of property and economic advantage, which seem to me analytically different in their relationship to capabilities. Take, for example, the right to a certain level of income, or the right to shelter and housing. These are rights that can be analyzed in a number of distinct ways, in terms of resources, or utility, or capabilities. We could think of the right to a decent level of living as a right to a certain level of resources; or, less plausibly, as a right to a certain level of satisfaction; or as a right to attain a certain level of capability to function.

Once again, we must distinguish the use of the term "right" in the sentence "A has a right to X," from its use in the sentence "Country C gives citizens the right to X." All human beings may arguably have a right to something in the first sense, without being in countries that secure these rights. If a decent living standard is a human right, then American citizens have that right although their state does not give them, or secure to them, such a right. So far, then, we have the same distinctions on our hands that we did in the case of the political liberties. But the point I am making is that at the second level, the analysis of "Country C secures to its citizens the right to a decent living standard" may plausibly take a wider range of forms than it does for the political and religious liberties, where it seems evident that the best way to think of the secured right is as a capability. The material rights may, by contrast, plausibly be analyzed in terms of resources, or possibly in terms of utility.

Here again, however, I think it is valuable to understand these rights, insofar as we decide we want to recognize them, in terms of capabilities. That it, if we think of a right to a decent level of living as a right to a certain quantity of resources, then we get into the very problems I have pointed to: that is, giving the resources to people does not always bring differently situated people up to the same level of functioning. If you have a group of people who are traditionally marginalized, you are probably going to have to expend more resources on them to get them up to the same living standard—in capability terms—than you would for a group of people who are in favorable social situations.

Analyzing economic and material rights in terms of capabilities would thus enable us to understand, as we might not otherwise, a rationale we might have for spending unequal amounts of money on the disadvantaged, or creating special programs to assist their transition to full capability. The Indian government has long done this. Indeed, affirmative action in this sense for formerly despised caste and tribal groups was written into the constitution itself, and it has played a crucial role in creating the situations we have today, in which lower-caste required this type of affirmative action. If we think of these economic rights asking the question—"What are people actually able to do and to be?"—then I think we have a better way of understanding what it is really to put people securely in possession of those rights, to make them able really to function in those ways, not just to have the right on paper.

If we have the language of capabilities, do we still need, as well, the language of rights? The language of rights still plays, I believe, four important roles in public discourse, despite its unsatisfactory features. When used in the first way, as in the sentence "A has a right to have the basic political liberties secured to her by her government," rights language reminds us that people have justified and urgent claims to certain types of urgent treatment, no matter what the world around them has done about that. I have suggested that this role of rights language lies very close to what I have called "basic capabilities," in the sense that the justification for saying that people have such natural rights usually proceeds by pointing to some capability-like feature of persons that they actually have, on at least a rudimentary level, no matter what the world around them has done about that. And I actually think that without such a justification the appeal to rights is quite mysterious. On the other hand, there is no doubt that one might recognize the basic capabilities of people and yet still deny that this entails that they have rights, in the sense of justified claims, to certain types of treatment. We know that this inference has not been made through a great deal of the world's history, though it is false to suppose that it only was made in the West, or that it only began in the Enlightenment.[65] So, appealing to rights communicates more than appealing to basic capabilities: it says what normative conclusions we draw from the fact of the basic capabilities.

Even at the second level, when we are talking about rights guaranteed by the state, the language of rights places great emphasis on the importance and the basic role of these things. To say, "Here's a list of things that people ought to be able to do and to be" has only a vague normative resonance. To say, "Here is a list of fundamental rights," means considerably more. It tells people right away that we are dealing with an especially urgent set of functions, backed up by a sense of the justified claim that all humans have to such things, by virtue of being human.

Third, rights language has value because of the emphasis it places on people's choice and autonomy. The language of capabilities, as I have said, was designed to leave room for choice, and to communicate the idea that there is a big difference between pushing people into functioning in ways you consider valuable and leaving the choice up to them. At the same time, if we have the language of rights in play as well, I think it helps us to lay extra emphasis on this very important fact: that what one ought to think of as the benchmark are people's autonomous choices to avail themselves of certain opportunities, and not simply their actual functionings.

Finally, in the areas where there is disagreement about the proper analysis of right talk—where the claims of utility, resources, and capabilities are still being worked out—the language of rights preserves a sense of the terrain of agreement, while we continue to deliberate about the proper type of analysis at the more specific level.

One further point should be made. I have discussed one particular view about human capabilities and functioning, my own, and I have indicated its relationship to Sen's very similar view. But of course there are many other ways in which one might construct a view based on the idea of human functioning and capability without bringing capabilities nearly so close to rights. As I have suggested, the view Sen and I share is a liberal view of human capabilities, which gives a strong priority to traditional political and religious liberties, and which focuses on capability as the goal precisely in order to leave room for choice. In addition, as I have more recently stressed, the items on my list of basic capabilities are to be regarded as the objects of a specifically political consensus, rather like a Rawlsian list of primary goods, and not as a comprehensive conception of the good.

A capabilities theorist might construct a view that departed from our view in all of these ways. First, the content of the list might be different: it might not give the same importance to the traditional liberal freedoms. Second, government might be given much more latitude to shoot directly for functioning as a goal, and to penalize people who do not exhibit the desired mode of functioning. Such, indeed, is the strategy of some natural-law thinkers in the Catholic tradition, and in this regard they are closer to Aristotle himself than I am.[66] In that sense, as I have written, they construe the account of the human good as a source of public *discipline* on the choices of citizens, whereas we construe the good as an account of *freedoms* citizens have to pursue a variety of different plans of life. Finally, one might think of the account of human functioning as a comprehensive conception of human flourishing for both public and private purposes, rather than as the object of a specifically political consensus. Again, natural law theorists sometimes understand the view this way, as does Aristotle himself—although some Catholic thinkers have themselves adopted a political-liberal interpretation of their tradition.[67] Insofar as any of these alternatives are pursued, the relationship between capabilities and rights will shift accordingly.

Notes

1. For one excellent recent account, with discussions of other views, see Alan Gewirth, *The Community of Rights* (1996).

2. For just one example, this is the view of Thomas Paine. See Thomas Paine, *Rights of Man—Common Sense* 80-85 (Alfred A, Knopf, 1994) (quoting and discussing the French Declaration of the Rights of Man and of Citizens); id. At 114 (insisting that rights, so conceived, should be the foundation of a nation's prosperity). Such views ultimately derive from ancient Greek and Roman Stoic views of natural law. The Latin word *ius* can be translated either as "right" or as "law;" Grotius already discussed the manifold applications of *ius*. See Hugo Grotius, *De Iure Belli Ac Pacis* (*On the Law of War and Peace*.)

3. The most influential exemplar of such a view, followed by most later theorists, is Cicero. See M. Tulli Ciceronis, *De Officiis* (*On Duties*), bk. 1, paras. 11-14 (Oxford University Press, 1994) (distinguishing humans from beasts by reference to rationality and language); id. Paras. 20-41 (deriving duties from this).

4. See Peter Singer, *Animal Liberation* (2d ed. 1990).

5. This view is most influentially found in Kant. See Immanuel Kant, *The Metaphysics of Morals*, in *Kant: Political Writings* 132-35 (Hans Reiss ed. & H.B. Nisbet trans., Cambridge University Press, 2d enlarged ed., 1991) (1798) (defining right and the theory of right with reference to law and the state).

6. An influential example of the first approach is Robert Nozick, *Anarchy, State, and Utopia* 26-53 (1974) (Chapter 3: Moral Constraints and the State), arguing that rights supply moral constraints on state action. See also Samuel Scheffler, *The Rejection of Consequentialism* (rev. ed., 1994) (developing a theory of rights as side constraints). For the second approach, see, for example, Amartya Sen, "Rights as Goals," in *Equality and Discrimination: Essays in Freedom and Justice* (Stephen Guest & Alan Milne, eds., 1985) [hereinafter "Rights as Goals"], developing an account of rights as among the goals of public action.

7. See Amartya Sen, "Equality of What?," *The Tanner Lectures on Human Values* 195 (Sterling M. McMurrin, ed., 1980), reprinted in *Choice, Welfare and Measurement* 353 (1982) [hereinafter "Equality of What"] (arguing that the most relevant type of equality for political purposes is equality of capability); see also Amartya Sen, *Inequality Reexamined*, passim (1992) [hereinafter *Inequality Reexamined*] (making the same case in more detail); Richard J. Arneson, "Equality and Equal Opportunity for Welfare," 56 *Phil. Stud.* 77 (1989) (defending equality of opportunity for welfare); G.A. Cohen, "On the Currency of Egalitarian Justice," 99 *Ethics* 906, 920-21 (1989) (arguing that the right thing to equalize is "access to advantage"); Ronald Dworkin, "What Is Equality? Part 1: Equality of Welfare," 10 *Phil. & Pub. Aff.* 185 (1981) (discussing distributional equality); Ronald Dworkin, "What Is Equality? Part 2: Equality of Resources," 10 *Phil. &*

Pub. Aff. 283 (1981) (arguing that the right thing to equalize are resources, and defining a suitable conception of equality of resources); John E. Roemer, "Equality of Resources Implies Equality of Welfare," 101 *Q. J. Econ.* 751 (1986) (arguing that, suitably understood, equality of resources implies equality of welfare).

8. See, e.g., Bernard Williams, "The Standards of Living: Interests and Capabilities," in *The Standard of Living* 94, 100 (Geoffrey Hawthorn, ed., 1987) (arguing for an approach to basic human rights through basic capabilities).

9. See, e.g., United Nations Programme, *Human Development Report 1996*; United Nations Programme, *Human Development Report 1993* [*hereinafter Human Development Report 1993*].

10. The report's primary measure of quality of life is the "human development index" ("HDI"). *Human Development Report 1993*, supra note 9, at 10. HDI is a composite of three basic components of human development: longevity (measure by life expectancy), knowledge (measured by a combination of adult literacy and mean years of schooling), and standard of living (measured by income relative to the poverty level). id. At 100. For a standard definition of capabilities, see Amartya Sen, "Capability and Well-Being," in *The Quality of Life* 30-31 (Martha Nussbaum & Amartya Sen, eds., 1993), explaining the choice of the term and its relationship to other basic concepts.

11. See Martha C. Nussbaum, "Nature, Function, and Capability: Aristotle on Political Distribution," in [Supplementary Volume] *Oxford Studies in Ancient Philosophy* 145 (Julia Annas & Robert H. Grimm eds., 1988) [hereinafter "Nature, Function, and Capability"].

12. See Martha Nussbaum, "Aristotelian Social Democracy," in *Liberalism and the Good* 203 (R. Bruce Douglass et al, eds., 1990) [hereinafter "Aristotelian Social Democracy"]; Martha C. Nussbaum, "Aristotle on Human Nature and the Foundations of Ethics," in *World, Mind, and Ethics: Essays on the Ethical Philosophy of Bernard Williams* 86 (J.E.J. Altham & Ross Harrison eds., 1995) [hereinafter "Human Nature"]; Martha C. Nussbaum, "Human Capabilities, Female Human Beings," in *Women, Culture, and Development* 61(M. Nussbaum &J. Glover, eds., 1995) {hereinafter "Human Capabilities"]; Martha Nussbaum, "Non-Relative Virtues: An Aristotelian Approach," in *The Quality of Life*, supra note 10, at 242; Martha C. Nussbaum, "Human Functioning and Social Justice: In Defense of Aristotelian Essentialism," 20 *Pol. Theory* 202 (1992) [hereinafter "Human Functioning"]; Martha C. Nussbaum, "The Good as Discipline, The Good as Freedom," in *The Ethics of Consumption and Global Stewardship* 312 (D. Crocker & T. Linden, eds., forthcoming 1998) (manuscript on file with the Fordham Law Review) [hereinafter "The Good as Discipline, The Good as Freedom"]; Martha C. Nussbaum, *Sex and Social Justice* (forthcoming 1998) (Chapter 1: Women and Cultural Universals) (manuscript on file with the Fordham Law Review) [hereinafter "Women and Cultural Universals"].

13. See, for example, *Inequality Reexamined*, supra note 7, which also contains his most recent formulation of the approach.

14. A good summary of our approaches, and the similarities and differences

between Sen's and my views, is in David A. Crocker, "Functioning and Capability: The Foundations of Sen's and Nussbaum's Development Ethic," 20 *Pol. Theory* 584 (1992) [hereinafter "Functioning and Capability: Part 1"], and David A. Crocker, "Functioning and Capability: The Foundations of Sen's and Nussbaum's Development Ethic, Part 2," in *Women, Culture, and Development*, supra note 12, at 153 [hereinafter "Functioning and Capability: Part 2"].

15. See Amartya Sen, "Capability and Well-Being," in *The Quality of Life*, supra note 10, at 30; Amartya Sen, *Commodities and Capabilities* (1985); "Equality of What?," supra note 7; Amartya Sen, "Gender Inequality and Theories of Justice," in *Women, Culture, and Development*, supra note 12, at 259 (hereinafter "Gender Inequality"]; Amartya Sen, "Well-Being, Agency and Freedom: The Dewey Lectures 1984," 82 *J. Phil.* 169 (1985) [hereinafter "Well-Being"].

16. See Amartya Sen, "Rights and Capabilities," in *Morality and Objectivity: A Tribute to J. L. Mackie* 130 (T. Honderich ed., 1985), reprinted in Amartya Sen, *Resources, Values and Development* 307-24 (1984) [hereinafter "Rights and Capabilities"]; "Rights as Goals," supra note 6; Amartya Sen, "Rights and Agency," 11 Phil. & Pub. Aff. 3 (1982) [hereinafter "Rights and Agency"].

17. See "Aristotelian Social Democracy," supra note 12, at 239.

18. See John Rawls, *Political Liberalism* (1993) [hereinafter *Political Liberalism*]; John Rawls, *A Theory of Justice* (1971) [hereinafter *A Theory of Justice*]. Sen discusses, and supports, the Rawlsian notion of the priority of liberty in "Freedoms and Needs," *New Republic*, Jan. 10 & 17, 1994, at 31-38 [hereinafter "Freedoms and Needs"]. I discuss the relationship between my own version of the capabilities view and Rawls's theory in "Aristotelian Social Democracy," supra note 12, and "The Good as Discipline, The Good as Freedom," supra note 12. In "The Good as Discipline, The Good as Freedom," I emphasize the liberal roots of my own Aristotelianism, contrasting my view with two non-liberal forms of Aristotelianism.

19. This is my term from "Aristotelian Social Democracy," supra note 12, at 217, contrasting with Rawls's "thin theory of the good." *A Theory of Justice,* supra note 18, at 395-99.

20. See "Human Capabilities," supra note 12, at 85.

21. Id. At 84.

22. Id. At 84-85.

23. "Women and Cultural Universals," supra note 12, at 25-26.

24. For the close relationship between the capabilities approach and Enlightenment liberalism, see "Freedoms and Needs," supra note 18, and "The Good as Discipline, The Good as Freedom," supra note 12.

25. I put things this way because the most prominent anti-liberal natural law theorists do not explicitly reject rights language, see John Finnis, *Natural Law and Natural Rights* (1980), and Robert P. George, *Making Men Moral: Civil Liberties and Public Morality* (1993); and the most prominent Catholic opponent of rights language does not endorse the capabilities approach, see Mary Ann Glendon, *Rights Talk: The Impoverishment of Political Discourse* (1991); but the

combination is easy enough to imagine.

26. See "Rights and Capabilites," supra note 16, at 310-12.

27. A valuable beginning, bringing together all that Sen and I have said on the topic, is in "Functioning and Capabilities: Part 2," supra note 14, at 186-91.

28. For discussion of this approach, see "Equality of What?," supra note 7, at 358-64.

29. See *A Theory of Justice*, supra note 18; Amartya Sen & Bernard Williams, "Introduction," to *Utilitarianism and Beyond* 1, 4-5 (Amartya Sen & Bernard Williams, eds., 1982) (arguing that utilitarianism views people simply as locations of their respective utilities).

30. See *A Theory of Justice*, supra note 18, at 179-83 (arguing that utilitarianism treats people as means, rather than as ends).

31. See the discussion in Martha C. Nussbaum, "Plato on Commensurability and Desire," in *Love's Knowledge* 106 (1990) [hereinafter "Commensurability and Desire"], and Martha C. Nussbaum, "The Discernment of Perception: An Aristotelian Conception of Private and Public Rationality," in *Love's Knowledge*, supra, at 54 [hereinafter "Discernment of Perception"], arguing that the plurality and distinctness of the valuable things in life make any single metric a damaging distortion.

32. See "Discernment of Perception," supra note 31; "Commensurability and Desire," supra note 31; see also Martha C. Nussbaum, *The Fragility of Goodness* 290-317 (1986) (arguing that Aristotle was right to recognize a type of deliberation that does not rely on a single metric); Amartya Sen, *On Ethics and Economics* 62-63 (1987) [hereinafter *On Ethics and Economics*] (discussing plurality and non-commensurability); Amartya Sen, "Plural Utility," 81 *Proc. Aristotelian Soc'y* 193 (1981) [hereinafter "Plural Utility"] (arguing that the right way to think of utility is as a plurality of vectors).

33. See "Human Capabilities," supra note 12, at 85-86; *On Ethics and Economics*, supra note 32, at 63-64.

34. "Rights and Capabilites," supra note 16, at 309.

35. Id.

36. Id.

37. Id.

38. Id.

39. Id.

40. See John Elster, "Sour Grapes—Utilitarianism and the Genesis of Wants," in *Utilitarianism and Beyond*, supra note 29, at 219 (defining adaptive preferences and arguing that their existence poses insuperable problems for utilitarianism); Amartya K. Sen, "Gender and Cooperative Conflicts," in *Persistent Inequalities* 123 (Irene Tinker ,ed., 1990) (arguing that women frequently adjust their expectations to the low level of well-being they can achieve, and that on this account a bargaining model of the family is superior to a utilitarian account).

41. See Gary S. Becker, "Nobel Lecture: The Economic Way of Looking at Behavior," in *The Essence of Becker* 633, 636-37 (Ramón Febrero & Pedro. S.

Schwartz, eds., 1995) (arguing that the beliefs of employers, teachers, and others that minorities are less productive can be self-fulfilling, causing minorities to underinvest in education and work skills, thus becoming less productive than they would otherwise have been).

42. *A Theory of Justice*, supra note 18, at 62, 90-95, 396-97. More recently, Rawls has qualified his view by stating that the primary goods are to be seen not as all-purpose means, but as the needs of citizens understood from a political point of view, in connection with the development and expression of their "moral powers." He has stressed that the account of the moral powers—of forming and revising a life plan—is itself an important part of the political theory of the good. See *Political Liberalism*, supra note 18, at 178-90.

43. *Political Liberalism*, supra note 18, at 181.

44. *A Theory of Justice*, supra note 18, at 97-98 (discussing different ways of defining the least well off—both favored approaches focus on income and wealth as indicators).

45. *Political Liberalism*, supra note 18, at 187-88.

46. See "Equality of What?," supra note 7, at 364-67; "Gender Inequality," supra note 15, at 263-66.

47. Sen has insisted, however, that happiness is "a momentous functioning," in "Well-Being," supra note 15, at 200, and I have insisted that emotional functioning is one of the important types of functioning we should consider. See Martha C. Nussbaum, "Emotions and Women's Capabilities," in *Women, Culture, and Development*, supra note 12, at 360.

48. See "Human Capabilites," supra note 12, at 85-86; "Plural Utility," supra note 32.

49. In this sense, the approach takes its inspiration from Marx's discussion of fully human functioning in several early works in which he was in turn much influenced by Aristotle. For discussion of these links, see "Human Nature," supra note 12, at 119-20.

50. See, e.g., Jean Drèze & Amartya Sen, *India: Economic Development and Social Opportunity* 13-16, 109-39 (1995) (discussing the relationship between health and education and other capabilities); id. At 155-78 (discussing the relationship between gender inequality and women's functioning and capability). For an enumeration of all the examples Sen has given in a variety of different works, see "Functioning and Capability: Part 1," supra note 14, and "Functioning and Capability: Part 2," supra note 14.

51. This is especially evident in "Human Nature," supra note 12, at 90-95.

52. See "Human Capabilities," supra note 12, at 67-72, 93-95; "Human Functioning," supra note 12; "Women and Cultural Universals," supra note 12, at 12-20.

53. *Political Liberalism*, supra note 18, passim.

54. The primary changes are a greater emphasis on bodily integrity, a focus on dignity and non-humiliation, and an emphasis on control overr one's environment. Oddly, these features of human "self-sufficiency" are the ones most often

criticized by Western feminists as "male" and "Western"—one reason for their more muted role in earlier versions of the list. See Martha C. Nussbaum, "The Feminist Critique of Liberalism," *The Lindley Lecture*, University of Kansas (1997), also in *Sex and Social Justice*, supra note 12.

55. See "Aristotelian Social Democracy," supra note 12, at 226-28; "Human Nature," supra note 12, at 102-20.

56. See "Human Nature," supra note 12, at 119-20 (discussing Marx).

57. See Martha C. Nussbaum, "Religion and Women's Human Rights," in *Religion and Contemporary Liberalism* 93, 107-10 (Paul J. Weithman, ed., 1997) [hereinafter "Religion and Women's Human Rights"]; Martha Nussbaum, "Double Moral Standards?," *Boston Review*, October-November 1996, at 28, 30 (replying to Yael Tamir's "Hands Off Clitoridectomy," *Boston Re*view, Summer 1996, at 21-22).

58. See "Human Capabilities," supra note 12, at 88 (discussing the basic capabilities); "Nature, Function, and Capability," supra note 11, at 160-64 (referring to Aristotle's similar distinctions). Sen does not use these three levels explicitly, although many things he says assume some such distinctions.

59. This distinction is related to Rawls's distinction between social and natural primary goods. *A Theory of Justice*, supra note 18, at 62. Whereas he holds that only the social primary goods should be on the list, and not the natural (such as health and imagination), we say that the social basis of the natural primary goods should most emphatically be on the list.

60. Though in one form Aristotle had it too. See "Human Nature," supra note 12, at 110-20.

61. See *A Theory of Justice*, supra note 18, at 251-57; "Freedoms and Needs," supra note 18, at 38.

62. Cf. "Freedoms and Needs," supra note 18, at 38 ("The importance of political rights for the understanding of economic needs turns ultimately one seeing human beings as people with rights to exercise, not as parts of a 'stock' or 'population' that passively exists and must be looked after. What matters, finally, is how we see each other.").

63. This way of thinking derives from the ancient Stoic tradition, continued through Cicero and on into Grotius and Kant. See Martha C. Nussbaum, "Kant and Stoic Cosmopolitanism," 5 *J. Pol. Phil.* 1 (1997) [hereinafter "Kant and Stoic Cosmopolitanism"]; Martha C. Nussbaum, "The Incomplete Feminism of Musonius Rufus: Platonist, Stoic, and Roman," paper presented at the *Conference on Gender and Sexual Experience in Ancient Greece and Rome*, Finnish Academy in Rome (June 22-25, 1997) (on file with the Fordham Law Review).

64. "Religion and Women's Human Rights," supra note 57, at 121-26 (reviewing this situation). Typically, only small and unpopular religions get their laws thrown out. Thus, the Christian inheritance law—or one of them, since Christians in India are governed by a bewildering variety of different systems of Christian law—was declared unconstitutional on grounds of sex equality, but the attempt to set aside a part of the Hindu marriage act on these grounds was

reversed at the Supreme Court level. id. at 108.

65. On Indian discussions of religious pluralism and liberty, see Amartya Sen, "Human Rights and Asian Values," *New Republic*, July 14 & 21, 1997, at 33-40. For related discussion of Indian conceptions of pluralism, see Amartya Sen, "Tagore and His India," *New York Review of Books*, June 26, 1997, at 55-56. On the Greek and Roman origins of ideas of human rights, see Fred D. Miller, Jr., *Nature, Justice, and Rights in Aristotle's Politics* (1995), arguing that Aristotle's political theory contains the basic ingredients of a theory of rights; "Nature, Function, and Capability," supra note 11, arguing that Aristotle's political theory contains the view that the job of politics is to distribute to citizens the things that they need for a flourishing life; "Kant and Stoic Cosmopolitanism," supra note 64, arguing that Kant's view of basic human rights is in many ways indebted to the views of the Greek and Roman Stoics.

66. See Finnis, supra note 25; George, supra note 25. For a detailed discussion of differences between the Sen/Nussbaum view and those views in a range of areas of public policy, see "The Good as Discipline, The Good as Freedom," supra note 12.

67. For an eloquent example, see Jacques Maritain, "Truth and Human Fellowship," in *On the Use of Philosophy: Three Essays* 16, 24-29 (1961).

QUESTIONS FOR REFLECTION

1. What are the central human capabilities identified by Nussbaum? Do you think there are others that could be added to the list? Taken off the list?

2. Why does Nussbaum argue that capability and not functioning is the goal of public policy? Do you agree?

3. What, according to Nussbaum, are the "four important roles" that rights play in public policy discourse? How exactly do human rights relate to capabilities?

21. RICHARD RORTY

Richard Rorty (1931-) is professor of Philosophy at Stanford University, having taught previously at the University of Virginia. Rorty's numerous writings include the books *Philosophy and the Mirror of Nature* (1979), *Contingency, Irony, and Solidarity* (1989), and *Philosophy and Social Hope* (1999). Rorty has characterized his philosophy as "neo-pragmatism," an anti-metaphysical variety of philosophy influenced by classical American pragmatists such as John Dewey, but also by Continental thinkers such as Friedrich Nietzsche and Jacques Derrida. One of the primary themes of Rorty's philosophy is that the traditional philosophical pursuit of ultimate, objective, foundational knowledge is misguided and ineffective. In the following essay, Rorty denies that traditional moral theory, particularly of the kind developed by Kant, can lead to practical ethical and political action. On the issue of human rights, Rorty suggests that solidarity is a more pragmatic alternative which can be achieved by means of a "sentimental education" that uses detailed stories to produce feelings of sympathy for others.

Text—Human Rights, Rationality, and Sentimentality

In a report from Bosnia some months ago,[1] David Rieff said "To the Serbs, the Muslims are no longer human.... Muslim prisoners, lying on the ground in rows, awaiting interrogation, were driven over by a Serb guard in a small delivery van." This theme of dehumanization recurs when Rieff says

> A Muslim man in Bosansi Petrovac...[was] forced to bite off the penis of a fellow-Muslim.... If you say that a man is not human, but the man looks like you and the only way to identify this devil is to make him drop his trousers—Muslim men are cir-

> cumcised and Serb men are not—it is probably only a short step, psychologically, to cutting off his prick.... There has never been a campaign of ethnic cleansing from which sexual sadism has gone missing.

The moral to be drawn from Rieff's stories is that Serbian murderers and rapists do not think of themselves as violating human rights. For they are not doing these things to fellow human beings, but *Muslims*. They are not being inhuman, but rather are discriminating between the true humans and the pseudohumans. They are making the same sort of distinction as the Crusaders made between humans and infidel dogs, and the Black Muslims make between humans and blue-eyed devils. The founder of my university was able both to own slaves and to think it self-evident that all men were endowed by their creator with certain inalienable rights. He had convinced himself that the consciousness of Blacks, like that of animals, "participate[s] more of sensation than reflection."[2] Like the Serbs, Mr. Jefferson did not think of himself as violating *human* rights.

The Serbs take themselves to be acting in the interests of true humanity by purifying the world of pseudohumanity. In this respect, their self-image resembles that of moral philosophers who hope to cleanse the world of prejudice and superstition. This cleansing will permit us to rise above our animality by becoming, for the first time, wholly rational and thus wholly human. The Serbs, the moralists, Jefferson, and the Black Muslims all use the term "men" to mean "people like us." They think the line between humans and animals is not simply the line between featherless bipeds and all others. They think the line divides some featherless bipeds from others: There are animals walking about in humanoid form. We and those like us are paradigm cases of humanity but those too different from us in behavior or custom are, at best, borderline cases. As Clifford Geertz puts it, "Men's most importunate claims to humanity are cast in the accents of group pride."[3]

We in the safe, rich, democracies feel about the Serbian torturers and rapists as they feel about their Muslim victims: They are more like animals than like us. But we are not doing anything to help the Muslim women who are being gang raped or the Muslim men who are being castrated, any more than we did anything in the thirties when the Nazis were amusing themselves by torturing Jews. Here in the safe countries we find ourselves saying things like "That's how things have always been in the Balkans," suggesting that, unlike us, those people are used to being raped and castrated. The contempt we always feel for losers—Jews in the thirties, Muslims now—combines with our disgust at the winners' behavior to produce the semiconscious attitude: "a plague on both your houses." We think of the Serbs or the Nazis as animals, because ravenous beasts of prey are animals. We think of the Muslims or the Jews being herded into concentration camps as animals, because cattle are animals. Neither sort of animal is very much like us, and there seems no point in human beings getting involved in quarrels between animals.

The human-animal distinction, however, is only one of the three main ways in which we paradigmatic humans distinguish ourselves from borderline cases. A second is by invoking the distinction between adults and children. Ignorant and superstitious people, we say, are like children; they will attain true humanity only if raised up by proper education. If they seem incapable of absorbing such education, that shows they are not really the same kind of being as we educable people are. Blacks, the whites in the United States and in South Africa used to say, are like children. That is why it is appropriate to address Black males, of whatever age, as "boy." Women, men used to say, are permanently childlike; it is therefore appropriate to spend no money on their education, and to refuse them access to power.

When it comes to women, however, there are simpler ways of excluding them from true humanity: for example, using "man" as a synonym of "human being." As feminists have pointed out, such usages reinforce the average male's thankfulness that he was not born a woman, as well as his fear of the ultimate degradation: feminization. The extent of the latter fear is evidenced by the particular sort of sexual sadism Rieff describes. His point that such sadism is never absent from attempts to purify the species or cleanse the territory confirms Catharine MacKinnon's claim that, for most men, being a woman does not count as a way of being human. Being a nonmale is the third way of being nonhuman. There are several ways of being nonmale. One is to be born without a penis; another is to have one's penis cut or bitten off; a third is to have been penetrated by a penis. Many men who have been raped are convinced that their manhood, and thus their humanity, has been taken away. Like racists who discover they have Jewish or Black ancestry, they may commit suicide out of sheer shame, shame at no longer being the kind of featherless biped that counts as human.

Philosophers have tried to clear this mess up by spelling out what all and only the featherless bipeds have in common, thereby explaining what is essential to being human. Plato argued that there is a big difference between us and the animals, a difference worthy of respect and cultivation. He thought that human beings have a special added ingredient which puts them in a different ontological category than the brutes. Respect for this ingredient provides a reason for people to be nice to each other. Anti-Platonists like Nietzsche reply that attempts to get people to stop murdering, raping, and castrating each other are, in the long run, doomed to fail—for the real truth about human nature is that we are a uniquely nasty and dangerous kind of animal. When contemporary admirers of Plato claim that all featherless bipeds—even the stupid and childlike, even the women, even the sodomized—have the same inalienable rights, admirers of Nietzsche reply that the very idea of "inalienable human rights" is, like the idea of a special added ingredient, a laughably feeble attempt by the weaker members of the species to fend off the stronger.

As I see it, one important intellectual advance made in our century is the steady decline in interest in the quarrel between Plato and Nietzsche. There is a growing willingness to neglect the question "What is our nature?" and to substitute the question "What can we make of ourselves?" We are much less inclined than our ancestors were to take "theories of human nature" seriously, much less inclined to take ontology or history as a guide to life. We have come to see that the only lesson of either history or anthropology is our extraordinary malleability. We are coming to think of ourselves as the flexible, protean, self-shaping, animal rather than as the rational anima or the cruel animal.

One of the shapes we have recently assumed is that of a human rights culture. I borrow the term "human rights culture" from the Argentinean jurist and philosopher Eduardo Rabossi. In an article called "Human Rights Naturalized," Rabossi argues that philosophers should think of this culture as a new, welcome fact of the post-Holocaust world. They should stop trying to get behind or beneath this fact, stop trying to detect and defend its so-called "philosophical presuppositions." On Rabossi's view, philosophers like Alan Gewirth are wrong to argue that human rights cannot depend on historical facts. "My basic point," Rabossi says, is that "the world has changed, that the human rights phenomenon renders human rights foundationalism outmoded and irrelevant."[4]

Rabossi's claim that human rights foundationalism is *outmoded* seems to me both true and important; it will be my principal topic in this lecture. I shall be enlarging on, and defending, Rabossi's claim that the question whether human beings really have the rights enumerated in the Helsinki Declaration is not worth raising. In particular, I shall be defending the claim that nothing relevant to moral choice separates human beings from animals except historically contingent facts of the world, cultural facts.

This claim is sometimes called "cultural relativism" by those who indignantly reject it. One reason they reject it is that such relativism seems to them incompatible with the fact that our human rights culture, the culture with which we in this democracy identify ourselves, is morally superior to other cultures. I quite agree that ours is morally superior, but I do not think this superiority counts in favor of a universal human nature. It would only do so if we assumed that a moral claim is ill-founded if not backed up by knowledge of a distinctively human attribute. But it is not clear why "respect for human dignity"—our sense that the differences between Serb and Muslim, Christian and infidel, gay and straight, male and female should not matter—must presuppose the existence of any such attribute.

Traditionally, the name of the shared human attribute which supposedly "grounds" morality is "rationality." Cultural relativism is associated with irrationalism because it denies the existence of morally relevant transcultural facts. To agree with Rabossi one must, indeed, be irrationalist in that sense. But one need not be irrationalist in the sense of ceasing to make one's web of belief as coherent, and as perspicuously structured, as possible. Philosophers like myself, who think of rationality as simply the attempt at such coherence, agree with Rabossi that foundationalist projects are outmoded. We see our task as a matter of making our own culture—the human rights culture—more self-conscious and more powerful, rather than of demonstrating its superiority to other cultures by an appeal to something transcultural.

We think that the most philosophy can hope to do is summarize our culturally influenced intuitions about the right thing to do in various situations. The summary is effected by formulating a generalization from which these intuitions can be deduced, with the help of noncontroversial lemmas. That generalization is not supposed to ground our intuitions, but rather to summarize them. John Rawls's "Difference Principle" and the US Supreme Court's construction, in recent decades, of a constitutional "right to privacy" are examples of this kind of summary. We see the formulation of such summarizing generalizations as increasing the predictability, and thus the power and efficiency, of our institutions, thereby heightening the sense of shared moral identity which brings us together in a moral community.

Foundationalist philosophers, such as Plato, Aquinas, and Kant, have hoped to provide independent support for such summarizing generalizations. They would like to infer these generalizations from further premises, premises capable of being known to be true independently of the truth of the moral intuitions which have been summarized. Such premises are supposed to justify our intuitions, by providing premises from which the content of those intuitions can be deduced. I shall lump all such premises together under the label "claims to knowledge about the nature of human beings." In this broad sense, claims to know that our moral intuitions are recollections of the Form of the Good, or that we are the disobedient children of a loving God, or that human beings differ from other kinds of animals by having dignity rather than mere value, are all claims about human nature. So are such counterclaims as that human beings are merely vehicles for selfish genes, or merely eruptions of the will to power.

To claim such knowledge is to claim to know something which, though not itself a moral intuition, can *correct* moral intuitions. It is essential to this idea of moral knowledge that a whole community might come to know that most of their most salient intuitions about the right thing to do were wrong. But now suppose we ask: *Is* there this sort of knowledge? What kind of question is that? On the traditional view, it is a philosophical question, belonging to a branch of epistemology known as "metaethics." But on the pragmatist view which I favor, it is a question of efficiency, of how best to grab hold of history—how best to bring about the utopia sketched by the Enlightenment. If the activities of those who attempt to achieve this sort of knowledge seem of little use in actualizing this utopia, that is a reason to think there is no such knowledge. If it seems that most of the work of changing moral intuitions is being done by manipulating our feelings rather than increasing our knowledge, that will be a reason to think that there is no knowledge of the sort which philosophers like Plato, Aquinas, and Kant hoped to acquire.

This pragmatist argument against the Platonist has the same form as an argument for cutting off payment to the priests who are performing purportedly war-winning sacrifices—an argument which says that all the real work of winning the war seems to be getting done by the generals and admirals, not to mention the foot soldiers. The argument does not say: Since there seem to be no gods, there is probably no need to support the priests. It says instead: Since there is apparently no need to support the priests, there probably are no gods. We pragmatists argue from the fact that the emergence of the human rights culture seems to owe nothing to increased moral knowledge, and everything to hearing sad and sentimental stories, to the conclusion that there is probably no knowledge of the sort Plato envisaged. We go on to argue: Since no useful work seems to be done by insisting on a purportedly ahistorical human nature, there probably is no such nature, or at least nothing in that nature that is relevant to our moral choices....

The question "What is Man?" in the sense of "What is the deep ahistorical nature of human beings?" owed its popularity to the standard answer to that question: We are the *rational* animal, the one which can know as well as merely feel. The residual popularity of this answer accounts for the residual popularity of Kant's astonishing claim that sentimentality has nothing to do with morality, that there is something distinctively and transculturally human called "the sense of moral obligation" which has nothing to do with love, friendship, trust, or social solidarity. As long as we believe *that*, people like Rabossi are going to have a tough time convincing us that human rights foundationalism is an outmoded project.

To overcome this idea of a *sui generis* sense of moral obligation, it would help to stop answering the question "What makes us different from the other animals?" by saying "We can know, and they can merely feel." We should substitute "We can feel *for each other* to a much greater extent than they can." This substitution would let us disentangle Christ's suggestion that love matters more than knowledge from the neo-Platonic suggestion that knowledge of the truth will make us free. For as long as we think that there is an ahistorical power which makes for righteousness—a power called truth, or rationality—we shall not be able to put foundationalism behind us.

The best, and probably the only, argument for putting foundationalism behind us is the one I have already suggested: It would be more efficient to do so, because it would let us concentrate our energies on manipulating sentiments, on sentimental education. That sort of education sufficiently acquaints people of different kinds with one another so that they are less tempted to think of those different from themselves as only quasi-human. The goal of this manipulation of sentiment is to expand the reference of the terms "our kind of people" and "people like us."

All I can do to supplement this argument from increased efficiency is to offer a suggestion about how Plato managed to convince us that knowledge of universal truths mattered as much as he thought it did. Plato thought that the philosopher's task was to answer questions like "Why should I be moral? Why is it rational to be moral? Why is it in my interest to be moral? Why is it in the interest of human beings as such to be moral?" He thought this because he believed the best way to deal with people like Thrasymachus and Callicles was to demonstrate to them that they had an interest of which they were unaware, an interest in being rational, in acquiring self-knowledge. Plato thereby saddled us with a distinction between the true and the false self. That distinction was, by the time of Kant, transmuted into a distinction between categorical, rigid, moral obligation and flexible, empirically determinable, self-interest. Contemporary moral philosophy is still lumbered with this opposition between self-interest and morality, an opposition which makes it hard to realize that my pride in being a part of the human rights culture is no more external to my self than my desire for financial success.

It would have been better if Plato had decided, as Aristotle was to decide, that there was nothing much to be done with people like Thrasymachus and Callicles, and that the problem was how to avoid having children who would be like Thrasymachus and Callicles. By insisting that he could re-educate people who had matured without acquiring appropriate moral sentiments by invoking a higher power than sentiment, the power of reason, Plato got moral philosophy off on the wrong foot. He led moral philosophers to concentrate on the rather rare figure of the psychopath, the person who has no concern for any human being other than himself. Moral philosophy has systematically neglected the much more common case: the person whose treatment of a rather narrow range of featherless bipeds is morally impeccable, but who remains indifferent to the suffering of those outside this range, the ones he or she thinks of as pseudohumans.[5]

Plato set things up so that moral philosophers think they have failed unless they convince the rational egotist that he should not be an egotist—convince him by telling him about his true, unfortunately neglected, self. But the rational egotist is not the problem. The problem is the gallant and honorable Serb who sees Muslims as circumcised dogs. It is the brave soldier and good comrade who loves and is loved by his mates, but who thinks of women as dangerous, malevolent whores and bitches.

Plato thought that the way to get people to be nicer to each other was to point out what they all had in common—rationality. But it does little good to point out, to the people I have just described, that many Muslims and women are good at mathematics or engineering or jurisprudence. Resentful young Nazi toughs were quite aware that many Jews were clever and learned, but this only added to the pleasure they took in beating them up. Nor does it do much good to get such people to read Kant, and agree that one should not treat rational agents simply as means. For everything turns on who counts as a fellow human being, as a rational agent in the only relevant sense—the sense in which rational agency is synonymous with membership in *our* moral community.

For most white people, until very recently, most Black people did not so count. For most Christians, up until the seventeenth century or so, most heathen did not so count. For the Nazis, Jews did not so count. For most males in countries in which the average annual income is under four thousand dollars, most females still do not so count. Whenever tribal and national rivalries become important, members of rival tribes and nations will not so count. Kant's account of the respect due to rational agents tells you that you should extend the respect you feel for people like yourself to all featherless bipeds. This is an excellent suggestion, a good formula for secularizing the Christian doctrine of the brotherhood of man. But it has never been backed up by an argument based on neutral premises, and it never will be. Outside the circle of post-Enlightenment European culture, the circle of relatively safe and secure people who have been manipulating each others' sentiments for two hundred years, most people are simply unable to understand why membership in a biological species is supposed to suffice for membership in the moral community. This is not because they are insufficiently rational. It is, typically, because they live in a world in which it would be just too risky—indeed, would often be insanely dangerous—to let one's sense of moral community stretch beyond one's family, clan, or tribe.

To get whites to be nicer to Blacks, males to females, Serbs to Muslims, or straights to gays, to help our species link up into what Rabossi calls a "planetary community" dominated by a culture of human rights, it is of no use whatever to say, with Kant: Notice that what you have in common, your humanity, is more important than these trivial differences. For the people we are trying to convince will rejoin that they notice nothing of the sort. Such people are *morally* offended by the suggestion that they should treat someone who is not kin as if he were a brother, or a nigger as if he were white, or a queer as if he were normal, or an infidel as if she were a believer. They are offended by the suggestion that they treat people whom they do not think of as human as if they were human. When utilitarians tell them that all pleasures and pains felt by members of our biological species are equally relevant to moral deliberation, or when Kantians tell them that the ability to engage in such deliberation is sufficient for membership in the moral community, they are incredulous. They rejoin that these philosophers seem oblivious to blatantly obvious moral distinctions, distinctions any decent person will draw.

This rejoinder is not just a rhetorical device, nor is it in any way irrational. It is heartfelt. The identity of these people, the people whom we should convince to join our Eurocentric human rights culture, is bound up with their sense of who they are *not*. Most people—especially people relatively untouched by the European Enlightenment—simply do not think of themselves as, first and foremost, a human being. Instead, they think of themselves as being a certain *good* sort of human being—a sort defined by explicit opposition to a particularly bad sort. It is crucial for their sense of who they are that they are *not* an infidel, *not* a queer, *not* a woman, *not* an untouchable. Just insofar as they are impoverished, and as their lives are perpetually at risk, they have little else than pride in not being what they are not to sustain their self-respect. Starting with the days when the term "human being" was synonymous with "member of our tribe," we have always thought of human beings in terms of paradigm members of the species. We have contrasted *us*, the *real* humans, with rudimentary, or perverted, or deformed examples of humanity.

We Eurocentric intellectuals like to suggest that we, the paradigm humans, have overcome this primitive parochialism by using that paradigmatic human faculty, reason. So we say that failure to concur with us is due to "prejudice." Our use of these terms in this way may make us nod in agreement when Colin McGinn tells us, in the introduction to his recent book,[6] that learning to tell right from wrong is not as hard as learning French. The only obstacles to agreeing with his moral views, McGinn explains, are "prejudice, vested interest and laziness."

One can see what McGinn means: If, like many of us, you teach students who have been brought up in the shadow of the Holocaust, brought up believing that prejudice against racial or religious groups is a terrible thing, it is not very hard to convert them to standard liberal views about abortion, gay rights, and the like. You may even get them to stop eating animals. All you have to do is convince them that all the arguments on the other side appeal to "morally irrelevant" considerations. You do this by manipulating their sentiments in such a way that they imagine themselves in the shoes of the despised and oppressed. Such students are already so nice that they are eager to define their identity in nonexclusionary terms. The only people they have trouble being nice to are the ones they consider irrational—the religious fundamentalist, the smirking rapist, or the swaggering skinhead

Producing generations of nice, tolerant, well-off, secure, other-respecting students of this sort in all parts of the world is just what is needed—indeed *all* that is needed—to achieve an Enlightenment utopia. The more youngsters like this we can raise, the stronger and more global our human rights culture will become. But it is not a good idea to encourage these students to label "irrational" the intolerant people they have trouble tolerating. For that Platonic-Kantian epithet suggests that, with only a little more effort, the good and rational part of these other people's souls could have triumphed over the bad and irrational part. It suggests that we good people know something these bad people do not know, and that it is probably their own silly fault that they do not know it. All they have to do, after all, is to think a little harder, be a little more self-conscious, a little more rational.

But the bad people's beliefs are not more or less "irrational" than the belief that race, religion, gender, and sexual preference are all morally irrelevant—that these are all trumped by membership in the biological species. As used by moral philosophers like McGinn, the term "irrational behavior" means no more than "behavior of which we disapprove so strongly that our spade is turned when asked *why* we disapprove of it." It would be better to teach our students that these bad people are no less rational, no less clearheaded, no more prejudiced, than we good people who respect otherness. The bad people's problem is that they were not so lucky in the circumstances of their upbringing as we were. Instead of treating as irrational all those people out there who are trying to find and kill Salman Rushdie, we should treat them as deprived.

Foundationalists think of these people as deprived of truth, of moral knowledge. But it would be better—more specific, more suggestive of possible remedies—to think of them as deprived of two more concrete things: security and sympathy. By "security" I mean conditions of life sufficiently risk-free as to make one's difference from others inessential to one's self-respect, one's sense of worth. These conditions have been enjoyed by Americans and Europeans—the people who dreamed up the human rights culture—much more than they have been enjoyed by anyone else. By "sympathy" I mean the sort of reaction that the Athenians had more of after seeing Aeschylus' *The Persians* than before, the sort that white Americans had more of after reading *Uncle Tom's Cabin* than before, the sort that we have more of after watching TV programs about the genocide in Bosnia. Security and sympathy go together, for the same reasons that peace and economic productivity go together. The tougher things are, the more you have to be afraid of, the more dangerous your situation, the less you can afford the time or effort to think about what things might be like for people with whom you do not immediately identify. Sentimental education only works on people who can relax long enough to listen.

If Rabossi and I are right in thinking human rights foundationalism outmoded, then Hume is a better advisor than Kant about how we intellectuals can hasten the coming of the Enlightenment utopia for which both men yearned. Among contemporary philosophers, the best advisor seems to me to be

Annette Baier. Baier describes Hume as "the woman's moral philosopher" because Hume held that "corrected (sometimes rule-corrected) sympathy, not law-discerning reason, is the fundamental moral capacity."[7] Baier would like us to get rid of both the Platonic idea that we have a true self, and the Kantian idea that it is rational to be moral. In aid of this project, she suggests that we think of "trust" rather than "obligation" as the fundamental moral notion. This substitution would mean thinking of the spread of the human rights culture not as a matter of our becoming more aware of the requirements of the moral law, but rather as what Baier calls "a progress of sentiments."[8] This progress consists in an increasing ability to see the similarities between ourselves and people very unlike us as outweighing the differences. It is the result of what I have been calling "sentimental education." The relevant similarities are not a matter of sharing a deep true self which instantiates true humanity, but are such little, superficial, similarities as cherishing our parents and our children—similarities that do not interestingly distinguish us from many nonhuman animals....

If one follows Baier's advice one will not see it as the moral educator's task to answer the rational egotist's question "Why should I be moral?" but rather to answer the more frequently posed question "Why should I care about a stranger, a person who is no kin to me, a person whose habits I find disgusting?" The traditional answer to the latter question is "Because kinship and custom are morally irrelevant, irrelevant to the obligations imposed by the recognition of membership in the same species." This has never been very convincing, since it begs the question at issue: whether mere membership is, in fact, a sufficient surrogate for closer kinship. Furthermore, that answer leaves one wide open to Nietzsche's discomfiting rejoinder: *That* universalistic notion, Nietzsche will sneer, would only have crossed the mind of a slave—or, perhaps, the mind of an intellectual, a priest whose self-esteem and livelihood both depend on getting the rest of us to accept a sacred, unarguable, unchallengeable paradox.

A better sort of answer is the sort of long, sad, sentimental story which begins "Because this is what it is like to be in her situation—to be far from home, among strangers," or "Because she might become your daughter-in-law," or "Because her mother would grieve for her." Such stories, repeated and varied over the centuries, have induced us, the rich, safe, powerful, people, to tolerate, and even to cherish, powerless people—people whose appearance or habits or beliefs at first seemed an insult to our own moral identity, our sense of the limits of permissible human variation.

To people who, like Plato and Kant, believe in a philosophically ascertainable truth about what it is to be a human being, the good work remains incomplete as long as we have not answered the question "Yes, but am I under a *moral obligation* to her?" To people like Hume and Baier, it is a mark of intellectual immaturity to raise that question. But we shall go on asking that question as long as we agree with Plato that it is our ability to know that makes us human.

Plato wrote quite a long time ago, in a time when we intellectuals had to pretend to be successors to the priests, had to pretend to know something rather esoteric. Hume did his best to josh us out of that pretense. Baier, who seems to me both the most original and the most useful of contemporary moral philosophers, is still trying to josh us out of it. I think Baier may eventually succeed, for she has the history of the last two hundred years of moral progress on her side. These two centuries are most easily understood not as a period of deepening understanding of the nature of rationality or of morality, but rather as one in which there occurred an astonishingly rapid progress of sentiments, in which it has become much easier for us to be moved to action by sad and sentimental stories.

This progress has brought us to a moment in human history in which it is plausible for Rabossi to say that the human rights phenomenon is a "fact of the world." This phenomenon may be just a blip. But it may mark the beginning of a time in which gang rape brings forth as strong a response when it happens to women as when it happens to men, or when it happens to foreigners as when it happens to people like us.

Notes

1. "Letter from Bosnia," *New Yorker*, November 23, 1992, 82-95.

2. "Their griefs are transient. Those numberless afflictions, which render it doubtful whether heaven has given life to us in mercy or in wrath, are less felt, and sooner forgotten with them. In general, their existence appears to participate more of sensation than reflection. To this must be ascribed their disposition to sleep when abstracted from their diversions, and unemployed in labor. An animal whose body is at rest, and who does not reflect must be disposed to sleep of course." Thomas Jefferson, "Notes on Virginia," *Writings*, Lipscomb and Bergh, eds., (Washington, DC: 1905), 1: 194.

3. Geertz, "Thick Description" in his *The Interpretation of Culture* (New York: Basic Books, 1973), 22.

4. Rabossi also says that he does not wish to question "the idea of a rational foundation of morality." I am not sure why he does not. Rabossi may perhaps mean that in the past—for example, at the time of Kant—this idea still made a kind of sense, but it makes sense no longer. That, at any rate, is my own view. Kant wrote in a period when the only alternative to religion seemed to be something like science. In such a period, inventing a pseudoscience called "the system of transcendental philosophy"—setting the stage for the show-stopping climax in which one pulls moral obligation out of a transcendental hat—might plausibly seem the only way of saving morality from the hedonists on one side and the priests on the other.

5. Nietzsche was right to remind us that "these same men who, amongst themselves, are so strictly constrained by custom, worship, ritual gratitude and by mutual surveillance and jealousy, who are so resourceful in consideration, tenderness, loyalty, pride and friendship, when once they step outside their circle become little better than uncaged beasts of prey." *The Genealogy of Morals*, trans. Golffing (Garden City, NY: Doubleday, 1956), 174.

6. Colin McGinn, *Moral Literacy: or, How to Do the Right Thing* (London: Duckworth, 1992), 16.

7. Baier, "Hume, the Women's Moral Theorist?," in Eva Kittay and Diana Meyers, eds., *Women and Moral Theory* (Totowa, NJ: Rowman and Littlefield, 1987), 40.

8. Baier's book on Hume is entitled *A Progress of Sentiments: Reflections on Hume's Treatise* (Cambridge, MA: Harvard University Press, 1991). Baier's view of the inadequacy of most attempts by contemporary moral philosophers to break with Kant comes out most clearly when she characterizes Allan Gibbard (in his book *Wise Choices, Apt Feelings*) as focusing "on the feelings that a patriarchal religion has bequeathed to us," and says that "Hume would judge Gibbard to be, as a moral philosopher, basically a divine disguised as a fellow expressivist" (312).

Questions for Reflection

1. Why does Rorty claim that knowledge about human nature is neither necessary nor useful for the existence of human rights? Do you agree or disagree?

2. According to Rorty, sentimental storytelling is more effective at furthering a human rights culture than is the search for moral knowledge. Can you identify any examples from your own experience that support Rorty's claim?

3. What do you think are the positive features of Rorty's idea of a sentimental education? What do you think are its negative features?

22. JACQUES DERRIDA

Jacques Derrida (1930-) is Directeur d'Études at the École des Hautes Études en Sciences Sociales in Paris, and Professor of French and Comparative Literature at the University of California-Irvine. Born in Algeria and educated at the École Normale Supérieure in Paris, Derrida made his reputation beginning in the late 1960s by developing his critical philosophy of deconstruction. Inspired by the works of Nietzsche and Martin Heidegger, deconstruction aims to expose the binary oppositions which pervade traditional metaphysics—such as "true" and false," "essence" and "appearance," and "good" and "evil"—and reveal how language is a system of differences and multiple interpretations. Throughout his many works, which include *Of Grammatology* (1967), *Margins of Philosophy* (1972) and *The Other Heading* (1991), Derrida has insisted that deconstruction also seeks to deepen our understanding of ethical and political responsibility. In the following selection, Derrida addresses how current forms of technology, economic globalization, and expanded militarism present difficult challenges for democracy and justice around the globe. In particular, the apparent "triumph" of capitalism following the end of the Cold War reveals the dangers of an international system that continues to expand without critical resistance or humane alternatives.

Text—Wears and Tears (Tableau of an Ageless World)

The time is out of joint. The world is going badly. It is worn but its wear no longer counts. Old age or youth—one no longer counts in that way. The world has more than one age. We lack the measure of the measure. We no longer realize the wear, we no longer take account of it as of a single age in the progress of history. Neither maturation, nor crisis, nor even agony. Something else. What is happening is happening to age itself, it strikes a blow at the teleological order of history. What is coming, in which the untimely appears, is happening to time but it does not happen in time. Contretemps. *The time is out of joint.* Theatrical speech, Hamlet's speech before the theater of the world, of history, and of politics. The age is off its hinges. Everything, beginning with time, seems out of kilter, unjust, dis-adjusted. The world is going very badly, it wears as it grows....

This wearing in expansion, in growth itself, which is to say in the becoming worldwide [*mondialization*] of the world, is not the unfolding of a normal, normative, or normed process. It is not a phase of development, one more crisis, a growth crisis because growth is what is bad ("it wears as it grows"); it is no longer an end-of-ideologies, a last crisis-of-Marxism, or a new crisis-of-capitalism.

The world is going badly, the picture is bleak, one could say almost black. Let us form an hypothesis. Suppose that, for lack of time (the spectacle or the tableau is always "for lack of time"), we propose simply to paint, like the Painter in *Timon of Athens*. A black picture on a blackboard. Taxonomy or freeze-frame image. Title: "The time is out of joint" or "What is going so badly today in the world." We would leave this banal title in its neutral form so as to avoid speaking of crisis, a very insufficient concept, and so as to avoid deciding between the bad as suffering and the bad as wrong or as crime....

But what is one to think today of the imperturbable thoughtlessness that consists in singing the triumph of capitalism or of economic and political liberalism, "the universalization of Western liberal democracy as the endpoint of human government," the "end of the problem of social classes"? What cynicism of good conscience, what manic disavowal could cause someone to write, if not believe, that "everything that stood in the way of the reciprocal recognition of human dignity, always and everywhere, has been refuted and buried by history"?

Provisionally and for the sake of convenience, let us rely on the outdated opposition between civil war and international war. Under the heading of civil war, is it still necessary to point out that liberal democracy of the parliamentary form has never been so much in the minority and so isolated in the world? That it has never been in such a state of dysfunction in what we call the Western democracies? Electoral representativity or parliamentary life is not only distorted, as was always the case, by a great number of socio-economic mechanisms, but it is exercised with more and more difficulty in a public space profoundly upset by techno-tele-media apparatuses and by new rhythms of information and communication, by the devices and the speed of forces represented by the latter, but also and consequently by the new modes of appropriation they put to work.... This transformation does not affect only facts but the concept of such "facts." The very concept of the event. The relation between deliberation and decision, the very functioning of government has changed, not only in its technical conditions, its time, its space, and its speed, but, without anyone having really idealized it, in its concept. Let us recall the technical, scientific, and economic transformations that, in Europe, after the First World War, already upset the topological structure of the *res publica*, of public space, and of public opinion. They affected not only this topological *structure*, they also began to make problematic the very presumption of the topographical, the presumption that there was a *place*, and thus an identifiable and stabilizable body for public speech, the public thing, or the public cause, throwing liberal, parliamentary, and capitalist democracy into crisis, as is often said, and opening thereby the way for three forms of totalitarianism which then allied, fought, or combined with each other in countless ways. Now, these transformations are being amplified beyond all measure today.... Under the heading of international or civil-international war, is it still necessary to point out the economic wars, national wars, wars among minorities, the unleashing of racisms and xenophobias, ethnic conflicts, conflicts of culture and religion that are tearing apart so-called democratic Europe and the world today? Entire regiments of ghosts have returned, armies from every age, camouflaged by the archaic symptoms of the paramilitary and of the postmodern excess of arms (information technology, panoptical surveillance via satellite, nuclear threat, and so forth). Let us accelerate things. Beyond these two types of war (civil and international) whose dividing line cannot even be distinguished any longer, let us blacken still more the picture of this wearing down beyond wear. Let us name with a single trait that which could risk making the euphoria of liberal-democrat capitalism resemble the blindest and most delirious of hallucinations, or even an increasingly glaring hypocrisy in its formal or juridicist rhetoric of human rights. It will not be a matter of merely accumulating, as Fukuyama might say, "empirical evidence," it will not suffice to point one's finger at the mass of undeniable facts that this picture could describe or denounce. The question posed too briefly would not even be that of the analysis with which one would then have to proceed in all these directions, but of the *double interpretation*, the concurrent readings that the picture seems to call for and to oblige us to associate. If one were permitted to name these plagues of the "new world order" in a ten-word telegram, one might perhaps choose the following ten words.

1. Unemployment, that more or less well-calculated deregulation of a new market, new technologies, new worldwide competitiveness, would no doubt, like labor or production, deserve another name today. All the more so in that tele-work inscribes there a new set of givens that perturbs both the methods of traditional calculation and the conceptual opposition between work and non-work, activity, employment, and their contrary. This regular deregulation is at once mastered, calculated, "socialized" (that is, most often disavowed), and irreducible to prediction—like suffering itself, a suffering that suffers still more, and more obscurely, for having lost its habitual models and language once it no longer recognizes itself in the old word unemployment and in the scene that word named for so long. The function of social inactivity, of non-work or of underemployment is entering into a new era. It calls for another politics. And another concept. The "new unemployment" no more resembles unemployment, in the very forms of its experience and its calculation, than what in France is called the "new poverty" resembles poverty

2. The massive exclusion of homeless citizens from any participation in the democratic life of States, the expulsion or depor-

tation of so many exiles, stateless persons, and immigrants from a so-called national territory already herald a new experience of frontiers and identity—whether national or civil.

3. The ruthless economic war among the countries of the European Community themselves, between them and the Eastern European countries, between Europe and the United States, and between Europe, the United States, and Japan. This war controls everything, beginning with the other wars, because it controls the practical interpretation and an inconsistent and unequal application of international law. There have been too many examples in the last decade or more.

4. The inability to master the contradictions in the concept, norms, and reality of the free market (the barriers of a protectionism and the interventionist bidding wars of capitalist States seeking to protect their nationals, or even Westerners or Europeans in general, from cheap labor, which often has no comparable social protection). How is one to save one's own interests in the global market while claiming to protect one's "social advantages" and so forth?

5. The aggravation of the foreign debt and other connected mechanisms are starving or driving to despair a large portion of humanity. They tend thus to exclude it simultaneously from the very market that this logic nevertheless seeks to extend. This type of contradiction works through many geopolitical fluctuations even when they appear to be dictated by the discourse of democratization or human rights.

6. The arms industry and trade (whether it be "conventional" arms or at the cutting edge of tele-technological sophistication) are inscribed in the normal regulation of the scientific research, economy, and socialization of labor in Western democracies. Short of an unimaginable revolution, they cannot be suspended or even cut back without running major risks, beginning with the worsening of the said unemployment. As for arms trafficking, to the (limited) degree that it can still be distinguished from "normal" commerce, it remains the largest in the world, larger than the drug traffic, from which it is not always dissociated.

7. The spread ("dissemination") of nuclear weapons, main-

tained by the very countries that say they want to protect themselves from it, is no longer even controllable, as was the case for a long time, by statist structures. It exceeds not only statist control but every declared market.

8. Inter-ethnic wars (have there ever been another kind?) are proliferating, driven by an *archaic* phantasm and concept, by a *primitive conceptual phantasm* of community, the nation-State, sovereignty, borders, native soil and blood. Archaism is not a bad thing in itself, it doubtless keeps some irreducible resource. But how can one deny that this conceptual phantasm is, so to speak, made more outdated than ever, in the very *ontopology* it supposes, by tele-technic dis-location? (By *ontopology* we mean an axiomatics linking indissociably the ontological value of present-being [*on*] to its *situation*, to the stable and presentable determination of a locality, the *topos* of territory, native soil, city, body in general). For having spread in an unheard-of fashion, which is more and more differentiated and more and more accelerated (it is acceleration itself, beyond the norms of speed that have until now informed human culture), the process of dislocation is no less arch-originary, that is, just as "archaic" as the archaism that it has always dislodged. This process is, moreover, the positive condition of the stabilization that it constantly relaunches. All stability in a place being but a stabilization or a sedentarization, it will have to have been necessary that the local differ*a*nce, the spacing of a displacement gives the movement its start. And gives place and gives rise [*donne lieu*]. All national rootedness, for example, is rooted first of all in the memory or the anxiety of a displaced—or displaceable—population. It is not only time that is "out of joint," but space, space in time, spacing.

9. How can one ignore the growing and undelimitable, that is, worldwide power of those super-efficient and properly capitalist phantom-States that are the mafia and the drug cartels on every continent, including in the former so-called socialist States of Eastern Europe? These phantom-States have infiltrated and banalized themselves everywhere, to the point that they can no longer be strictly identified. Nor even sometimes clearly dissociated from the processes of democratization.... All these infiltra-

tions are going through a "critical" phase, as one says, which is no doubt what allows us to talk about them or to begin their analysis. These phantom-States invade not only the socio-economic fabric, the general circulation of capital, but also statist or inter-statist institutions.

10. For above all, above all, one would have to analyze the present state of international law and of its institutions. Despite a fortunate perfectibility, despite an undeniable progress, these international institutions suffer from at least two limits. The first and most radical of the two stems from the fact that their norms, their charter, the definition of their mission depend on a certain historical culture. They cannot be dissociated from certain European philosophical concepts, and notably from a concept of State or national sovereignty whose genealogical closure is more and more evident, not only in a theoretico-juridical or speculative fashion, but concretely, practically, and practically quotidian. Another limit is strictly linked to the first: This supposedly universal international law remains, in its application, largely dominated by particular nation-States. Almost always their techno-economic and military power prepares and applies, in other words, *carries* the decision. As one says in English, it *makes the decision*. Countless examples, recent or not so recent, would amply demonstrate this, whether it is a question of deliberations and resolutions of the United Nations or of the putting into practice or the "enforcement" of these decisions: the incoherence, discontinuity, inequality of States before the law, the hegemony of certain States over military power in the service of international law, this is what, year after year, day after day, we are forced to acknowledge.

These facts do not suffice to disqualify international institutions. Justice demands, on the contrary, that one pay tribute to certain of those who are working within them in the direction of the perfectibility and emancipation of institutions that must never be renounced. However insufficient, confused, or equivocal such signs may still be, we should salute what is heralded today in the reflection on the right of interference or intervention in the name of what is obscurely and sometimes hypocritically called the *humanitarian*, thereby limiting the sovereignty of the State in certain conditions. Let us salute such signs even as one remains vigilantly on guard against the manipulations or appropriations to which these novelties can be subjected.

Let us return now to the immediate vicinity of the subject of our conference. My subtitle, "the New International," refers to a profound transformation, projected over a long term, of international law, of its concepts, and its field of intervention. Just as the concept of human rights has slowly been determined over the course of centuries through many socio-political upheavals (whether it be a matter of the right to work or economic rights, of the rights of women and children, and so forth), likewise international law should extend and diversify its field to include, if at least it is to be consistent with the idea of democracy and of human rights it proclaims, the *worldwide* economic and social field, beyond the sovereignty of States and of the phantom-States we mentioned a moment ago. Despite appearances, what we are saying here is not simply anti-statist: in given and limited conditions, the super-State, which might be an international institution, may always be able to limit the appropriations and the violence of certain private socio-economic forces. But without necessarily subscribing to the whole Marxist discourse (which, moreover, is complex, evolving, heterogeneous) on the State and its appropriation by a dominant class, on the distinction between State power and State apparatus, on the end of the political, on "the end of politics" or on the withering away of the State, and, on the other hand, without suspecting the juridical idea in itself, one may still find inspiration in the Marxist "spirit" to criticize the presumed autonomy of the juridical and to denounce endlessly the *de facto* take-over of international authorities by powerful Nation-States, by concentrations of techno-scientific capital, symbolic capital, and financial capital, of State capital and private capital. A "new international" is being sought through these crises of international law; it already denounces the limits of a discourse on human rights that will remain inadequate, sometimes hypocritical, and in any case formalistic and inconsistent with itself as long as the law of the market, the "foreign debt," the inequality of techno-scientific, military, and economic development maintain an effective inequality as monstrous as that which prevails today, to a greater extent than ever in the history of humanity. For it must be cried out, at a time when some have the audacity to neo-evangelize in the name of the ideal of a liberal democracy that has finally realized itself as the ideal of human history: never have violence, inequality, exclusion, famine, and thus economic oppression affected as many human beings in the history of the earth and of humanity. Instead of singing the advent of the ideal of liberal democracy and of the capitalist market in the euphoria of the end of history, instead of celebrating the "end of ideologies" and the end of the great emancipatory discourses, let us never neglect this obvious macroscopic fact, made up of innumerable singular sites of suffering: no degree of progress allows one to ignore that never before, in absolute figures, never have so many men, women, and children been subjugated, starved, or exterminated on the earth....

...If my subtitle specified the *State of the debt*, it was also in view of problematizing the concept of the State or the state, with or without capital initial, and in *three ways*.

First of all, we have said it often enough, one cannot *establish* the *state* of a debt, for example as regards Marx and Marxism, as one would a balance sheet or an exhaustive record, in a static and statistical manner. These accounts cannot be tabulated. One makes oneself accountable by an engagement that selects, interprets, and orients. In a practical and performative manner, and by a decision that begins by getting caught up, like a responsibility, in the snares of an injunction that is already multiple, heterogeneous, contradictory, divided....

Secondly, another debt, all the questions concerning democracy, the universal discourse on human rights, the future of humanity, and so forth, will give rise only to formal, right-thinking, and hypocritical alibis as long as the "foreign Debt" has not been treated head-on, in as responsible, consistent, and systematic manner as possible. With this name or with this emblematic figure, we are pointing to the *interest* and first of all the interest of capital in general, an interest that, in the order of the world today, namely the worldwide market, holds a mass of humanity under its yoke and in a new form of slavery. This happens and is authorized always in the statist or inter-statist forms of an organization. Now, these problems of the foreign Debt—and everything that is metonymized by this concept—will not be treated without at least the spirit of the Marxist critique, the critique of the market, of the multiple logics of capital, and of that which links the State and international law to this market.

Thirdly, lastly, and consequently, a profound and critical re-elaboration of the concepts of the State, of the nation-State, of national sovereignty, and of citizenship must correspond to a phase of decisive mutation. The latter would be impossible without vigilant and systematic reference to a Marxist problematic, if not to the Marxist conclusions regarding the State, the power of the State, and the State apparatus, the illusions of its legal autonomy as concerns socio-economic forces, but also regarding new forms of a withering or rather a reinscription, a re-delimitation of the State in a space that it no longer dominates and that moreover it never dominated by itself.

Questions for Reflection

1. Derrida identifies ten problems of the so-called "new world order." Do you agree that these are problems? Which problems on the list do you find most disturbing?
2. According to Derrida, what dangers does the globalization of capitalism present to human rights? How does he propose that we respond to those dangers?
3. In what ways is Derrida's position regarding human rights similar to that of Marx? In what ways are they different?

FURTHER READINGS FOR SECTION 3

Brandt, Richard B. "The Concept of a Moral Right and Its Function." *Journal of Philosophy* 80 (1983): 29-45.

Cornell, Drucilla, Michael Rosenfield, and David G. Carlson, eds. *Deconstruction and the Possibility of Justice*. New York: Routledge, 1993.

Dworkin, Ronald. *Taking Rights Seriously*. Cambridge, MA: Harvard University Press, 1977.

Forst, Rainer. "The Basic Right to Justification: Toward a Constructivist Conception of Human Rights." *Constellations* 6 (1999): 35-60.

Gaete, Rolando. "Postmodernism and Human Rights: Some Insidious Questions." *Law and Critique* 2 (1991): 140-70.

Gewirth, Alan. "The Basis and Content of Human Rights." In J. Roland Pennock and John W. Chapman, eds. *Human Rights: NOMOS XXIII*. New York: New York University Press, 1981.

——. *Human Rights: Essays on Justification and Applications*. Chicago: University of Chicago Press, 1982.

Hayden, Patrick. "Sentimentality and Human Rights: Critical Remarks on Rorty." *Philosophy in the Contemporary World* 6 (1999): 59-66.

Hughes, Cheryl L. "Reconstructing the Subject of Human Rights." *Philosophy and Social Criticism* 25 (1999): 47-60.

Levinas, Emmanuel. *Outside the Subject*, trans. Michael B. Smith. Stanford: Stanford University Press, 1994.

Li, Xiaorong. "Postmodernism and Universal Human Rights: Why Theory and Reality Don't Mix." *Free Inquiry*, Fall 1998: 28-31.

Lomasky, Loren. *Persons, Rights, and the Moral Community*. Oxford: Oxford University Press, 1987.

Lyons, David. "The Correlativity of Rights and Duties." *Nous* 4 (1970): 45-55.

Martin, Rex. "Human Rights and Civil Rights." *Philosophical Studies* 37 (1980): 391-403.

Mineau, Andre. "Human Rights and Nietzsche." *History of European Ideas* 11 (1989): 877-82

Nickel, James W. *Making Sense of Human Rights*. Berkeley and Los Angeles: University of California Press, 1987.

Nino, Carlos Santiago. *The Ethics of Human Rights*. Oxford: Clarendon Press, 1991.

Rawls, John. *A Theory of Justice*. Revised Edition. Cambridge, MA: Harvard University Press, 1971, 1999.

Raz, Joseph. "On the Nature of Rights." *Mind* XCIII (1984): 194-214.

Sen, Amartya. "Rights and Agency." *Philosophy and Public Affairs* 11 (1981): 3-39.

Shue, Henry. *Basic Rights*. Second Edition. Princeton, NJ: Princeton University Press, 1996.

Sumner, L.W. *The Moral Foundation of Rights*. Oxford: Clarendon Press, 1987.

Section 4:

NON-WESTERN PERSPECTIVES

23. CONFUCIUS

Confucius (551-479 BC) is one of the most influential philosophers in the Eastern tradition. Confucius not only operated his own school of learning, he also received several appointments in government, including that of minister of justice for the State of Lu. Confucius developed an enduring reputation as a sage with a deep love of wisdom and virtue, a reputation which attracted a number of disciples in much the same fashion as did Socrates in ancient Athens. Confucius' teachings are recorded in the *Analects*, compiled by his disciples and their students. It is generally recognized that "benevolence" is the core idea of Confucian philosophy. For Confucius benevolence finds its expression through the performance of *li*, which refers to rituals of etiquette or propriety between human beings, including behavior of mutual respect and civility that government officials should cultivate within themselves. Even though Confucius taught that government should be benevolent, his ethical teachings place great stress on the hierarchical relationship of individuals in society and on the demands of obedience. In a virtuous state, Confucius emphasized that all people have a duty to contribute to its unity and harmony. Thus, Confucius cannot be considered an advocate of what we now think of as the human rights claims of individuals against governing authorities. In the following excerpts from the *Analects*, several of Confucius' observations on ethics are presented, providing a glimpse into his still-influential views on obligation, political power, and social order.

Text—The Analects

Reprinted from The Chinese Classics, Volume I, *edited and translated by James Legge. Oxford: Clarendon Press, 1893.*

1:2. The philosopher Yu said, "They are few who, being filial and fraternal, are fond of offending against their superior. There have been none who, not liking to offend against their superiors, have been fond of stirring up confusion.

"The superior man bends his attention to what is radical.

That being established, all practical courses naturally grow up. Filial piety and fraternal submission!—are they not the root of all benevolent actions?"

1:4. The philosopher Tsang said, "I daily examine myself on three points:—whether, in transacting business for others, I may have been not faithful;—whether, in intercourse with friends, I may have been not sincere;—whether I may have not mastered and practiced the instructions of my teacher."

1:6. The master said, "A youth, when at home, should be filial, and, abroad, respectful to his elders. He should be earnest and truthful. He should overflow in love to all, and cultivate the friendship of the good. When he has time and opportunity, after the performance of these things, he should employ them in polite studies."

1:7. Tsze-hsia said, "If a man withdraws his mind from the love of beauty, and applies it as sincerely to the love of the virtuous; if, in serving his parents, he can exert his utmost strength; if, in serving his prince, he can devote his life; if, in his intercourse with his friends, his words are sincere:—although men say that he has not learned, I will certainly say that he has."

2:4. The Master said, "At fifteen, I had my mind bent on learning.

"At thirty, I stood firm.

"At forty, I had no doubts.

"At fifty, I knew the decrees of Heaven.

"At sixty, my ear was an obedient organ *for the reception of truth.*

"At seventy, I could follow what my heart desired, without transgressing what was right."

4:15. The Master said, "Shan, my doctrine is that of an all-pervading unity." The disciple Tsang replied, "Yes."

The Master went out, and the other disciples asked, saying, "What do his words mean?" Tsang said, "The doctrine of our master is to be true to the principles of our nature and the benevolent exercise of them to others,—this and nothing more."

4:16. The Master said, "The mind of the superior man is conversant with righteousness; the mind of the mean man is conversant with gain."

4:17. The Master said, "When we see men of worth, we should think of equaling them; when we see men of a contrary character, we should turn inwards and examine ourselves."

4:18. The Master said, "In serving his parents, a son may remonstrate with them, but gently; when he sees that they do not incline to follow his advice, he shows an increased degree of reverence, but does not abandon his purpose; and should they punish him, he does not allow himself to murmur."

4:24. The Master said, "The superior man wishes to be slow in his speech and earnest in his conduct."

4:25. The Master said, "Virtue is not left to stand alone. He who practices it will have neighbors."

5:11. Tsze-kung said, "What I do not wish men to do to me, I also wish not to do to men." The Master said, "Tsze, you have not attained that."

6:20. Fan Ch'ih asked what constituted wisdom. The Master said, "To give one's self earnestly to the duties due to men, and, while respecting spiritual beings, to keep aloof from them, may be called wisdom." He asked about perfect virtue. The Master said, "The man of virtue makes the difficulty to be overcome his first business, and success only a subsequent consideration;—this may be called perfect virtue."

6:25. The Master said, "The superior man, extensively studying all learning, and keeping himself under the restraint of the rules of propriety may thus likewise not overstep what is right."

6:27. The Master said, "Perfect is the virtue which is according to the Constant Mean! Rare for a long time has been its practice among the people."

6:28. Tsze-kung said, "Suppose the case of a man extensively conferring benefits on the people, and able to assist all, what would you say of him? Might he be called perfectly virtuous?" The Master said, "Why speak only of virtue in connection with him? Must he not have the qualities of a sage? Even Yao and Shun were still solicitous about this.

"Now the man of perfect virtue, wishing to be established himself, seeks also to establish others; wishing to be enlarged himself, he seeks also to enlarge others.

"To be able to judge of others by what is nigh in ourselves;—this may be called the art of virtue."

7:27. The Master said, "There may be those who act without knowing why. I do not do so. Hearing much and selecting what is good and following it; seeing much and keeping it in memory—this is the Second style of knowledge."

8:2. The Master said, "Respectfulness, without the rules of propriety, becomes laborious bustle; carefulness, without the rules of propriety, becomes timidity; boldness, without the rules of propriety, becomes insubordination; straightforwardness, without the rules of propriety, becomes rudeness.

"When those who are in high stations perform well all their duties to their relations, the people are aroused to virtue. When old friends are not neglected by them, the people are preserved from meanness."

8:13. The Master said, "With sincere faith he unites the love of learning; holding firm to death, he is perfecting the excellence of his course.

"Such a one will not enter a tottering state, nor dwell in a disorganized one. When right principles of government prevail in the kingdom, he will show himself; when they are prostrated, he will keep concealed.

"When a country is well governed, poverty and a mean condition are things to be ashamed of. When a country is ill governed, riches and honor are things to be ashamed of."

9:24. The Master said, "Hold faithfulness and sincerity as first principles. Have no friends not equal to yourself. When you have faults, do not fear to abandon them."

12:1. Yen Yüan asked about perfect virtue. The Master said, "To subdue one's self and return to propriety, is perfect virtue. If a man can for one day subdue himself and return to propriety, all under heaven will ascribe perfect virtue to him. Is the practice of perfect virtue from a man himself, or is it from others?"

Yen Yüan said, "I beg to ask the steps of that process." The Master replied, "Look not at what is contrary to propriety; listen not to what is contrary to propriety; speak not what is contrary to propriety; make no movement which is contrary to propriety." Yen Yüan then said, "Though I am deficient in intelligence and vigor, I will make it my business to practice this lesson."

12:2. Chung-kung asked about perfect virtue. The Master said, "It is, when you go abroad, to behave to everyone as if you were receiving a great guest; to employ the people as if you were assisting at a great sacrifice; not to do to others as you would not wish done to yourself; to have no murmuring against you in the country, and none in the family." Chung-kung said, "Though I am deficient in intelligence and vigor, I will make it my business to practice this lesson."

12:15. The Master said, "By extensively studying all learning, and keeping himself under the restraint of the rules of propriety, *one* may thus likewise not err from what is right."

12:17. Chi K'ang asked Confucius about government. Confucius replied, "To govern means to rectify. If you lead on the people with correctness, who will dare not to be correct?"

13:6. The Master said, "When a prince's personal conduct is correct, his government is effective without the issuing of orders. If his personal conduct is not correct, he may issue orders, but they will not be followed."

13:11. The Master said, "'If good men were to govern a country in succession for a hundred years, they would be able to transform the violently bad, and dispense with capital punishments.' True indeed is this saying!"

13:13. The Master said, "If a minister make his own conduct correct, what difficulty will he have in assisting in government? If he cannot rectify himself, what has he to do with rectifying others?"

13:16. The duke of Sheh asked about government.

The Master said, "Good government obtains when those who are near are made happy, and those who are far off are attracted."

14:36. Someone said, "What do you say concerning the principle that injury should be recompensed with kindness?"

The Master said, "With what then will you recompense kindness?"

"Recompense injury with justice, and recompense kindness

with kindness."

15:17. The Master said, "The superior man in everything considers righteousness to be essential. He performs it according to the rules of propriety. He brings it forth in humility. He completes it with sincerity. This is indeed a superior man."

15:23. Tsze-kung asked, saying, "Is there one word which may serve as a rule of practice for all one's life?" The Master said, "Is not RECIPROCITY such a word?" What you do not want done to yourself, do not do to others."

17:6. Tsze-chang asked Confucius about perfect virtue. Confucius said, "To be able to practice five things everywhere under heaven constitutes perfect virtue." He begged to ask what they were, and was told, "Gravity, generosity of soul, sincerity, earnestness, and kindness. If you are grave, you will not be treated with disrespect. If you are generous, you will win all. If you are sincere, people will repose trust in you. If you are earnest, you will accomplish much. If you are kind, this will enable you to employ the services of others."

Questions for Reflection

1. According to Confucius, how is it possible to form good government? Do you agree or not that piety and submission toward the state is necessary for good government?
2. What rules of propriety do you think are important for leading a virtuous life?
3. Which do you think it is better to emphasize: the rights of individuals, or the duties of individuals? Do they both produce the same kinds of results? What relationships do you see between rights and duties?

24. MO TZU

Mo Tzu (470-391 BC) is another important Chinese philosopher. Initially an advocate of Confucius' teachings, Mo Tzu later rejected Confucianism because of its overemphasis of filial obligation and state hierarchy. Mo Tzu then founded his own school of philosophy known as Moism, which stresses the need to administer justice impartially. In the selection included here, Mo Tzu argues that people's suffering is due to a single primary cause, namely, that people love others only partially. In Mo Tzu's view, conflict and injustice exist because humans tend to love only some people, while hating or neglecting others. The way to overcome injustice, Mo Tzu contends, is to act upon a motivation of universal love. All of us, including the rulers of states, should regard others' suffering as our own and therefore seek to end the suffering of all by practicing universal mutual love.

Text—Universal Love

Reprinted from The Chinese Classics, Volume II, *edited and translated by James Legge. Oxford: Clarendon Press, 1895.*

CHAPTER I

It is the business of the sages to effect the good government of the world. They must know, therefore, whence disorder and confusion arise, for without this knowledge their object cannot be effected. We may compare them to a physician who undertakes to cure men's diseases:—he must ascertain whence a disease has arisen, and then he can assail it with effect, while, without such knowledge, his endeavors will be in vain. Why should we except the case of those who have to regulate disorder from this rule? They must know whence it has arisen, and then they can regulate it.

It is the business of the sages to effect the good government of the world. They must examine therefore into the cause of disorder; and when they do so they will find that it arises from the want of mutual love. When a minister and a son are not filial to their sovereign and their father, this is what is called disorder. A son loves himself, and does not love his father;—he therefore wrongs his father, and seeks his own advantage: a younger brother loves himself and does not love his elder brother;—he therefore wrongs his elder brother, and seeks his own advantage: a minister loves himself, and does not love his sovereign;—he therefore wrongs his sovereign, and seeks his own advantage:—all these are cases of what is called disorder. Though it be the father who is not kind to his son, or the elder brother who is not kind to his younger brother, or the sovereign who is not gracious to his minister:—the case comes equally under the general name of disorder. The father loves himself, and does not love his son:—he therefore wrongs his son, and seeks his own advantage: the elder brother loves himself, and does not love his younger brother;—he therefore wrongs his younger brother, and seeks his own advantage: the sovereign loves himself, and does not love his minister;—he therefore wrongs his minister, and seeks his own advantage. How do these things come to pass? They all arise from the want of mutual love. Take the case of any thief or robber:—it is just the same with him. The thief loves his own house, and does not love his neighbour's house:—he therefore steals from his neighbour's house to benefit his own: the robber loves his own person, and does not love his neighbour;—he therefore does violence to his neighbour to benefit himself. How is this? It all arises from the want of mutual love. Come to the case of great officers throwing each other's Families into confusion, and of princes attacking one another's States:—it is just the same with them. The great officer loves his own Family, and does not love his neighbour's;—he therefore throws the neighbour's Family into disorder to benefit his own: the prince loves his own State, and does not love his neighbour's:—he therefore attacks his neighbour's State to benefit his own. All disorder in the kingdom has the same explanation. When we examine into the cause of it, it is found to be the want of mutual love.

Suppose that universal, mutual love prevailed throughout the kingdom;—if men loved others as they love themselves, disliking to exhibit what was unfilial.... And moreover would there be those who were unkind? Looking on their sons, younger brothers, and ministers as themselves and disliking to exhibit what was unkind...the want of filial duty would disappear. And would there be thieves and robbers? When every man regarded his neighbour's house as his own, who would be found to steal? When everyone regarded his neighbour's person as his own, who would be found to rob? Thieves and robbers would disappear. And would there be great officers throwing one another's Families into confusion, and princes attacking one another's States? When officers regarded the families of others as their own, what one would make confusion? When princes regarded other States as their own, what one would begin an attack? Great officers throwing one another's Families into confusion, and princes attacking one other's States, would disappear.

If, indeed, universal, mutual love prevailed throughout the kingdom; one State not attacking another, and one Family not throwing another into confusion; thieves and robbers nowhere existing; rulers and ministers, fathers and sons, all being filial and kind:—in such condition the nation would be well governed. On this account, how many sages, whose business it is to effect the good government of the kingdom, do but prohibit hatred and advise to love? On this account it is affirmed that universal mutual love throughout the country will lead to its happy order, and that mutual hatred leads to confusion. This was what our master, philosopher Mo, meant, when he said, "We must above all inculcate the love of others."

CHAPTER III

Our Master, the philosopher Mo, said, "The business of benevolent men requires that they should strive to stimulate and promote what is advantageous to the kingdom, and to take away what is injurious to it."

Speaking, now, of the present time, what are to be accounted the most injurious things to the kingdom? They are such as the attacking of small States by great ones; the inroads on small Families by great ones; the plunder of the weak by the strong; the oppression of the few by the many; the scheming of the crafty against the simple; the insolence of the noble to the mean. To the same class belong the ungraciousness of rulers, and the disloyalty of ministers; the unkindness of fathers, and the want of filial duty on the part of sons. Yea, there is to be added to these the conduct of the mean men, who employ their edged weapons and poisoned stuff, water and fire, to rob and injure one another.

Pushing on the inquiry now, let us ask whence all these injurious things arise. Is it from loving others and advantaging others? It must be answered "No"; and it must likewise be said, "They arise clearly from hating others and doing violence to others." If it be further asked whether those who hate and do violence to others hold the principle of loving all, or that of making distinctions, it must be replied, "They make distinctions." So then, it is the principle of making distinctions between man and man, which gives rise to all that is most injurious in the kingdom. On this account we conclude that the principle is wrong.

Our Master said, "He who condemns others must have means whereby to change them." To condemn men, and have no means of changing them, is like saving them from fire by plunging them in water. A man's language in such a case must be improper. On this account our Master said, "There is the principle of loving all, to take the place of that which makes distinctions." If, now, we ask, "And how is it that universal love can change the consequences of that other principle which makes distinctions?" the answer is, "If princes were as much for the States of others as for their own, what one among them would raise the forces of his State to attack that of another?—he is for that other as much as for himself. If they were for the capitals of others as much as for their own, what one would raise the forces of his capital to attack that of another?—he is for that as much as for his own. If chiefs regarded the families of others as their own, what one would lead the power of his Family to throw that of another into confusion?—he is for that other as much as for himself. If, now, States did not attack, nor holders of capitals smite, one another, and if

Families were guilty of no mutual aggressions, would this be injurious to the kingdom, or its benefit? It must be replied, "This would be advantageous to the kingdom." Pushing on the inquiry, now, let us ask whence all these benefits arise. Is it from hating others and doing violence to others? It must be answered, "No"; and it must likewise be said, "They arise clearly from loving others and doing good to others." If it be further asked whether those who love others and do good to others hold the principle of making distinctions between man and man, or that of loving all, it must be replied, "They love all." So then it is this principle of universal mutual love which really gives rise to all that is most beneficial to the nation. On this account we conclude that that principle is right.

Our Master said, a little while ago, "The business of benevolent men requires that they should strive to stimulate and promote what is advantageous to the kingdom, and to take away what is injurious to it." We have now traced the subject up, and found that it is the principle of universal love which produces all that is most beneficial to the kingdom, and the principle of making distinctions which produces all that is injurious to it. On this account what our Master said, "The principle of making distinctions between man and man is wrong, and the principle of universal love is right," turns out to be correct as the sides of a square.

If, now, we just desire to promote the benefit of the kingdom, and select for that purpose the principle of universal love, then the acute ears and piercing eyes of people will hear and see for one another; and the strong limbs of people will move and be ruled for one another; and men of principle will instruct one another. It will come about that the old, who have neither wife nor children, will get supporters who will enable them to complete their years; and the young and weak, who have no parents, will yet find helpers that shall bring them up. On the contrary, if this principle of universal love is held not to be correct, what benefits will arise from such a view? What can be the reason that the scholars of the kingdom, whenever they hear of this principle of universal love, go on to condemn it? Plain as the case is, their words in condemnation of this principle do not stop;—they say

"It may be good, but how can it be carried into practice?"

Our Master said, "Supposing that it could not be practiced, it seems hard to go on likewise to condemn it. But how can it be good, and yet incapable of being put into practice?"

Let us bring forward two instances to test the matter—Let anyone suppose the case of two individuals, the one of whom shall hold the principle of making distinctions, and the other shall hold the principle of universal love. The former of these will say, "How can I be for the person of my friend as much as for my own person? How can I be for the parents of my friend as much as for my own parents?" Reasoning in this way, he may see his friend hungry, but he will not feed him; cold, but he will not clothe him; sick, but he will not nurse him; dead, but he will not bury him. Such will be the language of the individual holding the principle of distinction, and such will be his conduct. He will say, "I have heard that he who wishes to play a lofty part among men, will be for the person of his friend as much as for his own person, and for the parents of his friend as much as for his own parents. It is only thus that he can attain his distinction?" Reasoning in this way, when he sees his friend hungry, he will feed him; cold, he will clothe him; sick, he will nurse him; dead, he will bury him. Such will be the language of him who holds the principle of universal love, and such will be his conduct.

The words of the one of these individuals are a condemnation of those of the other, and their conduct is directly contrary. Suppose now that their words are perfectly sincere, and that their conduct will be carried out,—that their words and actions will correspond like the parts of a token, every word being carried into effect; and let us proceed to put the following questions on the case:—Here is a plain in the open country, and an officer, with coat of mail, gorget, and helmet, is about to take part in a battle to be fought in it, where the issue, whether for life or death, cannot be foreknown; or here is an officer about to be dispatched on a distant commission from Pa to Yueh, or from Ch'i to Ching, where the issue of the journey, going and coming, is quite uncertain—on either of these suppositions, to whom will the officer entrust the charge of his house, the support of his parents, and the care of his wife and children?—to one who holds the principle of universal love? or to one who holds that which makes distinctions? I apprehend there is no one under heaven, man or woman, however stupid, though he may condemn the principle of universal love, but would at such a time make one who holds it the subject of his trust. This is in words to condemn the principle, and when there is occasion to choose between it and the opposite, to approve it;—words and conduct are here in contradiction. I do not know how it is that throughout the kingdom scholars condemn the principle of universal love, whenever they hear it.

Plain as the case is, their words in condemnation of it do not cease, but they say, "This principle may suffice perhaps to guide in the choice of an officer, but it will not guide in the choice of a sovereign."

Let us test this by taking two illustrations:—Let anyone suppose the case of two sovereigns, the one of whom shall hold the principle of mutual love, and the other shall hold the principle which makes distinctions. In this case, the latter of them will say, "How can I be as much for the persons of all my people as for my own? This is much opposed to human feelings. The life of man upon the earth is but a very brief space; it may be compared to the rapid movement of a team of horses whirling past a small chink." Reasoning in this way, he may see his people hungry, but he will not feed them; cold, but he will not clothe them; sick, but he will not nurse them; dead, but he will not bury them. Such will be the language of the sovereign who holds the principle of distinctions, and such will be his conduct. Different will be the language and conduct of the other who holds the principle of universal love. He will say, "I have heard that he who would show himself a virtuous and intelligent sovereign, ought to make his people the first consideration, and think of himself only after them." Reasoning in this way, when he sees any of the people hungry, he will feed them; cold he will clothe them; sick, he will nurse them; dead, he will bury them. Such will be the language of the sovereign who holds the principle of universal love, and such his conduct. If we compare the two sovereigns, the words of the one are condemnatory of those of the other, and their actions are opposite. Let us suppose that their words are equally sincere, and that their actions will make them good—that their words and actions will correspond like the parts of a token, every word being carried into effect; and let us proceed to put the following questions on the case:—Here is a year when a pestilence walks abroad among the people; many of them suffer from cold and famine; multitudes die in the ditches and water-channels. If at such a time they might make an election between the two sovereigns whom we have supposed, which would they prefer? I apprehend there is no one under heaven, however stupid, though he may condemn the principle of universal love, but would at such a time prefer to be under the sovereign who holds it. This is in words to condemn the principle, and, when there is occasion to choose between it and the opposite, to approve it;—words and conduct are here in contradiction....

How is that the scholars throughout the kingdom condemn this universal love, whenever they hear of it? Plain as the case is, the words of those who condemn the principle of universal love do not cease. They say, "It is not advantageous to the entire devotion to parents which is required:—it is injurious to filial piety." Our Master said, "Let us bring this objection to the test:—A filial son, having the happiness of his parents at heart, considers how it is to be secured. Now, does he, so considering, wish men to love and benefit his parents? or does he wish them to hate and injure his parents?" On this view of the question, it must be evident that he wishes men to love and benefit his parents. And what must he himself first do in order to gain this object? If I first address myself to love and benefit men's parents, will they for that return love and benefit to my parents? or if I first address myself to hate men's parents, will they for that return love and benefit to my parents? It is clear that I must first address myself to love and benefit men's parents, and they will return to me love and benefit to my parents. The conclusion is that a filial son has no alternative.—He must address himself in the first place to love and do good to the parents of others. If it be supposed that this is an accidental course, to be followed on emergency by a filial son, and not sufficient to be regarded as a general rule, let us bring it to the test to what we find in the Books of the ancient kings.—It is said in the Ta Ya,

Every word finds its answer;
Every action its recompense
He threw me a peach;
I returned him a plum.

These words show that he who loves others will be loved, and that he who hates others will be hated. How is it that the scholars throughout the kingdom condemn the principle of universal love, when they hear it?....

...And now, as to universal mutual love, it is an advantageous thing and easily practiced—beyond all calculation. The only reason why it is not practiced is, in my opinion, because superiors do not take pleasure in it. If superiors were to take pleasure in it, stimulating men to it by rewards and praise, and awing them from opposition to it by punishments and fines, they would, in my opinion, move to it—the practice of universal mutual love, and the interchange of mutual benefits—as fire rises upwards, and as water flows downwards:—nothing would be able to check them. This universal love was the way of the sage kings; it is the principle to secure peace for kings, dukes, and great men; it is the means to secure plenty of food and clothes for the myriads of the people. The best course for the superior man is to well understand the principle of universal love, and to exert himself to practice it. It requires the sovereign to be gracious, and the minister to be loyal; the father to be kind and the son to be filial; the elder brother to be friendly, and the younger to be obedient. Therefore the superior man,—with whom the chief desire is to see gracious sovereigns and loyal ministers; kind fathers and filial sons; friendly elder brothers and obedient younger ones—ought to insist on the indispensableness of the practice of universal love. It was the way of the sage kings; it would be the most advantageous thing for the myriads of the people.

Questions for Reflection

1. Mo Tzu contends that it is selfishness and partiality that leads to conflict and oppression. Do you think that partiality—for ourselves, our friends and families, and our own countries—is a natural tendency? Do you think it is harmful or beneficial?

2. Mo Tzu advocates universal mutual love as the way to eliminate conflict and disorder in society. Is it possible to practice universal love? Is universal mutual love an inherent feature of universal human rights? Why or why not?

3. How does Mo Tzu's argument about universal mutual love compare to Cicero's argument about natural law? How does it compare to Hobbes' argument about natural law?

25. THE BUDDHA

"Buddha" is a Sanskrit word that means "Enlightened One" and is the title conferred on Siddhartha Gautama (563 BC-483 BC). Born to a royal family in what is now modern Nepal, Siddhartha lived a sheltered and extravagant life as a prince. At the age of twenty-nine, he ventured outside the royal palace and discovered the suffering of the poor, the ill, and the aged all around him. The next day Siddhartha left his family and kingdom to lead an ascetic life and determine a way to relieve the suffering of humans. He spent the next six years studying with various sages and following different ascetic practices, yet remaining unsatisfied with their teachings. One evening he sat alone under a Bodhi tree and resolved to meditate until he discovered how to overcome suffering. After purifying his mind, Siddhartha attained enlightenment and henceforth was called the Buddha. For the remainder of his life the Buddha taught others in an effort to help them reach enlightenment, and from his teachings Buddhism spread throughout Asia and much of the world. The core of the Buddha's teachings is called the "Middle Way," which prescribes the search for balance and the avoidance of extremes. This teaching is contained in the following selection on the "Four Noble Truths": the omnipresence of suffering; its cause, desire; the elimination of suffering by the elimination of desire; and the "Eightfold Path." The release or freedom from suffering can be attained by following the Eightfold Path, comprising Right view, Right aspirations, Right speech, Right conduct, Right livelihood, Right effort, Right mindfulness, and Right contemplation.

Text—Foundation of the Kingdom of Righteousness

Reprinted from The Sacred Books of the East, *Vol. XI. Translated by T. W. Rhys Davids. Oxford: Clarendon, 1881.*

Reverence to the Blessed One, the Holy One, the Fully-Enlightened One.

1. Thus have I heard. The Blessed One was once staying at

Benares, at the hermitage called Migadaya. And there the Blessed One addressed the company of the five Bhikkhus, and said:

2. "There are two extremes, O Bhikkhus, which the man who has given up the world ought not to follow—the habitual practice, on the one hand, of those things whose attraction depends upon the passions, and especially of sensuality—a low and pagan way (of seeking satisfaction) unworthy, unprofitable, and fit only for the worldly-minded—and the habitual practice, on the other hand, of asceticism (or self-mortification), which is painful, unworthy, and unprofitable.

3. "There is a middle path, O Bhikkhus, avoiding these two extremes, discovered by the Tathagata—a path which opens the eyes, and bestows understanding, which leads to peace of mind, to the higher wisdom, to full enlightenment, to Nirva*n*a!

4. "What is that middle path, O Bhikkhus, avoiding these two extremes, discovered by the Tathagata—that path which opens the eyes, and bestows understanding, which leads to peace of mind, to the higher wisdom, to full enlightenment, to Nirva*n*a? Verily! it is this noble eightfold path; that is to say:

"Right views;
Right aspirations;
Right speech;
Right conduct;
Right livelihood ;
Right effort;
Right mindfulness; and
Right contemplation.

"This, O Bhikkhus, is that middle path, avoiding these two extremes, discovered by the Tathagata—that path which opens the eyes, and bestows understanding, which leads to peace of mind, to the higher wisdom, to full enlightenment, to Nirva*n*a!

5. "Now this, O Bhikkhus, is the noble truth concerning suffering.

"Birth is attended with pain, decay is painful, disease is painful, death is painful. Union with the unpleasant is painful, painful is separation from the pleasant; and any craving that is unsatisfied, that too is painful. In brief, the five aggregates which spring from attachment (the conditions of individuality and their cause) are painful.

"This then, O Bhikkhus, is the noble truth concerning suffering.

6. "Now this, O Bhikkhus, is the noble truth concerning the origin of suffering.

"Verily, it is that thirst (or craving), causing the renewal of existence, accompanied by sensual delight, seeking satisfaction now here, now there—that is to say, the craving for the gratification of the passions, or the craving for (a future) life, or the craving for success (in this present life).

"This then, O Bhikkhus, is the noble truth concerning the origin of suffering.

7. "Now this, O Bhikkhus, is the noble truth concerning the destruction of suffering.

"Verily, it is the destruction, in which no passion remains, of this very thirst; the laying aside of, the getting rid of, the being free from, the harbouring no longer of this thirst.

"This then, O Bhikkhus, is the noble truth concerning the destruction of suffering.

8. "Now this, O Bhikkhus, is the noble truth concerning the way which leads to the destruction of sorrow. Verily! it is this noble eightfold path; that is to say:

"Right views;
Right aspirations;
Right speech;
Right conduct;
Right livelihood;
Right effort;
Right mindfulness; and
Right contemplation.

"This then, O Bhikkhus, is the noble truth concerning the destruction of sorrow.

9. "That this was the noble truth concerning sorrow, was not, O Bhikkhus, among the doctrines handed down, but there arose within me the eye (to perceive it), there arose the knowledge (of its nature), there arose the understanding (of its cause), there arose

the wisdom (to guide in the path of tranquillity), there arose the light (to dispel darkness from it).

Questions for Reflection

1. According to the Buddha, what is the cause of suffering? Can you identify any cravings that are a source of suffering?
2. What is the relationship between the elimination of suffering and the Eightfold Path? What do you think each of the categories of the Eightfold path means in terms of specific ways of living?
3. How might practicing the categories of the Eightfold Path contribute to universal love and compassion for all living things?

26. DALAI LAMA

Tenzin Gyatso (1935-), the Fourteenth Dalai Lama, was born into a poor peasant family in Takster village, eastern Tibet. "Dalai Lama" is a Tibetan phrase meaning "Ocean of wisdom and compassion," and is the title bestowed upon the head of the Yellow Hat monks, the dominant sect in Tibetan Buddhism. Since the thirteenth century, a succession of Dalai Lamas have been the spiritual and temporal rulers of Tibet. Each Dalai Lama is a reincarnation of the previous one, and successors are discovered through the use of signs, portents, and tests. As a small child, Tenzin Gyatso was recognized as the fourteenth incarnation of the Dalai Lama, and from the age of six began a rigorous training as a Buddhist monk. His education included the study of logic, Buddhist philosophy and metaphysics, ethics, as well as science. At the age of 16, he assumed political power of Tibet and for the next nine years attempted to negotiate the withdrawal of the communist Chinese army, which had invaded Tibet in 1950. In 1959, the Chinese crushed an attempted rebellion by the Tibetans and the Dalai Lama was forced to flee across the Himalayas to neighboring India. Since that time he has been the leader of the Tibetan government-in-exile, working tirelessly for the cause of a free Tibet. The Dalai Lama is recognized internationally as an advocate of human rights, non-violence, compassion, and personal responsibility, and he received the 1989 Nobel Peace Prize for his work. In the following selection, the Dalai Lama provides a clear statement of his ethical and spiritual principles as they relate to the need for universal human rights.

Text—Human Rights and Universal Responsibility

Speech presented to The United Nations World Conference on Human Rights, Vienna, Austria, 15 June, 1993. Reprinted by permission of the Office of Tibet and His Holiness the Dalai Lama.

Our world is becoming smaller and ever more interdependent with the rapid growth in population and increasing contact between people and governments. In this light, it is important to reassess the rights and responsibilities of individuals, peoples and nations in relation to each other and to the planet as a whole. This World Conference of organizations and governments concerned about the rights and freedoms of people throughout the world reflects the appreciation of our interdependence.

No matter what country or continent we come from we are all basically the same human beings. We have the common human needs and concerns. We all seek happiness and try to avoid suffering regardless of our race, religion, sex or political status. Human beings, indeed all sentient beings, have the right to pursue happiness and live in peace and in freedom. As free human beings we can use our unique intelligence to try to understand ourselves and our world. But if we are prevented from using our creative potential, we are deprived of one of the basic characteristics of a human being. It is very often the most gifted, dedicated and creative members of our society who become victims of human rights abuses. Thus the political, social, cultural and economic developments of a society are obstructed by the violations of human rights. Therefore, the protection of these rights and freedoms are of immense importance both for the individuals affected and for the development of the society as a whole.

It is my belief that the lack of understanding of the true cause of happiness is the principal reason why people inflict suffering on others. Some people think that causing pain to others may lead to their own happiness or that their own happiness is of such importance that the pain of others is of no significance. But this is clearly shortsighted. No one truly benefits from causing harm to another being. Whatever immediate advantage is gained at the expense of someone else is short-lived. In the long run causing others misery and infringing upon their peace and happiness creates anxiety, fear and suspicion for oneself.

The key to creating a better and more peaceful world is the development of love and compassion for others. This naturally means we must develop concern for our brothers and sisters who are less fortunate than we are. In this respect, the non-governmental organizations have a key role to play. You not only create awareness for the need to respect the rights of all human beings, but also give the victims of human rights violations hope for a better future.

When I traveled to Europe for the first time in 1973, I talked about the increasing interdependence of the world and the need to develop a sense of universal responsibility. We need to think in global terms because the effects of one nation's actions are felt far beyond its borders. The acceptance of universally binding standards of Human Rights as laid down in the Universal Declaration of Human Rights and in the International Covenants of Human Rights is essential in today's shrinking world. Respect for fundamental human rights should not remain an ideal to be achieved but a requisite foundation for every human society.

When we demand the rights and freedoms we so cherish we should also be aware of our responsibilities. If we accept that others have an equal right to peace and happiness as ourselves do we not have a responsibility to help those in need? Respect for fundamental human rights is as important to the people of Africa and Asia as it is to those in Europe or the Americas. All human beings, whatever their cultural or historical background, suffer when they are intimidated, imprisoned or tortured. The question of human rights is so fundamentally important that there should be no difference of views on this. We must therefore insist on a global consensus not only on the need to respect human rights world wide but more importantly on the definition of these rights.

Recently some Asian governments have contended that the standards of human rights laid down in the Universal Declaration of Human Rights are those advocated by the West and cannot be applied to Asia and others parts of the Third World because of differences in culture and differences in social and economic development. I do not share this view and I am convinced that the majority of Asian people do not support this view either, for it is the inherent nature of all human beings to yearn for freedom, equality and dignity, and they have an equal right to achieve that. I do not see any contradiction between the need for economic development and the need for respect of human rights. The rich diversity of cultures and religions should help to strengthen the fundamental human rights in all communities. Because underlying this diversity are fundamental principles that bind us all as members of the same human family. Diversity and traditions can never justify the violations of human rights. Thus discrimination of persons from a different race, of women, and of weaker sections of society may be traditional in some regions, but if they are inconsistent with universally recognized human rights, these forms of behavior must change. The universal principles of equality of all human beings must take precedence.

It is mainly the authoritarian and totalitarian regimes who are opposed to the universality of human rights. It would be absolutely wrong to concede to this view. On the contrary, such regimes must be made to respect and conform to the universally accepted principles in the larger and long term interests of their own peoples. The dramatic changes in the past few years clearly indicate that the triumph of human rights is inevitable.

There is a growing awareness of peoples' responsibilities to each other and to the planet we share. This is encouraging even though so much suffering continues to be inflicted based on chauvinism, race, religion, ideology and history. A new hope is emerging for the downtrodden, and people everywhere are displaying a willingness to champion and defend the rights and freedoms of their fellow human beings.

Brute force, no matter how strongly applied, can never subdue the basic human desire for freedom and dignity. It is not enough, as communist systems have assumed, merely to provide people with food, shelter and clothing. The deeper human nature needs to breathe the precious air of liberty. However, some governments still consider the fundamental human rights of its citizens an internal matter of the state. They do not accept that the fate of a people in any country is the legitimate concern of the entire human family and that claims to sovereignty are not a license to mistreat one's citizens. It is not only our right as members of the global human family to protest when our brothers and sisters are being treated brutally, but it is also our duty to do whatever we can to help them.

Artificial barriers that have divided nations and peoples have fallen in recent times. With the dismantling of Berlin wall the East-West division which has polarized the whole world for decades has now come to an end. We are experiencing a time filled with hope and expectations. Yet there still remains a major gulf at the heart of the human family. By this I am referring to the North-South divide. If we are serious in our commitment to the fundamental principles of equality, principles which, I believe, lie at the heart of the concept of human rights, today's economic disparity can no longer be ignored. It is not enough to merely state that all human beings must enjoy equal dignity. This must be translated into action. We have a responsibility to find ways to achieve a more equitable distribution of world's resources.

We are witnessing a tremendous popular movement for the advancement of human rights and democratic freedom in the world. This movement must become an even more powerful moral force, so that even the most obstructive governments and armies are incapable of suppressing it. This conference is an occasion for all of us to reaffirm our commitment to this goal. It is natural and just for nations, peoples and individuals to demand respect for their rights and freedoms and to struggle to end repression, racism, economic exploitation, military occupation, and various forms of colonialism and alien domination. Governments should actively support such demands instead of only paying lip service to them.

As we approach the end of the Twentieth Century, we find that the world is becoming one community. We are being drawn together by the grave problems of over population, dwindling natural resources, and an environmental crisis that threaten the very foundation of our existence on this planet. Human rights, environmental protection and great social and economic equality, are all interrelated. I believe that to meet the challenges of our times, human beings will have to develop a greater sense of universal responsibility. Each of us must learn to work not just for one self, one's own family or one's nation, but for the benefit of all humankind. Universal responsibility is the is the best foundation for world peace.

This need for co-operation can only strengthen humankind,

because it helps us to recognize that the most secure foundation for a new world order is not simply broader political and economic alliances, but each individual's genuine practice of love and compassion. These qualities are the ultimate source of human happiness, and our need for them lies at the very core of our being. The practice of compassion is not idealistic, but the most effective way to pursue the best interests of others as well as our own. The more we become interdependent the more it is in our own interest to ensure the well-being of others.

I believe that one of the principal factors that hinder us from fully appreciating our interdependence is our undue emphasis on material development. We have become so engrossed in its pursuit that, unknowingly, we have neglected the most basic qualities of compassion, caring and cooperation. When we do not know someone or do not feel connected to an individual or group, we tend to overlook their needs. Yet, the development of human society requires that people help each other.

I, for one, strongly believe that individuals can make a difference in society. Every individual has a responsibility to help more our global family in the right direction and we must each assume that responsibility. As a Buddhist monk, I try to develop compassion within myself, not simply as a religious practice, but on a human level as well. To encourage myself in this altruistic attitude, I sometimes find it helpful to imagine myself standing as a single individual on one side, facing a huge gathering of all other human beings on the other side. Then I ask myself, 'Whose interests are more important?' To me it is quite clear that however important I may feel I am, I am just one individual while others are infinite in number and importance.

Thank you.

Questions for Reflection

1. According to the Dalai Lama, suffering and human rights abuses are caused by peoples' misunderstanding of the cause of happiness. In what ways do people misunderstand the cause of happiness? What is the relationship between happiness and the cessation of suffering?

2. How does the Dalai Lama respond to the debate about universality and cultural relativism? Do you agree with him? Why or why not?

3. What important differences and similarities can you identity between the ethical attitudes expressed by the Buddha and the Dalai Lama and those of the Western scholars presented in the previous sections?

27. KWASI WIREDU

Born in Ghana, Kwasi Wiredu (1931-) is Professor of Philosophy at the University of South Florida. He was Professor and Head of the Department of Philosophy at the University of Ghana for a number of years. The author of *Philosophy and an African Culture* (1980) and of *Cultural Universals and Particulars: An African Perspective* (1996), Wiredu is a leading figure in the study of African philosophical traditions. In the following essay, Wiredu examines the cultural traditions of the Akan peoples of West Africa in order to determine whether those traditions are compatible with international human rights standards. Through an explanation of several aspects of Akan value systems and institutional practices, Wiredu contends that the Akan have notions of human dignity and justice quite similar to those expressed by contemporary human rights standards. Moreover, our conceptions and formulations of human rights may be enriched by the moral values—such as those of communal cooperation and social responsibility—found in traditional African societies.

Text—An Akan Perspective on Human Rights

A right is a claim that people are entitled to make on others or on society at large by virtue of their status. Human rights are claims that people are entitled to make simply by virtue of their status as human beings. The question naturally arises, what is it about a human being that makes him or her entitled to make the latter kind of claim? I intend to explore the answer to this question, which is found in Akan thought, by looking principally at the Akan conception of a person.

The word *Akan* refers both to a group of intimately related languages found in West Africa and to the people who speak them. This ethnic group lives predominantly in Ghana and in parts of adjoining Cote d'Ivoire. In Ghana they inhabit most of the southern and middle belts and account for about half the national population of 14 million. Best known among the Akan subgroup are the Ashantis. Closely cognate are the Denkyiras, Akims, Akuapims, Fantes, Kwahus, Wassas, Brongs, and Nzimas, among others.[1]

All these groups share the same culture not only in basics but also in many details. Although the cultural affinities of the various Akan subgroups with the other ethnic groups of Ghana are not on the same scale as among themselves, any divergences affect only details. Indeed, viewed against the distant cultures of the East and West, Akan culture can be seen to have such fundamental commonalities with other African cultures as to be subsumable under "African culture" as a general cultural type.

The Akan Conception of a Person

The Akan conception of a person has both descriptive and normative aspects that are directly relevant not only to the idea that there are human rights but also to the question of what those rights are. In this conception a person is the result of the union of three elements, not necessarily sharply disparate ontologically though each is different from the other. There is the life principle (*okra*), the blood principle (mogya), and what might be called the personality principle (*sunsum*). The first, the *okra*, is held to come directly from God. It is supposed to be an actual speck of God that he gives out of himself as a gift of life along with a specific destiny. The second, the *mogya* (literally, blood) is held to come from the mother and is the basis of lineage, or more extensively, clan identity. The third, the *sunsum*, is supposed to come from the father, but not directly. In the making of a baby, the father contributes *ntoro* (semen), which combines, according to the Akans, with the blood of the mother to constitute, in due course, the frame of the human being to come. The inherited characteristics of the new arrival are, of course, taken to be attributable to both parents. But the father's input is believed to give rise to a certain immanent characteristic of the individual, called the *sunsum*, which is the kind of personal presence that he has, the unique impression that he communicates to others. This is one meaning of the word *sunsum*. In this sense, *sunsum* is not an entity; it is, rather, a manner of being. But it is assumed that there must be something in the person that is the cause of the characteristic in question. It is in this sense that *sunsum* names a constituent of the human person.

By virtue of possessing an *okra*, a divine element, every person has an intrinsic value, the same in each, which he does not owe to any earthly circumstance. Associated with this value is a concept of human dignity, which implies that every human being is entitled in an equal measure to a certain basic respect. In support of this the Akans say, "Every one is the offspring of God; no one the offspring of the earth." Directly implied in the doctrine of *okra* is the right of each person, as the recipient of a destiny, to pursue that unique destiny assigned to him by God. In more colloquial language everyone has the right to do his own thing, with the understanding, of course, that ultimately one must bear the consequences of one's own choices. This might almost be called the metaphysical right of privacy. It is clinched with the maxim "Nobody was there when I was taking my destiny from my God."

Through the possession of an *okra*, *mogya*, and *sunsum* a person is situated in a network of kinship relations that generate a system of rights and obligations. Because the Akans are matrilineal, the most important kinship group is the lineage, which may be pictured as a system of concentric circles of matrilineal kinship relationship that, at its outermost reaches, can include people in widely separated geographic regions. In these outermost dimensions a lineage becomes a clan. Its innermost circle comprises the grandmother, the mother, the mother's siblings, her own children, and the children of her sisters. To this group, with the mother as the principal personage, belongs the duty of nursing an Akan newborn. The Akans have an acute sense of the dependency of a human being. On first appearance in this world, one is totally defenseless and dependent. This is the time when there is the greatest need for the care and protection of others and also, to the Akan mind, the time of the greatest right to that help; but this right never deserts a human being, for one is seen at all times as insufficient unto oneself. The logic of this right may be simply phrased: a genuine human need carries the right to satisfaction. The right to be nursed, then, is the first human right. In the fullness of time it will be transformed dialectically into a duty, the duty to nurse one's mother in her old age. "If your mother nurses you to grow your teeth," says an Akan adage, "you nurse her to lose hers." But there is another aspect to the nurturing of a human being—he or she needs to be instructed in the arts of gainful living—and this function the Akans ascribe to the father. To the father, then, attaches the duty to provide the child with character training, general education, and career preparation.

Through an individual's *ntoro*, the element contributed to each biological makeup by the father, one acquires a certain social link to a patrilineal kinship group, which, however, is much less important than one's matrilineal affiliations except for this: from the father's sister the child has the right to receive sexual education.

Earning a livelihood in traditional Akan society presupposed the possession of one basic resource: land. In an agricultural society like traditional Akan society, education profited a person little unless he could count on some land, land to till and land on which to build. It is in this connection that we see an Akan person's most cherished positive right, the right to land. This right he has by virtue of his membership in a lineage; it is a claim that he has primarily on his lineage, but because of the statewide significance of land, it is also, as I will explain later, a right that he could claim against the state.

We have already mentioned some quite important rights. These are rights, in the Akan perception of things, that people have simply because they are human beings. They are entitlements entailed by the intrinsic sociality of the human status. In viewing a human being in this light, the Akans perhaps went beyond Aristotle's maxim that man is by nature a political animal. To the Akans, a human being is already social at conception, for the union of the blood principle and the personality principle already defines a social identity. A person is social in a further sense. The social identity just alluded to is a kinship identity. But a person lives, moves, and has his being in an environment that includes people outside the kin group. He lives in a town and has to relate to that environment in definite ways. A well-known Akan maxim asserts that when a human being descends upon the earth from above, he lands in a town. Membership in town and state brings with it a wider set of rights and obligations embracing the whole race of humankind, for the possession of the *okra*, the speck of God in man, is taken to link all human beings together in one universal family. The immediate concerns here, however, are with the rights of man in the context of Akan society. In that society an individual's status as a person is predicated upon the fulfillment of certain roles that have a reference to circles of relationships transcending the kin group. There is an ambiguity here in the use of the word *person*, the resolution of which will bring us to the normative conception of a person.

In one sense the Akan word *onipa* translates into the English word person in the sense of a human being, the possessor of *okra*, *mogya*, and *sunsum*. In this sense everyone is born as a person, an *onipa*. This is the descriptive sense of the word. But there is a further sense of the word *onipa* in which to call an individual a person is to commend him; it implies the recognition that he has attained a certain status in the community. Specifically, it implies that he has demonstrated an ability through hard work and sober thinking to sustain a household and make contributions to the communal welfare. In traditional Akan society, public works were always done through communal labor. Moreover, the defense of the state against external attack was the responsibility of all. Good contributions toward these ends stamped an individual in the community as an *onipa*. Inversely, consistent default distanced him from that title. In this sense, personhood is not something you are born with but something you may achieve, and it is subject to degrees, so that some are more *onipa* than others, depending on the degree of fulfillment of one's obligations to self, household, and community.

On the face of it, the normative layer in the Akan concept of person brings only obligations to the individual. In fact, however these obligations are matched by a whole series of rights that accrue to the individual simply because he lives in a society in which everyone has those obligations. It is useful in this regard to recall the fact, noted earlier, that the Akans viewed a human being as essentially dependent. From this point of view, human society is seen as a necessary framework of mutual aid for survival and, beyond that, for the attainment of reasonable levels of well-being. A number of Akan sayings testify to this conception, which is at the root of Akan communalism. One is to the effect that a human being is not a palm tree so as to be sufficient unto himself. (The Akans were highly impressed by the number of things that could be got from a palm tree, not the least memorable among them being palm nut soup and palm wine.) A second saying points out that to be human is to be in need of help. Literally it says simply "a human being needs help" (*onipa hyia mmoa*). The Akan verb *hyia* means "is in need of." In this context it also has the connotation of merits, "is entitled to," so that the maxim may also be interpreted as asserting that a human being, simply because he is a human being, is entitled to help from others. A further saying explains that it is because of the need to have someone blow out the speck of dust in one's eye that antelopes go in twos. This saying obviously puts forward mutual aid as the rationale of society.

Although the rights deriving from the general human entitlement to the help of their kind did not have the backing of state sanctions, they were deeply enough felt in Akan society. In consequence, such rights may be said to have enjoyed the strong backing of public opinion, which in communalistic societies cannot be taken lightly. However, at this stage rights that appertain to political existence must be looked at. If, as the Akans said, when a human being descends upon the earth, he lands in a town, the point is that he becomes integrated into a particular social and political structure. The specifics of that structure will determine his rights and obligations.

The Akan Political System

The importance of kinship relations in Akan society has already been noted. This grouping provides the basic units of political organization. These units are the lineages. A lineage, to be sure, is all the individuals in a town who are descended from one ancestress. A clan includes all the lineages united by a common maternal ancestry. It is too large and too scattered to be the unit of political organization in spite of the real feelings of brotherhood (and sisterhood) that exist among its members. In every town there would be quite a manageable number of lineages. Each of them had a head, called *Abusuapanyin* (elder of the lineage), who was elected by the adult members of the group. Age was an important qualification for this position—just reflect on the title "elder"—but so also was wisdom, eloquence, integrity, and, in earlier times, fighting competence. The last qualification calls for a word of explanation. Every head of lineage was, ex officio, a military leader who led his lineage in a particular position in the battle formation of the Akan army. This was not a professional army but rather a citizen force....

But if every Akan was thus obligated by birth to contribute to defense in one way or another, there was also the complementary fact that he had a right to the protection of his person, property, and dignity, not only in his own state but also outside it. And states were known to go to war to secure the freedom of their citizens abroad or avenge their mistreatment.

The ruling body of an Akan town was a council consisting of the lineage heads with the chief of the town in the capacity of chairman. The functions of the council were to preserve law, order, and peace in the town, to ensure its safety, and to promote its welfare. The office of a chief is hereditary but also partly elective. Some sort of an election is necessary because at any one time there are several people belonging to the royal lineage who are qualified by birth to be considered. The queen of the town (strictly, the queen mother) has the prerogative of selecting the best-qualified candidate, all things considered, but the final decision does not come until the council has assessed the candidate and indicated its approval. Such an approval, if forthcoming, seals the election, provided an objection is not voiced by the populace.

This last proviso is of special significance for the question of human rights, as shown later. In every town there was an unofficial personage recognized as the chief of the general populace. He was called *Nkwankwaahene* (literally, the chief of the young men) and functioned as the spokesman of the populace. His position is described here as unofficial simply because unlike most Akan political offices, it had nothing to do with his lineage; moreover, he was not a member of the chief's council. However, he had the right to make representations before the council on behalf of the young men of the town. In particular, if there were objections to a proposed chief among the populace, he made very forthright representations that, as a rule, prevailed. This is in conformity with the Akan principle that royals do not install a chief; it is those who have to serve him who do.

Beyond the political organization of the Akan town, a certain collection of towns constituted a division (*Oman*, literally, state) with a divisional council consisting of paramount chiefs. In an Akan territory of the proportions of Ashanti, paramount chiefs from a number of divisional councils served also as members of a confederacy council, which held sway over the whole nation.

Rights of Political Participation

This brings us, naturally, to political rights. It is clear from the foregoing that in principle citizens had a say, first in the question of who would exercise political power over them, and second in the issue of what specific policies were to be implemented in the town and, derivatively, in the state and nation. They had two avenues in this matter. They could work through their lineage head, who was in duty bound to consult them on all matters due for decision at the council, and they could work through the spokesman of the populace. The chief had absolutely no right to impose his own wishes on the elders of the council. On the contrary, all decisions of the council were based on consensus. The elders would keep on discussing an issue till consensus was reached, a method that contrasts with the decision by majority vote that prevails in modern democracies. The rationale of decision by consensus, as can easily be inferred, was to forestall the trivialization of the right of the minority to have an effect on decisionmaking.

Once a decision had been reached in council by consensus, it became officially the decision of the chief, regardless of his own opinion. That opinion would already have been given consideration at the discussion stage, but no one encouraged him in any illusions of infallibility. Nevertheless, the chief was never contradicted in public, since he was a symbol of the unity of the council and was also perceived as the link between the community and its hallowed ancestors. Because of the great pains taken to achieve consensus, the council took a very severe view of a member who subjected any of its decisions to criticism in public. The leader of the populace was in a different position. Not being privy to the deliberations of the council, he had the fullest right to criticize any decisions unacceptable to his constituency, as did the members of that constituency. One thing then is clear here. The people's freedom of thought and expression went beyond the devices of any chief or council.

Nor was there ever a doubt about the right of the people, including the elders, to dismiss a chief who tried to be oppressive. A cherished principle of Akan politics was that those who served the chief could also destool him. (The stool was the symbol of chiefly status, and so the installation of a chief was called enstoolment and his dismissal destoolment.) This was a process governed by well-defined rules. Charges had to be filed before appropriate bodies and thorough investigations made before a decision to destool or retain a chief was reached. Actually, as Abraham remarked, among the Akans "kingship was more a sacred office than a political one."[2] The chief was regarded as the spiritual link between the people and their ancestors and was for this reason approached with virtual awe. But this did not translate into abject subservience when it came to political matters. Here the chief had to play the game according to the rules whereby he was always to act in conformity with the decisions of the council and eschew any wayward style of life. So long as he did so, he was held to be sacrosanct, but as soon as he violated this compact, he lost that status and could experience a rough time. When this factor is taken into account, the representative character of the Akan system looms even larger. The real power was in the hands of the elected elders of the various lineages. This conforms to the principle that people have a right to determine who shall exercise political power over them and for how long.

That principle links up with another important feature of the Akan constitution: its decentralization. At every level of political organization, the groups involved enjoyed self-government. Thus the lineage, together with its head, conducted its affairs without interference from any higher authorities so long as the issues did not have townwide or statewide reverberations. Similarly, the town and the division handled all issues pertaining exclusively to their domains. Apparent here is the Akan conception of a right due to all human beings, that is, the right of self-government.

This right of self-government was particularly important in the administration of justice. Because all kinds of cases arising in the internal affairs of a lineage or sometimes in interlineage affairs were left to lineage personnel to settle on a household-to-household basis rather than in the more formalized and adversarial atmosphere of a chief's court, many potentially divisive problems between people could be solved painlessly, often through mere verbal apologies or minor compensations. A salutary by-product of this personalized way of settling cases was that it often brought a reinforcement of neighborhood good will. This is not to suggest, though, that the official, state-level reaction to issues of wrongdoing and the like was excessively retributive. On the contrary, often the aim was to reestablish satisfactory relations between person and person or person and the ancestors through compensatory settlements and pacificatory rituals.

The Right to a Trial

There are some interesting aspects of the Akan approach to punishment and related issues that could be gone into here, but from the point of view of human rights, the most important observation is that it was an absolute principle of Akan justice that no human being could be punished without trial. Neither at the lineage level nor at any other level of Akan society could a citizen be subjected to any sort of sanctions without proof of wrongdoing. This principle was so strongly adhered to that even a dead body was tried before posthumous punishment was symbolically meted out to him. The best-known example of this sort of procedure was the reaction to a suicide apparently committed to evade the consequences of evil conduct. The dead person was meticulously tried. If guilt was established, the body was decapitated. If the motive behind the suicide remained obscure, it was assumed to be bad and had the same result.[3] If the right of the dead to trial before punishment was recognized, could the living have been entitled to less courtesy? The modern misdeeds, on the part of certain governments both inside and outside Africa, of imprisoning citizens without trial would have been inconceivable in a traditional Akan setting, not only because there were no such institutions as prisons but also because the principle of such a practice would have been totally repugnant to the Akan mentality....

The Right to Land

As noted earlier, any human being was held, by virtue of his blood principle (*mogya*), to be entitled to some land. For the duration of his life any Akan had the right to the use of a piece of the lineage land. However, land was supposed to belong to the whole lineage, conceived as including the ancestors, the living members, and those as yet to be born. For this reason, in traditional times the sale of land was prohibited. And the prohibition was effective. But our ancestors reckoned without the conquering power of modern commercialism. Land sale is now a thriving racket in which chiefs yield no ground to commoners. As a foreseeable consequence, there are now many Akans and others who have no land to till. Here then, sadly, is a human right, recognized of old, that seems to have been devoured by advancing time....

Religious Freedom

My previous mention of the right to freedom of thought and expression referred to political issues. It is relevant, however, to ask whether the Akan system supported freedom of thought and expression in such areas as religion and metaphysics.

To consider religion first, there was no such thing as an institutionalized religion in Akan land. Religion consisted simply of belief and trust in and reverence for a Supreme Being regarded as the architect of the cosmos. The Akans took it to be obvious even to children that such a being existed—witness the saying: "No one shows God to a child" (*Obi nykyere akwadaa Nyame*). However, I know of no sentiment in the Akan corpus of proverbs, epigrams, tales, and explicit doctrines that lends the slightest support to any abridgement of the freedom of thought or expression. As a matter of fact, skeptics with respect to religious and other issues (*akyinyefo*, literally, debater) were known in Akan society, but no harm seems to have befallen them.

The belief in the assortment of extrahuman forces (including the ancestors) that is so often mentioned in connection with Akan, and in general with African, religion does not seem to me to belong properly to the field of religion. Be that as it may, one must concede that any person in Akan traditional society disagreeing fundamentally with this worldview would have had a serious sense of isolation. Almost every custom or cultural practice presupposed beliefs of that sort. Yet if he was prepared to perform his civic duties without bothering about any underlying beliefs, he could live in harmony with his kinsmen in spite of his philosophical nonconformism. Here again, one may observe that persecution on grounds of belief is unheard of in Akan society.

The conflict between Christian missionaries and the chiefs of Ashanti in the early years of this century, when the campaign to convert the people of Ghana to the Christian faith was getting under way, provides an illuminating case study. In that conflict the Ashanti chiefs remained remarkably forbearing, merely insisting that all Ashantis, irrespective of their religious persuasion, should obey customary law. By contrast, the missionaries, without challenging the authority of the chiefs over the Ashanti people, objected to the participation of Ashanti Christians in any activities that seemed to be based on beliefs they regarded as incompatible with their faith, beliefs which they called fetish.

Intellectually this issue has not been resolved even to this day, but the force of circumstances has seemed to give the upper hand now to one party, now to the other. By the 1930s and 1940s Christianity was in the ascendancy, and many of the chiefs themselves, including, a little later, the king of Ashanti, had become converts. Neither the psychology, nor the logic, nor the theology of such conversions was free from paradox. But it ensured the easing of the conflict by virtue of accommodations from the side of the Ashanti authorities. Then came political independence, and with it a certain reassertion of cultural identity on the part of the people and, complementarily, greater tolerance for African ways on the part of the Christian dignitaries, both foreign and native. As a result, practices like traditional drumming and the pouring of libation to the ancestors, which a few decades ago were proscribed by the missionaries for being fetish, are now commonplace among Christians, sometimes even on occasions of Christian worship. In fact, one even hears of the Africanization of Christianity from some high-minded church circles. Evidently the wheel has turned 180 degrees, or nearly so.

In all this, two things stand out as indicative of the Ashanti (and, generally, Ghanaian) tolerance for different beliefs. First, there is the fact that a great many Ashantis, commoners and chiefs alike, found a way to embrace the new beliefs, while not erasing the older ones from their consciousness.[4] But second, and even more important, the Ashantis from the beginning were not much exercised about what actually went on in the minds of people in matters having to do with such things as their worldview. Their main concern regarding the early Ashanti converts was simply with their actual civic conduct. You can get people to do or not do specific things, reasoned the Akans, but you cannot guarantee that they will think particular thoughts. Hence the futility, from their point of view, of trying to interfere with freedom of thought. Confronted with any such attempt, an Akan would typically say to himself or to a confidant: *Me kose kose wo mitirm*, meaning "My real thoughts are in my own head," which by interpretation means, "I carry in my own person proof of the futility of any attempt to control people's thinking." Not only, then, is it wrong from the Akan standpoint to try to curtail freedom of thought; it is by and large futile.

From their tolerant attitude toward other people's religious beliefs, it is sufficiently clear that the Akans made no exceptions about subject matter in the question of the freedom of thought. When they said "two heads are better than one" and "one head does not hold council" in extolling the virtues of consultation, they were not thinking of politics alone. They were aware that other minds always have the potential to bring to light new aspects of things familiar or recondite. In metaphysical matters they left little doubt of their sense of the presumptuousness of dogmatism, for their metaphysicians often spoke in paradoxes and riddles, purposely inviting individual speculative ingenuity. Witness, for example, the following poser from a metaphysical drum text:

> Who gave word to Hearing
> For Hearing to have told the Spider
> For the Spider to have told the maker of the world
> For the maker of the world to have made the world?

Conclusion

In summary, one finds a veritable harvest of human rights. Akan thought recognized the right of a newborn to be nursed and educated, the right of an adult to a plot of land from the ancestral holdings, the right of any well-defined unit of political organization to self-government, the right of all to have a say in the enstoolment or destoolment of their chiefs or their elders and to participate in the shaping of governmental policies, the right of all to freedom of thought and expression in all matters, political, religious, and metaphysical, the right of everybody to trial before punishment, the right of a person to remain at any locality or to leave, and so on. Although frequently people who talk of human rights have political rights uppermost in their minds, some human rights do not fall within the purview of any constituted authority. In the last analysis, a people's conception of human rights will reflect their fundamental values, and not all such values will ever acquire the backing of institutional authority. In any case this discussion does not pretend to have disclosed all the human rights generated by Akan values.

Again, it is probably needless to point out that my outline of human rights is a portrayal of Akan principles rather than an assessment of Akan practice. One can assume, a priori, that in actual practice the reality must have been some sort of a mixture of both the pursuit and the perversion of precept....

Probably every culture can be viewed as a matrix of forces and tendencies of thought and practice not always mutually compatible. The characterization of cultural traits, therefore, frequently has to take cognizance of countervailing factors. Nevertheless, the bent of a culture will, if anything, stand out in heightened relief in the full view of such facts. On the question of human rights it can justly be said that, notwithstanding any contrary tendencies, the principles of human rights enumerated here did motivate predominantly favorable practices in traditional Akan society. Moreover, from the perspective of those principles one can check how faithful certain claims in contemporary African politics are to at least one African tradition. Regrettably, I must content myself here with only one, brief, illustration.

Many African governments today are based upon the one-party system. There are both critics and defenders of that system in Africa, and in the resulting controversy human rights have almost always been at issue. In some one-party apologetics the suggestion is made not only that the system is hospitable to all the desirable human rights but also that traditional African systems of government were of the one-party variety, in a full-blown or an embryonic form. As far at least as the Akan tradition is concerned, I hope that this discussion demonstrates that both claims are contrary to fact. Although the Akan system was not of a multiparty type, it was not a one-party type either. The decisive reason that the Akan system is antithetical to the one-party system is that no such system can survive the right of the populace, organized under their own spokesman, to question the decisions of the ruling body or to demand the dismissal of its leader. Since the traditional system featured this right, it was neither a one-party system nor even a simulacrum of it. For the same reason it is not true that the one-party system is compatible with all human rights. On this showing, our traditional systems require close analysis from the point of view of contemporary existential concerns. Human rights are certainly among the most urgent of these concerns. That Africa has suffered human rights deprivations from various causes in the past, including particularly the transatlantic slave trade and colonialism, is well-known history. It is surely an agonizing reflection that, aside from the vexatious case of apartheid, the encroachments on human rights in Africa in recent times have usually come from African governments themselves. To a certain extent the exigencies of postindependence reconstruction may account for this. But they cannot justify it. Nor, as just pointed out in the matter of the one-party system, can they be rationalized by appeal to any authentic aspect of African traditional politics, at least in the Akan instance. How to devise a system of politics that, while being responsive to the developments of the modem world, will reflect the best traditional thinking about human rights (and other values) is one of the profoundest challenges facing modem Africans. A good beginning is to become informed about traditional life and thought.

Notes

1. The Akans have, historically, been the subject of some famous anthropological, linguistic, and philosophical studies by foreign scholars such as R. S. Rattray, *Ashanti* (Oxford University Press, 1923), and *Religion and Art in Ashanti* (Oxford University Press,1927); J. G. Christaller, *Dictionary of the Asante and Fante Language Called Tshi (Twi)*, 2d ed. (Basel, 1933); and E. L. Mayerowitz, *The Sacred State of the Akan* (London: Faber and Faber, 1951); and native scholars such as Casely Hayford, *Gold Coast Native Institutions* (London: Sweet and Maxwell, 1903); J. B. Danquah, *The Akan Doctrine of God* (London, 1946); and K. A. Busia, *The Position of the Chief in the Modern Political System of Ashanti* (London: Frank Cass, 1951). Two important recent philosophical studies are W. E. Abraham, *The Mind of Africa* (University of Chicago Press, 1962): and Kwame Gyekye, *An Essay on African Philosophical Thought: The Akan Conceptual Scheme* (Cambridge University Press, 1987).

2. Abraham, *Mind of Africa*, p. 77.

3. See, for example, Busia, *Position of the Chief*, pp. 66, 70-71.

4. Other Ashantis extended the same courtesy to Islam.

Questions for Reflection

1. What features of the Akan conception of a person are relevant to the recognition of human rights?

2. Compare the rights of political participation in the Akan community to the rights of political participation in your own community. In what ways are your rights similar to or different from those of the Akan?

3. Wiredu claims that the traditional life and thought of the Akan is compatible with human rights. Do you agree that the Akan conceptions of human rights can be reconciled with Western conceptions? Why or why not?

28. ABDULLAHI AHMED AN-NA'IM

Abdullahi Ahmed An-Na'im (1946-) is Charles Howard Candler Professor of Law, and Fellow of the Law and Religion Program at Emory University. Born and educated in Sudan, as well as at the universities of Cambridge and Edinburgh, An-Na'im is an internationally recognized scholar of Islam and human rights, and human rights in cross-cultural perspectives. He has published numerous articles and books on these topics, including *Toward an Islamic Reformation: Civil Liberties, Human Rights and International Law* (1990) and *Human Rights in Cross-Cultural Perspectives: A Quest for Consensus* (1992). In the article included here, An-Na'im examines the implications of Shari'a, or Islamic religious law, for Muslim recognition of international human rights standards. An-Na'im argues that a number of inconsistencies between Shari'a and human rights standards can be eliminated through a critical analysis of Muslim scriptural imperatives.

Text—Human Rights in the Muslim World

From Abdullahi Ahmed An-Na'im, "Human Rights in the Muslim World: Socio-Political Conditions and Scriptural Imperatives," Harvard Human Rights Law Journal *3 (1990).*

INTRODUCTION

Historical formulations of Islamic religious law, commonly known as Shari'a, include a universal system of law and ethics and purport to regulate every aspect of public and private life. The power of Shari'a to regulate the behavior of Muslims derives from its moral and religious authority as well as the formal enforcement of its legal norms. As such, Shari'a influences individual and collective behavior in Muslim countries through its role in the socialization processes of such nations regardless of its status in their formal legal systems. For example, the status and rights of women in the Muslim world have always been significantly influenced by Shari'a, regardless of the degree of Islamization in public life. Of course, Shari'a is not the sole determinant of human behavior nor the only formative force behind social and political institutions in Muslim countries.

In this Article, I explore the implications of Shari'a for the status of human rights in the Muslim world. After briefly discussing my methodological choice in Part I, in Part II I explain Shari'a and the human rights violations which result from the dominant interpretation of Shari'a. In Part III, I describe some of the political and social forces which translate this scriptural interpretation into action. In Part IV, I analyze in some detail the impact of Shari'a and Islamization on the status and rights of women in Muslim communities. And in Part V, I argue that human rights reform requires reinterpretation of Shari'a and I offer one possible reformulation.

I conclude that human rights advocates in the Muslim world must work within the framework of Islam to be effective. They need not be confined, however, to the particular historical interpretations of Islam known as Shari'a. Muslims are obliged, as a matter of faith, to conduct their private and public affairs in accordance with the dictates of Islam, but there is room for legitimate disagreement over the precise nature of these dictates in the modern context. Religious texts, like all other texts, are open to a variety of interpretations. Human rights advocates in the Muslim world should struggle to have their interpretations of the relevant texts adopted as the new Islamic scriptural imperatives for the contemporary world.

A. *Cultural Legitimacy for Human Rights*

The basic premise of my approach is that human rights violations reflect the lack or weakness of cultural legitimacy of international standards in a society. Insofar as these standards are perceived to be alien to or at variance with the values and institutions of a people, they are unlikely to elicit commitment or compliance. While cultural legitimacy may not be the sole or even primary determinant of compliance with human rights standards, it is, in my view, an extremely significant one. Thus, the underlying causes of any lack or weakness of legitimacy of human rights standards must be addressed in order to enhance the promotion and protection of human rights in that society.

Some commentators have focused on this lack of cultural legitimacy of international standards in the non-Western world to challenge the basic validity of international human rights standards. In fact, conduct which would amount to human rights violations under existing international standards has been justified precisely because these standards were perceived to be culturally illegitimate. This cultural illegitimacy, it is argued, derives from the historical conditions surrounding the creation of the particular human rights instruments. Most African and Asian countries did not participate in the formulation of the Universal Declaration of Human Rights because, as victims of colonization, they were not members of the United Nations. When they did participate in the formulation of subsequent instruments, they did so on the basis of an established framework and philosophical assumptions adopted in their absence. For example, the preexisting framework and assumptions favored individual civil and political rights over collective solidarity rights, such as a right to development, an outcome which remains problematic today. Some authors have gone so far as to argue that inherent differences exist between the Western notion of human rights as reflected in the international instruments and non-Western notions of human dignity. In the Muslim world, for instance, there are obvious conflicts between Shari'a and certain human rights, especially of women and non-Muslims.

Concern for the lack of universal participation in formulating international human rights instruments does not lead me to invalidate those existing instruments. On the contrary, for the purposes of this study, I take the International Bill of Human Rights as the source of these standards. It is true that not all Muslim countries have endorsed or ratified these instruments, but neither have they publicly repudiated them. The human rights idea is too powerful and popular now for any government to oppose openly. The governments of Muslim countries are no exception to this general rule. In this discussion, I focus on the principles of legal equality and nondiscrimination contained in many human rights instruments. These principles relating to gender and religion are particularly problematic in the Muslim world.

I adopt a constructive approach to the problem of the cultural legitimacy of human rights norms. This approach posits that such problems can be overcome through a process of reinterpreting the fundamental sources of the Islamic tradition. The proposed new interpretation will have to be undertaken in a sensitive, legitimate manner, and time will be required for its acceptance and implementation by the population at large. The availability of such reinterpretation is a vital prelude to the political struggle which is integral to the whole process. The reformulation I offer in the final part of this Article is but a brief presentation of my arguments for a reinterpretive approach which I have explored in more detail elsewhere. In the final part of this Article, I offer a brief presentation of the thesis and the prospects of its implementation in the Muslim world today.

II. ISLAM, SHARI'A AND HUMAN RIGHTS

In this part, I first discuss the formation of the Shari'a and address the impact which Shari'a has had upon the thinking and conduct of Muslims. I conclude with a discussion of recent mounting pressure in Muslim countries to adopt the Shari'a as their formal legal systems.

A. *The Development and Current Application of Shari'a*

To the over nine hundred million Muslims of the world, the Qur'an is the literal and final word of God and Muhammad is the final Prophet. During his mission, from 610 A.D. to his death in 632 A.D., the Prophet elaborated on the meaning of the Qur'an and supplemented its rulings through his statements and actions. This body of information came to be known as Sunna. He also established the first Islamic state in Medina around 622 A.D. which emerged later as the ideal model of an Islamic state. In addition, the practices of the first four caliphs, successors of the Prophet, are also binding or at least highly authoritative for the ninety percent of Muslims commonly known as Sunnis. In contradistinction, the Shi'a minority insists that the fourth caliph Ali (the Prophet's cousin and son-in-law) and his descendants from Fatima, the Prophet's daughter, were the only rightful *imams*, leaders of the Muslim community

While the Qur'an was collected and recorded soon after the Prophet Muhammad's death, it took almost two centuries to collect, verify, and record the Sunna. Because it remained an oral tradition for a long time during a period of exceptional turmoil in Muslim history, some Sunna reports are still controversial in terms of both their authenticity and relationship to the Qur'an.

Because Shari'a is derived from Sunna as well as the Qur'an, its development as a comprehensive legal and ethical system had to await the collection and authentication of Sunna. Shari'a was not developed until the second and third centuries of Islam. The concept itself, in the sense of a unified body of law, was a relatively late development. The first generation of Muslim legal scholars worked independently in various centers, discussing their views on the meaning of the Qur'an and Sunna and issuing individual opinions upon request.

Shari'a, therefore, was constructed by Muslim jurists over a long period of time and did not become a comprehensive legal and ethical system until well into the third century of Islam. The jurists who founded the main schools of Islamic jurisprudence that are followed by the vast majority of modern Muslims did their founding work between the middle of the eighth century and the middle of the ninth century, one to two hundred years after the Prophet's death. In fact, the techniques and methods for the derivation of general principles and specific rules of Shari'a, such as *ijma* (consensus) and *qiyas* (analogy), were not settled until the time of Shafi'i who died in 819.

Shari'a is not a formally enacted legal code. It consists of a vast body of jurisprudence in which individual jurists express their views on the meaning of the Qur'an and Sunna and the legal implications of those views. Although most Muslims believe Shari'a to be a single logical whole, there is significant diversity of opinion not only among the various schools of thought, but also among the different jurists of a particular school. The original founding jurists themselves were not attempting during the second and third centuries of Islam to establish permanent opinions of general application.

Furthermore, Muslim jurists were primarily concerned with the formulation of principles of Shari'a in terms of moral duties sanctioned by religious consequences rather than with legal obligations and rights and specific temporal remedies. They categorized all fields of human activity as permissible or impermissible and recommended or reprehensible. In other words, Shari'a addresses the conscience of the individual Muslim, whether in a private, or public and official, capacity, and not the institutions and corporate entities of society and the state. Each Muslim is in theory entitled to follow whatever view is acceptable to his or her private conscience. As a general rule, Muslims to the present day tend to identify themselves as observers of one or another of the established schools of thought. One is entitled to choose not only from among the various views available within his or her school of thought, but also from those views available within other schools. In accordance with this principle, modern official legal reforms in the Muslim world have employed a technique known as *talfiq*: constructing a composite general principle or specific rule from a variety of sources regardless of whether they belong to the same school of thought.

Shari'a, as a religious and moral body of principles and directives, has had and continues to have a significant impact on the thinking and behavior of Muslims. It forms an integral part of the socialization of every Muslim child and is one of the primary forces behind the Institutions and customs of the vast majority of Muslim societies.

Whatever may have been the historical status of Shari'a as the legal system of Muslim countries, the scope of its application in the public domain has diminished significantly since the middle of the nineteenth century. Due to both internal factors and external influence, Shari'a principles had been replaced by European law governing commercial, criminal, and constitutional matters in almost all Muslim countries. Only family law and inheritance continued to be governed by Shari'a. Even countries such as Saudi Arabia which claim always to have maintained Shari'a as their sole legal system have enacted numerous "regulations" based on European law and practice in the commercial and public administration fields.

Recently, many Muslims have challenged the gradual weakening of Shari'a as the basis for their formal legal systems. Most Muslim countries have experienced mounting demands for the immediate application of Shari'a as the sole, or at least primary, legal system of the land. These movements have either succeeded in gaining complete control, as in Iran, or achieved significant success in having aspects of Shari'a introduced into the legal system, as in Pakistan and the Sudan. Governments of Muslim countries generally find it difficult to resist these demands out of fear of being condemned by their own populations as anti-Islamic. Therefore, it is likely that this so-called Islamic fundamentalism will achieve further successes in other Muslim countries.

The possibility of further Islamization may convince more people of the urgency of understanding and discussing the relationship between Shari'a and human rights, because Shari'a would have a direct impact on a wider range of human rights issues if it became the formal legal system of any country. To my mind, however, this need is urgent regardless of the official status of Shari'a. As a Muslim, I appreciate the extralegal power that Shari'a has on the minds and hearts of Muslims. Given this power, it is difficult to see how Muslim governments can honor their obligations to promote and protect human rights, even if they wish to do so, where those obligations are perceived to be contrary to Shari'a.

The above survey of the development and nature of Shari'a clearly indicates that Shari'a, as a unified body of moral and legal principles derived from both the Qur'an and Sunna, reflects specific historical interpretations of the scriptural imperatives of Islam. Other interpretations are possible and were in fact anticipated by the founding jurists of Shari'a themselves. Although modern Muslim reformers have expressed some support for this proposition, usually in more moderate terms, very little has been done to develop an adequate reform technique. I believe that a modern version of Islamic law can and should be developed. Such a modern "Shari'a" could be, in my view, entirely consistent with current standards of human rights. These views, however, are appreciated by only a tiny minority of contemporary Muslims. To the overwhelming majority of Muslims today, Shari'a is the sole valid interpretation of Islam, and as such ought to prevail over any human law or policy.

B. *Shari'a and Human Rights*

In this part, I illustrate with specific examples how Shari'a conflicts with international human rights standards. Specifically, I will focus on discrimination against women and non-Muslims. Some contemporary Muslim authors have claimed that Shari'a is fully consistent with and has always protected human rights. Ali A. Wafi, for example, contends that "the most important human rights can be classified" into five principal rights relating to five kinds of liberty: "religious liberty; liberty of opinion and expression; liberty of work; liberty of instruction and culture; and civil liberty." Wafi cites general Islamic sources in support of each liberty and concludes that "Islam" provided for that particular liberty. I find this approach to be both simplistic and misleading. It is simplistic in its classification of human rights and failure to consider conceptual and structural aspects of the modern human rights movement. According to Wafi, civil liberty is the right to conclude contracts, shoulder civil obligations and to dispose freely of property. This is hardly an adequate description of civil liberty as a human right even in the most formal and minimal sense. Wafi's approach is also misleading because it is highly selective and fails to mention other Islamic sources which contradict his contentions in relation to each of the five liberties. He fails to mention the ways in which jurists of Shari'a interpreted these sources and the manner in which Muslim states applied those interpretations through the ages.

The claim that Shari'a is fully consistent with and has always protected human rights is problematic both as a theoretical and a practical matter. As a theoretical matter, the concept of human rights as rights to which every human being is entitled by virtue of being human was unknown to Islamic jurisprudence or social philosophy until the last few decades and does not exist in Shari'a. Many rights are given under Shari'a in accordance with a strict classification based on faith and gender and are not given to human beings as such. As a practical matter, fundamental inconsistencies exist between Shari'a as practiced in Muslim countries and current standards of human rights. For example, many aspects of Shari'a discriminate against women and violate their fundamental human rights. I will discuss this further in Part IV. Three other specific examples of human rights violations can be cited here to illustrate the point.

Although slavery was formally abolished in all Muslim countries through secular law, the institution itself remains lawful under Shari'a to the present day. It is true that Islam originally discouraged slavery by restricting the "legitimate" sources of slaves and encouraging their emancipation, but it did not directly prohibit slavery and the institution of slavery has never been abolished under Shari'a. In fact, treatises on Shari'a discuss at length contractual and other arrangements relating to slaves. In my view, the original intention of Islam was to eliminate slavery in due course, but that intention has never been realized through Shari'a.

The second example is the Shari'a law of apostasy. According to Shari'a, a Muslim who repudiates his faith in Islam, whether directly or indirectly, is guilty of a capital offense punishable by death. This aspect of Shari'a is in complete conflict with the fundamental human right of freedom of religion and conscience. The apostasy of a Muslim may be inferred by the court from the person's views or actions deemed by the court to contravene the basic tenets of Islam and therefore be tantamount to apostasy, regardless of the accused's personal belief that he or she is a Muslim.

The Shari'a law of apostasy can be used to restrict other human rights such as freedom of expression. A person may be liable to the death penalty for expressing views held by the authorities to contravene the official view of the tenets of Islam. Far from being an historical practice or a purely theoretical danger, this interpretation of the law of apostasy was applied in the Sudan as recently as 1985, when a Sudanese Muslim reformer was executed because the authorities deemed his views to be contrary to Islam.

A third and final example of conflict between Shari'a and human rights relates to the status and rights of non-Muslims. Shari'a classifies the subjects of an Islamic state in terms of their religious beliefs: Muslims, *ahl al-Kitab* or believers in a divinely revealed scripture (mainly Christian and Jews), and unbelievers. In modern terms, Muslims are the only full citizens of an Islamic state, enjoying all the rights and freedoms granted by Shari'a and subject only to the limitations and restrictions imposed on women. *Ahl al-Kitab* are entitled to the status of *dhimma*, a special compact with the Muslim state which guarantees them security of persons and property and a degree of communal autonomy to practice their own religion and conduct their private affairs in accordance with their customs and laws. In exchange for these limited rights, *dhimmis* undertake to pay *jizya* or poll tax and submit to Muslim sovereignty and authority in all public affairs. Unbelievers may be granted *aman* or safe conduct which secures their persons and property for the duration of the *aman* period. Moreover, unbelievers that are permanent residents of an Islamic state may be recognized as *dhimmis*.

According to this scheme, non-Muslim subjects of an Islamic state can aspire only to the status of *dhimma*, under which they would suffer serious violations of their human rights. *Dhimmis* are not entitled to equality with Muslims. Their lives are evaluated as inferior in monetary terms as well: they are not entitled to the same amount of *diya* or financial compensation for homicide or bodily harm as Muslims. The reputation of a *dhimmi* is not protected by Shari'a on equal terms with that of a Muslim since the *hadd* of *qadhf*, the special criminal penalty for an unproven accusation of fornication, does not apply unless the victim is a Muslim. In the private law of, discrimination against non-Muslims includes the rule that a Muslim man may marry a *dhimmi* woman but a *dhimmi* man may not marry a Muslim woman.

Some of these restrictions against non-Muslims have not been enforced in most Muslim countries for some time, but they all remain part of Shari'a, and consequent violations of the human rights of non-Muslims recently have occurred in some modern Muslim countries. Not only are these human rights violations committed against those who identify themselves as non-Muslims, such as the Copts of Egypt, but they are also committed against minority Muslim sects which are deemed by the majority to be apostates from Islam, such as the Ahmadis of Pakistan. Members of these minorities are not only persecuted by governments, but are also frequently attacked and murdered by mobs unfettered by legal restrictions.

The broader implications of the law of apostasy are also relevant to understanding the status and rights of other minority sects, such as the Shi'a of Pakistan and Saudi Arabia, who do not conform to orthodox Sunni beliefs dominant in those countries. Serious human rights violations are committed against these minorities by official and private actors....

IV. A CASE STUDY: THE ISLAMIC DIMENSION OF THE STATUS OF WOMEN

Given the rising tide of Islamization in Muslim countries and its call for wider recognition of Shari'a as the primary legal basis of Muslim nations, concerns about Shari'a's conflict with human rights standards must be addressed. Such conflict and tension between historical formulations of Shari'a and modern standards of human rights is readily illustrated by the situation of women in Muslim countries today. The status and rights of women are a major human rights concern in all parts of the world: women are consistently oppressed, discriminated against, and denied their rightful equality with men. Although the situation has recently improved in some developed countries, I believe that it is by no means satisfactory anywhere in the world today. The present focus on Muslim violations of the human rights of women does not mean that these are peculiar to the Muslim world. As a Muslim, however I am particularly concerned with the situation in the Muslim world and wish to contribute to its improvement.

The following discussion is organized in terms of the status and rights of Muslim women in the private sphere, particularly within the family, and in public fora, in relation to access to work and participation in public affairs. This classification is recommended for the Muslim context because the personal law aspects of Shari'a, family law and inheritance, have been applied much more consistently than the public law doctrines. The status and rights of women in private life have always been significantly influenced by Shari'a regardless of the extent of Islamization of the public debate.

A. *Shari'a and the Human Rights of Women*

This part begins with a brief survey of general principles and rules of Shari'a which are likely to have a negative impact on the status and rights of Muslim women. This includes general principles which affect the socialization of both men and women and the orientation of society at large as well as legal rules in the formal sense. The most important general principle of Shari'a influencing the status and rights of women is the notion of *qawama*. *Qawama* has its origin in verse 4:34 of the Qur'an: "Men have *qawama* [guardianship and authority] over women because of the advantage they [men] have over them [women] and because they [men] spend their property in supporting them [women]." According to Shari'a interpretations of this verse, men as a group are the guardians of and superior to women as a group, and the men of a particular family are the guardians of and superior to the women of that family.

This notion of general and specific *qawama* has had far reaching consequences for the status and rights of women in both the private and public domains. For example, Shari'a provides that women are disqualified from holding general public office, which involves the exercise of authority over men, because, in keeping with the verse 4:34 of the Qur'an, men are entitled to exercise authority over women and not the reverse.

Another general principle of Shari'a that has broad implications for the status and rights of Muslim women is the notion of *al-hijab*, the veil. This means more than requiring women to cover their bodies and faces in public. According to Shari'a interpretations of verses 24:31, 33:33, 33:53, and 33:59 of the Qur'an, women are supposed to stay at home and not leave it except when required to by urgent necessity. When they are permitted to venture beyond the home, they must do so with their bodies and faces covered. *Al-hijab* tends to reinforce women's inability to hold public office and restricts their access to public life. They are not supposed to participate in public life, because they must not mix with men even in public places.

In addition to these general limitations on the rights of women under Shari'a, there are a number of specific rules in private and public law that discriminate against women and highlight women's general inferiority and inequality. In family law for example, men have the right to marry up to four wives and the power to exercise complete control over them during marriage, to the extent of punishing them for disobedience if the men deem that to be necessary. In contrast, the co-wives are supposed to submit to their husband's will and endure his punishments. While a husband is entitled to divorce any of his wives at will, a wife is not entitled to a divorce, except by judicial order on very specific and limited grounds. Another private law feature of discrimination is found in the law of inheritance, where the general rule is that women are entitled to half the share of men.

In addition to their general inferiority under the principle of *qawama* and lack of access to public life as a consequence of the notion of *al-hijab*, women are subjected to further specific limitations in the public domain. For instance, in the administration of justice, Shari'a holds women to be incompetent witnesses in serious criminal cases, regardless of their individual character and knowledge of the facts. In civil cases where a woman's testimony is accepted, it takes two women to make a single witness. *Diya*, monetary compensation to be paid to victims of violent crimes or to their surviving kin, is less for female victims than it is for male victims.

The private and public aspects of Shari'a overlap and interact. The general principles of *qawama* and *al-hijab* operate at the public as well as the private levels. Public law discrimination against women emphasizes their inferiority at home. The inferior status and rights of women in private law justify discrimination against them in public life. These overlapping and interacting principles and rules play an extremely significant role in the socialization of both women and men. Notions of women's inferiority are deeply embedded in the character and attitudes of both women and men from early childhood.

This does not mean that the whole of Shari'a has had a negative impact on the status and rights of women. Relatively early on, Shari'a granted women certain rights of equality which were not achieved by women in other legal systems until recently. For example, from the very beginning, Shari'a guaranteed a woman's independent legal personality to own and dispose of property in her own right on equal footing with men, and secured for women certain minimum rights in family law and inheritance long before other legal systems recognized similar rights.

These theoretical rights under Shari'a, however, may not be realized in practice. Other Shari'a rules may hamper or inhibit women from exercising these rights in some societies. According to one author, "while legally recognized as 'economic persons' to whom property is transmitted, Muslim women are constrained from acting out economic roles because of other legal, as well as ideological, components of Muslim female status." Customary practice in certain rural Muslim communities in Iran and Indonesia denies women their rightful inheritance under Shari'a. While the strict application of Shari'a would improve the status and rights of women in comparison to customary practice in these situations, the position of women under Shari'a would nevertheless fall short of the standards set by international human rights instruments.

This is Shari'a doctrine as it is understood by the vast majority of Muslims today. Significant possibilities exist for reform, but to undertake such reforms effectively, we must be clear on what Shari'a *is* rather than what it can or ought to be. Some Muslim feminists emphasize the positive aspects of Shari'a while overlooking the negative aspects. Others restrict their analysis to the Qur'an, and select only verses favoring the status of women while overlooking other parts and failing to take into account the ways in which the parts they select have been interpreted by the Shari'a jurists. Neither approach is satisfactory. Shari'a is a complex and integrated whole and must be perceived as such. The status and rights of Muslim women are affected by the negative as well as the positive aspects of Shari'a. In fact, its negative aspects may receive greater emphasis than its positive aspects in some Muslim societies today. Moreover, Shari'a jurists have developed specific jurisprudential techniques which control and limit prospects of reform within the framework of Shari'a. As will be explained in the final section on Islamic reform and human rights, modernist Muslims may need to challenge and change those techniques before they can implement significant reforms....

V. ISLAMIC REFORM AND HUMAN RIGHTS

I have referred several times in this Article to the need for Islamic reform to protect and promote human rights in the Muslim world. Such reform must be *sufficient* to resolve human rights problems with Shari'a while maintaining *legitimacy* from the Islamic point of view. On the one hand, reform efforts which fall short of resolving the serious human rights problems indicated earlier may not be worth pursuing. On the other hand, it is futile to advocate reforms which are unlikely to be acceptable to Muslims as criteria of Islamic reform.

Islamic reform needs must be based on the Qur'an and Sunna, the primary sources of Islam. Although Muslims believe that the Qur'an is the literal and final word of God, and Sunna are the traditions of his final Prophet, they also appreciate that these sources have to be understood and applied through human interpretation and action. As I have pointed out above, these sources have been interpreted by the founding jurists of Shari'a and applied throughout Muslim history. Because those interpretations were developed by Muslim jurists in the past, it should be possible for modern Muslim jurists to advance alternative interpretations of the Qur'an and Sunna.

A. *An Adequate Reform Methodology*

I have elsewhere argued extensively for this position and advanced a specific reform methodology which I believe would achieve the necessary degree of reform. The basic premise of my position, based on the work of the late Sudanese Muslim reformer *Ustadh* Mahmoud Mohamed Taha, is that the Shari'a reflects a historically-conditioned interpretation of Islamic scriptures in the sense that the founding jurists had to understand those sources in accordance with their own social, economic, and political circumstances. In relation to the status and rights of women, for example, equality between men and women in the eighth and ninth centuries in the Middle East, or anywhere else at the time, would have been inconceivable and impracticable. It was therefore natural and indeed inevitable that Muslim jurists would understand the relevant texts of the Qur'an and Sunna as confirming rather than repudiating the realities of the day.

In interpreting the primary sources of Islam in their historical context, the founding jurists of Shari'a tended not only to understand the Qur'an and Sunna as confirming existing social attitudes and institutions, but also to emphasize certain texts and "enact" them into Shari'a while de-emphasizing other texts or interpreting them in ways consistent with what they believed to be the intent and purpose of the sources. Working with the same primary sources, modern Muslim jurists might shift emphasis from one class of texts to the other, and interpret the previously enacted texts in ways consistent with a new understanding of what is believed to be the intent and purpose of the sources. This new understanding would be informed by contemporary social, economic, and political circumstances in the same way that the "old" understanding on which Shari'a jurists acted was informed by the then prevailing circumstances. The new understanding would qualify for Islamic legitimacy, in my view, if it is based on specific texts in opposing the application of other texts, and can be shown to be in accordance with the Qur'an and Sunna as a whole.

For example, the general principle of *qawama*, the guardianship and authority of men over women under Shari'a, is based on verse 4:34 of the Qur'an quoted earlier. This verse presents *qawama* as a consequence of two conditions: men's advantage over and financial support of women. The fact that men are generally physically stronger than most women is not relevant in modern times where the rule of law prevails over physical might. Moreover, modern circumstances are making the economic independence of women from men more readily realized and appreciated. In other words, neither of the conditions—advantages of physical might or earning power—set by verse 4:34 as the justification for the *qawama* of men over women is tenable today.

The fundamental position of the modern human rights movement is that all human beings are equal in worth and dignity, regardless of gender, religion, or race. This position can be substantiated by the Qur'an and other Islamic sources, as understood under the radically transformed circumstances of today. For example, in numerous verses the Qur'an speaks of honor and dignity for "humankind" and "children of Adam," without distinction as to race, color, gender, or religion. By drawing on those sources and being willing to set aside archaic and dated interpretations of other sources, such as the one previously given to verse 4:34 of the Qur'an, we can provide Islamic legitimacy for the full range of human rights for women.

Similarly, numerous verses of the Qur'an provide for freedom of choice and non-compulsion in religious belief and conscience. These verses have been either de-emphasized as having been "overruled" by other verses which were understood to legitimize coercion, or "interpreted" in ways which permitted such coercion. For example, verse 9:29 of the Qur'an was taken as the foundation of the whole system of *dhimma*, and its consequent discrimination against non-Muslims. Relying on those verses which extol freedom of religion rather than those that legitimize religious coercion, one can argue now that the *dhimma* system should no longer be part of Islamic law and that complete equality should be assured regardless of religion or belief. The same argument can be used to abolish all negative legal consequences of apostasy as inconsistent with the Islamic principle of freedom of religion.

Reference has been made to the possible need to challenge some jurisprudential techniques of Shari'a in order to implement the necessary degree of reform. One of the main mechanisms for development and reform within the framework of Shari'a is *ijtihad*—independent juristic reasoning to provide for new principles and rules of Shari'a in situations on which the Qur'an and Sunna were silent. By virtue of its rationale and textual support, *ijtihad* was not supposed to be exercised in any matter governed by clear and categorical texts of Qur'an and/or Sunna because that would amount to substituting juristic reasoning for the fundamental sources of Islam. According to the prevailing view in Shari'a, *ijtihad* should not be exercised even in matters settled through *ijma*, consensus.

Some of the problematic aspects of Shari'a identified in this Article, however, are based on clear and categorical texts of Qur'an and Sunna. To achieve the necessary degree of reform, I would therefore suggest that the scope of *ijtihad* be expanded to enable modern Muslim jurists not only to change rules settled through *ijma*, but also to substitute previously enacted texts with other, more general, texts of Qur'an and Sunna despite the categorical nature of the prior texts. This proposal is not as radical as it may seem because the proposed new rule would also be based on the Qur'an or Sunna, albeit on a new interpretation of the text. For example, the above-mentioned categorical verse 9:29 regulating the status of non-Muslims would be superseded by the more general verses providing for freedom of religion and inherent dignity of all human beings without distinction as to faith or belief.

I believe that the choice of texts to be implemented as modern Islamic Shari'a is systematic and not arbitrary; it is based on the timing and circumstances of revelation as well as the relationship of the text to the themes and objectives of Islam as a whole. Moreover, I maintain that the proposed reinterpretation is consistent with normal Arabic usage and apparent sense of the text. It is neither contrived nor strained. The ultimate test of legitimacy and efficacy is, of course, acceptance and implementation by Muslims throughout the world.

B. *Prospects for Acceptance and Likely Impact of the Proposed Reform*

In addition to this methodology's own Islamic legitimacy and cohesion, at least two main factors are likely to affect the acceptance and implementation of this or any other reform. It must be timely, addressing urgent concerns and issues facing Muslim societies, and it must be disseminated and discussed in Muslim countries. I believe that my proposal will be acceptable to Muslim peoples if offered in an effective and organized manner. Paradoxical as it may seem, I suspect that the proposal may face difficulties of dissemination and discussion precisely because it is timely.

This proposal is timely because Muslims throughout the world are sensitive to charges that their religious laws and cultural traditions permit and legitimize human rights violations; hence the efforts of contemporary Muslim authors to dispel such allegations. Governments of Muslim countries, like many other governments, formally subscribe to international human rights instruments because, in my view, they find the human rights idea an important legitimizing force both at home and abroad. Moreover, as explained earlier, many emerging women's organizations and modernist forces are now asserting and articulating their demands for justice and equality in terms of international human rights standards.

Nevertheless, the proposed reform will probably be resisted because it challenges the vested interests of powerful forces in the Muslim world and may upset male-dominated traditional political and social institutions. These forces probably will try to restrict opportunities for a genuine consideration of this reform methodology. It is equally likely that they will attempt to obstruct its acceptance and implementation in the name of Islamic orthodoxy. Proponents of Shari'a will also resist it because it challenges their view of the good Muslim society and the ideal Islamic state.

Consequently, the acceptance and implementation of this reform methodology will involve a political struggle within Muslim nations as part of a larger general struggle for human rights. I would recommend this proposal to participants in that struggle who champion the cause of justice and equality for women and non-Muslims, and freedom of belief and expression in the Muslim world. Given the extreme importance of Islamic legitimacy in Muslim societies, I urge human rights advocates to claim the Islamic platform and not concede it to the traditionalist and fundamentalist forces in their societies. I would also invite outside supporters of Muslim human rights advocates to express their support with due sensitivity and genuine concern for Islamic legitimacy in the Muslim world.

Questions for Reflection

1. What does An-Na'im mean when he refers to "cultural legitimacy" as a problem for the enforcement of international human rights standards?
2. What examples does An-Na'im provide to demonstrate how Shari'a and human rights conflict? In what ways must Shari'a be reformed, according to An-Na'im, if human rights are to be effectively protected in Muslim countries?
3. How would you evaluate the chances of reconciling Shari'a with international human rights standards? Do you think it is right that the Islamic religious tradition be reinterpreted so that it agrees with international standards?

FURTHER READINGS FOR SECTION 4

Am-Na'im, Abdullahi Ahmed, ed. *Human Rights in Cross-Cultural Perspectives: A Quest for Consensus*. Philadelphia: University of Pennsylvania Press, 1992.

Am-Na'im, Abdullahi Ahmed, and Francis M. Deng, eds. *Human Rights in Africa: Cross-Cultural Perspectives*. Washington, DC: Brookings Institution Press, 1990.

Cobbah, Josiah A.M. "African Values and the Human Rights Debate: An African Perspective." *Human Rights Quarterly* 9 (1987): 309-31.

Howard, Rhoda. "Is There an African Concept of Human Rights?" In *Foreign Policy and Human Rights*, R.J. Vincent, ed. Cambridge: Cambridge University Press, 1986.

Hsiung, James C., ed. *Human Rights in East Asia: A Cultural Perspective*. New York: Paragon House, 1985.

Inada, Kenneth K. "The Buddhist Perspective on Human Rights." In *Human Rights in Religious Traditions*, Arlene Swidler, ed. New York: Pilgrims Press, 1982.

Keown, Damien. "Are There 'Human Rights' in Buddhism?" *Journal of Buddhist Ethics* 2 (1995): 3-27.

Moosa, Najma. "Human Rights in Islam." *South African Journal on Human Rights* 14 (1998): 508-524.

Olayiwola, Abdur Rahman. "Human Rights in Islam." *The Islamic Quarterly* 36 (1992): 262-79.

Welch, Claude E., Jr., and Virginia A. Leary, eds. *Asian Perspectives on Human Rights*. Boulder: Westview Press, 1990.

Section 5:

DOCUMENTS FOR PART ONE

29. THE ENGLISH BILL OF RIGHTS (1689)

Whereas the Lords Spiritual and Temporal and Commons assembled at Westminster, lawfully, fully and freely representing all the estates of the people of this realm, did upon the thirteenth day of February in the year of our Lord one thousand six hundred eighty-eight present unto their Majesties, then called and known by the names and style of William and Mary, prince and princess of Orange, being present in their proper persons, a certain declaration in writing made by the said Lords and Commons in the words following, viz:

Whereas the late King James the Second, by the assistance of divers evil counsellors, judges and ministers employed by him, did endeavour to subvert and extirpate the Protestant religion and the laws and liberties of this kingdom;

By assuming and exercising a power of dispensing with and suspending of laws and the execution of laws without consent of Parliament;

By committing and prosecuting divers worthy prelates for humbly petitioning to be excused from concurring to the said assumed power;

By issuing and causing to be executed a commission under the great seal for erecting a court called the Court of Commissioners for Ecclesiastical Causes;

By levying money for and to the use of the Crown by pretence of prerogative for other time and in other manner than the same was granted by Parliament;

By raising and keeping a standing army within this kingdom in time of Peace without consent of Parliament, and quartering soldiers contrary to law;

By causing several good subjects being Protestants to be disarmed at the same time when papists were both armed and employed contrary to law;

By violating the freedom of election of members to serve in parliament;

By prosecutions in the Court of King's Bench for matters and causes cognizable only in parliament, and by divers other arbitrary and illegal courses;

And whereas of late years partial corrupt and unqualified persons have been returned and served on juries in trials, and particularly divers jurors in trials for high treason which were not freeholders;

And excessive bail hath been required of persons committed in criminal cases to elude the benefit of the laws made for the liberty of the subjects;

And excessive fines have been imposed;

And illegal and cruel punishments inflicted;

And several grants and promises made of fines and forfeitures before any conviction or judgment against the persons upon whom the same were to be levied;

All which are utterly and directly contrary to the known laws and statutes and freedom of this realm;

And whereas the said late King James the Second having abdicated the government and the throne being thereby vacant, his Highness the prince of Orange (whom it hath pleased Almighty God to make the glorious instrument of delivering this kingdom from popery and arbitrary power) did (by the advice of the Lords Spiritual and Temporal and divers principal persons of the Commons) cause letters to be written to the Lords Spiritual and Temporal being Protestants, and other letters to the several counties, cities, universities, boroughs and Cinque ports, for the choosing of such persons to represent them as were of right to be sent to Parliament, to meet and sit at Westminster upon the two and twentieth day of January in year one thousand six hundred eighty and eight, in order to such an establishment as that their religion, laws and liberties might not again be in danger of being subverted, upon which letters elections having been accordingly made;

And thereupon the said Lords Spiritual and Temporal and Commons, pursuant to their respective letters and elections, being now assembled in a full and free representative of this nation, taking into their most serious consideration the best means for attaining the ends aforesaid, do in the first place (as their ancestors in like case have usually done) for the vindicating and asserting their ancient rights and liberties declare:

That the pretended power of suspending of laws or the execution of laws by regal authority without consent of Parliament is illegal;

That the pretended power of dispensing with laws or the execution of laws by regal authority, as it hath been assumed and exercised of late, is illegal;

That the commission for erecting the late Court of Commissioners for Ecclesiastical Causes, and all other commissions and courts of like nature, are illegal and pernicious;

That levying money for or to the use of the Crown by pretence of prerogative, without grant of Parliament, for longer time, or in other manner than the same is or shall be granted, is illegal;

That it is the right of the subjects to petition the king, and all commitments and prosecutions for such petitioning are illegal;

That the raising or keeping a standing army within the kingdom in time of peace, unless it be with consent of Parliament, is against law;

That the subjects which are Protestants may have arms for their defence suitable to their conditions and as allowed by law;

That election of members of Parliament ought to be free;

That the freedom of speech and debates or proceedings in Parliament ought not to be impeached or questioned in any court or place out of Parliament;

That excessive bail ought not to be required, nor excessive fines imposed, nor cruel and unusual punishments inflicted;

That jurors ought to be duly impanelled and returned, and jurors which pass upon men in trials for high treason ought to be freeholders;

That all grants and promises of fines and forfeitures of particular persons before conviction are illegal and void;

And that for redress of all grievances, and for the amending, strengthening and preserving of the laws, Parliaments ought to be held frequently.

And they do claim, demand and insist upon all and singular the premises as their undoubted rights and liberties, and that no declarations, judgments, doings or proceedings to the prejudice of the people in any of the said premises ought in any wise to be drawn hereafter into consequence or example; to which demand of their rights they are particularly encouraged by the declaration of his Highness the prince of Orange as being the only means for obtaining a full redress and remedy therein. Having therefore an entire confidence that his said Highness the prince of Orange will perfect the deliverance so far advanced by him, and will still preserve them from the violation of their rights which they have here asserted, and from all other attempts upon their religion, rights and liberties, the said Lords Spiritual and Temporal and Commons assembled at Westminster do resolve that William and Mary, prince and princess of Orange, be and be declared king and queen of England, France and Ireland and the dominions thereunto belonging.

Now in pursuance of the premises, the Lords Spiritual and Temporal and Commons in Parliament assembled...do pray that...all and singular the rights and liberties asserted and claimed in the said declaration are the true, ancient and indubitable rights and liberties of the people of this kingdom, and...shall be firmly and strictly holden and observed...and all officers and ministers whatsoever shall serve Their Majesties and their successors according to the same in all times to come.

30. DECLARATION OF INDEPENDENCE OF THE UNITED STATES OF AMERICA (1776)

When in the Course of Human Events it becomes necessary for one people to dissolve the political bands which have connected them with another, and to assume among the Powers of the earth, the separate and equal station to which the Laws of Nature and of Nature's God entitle them, a decent respect to the opinions of mankind requires that they should declare the causes which impel them to the separation.

We hold these truths to be self-evident, that all men are created equal, that they are endowed by their Creator with certain unalienable Rights, that among these are Life, Liberty and the pursuit of Happiness.

That to secure these rights, Governments are instituted among Men, deriving their just powers from the consent of the governed, That whenever any Form of Government becomes destructive of these ends, it is the Right of the People to alter or to abolish it, and to institute a new Government, laying its foundation on such principles, and organizing its powers in such form, as to them shall seem most likely to effect their Safety and Happiness. Prudence, indeed, will dictate that Governments long established should not be changed for light and transient causes; and accordingly all experience hath shown, that mankind are more disposed to suffer, while evils are sufferable, than to right themselves by abolishing the forms to which they are accustomed. But when a long train of abuses and usurpations, pursuing invariably the same Object evinces a design to reduce them under absolute Despotism, it is their right, it is their duty, to throw off such Government, and to provide new Guards for their future security.—Such has been the patient sufferance of these Colonies; and such is now the necessity which constrains them to alter their former Systems of Government. The history of the present King of Great Britain is a history of repeated injuries and usurpations, all having in direct object the establishment of an absolute Tyranny over these States. To prove this, let Facts be submitted to a candid world.

He has refused his Assent to Laws, the most wholesome and necessary for the public good.

He has forbidden his Governors to pass Laws of immediate and pressing importance, unless suspended in their operation till his Assent should be obtained; and when so suspended, he has utterly neglected to attend to them.

He has refused to pass other Laws for the accommodation of large districts of people, unless those people would relinquish the right of Representation in the Legislature, a right inestimable to them and formidable to tyrants only.

He has called together legislative bodies at places unusual, uncomfortable, and distant from the depository of their Public Records, for the sole purpose of fatiguing them into compliance with his measures.

He has dissolved Representative Houses repeatedly, for opposing with manly firmness his invasions on the rights of the people.

He has refused for a long time, after such dissolutions, to cause others to be elected; whereby the Legislative Powers, incapable of Annihilation, have returned to the People at large for their exercise; the State remaining in the mean time exposed to all the dangers of invasion from without, and convulsions within.

He has endeavored to prevent the population of these States; for that purpose obstructing the Laws of Naturalization of Foreigners; refusing to pass others to encourage their migrations hither, and raising the conditions of new Appropriations of Lands.

He has obstructed the Administration of Justice, by refusing his Assent to Laws for establishing Judiciary Powers.

He has made Judges dependent on his Will alone, for the tenure of their offices, and the amount and payment of their salaries.

He has erected a multitude of New Offices, and sent hither swarms of Officers to harass our People, and eat out their substance.

He has kept among us, in times of peace, Standing Armies without the Consent of our legislature.

He has affected to render the Military independent of and superior to the Civil Power.

He has combined with others to subject us to a jurisdiction foreign to our constitution, and unacknowledged by our laws; giving his Assent to their acts of pretended legislation: For quartering large bodies of armed troops among us: For protecting them, by a mock Trial, from Punishment for any Murders which they should commit on the Inhabitants of these States: For cutting off our trade with all parts of the world: For imposing Taxes on us without our Consent: For depriving us in many cases, of the benefits of Trial by Jury: For transporting us beyond Seas to be tried for pretended offences: For abolishing the free System of English Laws in a neighboring Province, establishing therein an Arbitrary government, and enlarging its Boundaries so as to render it at once an example and fit instrument for introducing the same absolute rule into these Colonies: For taking away our Charters, abolishing our most valuable Laws, and altering fundamentally the Forms of our Governments: For suspending our own Legislature, and declaring themselves invested with Power to legislate for us in all cases whatsoever.

He has abdicated Government here, by declaring us out of his Protection and waging War against us.

He has plundered our seas, ravaged our Coasts, burnt our towns, and destroyed the lives of our people.

He is, at this time, transporting large armies of foreign mercenaries to complete the works of death, desolation and tyranny, already begun with circumstances of Cruelty and perfidy scarcely paralleled in the most barbarous ages, and totally unworthy the Head of a civilized nation.

He has constrained our fellow Citizens taken Captive on the high Seas to bear Arms against their Country, to become the executioners of their friends and Brethren, or to fall themselves by their Hands.

He has excited domestic insurrections amongst us, and has

endeavored to bring on the inhabitants of our frontiers, the merciless Indian Savages, whose known rule of warfare, is an undistinguished destruction of all ages, sexes and conditions.

In every stage of these Oppressions We have Petitioned for Redress in the most humble terms: Our repeated Petitions have been answered only by repeated injury. A Prince, whose character is thus marked by every act which may define a Tyrant, is unfit to be the ruler of a free People.

Nor have We been wanting in attentions to our British brethren. We have warned them from time to time of attempts by their legislature to extend an unwarrantable jurisdiction over us. We have reminded them of the circumstances of our emigration and settlement here. We have appealed to their native justice and magnanimity, and we have conjured them by the ties of our common kindred to disavow these usurpations, which, would inevitably interrupt our connections and correspondence. They too have been deaf to the voice of justice and of consanguinity. We must, therefore, acquiesce in the necessity, which denounces our Separation, and hold them, as we hold the rest of mankind, Enemies in War, in Peace Friends.

We, therefore, the Representatives of the United States of America, in General Congress, Assembled, appealing to the Supreme Judge of the world for the rectitude of our intentions, do, in the Name, and by Authority of the good People of these Colonies, solemnly publish and declare, That these United Colonies are, and of Right ought to be Free and Independent States; that they are Absolved from all Allegiance to the British Crown, and that all political connection between them and the State of Great Britain, is and ought to be totally dissolved; and that as Free and Independent States, they have full power to levy War, conclude Peace, contract Alliance, establish Commerce, and to do all other Acts and Things which Independent States may of right do. And for the support of this Declaration, with a firm reliance on the Protection of Divine Providence, we mutually pledge to each other our Lives, our Fortunes and our sacred Honor.

31. THE BILL OF RIGHTS OF THE UNITED STATES OF AMERICA (1791)

Articles in Addition to, and Amendment of, the Constitution of the United States of America, proposed by Congress, and ratified by the Legislatures of the Several States pursuant to the Fifth Article of the Original Constitution:

Amendment I

Congress shall make no law respecting an establishment of religion, or prohibiting the free exercise thereof; or abridging the freedom of speech, or of the press; or the right of the people peaceably to assemble, and to petition the Government for a redress of grievances.

Amendment II

A well-regulated militia, being necessary to the security of a free State, the right of the people to keep and bear arms, shall not be infringed.

Amendment III

No soldier shall, in time of peace, be quartered in any house, without the consent of the owner, nor in time of war, but in a manner to be prescribed by law.

Amendment IV

The right of the people to be secure in their persons, houses, papers, and effects, against unreasonable searches and seizures, shall not be violated, and no warrants shall issue, but upon probable cause, supported by oath or affirmation, and particularly describing the place to be searched, and the persons or things to be seized.

Amendment V

No person shall be held to answer for a capital, or otherwise infamous crime, unless on a presentment or indictment of a Grand Jury, except in cases arising in the land or naval forces, or in the militia, when in actual service, in time of war or public danger; nor shall any person be subject for the same offense to be twice put in jeopardy of life or limb; nor shall be compelled in any criminal case to be a witness against himself, nor be deprived of life, liberty, or property, without due process of law; nor shall private property be taken for public use, without just compensation.

Amendment VI

In all criminal prosecutions, the accused shall enjoy the right to a speedy and public trial, by an impartial jury of the State and district wherein the crime shall have been committed, which districts shall have been previously ascertained by law, and to be informed of the nature and cause of the accusation; to be confronted with the witnesses against him; to have compulsory process for obtaining witnesses in his favor, and to have the assistance of counsel for his defense.

Amendment VII

In suits at common law, where the value in controversy shall exceed twenty dollars, the right of trial by jury shall be preserved, and no fact tried by a jury shall be otherwise reexamined in any court of the United States, than according to the rules of the common law.

Amendment VIII

Excessive bail shall not be required, nor excessive fines imposed, nor cruel and unusual punishments inflicted.

Amendment IX

The enumeration in the Constitution of certain rights shall not be construed to deny or disparage others retained by the people.

Amendment X

The powers not delegated to the United States by the Constitution, nor prohibited by it to the States, are reserved to the States respectively, or to the people.

Amendment XIII (1868)

1. Neither slavery nor involuntary servitude, except as a punishment for crime whereof the party shall have been duly convicted, shall exist within the United States, or any place subject to their jurisdiction.

2. Congress shall have power to enforce this article by appropriate legislation.

Amendment XV (1870)

1. The right of citizens of the United States to vote shall not be denied or abridged by the United States or by any State on account of race, color, or previous condition of servitude.

2. The Congress shall have power to enforce this article by appropriate legislation.

Amendment XIX (1920)

1. The right of citizens of the United States to vote shall not be denied or abridged by the United States or by any State on account of sex.

2. The Congress shall have power to enforce this article by appropriate legislation.

32. FRENCH DECLARATION OF THE RIGHTS OF MAN AND OF THE CITIZEN (1789)

The representatives of the French people, formed into a National Assembly, considering that ignorance, disregard or contempt of the rights of man are the sole causes of public misfortunes and of the corruption of governments, have resolved to set forth in a solemn declaration the natural, inalienable and sacred rights of man, in order that this declaration, continually before all members of the body politic, may be a perpetual reminder of their rights and duties; in order that the acts of the legislative power and those of the executive power, since they may constantly be compared with the aim of every political institution, may thereby be more respected; in order that the demands of the citizens, founded henceforth on simple and incontestable principles, may always be directed towards the maintenance of the Constitution and the welfare of all. Accordingly, the National Assembly recognizes and proclaims, in the presence and under the auspices of the Supreme Being, the following rights of man and of the citizen:

1. Men are born and remain free and equal in rights. Social distinctions may be based only upon considerations of general usefulness.

2. The aim of every political association is the preservation of the natural and inalienable rights of man. These rights are liberty, property, security, and resistance to oppression.

3. The source of all sovereignty resides essentially in the nation; no body, no individual may exercise authority not emanating expressly therefrom.

4. Liberty consists of the power to do whatever is not injurious to others; thus, the exercise of the natural rights of every man has for its limits only those that assure other members of

society the enjoyment of those same rights. These limits may be determined only by law.

5. The law has the right to forbid only those actions which are injurious to society. Whatever is not forbidden by law may not be prevented, and no one may be constrained to do what it does not command.

6. The law is the expression of the general will. All citizens have the right to participate personally, or through their representatives, in its formation. The law must be the same for all, whether it protects or punishes. All citizens, being equal before it, are equally admissible to all high offices, public positions, and employments, according to their capacities and without other distinction than that of their virtues and talents.

7. No man may be accused, arrested or detained, except in the cases determined by law and according to the procedures which it has prescribed. Those who solicit, expedite, execute, or cause to be executed arbitrary orders must be punished; but any citizen summoned or apprehended in pursuance of the law must obey immediately; he renders himself culpable by resistance.

8. The law is to establish only penalties that are absolutely and obviously necessary; and no one may be punished except by virtue of a law established and promulgated prior to the offence and legally applied.

9. Since every man is presumed innocent until declared guilty, if arrest be deemed indispensable, all unnecessary severity for securing the suspect must be severely repressed by law.

10. No one is to be persecuted because of his opinions, even religious ones, provided their manifestation does not disturb the public order established by law.

11. Free communication of ideas and opinions is one of the most precious of the rights of man. Consequently, every citizen may speak, write and print freely; yet he may have to answer for the abuse of that liberty in the cases determined by law.

12. The guarantee of the rights of man and of the citizen necessitates a public force; this force is, therefore, instituted for the advantage of all and not for the particular use of those to whom it is entrusted.

13. For the maintenance of the public force and for the expenses of administration, a common tax is indispensable; it must be assessed equally among all citizens in proportion to their means.

14. All citizens have the right to ascertain, by themselves or through their representatives, the necessity of the public tax, to consent to it freely, to supervise its use and to determine its amount, assessment basis, collection and duration.

15. Society has the right to require of every public official an accounting of his administration.

16. Any society in which the guarantee of rights is not assured, or the separation of powers not determined, has no constitution at all.

17. Since property is an inviolable and sacred right, no one may be deprived thereof unless a legally established public necessity obviously requires it, and on condition of just and prior compensation.

33. UNIVERSAL DECLARATION OF HUMAN RIGHTS (1948)

Preamble

Whereas recognition of the inherent dignity and of the equal and inalienable rights of all members of the human family is the foundation of freedom, justice and peace in the world,

Whereas disregard and contempt for human rights have resulted in barbarous acts which have outraged the conscience of mankind, and the advent of a world in which human beings shall enjoy freedom of speech and belief and freedom from fear and want has been proclaimed as the highest aspiration of the common people,

Whereas it is essential, if man is not to be compelled to have recourse, as a last resort, to rebellion against tyranny and oppression, that human rights should be protected by the rule of law,

Whereas it is essential to promote the development of friendly relations between nations,

Whereas the peoples of the United Nations have in the Charter reaffirmed their faith in fundamental human rights, in the dignity and worth of the human person and in the equal rights of men and women and have determined to promote social progress and better standards of life in larger freedom,

Whereas Member States have pledged themselves to achieve, in co-operation with the United Nations, the promotion of universal respect for and observance of human rights and fundamental freedoms,

Whereas a common understanding of these rights and freedoms is of the greatest importance for the full realization of this pledge,

Now, Therefore
The General Assembly

Proclaims this Universal Declaration of Human Rights as a common standard of achievement for all peoples and all nations, to the end that every individual and every organ of society, keeping this Declaration constantly in mind, shall strive by teaching and education to promote respect for these rights and freedoms and by progressive measures, national and international, to secure their universal and effective recognition and observance, both among the peoples of Member States themselves and among the peoples of territories under their jurisdiction.

Article 1. All human beings are born free and equal in dignity and rights. They are endowed with reason and conscience and should act towards one another in a spirit of brotherhood.

Article 2. Everyone is entitled to all the rights and freedoms set forth in this Declaration, without distinction of any kind, such as race, colour, sex, language, religion, political or other opinion, national or social origin, property, birth or other status.

Furthermore, no distinction shall be made on the basis of the political, jurisdictional or international status of the country or territory to which a person belongs, whether it be independent, trust, non-self-governing or under any other limitation of sovereignty.

Article 3. Everyone has the right to life, liberty and security of person.

Article 4. No one shall be held in slavery or servitude; slavery and the slave trade shall be prohibited in all their forms.

Article 5. No one shall be subjected to torture or to cruel, inhuman or degrading treatment or punishment.

Article 6. Everyone has the right to recognition everywhere as a person before the law.

Article 7. All are equal before the law and are entitled without any discrimination to equal protection of the law. All are entitled to equal protection against any discrimination in violation of this Declaration and against any incitement to such discrimination.

Article 8. Everyone has the right to an effective remedy by the competent national tribunals for acts violating the fundamental rights granted him by the constitution or by law.

Article 9. No one shall be subjected to arbitrary arrest, detention or exile.

Article 10. Everyone is entitled in full equality to a fair and public hearing by an independent and impartial tribunal, in the determination of his rights and obligations and of any criminal charge against him.

Article 11.-1. Everyone charged with a penal offence has the right to be presumed innocent until proved guilty according to law in a public trial at which he has had all the guarantees necessary for his defence.

2. No one shall be held guilty of any penal offence on account of any act or omission which did not constitute a penal offence, under national or international law, at the time when it was committed. Nor shall a heavier penalty be imposed than the one that was applicable at the time the penal offence was committed.

Article 12. No one shall be subjected to arbitrary interference with his privacy, family, home or correspondence, nor to attacks upon his honour and reputation. Everyone has the right to the protection of the law against such interference or attacks.

Article 13.-1. Everyone has the right to freedom of movement and residence within the borders of each state.

2. Everyone has the right to leave any country, including his own, and to return to his country.

Article 14.-1. Everyone has the right to seek and to enjoy in other countries asylum from persecution.

2. This right may not be invoked in the case of prosecutions genuinely arising from non-political crimes or from acts contrary to the purposes and principles of the United Nations.

Article 15.-1. Everyone has the right to a nationality.

2. No one shall be arbitrarily deprived of his nationality nor denied the right to change his nationality.

Article 16.-1. Men and women of full age, without any limitation due to race, nationality or religion, have the right to marry and to found a family. They are entitled to equal rights as to marriage, during marriage and at its dissolution.

2. Marriage shall be entered into only with the free and full consent of the intending spouses.

3. The family is the natural and fundamental group unit of society and is entitled to protection by society and the State.

Article 17.-1. Everyone has the right to own property alone as well as in association with others.

2. No one shall be arbitrarily deprived of his property.

Article 18. Everyone has the right to freedom of thought, conscience and religion; this right includes freedom to change his religion or belief, and freedom, either alone or in community with others and in public or private, to manifest his religion or belief in teaching, practice, worship and observance.

Article 19. Everyone has the right to freedom of opinion and expression; this right includes freedom to hold opinions without interference and to seek, receive and impart information and ideas through any media and regardless of frontiers.

Article 20.-1. Everyone has the right to freedom of peaceful assembly and association.

2. No one may be compelled to belong to an association.

Article 21.-1. Everyone has the right to take part in the government of his country, directly or through freely chosen representatives.

2. Everyone has the right of equal access to public service in his country.

3. The will of the people shall be the basis of the authority of government; this will shall be expressed in periodic and genuine elections which shall be by universal and equal suffrage and shall be held by secret vote or by equivalent free voting procedures.

Article 22. Everyone, as a member of society, has the right to social security and is entitled to realization, through national effort and international co-operation and in accordance with the organization and resources of each State, of the economic, social and cultural rights indispensable for his dignity and the free development of his personality.

Article 23.-1. Everyone has the right to work, to free choice of employment, to just and favourable conditions of work and to protection against unemployment.

2. Everyone, without any discrimination, has the right to equal pay for equal work.

3. Everyone who works has the right to just and favourable remuneration ensuring for himself and his family an existence worthy of human dignity, and supplemented, if necessary, by other means of social protection.

4. Everyone has the right to form and to join trade unions for the protection of his interests.

Article 24. Everyone has the right to rest and leisure, including reasonable limitation of working hours and periodic holidays with pay.

Article 25.-1. Everyone has the right to a standard of living adequate for the health and well-being of himself and of his family, including food, clothing, housing and medical care and necessary social services, and the right to security in the event of unemployment, sickness, disability, widowhood, old age or other lack of livelihood in circumstances beyond his control.

2. Motherhood and childhood are entitled to special care and assistance. All children, whether born in or out of wedlock, shall enjoy the same social protection.

Article 26.-1. Everyone has the right to education. Education shall be free, at least in the elementary and fundamental stages. Elementary education shall be compulsory. Technical and professional education shall be made generally available and higher education shall be equally accessible to all on the basis of merit.

2. Education shall be directed to the full development of the human personality and to the strengthening of respect for human rights and fundamental freedoms. It shall promote understanding, tolerance and friendship among all nations, racial or religious groups, and shall further the activities of the United Nations for the maintenance of peace.

3. Parents have a prior right to choose the kind of education that shall be given to their children.

Article 27.-1. Everyone has the right freely to participate in the cultural life of the community, to enjoy the arts and to share in scientific advancement and its benefits.

2. Everyone has the right to the protection of the moral and

material interests resulting from any scientific, literary or artistic production of which he is the author.

Article 28. Everyone is entitled to a social and international order in which the rights and freedoms set forth in this Declaration can be fully realized.

Article 29.-1. Everyone has duties to the community in which alone the free and full development of his personality is possible.

2. In the exercise of his rights and freedoms, everyone shall be subject only to such limitations as are determined by law solely for the purpose of securing due recognition and respect for the rights and freedoms of others and of meeting the just requirements of morality, public order and the general welfare in a democratic society.

3. These rights and freedoms may in no case be exercised contrary to the purposes and principles of the United Nations.

Article 30. Nothing in this Declaration may be interpreted as implying for any State, group or person any right to engage in any activity or to perform any act aimed at the destruction of any of the rights and freedoms set forth herein.

34. AFRICAN CHARTER ON HUMAN AND PEOPLES' RIGHTS

Preamble

The African States members of the Organization of African Unity, parties to the present convention entitled "African Charter on Human and Peoples' Rights,"

Recalling Decision 115 (XVI) of the Assembly of Heads of State and Government at its Sixteenth Ordinary Session held in Monrovia, Liberia, from 17 to 20 July 1979 on the preparation of a "preliminary draft on an African Charter on Human and Peoples' Rights providing *inter alia* for the establishment of bodies to promote and protect human and peoples' rights";

Considering the Charter of the Organization of African Unity, which stipulates that "freedom, equality, justice and dignity are essential objectives for the achievement of the legitimate aspirations of the African peoples";

Reaffirming the pledge they solemnly made in Article 2 of the said Charter to eradicate all forms of colonialism from Africa, to coordinate and intensify their cooperation and efforts to achieve a better life for the peoples of Africa and to promote international cooperation having due regard to the Charter of the United Nations and the Universal Declaration of Human Rights;

Taking into consideration the virtues of their historical tradition and the values of African civilization which should inspire and characterize their reflection on the concept of human and peoples' rights; Recognizing on the one hand, that fundamental human rights stem from the attributes of human beings which justifies their national and international protection and on the other hand that the reality and respect of peoples' rights should necessarily guarantee human rights;

Considering that the enjoyment of rights and freedoms also implies the performance of duties on the part of everyone;

Convinced that it is henceforth essential to pay a particular attention to the right to development and that civil and political rights cannot be dissociated from economic, social and cultural rights in their conception as well as universality and that the satisfaction of economic, social and cultural rights ia a guarantee for the enjoyment of civil and political rights;

Conscious of their duty to achieve the total liberation of Africa, the peoples of which are still struggling for their dignity and genuine independence, and undertaking to eliminate colonialism, neo-colonialism, apartheid, zionism and to dismantle aggressive foreign military bases and all forms of discrimination, particularly those based on race, ethnic group, color, sex, language, religion or political opinions;

Reaffirming their adherence to the principles of human and peoples' rights and freedoms contained in the declarations, conventions and other instrument adopted by the Organization of African Unity, the Movement of Non-Aligned Countries and the United Nations;

Firmly convinced of their duty to promote and protect human and peoples' rights and freedoms taking into account the importance traditionally attached to these rights and freedoms in Africa;

Have agreed as follows:

PART I: RIGHTS AND DUTIES

Chapter I—Human and Peoples' Rights

Article 1. The Member States of the Organization of African Unity parties to the present Charter shall recognize the rights, duties and freedoms enshrined in this Chapter and shall undertake to adopt legislative or other measures to give effect to them.

Article 2. Every individual shall be entitled to the enjoyment of the rights and freedoms recognized and guaranteed in the present Charter without distinction of any kind such as race, ethnic group, color, sex, language, religion, political or any other opinion, national and social origin, fortune, birth or other status.

Article 3.-1. Every individual shall be equal before the law.

2. Every individual shall be entitled to equal protection of the law.

Article 4. Human beings are inviolable. Every human being shall be entitled to respect for his life and the integrity of his person. No one may be arbitrarily deprived of this right.

Article 5. Every individual shall have the right to the respect of the dignity inherent in a human being and to the recognition of his legal status. All forms of exploitation and degradation of man particularly slavery, slave trade, torture, cruel, inhuman or degrading punishment and treatment shall be prohibited.

Article 6. Every individual shall have the right to liberty and to the security of his person. No one may be deprived of his freedom except for reasons and conditions previously laid down by law. In particular, no one may be arbitrarily arrested or detained.

Article 7.-1. Every individual shall have the right to have his cause heard. This comprises: (a) the right to an appeal to competent national organs against acts of violating his fundamental rights as recognized and guaranteed by conventions, laws, regulations and customs in force; (b) the right to be presumed innocent until proved guilty by a competent court or tribunal; (c) the right to defence, including the right to be defended by counsel of his choice; (d) the right to be tried within a reasonable time by an impartial court or tribunal.

2. No one may be condemned for an act or omission which did not constitute a legally punishable offence at the time it was committed. No penalty may be inflicted for an offence for which no provision was made at the time it was committed. Punishment is personal and can be imposed only on the offender.

Article 8. Freedom of conscience, the profession and free practice of religion shall be guaranteed. No one may, subject to law and order, be submitted to measures restricting the exercise of these freedoms.

Article 9.-1. Every individual shall have the right to receive information.

2. Every individual shall have the right to express and disseminate his opinions within the law.

Article 10.-1. Every individual shall have the right to free association provided that he abides by the law.

2. Subject to the obligation of solidarity provided for in 29 no one may be compelled to join an association.

Article 11. Every individual shall have the right to assemble freely with others. The exercise of this right shall be subject only to necessary restrictions provided for by law in particular those enacted in the interest of national security, the safety, health, ethics and rights and freedoms of others.

Article 12.-1. Every individual shall have the right to freedom of movement and residence within the borders of a State provided he abides by the law.

2. Every individual shall have the right to leave any country including his own, and to return to his country. This right may only be subject to restrictions, provided for by law for the protection of national security, law and order, public health or morality.

3. Every individual shall have the right, when persecuted, to seek and obtain asylum in other countries in accordance with laws of those countries and international conventions.

4. A non-national legally admitted in a territory of a State Party to the present Charter, may only be expelled from it by virtue of a decision taken in accordance with the law.

5. The mass expulsion of non-nationals shall be prohibited. Mass expulsion shall be that which is aimed at national, racial, ethnic or religious groups.

Article 13.-1. Every citizen shall have the right to participate freely in the government of his country, either directly or through freely chosen representatives in accordance with the provisions of the law.

2. Every citizen shall have the right of equal access to the public service of his country.

3. Every individual shall have the right of access to public property and services in strict equality of all persons before the law.

Article 14. The right to property shall be guaranteed. It may only be encroached upon in the interest of public need or in the general interest of the community and in accordance with the provisions of appropriate laws.

Article 15. Every individual shall have the right to work under equitable and satisfactory conditions, and shall receive equal pay for equal work.

Article 16.-1. Every individual shall have the right to enjoy the best attainable state of physical and mental health.

2. States parties to the present Charter shall take the necessary measures to protect the health of their people and to ensure that they receive medical attention when they are sick.

Article 17.-1. Every individual shall have the right to education.

2. Every individual may freely, take part in the cultural life of his community.

3. The promotion and protection of morals and traditional values recognized by the community shall be the duty of the State.

Article 18.-1. The family shall be the natural unit and basis of society. It shall be protected by the State which shall take care of its physical health and moral.

2. The State shall have the duty to assist the family which is the custodian of morals and traditional values recognized by the community.

3. The State shall ensure the elimination of every discrimination against women and also ensure the protection of the rights of the woman and the child as stipulated in international declarations and conventions.

4. The aged and the disabled shall also have the right to special measures of protection in keeping with their physical or moral needs.

Article 19. All peoples shall be equal; they shall enjoy the same respect and shall have the same rights. Nothing shall justify the domination of a people by another.

Article 20.-1. All peoples shall have the right to existence. They shall have the unquestionable and inalienable right to self-determination. They shall freely determine their political status and shall pursue their economic and social development according to the policy they have freely chosen.

2. Colonized or oppressed peoples shall have the right to free themselves from the bonds of domination by resorting to any means recognized by the international community.

3. All peoples shall have the right to the assistance of the States parties to the present Charter in their liberation struggle against foreign domination, be it political, economic or cultural.

Article 21.-1. All peoples shall freely dispose of their wealth and natural resources. This right shall be exercised in the exclusive interest of the people. In no case shall a people be deprived of it.

2. In case of spoliation the dispossessed people shall have the right to the lawful recovery of its property as well as to an adequate compensation.

3. The free disposal of wealth and natural resources shall be exercised without prejudice to the obligation of promoting international economic cooperation based on mutual respect, equitable exchange and the principles of international law.

4. States parties to the present Charter shall individually and collectively exercise the right to free disposal of their wealth and natural resources with a view to strengthening African unity and solidarity.

5. States parties to the present Charter shall undertake to eliminate all forms of foreign economic exploitation particularly that practiced by international monopolies so as to enable their peoples to fully benefit from the advantages derived from their national resources.

Article 22.-1. All peoples shall have the right to their economic, social and cultural development with due regard to their freedom and identity and in the equal enjoyment of the common heritage of mankind.

2. States shall have the duty, individually or collectively, to ensure the exercise of the right to development.

Article 23.-1. All peoples shall have the right to national and international peace and security. The principles of solidarity and friendly relations implicitly affirmed by the Charter of the United

Nations and reaffirmed by that of the Organization of African Unity shall govern relations between States.

2. For the purpose of strengthening peace, solidarity and friendly relations, States parties to the present Charter shall ensure that: (a) any individual enjoying the right of asylum under 12 of the present Charter shall not engage in subversive activities against his country of origin or any other State party to the present Charter; (b) their territories shall not be used as bases for subversive or terrorist activities against the people of any other State party to the present Charter.

Article 24. All peoples shall have the right to a general satisfactory environment favorable to their development.

Article 25. States parties to the present Charter shall have the duty to promote and ensure through teaching, education and publication, the respect of the rights and freedoms contained in the present Charter and to see to it that these freedoms and rights as well as corresponding obligations and duties are understood.

Article 26. States parties to the present Charter shall have the duty to guarantee the independence of the Courts and shall allow the establishment and improvement of appropriate national institutions entrusted with the promotion and protection of the rights and freedoms guaranteed by the present Charter.

Chapter II—Duties

Article 27.-1. Every individual shall have duties towards his family and society, the State and other legally recognized communities and the international community.

2. The rights and freedoms of each individual shall be exercised with due regard to the rights of others, collective security, morality and common interest.

Article 28. Every individual shall have the duty to respect and consider his fellow beings without discrimination, and to maintain relations aimed at promoting, safeguarding and reinforcing mutual respect and tolerance.

Article 29. The individual shall also have the duty:

1. To preserve the harmonious development of the family and to work for the cohesion and respect of the family; to respect his

parents at all times, to maintain them in case of need;

2. To serve his national community by placing his physical and intellectual abilities at its service;

3. Not to compromise the security of the State whose national or resident he is;

4. To preserve and strengthen social and national solidarity, particularly when the latter is threatened;

5. To preserve and strengthen the national independence and the territorial integrity of his country and to contribute to its defence in accordance with the law;

6. To work to the best of his abilities and competence, and to pay taxes imposed by law in the interest of the society;

7. to preserve and strengthen positive African cultural values in his relations with other members of the society, in the spirit of tolerance, dialogue and consultation and, in general, to contribute to the promotion of the moral well being of society;

8. To contribute to the best of his abilities, at all times and at all levels, to the promotion and achievement of African unity.

PART TWO

Introduction to Part Two:

CONTEMPORARY ISSUES

As the readings in Part One demonstrate, the idea of human rights has received a great deal of attention from scholars around the world. Thinkers of many different persuasions have sought to provide answers to questions concerning what is meant by human rights, what are the sources of human rights, and which rights are human rights. Yet the considerable theoretical analysis of human rights surveyed in Part One does not exhaust the subject. The philosophical exploration of fundamental conceptual issues is pertinent, of course, in the quest to develop human rights in the international context, in order to achieve a more just world order. This quest necessarily engages with difficult human rights issues that are social, political, and legal in nature. The readings contained in Part Two are intended to illuminate the connections between theory and practice that define the contemporary struggle for human rights by looking at a number of specific debates and problems.

Prior to the end of World War II, even before the full extent of Nazi atrocities became widespread public knowledge, the leaders of the democratic states fighting against the Axis coalition of Germany and Japan portrayed their efforts as attempts to halt the spread of totalitarian threats to freedom and human rights. Speaking to the US Congress in his State of the Union Address of January, 1941, President Franklin D. Roosevelt proclaimed:

> In the future days, which we seek to make secure, we look forward to a world founded upon four essential human freedoms.
>
> The first is freedom of speech and expression—everywhere in the world.
>
> The second is freedom of every person to worship God in his own way—everywhere in the world.

> The third is freedom from want—which, translated into world terms, means economic understandings which secure to every nation a healthy peacetime life for its inhabitants—everywhere in the world.
>
> The fourth is freedom from fear—which, translated into world terms, means a world-wide reduction of armaments to such a point and in such a thorough fashion that no nation will be in a position to commit an act of physical aggression against any neighbor—anywhere in the world.
>
> That is no vision of a distant millennium. It is a definite basis for a kind of world attainable in our time and generation. That kind of world is the very antithesis of the so-called new order of tyranny which the dictators seek to create with the crash of a bomb.
>
> To that new order we oppose the greater conception—the moral order....
>
> Freedom means the supremacy of human rights everywhere. Our support goes to those who struggle to gain those rights or keep them.[1]

The "four freedoms" identified by Roosevelt became the basic standards for the formal elaboration of international human rights undertaken by the United Nations following World War II. The United Nations was founded in 1945 when 51 of the world's states sent representatives to San Francisco to establish a new collective-security organization. The UN Charter explains that the fundamental objectives of the UN are to "save succeeding generations from the scourge of war," and to "reaffirm faith in fundamental human rights, in the dignity and worth of the human person, in the equal rights of men and women and of nations large and small."

Although the Charter refers to human rights in several places it does not define what those rights are. Thus, one of the first tasks the United Nations assumed was to produce a document that would specifically stipulate international human rights norms. The result was the Universal Declaration of Human Rights (UDHR), which was unanimously adopted by the UN General Assembly on December 10, 1948. Because the UDHR is a resolution and not a treaty, it is not legally binding. However, over time the Universal Declaration has become a part of customary international law. In addition, the UDHR has been supplemented by two treaties that give human rights binding force in international law, both adopted by the General Assembly in 1966: (1) the International Covenant on Civil and Political Rights, and (2) the International Covenant on Economic, Social and Cultural Rights. These three documents, plus various associated human rights instruments, are known collectively as the International Bill of Human Rights. With the production of these formal human rights agreements the international political system has increasingly recognized that the rights and dignity of each human being ought to be respected and protected. Just as important, it is now the case that violations of human rights by governments are considered matters of international action and concern, justifying investigation, diplomatic pressure, economic sanctions and, perhaps, military intervention.

Clearly, the past fifty years have seen remarkable developments in the movement to codify and enforce robust human rights standards. Despite this international attention to human rights, though, a number of problematic issues either remain unresolved or have arisen due to changes in world politics. One such issue concerns the alleged universal nature of human rights. As we have seen, human rights are supposed to be the rights that all humans have simply because they are human. In this view, human rights belong to all persons, in all places, at all times. This position, referred to as *universalism*, endorses the universal character of human rights norms. A contrary position, referred to as *relativism*, sees moral norms as historically and culturally determined, rather than as universal. With regard to human rights, relativists contend that each society is the proper source of judgments about which rights and duties are legitimate. Thus, human rights may differ from one society to another. The debate between universalism and relativism has been prominent for a number of years and points to the tensions that can exist between the desire to respect the rights of every individual, regardless of their race, sex, religion and nationality, and the desire to respect differences between cultures and nations that may not be easily reconciled with the universal prescriptions of human rights.

The cultural particularities of peoples and nations present another difficulty for contemporary human rights. Since the adoption of the Universal Declaration the number of states in the world has increased dramatically, from around 60 to nearly 200, due to the process of decolonization that ended Western colonial rule throughout Asia and Africa. Decolonization was spurred on by assertions of the rights not only of individuals but also of peoples, that is, of the collective rights of communities. The rights of peoples became integral to secessionist or autonomy movements which sought to claim their right to self-determination. As a result an important human rights issue emerged that focuses on minority groups and indigenous cultures that face the threatened or actual violation of their right to exist *as a group* by some government or other dominant cultural group. How well traditional conceptions of human rights, which tend to focus on individual rights rather than collective rights, are able to address these concerns remains an issue within the human rights movement.

The right of self-determination in connection with the claims of distinct ethnic groups poses another significant human rights problem. Most nations of the world today are ethnically diverse, composed of numerous ethnic minorities as well as dominant ethnic groups. In the postcolonial and post-Cold War era, ethnic conflicts have become increasingly widespread. Many ethnic communities are disaffected, either resentful of historical dominations and oppressions carried out by other ethnic groups or fearful that their cultural distinctness is being jeopardized by competing populations. Some cultural communities have attempted to assert their right to self-determination within existing states, even resorting to force in pursuit of their autonomy.[2] Tragic expressions of such ethnic conflict can be found in the Rwandan genocide of 1994 and in the brutal campaigns of "ethnic cleansing" throughout the former Yugoslavia since the early 1990s.

Ethnic cleansing is the genocidal effort to "purify" a territory through the intentional murder and forced migration of one ethnic group by another. Because ethnic cleansing constitutes a massive violation of human rights, and since the United Nations criminalized genocide with the 1948 Convention on the Prevention and Punishment of the Crime of Genocide, the issue is raised as to what obligations the international community has when genocide occurs. One possible response, which has gained greater support over the past decade, is to resort to international military intervention. Intervention can be justified on both humanitarian grounds—to prohibit the violation of people's rights; to provide necessary goods such as food, shelter and medical assistance; and to help repatriate civilian refugees displaced by conflict—and security grounds—to prevent the conflict from escalating across borders into neighboring states. Nevertheless, the possibility of intervention raises several questions for an international political system built around the sovereignty of independent states: Do the norms of international human rights law override the domestic laws of sovereign states? Who will enforce the international norms, and how? And, what happens after the intervention has taken place?

Another important issue in contemporary world politics and human rights concerns the treatment and status of women. The universal character of human rights requires that all human rights be secured equally for men and women. Unfortunately, women around the world still are consistently denied many of their rights simply because of their gender. This is true not only in many developing countries where traditional social roles and cultural values often conflict with the ideals of gender equality, but also in industrialized nations where women are discriminated against in both overt and covert fashion. Violations of women's human rights take many forms: women have less access to education and training, so that illiteracy is much higher among women than men; women are paid less than men for the same jobs and the majority of the unemployed are women, leaving them in a subordinate social and economic status; women continue to be subjected to violence resulting in physical, sexual and psychological harm, in the home (domestic abuse), the workplace (sexual harassment), the community (rape, prostitution, slavery), and by the state (abuse in prisons and rape as a form of political violence or genocide). While steps have been taken to address the specific problems facing women in their search for equal rights, such as the 1979 Convention on the Elimination of All Forms of Discrimination against Women, violations of the rights of women continue to be a common affront to their human dignity.

Sex discrimination can be based not only on a person's gender but also on their sexual orientation. One frequently overlooked yet prevalent form of discrimination that results in human rights violations is specific to or primarily directed against gays and lesbians. Because of the deep biases against homosexuality that characterize many traditional social, cultural, and religious beliefs, this is an issue that demands special awareness and sensitivity if the rights of gays and lesbians are to be acknowledged as human rights. As it is now, there is no comprehensive legally binding document that protects the rights of gays and lesbians. Nevertheless, recognition is growing that homosexuals are often targeted by practices that harm their physical and mental well-being and deny them their human rights to dignity and equality. With continued education, good will, sensitivity, direct condemnation of discrimination and acts of violence, and increased accountability on the part of governments, the goal of equal human rights for all can be realized.

The final area of concern examined in Part Two focuses on emerging claims that the right to a healthy environment is a fundamental human right. Among the rights recognized by the existing international covenants are the right to life and liberty; the right to security of the person; the right to decent housing and to an adequate standard of living; the right to health care, to education, and to property. These rights, and others not named here, represent the minimum social, economic, and political standards that human beings require—and are entitled to—for a life of dignity. In recent years, however, some human rights theorists and advocates have pointed out that human life exists within the context of a natural environment and, therefore, that human rights depend upon the continued existence of a safe, healthy environment. While this may seem an obvious point, nevertheless, the destruction and degradation of the environment by human beings continue at a ferocious pace. As forests decrease, deserts spread, arable land and fisheries deteriorate, the ozone is depleted, and the air and water become poisoned, the worth of our human rights also declines.

Furthermore, environmental destruction contributes either directly or indirectly to violations of human rights. When resources shrink and become more scarce, violence between individuals and states over those resources becomes more likely. Degrading environments can lead to droughts, famines, civil unrest, and the displacement of peoples from their customary lands and homes. And, perversely, since scarce natural resources become more valuable "commodities," economic exploitation by powerful corporations and corrupt governments places women, children, indigenous and other powerless groups at risk for abuse. Given these dangers grounded on the interrelatedness of humanity and the environment, attempts have been made to articulate a specific human right to a healthy, sustainable environment. Unless such a right is recognized and protected, it is argued, we will not be able to adequately protect our other basic human rights—those of our own as well as of future generations. And as the Universal Declaration itself proclaims, the protection of our basic freedoms and human rights represents "the highest aspiration of the common people." The essays in Part Two give clear expression to this aspiration in all its complex forms.

Notes

1. W. Ebenstein, ed. *Man and the State* (New York: Rinehart & Co., 1947), p. 81.

2. See Theodore R. Gurr, *Minorities at Risk: A Global View of Ethnopolitical Conflicts* (Washington, DC: United States Institute of Peace Press, 1993), and Donald Horowitz, *Ethnic Groups in Conflict* (Berkeley: University of California Press, 1985).

Section 6:

UNIVERSALISM AND RELATIVISM

35. FERNANDO R. TESÓN

Fernando Tesón (1950-) is Professor of Law at Arizona State University and a former diplomat in the Argentine Foreign Service. A specialist in international law, human rights, and comparative law, Tesón has published numerous articles in major international law journals and is the author of *Humanitarian Intervention: An Inquiry into Law and Morality* (1996) and *The Philosophy of International Law* (1998). In the following essay, Tesón examines the issue of cultural diversity with regard to the universality of human rights. In particular, Tesón questions whether differences from society to society are at variance with the prescriptions of human rights standards contained in international law. Tesón concludes that theories of cultural relativism are not justified by the fact of cultural diversity, and that universal human rights standards are needed to eliminate the discriminatory implications of relativism.

Text—International Human Rights and Cultural Relativism

Reprinted from Fernando R. Tesón, "International Human Rights and Cultural Relativism," Virginia Journal of International Law *25, no. 4 (1985): 869-98.*

I. INTRODUCTION

We are witnessing an unequivocal process of universalization of the concern for human dignity. As international law becomes more responsive to the demands for individual freedom, however, it necessarily challenges the validity of certain state practices reflecting geographical and cultural particularities. The tension between national sovereignty and the enforcement of international human rights standards is highlighted when governments point to national cultural traditions to justify failures to comply with international law. States espousing such positions have found invaluable allies not only in Third World writers,[1] but also among Western legal scholars,[2] anthropologists, and philosophers.[3]

"Cultural relativism" is not a term of art, nor even a legal term. It has been borrowed from anthropology and moral philosophy, a fact that has several consequences. First, because an intimate link exists between the moral and legal dimensions of relativism, both the philosophical aspects of relativism and the status of that doctrine in positive international law will be discussed. Second, the theory of cultural relativism has several different possible meanings. While the core idea of cultural relativism will be discussed and critiqued, arguments that relativists could or should advance will also occasionally be anticipated, even though such arguments may not yet have been articulated by relativist scholars or governments.

In the context of the debate about the viability of international human rights, cultural relativism may be defined as the position according to which local cultural traditions (including religious, political, and legal practices) properly determine the existence and scope of civil and political rights enjoyed by individuals in a given society.[4] A central tenet of relativism is that no transboundary legal or moral standards exist against which human rights practices may be judged acceptable or unacceptable.[5] Thus, relativists claim that substantive human rights standards vary among different cultures and necessarily reflect national idiosyncracies. What may be regarded as a human rights violation in one society may properly be considered lawful in another, and Western ideas of human rights should not be imposed upon Third World societies. Tolerance and respect for self-determination preclude cross-cultural normative judgments. Alternatively, the relativist thesis holds that even if, as a matter of customary or conventional international law, a body of substantive human rights norms exists, its meaning varies substantially from culture to culture.[6]

The critique advanced here of cultural relativism shall be limited in several important ways. First, the paper will only deal with violations of civil and political rights—the so-called "first generation" rights. Cultural relativism will not be analyzed in relation to other human rights that may be part of international law, such as the socioeconomic or "second generation" rights.[7] Second, cultural relativism must be distinguished from the thesis that governments, especially those of the Third World, may suppress, delay or suspend civil and political rights in an effort to achieve a just economic order. While the issue of whether socioeconomic rights should in certain situations have priority over civil and political rights has received a great deal of attention in human rights literature,[8] it differs from the problems raised by cultural relativism *stricto sensu*.[9]

The discussion here will be further circumscribed by two assumptions which have solid foundations in international law. The first assumption is that human rights are a substantive part of international law, not only as a matter of treaty, but also as part of customary law. It follows that arguments premised upon the exclusively municipal nature of human rights law are inconsistent with present international law. The cultural relativist may, but need not, disagree with this assumption. He need only hold that the various freedoms have different meanings when applied to different societies. Some relativists would even agree that a few basic human rights, such as the right to life and the freedom from torture, are absolute in the sense that even cultural traditions may not override them. But relativists do not regard other rights, such as the right to physical integrity, the right to participate in the election of one's government, the right to a fair trial, freedom of expression, freedom of association, freedom of movement, or the prohibition of discrimination, as required by international law.[10] While I assume that the core meaning of international human rights law encompasses rights beyond the right to life and to freedom from torture, I do not attempt to prove this assumption. Rather, my main thesis can be condensed into the following two propositions:

a) If there is an international human rights standard—the exact scope of which is admittedly difficult to ascertain—then its meaning remains uniform across borders.

b) Analogously, if there is a possibility of meaningful moral discourse about rights, then it is universal in nature and applies to all human beings despite cultural differences.

The second assumption made in this paper is that an obligation in international law indeed exists to respect the cultural identities of peoples, their local traditions, and customs. For example, the classical international law on the treatment of aliens has long recognized that Westerners cannot expect to enjoy Western judicial procedures in non-Western states. Arbitral tribunals have consistently refused to accept the claim that partially nonadversary criminal procedures violate the international minimum standard concerning the right to a fair trial.

However, to say that cultural identities should be respected does not mean that international human rights law lacks a substantive core. Such a core can be gleaned from international human rights treaties, both regional and universal, and diplomatic practice, including the relevant practices of international organizations, Indeed, human rights treaties offer a surprisingly uniform articulation of human rights law. They may safely be used as a reference, regardless of how many or which states are parties. The rights, *inter alia*, to life, to physical integrity, to a fair trial, freedom of expression, freedom of thought and religion, freedom of association, and the prohibition against discrimination are all rights upon which international instruments agree. Unless one wishes to give up the very notion of an international law of human rights altogether, these rights should have essentially the same meaning regardless of local traditions....

A. *Moral Philosophy and Human Rights Law*

The law of human rights borrows its language from moral philosophy. From its inception at the end of World War II, the modern international law of human rights has been indissolubly linked with the moral concerns prompted by the Nazi horrors. The statesmen who drafted the UN Charter were motivated in part by the moral imperative to restore human dignity and give it legal status, and indeed that moral concern permeates the subsequent development of human rights law.

At the same time, the framers of the Charter also worried about problems of conflict avoidance, peace, security, and maintaining the balance of power. Paradoxically, while national sovereignty continues to be strongly asserted both inside and outside the confines of the United Nations, human rights law has developed impressively. Indeed, reconciling national sovereignty and the international law of human rights remains one of the central challenges of our times.[11] Despite serious problems of enforcement, the dynamism of human rights groups throughout the world and the pressure exerted on delinquent governments by democratic nations has achieved remarkable results, demonstrating that the belief in human rights is not a mere illusion created by scholars, but an effective and living tool for political reform.

Another reason for focusing on moral philosophy is that the concern for human rights did not grow from a desire to force governments to comply with the law "as it is." The world regards human rights violations as a moral wrong of the most serious nature, and presumably continues to condemn such practices even though technically the accused government has not violated any unambiguous positive international obligation. Given the intimate historical and conceptual connection between international human rights law and morality and the current emphasis of some writers on relativism as a supposed basis of the contemporary world order, it is important to examine the conclusions about cultural relativism that can be gleaned from moral philosophy.[12]

B. *Descriptive, Metaethical, and Normative Relativism*

To analyze the moral status of relativism, several types of relativism must be carefully distinguished.[13] First, different societies have different perceptions of right and wrong. This assertion—which may be called "descriptive" relativism—finds support among anthropologists who consider themselves relativists.[14] Although descriptive relativism has been challenged, its validity may be conceded for the purposes of the present analysis.

The second type of relativism, "metaethical" relativism, asserts that it is impossible to discover moral truth. Metaethical relativism may take the form of a thesis about the meaning of moral terms. The relativist can adopt either some version of emotivism[15] or a straight nihilist position.[16] A milder version of metaethical relativism contends that there is no valid method for moral reasoning—that is, no method that would have, on moral matters, the same persuasive force as scientific method.

Finally, "normative" relativism asserts that persons, depending on their cultural attachments, ought to do different things and have different rights. This is the version of relativism equivalent to the one discussed in Part II of this study. It should be clear that descriptive and metaethical relativism do not logically entail normative relativism. Descriptive relativism operates at a different logical level than its normative counterpart. The anthropologist or descriptive relativist says that different cultures in fact have different conceptions of morality. The normative relativist asserts that individuals of different cultures have different rights, and that they ought to do or to abstain from doing different things. It is therefore perfectly possible for the descriptive relativist to concede that different societies have different social practices and conflicting views about morality and yet consider some practices or views morally preferable to others.

The relationship between metaethical and normative relativism is more complex, but the two theories are still logically distinguishable. The metaethical relativist doubts the possibility of demonstrating the correctness of any particular moral principle. As a matter of moral decision, he may reject normative relativism while denying that any moral principle or system is demonstrably correct. To create a framework within which to make moral judgments, the metaethical relativist nevertheless has an option: he may subscribe to the "reflective equilibrium" method suggested by John Rawls.[17] Rawls devised a framework within which to make meaningful moral judgments without encountering the problem of demonstration. He suggests that moral conclusions may be reached by checking one's moral intuitions against one's moral principles with the crucial proviso that both be subject to modification.[18] At the very least, Rawls demonstrates that it is unnecessary to have an infallible method of discovering moral truth in order to speak about the rights all people should enjoy.

C. *Critique of Normative Relativism*

As a moral theory, normative relativism cannot withstand scrutiny.[19] First, its straightforward formulation reflects a fundamental incoherence. It affirms at the same time that (a) there are no universal moral principles; (b) one ought to act in accordance with the principles of one's own group; and (c), (b) is a universal moral principle. David Lyons demonstrated that the typical anthropologists' version of relativism ("an act is right if, and only if, it accords with the norms of the agent's group") does not validate conflicting moral judgments, because each group is regarded as a separate moral realm.[20] Consequently, the incoherence attached to normative relativism springs from the fact that the very assertion of universal relativism is self-contradictory, not from the fact that it validates conflicting substantive moral judgments. If it is true that no universal moral principles exist, then the relativist engages in self-contradiction by stating the universality of the relativist principle. As Bernard Williams observed, this is a "logically unhappy attachment of a nonrelative morality of toleration or noninterference to a view of morality as relative."[21]

However, this objection over the incoherence of normative relativism is not decisive. Normative relativism can be reformulated to avoid the threat of incoherence as follows: (a) there are no universal moral principles, save one; (b) one ought to act in accordance with the principles of one's own group; and (c) the only universal moral principle is (b). Yet, if the normative relativist is also a metaethical relativist, he cannot justify why (b) is a universal moral principle. If the relativist has a method of discovering universal moral principles—for example, Rawls' "reflective equilibrium" or the utilitarian principle—then it is difficult to see why the only principle yielded by such method would be (b) above. Thus, this new version of relativism avoids inconsistency, but it is epistemologically weak.

A second problem with normative relativism is that it overlooks an important feature of moral discourse, its *universalizability*.[22] Independently of substantive morals, when we talk about right and wrong or rights and duties, and act accordingly, we are logically committed to "act in accordance with the generic rights of

[our] recipients as well as of [our]selves," on pain of self-contradiction.[23] This not only means that we cannot make exceptions in our own favor, but also that individuals must be treated as equally entitled to basic rights regardless of contingent factors such as their cultural surroundings. The requirement of universalizability may be thought of as having a logical nature, or alternatively, as being a requirement of moral plausibility.[24] If the first approach is correct, the relativist simply refuses to engage in meaningful moral discourse. Under the second approach, the relativist endorses the highly implausible position that in moral matters we can pass judgments containing proper names, and that consequently we may make exceptions in our own favor.

The relativist has two responses to the universalizability argument. First, the relativist may argue that belonging to different communities is a morally relevant circumstance. Universalizability, he would argue, is not violated when individuals are situated in different factual conditions. To say that if A ought to do X in circumstances C, then B also ought to do X in circumstances C, presupposes a similarity of circumstances. If such circumstances vary substantially, that is, if cultural traditions, creeds, and practices differ, then we would not violate the universalizability requirement by holding that individuals who belong to different cultures ought to have different basic rights.[25] Sometimes relativists articulate this position in the form of an attack on the assertion of the existence of abstract rights, as opposed to the assertion of concrete rights and duties in materially defined social conditions.

Such arguments are flawed, however, because the fact that one belongs to a particular social group or community is not a *morally* relevant circumstance. The place of birth and cultural environment of an individual are not related to his moral worth or to his entitlement to human rights. An individual cannot be held responsible for being born in one society rather than in another, for one "deserves" neither one's cultural environment nor one's place of birth. There is nothing, for example, in the nature of a Third World woman that makes her less eligible for the enjoyment of human rights (though she may, of course, consensually waive her rights) than a woman in a Western democracy.[26] If the initial conditions are not morally distinguishable, the requirement of universalizability fully applies to statements about individual rights, even where the agents are immersed in different cultural environments.

The relativist's first objection to universalizability also confuses the circumstances in which one learns moral concepts with the *meaning* of those concepts. A person who learns a moral concept (such as that of "wrong") by applying it in fact situations peculiar to his culture, is perfectly able to apply that concept to a set of facts he has never encountered before. As Bernard Williams said in his most recent work:

> The fact that people can and must react when they are confronted with another culture, and do so by applying their existing notions—also by reflecting on them—seems to show that the ethical thought of a given culture can always stretch beyond its boundaries. Even if there is no way in which divergent ethical beliefs can be brought to converge by independent inquiry or rational argument, this fact will not imply relativism. Each outlook may still be making claims it intends to apply to the whole world, not just to that part of it which is its "own world."[27]

By claiming that moral judgments only have meaning within particular cultures, the relativist underestimates the ability of the human intellect to confront, in a moral sense, new situations.

The relativist's second objection to universalizability has a logical nature. As noted above, the relativist may contend that (a) his only principle is that culture determines human rights; and (b), (a) is universal. The relativist thus universalizes a principle. But the requirement of universalizability applies to *substantive* moral statements, which (a) is not. The principle that culture determines human rights is a principle of *renvoi*; that is, it refers us to different normative systems in order to determine the rights of individuals. The principle does not establish rules governing the rights of any particular individual. Universalizability requires that *if* we make a statement about the right of X to freedom of thought, we are committed to grant that right to Y under similar, morally relevant circumstances. Because the relativist principle does not address issues of substantive morality in this respect, it is not susceptible to being universalized in the same way. The violation of universalizability becomes apparent when one translates the relativist principle into substantive moral statements (i.e., X, who lives in culture C1, has the right R; while Y, who lives in culture C2, does not have the right R). In other words, the relativist principle may be regarded as *metamoral*, even where it is asserted as the basis of normative morality.

Third, normative relativism runs counter to the principle that persons have moral worth *qua* persons and must be treated as ends in themselves, not as functions of the ends of others—a non-trivial version of the Kantian principle of autonomy. This principle of moral worth forbids the imposition upon individuals of cultural standards that impair human rights. Even if relativists could show that authoritarian practices are somehow required by a community—a claim which in many cases remains to be proven—they would still fail to explain why individuals should surrender their basic rights to the ends of the community. If women in Moslem countries are discriminated against, it is not enough to say that a tradition, no matter how old and venerable, requires such discrimination. The only defense consistent with the principle of autonomy would be a showing that each subjugated woman consented to waive her rights. However, because of the mystical and holistic assumptions underlying relativism, presumably the relativist would not regard such a test as relevant or necessary.

Quite apart from the moral implausibility of normative relativism, it is worth noting the extreme conservatism of the doctrine.[28] Normative relativism tells us that if a particular society has always had authoritarian practices, it is morally defensible that it continue to have them. It works as a typical argument of authority: it has always been like this, this is our culture, so we need not undertake any changes. In the final analysis, normative relativism thus conceived amounts to the worst form of moral and legal positivism: it asserts that the rules enacted by the group are necessarily correct as a matter of critical morality. If there is a particularly unfit domain for arguments of authority, it is surely that of human rights.

Admittedly, the force of the moral critique of relativism articulated here depends on the intuitive acceptance of certain moral premises. The relativist can successfully resist the attack by rejecting metaethical relativism so as to avoid logical incoherence, denying that universalizability is an ingredient of moral judgments, and rejecting the principle of autonomy. But this is a high price to pay. Normative relativism would then be a poor and implausible moral doctrine, and it is doubtful that many relativists, upon careful reflection, would accept the harsh implications. Furthermore, cultural relativism as defined in the first part of this article expressly or impliedly assumes the validity of normative relativism. Not only does positive international law fail to provide any basis for the relativist doctrine, but the underlying philosophical structure of relativism also reveals profound flaws.

IV. TWO BY-PRODUCTS OF RELATIVISM: ELITISM AND CONSPIRACY

In this Part I will briefly consider two doctrines closely associated with relativism. The first theory asserts that one can appropriately honor human rights in certain societies, usually the most sophisticated ones, but not in others, on account, for example, of the latter's insufficient economic development. This doctrine, which can be called "elitism," necessarily follows from relativism. The second theory states that the law of human rights results from a conspiracy of the West to perpetuate imperialism. The "conspiracy theory," by contrast, does not follow inevitably from, and is not required by, cultural relativism.

A. *The Elitist Theory of Human Rights*

During the dark years of the military dictatorship in Argentina, one commonly heard many well-intentioned commentators exclaiming: "It is really a shame! Argentina, a country that springs from Western tradition, cannot be excused for not respecting human rights." The statement implies that countries that do not spring from a Western tradition may somehow be excused from complying with the international law of human rights. This elitist theory of human rights holds that human rights are good for the West but not for much of the non-Western world. Surprisingly, the elitist theory of human rights is very popular in the democratic West, not only in conservative circles but also, and even more often, among liberal and radical groups. The right-wing version of elitism embodies the position, closely associated with colonialism, that backward peoples cannot govern themselves and that democracy only works for superior cultures. The left-wing version, often articulated by liberals who stand for civil rights in Western countries but support leftist dictatorships abroad, reflects a belief that we should be tolerant of and respect the cultural identity and political self-determination of Third World countries (although, of course, it is seldom the people who choose to have dictators; more often the dictators decide for them).

The position of relativist scholars who are human rights advocates illustrates an eloquent example of concealed elitism. Such persons find themselves in an impossible dilemma. On the one hand they are anxious to articulate an international human rights standard, while on the other they wish to respect the autonomy of individual cultures. The result is a vague warning against "ethnocentrism," and well-intentioned proposals that are deferential to tyrannical governments and insufficiently concerned with human suffering. Because the consequence of either version of elitism is that certain national or ethnic groups are somehow less entitled than others to the enjoyment of human rights, the theory is fundamentally immoral and replete with racist overtones.

B. *The Conspiracy Theory of Human Rights*

The final aspect of relativism to be discussed is what Karl Popper might describe as "the conspiracy theory of human rights."[29] This theory asserts that human rights are a Macchiavelian creation of the West calculated to impair the economic development of the Third World. Starting from the Marxist assumption that civil and political rights are "formal" bourgeois freedoms that serve only the interests of the capitalists,[30] the conspiracy theory holds that human rights serve the same purpose in the international arena. It sees them as instruments of domination because they are indissolubly tied to the right to property, and because in the field of international economic relations, the human rights movement fosters free and unrestricted trade which seriously hurts the economies of Third World nations. Furthermore, proponents of the conspiracy theory charge that human rights advocacy amounts to moral imperialism. In short, "the effect, if not the design, of such an exclusive political preoccupation [is] to leave the door open to the most ruthless and predatory economic forces in international society."[31]

The conspiracy theory, however, fails to justify the link between the support for human rights and support for particular property rights or trade policies—a fundamental flaw. The argument made in this paper does not presuppose or imply any position in this regard. Moreover, to claim that civil and political rights must be suppressed as a necessary condition for the improvement of Third World economies grossly distorts the facts. As Louis Henkin put it:

> [H]ow many hungry are fed, how much industry is built, by massacre, torture, and detention, by unfair trials and other injustices, by abuse of minorities, by denials of freedoms of conscience, by suppression of political association and expression?[32]

The contention that the West imposed human rights on the world and that "poor peoples" do not care about freedom is clearly a myth.[33] First, it contradicts the plain fact that a growing awareness exists in the Third World about the need for reinforcing the respect for human rights. Second, even if, *gratia argumentandi*, some Western plot created human rights philosophy, that fact alone would not necessarily undermine its moral value. Conspiracy theories (such as vulgar Marxism, "ideologism," and Critical Legal Studies) assert that the true explanation of a phenomenon consists of discovering the groups of people or hidden interests which are interested in the occurrence of the phenomenon and which have plotted to bring it about.[34] To be sure, conspiracies do occur. As Popper conclusively showed, however, the fact that conspiracies rarely succeed ultimately disproves the conspiracy theory. Social life is too complex and the unforeseen consequences of social action too many to support conspiracy as the explanation of every social phenomenon.[35] Institutions originally designed for a certain purpose often turn against their creators. Thus, even if the law of human rights was originally conceived as an ideological tool against communism, today human rights have achieved a universal scope and inspire the struggle against all types of oppression.[36] In other words, the circumstances surrounding the origins of human rights principles are irrelevant to their intrinsic value and cannot detract from their beneficial features.

V. CONCLUSION

The human rights movement has resisted the relativist attack by emphasizing that social institutions, including international law, are created by and for the individual. Consequently, as far as rights are concerned, governments serve as but the agents of the people. International norms aim to protect individuals, not governments, by creating concrete limits on how human beings may be treated.

I have suggested that cultural relativism is not, and ought not to be, the answer to human rights concerns. Supported neither by international law nor by independent moral analysis, cultural relativism exhibits strong discriminatory overtones and is to a large extent mistaken in its factual assumptions.

I also demonstrated that regardless of its historical origins, the international law of human rights cannot mean one thing to the West and another to the Third World. International human rights law embodies the imperfect yet inspired response of the international community to a growing awareness of the uniqueness of the human being and the unity of the human race. It also represents an eloquent body of norms condemning the effects of organized societal oppression on individuals. Fortunately, the Third World is now starting to play a role in the process of universalizing human rights. The significance of its new role will increase when governing elites cease to use authoritarian traditions as a shield against legitimate demands for basic human rights.

Notes

1. See, e.g., Wai, "Human Rights in Sub-Sahara Africa," in *Human Rights: Cultural and Ideological Perspectives* 1 (A. Pollis & P. Schwab, eds., 1979) (claiming that Western-oriented human rights notions embodied in the UN Charter and the Universal Declaration of Human Rights may not be applicable in non-Western areas); Mani, "Regional Approaches to the Implementation of Human Rights," 21 *Indian J. Int'l L.* 96, 97 (1981).

2. A recent work by E. McWhinney, *United Nations Law Making* (1984), bears the following subtitle: *Cultural and Ideological Relativism and International Law Making for an Era of Transition.*

3. See, e.g., M. Herskovits, *Man and His Works* 61-78 (1949); E. Westermarck, *Ethical Relativity* 183-219 (1932).

4. Many contemporary situations exemplify the tension between domestic cultural imperatives and international norms: mutilation and flogging as criminal punishment (see US Department of State, *Country Reports on Human Rights Practices* 1084 (1981); Marett, "Some Medical Problems Met in Saudi Arabia," 4 *U.S.A.F. Med. J.* 31, 36 (1953); the circumcision of women (see Dullea, "Female Circumcision a Topic at UN Parley," *New York Times*, July 18, 1980, at B4, col. 3.); the subjugation of women (see White, "Legal Reform as an Indicator of Women's Status in Muslim Nations," in *Women in the Muslim World* 52 (L. Beck & N. Keddie, eds., 1978); Marshall, "Tradition and the Veil: Female Status in Tunisia and Algeria," *Mod. African Stud.* 635, 632-37 (1981); and various authoritarian methods of government (see Note, "Human Rights Practices in the Arab States: The Modern Impact of Shari'a Values," 12 *Ga. J. Int'l & Comp. L.* 55, 92 (1981) (Shari'a values established a philosophical foundation for human rights abuses). All of these examples of contemporary practices, while clearly unlawful by international standards, are defended by some as being required or permitted by cultural traditions. See also the discussion of the Iranian position on human rights in E. McWhinney, supra note 2, at 210.

5. Since the main concern of international human rights is the position of the individual vis-à-vis the government, the expression "human rights practices" encompasses, in addition to governmental acts, actions by groups or individuals that governments tolerate or condone (e.g., religious practices carried out by the clergy and tolerated by the state).

6. See Pollis, "Liberal, Socialist and Third World Perspectives on Human Rights," in *Toward a Human Rights Framework* 1, 23 (A. Pollis & P. Schwab, eds., 1982) (arguing that human rights judgments ought to be determined "by the criteria set by the philosophic/ideological roots of particular states"); Said & Nasser, "The Use and Abuse of Democracy in Islam," in *International Human Rights: Contemporary Issues* 61 (J. Nelson & V. Green, eds., 1980) ("freedom exists in Islam as long as it serves the interest of the community").

7. For a complete though somewhat uncritical account of the evolution and meaning of different "generations" of rights in the United Nations, see Sohn, "The New International Law: Protection of the Rights of Individuals Rather

than States," 32 *Am. U. L. Rev.* 1 (1982). The so-called "third generation" of human rights are the "solidarity" rights. The advocacy of this new set of rights may represent an attempt to use the favorable emotive connections of human rights language to expand the "rights" of the state at the expense of individual rights. Cf. Alston, "A Third Generation of Solidarity Rights: Progressive Development or Obfuscation of International Human Rights Law?," 29 *Neth. Int'l L. Rev.* 307, 321 (1982) (proponents of such rights have a strong burden of proof to show that they are compatible with and do not devalue existing rights). See Forsythe, "Socioeconomic Human Rights: The United Nations, the United States and Beyond," 4 *Hum. Rts. Q.* 433, 434-45 (1982); Zalaquett, "An Interdisciplinary Approach to Development and Human Rights," 4 *B.C. Third World L. J.* 1, 28-31 (1983). Unlike "solidarity" rights, socioeconomic rights represent a positive force in the fight to enhance human dignity. However, the emergence of socioeconomic rights need not entail the demise or contraction of civil and political rights. It should be noted that authoritarian regimes, whether Marxist or not, invariably defend the priority of socioeconomic rights.

8. See Forsythe, supra, at 434. The UN majority appears to take the position that socioeconomic rights deserve as much attention as civil and political rights. See G.A. Res. 34/46, 34 UN GAOR Supp. (70th mtg.) at para 4, UN Doc. A/Res. 34/46 (1979). The philosophical literature has devoted considerable attention to the priority issue since the publication of John Rawls' *A Theory of Justice* (1971). Rawls suggests a "lexical" order between civil and political freedoms on the one hand and economic principles of justice on the other. Id. at 243-50. Some of the numerous responses to Rawls' solution of the priority problem include B. Barry, *The Liberal Theory of Justice* ch. 8 (1973), and Hart, "Liberty and Its Priority," in *Reading Rawls* 230 (N. Daniels, ed., 1975).

9. The position that socioeconomic rights should have priority over civil and political rights need not embrace cultural relativism. The relativist thesis states that cultural standards—and not economic development or the need to implement distributive justice—determine the extent and nature of human rights. A government that justifies human rights deprivations by appealing to economic priorities may well reject cultural relativism. Some of the arguments marshalled in this article, however, are also directed to the thesis of the priority of socioeconomic rights.

10. See Murphy, "Objections to Western Conceptions of Human Rights," 9 *Hofstra L. Rev.* 433 (1981).

11. Cf. Delbrueck, "International Protection of Human Rights and State Sovereignty," 57 *Ind. L. J.* 567 (1982) ("[T]he sovereign states not only are creating the international norms for the protection of human rights, but also are determining the process of their implementation—or nonimplementation—according to their sovereign will. Seen from this perspective, state sovereignty and the international protection of human rights appear to be incompatible.")

12. The relevance of moral inquiry to international law depends, of course, upon one's particular theory of the relation between law and morality. However, if

the relativist concedes that his theory is not supported by independent moral reasoning, he must conclude that cultural relativism, although technically legal, is immoral, and he is therefore logically committed to the reform of international law in the sense of eliminating the relativist defense.

13. See Brandt, "Ethical Relativism," in 3 *Encyclopedia of Philosophy* 75 (P. Edwards ed. 1967).

14. See, e.g., M. Herskovits, supra note 3, at 61-78.

15. Emotivism holds that moral propositions are no more than interjections or emotive utterances. See generally, A. J. Ayer, *Language, Truth and Logic* (1946); C. L. Stevenson, *Ethics and Language* (1944).

16. Nihilism, in this context, holds that moral terms lack any meaning whatsoever.

17. J. Rawls, supra note 8, at 48-51. Of course, the acceptance of reflective equilibrium as a plausible description of moral methodology is completely independent from (a) the acceptance of Rawls' contractarian justification for principles of social justice; (b) the acceptance of the principles themselves; or (c) the acceptance of his solution to the priority problem. For Rawls' view that "undeveloped" societies may fail to observe human rights in certain situations, see infra note 28.

18. J. Rawls, supra note 8, at 48.

19. Bernard Williams calls relativism "the anthropologists' heresy, possibly the most absurd view to have been advanced even in moral philosophy." B. Williams, *Morality: An Introduction to Ethics* 20 (1972).

20. Lyons, "Ethical Relativism and the Problem of Incoherence," 86 *Ethics*, at 104.

21. B. Williams, supra note 19, at 21. See also a profound criticism of relativism in B. Williams, *Ethics and the Limits of Philosophy*, ch. 9 (1985). 102.

22. The requirement of universalizability is usually traced to IV Immanuel Kant, *Critique of Practical Reason* § 436 (L. Beck, trans., 1949). It has been revived in recent philosophical literature, mainly by A. Gewirth, *Reason and Morality* (1978) and M. Singer, *Generalization in Ethics* (1961).

23. A. Gewirth, *Human Rights: Essays on Justification and Application* 52, 128-41 (1982).

24. See, e.g., J. Rawls, supra note 8, at 132 (principles apply to everyone by virtue of their being moral persons).

25. John Rawls asserts that in societies which have not attained certain minimal material conditions, individuals may be denied human rights. J. Rawls, supra note 8, at 151-52. This seems a surprising statement in the context of Rawls' impressive defense of the "rights" conception of justice. As Brian Barry put it (supra note 8, at 77):

> Why this should be so is not at all clear to me. Is there anything in the material condition of, say, a group of nomadic Bedouin seeking a bare subsistence from the desert or a population of poor peasant cultivators which prevents them from being able to use personal liberty?

In his most recent article, Rawls expressly refused to deal with the issue of whether his theory "can be extended to a general political conception for different kinds of societies existing under different historical and social conditions." Rawls, "Justice as Fairness: Political not Metaphysical," 14 *Phil. & Pub. Aff.* 223, 225 (1985). It would be unfair, however, to charge Rawls with yielding to relativism, since he expressly avoids "prejudging one way or the other." Id.

26. One must be careful not to overstate this exception. Dictators typically assert that they represent the people or that they have their support. Even if a particular dictator enjoys popular support, however, such support does not entitle him to oppress dissenters who have not consented to his rule. The majoritarian principle is thus useless when assessing human rights violations. See the discussion in J. Rawls, supra note 8, at 356-62.

27. B. Williams, supra note 21, at 159.

28. A similar point is made by Amy Gutmann in her response to modern critics of liberalism. Gutmann, "Communitarian Critics of Liberalism," 14 *Phil. & Pub. Aff.* 308, 309 (1985). As the text demonstrates, anti-liberal theories that emphasize the priority of communal values are necessarily relativist.

29. K. Popper, *The Open Society and Its Enemies* 94 (1966).

30. See, e.g., Marx, "On the Jewish Question," in *The Marx-Engels Reader* 42 (2d ed. Tucker 1978).

31. E. McWhinney, supra note 2, at 211.

32. L. Henkin, *The Rights of Man Today* 130 (1978).

33. Id.

34. K. Popper, supra note 29, at 94.

35. Id. at 95.

36. South Africa is a case in point. Maybe in 1948 the framers of the Universal Declaration of Human Rights did not intend for it to apply to the black majority in South Africa. Maybe they thought that democracy "among whites" was enough to comply with the Declaration. The international community has subsequently rejected that interpretation, however, and today the law and philosophy of human rights are the main bases for the claims for freedom by the black majority.

Questions for Reflection

1. Tesón directs his argument against the claims of normative relativism. Explain what normative relativism is, and evaluate Tesón's critique.

2. Do you believe that the fact of cultural diversity must lead to the doctrine of cultural relativism? Why or why not?

3. In what ways, if at all, should cultural differences be used to justify denying universal rights?

36. XIAORONG LI

Xiaorong Li (1958-) is a research scholar at the Institute for Philosophy and Public Policy, University of Maryland. She has been a visiting member at the Institute for Advanced Study, Princeton University, and the Vice-Chair of Human Rights in China since 1992. Li's work has focused primarily on human rights in the People's Republic of China. In this essay, Li considers the claim that the idea of universal human rights is a Western concept which emphasizes individuality at the expense of community, and is thus at odds with the values of Asian societies. While some theorists and politicians in Asia have sought to characterize the human rights of individuals as being foreign to the cultural traditions of Asian communities, Li argues that we must examine whether this claim is merely a rationalization on the part of authoritarian governments looking to rationalize their repression of citizens. Li suggests that human rights can have universal validity given an open dialogue across cultures on human rights standards.

Text—"Asian Values" and the Universality of Human Rights

Reprinted from Xiaorong Li, "'Asian Values' and the Universality of Human Rights," Report from the Institute for Philosophy and Public Policy *16, no. 2 (1996): 18–23. Reprinted by permission of the author.*

Orientalist scholarship in the nineteenth century perceived Asians as the mysterious and backward people of the Far East. Ironically, as this century draws to a close, leaders of prosperous and entrepreneurial East and Southeast Asian countries eagerly stress Asia's incommensurable differences from the West and demand special treatment of their human rights record by the international community. They reject outright the globalization of human rights and claim that Asia has a unique set of values, which, as Singapore's ambassador to the United Nations has urged, provide the basis for Asia's different understanding of human rights and justify the "exceptional" handling of rights by Asian governments.

Is this assertion of "Asian values" simply a cloak for arrogant regimes whose newly gained confidence from rapidly growing economic power makes them all the more resistant to outside criticism? Does it have any intellectual substance? What challenges has the "Asian values" debate posed to a human rights movement committed to globalism?

Though scholars have explored the understanding of human rights in various Asian contexts, the concept of "Asian values" gains political prominence only when it is articulated in government rhetoric and official statements. In asserting these values, leaders from the region find that they have a convenient tool to silence internal criticism and to fan anti-Western nationalist sentiments. At the same time, the concept is welcomed by cultural relativists, cultural supremacists, and isolationists alike, as fresh evidence for their various positions against a political liberalism that defends universal human rights and democracy. Thus, the "Asian values" debate provides an occasion to reinvigorate deliberation about the foundations of human rights, the sources of political legitimacy, and the relation between modernity and cultural identity.

This essay makes a preliminary attempt to identify the myths, misconceptions, and fallacies that have gone into creating an "Asian view" of human rights. By sorting out the various threads in the notions of "cultural specificity" and "universality," it shows that the claim to "Asian values" hardly constitutes a serious threat to the universal validity of human rights.

DEFINING THE "ASIAN VIEW"

To speak of an "Asian view" of human rights that has supposedly emanated from Asian perspectives or values is itself problematic: it is impossible to defend the "Asianness" of this view and its legitimacy in representing Asian culture(s). "Asia" in our ordinary language designates large geographic areas which house diverse political entities (states) and their people, with drastically different cultures and religions, and unevenly developed (or undeveloped) economies and political systems. Those who assert commonly shared "Asian values" cannot reconcile their claims with the immense diversity of Asia—a heterogeneity that extends to its people, their social-political practices and ethnic-cultural identities. Nonetheless, official statements by governments in the region typically make the following claims about the so-called "Asian view" of human rights:

Claim I: Rights are "culturally specific." Human rights emerge in the context of particular social, economic, cultural and political conditions. The circumstances that prompted the institutionalization of human rights in the West do not exist in Asia. China's 1991 White Paper stated that "[o]wing to tremendous differences in historical background, social system, cultural tradition and economic development, countries differ in their understanding and practice of human rights." In the Bangkok Governmental Declaration, endorsed at the 1993 Asian regional preparatory meeting for the Vienna World Conference on Human Rights, governments agreed that human rights "must be considered in the context of a dynamic and evolving process of international norm-setting, bearing in mind the significance of national and regional peculiarities and various historical, cultural, and religious backgrounds."

Claim II: The community takes precedence over individuals. The importance of the community in Asian culture is incompatible with the primacy of the individual, upon which the Western notion of human rights rests. The relationship between individuals and communities constitutes the key difference between Asian and Western cultural "values." An official statement of the Singapore government, *Shared Values* (1991), stated that "[a]n emphasis on the community has been a key survival value for Singapore." Human rights and the rule of law, according to the "Asian view," are individualistic by nature and hence destructive of Asia's social mechanism. Increasing rates of violent crime, family breakdown, homelessness, and drug abuse are cited as evidence that Western individualism (particularly the American variety) has failed.

Claim III: Social and economic rights take precedence over civil and political rights. Asian societies rank social and economic rights and "the right to economic development" over individuals' political and civil rights. The Chinese White Paper (1991) stated that "[t]o eat their fill and dress warmly were the fundamental demands of the Chinese people who had long suffered cold and hunger." Political and civil rights, on this view, do not make sense to poor and illiterate multitudes; such rights are not meaningful under destitute and unstable conditions. The right of workers to form independent unions, for example, is not as urgent as stability and efficient production. Implicit here is the promise that once people's basic needs are met—once they are adequately fed, clothed, and educated—and the social order is stable, the luxury of civil and political rights will be extended to them. In the meantime, economic development will be achieved more efficiently if the leaders are authorized to restrict individuals' political and civil rights for the sake of political stability.

Claim IV: Rights are a matter of national sovereignty. The right of a nation to self-determination includes a government's domestic jurisdiction over human rights. Human rights are internal affairs, not to be interfered with by foreign states or multinational agencies. In its 1991 White Paper, China stated that "the issue of human rights falls by and large within the sovereignty of each state." In 1995, the Chinese government confirmed its opposition to "some countries' hegemonic acts of using a double standard for the human rights of other countries...and imposing their own pattern on others, or interfering in the internal affairs of other countries by using 'human rights' as a pretext." The West's attempt to apply universal standards of human rights to developing countries is disguised cultural imperialism and an attempt to obstruct their development.

ELSEWHERE AND HERE

In this essay I address the first three claims that make up the "Asian view," particularly the argument that rights are "culturally specific." This argument implies that social norms originating in other cultures should not be adopted in Asian culture. But, in practice, advocates of the "Asian view" often do not consistently adhere to this rule. Leaders from the region pick and choose freely from other cultures, adopting whatever is in their political interest. They seem to have no qualms about embracing such things as capitalist markets and consumerist culture. What troubles them about the concept of human rights, then, turns out to have little to do with its Western cultural origin.

In any case, there are no grounds for believing that norms originating *elsewhere* should be inherently unsuitable for solving problems *here*. Such a belief commits the "genetic fallacy" in that it assumes that a norm is suitable only to the culture of its origin. But the origin of an idea in one culture does not entail its unsuitability to another culture. If, for example, there are good reasons for protecting the free expression of Asian people, free expression should be respected, no matter whether the idea of free expression originated in the West or Asia, or how long it has been a viable idea. And in fact, Asian countries may have now entered into historical circumstances where the affirmation and protection of human rights is not only possible but desirable.

In some contemporary Asian societies, we find economic, social, cultural, and political conditions that foster demands for human rights as the norm-setting criteria for the treatment of individual persons and the communities they form. National aggregate growth and distribution, often under the control of authoritarian governments, have not benefited individuals from vulnerable social groups—including workers, women, children, and indigenous or minority populations. Social and economic disparities are rapidly expanding. Newly introduced market forces, in the absence of rights protection and the rule of law, have further exploited and disadvantaged these groups and created anxiety even among more privileged sectors—professionals and business owners, as well as foreign corporations—in places where corruption, disrespect for property rights, and arbitrary rule are the norm. Political dissidents, intellectuals and opposition groups who dare to challenge the system face persecution. Meanwhile, with the expansion of communications technology and improvements in literacy, information about repression and injustice has become more accessible both within and beyond previously isolated communities; it is increasingly known that the notion of universal rights has been embraced by people in many Latin American, African, and some East and Southeast Asian countries (Japan, South Korea, Taiwan, and the Philippines). Finally, the international human rights movement has developed robust non-Western notions of human rights, including economic, social, and cultural rights, providing individuals in Asia with powerful tools to fight against poverty, corruption, military repression, discrimination, cultural and community destruction, as well as social, ethnic, and religious violence. Together, these new circumstances make human rights relevant and implementable in Asian societies.

CULTURE, COMMUNITY, AND THE STATE

The second claim, that Asians value community over individuality, obscures more than it reveals about community, its relations to the state and individuals, and the conditions congenial to its flourishing. The so-called Asian value of "community harmony" is used as an illustration of "cultural" differences between Asian and Western societies, in order to show that the idea of individuals' inalienable rights does not suit Asian societies. This "Asian communitarianism" is a direct challenge to what is perceived as the essence of human rights, i.e., its individual-centered approach, and it suggests that Asia's community-centered approach is superior.

However, the "Asian view" creates confusions by collapsing "community" into the state and the state into the (current) regime. When equations are drawn between community, the state and the regime, any criticisms of the regime become crimes against the nation-state, the community, and the people. The "Asian view" relies on such a conceptual maneuver to dismiss individual rights that conflict with the regime's interest, allowing the condemnation of individual rights as anti-communal, destructive of social harmony, and seditionist against the sovereign state.

At the same time, this view denies the existence of conflicting interests between the state (understood as a political entity) and communities (understood as voluntary, civil associations) in Asian societies. What begins as an endorsement of the value of community and social harmony ends in an assertion of the supreme status of the regime and its leaders. Such a regime is capable of dissolving any non-governmental organizations it dislikes in the name of "community interest," often citing traditional Confucian values of social harmony to defend restrictions on the right to free association and expression, and thus wields ever more pervasive control over unorganized individual workers and dissenters. A Confucian communitarian, however, would find that the bleak, homogeneous society that these governments try to shape through draconian practices—criminal prosecutions for "counterrevolutionary activities," administrative detention, censorship, and military curfew—has little in common with her ideal of social harmony.

Contrary to the "Asian view," individual freedom is not intrinsically opposed to and destructive of community. Free association, free expression, and tolerance are vital to the well-being of communities. Through open public deliberations, marginalized and vulnerable social groups can voice their concerns and expose the discrimination and unfair treatment they encounter. In a liberal democratic society, which is mocked and denounced by some Asian leaders for its individualist excess, a degree of separation between the state and civil society provides a public space for the flourishing of communities.

A FALSE DILEMMA

The third claim of the "Asian view," that economic development rights have a priority over political and civil rights, supposes that the starving and illiterate masses have to choose between starvation and oppression. It then concludes that "a full belly" would no doubt be the natural choice. Setting aside the paternalism of this assumption, the question arises of whether the apparent trade-off—freedom in exchange for food—actually brings an end to deprivation, and whether people must in fact choose between these two miserable states of affairs.

When it is authoritarian leaders who pose this dilemma, one should be particularly suspicious. The oppressors, after all, are well-positioned to amass wealth for themselves, and their declared project of enabling people to "get rich" may increase the disparity between the haves and the have-nots. Moreover, the most immediate victims of oppression—those subjected to imprisonment or torture—are often those who have spoken out against the errors or the incompetence of authorities who have failed to alleviate deprivation, or who in fact have made it worse. The sad truth is that an authoritarian regime can practice political repression and starve the poor at the same time. Conversely, an end to oppression often means the alleviation of poverty—as when, to borrow Amartya Sen's example, accountable governments manage to avert famine by heeding the warnings of a free press.

One assumption behind this false dilemma is that "the right to development" is a state's sovereign right and that it is one and the same as the "social-economic rights" assigned to individuals under international covenants. But the right of individuals and communities to participate in and enjoy the fruit of economic development should not be identified with the right of nation-states to pursue national pro-development policies, even if such policies set the stage for individual citizens to exercise their economic rights. Even when "the right to development" is understood as a sovereign state right, as is sometimes implied in the international politics of development, it belongs to a separate and distinct realm from that of "social-economic rights."

The distinction between economic rights and the state's right to development goes beyond the issue of who holds these particular rights. National development is an altogether different matter from securing the economic rights of vulnerable members of society. National economic growth does not guarantee that basic subsistence for the poor will be secured. While the right to development (narrowly understood) enables the nation-state as a unit to grow economically, social-economic rights are concerned with empowering the poor and vulnerable, preventing their marginalization and exploitation, and securing their basic subsistence. What the right of development, when asserted by an authoritarian state, tends to disregard, but what social-economic rights aspire to protect, is fair economic equality or social equity. Unfortunately, Asia's development programs have not particularly enabled the poor and vulnerable to control their basic livelihood, especially where development is narrowly understood as the creation of markets and measured by national aggregate growth rates.

A more plausible argument for ranking social and economic rights above political and civil rights is that poor and illiterate people cannot really exercise their civil-political rights. Yet the poor and illiterate may benefit from civil and political freedom by speaking, without fear, of their discontent. Meanwhile, as we have seen, political repression does not guarantee better living conditions and education for the poor and illiterate. The leaders who are in a position to encroach upon citizens' rights to express political opinions will also be beyond reproach and accountability for failures to protect citizens' social-economic rights.

Political-civil rights and social-economic-cultural rights are in many ways indivisible. Each is indispensable for the effective exercise of the other. If citizens' civil-political rights are unprotected, their opportunities to "get rich" can be taken away just as arbitrarily as they are bestowed; if citizens have no real opportunity to exercise their social-economic rights, their rights to political participation and free expression will be severely undermined. For centuries, poverty has stripped away the human dignity of Asia's poor masses, making them vulnerable to violations of their cultural and civil-political rights. Today, a free press and the rule of law are likely to enhance Asians' economic opportunity. Political-civil rights are not a mere luxury of rich nations, as some Asian leaders have told their people, but a safety net for marginalized and vulnerable people in dramatically changing Asian societies.

UNIVERSALITY UNBROKEN

The threat posed by "Asian values" to the universality of human rights seems ominous. If Asian cultural relativism prevails, there can be no universal standards to adjudicate between competing conceptions of human rights. But one may pause and ask whether the "Asian values" debate has created any really troubling threat to universal human rights—that is, serious enough to justify the alarm that it has touched off.

The answer, I argue, depends on how one understands the concepts of universality and cultural specificity. In essence, there are three ways in which a value can be universal or culturally specific. First, these terms may refer to the origin of a value. In this sense, they represent a claim about whether a value has developed only within specific cultures, or whether it has arisen within the basic ideas of every culture.

No one on either side of the "Asian values" debate thinks that human rights are universal with respect to their origin. It is accepted that the idea of human rights originated in Western traditions. The universalist does not disagree with the cultural relativist on this point—though they would disagree about its significance—and it is not in this sense that human rights are understood as having universality.

Second, a value may be culturally specific or universal with respect to its prospects for *effective (immediate) implementation.* That is, a value may find favorable conditions for its implementation only within certain cultures, or it may find such conditions everywhere in the world.

Now, I don't think that the universalist would insist that human rights can be immediately or effectively implemented in all societies, given their vastly different conditions. No one imagines that human rights will be fully protected in societies that are ravaged by violent conflict or warfare; where political power is so unevenly distributed that the ruling forces can crush any opposition; where social mobility is impossible, and people segregated by class, caste system, or cultural taboos are isolated and uninformed; where most people are on the verge of starvation and where survival is the pressing concern. The list could go on. However, to acknowledge that the prospects for effective implementation of human rights differ according to circumstances is not to legitimize violations under these unfavorable conditions, nor is it to deny the universal applicability or validity of human rights (as defined below) to all human beings no matter what circumstances they face.

Third, a value may be understood as culturally specific by people who think it is *valid* only within certain cultures. According to this understanding, a value can be explained or defended only by appealing to assumptions already accepted by a given culture; in cultures that do not share those assumptions, the validity of such a value will become questionable. Since there are few universally shared cultural assumptions that can be invoked in defense of the concept of human rights, the universal validity of human rights is problematic.

The proponents of this view suppose that the validity of human rights can only be assessed in an intracultural conversation where certain beliefs or assumptions are commonly shared and not open to scrutiny. However, an intercultural conversation about the validity of human rights is now taking place among people with different cultural assumptions; it is a conversation that proceeds by opening those assumptions to reflection and reexamination. Its participants begin with some minimal shared beliefs: for example, that genocide, slavery, and racism are wrong. They accept some basic rules of argumentation to reveal hidden presuppositions, disclose inconsistencies between ideas, clarify conceptual ambiguity and confusions, and expose conclusions based on insufficient evidence and oversimplified generalizations. In such a conversation based on public reasoning, people may come to agree on a greater range of issues than seemed possible when they began. They may revise or reinterpret their old beliefs. The plausibility of such a conversation suggests a way of establishing universal validity: that is, by referring to public reason in defense of a particular conception or value.

If the concept of human rights can survive the scrutiny of public reason in such a cross-cultural conversation, its universal validity will be confirmed. An idea that has survived the test of rigorous scrutiny will be reasonable or valid not just within the boundaries of particular cultures, but reasonable in a non-relativistic fashion. The deliberation and public reasoning will continue, and it may always be possible for the concept of human rights to become doubtful and subject to revision. But the best available public reasons so far seem to support its universal validity. Such public reasons include the arguments against genocide, slavery, and racial discrimination. Others have emerged from the kind of reasoning that reveals fallacies, confusions, and mistakes involved in the defense of Asian cultural exceptionalism.

Questions for Reflection

1. Li argues that relativist claims to internal self-determination are merely the rationalizations made by oppressive states for their efforts to control internal dissent. Do you agree?
2. Why is it important, as Li suggests, to distinguish between community and state? Are there relevant differences between Asian and Western notions of community when it comes to human rights?
3. Li discusses the argument made by some Asian states that it is necessary to restrict political and civil rights for the sake of economic development. Is such a trade-off really necessary?

37. CHARLES TAYLOR

Charles Taylor (1931-) was formerly Chichele Professor of Social and Political Theory at Oxford University, and is Emeritus Professor of Philosophy and Political Science at McGill University. Among Taylor's many articles and books are *Hegel and Modern Society* (1979), *Sources of the Self* (1989) and *The Ethics of Authenticity* (1992). Taylor is considered one of the leading theorists of communitarianism, which holds that contemporary liberal theory is based on an atomistic conception of the person that overlooks the importance of various forms of community for the realization of the moral and political capacities of human beings. In the following selection, Taylor considers how it might be possible to come to a global consensus on human rights standards, and what that consensus might look like. The preceding selections by Tesón and Li highlight some of the specific moral problems that follow from the arguments of cultural relativism. What Taylor attempts to give us is some indication of how it can be meaningful to speak of human rights in a culturally diverse world, by drawing upon both Western and Asian philosophies.

Text—A World Consensus on Human Rights?

What would it mean to come to a genuine, unforced international consensus on human rights? I suppose it would be something like what John Rawls describes in his *Political Liberalism* as an "overlapping consensus." That is, different groups, countries, religious communities, civilizations, while holding incompatible fundamental views on theology, metaphysics, human nature, and so on, would come to an agreement on certain norms that ought to govern human behavior. Each would have its own way of justifying this from out of its profound background conception. We would agree on the norms, while disagreeing on why they were the norms. And we would be content to live in this consensus, undisturbed by the differences of profound underlying belief.

The idea was already expressed in 1949 by Jacques Maritain: "I am quite certain that my way of justifying belief in the rights of man and the ideal of liberty, equality, fraternity is the only way with a firm foundation on truth. This does not prevent me from being in agreement on these practical convictions with people who are certain that their way of justifying them, entirely different from mine or opposed to mine...is equally the only way founded upon truth."

Is this kind of consensus possible? Perhaps because of my optimistic nature, I believe that it is. But we have to confess at the outset that it is not entirely clear around what the consensus would form, and we are only beginning to discern the obstacles we would have to overcome on the way there. I want to talk a little about both these issues here.

First, what would the consensus be on? One might have thought this was obvious: on human rights. That's what our original question was about. But right away there is a first obstacle. Rights talk has roots in Western culture. This is not to say that something very like the underlying norms expressed in schedules of rights don't turn up elsewhere. But they are not expressed in this language. We can't assume straight off, without further examination, that a future unforced world consensus could be formulated to the satisfaction of everyone in the language of rights. Maybe yes, maybe no. Or maybe: partially yes, partially no, as we come to distinguish some of the things that have been associated in the Western package.

This is not to say that we already have some adequate term for whatever universals we may discern among difference cultures. Jack Donnelly speaks of "human dignity" as a universal value. Yasuaki Onuma criticizes this term, pointing out that "dignity" has been a favorite term in the same Western philosophical stream that has elaborated human rights. He prefers to speak of the "pursuit of spiritual as well as material well-being" as the universal. Where "dignity" might be too precise and culture-bound a term, "well-being" might be too vague and general. Perhaps we are incapable at this stage of formulating the universal values in play here. Perhaps we shall always be incapable of this. This wouldn't matter, because what we need to formulate for an overlapping consensus is certain norms of conduct. And there does seem to be some basis for hoping that we can achieve at least some agreement on these norms. One can presumably find in all cultures condemnation of genocide, murder, torture, and slavery, as well as of, say "disappearances" and the shooting of innocent demonstrators. The deep underlying values supporting these common conclusions will, in the nature of the case, belong to the alternative, mutually incompatible justifications.

I have been distinguishing between norms of conduct and their underlying justification. The Western rights tradition in fact exists at both these levels. On one plane, it is a legal tradition, legitimating certain kinds of legal moves, and empowering certain kinds of people to make them. We could, and people sometimes do, consider this legal culture as the proper candidate for universalization, arguing that its adoption can be justified in more than one way. Then a legal culture entrenching rights would define the norms around which the world consensus would supposedly crystallize.

Now some people have trouble with this; for example, Lee Kwan Yew and those in East Asia who sympathize with him. They see something dangerously individualistic, fragmenting, dissolvent of community, in this Western legal culture. (Of course, they have particularly in mind—or in their sights—the United States.) But in their criticism of Western procedures, they also seem to be attacking the underlying philosophy of the West, which allegedly gives primacy to the individual, where supposedly a "Confucian" outlook would have a larger place for the community and the complex web of human relations in which each person stands.

For the Western rights tradition also carries certain views on human nature, society, and the human good that are elements of an underlying justification. It might help the discussion to distinguish these two levels, at least analytically, so that we can develop a more fine-grained picture of what our options are here. Perhaps, in fact, the legal culture could "travel" better if it could be separated from some of its underlying justifications. Or perhaps the reverse is true, that the underlying picture of human life might look less frightening if it could find expression in a different legal culture. Or maybe neither of these simple solutions will work (this is my hunch), but modifications need to be made in both; however, distinguishing the levels still helps, because the modifications are different on each level.

A good place to start the discussion would be to give a rapid portrait of the language of rights that has developed in the West and of the surrounding notions of human agency and the good. We could then proceed to identify certain centers of disagreement across cultures, and we might then see what, if anything, could be done to bridge these differences.

First, let's get at the peculiarities of the language of rights. As has often been pointed out, there is something rather special here. Many societies have held that it is good to ensure certain immunities or liberties to their members—or sometimes even to outsiders (think of the stringent laws of hospitality in many traditional cultures). Everywhere it is wrong to take human life, at least under certain circumstances and for certain categories of persons. Wrong is the opposite of right, and so this is in some sense in play here.

But a quite different sense of the word is invoked when we start to use the definite or indefinite articles or to put it in the plural and speak of "a right" or "rights" or when we start to attribute these to persons and speak of your rights or my rights. This is to introduce what has been called "subjective rights." Instead of saying that it is wrong to kill me, we begin to say that I have a right to life. The two formulations are not equivalent in all respects, because in the latter case the immunity or liberty is considered the property of someone. It is no longer just an element of the law that stands over and between all of us equally. That I have a right to life says more than that you shouldn't kill me. It gives me some control over this immunity. A right is something that in principle I can waive. It is also something I have a role in enforcing.

Some element of subjective right may exist in all legal systems. The peculiarity of the West was, first, that this idea played a bigger role in European medieval societies than elsewhere in history and, second, that it was the basis for the rewriting of Natural Law theory that marked the seventeenth century. The older notion that human society stands under a Law of Nature, whose origin was the Creator, and which was thus beyond human will, was now transposed. The fundamental law was reconceived as consisting of natural rights, attributed to individuals prior to society. At the origin of society stands a contract, which takes people out of a state of nature and puts them under political authority as a result of an act of consent on their part.

So subjective rights are not only crucial to the Western tradition; even more significant is the fact that they were projected onto Nature and formed the basis of a philosophical view of humans and their society, one that greatly privileges individuals' freedom and their right to consent to the arrangements under which they live. This view has been an important strand in Western democratic theory of the last three centuries.

We can see how the notion of (subjective) right both serves to define certain legal powers and also provides the master image for a philosophy of human nature, of individuals and their societies. It operates both as legal norm and as underlying justification.

Moreover, these two levels are not unconnected. The force of the underlying philosophy has brought about a steady promotion of the legal norm in our politico-legal systems; so that it now occupies pride of place in a number of contemporary polities. Charters of rights are now entrenched in the constitutions of several countries and also of the European Union. These are the basis of judicial review whereby the ordinary legislation of different levels of government can be invalidated on the grounds of conflict with fundamental rights.

So the modern Western discourse of rights involves, on one hand, a set of legal forms, by which immunities and liberties are inscribed as rights, with certain consequences for the possibility of waiver and for the ways in which they can be secured—whether these immunities and liberties are among those from time to time granted by duly constituted authority or among those that are entrenched in fundamental law.

And it involves, on the other hand, a philosophy of the person and of society, attributing great importance to the individual and making significant matters turn on his or her power of consent. In both these regards, it contrasts with many other cultures, including the pre-modern West: not that some of the same protections and immunities may not have been present, but in that they had a quite different basis.

When people protest against the Western rights model, they seem to have this whole package in mind. And we can therefore see how resistance to the Western discourse of rights might occur on more than one level. Some governments might resist the enforcement of widely accepted norms because they have an agenda that involves their violation (for example, the contemporary People's Republic of China). Others, however, are certainly ready, even eager, to espouse some universal norms, but they are made uneasy by the underlying philosophy of the human person in society. This seems to give pride of place to autonomous individuals, determined to demand their rights, even (indeed especially) in the face of widespread social consensus. How does this fit with the Confucian emphasis on close personal relationships, not only as highly valued in themselves but as a model for the wider society? Can people who imbibe the full Western human rights ethos, which (on one version anyway) reaches its highest expression in the lone courageous individual fighting against all the forces of social conformity for his rights, ever be good members of a "Confucian" society? And how does this ethic of demanding what is due to us fit with the Theravada Buddhist search for selflessness, for self-giving, and *dana* (generosity)?

Taking the rights package as a whole is not simply wrong, because the philosophy is plainly part of what has motivated the great promotion enjoyed by this legal form. But the misgivings expressed in the previous paragraph, which cannot be easily dismissed, show the potential advantages of distinguishing the elements and loosening the connection between the legal cultures of rights enforcement and the philosophical conceptions of human life by which they were originally nourished at their point of origin.

In fact, we can easily imagine situations in which, for all its interconnections, the package can be untied, and either the forms or the philosophy could be adopted alone, without the other. Of course, this might involve some adjustments in what was borrowed, but this inevitably happens whenever ideas and institutions developed in one area are taken up elsewhere.

It might help to structure our thinking if we made a tripartite distinction. What we are looking for, in the end, is a world consensus on certain norms of conduct, enforceable on governments. To be accepted in any given society, these would in each case have to repose on some widely acknowledged philosophical justification; and to be enforced in fact, they would have to find expression in legal mechanisms. One way of putting our central question might be this: what variations can we imagine in philosophical justifications or in legal forms that would still be compatible with a meaningful universal consensus on what really matters to us, the enforceable norms?

Following this line of thinking, it might help to understand a little better what exactly we want to converge onto in the world society of the future, as well as to measure our chances of getting there, if we imagine variations separately on the two levels.

This is a big agenda, and I don't propose to follow it out here in all its ramifications. I will just consider one example, a case where we can see an important difference with the Western philosophy of the human person. This will allow us to raise the issue of to what extent we could hope for a convergence on norms even with very different underlying justifications.

I'd like to recur to the Theravada Buddhist demurral before the anthropology of the rights-demanding individual, which I invoked earlier; and in particular, I want to look at the way this position has been articulated by an influential movement in Thailand. This society has seen in the last century a number of attempts to formulate reformed interpretations of the overwhelmingly majority religion. Some of these have attempted to find a basis in this Buddhism for democracy and human rights.

One main stream of reform consists of movements that (as they see it) attempt to purify Buddhism, to turn it away from a focus on ritual, on gaining merit, and even worldly success through blessings and acts of piety, and to focus more on what they see as the original goal of Enlightenment. The late Phutthathat (Buddhadasa) was a major figure in this regard. This stream tries to return to what it sees as the original core of Buddhist teaching, about the unavoidability of suffering, the illusion of the self, and the goal of Nirvana. It attacks what it sees as the "superstition" of those who seek potent amulets, the blessings of monks, and the like. It wants to separate the search for enlightenment from the seeking of merit through ritual. And it is very critical of the whole metaphysical structure of belief that has developed in mainstream Buddhism, about heaven, hell, gods, and demons, which play a large part in popular belief. It has been described by Sri Lankan anthropologist Gananath Obeyesekere as a "Protestant Buddhism."

It is this stream that seems to be producing new reflections on Buddhism as a basis for democratic society and practice. This is not to say that all of those concerned Buddhists, monks and lay, involved in democratic activism of one kind or another have been of this persuasion. But it is the reform stream that is concerned to develop a Buddhist vision of democratic society. One may see something paradoxical in this, in that this rather austere reformism is espoused by a relatively small elite, rather far removed from the religious outlook of the mass of the people. But the dedication of some members of this elite to democracy, equality, and human rights commands respect.

Phutthathat's reformism was the very opposite of a disengaged religion, unconcerned with the world. On the contrary, he and those inspired by him have always stressed that the path to enlightenment is inseparable from that of concern for all creatures: *metta* (loving kindness) and *karuna* (compassion). We can't really be concerned with our own liberation without also seeking that of others, just as any acts of injustice toward them redound to our own continued imprisonment in illusion. Saneh Chamarik quotes the Buddha: "Monks: Taking care of oneself means as well taking care of others. Taking care of others means as well taking care of oneself." This view leads to an activist concern for social justice and well-being. Phutthathat spoke of a "dhammic socialism." It is a spiritual stance that entails heightened standards of personal commitment and responsibility, of probity and dedication to duty, even of self-sacrifice and dedication to the poor and downtrodden. Following Obeyesekere's analogy, one would say that it is reminiscent in this respect of Max Weber's "asceticism" that led to responsible, disciplined social action.

But this concern is not necessarily democratic. It could also find expression in other modes of social action, including those that see the agency of reform as a minority with the right intentions. These modes are, after all, well rooted in Theravada Buddhist history, in particular in the paradigm model of the emperor Asoka as the ideally just ruler and upholder of *Dharma*. This is, indeed, one of the models on which the Thai monarchial state was based. The *dharmmaraja* is undoubtedly understood as an agency for good, for the welfare of the people, but he is not in any normal sense a democratic agency.

Phutthathat himself was not entirely clear on the issue of democratic agency. There has, however, been a democratic strand in this general movement. Panyanantha made a democratic application of Phutthathat's thought, for instance. And something similar could be said for Photirak and his Santi Asok movement. This has acquired additional political relevance recently, in that the charismatic leader of the Palang Dharma Party, Chamlong Srimuang, is a follower of Santi Asok.

Beyond these, there are followers of Phutthathat's reformism who are deeply committed to democracy, such as Sulak Sivaraksa and Saneh Charmarik. They and others in their milieu are highly active in the nongovernnmental organization (NGO) community. They are concerned with alternative models of development, which would be more ecologically sound, concerned to put limits to growth, critical of "consumerism," and conducive to social equality. The Buddhist commitment lies behind all these goals. As Sulak explains it, the Buddhist commitment to nonviolence entails a nonpredatory stance toward the environment and calls also for the limitation of greed, one of the sources of anger and conflict.

We can see here an agenda of universal well-being. But what specifically pushes to democracy, that is, to ensuring that people take charge of their own lives, rather than simply being the beneficiaries of benevolent rule? Two things seem to come together in this outlook to underpin a strong democratic commitment. The first is the notion, central to Buddhism, that ultimately each individual must take responsibility for his or her own Enlightenment. The second is a new application of the doctrine of nonviolence, which is now seen to call for a respect for the autonomy of each person, demanding in effect a minimal use of coercion in human affairs. This carries us far from the politics of imposed order, decreed by the wise minority, which has long been the traditional background to various forms and phases of military rule. It is also evident that this underpinning for democracy offers a strong support for human rights legislation. And that, indeed, is how it is understood by thinkers like Sulak.

There is an outlook here that converges on a policy of defense of human rights and democratic development, but that is rather different from the standard Western justifications of these. It isn't grounded on a doctrine of the dignity of human beings as something commanding respect. The injunction to respect comes rather as a consequence of the fundamental value of nonviolence, which also generates a whole host of other consequences (including the requirement for an ecologically responsible development and the need to set limits to growth). Human rights don't stand out, as they often do in the West, as a claim that is independent from the rest of our moral commitments or even sometimes in potential conflict with them.

Interestingly, this Buddhist conception provides an alternative way of linking together the agenda of human rights and that of democratic development. Whereas in the Western framework these go together because they are both seen as requirements of human dignity, and indeed, as two facets of liberty, a connection of a somewhat different kind is visible among Thai Buddhists of this reform persuasion. Their commitment to people-centered and ecologically sensitive development makes them strong allies of those communities of villagers who are resisting encroachment by the state and big business and fighting to defend their lands and forests. This means they are heavily engaged with a crucial part of the agenda of democratization in Thailand—decentralization, and in particular the recovery of local control over natural resources. They form a significant part of the NGO community committed to this agenda. Thus, a rather different route than that taken in the West has been traveled to a similar goal.

Other differences stand out. Because of its roots in a certain justice agenda, the politics of establishing rights in the West has often been surrounded by anger, indignation, and the imperative to punish historic wrongdoing. But from this Buddhist perspective comes a caution against the politics of anger, itself the potential source of new forms of violence.

My aim here is not to judge between these approaches, but to point out these differences as the source of a potentially fruitful exchange within a (one hopes) emerging world consensus on the practice of human rights and democracy. We can in fact see a convergence here on certain norms of action, however they may be entrenched in law. But what is unfamiliar to the Western observer is the entire philosophical basis, and its appropriate reference points, as well as the rhetorical bases of its appeal. In the West, both democracy and human rights have been furthered by the steady advance of a kind of humanism that stressed how humans stood out from the rest of the cosmos and had a higher status and dignity than anything else. This has its origins in Christianity, and also certain strands of ancient thought, but the distance is greatly exacerbated by what Weber describes as the disenchantment of the world, the rejection of a view of the cosmos as a meaningful order. The human agent stands out even more starkly from the mechanistic universe. For Pascal, the human being is a mere reed, but of incomparably greater significance than what threatens to crush it, because it is a thinking reed. Kant echoes some of the same reflections in his discussion of the sublime.

The human rights doctrine based on this humanism stresses

the importance of the human agent. It centers everything on him or her, makes his or her freedom and self-control a major value, something to be maximized. Consequently, in the Western mind, the defense of human rights seems indissolubly linked with this exaltation of human agency. It is because humans justifiably command all this respect and attention, at least in comparison to anything else, that their rights must be defended. The Buddhist philosophy that I have been describing starts from a quite different place, the demand of *ahimsa*, and yet seems to ground many of these same norms. (Of course, there will also be differences in the norms grounded, which raises its own problems, but for the moment I just want to note the substantial overlap.) The gamut of Western philosophical emotions, the exaltation of human dignity, the emphasis on freedom as the highest value, the drama of age-old wrongs righted in valor, all the things that move us in seeing *Fidelio* well performed, seem out of place in this alternative setting. And so do the models of heroism. The heroes of *ahimsa* are not forceful revolutionaries, not Cola di Rienzi or Garibaldi. And without the philosophy and the models, a whole rhetoric loses its basis.

This perhaps gives us an idea of what an unforced world consensus on human rights might look like. Agreement on norms, yes; but a profound sense of difference, of unfamiliarity, in the ideals, the notions of human excellence, the rhetorical tropes and reference points by which these norms become objects of deep agreement for us. To the extent that we can only acknowledge agreement with people who share the whole package, and are moved by the same heroes, the consensus will either never come or must be forced.

This is the situation at the outset, in any case, where consensus on some aspect of human rights has just been attained. Later, a process of mutual learning can follow, moving toward a "fusion of horizons" in Gadamer's term, where the moral universe of the other becomes less strange. And out of this will come further borrowings and the creation of new hybrid forms.

After all, something of this has already occurred with another stream of the philosophy of *ahimsa*, that of Gandhi.

Gandhi's practices of nonviolent resistance have been borrowed and adapted in the West, in the American civil rights movement, for example. And beyond that, they have become part of a world repertory of political practices, invoked in Manila in 1986 and in Prague in 1989, to name just two examples.

Also worthy of remark is one other facet of this case, which may be generalizable as well. An important part of the Western consciousness of human rights lies in the awareness of a historic achievement. The rights define norms of respect for human beings more radical and more exigent than have ever existed in the past. They offer in principle greater freedom, greater security from violence, from arbitrary treatment, from discrimination and oppression than humans have enjoyed at least in most major civilizations in history. In a sense they involve taking the rather exceptional treatment accorded to privileged people in the past and extending it to everyone. That is why so many of the landmarks of the historical development of rights were in their day instruments of elite privilege, starting with the Magna Carta.

Now there is a curious convergence in this respect with the strand of Reform Buddhism I have been describing. Here, too, there is the awareness that very exigent demands are being made, which go way beyond what the majority of ordinary believers recognize as required practices. Reform Buddhism is practiced by an elite, as has been the case with most of its analogues in history. But here, too, in developing a doctrine of democracy and human rights, Reform Buddhists are proposing to extend what has hitherto been a minority practice and entrench it in society universally. Here again there is a consciousness of the universalization of the highest of traditional minority practices.

It's as though, in spite of the difference in philosophy, this universalization of an exigent standard, which human rights practice at its best involves, was recognized as a valid move, and recreated within a different cultural, philosophical, and religious world. The hope for a consensus is that this kind of move will be made repeatedly.

Can it be? Will it be? It's too early to say; but perhaps we already dimly discern the direction in which we have to travel.[1]

Note

1. See the following sources on Buddhism: Chamarik, Senah, *Democracy and Development: A Cultural Perspective* (Bangkok: Local Development Institute, 1993); Gombrich, Richard and Gananath Obeyesekere, *Buddhism Transformed: Religious Change in Sri Lanka* (Princeton: Princeton University Press, 1988); Jackson, Peter. "Thai Buddhist Identity: Debates on the Traiphum Phra Ruang," in Craig Reynolds, ed., *National Identity and Its Defenders: Thailand 1939–1989* (Clayton, Victoria: Monash Papers on Southeast Asia number 25, 1991); Muntaborn, Vitit and Charles Taylor, *Roads to Democracy: Human Rights and Democratic Development in Thailand* (Bangkok and Montreal: International Centre for Human Rights and Democratic Development, July 1994); Siveraksa, Sulak, *Seeds of Peace: A Buddhist Vision for Renewing Society* (Berkeley and Bangkok: Parallax Press, 1992).

Questions for Reflection

1. In his argument for an international consensus on human rights, Taylor suggests that such a consensus is desirable because "we could agree on the norms, while disagreeing on why they were the right norms." What does Taylor mean by this? Why is this an important distinction?

2. Taylor contrasts the Western justification of human rights based on respect for the dignity of human beings, with the Buddhist justification based on well-being and nonviolence. In what ways are these two justifications different? Similar?

3. In light of the readings contained in this and in prior sections of the book, do you think it is likely that truly universal human rights norms can be agreed upon and enforced? Why or why not?

FURTHER READINGS FOR SECTION 6

Bielefeldt, Heiner. "Human Rights in a Multicultural World." *Jahrbuch für Recht und Ethik* 3 (1995): 283-294.

Brown, Chris. "Universal Human Rights: A Critique." *International Journal of Human Rights* 1 (1997): 41-65.

Davis, Michael C., ed. *Human Rights and Chinese Values*. Hong Kong: Oxford University Press, 1995.

Donnelly, Jack. "Cultural Relativism and Universal Human Rights." *Human Rights Quarterly* 6 (1984): 400-418.

Howard, Rhoda E. "Human Rights and Culture Wars: Globalization and the Universality of Human Rights." *International Journal* 53 (1997-98): 94-112.

Panikkar, Raimundo. "Is the Notion of Human Rights a Western Concept?" *Diogenes* 120 (1982): 75-102.

Renteln, Allison D. *International Human Rights: Universalism Versus Relativism*. Newbury Park, CA: Sage Publications, 1990.

Sen, Amartya. "Human Rights and Asian Values." In *Ethics & International Affairs*, Joel H. Rosenthal, ed. Second Edition. Washington, DC: Georgetown University Press, 1999.

Sweet, William. "Human Rights and Cultural Diversity." *International Journal of Applied Philosophy* 12 (198): 117-32.

Section 7:
MINORITY CULTURES AND GROUP RIGHTS

38. JAMES CRAWFORD

James Crawford (1948-) is Whewell Professor of International Law at Cambridge University, and a Member of the International Law Commission. A specialist in public international law and human rights, Crawford has authored books entitled *The Creation of States in International Law* (1979) and *The Rights of Peoples* (1988). In recent years claims to individual human rights have been increasingly supplemented by claims to collective or peoples' rights on the part of various communities, such as ethnic minorities and indigenous peoples. What Crawford draws our attention to in his essay is the way the term "peoples" must be understood as distinguished from individuals and states. Crawford also examines the types of collective or group rights that peoples might have in light of developments in international law.

Text—The Rights of Peoples: "Peoples" or "Governments"?

Reprinted from James Crawford, ed. The Rights of Peoples *(Oxford: Clarendon Press, 1988), 55-67.*

1. THE RIGHTS OF PEOPLES AND THE STRUCTURE OF INTERNATIONAL LAW

From the perspective of international law, the key feature of the phrase "rights of peoples" is not the term "rights", but the term "peoples." From a philosophical point of view, no doubt, the term "rights" is itself problematic. But lawyers, including international lawyers, are used to talking about rights, and so long as one accepts Hohfeld's point that one person's right must mean another person's duty, the term seems unremarkable even in the context of peoples' rights. Moreover, international law is familiar with the notion of "collective" rights. References to the State, the basic unit of international law, involve a reference to the social fact of a territorial community of persons with a certain political organization, in other words, a reference to a collectivity. In this sense, international law rules that confer rights on States confer collective rights. However, when international law attributes rights to States as social and political collectivities, it does so *sub modo*—that is to say, it does so subject to the rule that the actor on behalf of the State, and the agency to which other States are to look for the observation of the obligations of the State and which is entitled to activate its rights, is the government of the State. This basic rule drastically affects the point that the State *qua* community of persons has rights in international law, especially where the view or position taken by the government of a State diverges from the interests or wishes of the people of the State that government represents. And it is, so far at least, axiomatic that international law does not guarantee representative, still less democratic, governments.[1]

The proposition that the international law rights of States as communities of persons are moderated through a government (not necessarily representative, but legally the representative, of the people of the State) still represents the general rule. And it is that proposition which makes the term "peoples" in the phrase "rights of peoples" remarkable. Has international law taken up the task of conferring rights on groups or communities of people against the State which those people constitute, and against the government of the State? If so, it would be no great step for it to confer rights on those groups or communities as against other States and their governments. But the people of a State are—to put it mildly—at least as likely to have their rights violated by their own government as by the governments of other States. If the phrase "rights of peoples" has any independent meaning, it must confer rights on peoples against their own governments. In other words, if the only rights of peoples are rights against other States, and if there is no change to the established position that the government of the State represents "the State" (i.e. the people of the State) for all international purposes irrespective of its representativeness, then what is the point of referring to the rights in question as rights of peoples? Why not refer to them as the rights of States, in the familiar, well understood, though somewhat elliptical way?

I think it is more profitable to try to answer this question in the context of specific formulations of the "rights of peoples." Which of these rights are really rights of States in disguise? Which of them are really individual human rights—or aspirations to them? Which can properly be treated as rights of peoples, as distinct from individuals or States? And if they can so be treated, what is it that distinguishes them from the other two classes of rights? It should be stressed that these questions are independent of the actual status of any particular right as a matter of general international law, or, if (as I suspect) this is a different category, as one of the recognized body of "human rights." But the questions must be answered before we can make sense of the practice in relation to any asserted "right," so that to this extent at least, the issues are related.

2. A SURVEY OF "PEOPLES' RIGHTS"

Sieghart's compilation of general human rights texts[2] identifies six classes of "collective rights." For present purposes, these may be described as follows:

- self-determination and equality of rights
- rights relating to international peace and security
- permanent sovereignty over natural resources
- rights in relation to development
- rights in relation to the environment, and
- rights of minorities.

One cardinal omission from this list, from the point of view of the "rights of peoples," is the right of groups to exist, which may be conceived of, in the first place, as an obligation on the part of States not to engage in, or allow, genocidal acts.

In addition to these seven classes or categories, there are undoubtedly other asserted rights, or provisions in international texts which might be reformulated as "peoples rights," that could be added. Although the rights set out in Part III of the International Covenant on Economic, Social and Cultural Rights of 1966 are for the most part formulated in terms of individual rights, a number of them could be seen as having collective elements, including the right to form trade unions (art. 8), the right to a "continuous improvement of living conditions" (art. 11), and the rights in art. 15(1) with respect to "cultural life" and "the benefits of scientific progress and its applications." Nonetheless, the seven categories mentioned above are those which are sufficiently clearly formulated in terms of "collective" rights, and which have achieved recognition in at least one international human rights instrument in treaty form.[3] For the purposes of assessing the validity of the "rights of peoples" as a distinct concept or category, these seven seem a sufficient test.

The seven classes of "rights" under examination fall into two distinct categories. One immediately apparent category is the group of rights which in some respect deal with the existence and cultural or political continuation of groups. This category would include the right to self-determination, the rights of minorities, and the rights of groups to existence (i.e. as a minimum, not to be subjected to genocide).[4] But, it may be significant that the phrase "rights of peoples" tends to be used, at least by its proponents, primarily to refer to the other and more miscellaneous category of rights, concerned with a variety of issues relating to the economic development and the "coexistence" of peoples. This second category includes rights in respect of permanent sovereignty over natural resources, rights to development, to the environment and to international peace and security. However, one cannot exclude the first category in asking basic questions about the "rights of peoples", in particular because the three group rights referred to (self-determination, minorities, genocide) appear on their face to be "rights of peoples," and because each has gone through a considerable process of development in this century (and in the case of the rights of minorities, in earlier centuries also). By contrast the asserted rights in the second category are substantially new, and in most cases embryonic.

(1) Self-determination

The principle of self-determination has been one of the most vigorous, and vigorously disputed, collective or group rights in modern international law, and has generated a vast literature.[5]

The major focus for arguments about self-determination has of course been the question of decolonization, and it is controversial whether the principle of self-determination is restricted to cases of decolonization, or whether it can have consequences in terms of "metropolitan" States, including, for example, minority groups or peoples. As it happens, the term "self-determination of peoples" in the United Nations Charter occurs twice, in Art. 1 para. 2, and in Art. 55, in each case as part of the phrase "respect for the principle of equal rights and self-determination of peoples." In each case the context is quite distinct from questions of decolonization (which are dealt with in the Charter in Articles 73 and 76). In the United Nations Human Rights Covenants, the phrase has a similar tone of universality, although in each case it is described as a "right" rather than a "principle," and is dissociated from the term "equal rights." Thus Art. 1 para. 1 of both the Economic, Social and Cultural Rights Covenant, and the Civil and Political Rights Covenant, proclaims that:

> All peoples have the right of self-determination. By virtue of that right they freely determine their political status and freely pursue their economic, social and cultural development.

The link between self-determination and "economic, social and cultural development" is already explicit, and it is spelt out further by linking with self-determination in para. 2 the notion that "all peoples may, for their own ends, freely dispose of their natural wealth and resources.... In no case may a people be deprived of its own means of subsistence." Decolonization is only expressly referred to in para. 3 of Art. 1, and then in terms which imply that States parties to the Covenants may have obligations by reference to the notion of self-determination which extend beyond "Non-Self-Governing and Trust Territories."[6]

Whatever view is taken about the scope of the principle of self-determination in international law, from the point of view of the present enquiry the situation is clear. Self-determination is plainly a collective rather than an individual right, although obviously enough individuals are to be involved in the exercise of the right, and a majority of them at least will benefit directly from it in the sense of retaining or achieving a measure of self-government in accordance with their wishes or preferences. Secondly, self-determination is plainly to be thought of as a right of "peoples" rather than governments. To the extent that it applies, it qualifies the right of governments to dispose of the "peoples" in question in ways which conflict with their rights to self-determination.

(2) Genocide: The Right to Physical Existence

There can be no doubt that international law recognizes the obligation of States not to commit or condone genocide. This idea may be implicit in the notion of self-determination as expressed in Art. 1 para. 1 of the Human Rights Covenants, but it goes well beyond those provisions, because the "peoples" or "groups" protected by the rules about genocide include groups which would not be classed as beneficiaries of the right to self-determination. Article II of the Genocide Convention of 1948 describes the beneficiaries of the rule as any "national, ethnical [*sic*], racial or religious group" and proscribes certain acts committed against members of such groups with intent to destroy them in whole or in part.[7] It is true that the Genocide Convention is directed at offenders rather than victims; that is to say, the problem is treated in that Convention as a matter of the duties of "persons...whether they are constitutionally responsible rulers, public officials or private individuals" (Art. IV), rather than in terms of the rights of "national, ethnical, racial or religious groups." But plainly the definition of "genocide" can be regarded as having as its object the preservation of those groups, and in this sense it is meaningful to talk about their rights. It should be noted, however, that these rights are of a distinctly limited character, notwithstanding (or perhaps because of) the breadth of the notion of a "group" in the Convention. Thus the Convention only prohibits acts which involve or conduce to direct or indirect physical destruction of the group or a substantial part of it, whether by homicide, terrorism, mass deprivation, eugenics or forcible transfer of children. The Convention is not concerned with "cultural genocide" or what has been described as "ethnocide,"[8] in the sense of the destruction or disappearance of the distinctive values, traditions, or culture of a group, as distinct from the survival of the members of the group as individuals, and its continued existence as a group assuming its members so wish.[9]

(3) Rights of Minorities

As mentioned already, the notion that minority groups may have rights guaranteed to them as such is not a new one in international relations. Indeed, to the extent that minority rights are thought of as more than the product of the individual human rights of members of minority groups (including their rights to associate with each other), these rights were better protected under the international law of the pre-World War II period (in those cases where particular minorities were protected by treaties or other arrangements), than they are now under general human rights law.[10] The relevant provision of the International Covenant on Civil and Political Rights, Art. 27, hovers between being a mere extrapolation from the individual rights of members of a minority group, and being a genuinely "collective" right. Both the formulation of Art. 27 in terms of individual rights ("persons belonging to such minorities shall not be denied the right..."), and its association in international jurisprudence with notions of equality and non-discrimination, suggest that minority rights are not necessarily to be thought of as collective rights at all, in modern international law. The crucial issue is that of "minorities of minorities": if minority rights are genuinely collective, then it presumably follows that dissenting members of minority groups can be compelled to comply with the wishes of the majority of the group, in the same way that dissenting members of "peoples" with a right to self-determination can be compelled to accept a form of self government which the majority of that "people" have elected or accepted.[11]

One of the difficulties here is the underlying assumption that the category "minorities" bears some necessary relation to the category "peoples." This need not be so. A minority cannot cease to be a "people," if it is one, just because, as a result of demographic or territorial change or for some other reason, it becomes a majority of the national population of a State. By definition, a "minority" implies the existence of a "majority" (not necessarily a coherent one, since it could be made up by a collection of other minorities). By contrast, the notion of a "people" says nothing about the relationship of that people to other peoples inhabiting the same State or territory. Thus an individual might have rights as a member of a minority which coexist with rights that person enjoys as a member of (the same or a broader) group properly classified as a "people," for the purpose of the right to self-determination, or for some other purpose. One of the difficulties with nineteenth-century practice in the area of minorities was that it was seeking to protect what are logically and practically distinct values: the "collective" value of national existence or continuity or autonomy within a broader "multi-national" State or empire (a problem now partly at least subsumed under the category of self-determination), and the rights of individual members of minority groups to associate with each other, and to practice their culture, language or religion. The latter right is certainly capable of being thought of, and is perhaps best thought of, as in principle an individual one: no one can be forced to practice a religion. On this view the Human Rights Committee's treatment of Sandra Lovelace as a member of a "minority" under Art. 27 of the Civil and Political Rights Covenant[12] was not necessarily inconsistent with the view that the Indian group to which she claimed to belong, or other indigenous groups with a sufficiently distinctive character, might be "peoples" for the purposes of Art. 1 of the Covenant, that is to say, for the purposes of the right to self-determination. But in practice such claims are likely to be met with considerable hostility, especially from the "newly independent" States themselves, whose primary concern is stated to be nation building rather than respect for, or even tolerance of, the cultures and beliefs of local populations.[13]

(4) Rights to International Peace and Security

In this insecure and not particularly peaceful world, the idea that there might be individual or collective rights to international peace and security has a certain paradoxical quality. There have been various attempts since 1945 by legal means to address some of the causes of war, in particular measures prohibiting incitement to racial, national, or religious hatred, and a number of the international human rights instruments contain provisions requiring certain forms of incitement to "national, racial, or religious hatred," and "any propaganda for war" to be prohibited by law.[14] Article 23(1) Of the African Charter goes beyond this, and declares that:

> All peoples shall have the right to national and international peace and security. The principles of solidarity and friendly relations implicitly affirmed by the Charter of the United Nations and reaffirmed by that of the Organization of African Unity shall govern relations between States.

Article 23(2)(b) goes on to provide that the territory of States parties "shall not be used as bases for subversive or terrorist activities against the people of any other State party to the present Charter." Article 23 is of considerable interest in revealing the interplay, or perhaps one should say the confusion, between the notions of "people" and "State." The first sentence of Art. 23(1) declares a right of all peoples. The second sentence refers to principles of solidarity and friendly relations between States. But Art. 23(2), for the purpose of "strengthening peace, solidarity and friendly relations" imposes an obligation not to allow territory to be used as a base for subversive or terrorist activities against "the people of any other State party." Evidently the "people" referred to is assumed to be synonymous with the whole population of the State, at least for the purpose of Art. 23(2)(b). Moreover Art. 23(2)(b) might appear to allow "subversive or terrorist activities" against governments which are wholly unrepresentative of the "people" of the State, a proposition contradicted by the principles of international law expressly affirmed in the Charters of the United Nations and the Organization of African Unity, which principles Art. 23 had apparently earlier endorsed.

Of course, there is a practical relationship between the maintenance of general human rights, individual or collective, and the existence of a state of peace, if not friendly relations, between States. As a reference to this important though underlying reality, provisions such as Art. 23 of the African Charter, or for that matter Art. 28 of the Universal Declaration of Human Rights,[15] cannot be criticized. But to treat rights to international peace and security as distinct and independent, as it were "foreground" rights, whether individual or collective, raises questions of an altogether different kind. To say that States have the right to international peace and security is to repeat, in obverse, established and well-known duties such as those stated in Art. 2 para. 4 of the United Nations Charter. But to say, as Art. 23 of the African Charter does, that "peoples" have that right, even if in this context "peoples" means the populations of States as a whole, might appear to make a wide range of sensitive foreign policy questions justiciable in the African Commission of Human and Peoples Rights, particularly since Art. 23 makes no distinction between actions (e.g. invasion, military intervention) which themselves breach the peace, and actions, policies, or attitudes which have a more diffuse disruptive tendency. As is well known the United Nations Charter, and the international law founded on it, while acknowledging the link between respect for human rights and maintenance of international peace and security, placed a considerable priority upon avoiding outright conflict between States, whatever its origins, requiring underlying disputes to be settled by other means. Provisions such as Art. 23, in avoiding these distinctions and in conflating respect for human or peoples' rights and international peace and security, tend further to blur or confuse the basic premises upon which the Charter order was to be based. To be sure, there are other aspects of modern international relations and diplomacy having the same tendency, but it is by no means clear that debate on this central question is assisted by reformulating the issue in terms of peoples rights.

(5) Rights to Permanent Sovereignty over Natural Resources

The notion of permanent sovereignty over natural resources has gained considerable currency in the last two decades, and is recognized in the same terms both in the Civil and Political Rights Covenant, and in the Economic, Social and Cultural Rights Covenant. Article 1 para. 2 of both instruments provides that:[16]

> All peoples may, for their own ends, freely dispose of their natural wealth and resources without prejudice to any obligations arising out of international economic co-operation, based upon the principle of mutual benefit and international law. In no case may a people be deprived of its own means of subsistence.

The precedent for treating questions of permanent sovereignty over natural resources as rights of peoples, rather than as rights of States, is thus an established one. The African Charter is to that extent on firm ground when it elaborates upon the notion of permanent sovereignty in a similar, though more explicit, way. Article 21 provides that:[17]

> (1) All peoples shall freely dispose of their wealth and natural resources. This right shall be exercised in the exclusive interest of the people. In no case shall a people be deprived of it.
> (2) In case of spoliation the dispossessed people shall have the right to lawful recovery of its property as well as to an adequate compensation.
> (3) The free disposal of wealth and natural resources shall be exercised without prejudice to the obligation of promoting international economic co-operation based on mutual respect, equitable exchange and the principles of international law.

Despite the substantial body of support for rule or principle of permanent sovereignty over natural resources, there are difficulties in treating it as a collective right of peoples as distinct from States. In its application to States, the notion of "permanent sovereignty" (though something of an euphemism—States are not necessarily "permanently sovereign" but can be extinguished in a variety of ways) none the less makes reasonable sense as an extrapolation from underlying notions of sovereignty and independence. Agreements, whether on the international or municipal level, with respect to the use of natural resources do not extinguish a State's sovereignty over those resources while they remain within its territory. The notion of permanent sovereignty may also be concerned with establishing, or reaffirming, certain hierarchies of international law rules. For example, States may remain "sovereign" over their natural resources though their conduct in relation to those resources violates other principles of international law (e.g. in the context of expropriation of foreign-owned property).

So far "permanent sovereignty" fits sufficiently well within existing categories, whatever conclusions one arrives at as to the merits of particular issues. But introducing the notion that the "permanent sovereignty" is a sovereignty of "peoples" adds another dimension. If those "peoples" constitute a part only of the population of the State, then the notion of permanent sovereignty presumably limits the power of the national government freely to dispose of the natural resources of the region without the consent (or against the wishes or contrary to the interests) of the "people" in question. Alternatively, if the "people" is the whole population of the State, the principle apparently establishes that transactions entered into by or on behalf of the State and involving the disposal of natural resources are subject to subsequent scrutiny, and to invalidation or avoidance, if these turn out not to have been in the interests of the population. Moreover, such a rule can hardly make sense when it is limited to "foreign economic exploitation" (which to be effective cannot be wholly foreign: like charity, exploitation usually begins at home). Formulated in this way, the principle of permanent sovereignty over natural resources is certainly capable of operating as a guarantee of peoples against their own governments, limiting the capacity of governments for the time being in the interests of the community.[18] In the case of provisions such as Art. 21 of the African Charter, that would tend to make a State's natural resources policy justiciable in the African Commission on Human and Peoples Rights. No doubt the real point of provisions such as Art. 21, or Art. 1 para. 2 of the United Nations Human Rights Covenants, is that they provide a forensic basis for disputing existing contractual and other arrangements relating to natural resources. But thought of as a right of "peoples," the argument seems a dangerously double-edged one.

(6) The Right to Development

So far this is recognized as such in human rights treaties only in the African Charter, Art. 22 of which provides that:

> (1) All peoples shall have the right to their economic, social and cultural development with due regard to their freedom and identity and in the equal enjoyment of the common heritage of mankind.
> (2) States shall have the duty, individually or collectively, to ensure the exercise of the right to development.

Notwithstanding its scanty recognition in international human rights treaties, the notion of a right to development as a human or peoples' rights is very much at the center of the debate about peoples' rights.[19] For present purposes the analysis of the possible distinctions between a right to development as a peoples' right, and that right as a right of States, does not differ significantly from the situation with respect to the right of permanent sovereignty over natural resources. The right to development is, outside specific contexts and specific instruments (e.g. relating to development aid, or the distribution of benefits in the law of the sea regime), less well integrated into the body of international practice than the notion of permanent sovereignty.[20] So far as other States are concerned, the notion that "peoples" have a right to development does not appear to differ from the proposition that States have such a right. But the former proposition might have an independent content if its effect was to countermand deliberate governmental policies vis-à-vis the population of the State in question, leading designedly to non-development or to differential development of regions. It is difficult to believe that States would be interested to assert the illegitimacy of such policies on the part of another State against its own peoples (basic questions of racial discrimination or genocide apart), or that the "defaulting" governments themselves would be prepared to accept such assertions (whether or not accompanying the provision of development aid) as a matter of right. So far, the assessment of one leading African international lawyer seems accurate:[21]

> The right to development...appears not to have attained the definitive status of rule of law despite its powerful advocates. Its inclusion in the African Charter will be as effective as the Charter itself. The negative duty not to impede the development of States may go down well; the positive duty to aid such development, in the absence of specific accords, is a higher level of commitment that still rests on nonlegal considerations.

(7) Rights to the Environment

Much the same can be said of the notion of "rights to the environment," which are again reflected so far only in the African Charter. Article 24 provides that: "All peoples shall have the right to a general satisfactory environment favourable to their development."

Plainly we are here at the outer limits of the justiciability of rights of this general kind.[22]

3. SOME TENTATIVE CONCLUSIONS

So far I have only dealt with what might be called the concept of peoples' rights, and only by reference to those rights already recognized in international instruments in treaty form. That is a fair test in the longer term, whatever view one takes about General Assembly (or other international) resolutions. It would be possible to undertake the same analysis of other items in Alston's list, which includes such rights as:[23]

> the right not to be exposed to excessively and unnecessarily heavy, degrading, dirty and boring work; the right to identity with one's own work product, individually or collectively (as opposed to anonymity); the right to access to challenging work requiring creativity...the right to social transparency; the right to co-existence with nature; the right to be free to seek impressions from others (not only from the media); and the right to be free to experiment with alternative ways of life.

(Parenthetically, they are a remarkably Western, even bourgeois list!) But it is sufficient to draw conclusion from the seven classes of rights surveyed here.

Dealing first with the group rights associated with self-determination, the rights of minorities and related questions, the conventional view is that each of these is, as a collective right, still a rule of exception.[24] On the other hand, for the purposes of this inquiry, and without prejudice to questions of the scope of these rights, there is no difficulty in thinking of them as rights of peoples; some of them are also collective in character, that is to say, the beneficiary of the right is a group rather than its individual members.

So far as the other rights are concerned, as rights of States some are merely affirmative reformulations of existing duties. Others are merely contentious. As rights of peoples, their real content is with respect to the government of the State in question. No doubt this may not be intended by proponents of those rights, but if they do not intend it, perhaps they would do well to revert to more orthodox terminology. Whatever the case, these third generation rights as so interpreted seem consistent with basic concerns about equity between peoples and their governments which are by no means confined to the Third World. Whether such rights can be made internationally justiciable may be another question, although, as modern administrative law, and the experience with Bills of Rights in a number of countries, show, almost anything can be justiciable at a certain level, and given a sufficient political mandate to the adjudicating body. In the case of the African Charter, the mandate is to the African Commission on Human and Peoples' Rights, there being no African Court of Human Rights. It will be interesting to see—now that governments (not peoples) have ratified the African Charter and it is in force—to what extent the members of the African Commission turn out to be representatives of peoples, as distinct from representatives of governments.

Notes

1. Cf. the *Tinoco Arbitration* (1924) I RIAA 369. But the "right to have a democratic government representing all the citizens without distinction as to race, sex, belief or colour" is asserted by Art. 7 of the Algiers Declaration, and F. Rigaux comments that "le peuple est l'ensemble ou la majorité de la population d'un Etat dont un des droits fondamentaux est de n'être pas soumis au pouvoir d'une minorité." "Remarques Générales sur la Déclaration d'Alger" in A. Cassese

& E. Jouve (eds.), *Pour un Droit des Peuples. Essais sur la Déclaration d'Alger* (1978), 41, 46.

2. P. Sieghart, *The International Law of Human Rights* (1983), 367-78.

3. This is not to suggest that other instruments, such as General Assembly resolutions, may not be significant. But such resolutions do not create obligations even for States voting for them, however influential they may be as evidence or sources of argument.

4. Another "right" sometimes asserted in this context which would also fall into this category (if it is not merely a reformulation of the three "rights" referred to) is the "right to be different": cf. Art. 1(2) of the UNESCO Declaration on Race and Racial Prejudice, 27 November 1978: "All peoples have the right to be different, to consider themselves as different, and to be regarded as such." Principles of equality and non-discrimination are also relevant, though usually expressed as individual rather than group rights: cf. *Case Concerning Minority Schools in Albania* PCIJ Ser A/B No 64 (1935), 17.

5. See J. Crawford, *The Creation of States in International Law* (1979), 85-102 and works there cited.

6. Art. 1(3) provides that States parties "including those having responsibility for the administration of Non-Self-Governing and Trust Territories, shall promote the realisation of the right of self-determination...." (emphasis added).

7. 78 UNTS 277. See also L. Le Blanc, "The Intent to Destroy Groups in the Genocide Convention: The Proposed US Understanding" (1984) 78 *AJIL*, 369. The requirement of intent has led to arguments that the disappearance of indigenous groups as a more or less direct effect of government policies is not genocide because unintended: cf. id., 380-81 (Aché Indians in Paraguay).

8. Cf. P. Thornberry, "Is There a Phoenix in the Ashes? International Law and Minority Rights" (1980) 15 *Texas ILJ*, 421, 444.

9. On the other hand, acts of genocide as defined in the Convention may well take place with a view to the forced assimilation or destruction of the culture of a group, so that to this extent the two concepts are linked.

10. On the pre-World War II minorities treaties and their replacement by general human rights provisions after 1945 see e.g. J. B. Kelly, "National Minorities in International Law" (1973) 3 *Denver JILP*, 253.

11. As is the case of dissentients in the various UN-supervised plebiscites in trust and non-self-governing territories: see A. Rigo-Sureda, *The Evolution of the Right of Self-Determination* (1973).

12. GAOR 36th Sess., Supp. No 40 (A/36/40), Annex XVIII, 166.

13. Cf. the Human Rights Committee's reluctance to deal with an application brought on behalf of the Miqmaq Indians under the Optional Protocol to the ICCPR, alleging a violation of self-determination under Art. 1 of the Covenant: *Miqmaq Tribal Society v. Canada*, noted in (1984) 33 *Int Com Jurists Rev*, 45.

14. See e.g. ICCPR Art. 20 (1) ("any propaganda for war") (2) ("any advocacy of national, racial or religious hatred that constitutes incitement to discrimination, hostility or violence ..."). To similar effect Art. 13(5) Of the American

Convention on Human Rights of 1969. The African Charter contains no equivalent prohibition.

15. This provides that "Everyone is entitled to a social and international order in which the rights and freedoms set forth in this Declaration can be fully realised."

16. Art. 47 of the ICCPR (Art. 25 of the ICESCR) further states: "Nothing in the present Covenant shall be interpreted as impairing the inherent right of all peoples to enjoy and utilise fully and freely their natural wealth and resources."

17. Art 21(4) refers to the need to exercise this right "with a view to strengthening African unity and solidarity"; by contrast, Art 21(5) entails an obligation "to eliminate all forms of foreign economic exploitation," so as to maximise a people's benefits from their natural resources. Apparently, local economic exploitation has no such deleterious effects.

18. But, wholly exceptional situations apart, in the existing conditions of international relations the State acts through its government, and if a State's acts are ever to be definitive so too must the government's be.

19. e.g. H. G. Espiell, "The Right of Development as a Human Right" (1981) 16 *Texas ILJ*, 189. For a more objective account see Roland Rich, "The Right to Development: A Right of Peoples?" in J. Crawford (ed.), *The Rights of Peoples* (Oxford: Clarendon Press, 1988).

20. It is instructive in this context to compare the provisions of General Assembly Resolution 41/128, the Declaration on the Right to Development of 4 December 1986. The preambular paragraphs refer, in relation to development within particular States, to "the entire population and...all individuals," recall the rights of peoples to self-determination and to sovereignty over their natural wealth and resources, refer to various obstacles to "the complete fulfillment of human beings and of peoples," and specify that "the human person is the central subject of the development process and...the main participant and beneficiary of development." Article 1(1) describes the right to development as "an inalienable human right by virtue of which every human person and all peoples are entitled to participate in, contribute to and enjoy economic, social, cultural and political development, in which all human rights and fundamental freedoms can be fully realized." Article 1(2) states that "the human right to development...implies the full realization of the right of peoples to self-determination, which includes, subject to relevant provisions of both International Covenants on Human Rights, the exercise of their inalienable right to full sovereignty over all their natural wealth and resources." Clearly these provisions stop short of stating that the right to development is a collective right, or a right of peoples: the contrast between the "human right" to development in Art. 1(1) and the two rights of peoples referred to in Art. 1(2) is clear, and is continued in Art. 5 by the emphasis on the right of peoples to self-determination. The remaining articles refer to various responsibilities of States with respect to development, again without any implication that development is a collective or peoples' right.

21. U. O. Umozurike, "The African Charter on Human and People's Rights"

(1983) 77 *AJIL*, 902, 907.

22. See further W. P. Gormley, *Human Rights and Environment: The Need for International Co-operation* (1976). This is not to say that treaty provisions about the environment cannot be justiciable. But in the *Tasmanian Dam* case, the Australian High Court was obviously more comfortable with the specific obligation undertaken with respect to the region through its listing under the World Heritage Convention of 1974 than with the notion of an international obligation under Art. 4 and 5 of the Convention with respect to the natural heritage generally: *Commonwealth v. Tasmania* (1983) 46 ALR 625.

23. P. Alston, "Conjuring up New Human Rights: A Proposal for Quality Control" (1984) 78 *AJIL*, 607, 610-11 (where these are listed among 29 candidates).

24. But see Professor Brownlie's essay—"The Rights of Peoples in Modern International Law" in J. Crawford (ed.), *The Rights of Peoples*, supra note 19—for the suggestion that minority and indigenous rights are to be equated with the general principle of self-determination.

Questions for Reflection

1. According to Crawford, in what ways are "states" and "peoples" different under international law? What rights do states have? What rights do peoples have? Are the rights of states and the rights of peoples complementary or contradictory?

2. Under international law a people has the right to self-determination. What is the historical background to the right to self-determination? In what ways has self-determination promoted human rights? In what ways has self-determination hindered human rights? What examples can you find today of struggles for self-determination around the world?

3. The traditional conception of human rights is individualist, insofar as it regards human rights as the rights individuals have as human beings. The notion of peoples' rights refers to rights that are collective, held by groups of human beings rather than by individuals. What conceptual and ethical difficulties arise from thinking of human rights as collective or group rights? Do you agree that peoples' rights are human rights? Why or why not?

39. WILL KYMLICKA

Will Kymlicka (1962-) is Queen's National Scholar, Department of Philosophy, Queen's University. The author of *Liberalism, Community, and Culture* (1989), *Multicultural Citizenship: A Liberal Theory of Minority Rights* (1995) and *Finding Our Way: Rethinking Ethnocultural Relations in Canada* (1998), Kymlicka is one of the world's leading scholars on issues concerning the rights and status of minority cultures. In the essay that follows, Kymlicka considers the idea of group rights in relation to the traditional emphasis on individual rights and suggests that we need to distinguish between "good" and "bad" group rights. He then examines how the rights-claims of indigenous peoples present some difficulties for liberal societies committed to the ideal of individual equality, yet argues that such claims need not conflict with the human rights of all people to equality and dignity.

Text—The Good, the Bad, and the Intolerable: Minority Group Rights

Ethnocultural minorities around the world are demanding various forms of recognition and protection, often in the language of "group rights." Many commentators see this as a new and dangerous trend that threatens the fragile international consensus on the importance of individual rights. Traditional human rights doctrines are based on the idea of the inherent dignity and equality of all individuals. The emphasis on group rights, by contrast, seems to treat individuals as the mere carriers of group identities and objectives, rather than as autonomous personalities capable of defining their own identity and goals in life. Hence it tends to subordinate the individual's freedom to the group's claim to protect its historical traditions or cultural purity.

I believe that this view is overstated. In many cases, group rights supplement and strengthen human rights, by responding to potential injustices that traditional rights doctrine cannot address. These are the "good" group rights. There are cases, to be sure, where illiberal groups seek the right to restrict the basic liberties of their members. These are the "bad" group rights. In some cases, these illiberal practices are not only bad, but intolerable, and the larger society has a right to intervene to stop them. But in other cases, liberal states must tolerate unjust practices within a minority group. Drawing the line between the bad and the intolerable is one of the thorniest issues liberal democracies face.

I want to look at the relationship between group and individual rights in the context of the claims of indigenous peoples in North America. In both the United States and Canada, these peoples have various group rights. For example, they have rights of self-government, under which they exercise control over health, education, family law, policing, criminal justice, and resource development. They also have legally recognized land claims, which reserve certain lands for their exclusive use and provide guaranteed representation on certain regulatory bodies. And in some cases, they have rights relating to the use of their own language.

The situation of indigenous peoples is a useful example, I think, for several reasons. For one thing, they have been at the forefront of the movement toward recognizing group rights at the international level—reflected in the Draft Universal Declaration on Indigenous Rights at the United Nations. The case of indigenous peoples also shows that group rights are not a new issue. From the very beginning of European colonization, the "natives" fought for rights relating to their land, languages, and self-government. What has changed in recent years is not that indigenous peoples have altered their demands, but rather that these demands have become more visible, and that the larger society has started to listen to them.

Reflecting on this long history should warn us against the facile assumption that the demand for group rights is somehow a byproduct of current intellectual fashions, such as postmodernism, or of ethnic entrepreneurs pushing affirmative action programs beyond their original intention. On the contrary, the consistent historical demands of indigenous peoples suggests that the issue of group rights is an enduring and endemic one for liberal democracies.

Group rights, as I will use the term, refer to claims to something more than, or other than, the common rights of citizenship. The category is obviously very large and can be subdivided into any number of more refined categories, reflecting the different sorts of rights sought by different sorts of groups.

TWO KINDS OF GROUP RIGHTS

For my purposes, however, the most important distinction is between two kinds of group rights: one involves the claim of an indigenous group against its own members; the other involves the claim of an indigenous group against the larger society. Both of these can be seen as protecting the stability of indigenous communities, but they respond to different sources of instability. The first is intended to protect a group from the destabilizing impact of internal dissent (that is, the decision of individual members not to follow traditional practices or customs), whereas the second is intended to protect the group from the impact of external decisions (that is, the economic or political policies of the larger society). I will call the first "internal restrictions" and the second "external protections."

Both are "group rights," but they raise very different issues. Internal restrictions involve intra-group relations. An indigenous group may seek the use of state power to restrict the liberty of its own members in the name of group solidarity. For example, a tribal government might discriminate against those members who do not share the traditional religion. This sort of internal restriction raises the danger of individual oppression. Group rights in this sense can be invoked by patriarchal and theocratic cultures to justify the oppression of women and the legal enforcement of religious orthodoxy.

Of course, all forms of government involve restricting the liberty of those subject to their authority. In all countries, no matter how liberal and democratic, people are required to pay taxes to support public goods. Most democracies also require people to undertake jury duty or to perform some amount of military or community service, and a few countries require people to vote. All governments expect and sometimes require a minimal level of civic responsibility and participation from their citizens.

But some groups seek to impose much greater restrictions on the liberty of their members. It is one thing to require people to do jury duty or to vote, and quite another to compel people to attend a particular church or to follow traditional gender roles. The former are intended to uphold liberal rights and democratic institutions, the latter restrict these rights in the name of orthodoxy or cultural tradition. It is these latter cases that I have in mind when talking about internal restrictions.

Obviously, groups are free to require respect for traditional norms and authorities as terms of membership in private, voluntary associations. A Catholic organization can insist that its members be Catholics in good standing, and the same applies to voluntary religious organizations within indigenous communities. The problem arises when a group seeks to use *governmental* power, or the distribution of public benefits, to restrict the liberty of members.

On my view, such legally imposed internal restrictions are almost always unjust. It is a basic tenet of liberal democracy that whoever exercises political power within a community must respect the civil and political rights of its members, and any attempt to impose internal restrictions that violate this condition is unjust.

External protections, by contrast, involve *inter*-group relations. In these cases, the indigenous group seeks to protect its distinct existence and identity by limiting its vulnerability to the decisions of the larger society. For example, reserving land for the exclusive use of indigenous peoples ensures that they are not outbid for this resource by the greater wealth of outsiders. Similarly, guaranteeing representation for indigenous peoples on various public regulatory bodies reduces the chance that they will be outvoted on decisions that affect their community. And allowing indigenous peoples to control their own health care system ensures that critical decisions are not made by people who are ignorant of their distinctive health needs or their traditional medicines.

On my view, these sorts of external protections are often consistent with liberal democracy, and may indeed be necessary for democratic justice. They can be seen as putting indigenous peoples and the larger society on a more equal footing, by reducing the extent to which the former is vulnerable to the latter.

Of course, one can imagine circumstances where the sorts of external protections demanded by a minority group are unfair. Under the apartheid system in South Africa, for example, whites, who constituted less than 20 percent of the population, demanded 87 percent of the land mass of the country, monopolized all the political power, and imposed Afrikaans and English throughout the entire school system. They defended this in the name of reducing their vulnerability to the decisions of other larger groups, although the real aim was to dominate and exploit these groups.

However, the sorts of external protections sought by indigenous peoples hardly put them in a position to dominate others. The land claims, representation rights, and self-government powers sought by indigenous peoples do not deprive other groups of their fair share of economic resources or political power, nor of their language rights. Rather, indigenous peoples simply seek to ensure that the majority cannot use its superior numbers or wealth to deprive them of the resources and institutions vital to the reproduction of their communities. And that, I believe, is fully justified. So, whereas internal restrictions are almost inherently in conflict with liberal democratic norms, external protections are not—so long as they promote equality between groups rather than allowing one group to oppress another.

THE GROUP RIGHTS OF INDIGENOUS PEOPLES

Which sorts of claims are indigenous peoples making? This is not always an easy question to answer. Self-government rights can be used either to secure external protections or to impose internal restrictions, and some indigenous groups use these rights in both ways.

But most indigenous peoples seek group rights primarily for the external protections they afford. Most groups are concerned with ensuring that the larger society does not deprive them of the resources and institutions necessary for their survival, not with controlling the extent to which their own members engage in untraditional or unorthodox practices. Under these circumstances, there is no conflict between external protections and individual rights. Groups that have these external protections may fully respect the civil and political rights of their own members. Indeed, many indigenous groups have adopted their own internal constitutional bills of rights, guaranteeing freedom of religion, speech, press, conscience, association, and a speedy and public trial.

In these cases, group rights supplement, even strengthen, standard human rights. Far from limiting the basic civil and political rights of individual Indians, they help to protect the context within which those rights have their meaning and efficacy. The long history of European-indigenous relations suggests that even if indigenous peoples have citizenship rights in the mainstream society, they tend to be politically impotent and culturally marginalized.

Some readers might think that I am underestimating the illiberal tendencies of indigenous groups. I have argued that many Indian communities are committed to respecting the rights of their individual members. Why then are most indigenous peoples in the United States opposed to the idea that their internal decisions should be subject to judicial review under the US Bill of Rights?

This is an important question, which goes to the heart of the relationship between group and individual rights, and which is worth exploring in some depth. As part of their self-government, tribal councils in the United States have historically been exempted from the constitutional requirement to respect the Bill of Rights. Various efforts have been made by federal legislators to change this, most recently the 1968 Indian Civil Rights Act. According to this act, which was passed by Congress despite vociferous opposition from most Indian groups, tribal governments are now required to respect most (but not all) constitutional rights. However, there are still limits on judicial review of the actions of tribal councils. If a member of an Indian tribe feels that her rights have been violated by her tribal council, she can seek redress in a tribal court, but she cannot (except under exceptional circumstances) seek redress from the Supreme Court.

Indian groups remain strongly opposed to the 1968 Act, and would almost certainly resist any attempt to extend the jurisdiction of federal courts over Indian governments. Similarly, Indian bands in Canada have argued that their self-governing councils should not be subject to judicial review under the Canadian Charter of Rights and Freedoms. They do not want their members to be able to challenge band decisions in the courts of the mainstream society.

These limits on the application of constitutional bills of rights suggest that individuals or subgroups within Indian communities could be oppressed in the name of group solidarity or cultural purity. For example, concern has been expressed that Indian women in the United States and Canada might be discriminated against under certain systems of self-government, if these communities are exempt from the constitutional requirement of sexual equality. Demanding exemption from judicial review in the name of self-government, for many people, is a smokescreen behind which illiberal groups hide their oppressive practices.

Before jumping to this conclusion, however, we should consider the reasons why groups that believe in individual rights would nonetheless be distrustful of judicial review. In the case of indigenous peoples, these reasons are, I think, painfully obvious. After all, the federal courts have historically accepted and legitimated the colonization and dispossession of Indian peoples and lands. Why should Indians trust the federal courts to act impartially now?

But there are other, more specific concerns. Many Indians argue that their self-government needs to be exempt from the Bill of Rights, not in order to restrict the liberty of women or religious dissidents, but to defend the external protections of Indians vis-à-vis the larger society. Their special rights to land, or to hunting, or to group representation, which reduce their vulnerability to external economic and political decisions, could be struck down as discriminatory under the Bill of Rights. Such protections do not, in my view, violate equality. On the contrary, a powerful case could be made that they promote equality, by protecting Indians from unjust majority decisions. But Indians rightly worry that the Supreme Court could take a different and more formalistic view of equality rights.

Indian leaders also fear that white judges might interpret certain rights in culturally biased ways. For example, traditional Indian forms of consensual political decision making could be seen as denying democratic rights. These traditional procedures do not violate the underlying democratic principle of the Constitution—namely, that legitimate authority requires the consent of the governed, subject to periodic review. However, they do not use the particular method for securing consent envisioned by the Constitution—namely, periodic election of representatives. Rather, they rely on time-honored procedures for ensuring consensual decision making. Indian leaders worry that white judges will impose their own culturally specific form of democracy, without considering whether traditional Indian practices are an equally valid interpretation of democratic principles.

It is often difficult for outsiders to assess the likelihood that self-government for an indigenous minority will lead to the suppression of basic individual rights. The identification of oppression requires sensitivity to the specific context, particularly when dealing with other cultures, and so it is not surprising that Indians would want these questions settled in a forum where judges are familiar with the situation.

Hence many Indian leaders seek exemption from the Bill of Rights, but at the same time affirm their commitment to basic human rights and freedoms. They endorse the principles, but object to the particular institutions and procedures that the larger society has established to enforce these principles. They seek to create or maintain their own procedures for protecting rights, specified in tribal constitutions (some of which are based on the provisions of international protocols).

Of course, not all Indian groups accept the commitment to respect individual rights. One example of internal restrictions concerns freedom of religion on the Pueblo reservation. Because they are not subject to the Bill of Rights, tribal governments are not required to obey its strict separation of church and state. The Pueblo have, in effect, established a theocratic government that discriminates against those members who do not share the tribal religion. For example, housing benefits have been denied to members of the community who have converted to Protestantism. In this case, self-government powers are being used to limit the freedom of members to question and revise traditional practices.

The Pueblo also use sexually discriminatory membership rules. If female members marry outside the tribe, their children are denied membership. But if men marry outside the tribe, the children are members. Here again, the rights of individuals are being restricted to preserve a communal practice (although there is some debate about whether this membership rule is in fact the "traditional" one, or whether it was adopted by the Pueblo at the behest of the American government, which hoped thereby to minimize its financial obligations).

In other cases, tribal governments have become profoundly undemocratic, governed by strongmen who ignore traditional ideals of consensus and govern by a combination of intimidation and corruption.

In these cases, not surprisingly, members of the Indian community often seek some form of outside judicial review. These cases put liberals on the horns of a serious dilemma. This is no longer a case of whites imposing "our" norms on Indians, who would prefer to live by "their" norms. The problem, rather, is that Indians themselves are deeply divided, not only about their traditional norms, but also about the ability of their traditional decision-making procedures to deal with these divisions. In some cases, reformers seeking federal judicial review may form a sizable minority, if not a majority, within their community. For example, the Native Women's Association of Canada, worried about the danger of sexual discrimination on their reserves, has demanded that the decisions of Aboriginal governments be subject to the Canadian Charter.

THE LIMITS OF TOLERATION

How should liberal states respond in such cases? It is right and proper, I think, for liberals to criticize oppressive practices within indigenous communities, just as we should criticize foreign countries that oppress their citizens. These oppressive practices may be traditional (although many aren't), but tradition is not self-validating. Indeed, that an oppressive practice is traditional may just show how deep the injustice goes.

But should we intervene and impose a liberal regime on the Pueblo, forcing them to respect the religious liberty of Protestants and the sexual equality of women? Should we insist that indigenous governments be subject to the Bill of Rights, and that their decisions be reviewable by federal courts?

It's important here to distinguish two questions: (1) Are internal restrictions consistent with liberal principles? and (2) Should liberals impose their views on minorities that do not accept some or all of these principles? The first is the question of *identifying* a defensible liberal theory of group rights; the second is the question of *imposing* that theory.

The first question is easy: internal restrictions are illiberal and unjust. But the answer to the second question is less clear. That liberals cannot automatically impose their principles on groups that do not share them is obvious enough, I think, if the illiberal group is another country. The Saudi Arabian government unjustly denies political rights to women or non-Muslims. But it doesn't follow that liberals outside Saudi Arabia should forcibly intervene to compel the Saudis to give everyone the vote. Similarly, the German government unjustly denies political rights to the children and grandchildren of Turkish "guest-workers," born and raised on German soil. But it doesn't follow that liberals outside Germany should use force to compel Germany to change its citizenship laws.

What isn't clear is the proper remedy for rights violations. What third party (if any) has the authority to intervene in order to force the government to respect those rights? The same question arises when the illiberal group is a self-governing indigenous community within a single country. The Pueblo tribal council violates the rights of its members by limiting freedom of conscience and by employing sexually discriminatory membership rules. But what third party (if any) has the authority to compel the Pueblo council to respect those rights?

Liberal principles tell us that individuals have certain claims that their government must respect, such as individual freedom of conscience. But having identified those claims, we now face the very different question of imposing liberalism. If a particular government fails to respect those claims, who can legitimately step in and force compliance? (By "imposing" liberalism, I am referring to forcible intervention by a third party. Noncoercive intervention is a different matter, which I discuss below.)

The attitude of liberals toward imposing liberalism has changed over the years. In the international context, they have become increasingly skeptical about using force to compel foreign states to obey liberal principles. Many nineteenth-century liberals thought that liberal states were justified in colonizing and instructing foreign countries. Woodrow Wilson defended the American colonization of the Philippines in 1902 on the grounds that "they are children and we are men in these matters of government and justice." Contemporary liberals, however, have abandoned this doctrine as both imprudent and illegitimate, and sought instead to promote liberal values through persuasion and financial incentives.

In the case of self-governing indigenous minorities, however, liberals have been much more willing to endorse coercive intervention. Many American liberals assume that the Supreme Court has the legitimate authority to overturn any decisions of the Pueblo tribal council that violate individual rights. They commonly assume that to have a "right" means not only that legislators should respect one's claim, but also that there should be a system of judicial review to ensure that respect. Moreover, this judicial review should occur at a country-wide level. That is, in addition to the various state and tribal courts that review the laws of state and tribal governments, there should also be a Supreme Court to which all governments within the country are answerable. Indeed, many American liberals often talk as if it is part of the very meaning of "rights" that there should be a single court in each country with the authority to review the decisions of all governments within that country.

This is a very particularist understanding of rights. In some liberal countries (for example, Britain), there is a strong tradition of respecting individual rights, but there is no constitutional bill of rights and no basis for courts to overturn parliamentary decisions that violate individual rights. (The same was true in Canada until 1982.) In other countries, there is judicial review, but it is decentralized—that is, political subunits have their own systems of review, but there is no single bill of rights and no single court to which all levels of government are answerable. Indeed, this was true in the United States for a considerable period of time. Until the passage of the Fourteenth Amendment, state legislatures were answerable to state courts for the way they respected state constitutions, but were not answerable to the Supreme Court for respecting the Bill of Rights.

It's easy to see why American liberals are committed to giving the Supreme Court such wide authority. Historically, this sort of judicial review, backed up by federal troops, was required to overturn the racist legislation of Southern states, which state courts had upheld. Given the central role federal courts have played in the struggle against racism, American liberals developed a deep commitment to centralized judicial review. So when a question is raised about self-governing indigenous peoples, many liberals automatically support centralized review, even though these peoples were historically exempt from any such external intervention.

In short, contemporary liberals have become more reluctant to impose liberalism on foreign countries, but more willing to impose liberalism on indigenous minorities. This, I think, is inconsistent. Both foreign states and indigenous minorities form distinct political communities, with their own claims to self-government. Attempts to impose liberal principles by force are often perceived, in both cases, as a form of aggression or paternalistic colonialism. And, as a result, these attempts often backfire. The plight of many former colonies in Africa shows that liberal institutions are likely to be unstable when they are the products of external imposition rather than internal reform. In the end, liberal institutions can work only if liberal beliefs have been internalized by the members of the self-governing society, be it an independent country or an indigenous minority.

There are, of course, important differences between foreign states and indigenous minorities. Yet, in both cases, there is relatively little scope for legitimate coercive interference. Relations between the majority society and indigenous peoples should be determined by peaceful negotiation, not force. This means searching for some basis of agreement. The most secure basis would be agreement on fundamental principles. But if the two groups do not share basic principles, and cannot be persuaded to adopt the other's principles, they will have to rely on some more minimalist modus vivendi.

The resulting agreement may well exempt the indigenous minority from the Bill of Rights and judicial review. Indeed, such exemptions are often implicit in the historical treaties by which the minority entered the larger state. This means that the majority will sometimes be unable to prevent the violation of individual rights within the minority community. Liberals have to learn to live with this, just as they must live with illiberal laws in other countries.

It doesn't follow that liberals should stand by and do nothing. An indigenous government that rules in an illiberal way acts unjustly. Liberals have a right, and a responsibility, to speak out against such injustice. Hence, liberal reformers inside the culture should seek to promote their principles through reason and example, and liberals outside should lend their support. Since the most enduring forms of liberalization are those that result from internal reform, the primary focus for liberals outside the group should be to support liberals inside.

Moreover, there is an important difference between coercively imposing liberalism and offering incentives for liberal reforms. Again, this is clear in the international arena. For example, the desire of former communist countries to enter the European Community (EC) has provided leverage for Western democracies to push for liberal reforms in Eastern Europe. Membership in the EC is a powerful, but noncoercive, incentive for liberal reform. Similarly, many people thought that negotiations over the North American Free Trade Agreement provided an opportunity for Canada and the United States to pressure the Mexican government into improving its human rights record.

There are many analogous opportunities for a majority to encourage indigenous peoples, in a noncoercive way, to liberalize their internal constitutions. Of course there are limits to the appropriate forms of pressure. Refusing to extend trade privileges is one thing, imposing a total embargo or blockade is quite another. The line between incentive and coercion is not a sharp one, and where to draw it is a much-debated point in the international context.

Finally, and perhaps most important, liberals can push for the development and strengthening of international mechanisms for protecting human rights. Some Indian tribes have expressed a willingness to abide by international declarations of rights, and to answer to international tribunals about complaints of rights violations within their communities. They accept the idea that their governments, like all sovereign governments, should be accountable to international norms. Indeed, they have shown greater willingness to accept this kind of review than many nation-states, which jealously guard their sovereignty in domestic affairs. Most Indian tribes do not oppose all forms of external review. What they object to is being subject to the constitution of their conquerors, which they had no role in drafting, and being answerable to federal courts composed entirely of non-Indian justices.

This shows, I think, that the assumption of American liberals that there must be one court within each country that is the ultimate defender of individual rights is doubly mistaken, at least in the case of indigenous peoples. History has proven the value of holding all governments accountable for respecting human rights. But the appropriate forum for reviewing the actions of self-governing indigenous peoples may skip the federal level, as it were. Many indigenous groups would endorse a system in which their decisions are reviewed in the first instance by their own courts and then by an international court. Federal courts, dominated by the majority, would have little or no authority over them.

These international mechanisms could arise at the regional as well as global level. European countries have agreed to establish their own multilateral human rights tribunals. Perhaps North American governments and Indian tribes could agree to establish a similar tribunal, on which both sides are fairly represented.

This isn't to say that federal intervention to protect liberal rights is never justified. In cases of gross and systematic violation of human rights, such as slavery, genocide, torture, or mass expulsions, there are grounds for intervening in the internal affairs of an indigenous group. A number of factors are relevant here, including the severity of rights violations within the community, the degree of consensus on restricting individual rights, and the ability of dissenting members to leave the community if they so desire. For example, whether intervention is justified in the case of an Indian tribe that restricts freedom of conscience surely depends on whether it is governed by a tyrant who lacks popular support and prevents people leaving the community or whether the tribal government has a broad base of support and religious dissidents are free to leave.

I should note that my arguments here do not just apply to indigenous peoples. They also apply to other national minorities—that is, other nonimmigrant groups whose homeland has been incorporated into a larger state through conquest, colonization, or the ceding of territory from one imperial power to another. Nonindigenous national minorities include the Québécois in Canada and Puerto Ricans in the United States. These groups differ from indigenous peoples in many ways, but in all these cases, the role of the federal courts in reviewing the decisions of self-governing minorities should be settled by negotiation, not imposition.

Cases involving immigrant groups are quite different. It is more legitimate to compel respect for liberal principles. I do not think it is wrong for liberal states to insist that immigration entails accepting the state's enforcement of liberalism, so long as immigrants know this in advance, and nonetheless choose to come.

THINKING CREATIVELY ABOUT RIGHTS

I've argued that the group rights sought by indigenous peoples need not conflict with human rights, and that the relationship between the two must be assessed carefully on a case-by-case basis. Even when the two do conflict, we cannot assume automatically that the courts and constitutions of the larger society should prevail over the self-governing decisions of the indigenous group. Indigenous peoples have good reasons, and sound legal arguments, to reject federal review of their self-government.

We should, however, think creatively about new mechanisms for enforcing human rights that will avoid the legitimate objections indigenous peoples have to federal courts. My aim is not to undermine human rights but rather to find fairer and more effective ways to promote them.

As Joseph Carens puts it, "People are supposed to experience the realization of principles of justice through various concrete institutions, but they may actually experience a lot of the institution and very little of the principle." This is exactly how many indigenous peoples perceive the supreme courts of Canada and the United States. What they experience is not the principle of human dignity and equality, but rather a social institution that has historically justified their conquest and dispossession.

Moreover to focus exclusively on the danger of internal restrictions is often to miss the real source of injustice. The fact is that many indigenous groups feel compelled to impose internal restrictions because the larger society has denied them legitimate external protection. As Denise Réaume has noted, part of the "demonization" of other cultures is the assumption that they are naturally inclined to use coercion against their members. But insofar as some groups seem regrettably willing to use coercion to preserve traditional practices, this may be due, not to any innate illiberalism but to the fact that the larger society has failed to protect them. Unable to get protection for its lands and institutions, the minority turns to the only people it does have some control over, namely its own members. This tendency does not justify internal restrictions, but it suggests that before we criticize a minority for imposing restrictions on its members, we should first make sure we are respecting its legitimate group rights.

Our goal, therefore, should be to find new mechanisms that will protect *both* the individual and group rights of indigenous peoples. We need to think about effective mechanisms, acceptable to indigenous peoples, for holding their governments accountable for the way individual members are treated. But we need simultaneously to think about effective mechanisms for holding the larger society accountable for respecting the group rights of indigenous peoples. Focusing on the former while neglecting the latter is counterproductive and hypocritical.

Many indigenous peoples have looked to the United Nations, and its draft declaration on indigenous rights, as a possible forum for pursuing these twin forms of accountability. Unfortunately, both the Canadian and US governments have been reluctant to give any international body jurisdiction over the treaty rights, land claims, or self-government rights of indigenous peoples. Viewed in this light, the real obstacle to a more satisfactory balance of individual and group rights is not the refusal of indigenous peoples to accept external review, but rather the refusal of the larger society to accept restrictions on its sovereignty.

QUESTIONS FOR REFLECTION

1. In what ways does Kymlicka distinguish between "good" and "bad" group rights? Why is this distinction necessary?

2. How do you react to Kymlicka's assessment that the conflict between individual and group rights is, in large part, due to the refusal of state governments to limit their sovereignty? Would you support international treaties that would authorize restrictions on state sovereignty in order to strengthen the rights of indigenous peoples? What alternatives might you propose?

3. Given the arguments found in the selections by Crawford and Kymlicka, do you believe that group rights are needed to realize the goals of the international human rights movement? Are individual rights alone insufficient?

FURTHER READINGS FOR SECTION 7

Baker, Judith, ed. *Group Rights*. Toronto: University of Toronto Press, 1994.

Crawford, James, ed. *The Rights of Peoples*. Oxford: Clarendon Press, 1992.

Dinstein, Yoram. "Collective Human Rights of Peoples and Minorities." *International and Comparative Law Quarterly* 25 (1976): 102-120.

Halperin, Morton H., and David J. Scheffer with Patricia L. Small. *Self-Determination in the New World Order*. Washington, DC: Carnegie Endowment for International Peace, 1992.

Kukathas, Chandran. "Are There Any Cultural Rights?" *Political Theory* 20 (1992): 105-39.

Kymlicka, Will. *Multicultural Citizenship: A Liberal Theory of Minority Rights*. Oxford: Clarendon Press, 1995.

——, ed. *The Rights of Minority Cultures*. Oxford: Oxford University Press, 1995.

Margalit, Avishai and Joseph Raz. "National Self-Determination." *Journal of Philosophy* 87 (1990): 439-61.

Phillips, Allan and Allan Rosas, eds. *Universal Minority Rights*. Turku, Finland: University Institute for Human Rights, 1995.

Shapiro, Ian and Will Kymlicka, eds. *Ethnicity and Group Rights*. New York and London: New York University Press, 1997.

Section 8:
ETHNIC CLEANSING AND HUMANITARIAN INTERVENTION

40. JAMES W. NICKEL

James W. Nickel (1943-) is Professor of Philosophy at the University of Colorado. Nickel's fields of specialization are ethics, political philosophy, and philosophy of law. He has published extensively in these areas, including the book *Making Sense of Human Rights* (1987). In this essay Nickel discusses the concept of "ethnic cleansing," a term originally applied by Serbian nationalists in the early 1990s to their attempts to expel non-Serbs from areas of Bosnia. The Serb campaigns of ethnic cleansing typically involved the destruction of homes; the forced displacement of entire populations; the incarceration of men, women, and children in detention camps; the execution of political leaders, intellectuals, and teachers; the systematic rape of women; and the massacre of large groups of civilians. Nickels attempts to clarify the reasons why ethnic cleansing is morally wrong by focusing on five specific features of ethnic cleansing. Examination of these features, Nickels suggest, also allows us to identify cases in which certain narrow forms of ethnic cleansing might be morally tolerable.

Text—What's Wrong with Ethnic Cleansing?[1]

James W. Nickel, "What's Wrong with Ethnic Cleansing?," Journal of Social Philosophy *25/1 (1995): 5–15. Reprinted by permission of the* Journal of Social Philosophy.

The ethnic wars in Croatia and Bosnia-Herzegovina following the 1991 breakup of Yugoslavia have seen the use of detention, camps, massacres, torture, rape, and forced relocations of ethnic groups.[2] These events have brought the concept of *ethnic cleansing* into popular use. This concept describes the pursuit of greater ethnic purity within a country or region by relocating or killing all or most of the members of unwanted ethnic groups. An example of ethnic cleansing is described in the following passage:

> Palic, Yugoslavia, July 3, 1992.
>
> In a practice not seen in Europe since the end of World War II, the Serbian-led government of Yugoslavia chartered an 18-car train last week in an attempt to deport the entire population of a Muslim village to Hungary.
>
> Some 1,800 passengers, including 70 mothers carrying infants, were expelled from the east Bosnian village of Kozluk after two armored tanks crashed into the main square and Serb irregulars threatened to blow it up, according to the villagers....
>
> "They told us they could no longer assure us protection," said Mulaibisevic Mohmedalisa, 35. "They said this was part of an ethnically pure Serbian region, and it was inconvenient to have a Muslim village at a key road junction."[3]

This paper analyzes the concept of ethnic cleansing, attempts to deepen our understanding of why it generally merits harsh condemnation, and considers whether its milder forms are sometimes permissible.

I. THE CONCEPT OF ETHNIC CLEANSING

Ethnic cleansing always involves two key elements. One is that it attempts to eliminate a group from a country or region by killing or expelling all or most of its members. The other key element is that the goal of getting rid of the group is to attain greater ethnic homogeneity or "purity" within the country or region. (I will examine this goal below.)

The generic idea of ethnic cleansing is that of *attempting to eliminate or greatly reduce the size of an ethnic or national group in order to achieve greater homogeneity within a territory*. It is usually governments, or military groups, that attempt to do this.

No particular means of getting people to move is built into the notion of ethnic cleansing, so it is not necessarily the case that ethnic cleansing is violent or genocidal. Ethnic cleansing could proceed, for example, by paying all of the members of a minority group enough money to induce them to emigrate. But murder, violence, and terror are the *typical* means of ethnic cleansing.

We can distinguish between *genocidal* and *non-genocidal* forms of ethnic cleansing. The genocidal form endorses the goal of killing the unwanted group rather than driving it out, but typically recognizes that it would be difficult or impossible to kill all of the group's members. So the goal in practice comes to be killing many and expelling the rest. Non-genocidal ethnic cleansing often uses massacres as a means of getting the group to leave, but its purpose is not to destroy the group. Of course it is often very difficult to tell whether a case of ethnic cleansing is genocidal or not. And those ordering and carrying out the ethnic cleansing may not agree about its exact purposes.

International law has typically dealt with *forced relocation* or population transfers rather than ethnic cleansing.[4] One might think that these are the same thing, but it is dear from the preceding paragraphs that ethnic cleansing cannot be equated with forced relocation to achieve greater ethnic homogeneity. First, the genocidal form of ethnic cleansing need not involve relocation since it seeks to kill its victims rather than relocate them. Second, ethnic cleansing need not involve the use of force since offers of money or land can be used to induce an unwanted group to leave. The most we can say is that ethnic cleansing *usually* involves forced relocation.

We can distinguish between direct and indirect forms of forced relocation. When troops enter a village and compel its residents at gunpoint to board buses, this is directly forced relocation. But when people flee their homes from fear of massacres and atrocities that they believe to be coming their way, this is indirectly forced relocation.

A. *Near-relatives.* Ethnic cleansing is closely related to other notions such as *ethnic partition, forced relocation for purposes of territorial acquisition*, and *ethnic repatriation*. The first of these, ethnic partition, involves dividing a country into two (or more) ethnic regions or countries in a way that achieves a high degree of ethnic homogeneity on each side of the border without forcing anyone to move. We might call this *ethnic partition*. It does not necessarily involve ethnic cleansing, even though it has the same sorts of goals. Ethnic cleansing can be combined with ethnic partition in order to achieve greater ethnic homogeneity on one or both sides of the border than is possible without the stronger means that ethnic cleansing uses. Ethnic cleansing may also be used to eliminate geographically isolated ethnic enclaves such as small Moslem areas within generally Serbian regions.

Another near-relative of ethnic cleansing is forced relocation for purposes of territorial acquisition. Indigenous peoples have often been subjected to theft of their territory and relocation to reservations or other areas of the country. When acquisition of a group's territory is the only goal, relocation will focus on getting the people off all or most of the desired land but not on getting them out of the region or country. For example, mainstream Brazilians who want to steal the territory of Brazilian Indians typically have no objection to seeing those Indians live nearby or relocate to a large city like Manaus and join the Brazilian mainstream. Although forced relocation purely for purposes of territorial acquisition is not an instance of ethnic cleansing, it is objectionable for many of the same reasons.

A third near-relative of ethnic cleansing is *ethnic repatriation*, where this involves inducing, paying, or forcing expatriate citizens to return to the homeland. Hitler attempted, for example, to induce ethnic Germans living in Tyrolia and elsewhere to return to Germany. The goal seems not to have been the ethnic cleansing of Tyrolia but rather the return of ethnic Germans to their national homeland. If one takes ethnic purity within national states to be an important ideal, one may seek both to eliminate "outsiders" from one's own country and to avoid having one's own nationals live as minorities in other countries. If repatriation is forced or violent, it is objectionable for some of the same reasons as ethnic cleansing.

B. *Goals.* When a majority group (G1) ethnically cleanses another group (G2) from the country in which both groups live (G-land), an immediate goal of the G1s is always to avoid having to live together in G-land with the G2s, or with so many G2s. But this immediate goal can be sought in order to realize one or more of at least three different ultimate goals.

First, the G1s may despise the G2s because of historic grievances (real or imagined) or because they believe the G2s to be inferior or depraved. Because of these grievances or beliefs, the G1s do not wish to live together in G-land with the G2s, or at least not with many G2s. Pursuing this goal displays something akin to racism or bigotry.

Second, the G1s may wish to dissociate from the G2s in order to realize the nationalist ideal that every large ethnic group should have its own country, one in which it forms the overwhelming mass of the population. A defender of this ideal may concede that most countries will inevitably have some minority ethnic groups, but contend that these groups should be a small percentage of the population.

Third, the ultimate goal of the G1s may be to avoid ethnic conflict and civil war with the G2s by getting them out of G-land. If the G2s are destroyed or decimated, then they can't be the source of conflict or war (although destroying or decimating the G2s may cause conflicts with their sympathizers, co-religionists, or ethnic cousins). And if the G2s are expelled into G2-land, then future relations with them can be conducted across national boundaries. If good fences don't succeed in making good neighbors, they may at least succeed in creating a stable and manageable form of peaceful hostility or cold war.

It is obviously possible for the second or third goal to serve as a rhetorical cover for the first. Advocates of ethnic cleansing who are motivated by hatred and prejudice may recognize that few will share and consider legitimate their hatred and prejudice, and thus decide to defend ethnic cleansing in terms of a nationalist ideal or in terms of the promotion of stable peace between ethnic groups. We should also note that the implacable hostility between groups needed for the third goal to be plausible can be brought into existence as ethnic cleansing is used in pursuit of the first two goals. The typical methods of ethnic cleansing can create fear, destroy trust, and motivate reactive chauvinism between ethnic groups, thus bringing about the circumstances that make plausible the pursuit of separation as a means to peace.

II. WHY IS ETHNIC CLEANSING WRONG?

Ethnic cleansing is widely believed to be morally wrong, and there are at least two reasons commonly given in support of this view. One is that ethnic cleansing is typically genocidal or near-genocidal in its use of mass killing to destroy a group and to terrorize people into leaving their historic places of residence. The other is that forced relocations of populations are wrong and have been internationally condemned.[5] I think that these are valid reasons, but I submit that we will get a better understanding of what's wrong with ethnic cleansing if we look at it within a framework that has five headings:

(1) the legitimacy or illegitimacy of the goal;
(2) the mass killing and violence that are used to destroy the group or to force it to move;
(3) the lost territory and property;
(4) the hazards of the process of relocation; and,
(5) where the group ends up and whether it can create a successful life there.

I don't mean to suggest, however, that we can't in many actual cases obtain a justified condemnation of ethnic cleansing without taking such a comprehensive view. Information from one or two of these categories is often conclusive.

If these five categories identify the morally relevant features of ethnic cleansing, then the worst instances of ethnic cleansing would be ones in which:

(1) the desire to get rid of a group is motivated by hatred and a belief that its members are innately inferior or depraved;
(2) the cleansing is genocidal in that mass killing and large-scale violence are used not only to terrorize the unwanted group into leaving but also to destroy as many of its members as possible;
(3) no compensation is provided for lost territory, membership, and property;
(4) the mode of transport is extremely hazardous and causes many injuries and deaths along the way; and,
(5) the relocated group has no place to go and no assistance is provided for resettlement.

Let's look more closely at each one of these elements.

1. *Goals.* I suggested earlier that an immediate goal of ethnic cleansing is greater ethnic homogeneity or "purity," but that the ultimate goal may be: (1) avoiding coexistence in the same country with a group because its members are thought to be unfitting co-residents because of historic grievances or because of their alleged inferiority or depravity; (2) realizing the nationalist ideal that every large ethnic group should have its own country in which it forms the overwhelming mass of the population; or (3) avoiding ethnic conflict and civil war between two groups by getting one of them out of the country through partition and relocation.

I suggest that we should be extremely suspicious of the first two goals. The first, with its reliance on negative group stereotypes and belief in the inferiority and depravity of other groups, is uncomfortably close to racism and Nazism. The second, with its commitment to the nationalist ideal of ethnically homogenous states, seems ill-suited to today's world. Few states today are ethnically homogenous, and it is implausible to say that it is generally best to draw state boundaries so as to maximize the ethnic homogeneity of countries. Multiethnic and multinational societies have been successful in many places and it is far from clear that mono-ethnic arrangements are always best. Further, attempts to create mono-ethnic states often lead to violence and war. Yael Tamir suggests that the ideal of the homogenous national state should be renounced. She suggests that this ideal is a "pipedream," and that attempts to make this dream come true "inevitably lead to bloodshed."[6]

The third goal, which is to avoid further ethnic conflict or war by creating a more ethnically homogenous state, may be plausible in some circumstances. Ethnic tensions in Lebanon, Belgium, Canada, and Sri Lanka illustrate that it is often hard for two or more large ethnic groups to coexist amicably in a single country. But although these problems are real, they must be compared not with some ideal of tranquillity in a group's own country but rather with the conflict, problems, economic decline, and loss of life that are likely to occur in the process of partitioning and ethnically cleansing the country or region. If Yugoslavians had seen the full costs of partition and ethnic cleansing in advance, they might have been more willing to continue trying to manage the complicated politics of a multinational country.

Before leaving this discussion of possible goals of ethnic cleansing we should make clear that even if a goal is legitimate it may not be reachable by morally tolerable means. If the means are tolerable but costly, then a legitimate and valuable goal may be able to justify them. But not even a legitimate and valuable goal will justify genocidal means.

2. *Mass killing and violence as means.* Whether genocidal or not, ethnic cleansing typically involves very high levels of violence, injury, and death. Thus ethnic cleansing typically involves large-scale violations of very important human rights.[7] These include rights to life, to freedom from torture and degrading treatment, and to freedom from arbitrary arrest.

Even when ethnic cleansing pursues relocation rather than genocide, the kinds of coercion used are typically very severe. To get people to leave their historic place of residence it is frequently necessary to kill, torture, imprison, and rape many of them so as to terrorize the others into leaving. Consider Bogdan Denitch's description of events in Bosnia:

> Partition is the only answer that Croat and Serb nationalists will tolerate. However, it is impossible to have an ethnically based partition without massive transfers of population. These transfers will not be voluntary. Small townspeople and peasants do not readily leave their ancestral homes; they have to be terrorized out of their minds. Cantonization of Bosnia and the creation of nationally 'pure' states thus leads in a straight line to massacres, atrocities, looting, rape, and concentration camps as instruments of the new demographic policy.[8]

The peculiar horror of ethnic cleansing as we have seen it in Serbia, Croatia, and Bosnia is not that is it coercive but that the means of coercion are so severe, that coercion takes the form of massacres, rapes, torture, and confinement in harsh detention camps. Forcing someone to do something is generally bad, but forcing them to do something by threat of murderous violence is far worse.

3. *What's lost or left behind?* When a group is forcibly uprooted and moved, some valuable things will inevitably be left behind. These goods include not only individual holdings in land and buildings, but also collective holdings and citizenship. If a group has a historic territory, ethnic cleansing is likely to involve the loss of some or all of this territory—as well as the collectively held roads, rivers, bridges, and public places and buildings therein. And individuals will lose land, houses, buildings, businesses, and farms. These losses can be partially compensated in cash or by the provision of equivalent holdings elsewhere—although in fact compensation is seldom received by the victims of ethnic cleansing, and even when replacement territories are provided, they are seldom the equivalent of what was lost.[9]

The situation is not much different if the group's historic place was one that it shared with other ethnic groups—in the way that Serbs, Croats, and Muslims shared Sarajevo prior to the civil war. The cleansing of Serbs and Croats from Sarajevo will deprive them of their shares of these collectively held assets.

Ethnic cleansing often means the loss of nationality or citizenship as well. Jews who fled Germany in the thirties and forties lost their citizenship as Germans; they lost, along with their property, their membership in the German polity. Many were stateless—in the sense of having no country that was willing to accept them for permanent residence—at the end of the war.

It is possible, of course, that a group has no valid claim to membership or a share of collective assets. For example, the Brazilian government has on several recent occasions forcibly relocated mainstream Brazilian miners out of the territory of the Yanomano Indians. It is probably fair to say that these miners had no valid claim to the territory and property that they lost.

4. *Going.* Historic ways of moving people for purposes of ethnic cleansing include forced marches, train rides in freezing freight cars, and overcrowded boats. In Bosnia we have added United Nations truck convoys and chartered buses, trains, and airliners. Buses carrying civilians who were being removed from their villages were sometimes fired upon by snipers. As people flee war and terror, and leave behind most of their assets, they are exposed

to additional dangers including further violence, hunger, sickness, and death. Many who flee have no place to go, and thus end up spending long periods in refugee camps.

5. *Resettlement.* Once a relocated group has arrived at its destination, it faces the arduous task of rebuilding its economy, institutions such as schools, hospitals, and churches, and its government. Crucial to success in this is how many of its assets and talented people the group succeeded in saving and carrying with it. If the group did not receive or find a territory on which it could resettle, its members will face having to adapt to new countries as immigrants.

III. IS ETHNIC CLEANSING SOMETIMES PERMISSIBLE?

Ethnic cleansing, at least as I have defined it here, covers a very wide range of possible activities and situations. Cases of ethnic cleansing can range from ones that are genocidal to ones that are non-violent, and from ones that are motivated by hatred and prejudice to ones that are motivated by a sincere desire for a stable peace. Thus it wouldn't be surprising if some cases of ethnic cleansing were less bad than others, and if some instances were morally tolerable.

The analysis of the moral dimensions of ethnic cleansing that was offered earlier readily yields an account of which forms of ethnic cleansing are most likely to be morally tolerable. First, partition and ethnic cleansing are indispensable means to making possible a stable peace between antagonistic ethnic groups; second, the ethnic cleansing is both non-genocidal and largely non-violent, even though force may be used to induce people to move; third, fair replacements or compensation are provided for lost territory, membership, and property; fourth, the mode of transport is sufficiently safe that there are not large numbers of injuries and deaths as people are moved; and fifth, those relocated have places to go and adequate assistance is provided for resettlement.

These five items can be seen as providing the outline of an exception clause in an international norm prohibiting ethnic cleansing. The general idea of this exception is the following. We might be able to justify the coercion or force involved in ethnic cleaning if there were a compelling purpose and no major human rights violations or other major moral obstacles were present.

Most actual cases of ethnic cleansing will be unable to pass these tests. Ethnic cleansing seldom has a compelling purpose, and it almost always involves major violations of human rights. But there are cases, such as Bosnia today, where ethnic partition and relocation seem the only way out of civil war.

It may be questioned whether any exception to a prohibition of ethnic cleansing is needed. If the purpose of relocation is so compelling, won't the people facing relocation see this and move voluntarily? Certainly many people will, particularly if the general outline of future political arrangements is apparent and danger can be escaped by fleeing one's place of residence. But not all people will move; some will prefer a continuation of the war to their having to give up their historic place and see it occupied by an enemy group. Financial incentives, even if the funds to pay them were available, wouldn't persuade all of these people to move.

Could the five conditions for an exception to a general prohibition of ethnic cleansing be met as part of a peace settlement in Bosnia? As this is being written (1994), it seems likely that a settlement of the civil war in Bosnia will involve ethnic partition. In order for partition to work, members of one group, who reside in what is to become the territory of another group, will have to be relocated into the territory of their own group. It is likely that some of these people will refuse to move. Could they be justifiably relocated by force?

The first condition would be satisfied since there is a compelling purpose (stopping the war and achieving a stable peace) that can't be achieved by more acceptable means. The second condition, which requires mild means of forcing people to move, can't really be met because the threat of continued violence—and some would say Serbian aggression—is present. I'm uncertain about this, but perhaps the second condition should be qualified to allow for the use of partition and relocation as a means of getting out of severely deteriorated situations. The third condition, which requires adequate replacement for lost territory, property, and membership, will at best be partially satisfied. Each group will receive a territory, but it now seems likely that the Serbs in Bosnia will get about half of the territory even though they are only about thirty percent of the population. The fourth condition, which requires safe means of transfer, can perhaps be achieved substantially with United Nations assistance if a peace settlement is achieved. And the final condition, resettlement assistance, can be provided by the United Nations and by donations from countries and charitable organizations around the world.

The five tests proposed for any exception to the general prohibition of ethnic cleansing seem to do pretty well in this case. Although they don't give wholesale license to ethnic cleansing as a means to achieving peace through partition, they suggest that its milder form might be morally tolerable as a way of dealing with severely deteriorated situations.

IV. CONCLUSION

The idea of ethnic cleansing is an intelligible notion that can be defined clearly enough to be used alongside the notions of genocide and forced relocation in formulating international humanitarian and human rights norms. Further, it is possible to provide plausible explanations of why ethnic cleansing is generally abhorrent, and to identify the sorts of ethnic cleansing that might conceivably be justifiable.

Notes

1. This paper benefited from the comments of Charles Landesman and members of the audience at a Pacific Division APA session in 1994.

2. For a survey of these practices, see the Amnesty International Reports, *Bosnia-Herzegovina: Gross Abuses of Basic Human Rights* (October 1992), and *Bosnia-Herzegovina: Rape and Sexual Abuse by Armed Forces* (January 1993). See also Roy Gutman, *Witness to Genocide: The 1993 Pulitzer Prize-Winning Dispatches on the "Ethnic Cleansing" of Bosnia* (New York: Macmillan, 1993).

3. Gutman, *Witness to Genocide*, 20-22.

4. See Alfred M. De Zayas, "International Law and Mass Population Transfers," *Harvard International Law Review* 16 (1975): 207.

5. The *Geneva Convention Relative to the Protection of Civilian Persons in*

Time of War of August 12, 1949, contains in Article 49 an explicit prohibition of forced individual and group deportations during international war:

> Individual or mass forcible transfers, as well as deportations of protected person from occupied territory to the territory of the Occupying Power or to that of any other country, occupied or not, are prohibited, regardless of their motive.

6. Yael Tamir, *Liberal Nationalism* (Princeton, NJ: Princeton University Press, 1993): 16.

7. See Amnesty International, *Bosnia-Herzegovina: Gross Abuses of Basic Human Rights* (October 1992). See also James W. Nickel, *Making Sense of Human Rights* (Berkeley: University of California Press, 1987).

8. Bogdan Denitch, "Tragedy in Former Yugoslavia," *Dissent* (Winter 1993): 31.

9. There is also the question of whether relocated parties may legitimately occupy land or houses that have been made available through ethnic cleansing. Many Serbian refugees have been settled in lands that were taken from Croats and Muslims. See Iva Dominis and Ivo Bicanic, "Refugees and Displaced Persons in the Former Yugoslavia," *RFE/RL Research Report* 2 (January 1993): 1-4.

QUESTIONS FOR REFLECTION

1. Refer to Article 2 of the 1948 Convention on the Prevention and Punishment of the Crime of Genocide. In what ways does the definition of genocide contained in the Convention coincide with Nickel's definition of ethnic cleansing? In what ways are they different? Do you think the Convention adequately covers the concept of ethnic cleansing? Should it?

2. Explain Nickel's argument that it is possible to identify morally tolerable forms of ethnic cleansing. What factors distinguish morally tolerable and morally intolerable forms of ethnic cleansing? Do you agree with Nickel's argument? Why or why not?

3. What relationships can you identify between the issues of ethnic cleansing and the rights of indigenous and minority groups? Do the threats posed to indigenous peoples and minority cultures by the encroachment of larger, modernized societies constitute ethnic cleansing?

41. MICHAEL J. SMITH

Michael J. Smith (1951-) is Associate Professor of Government and Foreign Affairs at the University of Virginia, where he also directs the Program in Political and Social Thought. A specialist in international relations, US foreign policy and ethics in international politics, Smith is the author of *Realist Thought from Weber to Kissinger* (1989). Increasingly, Smith informs us, the international community is taking action—often employing military force—to deal with massive violations of human rights. The doctrine of "humanitarian intervention" recognizes the lawful use of force by one or more states to stop massive human rights violations, such as genocide and ethnic cleansing. Smith attempts to clarify, however, the various ethical and legal justifications either for or against humanitarian intervention. He concludes that universal human rights create obligations on the part of states to intervene when those rights are under large-scale threat, even though there are significant hurdles to overcome in making intervention effective.

Text—Humanitarian Intervention: An Overview of the Ethical Issues

Michael J. Smith, "Humanitarian Intervention: An Overview of the Ethical Issues," in Ethics & International Affairs: A Reader, *Joel H. Rosenthal, ed. (Washington, DC: Georgetown University Press, 1999), pp. 271-95. Reprinted by permission of the publisher.*

The capacity to focus on the issue of humanitarian intervention represents what Joel Rosenthal has noted as the maturation of the field of ethics and international affairs.[1] If nothing else, the debate surrounding this vexed issue has demonstrated that we have left behind the so-called oxymoron problem: there is no reason now to be defensive about bracketing the terms "ethics" and "international relations." One can hardly talk about Bosnia, Rwanda, Haiti, Somalia, or any cases of possible outside intervention, without recognizing from the very beginning that ethical dilemmas abound in the way we define our goals, our interests, and the means we use to pursue them. Even Samuel P. Huntington, not usually known to be a moralist, has asserted that "it is morally unjustifiable and politically indefensible that members of the [US] armed forces should be killed to prevent Somalis from killing one another."[2] Whether or not one agrees with that assertion (I do not), one may note that Professor Huntington speaks in terms of moral justification and regards his view of morality to be, in effect, self-evidently true. Thus even archrealists invoke morality in urging their preferred policies.

The discussion in this essay proceeds in three unequal stages. First, I present a brief and oversimple sketch of the objective and subjective changes in the broader milieu of international relations as they relate to humanitarian intervention. Second, and more substantially, I survey and analyze the arguments justifying or opposing the notion of humanitarian intervention from realist and liberal perspectives. Finally, I offer the beginnings of my own argument and consider the enormous difficulties of undertaking humanitarian intervention with any degree of effectiveness and consistency.

THE MILIEU

A New International Setting

What are some of the salient changes in the contemporary international system? Perhaps symptomatic of our current confusion is the absence of consensus even on what to call this new system. Is it unipolar? Balance-of-power? A globalized economic system and regional security system? The new world order? We agree only on the term "post-Cold War" and on the idea that we have no exact model for the kind of international system in which we find ourselves. The notion of unipolarity is not terribly helpful: the apparent single "pole," the United States, has shown singular reluctance to exert its military power, and functionally and economically the international system can hardly be described as unipolar. So, while apparently appealing, unipolarity doesn't work.

Realist analysts may struggle to find some sort of balance-of-power analogue, but this too is not terribly useful. Power is not fungible in the way that many realists following E. H. Carr have treated it, and much of contemporary international relations involves the intersection of the traditional realm of security and the modern arena of economic interdependence. But even theorists who emphasize the elusiveness of power or who have reclassified kinds of power have not as yet articulated a crystallized conception of the contemporary system.[3] In general, we continue to look for ways in which the contemporary system may or may not be the balance-of-power system of the nineteenth century, to identify what features of the Cold War system it still has, and to seek other historical models, but it is clear that we are in a system with many aspects we have never before encountered. Although nuclear weapons have not gone away, they no longer structure the international competition. We now have contending successor states within the former Soviet empire in the midst of profound political and economic transformations—transformations as yet incomplete and poorly understood. At the same time, a truly global economy now means that events in the stock markets of Seoul, Bangkok, or Hong Kong reverberate distortedly on Wall Street. In short, the model of billiard ball states combining and colliding in ways beloved of diplomatic history textbooks (and some realists) has given way to a kaleidoscope of factors including nationalism, ethnicity, and religion, as well as security and economics.

Perhaps our understanding of the international system was always over simplified: states were never billiard balls impermeable to transnational norms, influences, and activities. But the simplifications were defensible as a way to abstract the underlying logic of a system based on discrete sovereign states. Now, with the operational sovereignty of states systemically eroded, we know that no simple model encapsulates the complex reality of contemporary international relations.

If we shift our focus to the level of state actors, we may note some broad trends that at the same time undermine and affirm the idea of national sovereignty as the constituent principle of international society. Consider first the widely noted phenomenon of so-called failed or failing states, which are breaking down as a result of their inability to establish legitimacy with any degree of certainty. In addition, there are states, like Rwanda and Burundi, or Algeria, in which conflicts appear to be endemic or imminent or both. Such conflicts seem now to have greater salience.[4]

Finally, there is the phenomenon of so-called dangerous states: states that may, like Libya or North Korea, challenge the basic tenets of the society of states; states that for various reasons seek to bring attention to themselves through outrageous actions. Such states, because of the danger they pose for other states, may indeed make intervention necessary. For example, it is certainly an open question as to whether we should tolerate the overt acquisition of nuclear weapons by North Korea. When it invaded Kuwait, Iraq provided an occasion for a traditional collective security intervention of the sort envisaged by the framers of the League of Nations Covenant and the UN Charter. As I write this essay, Saddam Hussein's refusal to allow UN inspectors unfettered access to potential weapons sites in Iraq has triggered an international crisis. By the time it appears, we may well have seen another US-led military action against Iraq.

Then there are still cases of old-fashioned aggression, and it is not inconceivable that a state might simply attack another state or help itself to another bit of territory. How dangerous are such renegade states, and what ought we do about them? The overt acquisition of territory or goods by dangerous states will continue to provide a worry for those trying to enforce some version of international order. Together, all these factors at the state level seem to guarantee that we shall have no shortage of occasions for intervention.

A New Climate of Opinion

Thus the objective setting of the international system is not settled, and it is perhaps emblematic of this that we still refer to it as the post-Cold War system. And subjectively, on the issue of humanitarian intervention, we have seen a change even in the brief post-Cold War period in the prevalent attitude toward this issue. For a brief time, from about 1991 to 1993, there existed a sort of Dudley Do-Right euphoria, a sense that we could solve many problems throughout the world just by the use of goodwill and the dispatching of peacekeepers wherever they might be necessary. Thomas Franck characterized the time as an "exciting moment" in which we could begin to intervene on behalf of democratic legitimacy—to create democratically legitimate states everywhere.[5] There was indeed a large increase in the number of humanitarian operations.[6] Since 1993, and the perceived American debacle in Somalia, the attitude toward humanitarian intervention, especially in the United States, has become decidedly more cautious. The most immediate effect of this caution, of course, was the inaction (and worse) of the international community in the face of the conflict between the Hutus and Tutsis in Rwanda. Since then the brutal war in Bosnia, the absence of any international action in the conflict in Chechnya, and a kind of collective sense of shame at the failure of the international community to prevent or arrest the slaughter of tens of thousands of innocent civilians in Rwanda have all created a new climate of wariness about the whole issue of humanitarian intervention. The puzzled and ineffectual international response to the recurring massacres of villagers in Algeria reflects this same uncertainty.

Moreover, there was always a debate about whether humanitarian intervention is legal under international law. In an incisive review of the issue, Tom Farer concludes: "States will still have to choose between compliance with formal prohibitions [against intervention] and response to urgent moral appeals." Because international law is both "thinly institutionalized" and constantly evolving in ways that reflect emerging normative ideas, an appeal to the law itself cannot solve the underlying moral issues raised by humanitarian intervention.[7]

But such normative consensus is yet to emerge. Even sociologically, the events that may lead to humanitarian intervention are far from clear. Morally, substantively, the issues are deeply controversial. Is humanitarian intervention a rescue operation, a quick in and quick out, leaving the basic norms of sovereignty intact, or is it, rather, an attempt to address the underlying causes of the conflict and even to create the conditions for democracy? If the latter, then the model of going in and getting out quickly is obviously not appropriate. Even Michael Walzer, often criticized for the "statist" character of his theory in *Just and Unjust Wars*, has recently amended his rules for intervention. He now argues that there is an obligation to make sure the conditions that require the intervention in the first place do not simply resume once you leave.[8]

In terms of the subjective environment, there is some question as to whether or not international intervention for humanitarian causes is even moral. Both in the literature and in the pronouncements of leaders and actions of states, there is still a great deal of doubt and suspicion of unauthorized, unilateral intervention. This obviously reflects traditional international law and the traditional rules of a society of states. Recently, the United States has sought to gain multilateral authorization even for its unilateral actions, as was the case in Haiti and, to some extent, even in the Persian Gulf War. As Walzer suggests, there may still be situations in which autonomous unilateral intervention for humanitarian purposes is ethically justified, and certainly from the military point of view the formidable problems of command and control may be simplified when intervention is autonomous and unilateral.[9] But in general it seems that the old norms of sovereignty and nonintervention are still persuasive for states—at least in their official and quasi-official pronouncements.

What about collective intervention? Traditional international law has been hostile not only to unilateral intervention in domestic affairs but also to collective, coercive action, except in cases of threats to peace, breaches of peace, and overt aggression. The founding fathers of international law have always treated the concept as suspect. The most striking recent development has been some "creative exegesis" (Farer's phrase) on the part of international lawyers as exemplified in the willingness in the Security Council to broaden the traditional definition of threats to peace as a justification for intervention.[10] Was the intervention for the Kurds the application of a new principle of humanitarian intervention on behalf of oppressed minorities? Or was it a simple extension of a classical collective security operation against Iraq? Would it even have occurred if Iraq had not invaded Kuwait? The question is not entirely rhetorical, but almost. The relief action certainly did not recognize a right of Kurdish self-determination, as the United Nations has proclaimed its respect for Iraqi territorial integrity .

Many of the recent collective interventions in weak states have occurred at the formal request of the state concerned or of all parties involved. In its attempt to restore democracy in Haiti (and of course acting mainly by approving US intervention), the Organization of American States (OAS) moved into new territory by justifying collective intervention. Other UN interventions have mainly concerned emergency relief for violations of minority rights, the monitoring of elections, or more traditional-style peace-keeping missions. When the United Nations monitored elections in Nicaragua, the operation was explicitly connected to the Central American peace process rather than to concern for democracy per se or human rights. Whether Somalia and Cambodia will be exceptions or the first in a series of temporary takeovers of failed states will depend on the lessons being drawn from those two operations. So far the United Nations has resisted endorsing a general doctrine, proceeding, as is its wont, case by case. This means that the normative scene is still rather cloudy, and the extent to which we have moved beyond traditional norms is dubious. Even the definition of what constitutes threats to peace is ambiguous. Must an egregious violation of human rights that constitutes a "threat to peace" have an inescapable impact on interstate relations? Or are some violations in themselves, and virtually by definition, threats to peace? The "creative interpretation of its constitutional obligation to maintain peace and security" undertaken by the Security Council cannot by itself solve these ambiguities.[11] If all violations are defined as threats to peace, then the Security Council, in principle, could intervene in the affairs of any state; but if only violations that threaten interstate peace count, then many egregious violations (as, say, in Tibet or East Timor) could go unaddressed.

To summarize the relevance of the changes in the international milieu for humanitarian intervention: First, there is a lack of leadership and clear direction at the top of the system, either among the major states or in the institutions themselves. Former UN secretary-general Boutros Boutros-Ghali was probably out a little too far in front of the member states in his "Agenda for Peace"; his successor now labors to keep the organization financially afloat, especially in the face of US recalcitrance about its debt. The activist phase of interventions, at least in official pronouncements, has receded. Second, there will continue to be occasions for humanitarian interventions, and we will continue to be faced with dilemmas of rescue, peacekeeping, and peace making, to list the problems in ascending order of difficulty. Third, there is no real consensus on when or how to intervene in these conflicts or on who should do so. And fourth, it is also fair to say that such enthusiasm as may have existed for these types of operations from 1991 to 1993 seems by now to have evaporated.

A remark by David Rieff in a recent essay that Western states favor humanitarian intervention seems now to be singularly inapposite.[12] The United States is not about to embark on broad Wilsonian crusades. The two most recent instances of our intervention, in Haiti and Bosnia, were undertaken with evident reluctance. The title of the rather dyspeptic monograph written in 1978 by Ernst Haas, *Global Evangelism Rides Again*, now seems almost quaint.[13] As we close out the 1990s, global evangelism at best limps along, led by a motley if erudite array of philosophers and human-rights advocates. More typical is the remark of the freshman Republican member of Congress who, responding to President Clinton's belated speech justifying the Bosnian intervention, said she did not see any reason why we should be sending "our boys" to a country about which we know nothing to stop the fighting there.[14] It is doubtful that she knew how closely she was echoing Neville Chamberlain.

So what does this say? It tells us that we are unlikely to find guidance from leaders, either of major states or of institutions. International lawyers will continue to debate whether or not interventions are legal, and the prescriptions from the political scientists will remain murky. Where does this leave us? These are serious ethical problems that cannot be ignored, and ethicists must be willing to tread where lawyers and politicians fear to go. Thus, on to the arguments about humanitarian intervention itself.

HUMANITARIAN INTERVENTION

A provocative challenge to the very terms of the debate comes from Rieff, who says that in effect humanitarian intervention is just a sop to the Western conscience and that the rich nations are using it as a way to avoid dealing with the chronic and serious issues of poverty and misgovernment in Third World states.[15] This is a legitimate point, but I take it to be a kind of *cri de coeur* of a committed journalist who has seen some of the worst humanitarian disasters of the decade. The insight, or warning, should act only as the beginning, and not the end, of an argument. Extraordinary and excruciating dilemmas are raised by some of the situations we observe across the world, but throwing up one's hands at the horror of it all or raining down curses on all the world does not help us to address them.

There are various ways to characterize and categorize the positions in the debate, but I have no wish to impose a complicated taxonomy here. Stanley Hoffmann—and more recently Michael Doyle—divides the theoretical approaches to the issue into realist, Marxist, and liberal varieties.[16] One might also divide the theorists into statists, or people who look at states as the source of values, and cosmopolitans. This is the old distinction made famous some time ago by Hedley Bull in *The Anarchical Society*, where he discussed statist and universalist cosmopolitan conceptions of justice.[17] Today, however, the real debate is taking place mainly between realists and liberals.

Realist Arguments

As I have outlined elsewhere, realists, whether they reside in academia or in the military, are traditionally hostile to any intervention that is justified for allegedly ethical reasons.[18] They claim, in general, that there is a self-delusory quality to all ethical justifications regarding state actions. That is a larger argument, which

I have tried to address elsewhere.[19] But how does this argument play out when it comes to humanitarian intervention? Realists say two things that are partly incompatible. One is that states only act when it is in their interest to do so and that therefore when they engage in a humanitarian intervention they are really pursuing some other agenda. They may just be worried about prestige or image on the "soft" end of the interest calculus. Or they may have some actual "hard" interests involved, interests that are convenient to subsume under the category of "humanitarian." In any case, say realists, when states intervene for allegedly humanitarian reasons they do not seek disinterestedly to do the right thing; they have "real" interests at stake. However, there is also a kind of political assertion that is slightly incompatible with this one. It says that interventions work and are supported politically only when they are closely connected to real interests. But if the first assertion were true, then the second would not apply: states would act *only* when their interests were really engaged. Apparently states sometimes really do act in spite of the fact that their so-called national interests are not engaged to the degree that realists think they ought to be.

In addition to these not-quite compatible empirical assertions about why states act, realists also make what amounts to an ethical argument that states are necessarily self-interested creatures and are, by definition, unable to act in other than self-interested ways. To expect them to do so—to support genuinely humanitarian action—is to engage in self-delusion, error, and hypocrisy. Thus the best, indeed most ethical, thing to do is to hold on to a more concrete definition of interests and leave humanitarian interventions to *Medicins sans Frontieres*. Humanitarian intervention, therefore, is in a sense a chimera, or, as in Rieff's account, a sop to our collective conscience. Moreover, humanitarian crusades dilute the national purpose, say realists: Only when we recognize the inevitably self-interested character of all our policies can we think clearly about our interests. Realists developed this argument most fully in their opposition to the US intervention in Vietnam. People tend to forget that some of the earliest opponents of that intervention, which was by no means humanitarian, were realists like Hans Morgenthau, George Kennan, and Reinhold Niebuhr, all of whom thought that Vietnam was not a core American interest and that we were vainly seeking to project our anticommunism in ways quite inappropriate to the local conditions.

There is, nevertheless, a quasi-realist case for humanitarian intervention that some have made, and that is to define interests in terms of what Arnold Wolfers called "milieu goals."[20] That is, there is a realist case for structuring a more orderly international system and paying attention to the requirements of leadership by a great power. Realist arguments on behalf of intervention may even invoke credibility ("No one will take us seriously as a great power if we allow this to occur"). If the United States is to be believed about anything it is to do, the argument goes, it cannot allow a group of thugs in Haiti to thumb its nose at everything it says. This is an interesting redeployment of an argument originally made in a very different context. We heard it during the intervention in Vietnam, and we hear it recurringly in debates about how many nuclear weapons we need for what. The argument rests on a broad definition of national interest.

In addressing national interest, one can perhaps distinguish between imperatives and preferences, but even defining what is imperative to a state involves deploying ethical preferences.[21] The classical arguments, again, are made by Wolfers: even "survival" must be defined according to moral values. Consider the different choices made by Czechoslovakia in 1938 and Poland in 1939, when faced with Hitler's demands. The Czech and Polish leaders, like Marshal Petain and General de Gaulle in the France of 1940, defined "survival of the state" quite differently. Even the apparently starkest imperatives are not straightforward or objective. In the middle of the Vietnam War, Bruce Russett wrote *No Clear and Present Danger*, which for many was an annoying little book. It was annoying because it challenged settled beliefs about World War II, but it was also useful in that Russett showed that it is possible to make the case that there was no clear and present danger to the United States in 1941 and that we did not really need to fight the war the way we did. He argues that we could very well have survived without fighting the Germans or the Japanese. The point here is not to agree with that position but rather to note that values are built into the very notion of what constitutes an imperative. Russett showed that imperatives, even the apparently most obvious ones like resisting Nazi Germany and Tojo's Japan, are not self-evident. They are, in the prevailing jargon, "constructed." And therefore, when one is talking about humanitarian intervention, it is not necessarily helpful to distinguish between imperatives and preferences.

The key questions are, what constitutes an integrated definition of national interest, and what value should be placed on having an international system that acts to prevent the sort of brutal behavior we have been observing in the 1990s? These questions of course lead into order as a justification for intervention. There is a component of morality to order, after all, as well as a quasi-moral notion that imputes to great powers a responsibility to ensure a relatively orderly international system. The realist route to humanitarian intervention thus involves a conception of international society that requires us to define what constitutes acceptable behavior within it. Although this is founded on classical, "statist" values, it still provides a means of justifying humanitarian intervention. Thus one need not be a dewy-eyed idealist to think that there are times when humanitarian intervention can be justified on grounds that are fairly traditional and well connected to definitions of interest.

Liberal Arguments

Whereas liberals have traditionally valued self-determination, community, and shared history, as seen in Walzer's work, there is also within liberalism a more universalist conception of human rights in which sovereignty is a subsidiary and conditional value. Self-determination, after all, has been among the most abused of liberal values. Indeed Amir Pasic has shown in an essay on Bosnia how the liberal value of self-determination can and is used to create what he calls a "negative normative reality" that leads to acts of genocide and ethnic cleansing.[22] A deep fault line of liberal theory runs along the question of how a given community defines itself, what means it can use, what legitimate goals it can pursue to establish its conception of freedom and autonomy, and to what extent outsiders are legitimately a party to these conflicts when they get nasty. Most famously perhaps, and most familiarly, J. S. Mill and Walzer following him have asserted both the virtue and the necessity of Mill's argument of the "arduous struggle of self-help" as the way for a community to achieve freedom and autonomy. This sets the bar rather high, even for humanitarian intervention.

At the noninterventionist end of the liberal spectrum, we find again two sorts of claims—one ethical and one prudential. The ethical claim of the noninterventionists places high value on community in itself, on a notion of shared history—what Walzer calls the "thick" values in his 1995 book *Thick and Thin*.[23] These values are to be respected almost prima facie by outsiders. There is also an ethical component to the historical/empirical claim that unless freedom is "earned" by a people, it will not survive and endure. But what if "earning" communal autonomy and freedom means ethnic cleansing? And, if so, what does that imply for the rest of the international community in terms of its rights and/or obligations to intervene?

Related to the claim about community is a claim about the legitimating function of domestic political processes—apparently almost any domestic political process. In a perhaps unguarded passage in *The Anarchical Society*, Bull wrote that to the extent that the words of a despot are authenticated by a political process, one ought to weigh them more heavily than the pronouncements of, say, Bertrand Russell, Buckminster Fuller, or Norman Cousins (in perhaps descending order of profundity), none of whose pronouncements has been authenticated by any sort of process at all. The political claim is that, unlike individuals, at least spokesmen for states, even authoritarian states, have passed through some political process.

At the same time there may be an unconscious arrogance in assuming that the most extreme leader in a community is necessarily the "right" spokesperson for that community's aspirations. This is a point made well by the late political theorist Judith Shklar in her powerful essay "The Liberalism of Fear."[24] By what right is Radovan Karadzic accepted as the authoritative spokesperson of the Bosnian Serbs? It is not clear who has consulted the ordinary people there. Does Pat Robertson speak for all white, evangelical Christians? Or Louis Farrakhan for African Americans as a group? There is a tendency in an argument that privileges states and domestic political processes, however rudimentary, to overvalue the most extreme leader and to reward the people least supportive of peaceful accommodation. The so-called Parliament of Bosnian Serbs came into being solely at the behest of Karadzic and his supporters; its actions in the midst of the diplomacy to end the war in Bosnia conferred no conceivable legitimacy.

These ethical and practical arguments for nonintervention slide almost imperceptibly into prudential claims about order. A prudential concern for order tells us that we cannot license intervention everywhere to everyone who is of a mind to intervene. It would be a recipe for disaster in the international milieu. Not every violation can justify intervention. Pierre Laberge cites a play by Moliere in which a wife is suffering a beating at the hands of her husband. To the surprise of a well-meaning stranger who tries to intervene, the wife rudely rejects the offer of help. She tells him to mind his own business, that she and her husband will work out their problems.[25] Noninterventionist liberals make a similar claim: people should be left alone to work out their own governance.

What about the interventionist end of the liberal spectrum? Franck has written that in the light of recent orgies of genocide, Mill's position on the arduous struggle of self-help is a posture of insufferable insouciance.[26] Indeed, if one looks at what occurred even in a success story, South Africa, it is clear that success was the product of more than self-help. A combination of external sanctions and sustained action on the part of the international community sought to convince white South Africans that apartheid was deeply unacceptable, that South Africa would have to abandon it and grant full citizenship rights to the black majority if it were ever to join the international community of states as a fully acceptable member. This external pressure aided the undoubtedly more potent internal developments that ultimately led the remarkably peaceful transformation to occur. Intervention, after all, can involve more (or less) than sending troops. In the case of South Africa, it involved sustained sanctions at almost every level of international interaction. And many of these sanctions were the product of grassroots activism in the democratic states that were also trading partners, or sporting competitors, of the South African state.

In his deservedly standard treatment of the issue in *Just and Unjust Wars*, Walzer sought to avoid the extreme non- or interventionist positions. Since the book's publication in 1977, people on both sides of the debate have tried to claim him as an ally because his legalist paradigm rests on a tension between the statist and cosmopolitan positions. The book recognizes the pull of one side of an argument even when it lands on the other side. In effect, Walzer tries to ground the legalist paradigm of the rights of states in the rights of individuals—because the rights of states rest on the rights of individuals. But at the same time, states as members of international society are by definition entitled to presumptive legitimacy. The first reading of the rule is that we as outsiders must assume that another state is legitimate unless it has proved otherwise by actions that we cannot ignore. Walzer revises the absolute rule of nonintervention only when the absence of "fit" between people and regime is radically apparent. He cites interventions in civil wars involving secessionist movements; interventions to balance prior interventions; and—here is our focus—interventions to rescue peoples threatened by massacre, enslavement, and (in "The Politics of Rescue") by large-scale expulsion.

Walzer conceives of humanitarian intervention as a kind of international analogue to domestic law enforcement. Governments that engage in acts that allow us to intervene for humanitarian purposes are in effect criminal governments. Those who initiate massacres lose their right to participate in the normal, and even normally violent, processes of domestic self-determination. Governments and armies engaged in wholesale massacres of individuals are readily identifiable as criminal. Hence, humanitarian intervention comes closer than any other kind of intervention to what we commonly regard in domestic society as police work. But can one intervene unilaterally to stop an outlaw? Walzer prefers a collective action, but it seems that he does not insist on it. His discussion conceives of international humanitarian intervention as a rescue operation in which the intervenor goes in and then comes out. In "The Politics of Rescue," Walzer expresses willingness to allow members of the international community to stay a little longer, to move from what Hoffmann calls rescue to the restoration of peace.[27] He does not directly treat the murderous conflicts in failed states or the systematic terrorization of a population by another seeking its own version of self-determination, as in Bosnia. The model is still one of states acting as states to punish a particularly egregious member of the society of states. So the values of community, shared history, and culture—in general, the "thick" values—trump the universalist values of human rights, at least in Walzer's account.

A LIBERALISM OF HUMAN RIGHTS

I would like to sketch very briefly a version of liberalism that, at least ethically, makes the value of sovereignty subordinate to human rights claims.[28] This version rests on a view of liberalism that seeks to value both the universal and the communitarian aspects of the political doctrine. Most communitarian critiques of liberalism fail to recognize the extent to which liberals value community and how liberalism itself embodies a conception of the good. Such critiques take aim at the priority given to rights and try to show how this comes at the expense of the common good. But, in fact, liberalism does work to establish conditions in which individuals will be able to fulfill themselves and their projects, their vision of the good, while respecting the personality and personhood of the projects of others. This means that there are liberal virtues—tolerance is an important one—and also that there are limits to so-called liberal neutrality. At bottom, liberalism seeks to establish a form of social life free of moral coercion even in circumstances of deep social disagreement. A liberal polity is therefore fully entitled to place limits on projects that would impose moral coercion and hamper the ability of individuals to define and pursue their own idea of the good. The goal of a liberal political society is individual autonomy in a community of tolerance. Political society can be regarded as a combined product of history, with its vast share of accidents, upheavals, and manipulations, and of human choice. Thus it is both willed and historical. And very often, as we know from many studies, it is the sort of shared history that is sometimes invented, or re-created, by poets, philosophers, and the like.

Whatever its origins, the moral standing of a society rests on its ability to respect and to protect the rights of its members and on their consent, explicit or implicit, to its rules and institutions. Both the nation, which we define as a group that provides individuals with a sense of social identity and transcends other secular and often religious cleavages, and the state, which we define as a set of institutions that aims at providing individuals in a certain territory with order and a variety of resources, derive their moral standing and their rights from the will and the rights of the individuals that compose the nation and over whom the state rules. Political life is, as a whole, a ceaseless process of accommodation among the rights and duties of individuals within a nation, those of a national group, and those of the state. But here we would join forces with the broader liberal worldview. Neither the group nor the nation nor the state can be seen as possessing inherent rights. The rights they claim derive from individuals. When they define their rights and duties in a way that tramples the basic rights of individuals they forfeit their legitimacy. This version of liberalism recognizes that persons are social beings and that society, therefore, cannot be seen only as protector of private lives and activities from anarchy. Individuals often want to come together to achieve common purposes, to carry on grand designs, to build a common civil culture sounding all the usual communitarian hymns. Political society is not simply a market for free private enterprise. From a moral point of view we look at social groupings formed by persons as derivative and constructed and as drawing their legitimacy from the will and consent of these persons. Thus in international relations we treat the notion of the morality of states with suspicion. At the same time, we recognize that cosmopolitanism, however desirable it may be as a political goal, does not yet correspond to the choice of the great majority of states or individuals. But we would still insist that community is not a value that trumps all others.

In this conception of liberalism, then, the justification for state sovereignty cannot rest on its own presumptive legitimacy. Instead it must be derived from the individuals whose rights are to be protected from foreign oppression or intrusion and from their right to a safe, "sovereign" framework in which they can enforce their autonomy and pursue their interests. It follows, then, that a state that is oppressive and violates the autonomy and integrity of its subjects forfeits its moral claim to full sovereignty. Thus, a liberal ethics of world order subordinates the principle of state sovereignty to the recognition and respect of human rights. And when an illiberal state is attacked by another one, the defense and integrity of its independence against aggression must be accompanied by an international effort to improve its own human rights record. Steps have been taken for the international protection of human rights that move slowly and haltingly toward this goal. Here, obviously, we have in mind Kuwait. The principle of an individual's right to moral autonomy, or to put it differently, to the human rights enshrined in the Universal Declaration on Human Rights, should be recognized as the highest principle of world order, ethically speaking, with state sovereignty as a circumscribed and conditional norm.

What does this mean for humanitarian intervention? The answer is complex. We have still to maintain and even raise barriers to illegitimate intervention, define the areas, conditions, and procedures for legitimate ones, pay particular attention to both sets of cases and the special problems raised by coercion, particularly military coercion, and proceed as much as possible on a broad basis of consent. What does this mean in practice? I think we must maintain our suspicion of unilateral intervention, because it always contains a component of self-interest, and unilateral intervention risks almost by definition violating the autonomy of the target. Unilateral intervention should thus be presumptively illegitimate, but the presumption can be overridden. Would it have been wrong for the United States to act in Haiti even if it did not have OAS sanction? The point is arguable, but I believe that humanitarian intervention would nevertheless have been justifiable. A blanket requirement for multilateral approval or participation in a case of potential humanitarian intervention may have the unfortunate effect of ensuring that nothing is done. One could certainly argue that Rwanda was a case of "Well, I'll do it if you do it," with nobody willing to take the first step. Meanwhile, tens, even hundreds, of thousands of people were killed in a brutal, low-tech, and rather time-consuming way, largely by machetes. It is quite clear to most people who have studied this case that a modest deployment of international troops placed early and decisively could have prevented a large number of deaths. Because of cases like this, it does not seem reasonable to rule out unilateral action. At the same time, a collective process serves as a check on an individual state's tendency to intervene for self-interested purposes .

When could one intervene collectively? I think that we could build on the emerging consensus on threats to peace, breaches of peace, and acts of aggression—the traditional causes that allow us to intervene in interstate conflict. In domestic affairs the equivalent causes would be domestic policies and practices capable of leading to serious threats to peace, and in cases of egregious violations of human rights—even if those violations occurred entirely within the borders of a given state. A genocide is no less "a common threat to humanity"— the characterization of former UN secretary-general Boutros-Ghali—if it occurs within borders than if it crosses them. The basic principle that should guide international intervention is this: Individual state sovereignty can be overridden whenever the behavior of the state even within its own territory threatens the existence of elementary human rights abroad and whenever the protection of the basic human rights of its citizens can be assured only from the outside.

State sovereignty, in short, is a contingent value: its observance depends upon the actions of the state that invokes it. Members of the international community are not obliged to "respect the sovereignty" of a state that egregiously violates human rights. Why "egregiously"? The sad answer is that the world presents a far too rich array of human rights violations that might justify outside intervention. We must choose among the evils we seek to end. For much of the world, for example, capital punishment violates human rights. Yet few disinterested observers would urge or welcome the forcible landing of an international military force to prevent Virginia's next execution. However one regards capital punishment after due process of law, it cannot compare with the scale of violations that occurred in Rwanda or in the Cambodia of Pol Pot. As one analyst has observed, we currently possess "neither the capabilities nor the willingness to right all wrongs, even the relatively small number of wrongs that are deemed to warrant international action."[29] But as President Clinton put it in his speech justifying the NATO action in Bosnia: "We cannot stop all war for all time. But we can stop some wars.... There are times and places when our leadership can make the difference between peace and war."[30] Some judgement about the scale of evil, and about the capacity we have to end it, must be made.

This process of judgment should, in my view, be multinational. For all the flaws of the United Nations, it does provide a forum for international debate and for the emergence of consensus. And, as I have suggested, if taken as a general but not rigid rule of thumb, an insistence upon collective, multilateral intervention or, as in Haiti, collectively approved unilateral action can correct for self-interested interventions that are draped in a thin cloak of humanitarianism. At the same time, it may be necessary for a state to declare its intention to act on its own; if the cause is truly just, this very declaration may make collective action more possible. And the intervention may still be just even if its motives are mixed: the examples of India's intervention in the former East Pakistan and of Tanzania's in the Uganda of Idi Amin are often cited as unilateral interventions that nevertheless ended humanitarian disasters.[31]

What about the problem of consistency? Does the fact that we can do little, if anything, about human rights violations in

Tibet have implications for what can be done about human rights violations in Haiti or East Timor? Alas, it seems obvious that there simply won't be consistency, but what does that mean ethically? Is it more ethical to say that since I cannot do everything everywhere consistently I should do nothing? My own view is that the fact that one cannot do everything everywhere does not mean that one should not try to do anything anywhere.

A first stab at setting priorities for action might be to suggest humanitarian interventions where the threats to peace for neighboring states are indeed the greatest. One could also come up with a list that sets the potential costs of the intervention against what might actually be achieved. In short, we could seek to adapt the traditional criteria of the just war tradition to cases of humanitarian intervention. But this does require that we develop the means and capacities for acting in these ways.

I am not sympathetic to those who think that we must reserve our military for a single purpose lest it lose, so to speak, its "purity of essence," to quote a famous (movie) general.[32] It is not inconceivable to me that we can have dual-purpose military organizations. People can be trained to do more than one thing. We do have to address more seriously collective capacities. We have stopped talking about the UN standing force, and the Clinton administration has stopped trying to build up the collective capacities of the United Nations, apparently because the issue is regarded as a political loser. Nevertheless, there seems to me to be a clear ethical imperative to begin to develop means that are capable of addressing some of the problems that we have been seeing.

But as always in ethical arguments, ought implies can. It is clear that weighing in on the human rights side implies a willingness to intervene far more extensively than we are currently willing to do; and there are significant costs and dangers attached to this willingness. On the other hand, weighing in heavily on the side of traditional sovereignty and nonintervention entails a willingness to turn a blind eye to many outrages in the world. We could say, "Well, it is a pity that people are killing each other and it's true that there is something that we could do about it relatively easily, but it is actually occurring within a state so it's not our business." Surely one of the lessons of the Holocaust is that we should not allow this to occur again. And one of the benefits of the end of the Cold War is that we can now begin to address questions of endemic injustice and human suffering in ways that were not possible when the United States and the Soviet Union were worried about blowing each other up.

There remain formidable worries about the consistency and effectiveness of humanitarian intervention. But one has to begin working those out by deciding how much one is willing to overlook for the sake of sovereign independence. To claim that sovereignty is subsidiary to human rights is not to say that sovereignty is negligible or automatically weaker. Rather, claims to sovereignty are subsidiary in that they do not automatically trump other compelling claims. There may be times when prudence suggests doing something less, but I regard it still as a moral imperative to prevent or mitigate evil when one has the capacity to do so. Thus as an ethical imperative, the issue of humanitarian intervention demands our deepest attention and response.

Notes

1. Joel H. Rosenthal, ed., *Ethics and International Affairs: A Reader* (Washington, DC: Georgetown University Press, 1995), introduction.

2. Samuel P. Huntington, "New Contingencies, Old Roles," *Joint Forces Quarterly*, no. 2 (Autumn 1992), 338.

3. See Joseph S. Nye, *Bound to Lead: The Changing Nature of American Power* (New York: Basic Books, 1990), or, much earlier, Stanley Hoffmann, "Notes on the Elusiveness of Modern Power," *International Journal* 30 (Spring 1975), 183-206.

4. An exhaustive analysis of such conflicts can be found in Ted Robert Gurr, *Minorities at Risk: A Global View of Ethnopolitical Conflicts* (Washington, DC: US Institute of Peace Press, 1993). An alarmist, journalistic account is offered by Robert D. Kaplan, *The Ends of the Earth: A Journey at the Dawn of the 21st Century* (New York: Random House, 1996).

5. Thomas M. Franck, "The Emerging Right to Democratic Governance," *American Journal of International Law* 86 (January 1992), 46-91.

6. For an excellent summary of these operations, see the appendix prepared by Robert C. Johansen and Kurt Mills in Stanley Hoffmann, *The Ethics and Politics of Humanitarian Intervention* (Notre Dame, IN: University of Notre Dame Press, 1996), 101-15.

7. Tom J. Farer, "A Paradigm of Legitimate Intervention," in Lori Fisler Damrosch, ed., *Enforcing Restraint: Collective Intervention in Internal Conflicts* (New York: Council on Foreign Relations Press, 1993), 341.

8. Michael Waiter, "The Politics of Rescue," *Dissent* (Winter 1995), 41.

9. Michael Walzer, *Just and Unjust Wars* (New York: Basic Books, 1977), ch. 6.

10. Farer, "A Paradigm of Legitimate Intervention," 320, 330. On the "founding fathers," see J. L. Brierly, *The Law of Nations*, 6th ed. (New York: Oxford University Press, 1963), 403 ff., and Richard B. Lillich, ed., *Humanitarian Intervention and the United Nations* (Charlottesville: University Press of Virginia, 1973).

11. Farer, "A Paradigm of Legitimate Intervention," 330.

12. David Rieff, "The Lessons of Bosnia: Morality and Power," *World Policy Journal* (Spring 1995), 76-88.

13. Ernst B. Haas, *Global Evangelism Rides Again*, Institute of International Studies Policy Paper, no. 5 (Berkeley: University of California, 1978).

14. Quoted in the *New York Times*, November 28, 1995, A15.

15. Rieff, "The Lessons of Bosnia."

16. Hoffmann, "Notes on the Elusiveness of Modern Power" and Michael Doyle, *Ways of War and Peace* (New York: W. W. Norton, 1997).

17. Hedley Bull, *The Anarchical Society* (New York: Columbia University Press, 1977).

18. Michael J. Smith, "Ethics and Intervention," *Ethics and International Affairs* 3 (1989).

19. Michael J. Smith, *Realist Thought from Weber to Kissinger* (Baton Rouge: Louisiana State University Press, 1987).

20. See Arnold Wolfers, "Statesmanship and Moral Choice," in his *Discord and Collaboration* (Baltimore: Johns Hopkins Press, 1962).

21. Stanley Hoffmann, "Politics and Ethics of Military Intervention," *Survival* 37 (Winter 1995-96), 29-51; Wolfers, "Statesmanship and Moral Choice."

22. Amir Pasic, "Ethics and Reality: The Hard Case of Bosnia," paper presented at the International Studies Association meeting, San Diego, CA, April 1996.

23. Michael Walzer, *Thick and Thin: Moral Argument at Home and Abroad* (Notre Dame, IN: University of Notre Dame Press, 1995).

24. Judith N. Shklar, "The Liberalism of Fear," in Nancy Rosenblum, ed., *Liberalism and the Moral Life* (Cambridge, MA: Harvard University Press, 1989), 21-38.

25. Pierre Laberge, "Humanitarian Intervention: Three Ethical Positions," *Ethics and International Affairs* 9 (1995).

26. Franck, "The Emerging Right to Democratic Self-Governance."

27. Hoffmann, "Politics and Ethics of Military Intervention," 34-46.

28. The following passage draws on a manuscript in progress written with Stanley Hoffmann; hence the change to the first-person plural pronoun.

29. Franck, "The Emerging Right to Democratic Self-Governance."

30. President Clinton quoted in the *New York Times*, November 28, 1995, A12.

31. See Walzer, *Just and Unjust Wars*, 102-10.

32. I refer to the character in Stanley Kubrick's *Dr. Strangelove*, General Jack D. Ripper.

Questions for Reflection

1. Summarize the realist and liberal perspectives on the notion of humanitarian intervention. What do you agree with and disagree with in these two perspectives?

2. What argument does Smith offer in support of his claim that state sovereignty should not receive priority over human rights? Do you think that state sovereignty should always have priority? Why or why not?

3. What kinds of activities do you think call for humanitarian intervention? What forms of intervention do you think are appropriate? Should humanitarian intervention always be a collective effort on the part of the international community, or should an individual country have the right to intervene in order to prevent or stop violations of human rights in another country?

FURTHER READINGS FOR SECTION 8

Brown, Michael. *The International Dimensions of Internal Conflict.* Cambridge, MA: MIT Press, 1996.

Donnelly, Jack. "Human Rights, Humanitarian Intervention, and American Foreign Policy: Law, Morality and Politics." *Journal of International Affairs* 37 (1984): 311-28.

Falk, Richard. "The Challenge of Genocide and Genocidal Politics in an Era of Globalization." In *Human Rights in Global Politics*, Tim Dunne and Nicholas J. Wheeler, eds. Cambridge: Cambridge University Press, 1999.

Harff, Barbara. *Genocide and Human Rights: International Legal and Political Issues.* Denver, CO: University of Denver Press, 1984.

Human Rights Watch. *Slaughter Among Neighbors: The Political Origins of Communal Violence.* New Haven: Yale University Press, 1995.

Kuper, Leo. *The Prevention of Genocide.* Hew Haven: Yale University Press, 1985.

McMahan, Jeff. "Intervention and Collective Self-Determination." *Ethics & International Affairs* 10 (1996): 4-11.

Miller, Seumas. "Collective Responsibility, Armed Intervention and the Rwandan Genocide." *International Journal of Applied Philosophy* 12 (1998): 223-38.

Morsink, Johannes. "Cultural Genocide, the Universal Declaration, and Minority Rights." *Human Rights Quarterly* 21 (1999): 1009-1060.

Nardin, Terry and Jerome Slater. "Non-Intervention and Human Rights." *Journal of Politics* 48 (1986): 86-96.

Pease, Kelly Kate and David P. Forsythe. "Human Rights, Humanitarian Intervention, and World Politics." *Human Rights Quarterly* 15 (1993): 290-314.

Phillips, Robert L. and Duane L. Cade. *Humanitarian Intervention: Just War vs. Pacifism.* Lanham, MD: Rowman & Littlefield, 1996.

Ramsbotham, Oliver and Tom Woodhouse. *Humanitarian Intervention in Contemporary Conflict.* Cambridge: Polity Press, 1996.

Walzer, Michael. *Just and Unjust Wars.* New York: Basic Books, 1977.

Section 9:
WOMEN'S RIGHTS

42. ARATI RAO

Arati Rao has taught at Wellesley College and Columbia University, and her research focus is on feminist political theory and international human rights. She has published on a wide range of topics, including the family, culture, immigration, and law. In this essay, Rao examines how the status of women has become an issue in world politics. In her analysis she describes various cultural beliefs and practices that are injurious and unjust to women, such as wife battering and marital rape, many of which are traditionally features of the domestic realm to which women are exclusively relegated. Employing some of the critical insights of feminist theory, Rao argues for the necessity of strengthening international standards for women's rights, particularly since the abuses that many women suffer are often unrecognized in political systems dominated by patriarchal power relations.

Text—Right in the Home: Feminist Theoretical Perspectives on International Human Rights

Arati Rao, "Right in the Home: Feminist Theoretical Perspectives on International Human Rights," National Law School Journal *1 (1993): 62–81. Reprinted by permission of the author.*

In this article, I would like to extend the method and substance of Western feminist theoretical critiques of national legal systems to the field of international human rights. I use the issue of domestic violence, including marital rape, to test the responsiveness of the human rights framework to women's concerns. I am informed by the insights feminists have gained regarding rights-based legal approaches in my assessment of the value of the international human rights consensus for women. In emphasising the tensions inherent in the rights-based approach, I want to highlight various problematic epistemological assumptions and ontological slippages in international human rights discourse, to argue for the urgent need to reconceptualise human rights.

In India, as anywhere else, even the gross under reporting of violence against women cannot mask the magnitude and frequency of the crime. The pressures brought to bear on the victim, as well as her internalised constraints, make the reporting of violence difficult. Where the victim survives and lodges a complaint, the insufficient and often crime-reinforcing response of the selectively interventionist state makes a mockery of her desire for justice. Long-existing patterns of violence against women have become more deeply entrenched, and new forms of systematic abuse have emerged as ghastly accompaniments to modernisation.

The example of dowry harassment, often resulting in murder, is only one of several kinds of violence in the Indian home that illustrate the interlocking relationships between gender, ideology, socio-economic structures, and the patriarchal state. In India's dominant gender ideology, the criminal nature of dowry harassment is muddled by a number of cultural formulations, particularly of femaleness and the family, which circumscribes a world in which a woman's worth lies in direct relation to the amount of her dowry. For example, the definition of the woman as simultaneously a facilitator of wealth (when she brings dowry into her in-laws' household) and an economic liability (when her presence requires an accompanying dowry to offset her worthlessness to parents and in-laws alike), is representative of the mixed signals sent out by the dominant gender ideology—signals which the woman herself is encouraged to appropriate in her understanding of duty, humility, sacrifice, service and the like.

There are various grounds on which domestic violence such as dowry harassment can be condemned and ended; the assertion of the woman's rights is one approach that I would like to discuss. Like marital rape, dowry harassment too often receives the criminal protection of notions of familial roles and special obligations. In the following pages, I will examine the oppression and errors inherent in general formulations of "the family," and argue for changes in international perceptions of women's rights, if we are to successfully address violence against women in the home.

I. SUMMARY OF ARGUMENT

The widely-discussed androcentrism of the concept of human rights in its historical evolution and its contemporary forms has generated particularly serious difficulties for the recognition of women's rights. One important conceptual obstacle to gender justice is the notion of the division of society into public and private spheres. The acceptance of this notion pervades human rights discourse and activity, and undergirds the human rights focus on the public sphere. Since the two spheres are distinctly gendered, and unequally weighted by definition, it is difficult to conceptualise violations of women's rights in the private sphere in a fashion that is coherent as well as consistent with the language used to describe violations in the public sphere. The issues of domestic violence and abuse, particularly marital rape, bring to a head the philosophical inconsistencies that are internal to the international consensus on human rights. The normative privileging of the legally-recognised heterosexual family unit in international documents, such as the United Nations Declaration of Human Rights (1948), leaves unproblematised some of the most egregious human rights violations against women: those that occur as part of certain activities recognised as exclusively familial, and consequently are, by association, consonant with the definition of the institution of the family. The twin human rights assumptions of separate social spheres, and of the normatively privileged status of the family, rely on a mistaken notion of power as identifiable, quantifiable, and predominantly employed by the State. This mistake leads to further errors in identifying the locus of power, its direction and force, and its agents. In this approach, "domestic crime" becomes an oxymoron. Consequently, issues like marital rape place the conceptual framework of contemporary human rights under a strain so heavy that women-specific abuses may never be completely redressed unless and until the private realm is recognised as a legitimate area of human rights concern at the highest level, and is problematised as the crucial site of struggle for women's rights.

In expanding upon these points, I shall address the following four questions. What kinds of human activity are viewed as the legitimate scope of international human rights discourse? If some kinds of activity generally receive consideration before others, on what grounds are the priorities justified? How much room, if any, exists for the successful assertion of human rights claims in the lower-priority areas of human activity? What form are these claims permitted or compelled to take in their demand for redress?

In the following pages, I demonstrate that the epistemological foundations of the concept of human rights interact with some distinctly normative claims about different areas of human activity, to create a highly-charged atmosphere in which a gender-specific claim from women tends to give a shock to the system rather than get succor from it.

II. KNOWLEDGE-POWER RELATIONSHIPS

Feminist discussions of the androcentric nature of knowledge, and feminist critiques of the relationship between knowledge and social power, are valuable in assessing the limitations of some aspects of human rights discourse, particularly when they command a high degree of international consensus.[1] Certain androcentric realities form the backdrop against which my arguments unfold. These include firstly, the historical development of the concept of rights in the West in the service of certain subgroups in society (adult propertied male citizens) rather than of everyone; the subsequent appropriation of rights language by one oppressed group after another to the point at which the concept today purportedly applies to all human beings; the dominance of men in the drafting, refinement, interpretation, ratification, and implementation of international human rights; the late emergence of a widespread feminist effort to address gender-specific human rights abuses in women's lives.

The success of rights-based strategies in combating a variety of abuses is indisputable. Indisputable, too, is the attraction of rights language to many victims of oppression. Yet, rights as a concept, and as an approach, has come under fire from several directions, most notably from feminists. For example, the legal feminist thinker Ann Scales, extends the feminist critique of the

Western philosophical cannon to attack the primacy of the rights approach in law when she writes:

> The rights-based side of things, for all its grand abstraction, describes a pretty grim view of life on the planet. It treats individuals in society as isolated nomads, as natural adversaries who must each stake out his own territory and protect it with the sword/shield mechanism of "rights." This model of aggression is half of what is required for holocaust.[2]

At the same time, one must not be seduced by such stark depictions of rights-based individualism in its extreme form. Countering such critiques are feminist legal scholars like Frances Olsen, whose cautionary note below reminds us of the gendered oppression lurking behind the anti-individualistic alternative of "community":

> For many years women were forced into unequal and oppressive "community" under the control first of their fathers and then of their husbands.... Men force community upon women when they make sexual advances to coworkers and subordinates or pester women strangers with unwelcomed conversations. A rapist may believe he is seeking community with his victim, especially if she is his wife or social friend.[3]

Olsen goes on to suggest a way out of the unhelpful oppositional dichotomy of individual-community by linking both aspects of human existence in a mutually informing and sustaining relationship.

> The "women's rights" that we should support are an expression of the social practice of allowing women to resist forced community. The "bourgeois individualism" critique of rights is mistaken to the extent that it opposes this social practice. The critique is correct to the extent that it accepts the social practice but criticises a particular understanding of its underlying basis. The distinction is important; the social practice that allows women to resist forced community is itself the result of collective political activity.[4]

Such a carefully-articulated distinction is helpful in our search for concrete strategies to end domestic violence. Olsen's view emerges from an understanding of the law as neither wholly "male" nor steadfastly "anti-female." For critics like Olsen, the law is a complex, uncoordinated, contradictory, contextualised phenomenon, which has been imbued by patriarchal interests with the self-serving, false qualities of objectivity, rationality, abstraction and unity. This view of the law explains the coexistence of legal reform and legal victimisation. Such sensitivity to the epistemological complexity of institutional and personal relationships permits women to insist on immediate legal redress of their concerns, even as they demand a reconceptualising of gender issues in the law.

In international human rights circles, the issue of domestic violence against women has been muddled by the interventions of patriarchal ideology and practices. Globally, the husband's access to the wife's body for disciplinary and sexual purposes is generally acknowledged as consonant with the definition of marriage, thereby complicating any acknowledgement of wife-beating and marital rape as gender-specific crimes. Further, the assault by one privileged individual on another less-privileged, in an institution specifically defined as relational and communal, complicates the framing and assertion of an individualistic claim. After all, legal personhood is not universally guaranteed to a wife; in many societies, she is subsumed under the husband's legal person. Even where the legal standing of the wife as an individual is allowed, the tidal waves of preexisting judicial practices and social norms usually overwhelm her claim. Feminist activists have begun to demand that international pressure be brought to bear on countries that perpetuate this global pattern of abuse, and that the problem be addressed as a human rights violation at the highest international level.

Political theorist Jack Donnelly observes that "one typically has direct recourse to human rights claims only where legal or other remedies seem unlikely to work or have already failed.... In fact the special function of human rights virtually requires that they be claimed precisely when they are unenforceable by ordinary legal or political means."[5] Given that "all rights claims are a sort of 'last resort'," he reminds us that "claims of *human* rights are the final resort in the realm of rights."[6]

However, what if the courts of first as well as last resort do not, indeed cannot, recognise your human rights claims? What if the conceptual failures at the local level are replicated at the international level, whether they are failures of recognition of human rights or of addressing the violations thereof? What if the epistemological foundations of a community's unfair legal standards and social arrangements are reiterated in international laws and agreements? What if neither the existing conceptions of human rights, nor the normative understandings of human behaviour, serve the interest and well-being of significant numbers of people? What is the validity of a human rights approach if these people are readily identified as a group, such as "women," with particular needs and vulnerabilities, in *some* areas of concern, but not all?

Evidence of the worldwide increase in abuses particular to women's well-being is so alarming that existing theoretical analysis of a rights based legalistic approach must be extended immediately to the international rights community. For example, the patriarchy-enhancing "saneness" and "difference" principles, which the feminist legal theorist, Catharine MacKinnon, has identified in United States law, may be seen to be reiterated in content, as well as intent, in United Nations' declarations on human rights.[7]

Let me illustrate this "gender blindness," with the example of the definition of torture. The Convention Against Torture and Other Cruel, Inhuman or Degrading Treatment or Punishment (1984), recognises the integrity of the individual *qua* individual, and makes no reference to any gender-specificity in the purpose and practice of torture:

> For the purposes of this Convention, the term "torture" means any act by which severe pain or suffering, whether physical or mental, is intentionally inflicted on a person for such purposes as obtaining from him or a third person information or a confession, punishing him for an act he or a third person has committed or

> is suspected of having committed, or intimidating or coercing him or a third person, or for any reason based on discrimination of any kind, when such pain or suffering is inflicted by or at the instigation of or with the consent or acquiescence of a public official or other person acting in an official capacity. It does not include pain or suffering arising only from, inherent in or incidental to lawful sanctions.[8]

Amnesty International's earlier definition in its "Report on Torture" was equally deficient:

> Torture is the systematic and deliberate infliction of acute pain in any form by one person on another, or on a third person, in order to accomplish the purpose of the former against the will of the latter.... It can be safely stated that under all circumstances, regardless of the context in which it is used, torture is outlawed under the common law of mankind. This being so, its use may properly be considered to be a crime against humanity.[9]

Such gender-blindness is perplexing, given the vast body of feminist research that depicts the ways in which states themselves have developed a special agenda in the torture of women. This has been achieved by manipulating social factors that are specific to women's daily lives, such as religion, gender ideology, and social roles.[10]

Complicating this "gender sameness" approach is the coexisting "difference" approach, which recognises the particular circumstances of our unavoidably gendered human existence. The various documents which address general issues of gender discrimination as well as particular issues, such as trafficking in women, testify to the broad scope of this principle. Amnesty International's recent report, "Women in the Front Line," addresses human rights abuses that are particular to women, such as rape, sexual abuse, and violence related to pregnancy and childbearing.[11]

I would argue that the coexistence of these two approaches is uneasy at best, and counterproductive at worst. Even as the concept of human rights universalises, it obliterates; even where it acknowledges specificity, it insists on retaining established frameworks of general conceptualisation and analysis. Furthermore, all these documents restrict themselves to abuses in which the state is a visible actor, they do not address violations outside the state-citizen relationship.

However, many would argue that the emergence of discussion, and even international documents, on hitherto-unproblematised issues from the "private" realm sounds an encouraging note. The two examples most often cited are the rights of the child and the rights of women. Let me address one international document that has generated controversy despite its blandness: the 1979 Convention on the Elimination of All Forms of Discrimination Against Women (hereinafter CEDAW). Even among legal scholars who have demonstrated interest in women's rights, concern runs high regarding the interpretive extension of CEDAW into the private sphere. For example, while acknowledging the "rampant" discrimination against women in the private realm, Theodor Meron cautions:

> There is danger, however, that state regulation of interpersonal conduct may violate the privacy and associational rights of the individual and conflict with the principles of freedom of opinion, expression, and belief. Such regulation may require invasive state action to determine compliance, including inquiry into political and religious beliefs.[12]

In his argument against the "overbreadth" of the Convention, Meron particularly notes the added potential for conflict between women's rights and religious rights.

Offsetting this problematic acceptance of the primacy of already existing rights of already-privileged people over progress for women is the critical appraisal of "culture" found in numerous feminist writings. For example, MacKinnon points out that the concept of "culture" itself needs to be unpacked to reveal its structuring patriarchal power relations. In "Whose Culture? A Case Note on Martinez v. Santa Clara Pueblo (1983)," MacKinnon places the US Supreme Court's hands-off response to a Native American woman's demand for gender justice in her tribe, in the larger legal context of the Court's readiness to meddle in Native American affairs when they involve other issues, such as land ownership, mineral rights, or foreign relations.[13] MacKinnon also unmasks the complicity of male tribal leadership with the patriarchal state, which leaves Julia Martinez with no hope of receiving justice either from her community or from the state. In response to the Court's reading of tribal "culture" into what feminists would call a discriminatory practice, MacKinnon asks: "Is male supremacy sacred because it has become a tribal tradition?"[14]

Of course, there is a growing body of feminist thinking that takes a less radicalised view of the social construction of culture, in which minority writers dominate. For example, the African-American novelist, Toni Morrison, in an essay entitled, "Unspeakable Things Unspoken: The Afro-American Presence in American Literature," argues for a much more ambiguous and fluid relationship between the otherwise dichotomised roles of oppressor and oppressed, in which there is a mutually informing and even transformative process of interaction.[15] From this angle, women are involved in the construction of "culture", dominant or any other kind, to some degree—the exact nature and extent of which is the subject of feminist culture theory.

MacKinnon's analysis of Martinez gives the lie to Meron's fear of invasive state involvement, a fear which is shared by many legal scholars at the national, as well as international levels. Feminists have shown this fear to be a classic case of straining to keep the stable door closed long after the horse has bolted. State regulation of the "private" realm has long had a resounding impact on notions of family, sexuality, home and work.[16]

III. THE SPHERE(S) OF RIGHTS

"Private" and "public" derive from the common philosophical ancestor of the rights-based approach: liberalism. From the human rights perspective, it would be easy to assume a logical alliance between liberal ideology and feminist goals. As political theorist Carole Pateman points out:

> The roots of both doctrines lie in the emergence of individualism as general theory of social life; neither liberalism nor feminism is conceivable without some conception of individuals as free and equal beings, emancipated from the ascribed, hierarchical bonds of traditional society.[17]

Pateman and others are quick to point out the variety of opinion within the liberal camp itself on the nature of public and private, and the debatable validity of the constantly-shifting boundaries between the two spheres. However, even the slightest retention of the notion of different spheres of human activity—and the retention in liberal and lights ideology alike is far from slight—is open to the test of gender.

The separate spheres approach permits choices to be made between the two realms, as well as within each realm, on the issues central to liberal concerns, such as authority, freedom, rights, obligations. Now, in the best of all possible worlds, the mere existence of separate spheres would not result in inequality or injustice. However, the historical evolution of the separate spheres shows that they are unequally weighted in values and expectations, as well as normatively gendered. Further, despite all the tortuous arguments for the complementarity of the two spheres, in reality the male governs in each.

Along with other critiques, feminist theory has generated a voluminous body of literature on the relationships between gender, patriarchy, and the state. Feminist analysis of the public-private distinction shows the two spheres to be, in reality, "the two sides of the single coin of liberal-partriarchalism."[18] In liberalism, the state's role in carefully creating and strenuously maintaining the realm of the private is mystified, the state's structuring presence is disarmingly disowned. This mystification of reality is reinforced by the ideology of civil society which simply does not acknowledge civil society's very real division into gendered spheres of existence. As Nicos Poulantzas notes, "it is not the 'external' space of the modem family which shuts itself off from the state, but rather the state which, at the very time that it sets itself up as the public space, traces and assigns the site of the family."[19] Political theorist Zillah Eisenstein adds: "The division between public and private life, when it is identified, is spoken of as reflecting the development of the bourgeois liberal state, not the patriarchal ordering of the bourgeois state."[20] When the very rights language that governs the public realm eloquently excuses itself from the private, analysis of the family as *the* site of struggle for rights becomes even more urgent.

IV. THE FAMILY AS THE SITE OF STRUGGLE

Feminist theoretical discussion of the patriarchal bridge connecting, even as it attempts to separate, the two spheres suggests that analysis of the family is prior and fundamentally pre-emptive of analysis of other areas of human activity, such as the workplace. This overturns the conventional framework of analysis out of which the notion of rights has emerged. Here, the model of human nature is constructed around the denatured, dehistoricised, disembodied, disembedded, individual self. In the seventeenth century, English political theorist Thomas Hobbes urged: "Let us consider men...as if but even now sprung out of the earth, and suddenly, like mushrooms, come to full maturity, without all kind of engagement to each other."[21] Today, American philosopher John Rawls' theory-building enterprise is facilitated by the characterless creatures whose search for justice begins behind a "veil of ignorance" about themselves and each other.[22] While these approaches do not exhaust the range of rights thinking, they remain representative of the dominant strain of model-building in the rights tradition.

The construction of a rights framework in which the individual *qua* individual is the primary subject of inquiry, and which focuses on the activities of this individual in certain areas of (his) life and not others, relies on a false notion of the private realm. This construction bypasses the reality of the patriarchal framework within which the "two spheres" doctrine flourishes. In other words, the rights framework removes one kind of human being from the unavoidable particularities of our biological, relational, historicised, culture-bound, human existence and assigns paradigmatic privilege to *him,* even as it relegates another kind of human being to *her* paradigmatic secondary status. As Pateman observes, feminist insight "highlights the problem of the status of the 'natural' sphere of the family, which is presupposed by, yet seen as separate from and irrelevant to, the conventional relations of civil society." In reality, "the sphere of domestic life is at the heart of civil society rather than apart or separate from it."[23]

International consensus on the status of the family reifies these problems in the context of human rights. Article 16 of the United Nations Universal Declaration of Human Rights (1948) states:

> 1. Men and women of full age, without any limitation due to race, nationality, or religion, have the right to marry and to found a family. They are entitled to equal rights as to marriage, during marriage and at its dissolution.
> 2. Marriage shall be entered into only with the free and full consent of the intending spouses.
> 3. *The family is the natural and fundamental group unit of society and is entitled to protection by society and the State.* (emphasis added)

This formulation reappears in direct and indirect ways in subsequent human rights documents. For example, the sentence emphasised above is repeated in the International Covenant on Civil and Political Rights (1966), Article 23 (1); the "natural and fundamental" clause is repeated in the International Covenant on Economic, Social and Cultural Rights (1966), Article 10 (1). Furthermore, this particular definition influences virtually every single reference to the family in all important international human rights declarations and documents (e.g., maternity; childrearing; children born out of wedlock; marriage; divorce). While it is true that these carefully-worded documents have emerged out of long periods of intense consultation, negotiation, bargaining, and compromise, I suggest that even closer scrutiny from the feminist viewpoint will reveal conceptual stumbling blocks that seriously undermine the goals of the documents themselves. Let us look at what is enshrined in these documents and what is left out, to assess their implications for women.

There are several consequences of widespread international recognition of a particular form of the social institution of the family. While arguments can be made for the general value of such a form, as well as its drawbacks, this article will focus on only those aspects of the notion that have relevance for women's rights in the home.

Note the sentence from the Declaration, emphasised above. This is the *only* place in the entire Universal Declaration where society and the state are named as participants who are exhorted to take an active role in maintaining a social practice or institution, and where "the power of the state is invoked as a protective device."[24] This formal recognition of the state's role, and formal demand for the deployment of state power, in maintaining the family unit is nothing short of extraordinary, given that the person who is primarily identified with the family, the woman, is not conceptually central to human rights documents or discourse.

Fundamentally, since the "two spheres" theory defines the family as the woman's realm, her dissatisfaction with or departure from the family becomes conceptually problematic (even before we acknowledge her very real ideological and economic costs of leaving the family). When human rights violations occur within the family, the consequences of this particular definition of family as "natural" and "fundamental," as well as of this exhortation to the state, are extremely serious.

In an abusive situation, gender inequality emerges as one of the defining characteristics of this notion of the family. In the case of domestic violence, the normative standing of the family becomes a weapon to be used against the abused woman to assign responsibility and blame (and it usually is). For example, the raped wife can be censured for withholding the sexual access that is guaranteed the husband in many definitions of marriage (and she usually is). Her claim may be declared invalid in a legal system that relies upon this definition and consequently denies the possibility of rape within marriage (and it usually is). Agents of the state may be employed to send an abused woman back to the site of her abuse, the family, to "protect" its "natural" form and maintain family unity (and they usually are).

Yet, despite the difficulty of economic survival in a world where every aspect of existence is unequally weighted along gender lines, many of these women survive (along with many of their children). Given this reality, the formal acknowledgement of this one normative notion of "family" in international documents must be reassessed.

It could be argued that other formulations of "family" (for example, homosexual/communal) are not precluded by this definition, that creative interpretation is possible. I would counter by insisting that, since all significant references to family are related to this one notion, recognition of other notions of the family must be fought for and their diverse forms named, not assumed.

With this in mind, we can arrive at a broader understanding of the place of domestic violence in human rights discourse. The denial of conceptual reality to violence in the family, alongside the affirmation of the comprehensive rights of the husband over the wife, is part of the warp and woof of the notion of family, with a long and deeply-entrenched history in legislation, custom, and social practice.[25] Despite encouragement from law, religion, and culture to regard domestic violence as a private act committed between individuals, which warrants intervention from the state only in egregious instances, the evidence clearly implicates the state as an active and influential participant at all times. The man's inclination and ability to unleash violence on his female partner must be situated in the wider contexts of socially permissible behaviour and litigable acts.

V. THE CASE OF MARITAL RAPE

The issue of marital rape is a particularly strong test of the conceptual readiness of human rights to remedy crimes against women. Sexual assault within marriage is arguably the most mystified of abuses perpetrated against women. To borrow one of the phrases that heralded the women's movement in the United States in the 1960s, this is literally "the problem that has no name."[26]

The kind of rape recognised in international agreements itself has been scarcely analysed outside feminist circles.[27] Human rights writers who deploy notions of individual dignity and honour to condemn rape, perpetuate the kind of rape ideology that shunts questions of responsibility and instrumentality away from the patriarchal structure of society and on to the victim's psychological state. Yougindra Khushalani does this in applying the Civilian Geneva Convention, Article 3 (1949) and its Protocols I and II, 1977.[28] In Khushalani's approach, the indignity and dishonour that raped women feel is never problematised in order to understand exactly whose honour, dignity, autonomy, and property is violated in a rape. Nor is it clear why the crime is primarily defined in subjective psychological terms. Furthermore, in keeping with the purview of international human rights, Khushalani's inquiry is restricted to mass rape of women during armed conflict.

Given the narrow definitional and analytical focus on rape in human rights discourse, it is not surprising that rape in marriage has remained largely undiscussed. Legal, religious, and customary definitions of the institution of marriage lay the ground for the conceptual acknowledgement and legal admissibility of particular acts within marriage. Feminist scholarship has generated a wide array of materials on the institutions of marriage and the family, with critical analysis of their structuring principles, such as: restricted or exclusive right to sexual access; lines of transmission of property (including the human property of wives and children); establishment of legitimacy, which must precede all claims made on or against the parties to the marriage or family. As Pateman observes, feminists "have shown how the family is a major concern of the state and how, through legislation concerning marriage and sexuality and the policies of the welfare state, the subordinate status of women is presupposed and maintained by the power of the state."[29]

Diana Russell's influential study of rape in marriage in the United States demonstrates the conceptual and material difficulties in defining, acknowledging, and addressing the issue.[30] At one point, Russell argues that certain forms of human interaction in which women are the victims, such as domestic violence and marital rape, would qualify as torture. In this light one could note that, since international debate has been generated and agreement reached on human rights violations where the infliction of pain is evident, the infliction of pain in marital rape, with its short term as well as long term consequences that injure and dehumanise the woman, should not be excluded on the ground that it occurs in the private realm. The numbers of bodies broken and lives lost in reported domestic violence alone are staggering; the numbers of survivors of sexual assault within marriage very likely far exceed these. At a time when awareness and acknowledgement of women's vulnerability to abuse is widespread (CEDAW can boast of 110 signatories at the time of writing), the international silence on the issue of domestic violence stands in thunderous contrast to women's demands. The question is not: when will international agreement be reached? The question is: why has it not been reached yet?

Another important area of conceptual error in human rights thinking of women's issues is the notion of power that structures and prioritises human rights concerns. As long as the context for a human rights violation is one in which power emanates as a force from a single particular source, and is subsequently directed at one other entity, the kinds of abuses that are supported by society-wide mechanisms of policing and enforcement will be left in conceptual limbo. This is particularly true of violations in the private sphere, where the abdication of responsibility by the state is offset by the state-supported brutality of substitutes (the abusive husband who demands his "conjugal rights"; the police who do not respond to the woman's complaints; the legal system that does not address rape in terms consonant with the rape victim's experience; the judge who is permitted by law to give the husband custody of the very children whose safety is the woman's concern).

If human rights are seen to be protected and violated through the exercise of political power, and if only certain kinds of power fall within the scope of international human rights activities, then nothing short of a radical shift in the definition of power can permit any possible redress of violations that occur elsewhere. Only by fresh conceptual associations of knowledge, political power, and social practice can certain kinds of violence, such as marital rape, be given a name, and can their indubitably political nature be recognised....

VII. DIRECTIONS FOR DEBATE

The failure of the international rights community to break its silence on the most frequent and egregious violations of women's rights cannot, and indeed will not be allowed to continue. However, although women have begun to make serious demands in international meetings, disagreements on strategy have not been ironed out. The two most important issues run as follows:

First, it has been suggested that we extend existing documents like CEDAW, through creative interpretation and innovative application, to address domestic violence and even marital rape. We must hope that, with sufficient education, lobbying, publicity, and commitment, such rights claims can be asserted as well as recognised.

This is a serious and popular argument. However, the very attempt at extension is difficult to make, because it must run counter to the philosophical and conceptual focus on a different sphere of human existence, as discussed above. In addition, the task of interpretation lies in the hands of the same classes of persons who restricted, or agreed to restrict, the scope of human rights to the public sphere in the first place: international lawyers, diplomats and government officials. Creative interpretation, and still less creative implementation, is not a reliable strategy in the case of abuses in the private sphere. Furthermore, creative extensions, despite all their cunning, will generate the same kind of debate as the explicit naming of the crime. Therefore, the oft-stated rationale for simply extending CEDAW—to avoid the passion and chaos that very likely will attend debates on, say, a Convention on the Elimination of All Forms of Domestic Violence Against Women—is mistaken.

Second, it has been argued that there are various forms and levels of human rights activity. After all, social change continues to be effected by a variety of means at local, national, and regional levels, regardless of the legal status of asserted claims. Indeed, given the paramountcy of the domestic sphere as the site of violence against women, perhaps a state's resources may be deployed more favourably at the local level.

In response, I say the following: I agree that the pervasiveness and social embeddedness of the crime must be addressed at all levels. However, international debate and formal recognition of rights violations in the private sphere would make a tremendous difference. Restricting the battle to local women's groups and local human rights organisations will only maintain the splintered, uncoordinated nature of the struggle. Resources will continue to be scarce; information will remain unshared or duplicated; wide-ranging strategies will not be tested. Without international consensus and backing, funding will remain in short supply and energy will continue to be diverted to small-group survival. The argument regarding resource availability is bankrupt: As my discussion of the public-private dichotomy has shown, the state already had devoted vast resources to the maintenance of injustice in the private sphere; the state must be pressured to mobilise these resources to more productive ends.

In conclusion, I must insist that the problem is better understood as one of conceptual contradiction rather than as strategic inadequacy. It is imperative that human rights consensus and discourse, as they stand today, problematise the areas that critical supporters, such as feminists, have identified as contradictory and counterproductive. In this article, I have tried to demonstrate that, despite unavoidable tension and resistance, issues of domestic violence must be raised and debated with seriousness and honesty. In the process, the problems that will emerge will point out conceptual contradictions, and possible dead ends, that must be acknowledged and addressed. Only then can human rights make the leap from its present gains as a corrective practice for some to a transformative force for all.

Notes

1. See generally Jean Bethke Elshtain, *Public Man, Private Woman: Women in Social and Political Thought* (1981); Carol Gilligan, *In a Different Voice: Psychological Theory and Women's Development* (1982); Sandra Harding, *The Science Question in Feminism* (1986); Alison Jaggar, *Feminist Politics and Human Nature* (1983); Genevieve Lloyd, *The Man of Reason: "Male" and "Female" in Western Philosophy* (1984); Spike V. Peterson, "Whose Rights? A Critique of the 'Givens' in Human Rights Discourse," 15 *Alternatives* 303 (1990); Elizabeth V. Spelman,

Inessential Woman: Problems of Exclusion in Feminist Thought (1988).

2. Ann C. Scales, "The Emergence of Feminist Jurisprudence: An Essay" 95 *Yale Law Review* 1391 (1986).

3. Frances Olsen, "Statutory Rape: A Feminist Critique of Rights" 63:3 *Texas Law Review* 387, 393 (November 1984).

4. Id. at 394.

5. Jack Donnelly, *Universal Rights in Theory and Practice* 13 (1989).

6. Id.

7. See generally Catharine A. MacKinnon, *Feminism Unmodified: Discourses on Life and Law* (1987).

8. Convention Against Torture and Other Cruel, Inhuman or Degrading Treatment or Punishment, 1984, Part I, Article 1.

9. *Amnesty International Report of Torture*, London: Gerald Duckworth, 1973.

10. See Ximena Bunster-Burotto, "Surviving Beyond Fear: Women and Torture in Latin America," in *Women and Change in Latin America* (J. Nash and H. Safa, eds., 1985).

11. See *Women in the Front Line: Human Rights Violations Against Women, An Amnesty International Report*, 1991.

12. Theodor Meron, *Human Rights Law Making in the United Nations: A Critique of Instruments and Process* 62 (1986).

13. MacKinnon, supra note 7, at 63-69.

14. Id. at 67.

15. Toni Morrison, "Unspeakable Things Unspoken: The Afro-American Presence in American Literature" 27:1 *Michigan Quarterly Review* 1 (Winter 1989).

16. See generally Renate Bridenthal, Atina Grossman, and Marion Kaplan, *When Biology Became Destiny: Women in Weimar and Nazi Germany* (1984); Barbara Klugman, "The Politics of Contraception in South Africa" 13:3 *Women Studies International Forum* 261 (1990); Amina Mama, "Violence Against Black Women: Gender, Race and State Responses" 32 *Feminist Review* 30 (Summer 1989); Nira Yuval-Davis and Floya Anthias, *Woman-Nation-State* (1989).

17. Carole Pateman, *The Disorder of Women: Democracy, Feminism and Political Theory* 118 (1989).

18. Id. at 122.

19. Nicos Poulantzas, *State Power, Socialism* 66 (1978).

20. Zillah R. Eisenstein, *The Radical Future of Liberal Feminism* 223 (1981).

21. Thomas Hobbes, "Philosophical Rudiments Concerning Government and Society," in *The English Works of Thomas Hobbes, Volume II*, 109 (Sir William Molesworth, ed., 1966).

22. John Rawls, *A Theory of Justice* (1971).

23. Pateman, supra note 17, at 132-133.

24. Johannes Morsink, "Women's Rights in the Universal Delaration" 13 *Human Rights Quarterly* 229, 247 (1991).

25. Susan Schecter, *Women and Male Violence: The Visions and Struggles of the Battered Women's Movement* (1982).

26. Betty Friedan, *The Feminine Mystique* 15 (1963).

27. See Susan Brownmiller, *Against Our Will: Men, Women, and Rape* (1975).

28. See Yogingra Khushalani, *Dignity and Honour of Women as Basic and Fundamental Human Rights* (1982).

29. Pateman supra note 17, at 133.

30. See Diana Russell, *Rape in Marriage* (1982, reprint 1990).

QUESTIONS FOR REFLECTION

1. What does Rao mean when she refers to the "androcentrism of the concept of human rights"? Why is it important to note that the concept of human rights has traditionally been defined and interpreted by men?

2. According to Rao, what conceptual and ethical problems follow from the traditional division of the "private" and "public"? What consequences does this division have with respect to the family and to women in international human rights law?

3. The major international human rights documents—such as the Universal Declaration of Human Rights, the United Nations Charter, and the International Covenant on Civil and Political Rights—all seek to prevent racial, religious, and sexual discrimination. Why has it been necessary, then, to develop documents such as the 1979 Convention on the Elimination of All Forms of Discrimination Against Women? What specific obligations should states have under international law to eliminate discrimination against women?

43. CATHARINE A. MACKINNON

Catharine A. MacKinnon (1946-) is Elizabeth A. Long Professor of Law at the University of Michigan, Ann Arbor. Professor MacKinnon received a J.D. from Yale Law School in 1977 and a Ph.D. in Political Science from Yale University in 1987. Well-known for her work in feminist jurisprudence and political theory, MacKinnon is the author of numerous articles and books, including *Feminism Unmodified* (1984), *Toward a Feminist Theory of the State* (1989), and *Only Words* (1993). In this essay, MacKinnon contends that traditional human rights theory and practice have excluded women by failing to recognize that the pervasive occurrence of sexual and reproductive violence in women's lives are violations of human rights. Drawing upon reports of mass atrocities committed against Muslim and Croatian women during Serbian campaigns of ethnic cleansing in the former Yugoslavia, MacKinnon demonstrates how gendered aggression against women became an instrument of war and genocide: Muslim and Croatian women were raped both because of their gender and their ethnic or religious identity. MacKinnon goes on to argue that international human rights law has been unable or, worse, unwilling to acknowledge genocidal rape because such atrocities fall outside human rights standards established and enforced predominantly by men. Accountability for genocidal rape as a violation of women's human rights must, then, assume the priority it deserves within human rights law.

Text—Rape, Genocide, and Women's Human Rights

Human rights have not been women's rights—not in theory or in reality, not legally or socially, not domestically or internationally. Rights that human beings have by virtue of being human have not been rights to which women have had access, nor have violations of women as such been part of the definition of the violation of the human as such on which human rights law has traditionally been predicated.

This is not because women's human rights have not been violated. The eliding of women in the human rights setting happens in two ways. When women are violated like men who are otherwise like them—when women's arms and legs are cut and bleed like the arms and legs of men; when women, with men, are shot in pits and gassed in vans; when women's bodies are hidden with men's at the bottom of abandoned mines; when women's and men's skulls are sent from Auschwitz to Strasbourg for experiments—these atrocities are not marked in the history of violations of women's human rights. The women are counted as Argentinean or Honduran or Jewish—which, of course, they are. When what happens to women also happens to men, like being beaten and disappearing and being tortured to death, the fact that those it happened to are *women* is not registered in the record of human atrocity.

The other way violations of women are obscured is this: When no war has been declared, and life goes on in a state of everyday hostilities, women are beaten by men to whom we are close. Wives disappear from supermarket parking lots. Prostitutes float up in rivers or turn up under piles of rags in abandoned buildings. These atrocities are not counted as human rights violations, their victims as the *desaparecidos* of everyday life. In the record of human rights violations they are overlooked entirely, because the victims are women and what was done to them smells of sex. When a woman is tortured in an Argentine prison cell, even as it is forgotten that she is a woman, it is seen that her human rights are violated because what is done to her is also done to men. Her suffering has the dignity, and her death the honor, of a crime against humanity. But when a woman is tortured by her husband in her home, humanity is not violated. Here she is a woman—but *only* a woman. Her violation outrages the conscience of few beyond her friends.

What is done to women is either too specific to women to be seen as human or too generic to human beings to be seen as specific to women. Atrocities committed against women are either too human to fit the notion of female or too female to fit the notion of human. "Human" and "female" are mutually exclusive by definition; you cannot be a woman and a human being at the same time.

Women are violated in many ways in which men are violated. But women are also violated in ways men are not, or that are exceptional for men. Many of these sex-specific violations are sexual and reproductive.

Women are violated sexually and reproductively every day in every country in the world. The notion that these acts violate women's human rights has been created by women, not by states or governments. Women have created the idea that women have human rights out of a refusal to believe that the reality of violation we live with is what it means for us to be human—as our governments seem largely to believe.

Women have created the idea of women's human rights by refusing to abandon ourselves and each other, out of attachment to a principle of our own humanity—one defined against nearly everything around us, against nearly everything we have lived through, certainly not by transcending the reality of our violations, but by refusing to deny their reality as violations. In this project, women have learned that one day of real experience is worth volumes of all of their theories. If we believed existing approaches to human rights, we would not believe we had any. We have learned to look at the reality of women's lives first and to hold human rights law accountable to what we need, rather than to look at human rights law to see how much of what happens to women can be fit into it, as we are taught to do as lawyers.

In pursuit of this reality-based approach, consider one situation of the mass violation of women's human rights now occurring in the heart of Europe. In this campaign of extermination, which began with the Serbian invasion of Croatia in 1991 and exploded in the Serbian aggression against Bosnia and Herzegovina in 1992, evidence documents that women are being sexually and reproductively violated on a mass scale, as a matter of conscious policy, in pursuit of a genocide through war.

In October 1992 I received a communication from an American researcher of Croatian and Bosnian descent working with refugees and gathering information on this war. She said that Serbian forces had exterminated Croatians and Muslims in the hundreds of thousands "in an operation they've coined 'ethnic cleansing'"; that in this genocide thousands of Muslim and Croatian girls and women were raped and made forcibly pregnant in settings including Serbian-run concentration camps, of which "about twenty are solely rape/death camps for Muslim and Croatian women and children."[1] She had received reports of the making and use of pornography as part of the genocide. "One Croatian woman described being tortured by electric shocks and gang-raped in a camp by Serbian men dressed in Croatian uniforms who filmed the rapes and forced her to 'confess' on film that Croatians had raped her."[2] She also reported that some United Nations troops were targeting women:

> In the streets of Zagreb, UN troops often ask local women how much they cost. There are reports of refugee women being forced to sexually service the UN troops to receive aid. Tomorrow I talk to two survivors of mass rape—thirty men per day for over three months. We've heard the UN passed a resolution to collect evidence as the first step for a war crime trial, but it is said here that there is no precedent for trying sexual atrocities.[3]

Whether or not these practices are formally illegal—and it is easy to say with complacency that rape, prostitution, pornography, and sexual murder are illegal—they are widely permitted under both domestic and international law. They are allowed, whether understood, one man to another, as an excess of passion in peace or the spoils of victory in war, or as the liberties, civil or otherwise, of their perpetrators. They are legally rationalized, officially winked at, and in some instances formally condoned. Whether or not they are regarded as crimes, in no country in the world are they recognized as violations of the human rights of their victims.

This war exemplifies how existing approaches to violations

of women's human rights can serve to confuse who is doing what to whom and thus can cover up and work to condone atrocities. These atrocities also give an urgency, if any was needed, to the project of reenvisioning human rights so that violations of humanity include what happens to women.

The war against Croatia and Bosnia-Herzegovina, and their partial occupation, is being carried out by Serbian forces in collaboration with the Serbian regime in Belgrade, governing what remains of Yugoslavia. This is an international war. All the state parties have adopted relevant laws of nations that prohibit these acts; they are covered in any case by customary international law and *jus cogens*.[4] Yet so far nothing has been invoked to stop these abuses or to hold their perpetrators accountable. The excuses offered for this lack of action are illuminating.

In this war, the fact of Serbian aggression is beyond question, just as the fact of male aggression against women is beyond question, both here and in everyday life. "Ethnic cleansing" is a euphemism for genocide. It is a policy of ethnic extermination of non-Serbs with the aim of "all Serbs in one nation," a clearly announced goal of "Greater Serbia," of territorial conquest and aggrandizement. That this is a war against non-Serbian civilians, not between advancing and retreating armies, is also beyond question. Yet this war of aggression—once admitted to exist at all—has repeatedly been construed as bilateral, as a civil war or an ethnic conflict, to the accompaniment of much international head scratching about why people cannot seem to get along and a lot of pious clucking about the human rights violations of "all sides" as if they were comparable. This three-pronged maneuver is familiar to those who work with the issue of rape: blame women for getting ourselves raped by men we know, chastise us for not liking them very well afterward, and then criticize our lack of neutrality in not considering rapes of men to be a comparable emergency.

One result of this approach is that the rapes in this war are not grasped as either a strategy in genocide or a practice of misogyny, far less both at once. They are not understood as continuous both with this particular ethnic war of aggression and with the gendered war of aggression of everyday life. Genocide does not come from nowhere, nor does rape as a ready and convenient tool of it. Nor is a continuity an equation. These rapes are to everyday rape what the Holocaust was to everyday anti-Semitism. Without everyday anti-Semitism a Holocaust is impossible, but anyone who has lived through a pogrom knows the difference.

What is happening here is first a genocide, in which ethnicity is a tool for political hegemony; the war is an instrument of the genocide; the rapes are an instrument of the war. The Bosnian Serbs under the command of Radovan Karadzic do not control the state; their war is against the people and the democratically elected government of Bosnia-Herzegovina. If you control the state and want to commit genocide, as the Nazis did under the Third Reich, you do not need a war. You do it with the state mechanisms at hand. This is being done now, quietly, to Hungarians and Croatians in occupied eastern Croatia and in Vojvodina, formerly an autonomous region now annexed to Serbia.[5] This is virtually invisible to the world.

Now consider the situation of the Albanians in Kosova. They are surrounded; they are within a state. When Serbia moves on them militarily, going beyond the segregation and oppression they suffer now, it may not look like a war to anyone else. It will not cross international borders, the way much international law wants to see before it feels violated. But it will be another facet of the campaign to eliminate non-Serbs from areas targeted for "cleansing," a genocide.

To call such campaigns to exterminate non-Serbs "civil war" is like calling the Holocaust a civil war between German Aryans and German Jews. If and when the reality in Vojvodina comes out, or Albanians are "cleansed," perhaps that too will be packaged for Western consumption as ancient ethnic hatreds, a bog like Vietnam, or some other formulation to justify doing nothing about it.

In this genocide through war, mass rape is a tool, a tactic, a policy, a plan, a strategy, as well as a practice. Muslim and Croatian women and girls are raped, then often killed, by Serbian military men, regulars and irregulars in a variety of formations, in their homes, on hillsides, in camps—camps that used to be factories, schools, farms, mines, sports arenas, post offices, restaurants, hotels, or houses of prostitution. The camps can be outdoor enclosures of barbed wire or buildings where people are held, beaten, and killed and where women, and sometimes men, are raped. Sometimes the women are also raped after they are killed. Some of these camps are rape/death camps exclusively for women, organized like the brothels of what is called peacetime, sometimes in locations that were brothels before the war.

In the West, the sexual atrocities have been discussed largely as rape *or* as genocide, not as what they are, which is rape as genocide, rape directed toward women because they are Muslim or Croatian. It is as if people cannot think more than one thought at once. The mass rape is either part of a campaign by Serbia against non-Serbia, or an onslaught by combatants against civilians, or an attack by men against women, but never all at the same time. Or—this is the feminist version of the whitewash—these atrocities are presented as just another instance of aggression by all men against all women all the time. If this were the opening volley in a counteroffensive against rape as a war against all women, it would be one thing. But the way it works here is the opposite: to make sure that no one who cares about rape takes a side in *this* war against *these* particular rapes. It does not so much galvanize opposition to rape whenever and wherever it occurs, but rather obscures the fact that these rapes are being done by *some* men against *certain* women for specific reasons, here and now. The point seems to be to obscure, by any means available, exactly who is doing what to whom and why.

The result is that these rapes are grasped in either their ethnic or religious particularity, as attacks on a culture, meaning men, or in their sex specificity, meaning as attacks on women. But not as both at once. Attacks on women, it seems, cannot define attacks on a people. If they are gendered attacks, they are not ethnic; if they are ethnic attacks, they are not gendered. One cancels the other. But when rape is a genocidal act, as it is here, it is an act to destroy a people. What is done to women defines that distinction. Also, aren't women a people?

These rapes have also been widely treated as an inevitable by-product of armed conflict. Every time there is a war, there is rape. Of course rape does occur in all wars, both within and between all sides. As to rape on one's own side, aggression elsewhere is always sustained by corresponding levels of suppression and manipulation at home. Then, when the army comes back, it visits on the women at home the escalated level of assault the men were taught and practiced on women in the war zone. The United States knows this well from the war in Vietnam. Men's domestic violence against women of the same ethnicity escalated—including their skill at inflicting torture without leaving visible marks. But sexual aggression against Asian women through prostitution and pornography exploded in the United States: American men got a particular taste for violating them over there. This must be happening to Serbian women now.

Rape *is* a daily act by men against women; it is always an act of domination by men over women. But the role of these rapes in this genocidal war of aggression is a matter of fact, not of ideological spin. It means that Muslim and Croatian women are facing two layers of men on top of them rather than one, one layer engaged in exterminating the other, and two layers of justification—"just war" and "just life." Add the representation of this war as a civil war among equal aggressors, and these women are facing three times the usual number of reasons for the world to do nothing about it.

All the cover-ups ignore the fact that this is a genocide. The "civil war" cover-up obscures the role of Belgrade in invading first Croatia, then Bosnia-Herzegovina, and now in occupying parts of both. A civil war is not an invasion by another country. If this is a civil war, neither Croatia nor Bosnia-Herzegovina is a nation, but they are both recognized as such. In a civil war, aggression is mutual. This is not a reciprocal genocide. Muslims and Croatians are not advancing and retreating into and out of Serbia. They are not carrying out genocide against Serbs on their own territories. There are no concentration camps for Serbs in Sarajevo or Zagreb. The term "civil war" translates, in all languages, as "not my problem." In construing this situation as a civil war at bottom, the international community has defined it in terms of what it has been willing to do about it.

It is not that there are no elements of common culture here, at least as imposed through decades of Communist rule, meaning Serbian hegemony. It is not that there are no conflicts between or within sides, or shifting of sides in complex ways. It is not that the men on one side rape and the men on the other side do not. It is, rather, that none of these factors defines this emergency, none of them created it, none of them is driving it, and none of them explains it. Defining it in these terms is a smoke screen, a propaganda tool, whether sincere or cynical, behind which Serbia continues to expand its territory by exterminating people and raping women en masse.

The feminist version of the cover-up is particularly useful to the perpetrators because it seems to acknowledge the atrocities—which are hard to deny (although they do that too)—and appears to occupy the ground on which women have effectively aroused outrage against them. But its function is to exonerate the rapists and to deflect intervention. If all men do this all the time, especially in war, how can one pick a side in this one? And since all men do this all the time, war or no war, why do anything special about this now? This war becomes just a form of business as usual.[6] But genocide is not business as usual—not even for men.

This is often accompanied by a blanket critique of "nationalism," as if identification with the will to exterminate can be equated with identification with the will to survive extermination; as if an ethnic concept of nation (like the Serbian fascist one) is the same as a multiethnic concept of nation (like the Bosnian one); and as if those who are being killed because of the nation they belong to should find some loftier justification for staying alive than national survival.

Like all rape, genocidal rape is particular as well as part of the generic, and its particularity matters. This is ethnic rape as an official policy of war in a genocidal campaign for political control. That means not only a policy of the pleasure of male power unleashed, which happens all the time in so-called peace; not only a policy to defile, torture, humiliate, degrade, and demoralize the other side, which happens all the time in war; and not only a policy of men posturing to gain advantage and ground over other men. It is specifically rape under orders. This is not rape out of control. It is rape under control. It is also rape unto death, rape as massacre, rape to kill and to make the victims wish they were dead. It is rape as an instrument of forced exile, rape to make you leave your home and never want to go back. It is rape to be seen and heard and watched and told to others: rape as spectacle. It is rape to drive a wedge through a community, to shatter a society, to destroy a people. It is rape as genocide.

It is also rape made sexy for the perpetrators by the power of the rapist, which is absolute, to select the victims at will. They walk into rooms of captive women and point, "you, you, and you," and take you out. Many never return. It is rape made more arousing by the ethnic hostility against the designated "enemy," made to feel justified by the notion that it is "for Serbia," which they say as they thrust into the women and make them sing patriotic songs.[7] It is rape made to seem right by decades of lies about the supposed behavior of that enemy—years and years of propaganda campaigns, including in schools, full of historical lies and falsified data. In this effort, rapes and murders carried out by Serbs against non-Serbs are presented to the Serbian population on television as rapes and murders of Serbs by Muslims and Croats. The way in which pornography is believed in the men's bodies as well as in their minds gives this war propaganda a special potency.

This is also rape made especially exciting for the perpetrators by knowing that there are no limits on what they can do, by knowing that these women can and will be raped to death. Although the orders provide motivation enough, the rapes are made sexually enjoyable, irresistible even, by the fact that the women are about to be sacrificed, by the powerlessness of the women and children in the face of their imminent murder at the hands of their rapists. This is murder as the ultimate sexual act.

It will not help to say that this is violence, not sex, for the men involved. When the men are told to take the women away and not bring them back, first they rape them, then they kill them, and then sometimes rape them again and cut off their breasts and tear out their wombs.[8] One woman was allowed to live only as long as she kept her Serbian captor hard all night orally, night after night after night, from midnight to 5:00 A.M. What he got was sex for him. The aggression was the sex.

This is rape as torture as well as rape as extermination. In the camps, it is at once mass rape and serial rape in a way that is indistinguishable from prostitution. Prostitution is that part of everyday non-war life that is closest to what we see done to women in this war. The daily life of prostituted women consists of serial rape, war or no war. The brothel-like arrangement of the rape/death camps parallels the brothels of so called peacetime: captive women impounded to be passed from man to man in order to be raped.

This is also rape as a policy of ethnic uniformity and ethnic conquest, of annexation and expansion, of acquisition by one nation of other nations. It is rape because a Serb wants your apartment. Most distinctively, this is rape as ethnic expansion through forced reproduction. African American women were forcibly impregnated through rape under slavery. The Nazis required Eastern European women to get special permission for abortions if impregnated by German men. In genocide, it is more usual for the babies on the other side to be killed. Croatian and Muslim women are being raped, and then denied abortions, to help make a Serbian state by making Serbian babies.[10]

If this were racial rape, as Americans are familiar with it, the children would be regarded as polluted, dirty, and contaminated, even as they are sometimes given comparative privileges based on "white" blood. But because this is ethnic rape, lacking racial markers, the children are regarded by the aggressors as somehow clean and purified, as "cleansed" ethnically. The babies made with Muslim and Croatian women are regarded as Serbian babies. The idea seems to be to create a fifth column within Muslim and Croatian society of children—all sons?—who will rise up and join their fathers. Much Serbian fascist ideology simply adopts and adapts Nazi views. This one is the ultimate achievement of the Nazi ideology that culture is genetic.

The spectacle of the United Nations troops violating those they are there to protect adds a touch of the perverse. My correspondent added that some United Nations troops are participating in raping Muslim and Croatian women taken from Serb-run rape/death camps. She reports that "the UN presence has apparently increased the trafficking in women and girls through the opening of brothels, brothel-massage parlors, peep shows, and the local production of pornographic films."[11] There are also reports that a former United Nations Protection Force (UNPROFOR) commander accepted offers from a Serbian commander to bring him Muslim girls for sexual use.[12] All this is an example of the male bond across official lines. It pointedly poses a problem women have always had with male protection: who is going to watch the men who are watching the men who are supposedly watching out for us? Each layer of male protection adds a layer to violence against women. Perhaps intervention by a force of armed women should be considered.

Now, the use of media technology is highly developed. Before, the Nazis took pictures of women in camps, forced women into brothels in camps, and took pictures of naked women running to their deaths. They also created events that did not happen through media manipulation. In this war the aggressors have at hand the new cheap, mobile, accessible, and self-contained moving-picture technology. The saturation of what was Yugoslavia with pornography upon the dissolution of communism—pornography that was largely controlled by Serbs, who had the power—has created a population of men prepared to experience sexual pleasure in torturing and killing women. It also paved the way for the use on television of footage of actual rapes, with the ethnicity of the victims and perpetrators switched, to inflame Serbs against Muslims and Croatians.[13] In the conscious and open use of pornography, in making pornography of atrocities, in the sophisticated use of pornography as war propaganda, this is perhaps the first truly modern war.

Although these acts flagrantly violate provision after provision of international law, virtually nothing has been done about them for well over two years. Now the international machinery seems finally to be lumbering into action, even as more men, women, and children are being liquidated daily. To explain this slow response, it is important to consider that most human rights instruments empower states to act against states, not individuals or groups to act for themselves. This is particularly odd given that international human rights law recognizes only violations of human rights by state actors. In other words, only entities like those who do the harm are empowered to act to stop them. It would have seemed clear after 1945 that states often violate the rights of those who are not states and who have no state to act for them. The existing structure of international law was substantially created in response to this. Yet its architects could not bring themselves to empower individuals and groups to act against individuals, groups, or states when their human rights were violated.[14]

This problem is particularly severe for women's human rights because women are typically raped not by governments but by what are called individual men. The government just does nothing about it. This may be tantamount to being raped by the state, but it is legally seen as "private," therefore as not a human rights violation. In an international world order in which only states can violate human rights, most rape is left out. The role of the state in permitting women to be raped with impunity can be exposed, but the structural problem in addressing it remains.

There is a convergence here between ways of thinking about women and ways of thinking about international law and politics. The more a conflict can be framed as within a state—as a civil war, as domestic, as private—the less effective the human rights model becomes. The closer a fight comes to home, the more "feminized" the victims become, no matter what their gender, and the less likely it is that international human rights will be found violated, no matter what was done.[15] Croatia and Bosnia-Herzegovina are being treated like women,[16] women gang-raped on a mass scale. This is not an analogy; far less is it a suggestion that this rape is wrong only because the women belong to a man's state. It identifies the treatment of a whole polity by the treatment of the women there.[17]

In the structure of international human rights, based as it is on the interest of states in their sovereignty as such, no state has an incentive to break rank by going after another state for how it treats women—thus setting a standard of human rights treatment for women that no state is prepared to meet within its own borders or is willing to be held to internationally. When men sit in rooms, being states, they are largely being men. They protect each other; they identify with each other; they try not to limit each other in ways they themselves do not want to be limited. In other words, they do not represent women. There is no state we can point to and say, "This state effectively guarantees women's human rights. There we are free and equal."

In this statist structure, each state's lack of protection of women's human rights is internationally protected, and that is called protecting state sovereignty. A similar structure of insulation between women and accountability for their violations exists domestically. Raped women are compelled to go to the state; men make the laws and decide if they will enforce them. When women are discriminated against, they have to go to a human rights commission and try to get it to move. This is called protecting the community. It is the same with international human rights, only more so: only the state can hurt you, but to redress it you have to get the state to act for you. In international law there are a few exceptions to this, but in the current emergency in Bosnia-Herzegovina and Croatia they are of no use. Each state finds its reasons to do nothing, which can be read as not wanting to set a higher standard of accountability for atrocities to women than those they are prepared to be held to themselves.

Formally, wartime is an exception to the part of this picture that exempts most rape, because atrocities by soldiers against civilians are always considered state acts. The trouble has been that men do in war what they do in peace, only more so, so when it comes to women, the complacency that surrounds peacetime extends to wartime, no matter what the law says. Every country in this world has a legal obligation to stop the Serbian aggressors from doing what they are doing, but until Bosnia-Herzegovina went to the International Court of Justice and sued Serbia for genocide, including rape, no one did a thing.[18] In so doing, Bosnia-Herzegovina is standing up for women in a way that no state ever has. The survivors I work with also filed their own civil suit in New York against Karadzic for an injunction against genocide, rape, torture, forced pregnancy, forced prostitution, and other sex and ethnic discrimination that violates women's international human rights.[19]

A war crimes tribunal to enforce accountability for mass genocidal rape is being prepared by the United Nations.[20] There are precedents in the Tokyo trials after World War II for command responsibility for mass rape. Beyond precedent, the voices of the victims have been heard in the structuring of the new tribunal. To my knowledge, no one asked Jewish survivors how the trials at Nuremberg should be conducted, nor do I think the women raped in Nanking were asked what they needed in order to be able to testify about their rapes. The issue of accountability to victims has been raised here formally for the first time: How can we create a war crimes tribunal that is accessible to victims of mass sexual atrocity? What will make it possible for victims of genocidal rape to speak about their violations?

The genocidal rapes of this war present the world with an historic opportunity: that this becomes the time and place, and these the women, when the world recognizes that violence against women violates human rights. That when a woman is raped, the humanity of a human being is recognized to be violated. When the world says never again—not in war, not in peace—and this time means it.

Notes

*This lecture also appears in *Mass Rape: The War Against Women in Bosnia-Herzegovina* (Alexandra Stiglmayer, ed., 1994), published by the University of Nebraska Press. Earlier versions of this material were delivered at the United Nations World Conference on Human Rights, Vienna, on June 17, 1993, and at the Zagreb University Law School, Zagreb, on June 25, 1993. The intellectual and research collaboration of Natalie Nenadic and Asja Armanda, all the women of Kareta Feminist Group, and the survivors made this work possible.

1. Letter from Natalie Nenadic to the author from Zagreb, Croatia, Oct. 13, 1992 (on file with the *Harvard Women's Law Journal*).

2. Ibid.

3. Ibid.

4. See Theodor Meron, "Rape as a Crime under International Humanitarian Law," 87 *Am. J. Int'l Law* 424, 424-28 (1993) (rape as a crime against humanity under international law); "Letter from Jordan Paust," 88 *Am. J. Int'l Law* 88 (1994) (rape as genocide and other crimes under customary international law).

5. All otherwise unreferenced information on this war is taken directly from first-person accounts by survivors with whom I have worked, other than the information on Hungarians in Vojvodina, which comes from observations by other survivors.

6. See, e.g., Susan Brownmiller, "Making Female Bodies the Battlefield," in *Mass Rape: The War Against Women in Bosnia-Herzegovina* 180 (Alexandra Stiglmayer, ed., 1994).

7. Similar experiences are reported in Roy Gutman, *A Witness to Genocide*, 64-76, 164-67 (1993).

8. See S. Dzombic, "Go and Give Birth to Chetniks," *Vecernji List*, Nov. 25, 1992.

9. See Cora McRae v. Joseph Califano, 491 F. Supp. 630, 759 (E.D.N.Y.), *rev'd on other grounds sub nom.* Patricia Harris v. Cora McRae, 448 US 297 (1980).

10. See Dzombic, supra note 8.

11. Nenadic, supra note 1.

12. See Investigation Against General McKenzie, Vecernji List, Nov. 25, 1992.

13. See Catharine A. MacKinnon, "Turning Rape into Pornography: Postmodern Genocide," *Ms.*, July-Aug. 1993, at 24-30.

14. See generally Louis B. Sohn, "The New International Law: Protection of the Right of Individuals Rather than States," 32 *Am. U. L. Rev.* 1, 9-17 (1982) (outlining the evolution of human rights law after World War II); M. Tardu, *1 Human Rights: The International Petition System* 45 (1985) ("The potential of [divisive postwar] UN debates for conflict escalation was so obvious that all governments became fiercely determined to keep the process under their own control through rejecting individual complaint systems").

15. This insight was first expressed to me by Asja Armanda of Kareta Feminist Group.

16. For an analysis that "in 1991/1992, Croatia is a woman," see Katja Gattin, Kareta Feminist Group, Where have all the feminists gone? (1992) (unpublished paper, Zagreb) (on file with the *Harvard Women's Law Journal*).

17. On August 30, 1993, His Excellency Muhamed Sacirbey, ambassador and permanent representative of Bosnia and Herzegovina to the United Nations, brilliantly argued before the United Nations Security Council that Bosnia and Herzegovina is being gang-raped, forced into submission through the use of violence and aggression, including rape, deprived of means of self-defense, and

then treated as if it had been seduced—forced to embrace the consequences and denied legal relief. His Excellency Muhamed Sacirbey, Address at the United Nations Security Council (Aug. 30, 1993) (on file with the *Harvard Women's Law Journal*).

18. Application of the Convention on the Prevention and Punishment of the Crime of Genocide (Bosnia and Herzegovina v. Yugoslavia [Serbia and Montenegro]), 1993 I.C.J. 3 (April 8), reprinted in 32 I.L.M. 888 (1993) (order of provisional measures).

19. K. v. Radovan Karadziæ 93 Civ. 1163 (S.D.N.Y. 1993).

20. See S.C. Res. 827, UN SCOR, 3217th mtg., UN Dec. S/RES/827 (May 25, 1993); S.C. Res. 808, UN SCOR, 3175th mtg., UN Doc. S/RES/808 (Feb. 22, 1993).

Questions for Reflection

1. According to MacKinnon, how does gender-based violence constitute a distinct human rights problem? What factors can you think of that account for why women are at continuing risk for exploitation and abuse?

2. MacKinnon argues that the concept of human rights has been shaped too much by tradition and male power. How would you assess international attempts to enforce accountability for violations of women's human rights? In what ways do you think that human rights law can be changed to more effectively promote and protect the human worth and dignity of women?

3. In what ways is MacKinnon's analysis of genocidal rape similar to, or different from, James Nickel's critique of ethnic cleansing?

Further Readings for Section 9

Ashworth, Georgina. "The Silencing of Women." In *Human Rights in Global Politics*, Tim Dunne and Nicholas J. Wheeler, eds. Cambridge: Cambridge University Press, 1999.

Binion, Gayle. "Human Rights: A Feminist Perspective." *Human Rights Quarterly* 17 (1995): 509-526.

Boulware-Miller, Kay. "Female Circumcision: Challenges to the Practice as a Human Rights Violation." *Harvard Women's Law Journal* 8 (1985): 155-77.

Bunch, Charlotte. "Women's Rights as Human Rights: Toward a Re-Vision of Human Rights." *Human Rights Quarterly* 12 (1990): 486-98.

Eisler, Riane. "Human Rights: Toward an Integrated Theory for Action." *Human Rights Quarterly* 9 (1987): 287-308.

Engle, Karen. "International Human Rights and Feminism: When Discourses Meet." *Michigan Journal of International Law* 13 (1992): 517-610.

Nussbaum, Martha C. *Sex and Social Justice*. New York and Oxford: Oxford University Press, 1999.

Nussbaum, Martha C. and J. Glover, eds. *Women, Culture, and Development*. Oxford: Clarendon Press, 1995.

Okin, Susan Moller. "Feminism, Women's Human Rights, and Cultural Differences." *Hypatia* 13 (1998): 32-52.

Peters, Julie and Andrea Wolper, eds. *Women's Rights, Human Rights*. New York and London: Routledge, 1995.

Philipose, Liz. "The Laws of War and Women's Human Rights." *Hypatia* 11 (1996): 46-62.

Schuler, Margaret, ed. *Freedom from Violence: Women's Strategies from around the World*. New York: UNIFEM, 1992.

Tomasevski, Katarina. *Women and Human Rights*. London: Zed Books, 1993.

Section 10:
GAY AND LESBIAN RIGHTS

44. JACK DONNELLY

Jack Donnelly (1951-) is Andrew W. Mellon Professor, Graduate School of International Studies, University of Denver. The author of numerous articles and books, including *The Concept of Human Rights* (1985), *Universal Human Rights in Theory and Practice* (1989), and *International Human Rights* (1998), Donnelly is one of the world's most distinguished human rights scholars. In the essay included here, Donnelly critically discusses the continued exclusion of gays and lesbians from the international human rights agenda. Although much progress has been made in protecting human rights in the past fifty years sexual minorities have not yet been guaranteed the full equality to which all human beings are entitled. Donnelly examines several cases in which discrimination against minorities is no longer acceptable under human rights standards, such as with ethnic or religious minorities, and concludes with suggestions for how to include abuses against gays and lesbians within the contemporary human rights movement.

Text—Non-Discrimination and Sexual Orientation: Making a Place for Sexual Minorities in the Global Human Rights Regime[1]

Jack Donnelly, "Non-Discrimination and Sexual Orientation: Making a Place for Sexual Minorities in the Global Human Rights Regime," from Innovation and Inspiration: Fifty Years of the Universal Declaration of Human Rights, *Peter Baehr, Cees Flinterman, and Mignon Senders, eds. Amsterdam: Royal Netherlands Academy of Arts and Sciences, 1999. Reprinted by permission of the Royal Netherlands Academy of Arts and Sciences.*

The fiftieth anniversary of the Universal Declaration of Human Rights is an occasion for stocktaking. We can take considerable satisfaction in the immense progress that has been made in the development of multilateral norms and institutions, national and transnational activity by human rights NGOs, and bilateral human rights policies. But there have also been notable shortcomings. As a number of other chapters in this volume show, at the national level, all internationally recognized human rights are implemented unevenly in different countries, and often within particular countries as well. Internationally, multilateral institutions generally lack coercive enforcement powers. In this chapter, however, I want to look at a very different sort of shortcoming, namely, the continued exclusion of gay men, lesbians, and other sexual minorities from the full protection of international human rights norms.

1. THE RIGHT TO NONDISCRIMINATION

Human rights are the rights that one has simply as a human being. As such, they are necessarily equal rights. Each person either is or is not a human being, and thus has (or does not have) the same rights as all other human beings. As stated in Article 1 of the Universal Declaration of Human Rights, "All human beings are born free and equal in dignity and rights."

The right to protection against discrimination is an explicit guarantee of equal—and thus all—human rights for every person, despite the myriad other differences between human beings. As Article 2 of the Universal Declaration proclaims, "Everyone is entitled to all the rights and freedoms set forth in this Declaration, without distinction of any kind, such as race, colour, sex, language, religion, political or other opinion, national or social origin, property, birth or other status."

This statement, however, is in one important way seriously exaggerated. Everyone cannot be entitled to *all* human rights without distinction of any kind. States are not prohibited from taking into account *any* status differences. We are entitled only to protection against *invidious* discrimination, discrimination that tends to ill will or causes unjustifiable harm.

Social life is full of legitimate discriminations. Individuals, groups, and even public authorities often not merely recognize but legitimately act upon differences between groups of people.

For example, all societies restrict the rights of children, a distinction based on age or mental capacity. Distinctions of nationality are deeply embedded in international human rights regimes: individuals can claim human rights primarily against the government of which they are a national (or under whose jurisdiction they fall on the basis of residence). Those incarcerated for criminal behavior have a variety of their human rights legitimately restricted, on the basis of their past behavior.

The internationally recognized human right to nondiscrimination prohibits invidious public (or publicly supported or tolerated) discrimination that deprives target groups of the legitimate enjoyment of other rights. Although it may be hateful to choose one's friends on the basis of race, this is not an appropriate subject for regulation through anti-discrimination law. Only when friendships or social contacts systematically influence access to economic or political opportunities do they become a matter of legitimate state regulation. Likewise, discrimination in choice of marriage partners on the basis of family background, though cruel and hurtful, does not fall within the confines of the right to nondiscrimination unless it is publicly supported or required (as, for example, in laws against miscegenation).

But not even all illegitimate discriminations, thus defined, fall under a basic human right to nondiscrimination—if we insist on the idea that human rights are paramount rights. In particular, we need to focus our human rights attention on egregious or widespread systematic violations. Thus Article 2 of the Universal Declaration highlights race, color, sex, language, religion, political or other opinion, national or social origin, property, and birth. The notion of suspect classifications in American constitutional jurisprudence nicely captures this idea. Because we know that race, for example, has been the basis for invidious discrimination in the past, practices that categorize people on the basis of race are inherently suspect, and thus subject to particularly intensive scrutiny.[2]

Article 2.2 of the International Covenant on Economic, Social, and Cultural Rights provides a slightly more subtle statement of the underlying principle.

> The States Parties to the present Covenant undertake to guarantee that the rights enunciated in the present Covenant will be exercised without discrimination of any kind as to race, colour, sex, language, religion, political or other opinion, national or social origin, property, birth or other status.

The language of *distinction* of any kind is replaced by a prohibition of *discrimination* of any kind. And rather than present the enumerated grounds as examples of prohibited discrimination—"such as race..."—this formulation is exhaustive: "without discrimination...as to." (Flexibility is provided through the addition of "other status" at the end.)

In either formulation, however, the practical heart of the right is the list of explicitly prohibited grounds of invidious discrimination.[3] Strong and unambiguous protection requires explicit listing of the grounds of impermissible invidious discrimination. And appearance on the list is a reflection of extended and difficult, often violent, political struggles.

The right to nondiscrimination thus includes a central and inescapable historical element. Those whose equal rights are explicitly guaranteed protection against discrimination are members of groups that previously—but no longer—have been systematically (and probably officially) treated as less than full rights-holding members of the political community; that is, as in some sense less than fully human. The list of groups explicitly protected against discrimination provides a record of the successful struggles by excluded and despised groups to force full (or at least formally equal) inclusion in political society. And as additional forms of discrimination have come to be recognized as illegitimate, they have been added to our list of prohibited grounds.

2. NONDISCRIMINATION AND POLITICAL STRUGGLE

Consider the enumeration in Article 2 of the Declaration and Covenants. Protections against discrimination based on birth and social origin take us back to the beginning of the modern Western struggle for human rights against aristocratic privilege.

Most other societies as well have assigned rights in significant measure on the basis of birth. Today, however, we require that human rights be equally available to those born high or low on society's scale of social status and origins.

Birth, however, was only one ground of institutionalized discrimination in the assignment of basic rights. And in practice those who forced their social "betters" to recognize their equal rights actively denied the same rights to the substantial majority of the population. For example, John Locke used the universal language of natural rights, but developed a political theory that in practice aimed largely to protect the rights of propertied European males. Women, along with "savages," servants, and wage laborers of either sex, were not recognized as right holders.[4]

The history of human rights struggles over the past three centuries can be seen as a process of slowly, with immense difficulty, expanding the recognized subjects of human rights, group by despised group. Racist, bourgeois, Christian patriarchs again and again found natural rights arguments that they had used against aristocratic privilege turned against them in a struggle to incorporate new social groups into the realm of equal citizens entitled to participate in public and private life as equal and autonomous subjects and agents.

Having forced themselves into a position of social dominance, propertied white Christian European males were themselves forced to concede that differences of race, color, sex, language, religion, political or other opinion, national or social origin, and property are illegitimate grounds for differential basic rights. These previously accepted grounds of legal and political discrimination have been renounced. Today, through the right to nondiscrimination, we insist that such differences be treated as irrelevant in the assignment and enjoyment of rights. The state may no longer invidiously take these features into consideration when dealing with citizens and subjects.

Such changing conceptions of the criteria for full and equal membership in society have rested on and interacted with wider social, economic, and political transformations. For example, property restrictions on rights were often defended by arguing that those without property lacked the leisure required to develop their rational capacities sufficiently to be full participants in political society. The rise of mass literacy seriously undercut such arguments. Mass electoral politics, in which participation was conceived more as authorizing and reviewing the actions of others than as direct political decision making, also reduced the plausibility of such arguments.

The claim that the unpropertied lacked a sufficient "stake" in society to be allowed full political participation fell before changing conceptions of political membership, beginning with the American and French revolutions, the rise of popular armies, and growing nationalist sentiments. Legal discrimination based on an alleged lack of independence of the unpropertied gave way to social and economic changes associated with industrialization, particularly the increasingly impersonal relations between workers and employers and the general depersonalization of relations in urban areas. The implicit assumption of the coincidence of wealth and virtue was eroded by general processes of social leveling and mobility.

Likewise, women and non-whites were until well into this century widely seen as irreparably deficient in their rational or moral capacities, and thus incapable of exercising the full range of human rights. These racial and gender distinctions, however, were in principle subject to moral and empirical counter-arguments. Over the past several decades, dominant political ideas and practices in Western and nonwestern societies alike have been transformed by national and international movements to end slavery, and later colonialism; to grant women and racial minorities the vote; and to end discriminations based on race, ethnicity, and gender. A similar tale can be told in the case of Jews, nonconformist Christian sects, atheists, and other religious minorities.

In each case, a logic of full and equal humanity has overcome claims of group inferiority, bringing (at least formally) equal membership in society through explicitly guaranteed protections against discrimination. Signs of difference from the dominant mainstream that previously were seen as marks of moral inferiority and grounds for justifiable subordination have been excluded from the realm of legally and politically legitimate discriminations. Adherents of different, even despised, religions have come to be recognized as (nonetheless) fully human, and thus entitled to the same rights as other (dominant groups of) human beings. Africans, Arabs, and Asians have come to be recognized as no less human than white Europeans. And so forth.

Such an account emphasizes the progressive development of the right to nondiscrimination—and human rights more generally—through processes of social and political struggle. And it implicitly raises the question of other groups currently subject to discrimination, of victims of invidious public discrimination whose suffering remains legally and politically accepted. The remainder of this chapter focuses on those subject to discrimination because of their sexual behavior or orientation.

3. DISCRIMINATION AGAINST SEXUAL MINORITIES

Exactly how to characterize those subject to discrimination because of sexual behavior or orientation is a matter of controversy (as well as changing linguistic styles). "Homosexual" and "gay" have become relatively neutral and fairly inclusive terms in the American mainstream. Among activists in these communities, the formula of "gay, lesbian, bisexual, and transgendered (GLBT)" has considerable currency at the moment.[5] In addition to being more inclusive, this formulation has the virtue of emphasizing differences among those who engage in same sex erotic behavior or relationships. And by explicitly including transvestites and transsexuals it undermines conventional links between sex (defined by genitalia or chromosomes) and gender, sexual orientation, and personal identity.[6]

Following the logic laid out in the preceding section, however, I will adopt the language of sexual minorities. This terminology is even more inclusive, being open to any group (previously, presently, or in the future) stigmatized or despised as a result of sexual orientation, identity, or behavior.[7] Furthermore, the language of minorities explicitly focuses our attention on the issue of discrimination, and at least the possibility of political action to eliminate it.[8]

Sexual minorities are not merely people who engage in "deviant" sexual behavior—for example, fetishists of various types—or even those that adopt "deviant" (sexual) identities (e.g. "swingers"). They are those despised and targeted by "mainstream" society because of their sexuality, victims of systematic denials of rights because of their sexuality (and, in most cases, for transgressing gender roles). Like victims of racism, sexism, and religious persecution, they are human beings who have been identified by dominant social groups as somehow less than fully human, and thus not entitled to the same rights as "normal" people, "the rest of us."

Although it is unnecessary to spend much time documenting discrimination against sexual minorities, it is essential to emphasize the depth and scope of such discrimination in virtually all societies today. In many countries, the intimate behavior and loving relationships of sexual minorities are defined as crimes. They are singled out for official, quasi-official, and private violence. And in all countries, sexual minorities suffer under substantial civil disabilities.

In numerous countries—although only the United States among Western developed market economies—sexual relations among adult members of the same sex are legally prohibited. In Iran and Afghanistan, the proscribed penalty of death is regularly imposed.[9] In Zimbabwe, President Robert Mugabe has for the past three years pursued an unusually active and vocal campaign, claiming that "animals in the jungle are better than these people," and calling homosexuals "worse than dogs and pigs."[10] A number of gay men have been convicted and received lengthy prison sentences.

Such examples are (sadly) easily multiplied. In Romania, Mariana Cetiner was adopted by Amnesty International as a prisoner of conscience after her incarceration (solely) for homosexual activity. Less prominent, but no less characteristic, are Romanians Gabriel Presnac and Radu Vasiliu, who were beaten by police, prosecuted, and imprisoned for holding hands and kissing in public.[11] In India, where homosexual acts are punishable by life in prison, two men recently were arrested after attempting to be married in public, amid public calls by religious leaders for their execution.[12] China's first gay salon was closed by the authorities because it "was spreading erroneous points of view, and instead of opposing, advocating homosexuality."[13] And so forth.[14]

In addition to the direct threat of prosecution, criminalization leads to restrictions on a wide range of other rights. For example, freedoms of speech and association are limited by laws punishing advocating or organizing to engage in "criminal" behavior.[15]

The result often is a pervasive environment of fear in which jobs, housing, and social benefits are constantly at risk. In some cases, sexual minorities are targets of active intimidation. For example, in Petaling Jaya Selangor state in Malaysia, political authorities and religious leaders have supported and encouraged local vigilante groups hunting out immoral activities, including homosexuality, in their neighborhoods.[16] An ad in a state-sponsored Zimbabwean newspaper in 1997 read "CRUSADE AGAINST RAPISTS AND HOMOSEXUALS. God commands the death of sexual perverts. Our culture and traditional justice system condemns them to death. Our religion condemns them to death."[17]

Such attitudes regularly lead to violence. In some cases, it is quasi-official.[18]

Perhaps the most notorious example is "social cleansing" in Colombia, where a general climate of official and quasi-official political violence against "disposable" people has spilled over into death squad attacks on gays, lesbians, and transvestites.[19] In other countries, violence is tolerated but official involvement is more indirect. For example, in Brazil Luis Mott has documented over 100 murders based on sexual orientation every year for more than a decade.[20]

Even where violence against sexual minorities is regularly prosecuted, "gay bashing" is often sadly common.[21] Occasionally a case achieves widespread public prominence. For example, in the United States in the fall of 1998, Matthew Shepherd, a Wyoming college student, was brutally beaten and left to die, tied to a fence like a scarecrow, simply because he was gay. More often, it is lost in the everyday flow of crime,[22] or simply unreported.

Perhaps the most distressing feature of contemporary practice with respect to sexual minorities, however, is that gay men and lesbians in every country of the world, even where their behavior, orientation, or identity are neither illegal nor a common motive for violent assault, are subject to civil disabilities and pervasive social discrimination. The depth to which official discrimination runs is perhaps best illustrated by Fiji, which soon after it became only the second country in the world to prohibit discrimination on the basis of sexual orientation in its constitution, introduced legislation banning same sex marriages.

In most countries, sexual orientation is not an accepted ground for discrimination in employment,[23] housing, or access to public facilities and social services. With a few recent exceptions, same-sex couples are denied civil status, resulting in discrimination in inheritance, adoption, and social insurance. In the United States, where health insurance is provided principally through employers, same-sex partners may even be denied health care that would be routinely available were the couple male-female. Evan Wolfson nicely summarizes the contemporary American situation.

> Our society forbids gay people to marry, denies us equal pay for equal work, throws us off the job, forbids us from serving our country in the armed forces, refuses us health insurance, forces us into the closet, arrests us in our bedrooms, harasses our daily associations, takes away our children, beats and kills us in the streets and parks, smothers images of ourselves and others like us, and then tells us we are irresponsible, unstable, and aberrant.[24]

Even excluding violence and legal prohibition from this list, this still very partial accounting of the civil disabilities and social prejudice faced by sexual minorities is depressing.

Discrimination against sexual minorities even has an international dimension. Many countries deny entry to homosexuals as threats to public health or morals.[25] Qatar recently moved to deport foreign homosexuals, reportedly even using forced rectal examinations as "proof."[26] And only recently have a few countries begun to recognize sexual orientation or behavior as a grounds for asylum, which in international law requires establishing that one has a well founded fear of persecution were one to be returned "home."[27]

Such officially mandated or tolerated discrimination reflects deep currents of social prejudice against sexual minorities.... Here I address whether such social attitudes, no matter how widespread or deeply felt, justify continued exclusion of sexual orientation from the list of prohibited grounds for discrimination. I will argue that they do not. Or, to put the point more positively, gays, lesbians, and others of "deviant" sexuality are, as Evelyn Kallen nicely put it, "a stigmatized minority requiring [and deserving] protection."[28]

4. NATURE, (IM)MORALITY, AND PUBLIC MORALS

The common charge that homosexuality is "against nature" is hardly worth arguing against here. Most thoughtful analysts, at least outside of sociobiology, recognize that sexuality and sexual orientation are constructed sets of social roles.[29] Furthermore, appeals to natural law are largely outside of the discourse of international human rights. And many societies, including currently homophobic societies, have for extended periods tolerated, and even highly valued, (male) homoerotic relationships.

In the West, the best known examples come from ancient Greece.[30] But even the Christian tradition does not seem to have been consistently homophobic during its first millennium.[31] Melanesia, South Asia, and the Muslim Near East also have traditions of male homoerotic relations.[32]

Homoerotic relations in Asia are of special interest because of the prominence of arguments against homosexuality in recent debates over "Asian values." In Singapore and Malaysia in particular, homosexuality is regularity presented as a distinctively Western form of degeneracy by advocates of "Asia's different standard." In fact, however, male-male sexual relationships have a strong traditional basis in both China and Japan.[33] There even seems to be evidence of same sex marriage in Ming dynasty (1368-1644) Fujian.[34]

Nonetheless, as the evidence of discrimination reviewed in the preceding section clearly indicates, homosexuality is widely considered—by significant segments of society in all countries, and by most people in most countries—profoundly immoral. The language of perversion and degeneracy is standard.

Drawing on such attitudes, advocates of discrimination are likely to point to provisions in the International Human Rights Covenants that permit restrictions on a number of recognized rights on the grounds of "public morals." For example, Article 19 of the International Covenant on Civil and Political Rights permits restrictions on the right to freedom of expression that are "provide for by law and are necessary…for the protection of… public health or morals."[35] The problem with such arguments is that most if not all of the groups explicitly recognized as covered by the right to nondiscrimination were at one time also perceived to be a threat to public morals. Let me simply illustrate this point with some more or less randomly selected historical material from my own country concerning discrimination against those of African and Asian descent.

As is well known, slavery was explicitly permitted and racial discrimination not prohibited in the US Constitution and its Bill of Rights. In fact, for purposes of taxation and legislative representation, slaves—which James Madison described in *The Federalist Papers* (Number 54) as a mixture of persons and property and thus "divested of two fifths of the man"—counted as three-fifths of a person. And just one year after the founding of the republic, a 1790 statute confined naturalization to free white persons. This restriction remained formally on the statute books until 1952.

In the infamous Dred Scott case of 1857 (60 US [19 How.]), Chief Justice Taney held that even emancipated negroes do not "compose a portion of this people" and are not "constituent members of this sovereignty" but rather are a permanently "subordinate and inferior class of beings." From colonial times, Taney argued, "a perpetual and impassable barrier was intended to be erected between the white race and the one which they had reduced to slavery." In fact, he argued, throughout American history negroes had been considered by whites as "below them in the scale of created beings."

More than three quarters of a century later, Senator James O. Eastland, on the floor of the United States Senate, publicly proclaimed

> I believe in white supremacy, and as long as I am in the Senate I expect to fight for white supremacy, because I can see that if the amalgamation of whites and Negroes in this country is permitted, there will be a mongrel race.... The cultural debt of the colored peoples to the white race is such as to make the preservation of the white race a chief aim of the colored, if these latter but understood their indebtedness. That the colored race should seek to "kill the goose that lays the golden egg" is further proof that their inferiority, demonstrated so clearly in cultural attainments, extends to their reasoning processes in general.[36]

Making resistance to domination the decisive sign of inferiority is a rhetorical move as brilliant as it is frightening.

Turning to Asians, at the California Constitutional Convention of 1878-1879, a provision was proposed to prevent Chinese immigration in order to protect Californians "from moral and physical infection from abroad."[37]

> The Chinese bring with them habits and customs the most vicious and demoralizing.... They are, generally, destitute of moral principle. They are incapable of patriotism, and are utterly unfitted for American citizenship. Their existence here, in great numbers, is a perpetual menace to republican institutions, a source of constant irritation and danger to the public peace.[38]

Although federal preemption of immigration issues led to a somewhat more moderate statement of opposition to Asian immigration (on the ground that by federal law they were not eligible for naturalization),[39] the sentiment was widely shared.

In the same year, a California State Senate Special Committee

> on Chinese Immigration found that the Chinese seem to be antediluvian men renewed. Their code of morals, their forms of worship, and their maxims of life, are those of the remotest antiquity. In this aspect they stand as a barrier against which the elevating tendency of a higher civilization exerts itself in vain.... There can be no hope that any contact with our people, however long continued, will ever conform them to our institutions, enable them to comprehend or appreciate our form of government, or to assume the duties or discharge the functions of citizens.[40]

Almost half a century later, in 1921, V. S. McClatchy, publisher of the Sacramento Bee, the leading paper in California's state capital, delivered a speech in Honolulu where he argued that Japanese migrants were "an alien, unassimilable element" in the American population, "because their racial characteristics, heredity and religion prevent assimilation." McClatchy even went so far as to appeal to "the biological law which declares that races of widely different characteristics perpetuate through intermarriage, not their good, but their less desirable categories."[41] And as is well known, even US citizens of Japanese origin were forcibly interned in concentration camps in the American west during World War II.

Such examples could be readily multiplied, for other groups, and other countries. Jews have long been a special target of attack in the Western world. Women were almost universally considered morally inferior to men until well into the twentieth century—and in many places of the world, such attitudes persist as we move into a new century and millenium. In all such cases, certain marks of difference came to be constructed as "permissions-to-hate,"[42] grounds that authorized treating members of the group in question as less than fully human. Erik Erikson's notion of "psuedospeciation" nicely captures the dehumanizing logic, which we saw above in Mugabe's (unfavorable) comparison between gays and dogs.

Just to underscore the parallels with permissions to hate sexual minorities, consider an interim report of a US Senate subcommittee in 1950 investigating the issue of "Employment of Homosexuals and Other Sex Perverts in Government." The subcommittee's charge was "to determine the extent of the employment of homosexuals and other sex perverts in Government; to consider reasons why their employment by the Government is undesirable; and to examine into the efficacy of the methods used in dealing with the problem."[43] There was no question that these people were perverts who needed to be kept out of government (if they could not be fully purged from society). The only issue was whether enough reasons had been developed to achieve this unquestioned end and whether sufficiently strenuous efforts were being undertaken.[44]

The subcommittee found that employment was inappropriate because "first, they are generally unsuitable, and second, they constitute security risks." Their unsuitability, the subcommittee found, arose because "those who engage in overt acts of perversion lack the emotional stability of normal persons...sex perversion weakens the moral fiber of an individual to a degree that he is not suitable for a position of responsibility." And because homosexuals "frequently attempt to entice normal individuals to engage in perverted practices," and show a strong "tendency to gather other perverts about [them]," they must be rigorously sought out. "One homosexual can pollute a Government office."[45] This language of incorrigible degradation and fear of pollution strongly echoes the passages quoted above on Africans and Asians. The details are different, but the logic is the same.

Rather than continue to recount examples of this sordid history, let me simply conclude that popular beliefs about the inferiority or corruption of homosexuals and members of other sexual minorities simply cannot provide human rights grounds for continued discrimination. Even accepting, for the purposes of argument, that voluntary sexual relations among adults of the same sex and families headed by same-sex couples are a profound moral outrage, discrimination against sexual minorities cannot be justified from a human rights perspective. "Perverts," "degenerates," and "deviants"[46] have the same human rights as the morally pure, and should have those rights guaranteed by law. Members of sexual minorities are still human beings, no matter how deeply they are loathed by the rest of society. Therefore, they are entitled to equal protection of the law and the equal enjoyment of all internationally recognized human rights.

Human rights rest on the idea that *all* human beings have certain basic rights simply because they are human. Human rights do not need to be earned. And they cannot be lost because one holds beliefs or leads a particular lifestyle, no matter how repugnant most others in a society finds them.[47] How one chooses to lead one's life, subject only to minimum requirements of law and public order,[48] is a private matter—no matter how publicly one leads that life.

... [I]t is disheartening, if historically and sociologically understandable, to see leaders such as Mugabe, who came to power by opposing racist denials of his full humanity, resorting to vicious sexual hate mongering. But such resistance, however widespread, has no more moral force than past and present attitudes of racism, sexism, and religious intolerance. Just as other despised minorities have had to struggle against a dominant oppressive mainstream, ultimately forcing them to renounce their permissions to hate, homosexuals and other sexual minorities face just such a struggle today.

Popular attitudes of hatred and contempt are the problem to be overcome, not the solution to anything.[49] In the case of homosexuals and other sexual minorities, international human rights continues to express such morally indefensible popular sentiments rather than the true human rights logic of equality and nondiscrimination for *all*. Whatever the state of popular moral sentiments, we must remain committed to the overriding objective of "All human rights for all," the aptly chosen slogan of the High Commissioner for Human Rights for 1998, the fiftieth anniversary of the Universal Declaration.

5. STRATEGIES FOR INCLUSION

The moral and conceptual case for extending nondiscrimination protection to gay men, lesbians, and other sexual minorities is overwhelming. They are adult human beings exercising their rights of personal autonomy to speak and behave as they choose, and to associate, in public and private, with whom they choose, as they choose. But until the deep social prejudice against "perverts" is broken down, they will be subject to continued victimization and there is no real chance for explicit inclusion of sexual orientation among internationally prohibited grounds of discrimination.

As in most other areas of human rights, the central battle grounds are local and national. The international dimension of the human rights movement is, in general, supplementary to and supportive of national struggles. Nonetheless, it is the dimension to which this volume is devoted, and will be my focus here. In this final section I want to consider briefly some of the tactical and strategic issues involved in bringing sexual minorities under international nondiscrimination protections.

One special problem we face is that the authoritative international instruments, the International Human Rights Covenants, are largely fixed standards, reflecting attitudes of the 1950s and early 1960s, when no country had an active gay rights movement. In principle it is possible to "amend" the Covenants. It has been done once, in the Second Optional Protocol, outlawing the death penalty. But this process is extremely difficult. Even the process of supplementary norm creation, through a separate declaration (as, for example, was done from disappearances and the right to development) is not promising. In the short and medium run, there is no chance of anything even close to an international consensus on even a working text for a draft declaration on the rights of homosexuals.

If I am correct that explicit listing as a prohibited ground of discrimination really does make a significant difference, this relative inflexibility in the international human rights "legislative" mechanism of treaties drafted in the Commission on Human Rights, poses serious problems for sexual minorities. But explicit inclusion under Article 2 should be seen as the end point of a long struggle, rather than an immediate aim. For the next decade at least, and quite possibly longer, central attention needs to be focused elsewhere.

If the text can't be changed directly and explicitly, either through "amendment" or a new international declaration, we need to rely instead on "interpretation." Two obvious avenues suggested by Article 2: "other status" and "sex."

Sexual orientation is on its face an obvious case of an "other status" by which human beings are singled out for invidious discrimination. A campaign to emphasize these status disabilities can at least highlight the suffering publicly imposed on sexual minorities. This strategy may be particularly promising if some linkage can be established with struggles of those subject to discrimination on the basis of disability or age. The idea would be to emphasize that the list of explicitly prohibited grounds in Article 2 is illustrative, not exhaustive, and that there remain a number of other statuses that are still widely used to justify public discrimination. Even if successful, there is likely to remain an implication that discrimination against sexual minorities is in some way less important than discrimination against explicitly recognized groups. Nonetheless, recognition under the rubric of other status would represent considerable progress. And it might represent a step toward a separate declaration on the rights of homosexuals.

A more radical strategy of interpretative incorporation of gay rights would to be read "sex" in Article 2 to include sexual orientation. This was done by the Human Rights Committee in Toonen case.[50] Although a clever and provocative move, the Committee provided no grounds for such a finding. In its report, it simply stated, without further elaboration, "that in its view the reference to "sex" in articles 2, paragraph 1, and 26 is to be taken as including sexual orientation."[51] But this certainly was *not* what was intended at the time the provision was drafted; it is not even a widely held view even in legally "advanced" European countries. And it is substantively problematic. For example, sexual minorities are in many ways no more analogous to women than they are to religious minorities. Although involving issues of sex and gender, and although women and homosexuals share many similar experiences of victimization, sexual minorities also suffer in systematically different ways from women.

In addition to such problems, there are procedural problems with existing international mechanisms for interpretation. The

Human Rights Committee and the Committee on Economic, Social and Cultural Rights are not authorized to make authoritative interpretations (let alone act to enforce their understandings of the meaning of the Covenants). It is not even clear that these bodies are authorized to use what within the European regime is called "evolutive interpretation," a reading of the meaning of the text based on current understandings, rather than on those at the time of drafting (when sexual orientation clearly was not intended to be a prohibited ground).

The other principal source of interpretation in our decentralized international legal system is national legislatures and courts. These are authoritative—but only nationally. As part of a long term struggle, precedents set in one national jurisdiction may be drawn on by others. And as more and more national systems are changed, pressure for international changes may increase, and resistance may be eroded. In the short run, this is much better than nothing. But it is are only a start, not an ultimate solution. In the long run, we must work back up to the global dimension of Universal Declaration and the Covenants.

One other prominent place for international action should be noted. Article 17 of the International Covenant on Civil and Political Rights includes a right to privacy. Toonen brought his case against a Tasmanian sodomy law criminalizing consensual sex among members of the same sex. The Human Rights Committee found that "it is undisputed that adult consensual sexual activity in private is covered by the concept of 'privacy'."[52] Although perhaps true in this particular case, where Australia did not deny the private nature of the acts, such an understanding, as we have seen above, is anything but undisputed in many countries of the world. But precisely in such countries, privacy and the decriminalization of same sex relations would represent an important foot in the door.

The limited nature of the progress represented by mere decriminalization needs to be emphasized. It does nothing directly to eliminate civil disabilities, let alone address the roots of social prejudice. Real *protection* for sexual minorities must involve inclusion within the right to nondiscrimination (and probably also incorporation under the rubric of equal protection of the laws). But while struggling for that full protection and inclusion, an expanding sphere of privacy and protection against criminal prosecution are extremely valuable resources.

We have thus worked backward from an ultimate aim of explicit recognition as a prohibited ground of discrimination to the very minimal (and relatively intolerant) toleration of decriminalization of private same-sex relations. But if we think historically and politically, rather than conceptually and theoretically, we can reverse the direction of the flow and see an implicit strategy for achieving full inclusion.

Kees Waaldijk has found something very much like such a sequence in the European recognition of legal rights for homosexuals.

> The law in most countries seems to be moving on a line starting at (0) toal ban on homo-sex, then going through the process of (1) the decriminalisation of sex between adults, followed by (2) the equalisation of ages of consent, (3) the introduction of anti-discrimination legislation, and (4) the introduction of legal partnership. A fifth point on the line might be the legal rocognition of homosexual parenthood.[53]

The basic logic is one of gradual inclusion, beginning with decriminalization and moving through increasingly active measures of nondiscrimination in a wide range of areas of public activity.

Waaldijk identifies ten principal areas of legal change: touching, safety, organizations, leisure, information, nondiscrimination, services, employment, partnerships, and parenthood. And within each domain there is a similar functional logic of progress from minimal toleration through active recognition and support. For example, within the category of homosexual safety, he identifies three principal areas of activity, ranging from ending of official repression (e.g. police raids, safety in prisons, official registration), through the application of general laws to crimes against homosexuals, to special provisions to protect lesbians and gays. In the area of lesbian/gay organizations, progress can be measured from permission to organize, through official recognition as legal persons, to support from the authorities.[54]

Waaldijk's concluding advice bears for national activists bears repeating here.

> 1. Think of the legal recognition of homosexuality as a number of parallel developments in more than ten different fields.
> 2. Think of the developments in each field as a series of many small steps.
> 3. Look at the experiences in other countries to find out what these steps normally are, and what their standard sequence is.
> 4. Look at the experiences in other foreign countries to find out where, at this moment of time, political pressure for legal refrom can be most effectively applied.
> 5. Do not try too hard to make your legal system jump; be content with it only taking steps. But do keep the system walking.[55]

At the international level, similar advice seems warranted. Keep in mind the ideal of full explicit inclusion under international nondiscrimination law. But don't expect miracles. Take advantage of whatever avenues are available to transform international human rights norms in ways that can contribute to lifting the burden imposed on sexual minorities. Remain ready for a long struggle. And as the continuing problems of women, racial and ethnic minorities, and some religious minorities remind us, even after formal protection is granted, at the national, regional, or international level, the struggle for effective enjoyment of rights to nondiscrimination can remain a difficult one.

Notes

1. I thank Annelies Henstra and Rhoda Howard for helpful comments on an earlier draft. I also thank Matt Weinert for exemplary research assistance. And I owe a special debt to Kees Waaldijk, both for his formal remarks on this paper when it was originally delivered and for his generosity in sharing his considerable knowledge and highly developed conceptual insights on this topic.

2. Sexual orientation, however, has explicitly not been recognized as a suspect classification in the United States at the federal level. On current American legal practice and its shortcomings, see Evan Gerstmann, *The Constitutional Underclass: Gays, Lesbians, and the Failure of Class-Based Equal Protection* (Chicago: University of Chicago Press, 1999).

3. Although the inclusion of "other status" and "discrimination of any kind" in the international instruments also suggest a potentially expanding range of prohibited discriminations, they do so only abstractly. These formulations are too vague to carry much political or legal force.

4. In the United States, whose Declaration of Independence declared that all men are created equal and endowed by their creator with certain unalienable rights, "until 1815, only those white males who owned property or paid taxes could vote; not allowed to vote were white males who did not own property; all women; all African Americans, including nonslaves; and all Native Americans." Richard H. Ropers, and Dan J. Pence, *American Prejudice: With Liberty and Justice for Some* (New York: Plenum Press, 1995), p. 16.

5. "Queer" has been adopted by some radical homosexuals, inverting a term of "straight" abuse into a label of self-assertion and even prideful disdain. In a still homophobic society, however, this language, especially when used by "straights," remains problematic.

6. "Hermaphrodites" or "inter-sexuals"—understood as persons with a distinctive sexual identity; or at least more than those of physiologically "confused" or "problematic" sex—probably are also included, further problematizing the conventional dichotomy.

7. This language is itself controversial. Does engaging in same sex behavior make one homosexual, gay, or queer? It depends on one's definition. Must one incorporate same sex behavior or relations into one's identity to be a gay man or lesbian? How does sexual orientation interact with other orientation, identities, and behaviors?

8. The drawback of this language, as Kees Waaldijk has pointed out to me in private conversation, is that by including those engaging in despised sexual practices that are not related to gender roles, it moves away from the implicit emphasis on gender in the GLBT formulation. For example, were sado-masochists or rubber fetishists to be targets of systematic discrimination, they would fall under my definition of sexual minorities. I am not convinced, however, that discriminations based on sexual behavior but unrelated to gender should not, all things considered, be included. And to the extent that "sex" (sexual behavior) is part of the issue, as I believe it is, the alternative of "gender minorities," besides its rhetorical shortcomings, has its own conceptual problems.

9. On the Afghan practice of execution by collapsing a stone wall on the victims, see http://www.lgirtf.org/newsletters/Summer98/SU98-4.html. On Iran, where ILGA estimates over 800 sodomy executions, see http://www.qrd.org/qrd/world/asia/Iran/ILGA.asks.end.execution.of.homosexuals-08.06.97. See also James D. Wilets, "International Human Rights Law and Sexual Orientation," *Hastings International and Comparative Law Review* 18 (Fall 1994): 1-120, pp. 28-29.

10. http://www.qrd.org/qrd/world/wockner/news.briefs/210-05.04.98 and http://www.qrd.org/qrd/world/africa/zimbabwe/mugabe.renews.attacks. Such high level vilification seems to be spreading regionally, for example, to Namibia,

(http://www.iglhrc.org/news/features/1997_review.html) Zambia, (http://www.lgirtf.org/newsletters/Summer98/SU98-4.html) and Kenya (http://www.qrd.org/qrd/world/wockner/news.briefs/226-08.24.98).

11. See Amnesty International *Romania: A Summary of Human Rights Concerns* (AI INDEX: EUR 39/06/98) and http://www.iglhrc.org/world/easteurope/Romania1998Jan_2.html.

12. http://www.lgirtf.org/newsletters/Summer98/SU98-4.html

13. http://www.qrd.org/qrd/world/asia/china/china.cracks.down-5.31.93

14. Although the trend is toward decriminalization — for example, Ecuador and Kazakhstan were among the countries removing sodomy laws in 1997—the process is neither even nor universal. For example, Nicaragua *added* sodomy laws to its books in 1992, and they were upheld by the Supreme Court in 1996. In 1997, legislation was introduced in Nigeria to criminalize homosexuality. (http://www.iglhrc.org/news/features/1997_review.html) And in June 1998, despite intense European pressure, the Romanian Chamber of Deputies defeated legislation to decriminalize homosexuality. (http://www.qrd.org/qrd/world /wockner/news.briefs/219-07.06.98) Cyprus as well, although under intense regional pressure, has proposed to revise its laws against homosexuality in ways that Amnesty International has characterized as inadequate. See AI INDEX: EUR 17/02/98.

15. James D. Wilets, "Pressure from Abroad," *Human Rights* 21, Fall 1994), p. 22, and Wilets, "International Human Rights Law and Sexual Orientation," pp. 45-48, 76-81. For example, lesbian NGO delegates to the Beijing women's conference had published materials seized by Chinese authorities. (http://www.qrd.org/qrd/world/asia/china/censors.target.lesbians-wockner-09.07.95) In September 1998, Zambia's Home Affairs Minister, Peter Machungwa, threatened to arrest leaders of a newly formed movement of gays and lesbians, for illegal activity. And the registrar of societies, Herbert Nyendwa, indicated that he would not even consider their application. "The proposed gays' association will not be registered…it is an illegal activity." http://www.lgirtf. org/newsletters/Summer98/SU98-4.html and http://www.qrd.org/qrd/world/wockner/news.briefs/229-09.14.98

16. http://www.qrd.org/qrd/world/asia/malaysia/squads.target.gays-02.23.95. In Zimbabwe as well, the government has encouraged citizens to turn homosexuals over to the authorities. http://www.qrd.org/qrd/world/africa/zimbabwe/mugabe.renews.attacks

17. See http://www.qrd.org/qrd/world/africa/zimbabwe/homophobic.ad-03.03.97

18. In addition to the examples later in this paragraph, see Wilets, "International Human Rights Law and Sexual Orientation," pp. 29-34, 40-42.

19. Juan Pablo Ordoez, *No Human Being Is Disposable: Social Cleansing, Human Rights, and Sexual Orientation in Colombia* (San Francisco: International Gay and Lesbian Human Rights Commission, 1994).

20. Luiz R. B Mott, *Epidemic of Hate: Violations of the Human Rights of Gay Men, Lesbians, and Transvestites in Brazil* (San Francisco: International Gay

and Lesbian Human Rights Commision, 1996). For news reports on Mott's work, see http://www.qrd.org/qrd/world/americas/brazil/anti.gay.murders and http://www.qrd.org/qrd/world/americas/brazil/epidemic.of.hate.report-02.11.97.

21. See G. D. Comstock, *Violence Against Lesbians and Gays* (New York: Columbia University Press, 1991). Homosexual advances have even been accepted as excuses for manslaughter. For a discussion of US practice, see R. B. Mison, "Homophobia in Manslaughter: The Homosexual Advance as Insufficient Provocation," *California Law Review* 80, 1992): 133-178.

22. For recent illustrative examples from Jamaica, Latvia, and Italy, see http://www.qrd.org/qrd/world/americas/jamaica/jamaica.homophobia-UPI, http://www.qrd.org/qrd/world/wockner/news.briefs/209-04.27.98, http://www.qrd.org/qrd/world/wockner/news.briefs/200-02.23.98, and http://www.qrd.org/qrd/world/wockner/news.briefs/198-02.09.98.

23. Teachers in particular are regularly dismissed. For recent examples, see http://www.iglhrc.org/world/centralamerica/CostaRica1998May.html and http://www.qrd.org/qrd/world/wockner/news.briefs/208-04.20.98. In Thailand, homosexuals have been prohibited from entering the state teacher training colleges. (http://www.iglhrc.org/world/asia/Thailand1997Mar.html) Cheng Chung-cheng, a director of student affairs at the Ministry of Education in Taiwan recently said in a public meeting that "homosexuals should not pollute others with their relationships," and questioned whether they should have basic human rights. (http://www.qrd.org/qrd/world/asia/taiwan/gays.in.taiwan) For a recent discussion in the context of trade union activity, see Gerald Hunt, *Laboring for Rights: Unions and Sexual Orientation Across Nations* (Philadelphia: Temple University Press, 1999).

24. Evan Wolfson, "Civil Rights, Human Rights, Gay Rights: Minorities and the Humanity of the Different," *Harvard Journal of Law and Public Policy* 14 (Winter 1991): 21-39, pp. 31-33. Wolfson documents each of the denials in his list by references to recent American legal practice.

25. For example, the United States Supreme Court, in *Boutilier v. Immigration and Naturalization Service*, 387 US 118 (1967), upheld deportation of aliens on grounds that homosexuality counted as "afflicted with psychopathic personality" and thus excludable. This ruling remained in force until the Immigration Act of 1990. See Robert J. Foss, "The Demise of Homsexual Exclusion: New Possibilities for Gay and Lesbian Immigration," *Harvard Civil Rights-Civil Liberties Law Review* 29, Summer 1994): 439-475.

26. http://www.qrd.org/qrd/world/wockner/news.briefs/193-01.05.98.

27. In the United States, the first case was a Brazilian, Marcelo Tenorio, who was severely beaten and hospitalized in a gay bashing incident in Rio de Janeiro in 1989, refused a US visa, and then entered illegally in 1990. See Stuart Grider, "Sexual Orientation as Grounds for Asylum in the United States," *Harvard International Law Journal* 35 (Winter 1994): 213-224. A recently prominent case involved a gay Iranian refugee to Sweden, who received asylum in 1998

after initially being denied in 1996. See http://www.qrd.org/qrd/world/asia/iran/gay.iranian.granted.asylum.in.sweden-06.22.98. For more information, with a primarily American orientation, see http://www.glirtf.org. On Australia, see Peter De Waal, *When Only the Best Will Do: A Study of Lesbian and Gay Immigration* (Darlinghurst: GLITF NSW, 1998).

28. Evelyn Kallen, "Gay and Lesbian rights Issues: A Comparative Analysis of Sydney, Australia and Toronto, Canada," *Human Rights Quarterly* 18, no February 1996): 206-223, p. 209. See also Evelyn Kallen, *Label Me Human: Minority Rights of Stigmatized Canadians* (1989).

29. The most influential version of this argument is Michel Foucault, *The History of Sexuality. Volume I: An Introduction* (New York: Pantheon Books, 1978). For somewhat more mainstream presentations, see Edward Stein, ed., *Forms of Desire: Sexual Orientation and the Social Constructionist Controversy* (New York: Garland Publishing, 1990). With special referenced to the law, see Kristen Walker, "The Participation of the Law in the Construction of (Homo)Sexuality," *Law in Context* 12, (1994).

30. The standard scholarly study is K. Dover, *Greek Homsexuality*, Second ed. (Cambridge: Harvard University Press, 1986). See also Eva Cantarella, *Bisexuality in the Ancient World* (New Haven: Yale University Press, 1992) and, with explicit reference to contemporary debates, Martha Nussbaum, "Platonic Love and Colorado Law: The Relevance of Ancient Greek Norms to Modern Sexual Controversies," *Virginia Law Review* 80 (October 1994).

31. See, for example, John Boswell, *Christianity, Social Tolerance and Homosexuality: Gay People in Western Europe from the Beginning of the Christian Era to the Fourteenth Century* (Chicago: University of Chicago Press, 1980). More controversial is John Boswell, *Same-Sex Unions in Premodern Europe* (New York: Villard Books, 1994).

32. See, for example, Gilbert H. Herdt, ed., *Ritualized Homosexuality in Melanesia* (Berkeley: University of California Press, 1984); Rakesh Ratti, ed., *A Lotus of Another Color: An Unfolding of the South Asian Lesbian and Gay Experience* (Boston: Alyson Publications, 1993); and Arno Schmitt and Jehoeda Sofer, eds., *Sexuality and Eroticism Among Males in Moslem Societies* (New York: Harrington Park Press, 1992).

33. See, for example, Paul Gordon Schalow, "Male Love in Early Modern Japan: A Literary Depiction of the 'Youth'," *Hidden from History: Reclaiming the Gay and Lesbian Past*, M. B. Duberman, M. Vicinus and G. Chauncey, eds. (New York: New American Library, 1989); M. P. Lau, and M. L. Ng, "Homosexuality in Chinese Culture," *Culture, Medicine and Psychiatry* 13 (1989); Bret Hinsch, *Passions of the Cut Sleeve* (Berkeley: University of California Press, 1990); and Gary P. Leupp, *Male Colors: The Construction of Homosexuality in Tokugawa Japan* (Berkeley: University of California Press, 1995).

34. Bret Hinsch, *Passions of the Cut Sleeve* (Berkeley: University of California Press, 1990), pp. 127-134.

35. Similar limitations are allowed in Articles 12, 14, 18, 21, and 22.

36. Quoted in Stetson Kennedy, *Jim Crow Guide to the U.S.A.: The Laws, Customs and Etiquette Governing the Conduct of Nonwhites and Other Minorities as Second-Class Citizens* (London: Lawrence & Wishart Ltd., 1959), p. 32

37. Quoted in Benjamin B. Ringer, *"We the People" and Others: Duality and America's Treatment of Its Racial Minorities* (New York: Tavistock Publications, 1983), p. 590.

38. Quoted in Ibid., pp. 606-607.

39. When the law was changed in 1870 to permit naturalization of freed blacks, foreign-born Asians continued to be denied the right to American nationality. (The American Constitution explicitly grants American nationality to anyone born in the territory of the United States.)

40. Quoted in Ibid., p. 604.

41. V. S. McClatchy, "Assimilation of Japanese: Can They Be Moulded into American Citizens," *Four Anti-Japanese Pamphlets*, V. S. McClatchy, ed. (New York: Arno Press, 1979 [1921]), pp. 5, 10.

42. C. Vann Woodward, *The Strange Career of Jim Crow*, 2nd ed. (New York: Oxford University Press, 1966), p. 81.

43. Jonathan Katz, ed., *Government versus Homosexuals* (New York: Arno Press, 1975), p. 1. [81st Congress, 2d Session, Committee on Expenditures in the Executive Departments, Document No. 241, December 15 (legislative day, November 27), 1950.]

44. The committee, with a logic strikingly reminiscent of the red scare that was building at the same time, found that the government was insufficiently vigilant. The State Department, as during the McCarthy witch hunt, came in for special attack for allowing "known homosexuals" to resign for "personal reasons" without properly noting their homosexuality in their official personnel files. Ibid., p. 11.

45. Ibid., p. 4.

46. I trust it is clear that this language is not chosen to be inflammatory, or because it expresses my own views. In order to focus on the central issue of the justifiability of discrimination, I merely repeat, for the sake of argument, some standard moral condemnations of homosexuality.

47. I am implicitly assuming here that sexual orientation is "chosen" rather than given at birth, and thus more like religion than race—although, of course, racial identity is largely socially constructed. If homosexuality is "genetic," the case for discrimination is even more tenuous, and the appropriate analogy becomes more like race or even disability (another area of lingering legal discrimination in most countries).

48. For example, sexual relations with children may be legitimately prohibited—so long as same-sex and heterosexual relations are both prohibited.

49. I hasten to add, for those who have not yet read her chapter, that Howard shares this view. Although our two chapters were written entirely independently, there is considerable complementarity between her comparative and sociological perspective and my theoretical and international legal perspective.

50. Human Rights Committee, Communication 488/1992, submitted by Nicholas Toonen against Australia. UN Document CCPR/C/50/D/488/1992, 4 April 1994. http://www.unhchr.ch/html/menu2/8/oppro/vws488.htm

51. Ibid., par. 8.7.

52. Ibid., par. 8.2.

53 .Kees Waaldijk, "Standard Sequences in the Legal Recognition of Homosexuality: Europe's Past, Present, and Future," *Australasian Gay and Lesbian Law Journal* 4, no 4 1994): 50-72, pp. 51-52.

54. Ibid., pp. 69-72.

55. Ibid., p. 68.

QUESTIONS FOR REFLECTION

1. According to Donnelly, how does the principle of nondiscrimination justify recognition of the rights of gays and lesbians? Should we protect the rights of gays and lesbians even when doing so may conflict with widespread beliefs about the immorality of homosexuality? Does it make any difference whether those widespread beliefs are about gays and lesbians, or women, or ethnic and religious minorities?

2. What explains the reluctance of states to consider adopting international agreements that focus specifically on sexual orientation? What strategies does Donnelly suggest for strengthening recognition of the human rights of sexual minorities? Can you think of any others?

3. Donnelly mentions the highly-publicized case of Matthew Shepherd, the Wyoming college student who was murdered because he was gay. Does it matter *why*, morally and legally, Shepherd's killers murdered him? Must motives be taken into account in order to identify and condemn human rights violations?

45. MARTHA C. NUSSBAUM

A biographical sketch of Martha Nussbaum appears in section 3. In this essay, Nussbaum develops a framework for identifying the rights of gays and lesbians. Because of the extensive discrimination that continues against gays and lesbians, including violent forms of harassment and assault, gays and lesbians are particularly vulnerable to violations of their human rights. Unless there is a clear and direct recognition of the rights of gays and lesbians, Nussbaum argues, our societies will perpetuate acts of injustice against innocent individuals.

Text—Lesbian and Gay Rights

From The Liberation Debate, *M. Leahy and D. Cohn-Sherbok, eds. London and New York: Routledge, 1996. Reprinted by permission of the author.*

> Now in my own cases when I catch a guy like that I just pick him up and take him into the woods and beat him until he can't crawl. I have had seventeen cases like that in the last couple of years. I tell that guy if I catch him doing that again I will take him out to the woods and I will shoot him. I tell him that I carry a second gun on me just in case I find guys like him and that I will plant it in his hand and say that he tried to kill me and that no jury will convict me.

(Police officer in a large industrial city in the US, being interviewed about his treatment of homosexuals; Westley, "Violence and the Police," quoted in Comstock, 1991, pp. 90–5)

Whose rights are we talking about when we talk about "gay rights," and what are the rights in question? I shall take on, first, the surprisingly difficult task of identifying the people. Next, I shall discuss a number of the most important rights that are at issue, including: (1) the right to be protected against violence and, in general, the right to the equal protection of the law; (2) the right to have consensual adult sexual relations without criminal penalty; (3) the right to non-discrimination in housing, employment and education; (4) the right to military service; (5) the right to marriage and/or its legal benefits; (6) the right to retain custody of children and/or to adopt.

WHOSE RIGHTS?

This is no easy question. Legal and political disputes sometimes speak of "gays and lesbians," sometimes of "gays" only, sometimes of "gays, lesbians and bisexuals." Moreover, there are two different ways of defining these groups, each of which contains an internal plurality of frequently conflicting definitions. One broad class focuses on *conduct*, another on *orientation*.

Conduct first. Frequently, at least in American law, gay and lesbian people are taken to be all and only those people who commit "sodomy." Sodomy is usually defined today as a sex act in which the genital organs of one partner make contact with the mouth or anus of the other. (Earlier this was not the case: fellatio is a relatively late addition to US sodomy law and has never been counted "sodomy" in England: an 1885 statute criminalizing "gross indecency" between men was added to cover it. Female-female sex acts have never been illegal in Britain.) Obviously, however, this definition is both overinclusive and underinclusive: underinclusive because many gay males and lesbians have sex but do not commit these acts, especially in the age of AIDS; overinclusive because these acts are extremely common in male-female relations as well. The famous US case *Bowers v. Hardwick*, in which the Supreme Court upheld the constitutionality of a Georgia sodomy law, originally included a heterosexual couple as plaintiffs alongside Hardwick, since the Georgia law as written plainly covered them. (Their case was dismissed for lack of standing, since they were said to be in no danger of prosecution.) At one point, too, Hardwick's lawyers moved to disqualify any member of the Georgia attorney general's office who had ever committed sodomy. Had the motion succeeded, we could have expected a large number of heterosexual disqualifications. (More than seventy per cent of Americans, both male and female, have engaged in heterosexual oral sex during their lifetime; approximately one quarter have engaged in heterosexual anal sex

(Laumann *et al.*, 1994).)

More promising, then, would be a definition in terms of the biological sex of the actors: gays and lesbians are all and only those people who commit sex acts with partners of the same biological sex. Once again, however, there are problems: (1) what acts? and (2) how many such acts? Some accounts limit the acts to acts actually terminating in orgasm for one or both parties; some instead include all acts *intended* to induce orgasm in one or both parties (an elusive concept). But given the frequent lack of access to evidence about orgasmic reality or intent, the zeal of the American prosecutorial mind has found other more sweeping categorizations. Thus, the old US Army regulation under which Sgt. Perry Watkins, described by his commanding officer as "one of our most respected and trusted soldiers," was ejected from the military, referred to "bodily conduct between persons of the same sex, actively undertaken or passively permitted, with the intent to obtain or give sexual gratification." The act alleged in Watkins' discharge proceedings was described as "squeezing the knee of another male soldier." (All through his army career, as well as before it, Watkins publicly declared his sexual identity and practices; but his own evidence was considered insufficient, since he was suspected of trying to avoid military service.) The new US military policy goes still further, defining "homosexual conduct" as "a homosexual act, a statement that the member is homosexual or bisexual, or a marriage or attempted marriage to someone of the same gender"; hand-holding and kissing "in most circumstances" are explicitly mentioned as examples of "homosexual acts"—though it was determined that a person may visit a gay bar, march in a gay pride rally in civilian clothes or list a person of the same sex as an insurance beneficiary, without thereby committing a homosexual act (*Symposium*, 1993, p. 1802).

Frequently the law has considered the definition in terms of acts unsatisfactory—both because of the evident problem of vagueness and, more significantly, because many people who commit the prohibited acts are not the people against whom policy is really being directed. The US Army, for example, is well aware that many soldiers engage in same-sex sexual acts. (Watkins points out that he never had to approach any one for sex: once his reputation was established, all kinds of men who would never have called themselves "gay" came to him for oral sex—Humphrey, 1993, p. 370.) So the old policy, while specifying "homosexual act" in the loose way I have described, actually made the basis for discharge "homosexual orientation" rather than homosexual acts, used acts only as evidence of orientation and defined "orientation" in terms of the "desire" for any of the large menu of acts. (A still larger menu of evidentiary acts is used by the US Department of Defense: in a recent case membership of a gay organization was sufficient to brand one a "homosexual": cited in Rubenstein, 1993, *High Tech Gays*.)

Since such an account might prove overinclusive—presumably the men who repeatedly asked Watkins for sex desired what they got—Army policy allows that a soldier who has committed a homosexual act may escape discharge if he can show that the conduct was "a departure from the soldier's usual and customary behavior," that it is unlikely to recur because it is shown, for example, that the act occurred because of immaturity, intoxication, coercion, or a desire to avoid military service." Another section adds "curiousity" (sic) to the list of extenuating motives. The regulation expressly states that "The intent of this policy is to permit retention *only* of *nonhomosexual* soldiers who, because of extenuating circumstances engaged in, attempted to engage in, or solicited a homosexual act." (All citations from *Watkins v. United States Army*, original emphasis.) Still, there are problem cases. Think what the Army would say about one lover of Watkins', who, asked why he had sex with Watkins every day, replied, "Well, I like a good blow job, and the women downtown don't know how to suck dick worth a damn. But this man happens to suck mine better than anyone I have ever found in the world" (Humphreys, 1993, p. 371). We shall never know the Army's verdict, since Watkins did not name names. But the odds are that this man, who considered himself "straight," would be retained by some reading of the rules. (Curiosity, as Aristotle informs us, is a regular self-renewing part of our human equipment.)

We might suppose that we are dealing here with the stuff of

high comedy, or even farce. Such definitions, however, determine the course of many lives, not only in the military; and they create an atmosphere within which the violence endemic to American life can very easily direct itself against these people—whoever, more precisely, they are.

Can we ourselves define the category in a useful way? Any good definition should recognize that sexual orientation is itself multiple and complex. The biological sex of the partner may be just one part of what an individual desires in a partner. In many cultures, both historical and modern, biological sex is traditionally considered less salient than sexual role (e.g. the active or the passive) (Dover, 1986, *passim*; Nussbaum, 1994, *passim*). At the same time few real people would be willing to make love with any willing member of a given sex. Most people's "orientation" has other desiderata, often inscrutable and complex: persons of a certain ethnic type, or a certain level of intelligence, or a certain way of laughing or a certain resemblance to a parent. In many individuals and cultures, such desiderata are at least as revealing and interesting as biological sex. American culture's focus on the sex of the partners seems no more timeless than its equally obsessive focus on their race. (In the case of both homosexuality and miscegenation it has been similarly argued that "nature" forbids the unions in question: *Loving v. Virginia*.) However, to be crudely practical, let us define gays, lesbians and bisexuals, the class of persons with a "homosexual or bisexual orientation" (now the most common formulation in non-discrimination law), as those who stably and characteristically desire to engage in sexual conduct with a member or members of the same sex (whether or not they also desire sexual conduct with the opposite sex) and let us adopt a difficult-to-ascertain but not impossibly broad definition of same-sex conduct, namely that it is bodily conduct intended to lead to orgasm on the part of one or both parties. Notice, then, that we are talking about the rights both of people who frequently perform these acts and also of those who desire to but don't. "Stably and characteristically" is tricky still, but perhaps we can live with it, knowing that it excludes a person who experimented a few times in adolescence, or who hasn't desired such conduct for a good many years. On the other hand it includes people who regularly have sex with partners of both sexes, the so-called bi-sexuals. This definition clearly includes all the people against whom the Army policies are directed. Does it also include Watkins' friend, whom the Army would probably wish to retain? I think it should—he had regular access to women, but still re-peatedly chose Watkins; on the other hand, notice that his de-sire, completely impersonal and self-referential, had little to do with Watkins' sex—so he is in that way different from a person who has an actual *preference* for a partner of a certain sex. (It seems a bit odd for the Army to prefer him to Watkins, if indeed it would, just on the grounds of the total non-selectivity of his desire.) This definition, though it seems the best available at present, embodies no real understanding of people, and seems grossly inadequate as a conceptual basis for interference with real people's lives.

Why are lesbian and gay people as they are? (This question is rarely asked about heterosexuals, since that way of being is assumed to be neutral and natural.) Few questions in this area are more hotly disputed. There is considerable evidence in favour of some kind of biological explanation for sexual preference, though there are serious flaws with all the research done until now. But one thing that seems clear is that sexual orientation, if not innate, is formed very early in life, certainly before the age of ten, and after that time proves highly resistant to change, despite all the countless therapies that have been devised to change it. (It may, of course, not be exclusive, and, especially in these cases, it may alter with stages of life.) Another thing that is becoming increasingly clear from empirical research is that a child's sexual orientation is not a function of that of its parents or guardians (Posner, 1392, p. 418).

WHAT RIGHTS?

The right to be protected against violence

Gays, lesbians and bisexuals are targets of violence in America. Twenty-four per cent of gay men and ten per cent of lesbians, in a recent survey, reported some form of criminal assault because of their sexual orientation during the past year (as compared to general population assault rates in a comparable urban area of four per cent for women and six per cent for men). A Massachusetts study found that twenty-one per cent of lesbian and gay students, compared to five per cent of the entire student body, report having been physically attacked. An average of five recent US non-college surveys on anti-gay/lesbian violence show that thirty-three per cent of those surveyed had been chased or followed, twenty-three per cent had had objects thrown at them, eighteen per cent had been punched, hit, kicked or beaten, sixteen per cent had been victims of vandalism or arson, seven per cent had been spat on, and seven per cent had been assaulted with a weapon (data from Comstock, 1991, pp. 31-55). To live as a gay or lesbian in America is thus to live with fear. As one might expect, such violence is not unknown in the military. Most famous, but not unique, was the 1992 death of navy radioman Allen Schindler at the hands of three of his shipmates who, unprovoked, stalked and then fatally beat him—and later blamed their crime on the presence of gays in the military.

Who are the perpetrators? They are more likely than average assault perpetrators are to be strangers to their victims. Ninety-four per cent of them are male (as compared with eighty-seven per cent for comparable crimes of violence); forty-six per cent are under twenty-two years of age (as compared with twenty-nine per cent for comparable crimes); sixty-seven per cent are white. They do not typically exhibit what are customarily thought of as criminal attitudes. "Many conform to or are models of middle-class respectability" (Comstock, 1991, pp. 91-2). The arresting officer in a Toronto incident in which five youths beat a forty-year old gay man to death remarked, "If you went to [a shopping mall] and picked up any group of young males about the same age as these boys—that is what they were like. Average" (Comstock, 1991, p. 33). The data suggest that gay-beatings, including the most lethal, are often in essence "recreational": groups of adolescent men, bored and intoxicated, seek out gays not so much because they have a deep-seated hatred of them as because they recognize that this is a group society has agreed to dislike and not to protect fully (Comstock, 1991, p. 34). A California perpetrator of multiple anti-gay beatings, interviewed by Comstock, cited as reasons for his acts boredom, the desire for adventure, a belief in the wrongness of homosexuality and, finally, attraction to the men he and his friends attacked. He told Comstock that "[we] were probably attacking something within ourselves" (Comstock, 1991, pp. 171-2).

Physical assaults are crimes as defined by the laws of every state in the US. In that sense, the right to be protected against them is a right that gays and lesbians have already. But there is ample evidence that the police often fail to uphold these rights. They may indeed actively perpetrate violence against gays, in unduly violent behavior during vice arrests, etc. Such violence is illegal if it exceeds the requirements of arrest, but it is widely practiced. Even more common is the failure of police to come promptly to the aid of gays and lesbians who are being assaulted. A Canadian study finds that in fifty-six per cent of cases in which gays sought police protection the behaviour of the responding officers was "markedly unsatisfactory" (Comstock, 1991, pp. 151-62).

In numerous US jurisdictions, moreover, killers of gays have successfully pleaded "reasonable provocation," alleging that the revulsion occasioned by a (non-coercive and non-violent) homosexual advance, or even by witnessing gay sexual acts, justified a homicidal response; there is no corresponding tradition of a "heterosexual advance" defence. In a 1990 Pennsylvania case in which a drifter murdered two lesbians whom he saw making love in the woods, the court refused to allow this defence, saying that the law "does not recognize homosexual activity between two persons as legal provocation sufficient to reduce an unlawful killing...from murder to voluntary manslaughter" (*Commonwealth v. Carr*). This is, however, the exception rather than the rule (Mison, 1992).

There is a good case for linking rights involving protection against violence to other facets of gay experience as yet not universally recognized. As long as no laws protect gays against discrimination in other areas of life and guarantee their equal citizenship, as long as their sex acts can be criminalized, as long they are disparaged as second class citizens, we may expect the rights they do have to go on being underenforced, and violence against them to remain a common fact.

My discussion of violence has not addressed the emotional violence done to lesbians and gay people by the perception that they are hated and despised. This issue too can be addressed by law and public policy; for by enacting non-discrimination laws (such as the law recently enacted in my home state of Massachusetts, which forbids discrimination against lesbian and gay students in the school system) one can begin to alter the behaviour that causes this harm. Perhaps eventually one may alter attitudes themselves.

The right to have consensual adult sexual relations without criminal penalty

Consensual sexual relations between adult males were decriminalized in Britain in 1967. In the US, five states still criminalize only same-sex sodomy, while eighteen statutes (including the Uniform Code of Military Justice) criminalize sodomy for all. Five state sodomy laws have recently been judicially repealed, and, in addition, a Massachusetts law prohibiting "unnatural and lascivious act[s]." (But Massachusetts still has another law prohibiting "crime against nature," *Symposium*, 1993, p. 1774.) These laws are rarely enforced, but such enforcement as there is is highly selective, usually against same-sex conduct. Penalties are not negligible: the maximum penalty for consensual sodomy in Georgia is twenty years' imprisonment.

Although sodomy laws are, as I have argued, both under and overinclusive for same-sex conduct, it is frequently assumed that sodomy defines gay or lesbian sexual life. Thus the laws, in addition to their use in targeting the consensual activities of actual sodomites, can also be used to discriminate against gay and lesbian individuals who have never been shown to engage in the practices in question—as when Robin Shahar lost her job in the Georgia Attorney General's office for announcing a lesbian marriage. It was claimed that she could not be a reliable enforcer of the state's sodomy statute (*Shahar v. Bowers*). (All heterosexual intercourse outside marriage is criminal "fornication" in Georgia, and yet there is no evidence that Bowers ever denied employment to heterosexual violators of either that law or the sodomy law.)

The case against sodomy laws is strong. Rarity of enforcement creates a problem of arbitrary and selective police behaviour. Although neither all nor only homosexuals are sodomites, the laws are overwhelmingly used to target them; and the fact that some of their acts remain criminal is closely connected with the perception that they are acceptable targets of violence and with other social exclusions as well. For example, "[t]here is...a natural reluctance...to appoint to judicial positions people who have committed hundreds or even thousands of criminal acts" (Posner, 1992, p. 311)—unjustified as this reluctance may be, and also arbitrary, given that the judiciary is no doubt full of heterosexual perpetrators of sodomy and criminal fornication. (Laumann shows that the frequency of both oral and anal sex among heterosexuals increases with level of education, Laumann *et al*, 1994.)

Most important, such adult consensual sexual activity does no harm. There is thus no public benefit to offset the evident burdens these laws impose. As Judge Posner concludes, such laws "express an irrational fear and loathing of a group that has been subjected to discrimination" (1992, p. 346). We have no need of such laws in a country all too full of incitements to violence.

Should the age of consent be the same for same-sex as for opposite-sex activity? I am inclined to think that, in current American and European nations, 16 is a reasonable age for both. The biggest problem with age of consent law generally is the failure to discriminate between the act of two 15-year-olds and an act between a 30-year-old and a 15-year-old. In both same and opposite-sex relations, the law should (and often does) address itself to this issue.

The right to be free from discrimination in housing, employment and education

Gays, lesbians and bisexuals suffer discrimination in housing and employment. Many US states and local communities have responded to this situation by adopting non-discrimination laws. (Such laws have for some time been in effect in some European countries and in some Australian states.) Recently in the US, efforts have also been made to prevent local communities from so legislating, through referenda amending the state's constitution to forbid the passage of such a local law. The most famous example is that of Amendment 2 in the State of Colorado, which nullified anti-discrimination laws in three cities in the state, and prevented the passage of any new ones. I believe that there is no good argument for discrimination against gays and lesbians in housing and employment. (The repeated suggestion that such protection against discrimination would lead to quotas for this group and would therefore injure the prospects of other minorities was especially invidious and misleading; none of the local ordinances had even suggested quota policies.)

Along with the Supreme Court of Colorado (when it upheld a preliminary injunction against the law, laying the legal basis for the trial court judgement that found the law unconstitutional), I would make a further point. Such referenda, by depriving gays and lesbians of the right to organize at the local level to secure the passage of laws that protect them, thereby deprive them of equality with respect to the fundamental right of political participation. They, and they alone, have to amend the state constitution in order to pass a fair housing law in some town. Similar state laws have long been declared unconstitutional in the area of race. I believe that they are morally repugnant in this area as well.

The most serious issue that arises with regard to non-discrimination laws is that of religious freedom. Both institutions and individuals may sincerely believe that to be required to treat lesbians and gays as equal candidates for jobs (or as equal prospective tenants) is to be deprived of the freedom to exercise their religion. This argument seems more pertinent to some occupations than others. To hire someone as a teacher may plausibly be seen as conferring a certain role-model status on that person; to hire someone as an accountant can hardly be seen in this light. And it is not clear to me that a landlord's religious freedom is compromised by being forced to consider on an equal basis tenants he may deem immoral. (The US Supreme Court recently refused to hear an appeal of an Alaska decision against a landlord who refused to rent on religious grounds to an unmarried heterosexual couple.)

Various responses are possible. The Denver statute exempted religious organizations from its non-discrimination provisions. The American Philosophical Association refused to exempt religious institutions from its (non-binding) non-discrimination policy for hiring and promotion, except in the case of discrimination on the basis of religious membership. I believe that we should combine these two approaches: religious organizations should in some cases be allowed greater latitude to follow their own beliefs; but in publicly funded and in large professional organizations, with sexuality as with race, freedom to discriminate should be limited by shared requirements of justice. I recognize, however, that many people of good faith with deep religious convictions are likely to disagree.

Even in the sensitive area of education, there is no evidence to show that the presence of gay and lesbian teachers harms children or adolescents. Gays are at least no more likely, and in some studies less likely to molest children than are heterosexual males; nor is there evidence to show that knowing or respecting a gay person has the power to convert children to homosexuality (any more than being taught by heterosexuals has converted gay youths to heterosexuality). The sexual harassment of students or colleagues should be dealt with firmly wherever it occurs. Beyond that, what one's colleagues do in bed should be irrelevant to their employment.

One further educational issue remains: this is the right to have opportunities to learn about lesbian and gay people. This right is of special interest to lesbian and gay students, but it is also, importantly, a right of all students, all of whom are citizens and need to learn something about their fellow citizens, especially as potential voters in referenda such as the one in Colorado. The study of homosexuality—historical, psychological, sociological, legal, literary—is now a burgeoning field of research. Do students of various ages have the right to learn about this work? In the US the First Amendment makes a flat prohibition of such teaching unlikely (not impossible, since the First Amendment is not binding on private institutions), though teachers may be subtly penalized for introducing such material into their courses. In Britain, a 1986 law forbids local government to "intentionally promote homosexuality or publish material with the intention of promoting homosexuality" or to "promote the teaching in any maintained school of the acceptability of homosexuality as a pretended family relationship" (Local Government Act 1986, cited in *Symposium*, 1993, p. 7). This law would very likely be unconstitutional in the US. It is also, I think, morally repugnant for several reasons. First, it inhibits the freedom of enquiry. Second, it inhibits the freedom of political debate. Third, it creates just the sort of atmosphere of taboo and disgust that fosters discrimination and violence against gays and lesbians. Furthermore, I believe it to be counterproductive to the proponents' own ostensible goals of fostering morality as they understand it. For a moral doctrine to announce publicly that it needs to be backed up by informational restrictions of this sort is a clear confession of weakness. And Judge Richard Posner has cogently argued that such policies actually increase the likelihood that gay sex will be casual and promiscuous, presumably something the law's partisans wish to avoid. Deprived of the chance to learn about themselves in any way other than through action, Posner argues, young gay people will in all likelihood choose action earlier than they might have otherwise (Posner, 1392, p. 302). The atmosphere of concealment also makes courtship and dating difficult—so "they will tend to substitute the sex act, which can be performed in a very short time and in private, for courtship, which is public and protracted" (Posner, 1992, p. 302).

The right to military service

It is clear enough that gays and lesbians can serve with distinction in the military, since many of them have done so (Shilts, 1992, *passim*; Posner, 1992, p. 317). Furthermore, the armies of quite a few nations have successfully integrated open homosexuals into the service: France, Germany, Israel, Switzerland, Sweden, Denmark, Norway, Finland, the Netherlands, Belgium, Australia, Spain and recently Canada. As Posner writes, "The idea that homosexuals will not or cannot fight seems a canard, on a par with the idea that Jews or blacks will not or cannot fight" (Posner, 1992, p. 317). Nor are they security risks, if they openly announce their homosexuality. Nor are they to be excluded because they might commit acts of sexual harassment. (If this were so, in the wake of recent sexual harassment scandals in the US military we should first exclude all heterosexual males.) Sexual harassment should be dealt with firmly wherever it occurs; this has nothing to do with our issue.

The real issue that keeps coming up is that heterosexual males do not want to be forced to associate intimately with gay males, especially to be seen naked by them. The psychology of this intense fear of the gaze of the homosexual is interesting. (It has even been attempted as a legal defence in gay-bashing cases, under the description "homosexual panic".) This fear may have something to do with the idea expressed by Comstock's gay-basher, when he perceptively noted that his aggression assailed something within himself. It may also be connected with the thought that this man will look at me in the way I look at a woman—i.e. not in a respectful or personal way, but a way that says "I want to fuck you"—and that this gaze will somehow humiliate me. What should be noted, however, is that this fear goes away when it needs to, and quite quickly too. As a frequenter of health clubs, I note that in that setting both males and females undress all the time in front of other patrons, many of whom they can be sure are gay; frequently it is clear through conversation who the gays and lesbians are. Nonetheless, we do not observe an epidemic of muscular failure. Straight men do not leap off the treadmill or drop their barbells in panic. They know they cannot root out and eject these people, so they forget about the issue. Moving on, we note that openly gay officers have been included in the police forces of New York City, Chicago, San Francisco, Los Angeles and probably others by now, without incident. During wartime, moreover, when the need for solidarity and high morale is greatest, toleration of gay and lesbian soldiers has gone up, not down (see Shilts, 1992). It seems likely that gays could be integrated relatively painlessly into the US Armed Forces, if firm leadership were given from the top. The unfortunate fact, however, is that, here as with the harassment of women, high-ranking officers do not give the requisite leadership. As Judge Posner writes, "it is terrible to tell people they are unfit to serve their country, unless they really are unfit, which is not the case here" (Posner, 1992, p. 321).

The right to marriage and/or the legal and social benefits of marriage

Gays and lesbians in Denmark, Sweden and Norway can form a registered partnership that gives all the tax, inheritance and other civic benefits of marriage; similar legislation is soon to be passed in Finland. Many businesses, universities and other organizations within other nations, including the US, have extended their marriage benefits to registered same-sex domestic partners. Gay marriage is currently a topic of intense debate in Judaism and in every major branch of Christianity.

Why are marriage rights important to gays? Legally, marriage is a source of many benefits, including favourable tax, inheritance and insurance status; immigration rights; custody rights; the right to collect unemployment benefits if one partner quits a job to move to be where his or her partner has found employment; the spousal privilege exception when giving testimony; the right to bring a wrongful death action upon the negligent death of a spouse; the right to the privileges of next-of-kin in hospital visitations, decisions about burial, etc. (Mohr, 1994, pp. 72-3, Nava and Dawidoff, 1994, p. 155, citing Hawaii Supreme Court, *Baehr v. Lewin*). Many gays and lesbians have discovered in the most painful way that they lack these rights, although they may have lived together loyally for years.

Emotionally and morally, being able to enter a legally recognized form of marriage means the opportunity to declare publicly an intent to live in commitment and partnership. Although many lesbian and gay people consider themselves married and have frequently solemnized their commitment in ceremonies not recognized by the state, they still seek to do so in a recognized manner, because they attach importance to the public recognition of their union.

As the Norwegian Ministry of Children and Family Affairs writes, supporting Norway's 1933 law: "It can be detrimental for a person to have to suppress fundamental feelings concerning attachment and love for another person. Distancing oneself from these feelings or attempts to suppress them may destroy one's self-respect" (Norwegian Act on Registered Partnerships for Homosexual Couples, 1993). Noting that ninety-two per cent of gays and lesbians polled in a comprehensive Swedish survey were either part of a registered couple or stated that they would like to be, the Ministry concluded that the primary obstacle to stable marital unions in the gay community is "negative attitudes from the social environment."

These seem to be very plausible views. And yet gay marriage is widely opposed. On what grounds? On what account of marriage is it an institution that should remain closed to lesbians and gay men? The basis of marriage in the US and Europe is generally taken to be a stated desire to live together in intimacy, love and partnership, and to support one another, materially and emotionally, in the conduct of daily life. Of course many people enter marriage unprepared, and many marriages fail; but the law cannot and should not undertake a stringent enquiry into the character and behaviour of the parties before admitting them to the benefits of that status.

Many people do believe that a central purpose of marriage is to have and educate children. But (apart from the fact that many lesbian and gay people do have and raise children, whether their own from previous unions or conceived by artificial insemination within the relationship) nobody has seriously suggested denying marriage rights to post-menopausal women, to sterile individuals of any age or to people who simply know (and state) that they don't want children and won't have them. It therefore seems flatly inconsistent and unjust to deny these rights to other individuals who wish to form exactly this type of committed yet childless union.

No doubt the extension of marriage rights to gays and lesbians will change the way we think about "the family." On the other hand, "the family" has never been a single thing in western, far less in world, history, and its nuclear heterosexual form has been associated with grave problems of child abuse and gender inequality, so there is no reason to sentimentalize it as a morally perfect institution. Studies have shown that homosexual households have a more equal division of domestic labour than heterosexual ones (Blumstein and Schwartz, 1983). So they may even have valuable contributions to make to our understanding of what personal commitment and marital fairness are.

The right to retain custody of children and/or to adopt

Gays and lesbians have and raise children. In a 1970s California survey, twenty per cent of male homosexuals and more than a third of female homosexuals have been married (Posner, 1992, p. 417), and many of those have had children. Lesbian couples can have children through artificial insemination or sex with a male; a gay man can obtain a child through some sort of surrogacy arrangement. Should these things be (or remain) legal? Experience shows that children raised in homosexual households showed no differences from other groups, either in sexual orientation or in general mental health or social adjustment. Indeed, there was evidence that children raised by an unmarried heterosexual, woman had more psychological problems than others (Posner, 1992, p. 418). We need more research on these issues, clearly; samples have been small and have covered a relatively short time-span. But so far there is no evidence to justify a court in removing a child from its parent's custody on the grounds that he or she is living in a homosexual union. If one were to argue that such a child will inevitably be the target of social prejudice, no matter how well its parent is doing, it seems plausible that the Constitution will intervene to block that argument. In a 1984 case, *Palmore v. Sidoti*, in which a child was removed from its (white) mother's custody because she had remarried to a black man—grounds for change of custody being that such a child will suffer from public racial prejudice—the US Supreme Court returned custody to the child's mother, holding that the law may not give public legitimacy to private prejudices. This case was cited as a precedent in a 1985 Alaska decision granting custody to a gay parent (Mison, 1992, p. 175). In general, it seems especially important that children should not be removed from the custody of parents who love and care for them successfully, without compelling reason.

As for adoption and foster-parenting, I concur with Judge Posner that courts should take a case-by-case approach, rejecting a flat ban. Frequently, especially where foster-parenting is concerned, such a placement might be a child's best chance for a productive home life (Posner, 1992, p. 420). Once again, the reason for refusing a homosexual couple must not be the existence of public prejudice against homosexuality; and yet, no feature intrinsic to homosexuality as such has been demonstrated to have a detrimental effect on children.

COUNTERARGUMENTS: SCRUTON

It is frequently held, against gay rights of various sorts, that gay sex relationships are unusually likely to be promiscuous and/or superficial. This has rarely been claimed about lesbian relationships. But the image of the gay male bathhouse has often been paraded before voters as a scare image. What should we say about this?

To begin with, we have no reliable data. The only data about sexual behaviour in America that are even remotely reliable are those in the recent Laumann/Chicago survey (Laumann *et al*, 1994). Because of funding difficulties resulting from conservative Congressional opposition to the study, Laumann could not study a large enough sample of homosexuals to draw conclusions about their number of sex partners. His results show, however, that many if not most common beliefs in this general area are false, and that most types of people have far fewer sex partners than popular belief supposes. (The alleged promiscuity of black males, for example, turns out to be a complete myth: black males and white males have exactly the same number of lifetime sexual partners.)

One might well hold that a person's promiscuity is not the business of the law, unless he harms others, and should not have any relevance to deliberations about basic legal rights. But large numbers of people do think that the alleged connection between male homosexuality and promiscuity is pertinent to deliberations about such rights as the rights to marriage and adoption, and perhaps certain employment rights as well. So we should address these concerns.

First of all, we should insist that straight men are allowed to get married and to obtain the legal, emotional and religious benefits of marriage; gay men are not, and their stable committed unions have to fight against public denial and opprobrium. Furthermore, no evidence about the behaviour of a group that is currently the target of social opprobrium and violence is a very reliable predictor of the way in which those same people would behave in better social circumstances.

Next, we have to note that we are talking about males raised in a culture that has generally taught men to value self-sufficiency and the uncommitted state, women to value intimacy and commitment. It is not surprising that sometimes putting two males together doubles the "maleness" of the relationship—but should that be blamed on the same-sex character of the relationship, or its maleness? And is the remedy to be found (if one is wanted) in yet more measures against same-sex individuals, or in the reformation of the moral education of males?

In general, like any statistical argument, this cannot serve as a justification for denying any right to an entire group. If the mobility and assembly rights of all males were curtailed on the ground that males commit a high proportion of our society's violent crimes, we would view that as an outrage. So we should repudiate any attempt to deny rights to gays on grounds of the (alleged) promiscuity of some or even many gays. If the law wishes to discourage promiscuity, there are steps that can be taken without removing anyone's civil rights: tax incentives for married couples, public rhetoric of a hortatory sort, above all the legalization of gay and lesbian marriage. There is no need to target a group already targeted. It is inaccurate, and it is unjust.

An interesting variant of this argument, focusing on superficiality rather than promiscuity, has been made by my opponent Roger Scruton (Scruton, 1986, pp. 305-10). Scruton's argument is a pleasure to approach because it is expressed with a tentativeness and a lack of venom rare in these matters. The argument is as follows: when one makes love with someone of the opposite gender, one is dealing with a different, mysterious world; by contrast, the world of one's own gender is familiar and well known. (Scruton seems to me to give people undue credit for self-knowledge.) The willingness to put one's being at risk in the midst of a world so profoundly other is morally valuable and imparts depth to the relationship; same-sex relationships lack this risky openness, and this is connected with their (alleged) greater superficiality. This may help us to see that male gay sex (Scruton explicitly exempts lesbian relationships) is, if not perverted or depraved, still morally inferior.

A number of problems arise. First, Scruton uses the unclear notion of "gender," rather than the somewhat clearer notion of biological sex. This is important, since knowing one's own gender is supposed to be a matter of not just knowing what it's like to have a certain sort of genital organ, but of knowing a whole way of being in the world. But even within a single culture, most individuals will find in themselves in both conformity and nonconformity with any list of gender attributes one might construct. And even if one's attributes on the whole conform to the stereotype, one need not find the other gender's world unfamiliar, if one works with many people of that gender and has intimate friendships with some of them. I suspect, in fact, that Scruton's idea that the world of the female is mysterious to men (an idea I have heard from quite a number of men) is not easily separable from its cultural context, in which single sex education and the sparse representation of women in the professions have made it hard for men to have female friends.

Next, the argument is more sweeping than Scruton appears to realize, in two ways. First, if we follow it we shall be led to find superior moral value in any relationship in which a barrier of experiential difference is crossed. This ought to mean that relationships between the Chinese and the British, or the sighted and the blind or the aged and the youthful, have greater moral value than relationships between two Britons or two sighted people or two young people. I doubt that Scruton would actually hold this. I think Scruton is actually thinking not of qualitative differences of this sort, but of the mystery of intimacy with any world that is separate from one's own. But that is a challenge that exists in any intimate human relationship.

Second, if we really direct disapproval against those who are (for whatever reason) unwilling to be vulnerable and at risk in their sexual relationships, preferring contacts of a superficial sort, we will have to exclude from the targeted group many homosexuals, both female and male, and include many heterosexuals, well exemplified by Watkins' satisfied friend, whose desires were as superficial and narcissistic as anyone's could be. Indeed, attitudes just this self-centred, and even more possessive, have been common attitudes of men toward women throughout much of history.

Would it make any sense to say that people inclined to superficiality in sex could not serve in the armed forces? The US Navy's shameful Tailhook scandal (in which crude harassment of women was revealed as endemic to naval life) shows the broad sweep of promiscuous attitudes about sex, even at the highest levels of the services. Indeed, it appears that such attitudes are actively encouraged, in order to promote male group solidarity. It seems pathetic to lay all this at the door of the one group that is not allowed to serve and can least be blamed for the current situation. Where marriage rights are concerned, it might make *moral* sense to dissuade a person prone to superficial sexual contacts from marrying, given the likelihood that the partner might be disappointed. But surely this makes no *political* sense as a basis for the denial of the marriage licence. The enquiries that would then be required would be unmanageable and incredibly prone to abuse, vindictive ex-spouses offering testimony about their ex's superficial attitudes and his unwillingness to be "at risk" toward the "other," all to impede a marriage to the hated rival. Or, if a putative statistical correlation between (male) homosexuality and superficiality should be used as criterial, why not deny marriage licences to all males, on the grounds that they are far more likely than females to abuse their children? This is surely worse than superficiality. Where adoption is concerned, certainly let us look hard at the life of the individual couple—but let us look at the *individual* couple, and not assume beforehand what is perfectly false, that all and only same-sex couples are unsuitable. (Scruton already concedes the suitability of female couples, thus casting doubt on whether his argument is really about homosexuality at all.)

So: I think Scruton's argument gets at something deep about sex, when we take him to be talking about separateness or "otherness" rather than mere qualitative difference. But the argument seems to have no bearing on the legal issues before us.

I believe that the rights of lesbians and gays are a central issue of justice for our time. It is my hope that fifty years from now the current situation of this group of citizens will look just as irrational and as repugnant to a shared sense of justice as the situation of blacks in America in 1950 now looks to virtually all of us.

References

Comstock, G.D. *Violence Against Lesbians and Gay Men*. New York: Columbia University Press, 1991.

Dover, K. *Greek Homosexuality*. Second edition. Cambridge, MA: Harvard University Press, 1986.

Humphrey, M.A. "Interview with Perry Watkins." In W.B. Rubenstein, ed. *Lesbians, Gay Men, and the Law*. New York: The New Press, 1993.

Laumann, E. et al. *Sex in America*. Boston: Little Brown, 1994.

Mison, R.B. "Homophobia in Manslaughter: The Homosexual Advance as Insufficient Provocation." *California Law Review* 80 (1992).

Nava, M. and R. Dawidoff. *Created Equal: Why Gay Rights Matter to Americans*. New York: St. Martin's Press, 1994.

Nussbaum, M. "Platonic Love and Colorado Law: The Relevance of Ancient Greek Norms to Modern Sexual Controversies." *Virginia Law Review* 80 (1994).

Posner, R. *Sex and Reason*. Cambridge, MA: Harvard University Press, 1992.

Rubenstein, W.B., ed. *Lesbians, Gay Men, and the Law*. New York: The New Press, 1993.

Scruton, R. *Sexual Desire: A Moral Philosophy of Erotica*. New York: The Free Press, 1986.

Shilts, R. *Conduct Unbecoming: Lesbians and Gays in the US Military.* Harmondsworth: Penguin, 1992.
Symposium on Sexual Orientation and the Law, various authors. *Virginia Law Review* 79 (1993).

QUESTIONS FOR REFLECTION

1. What kinds of distinctive human rights violations are gays, lesbians, and bisexuals subjected to? Does the US military policy of discharging known homosexuals constitute a violation of their human rights?

2. Nussbaum suggests that by "enacting non-discrimination laws...one can begin to alter the behaviour that causes" physical and emotional harm to sexual minorities. Should government policies and governmental agencies be involved in transforming the behavior of citizens? Do you think it important to treat discriminatory behavior as a public, rather than merely private, matter?

3. What specific rights does Nussbaum identify with respect to gays and lesbians? Why are those rights significant? What kinds of things would have to change to bring about an international human rights system that is comprehensive in its approach to the rights of gays and lesbians?

FURTHER READINGS FOR SECTION 10

Breaking the Silence: Human Rights Violations Based on Sexual Orientation. London and New York: Amnesty International, 1997.

Comstock, Gary David. *Violence Against Lesbians and Gay Men.* New York: Columbia University Press, 1991.

Dorf, Julie and Gloria Careaga Pérez. "Discrimination and the Tolerance of Difference: International Lesbian Human Rights." In *Women's Rights, Human Rights,* Julie Peters and Andrea Wolper, eds. New York and London: Routledge, 1995.

Kaplan, Morris. "Autonomy, Equality, Community: The Question of Lesbian and Gay Rights." *Praxis International* 11 (1991): 195-213.

Mohr, Richard. *Gays/Justice.* New York: Columbia University Press, 1990.

Sanders, Douglas. "Getting Lesbian and Gay Issues on the International Human Rights Agenda." *Human Rights Quarterly* 18 (1996): 67-106.

Thomas, Michael. "Teetering on the Brink of Equality: Sexual Orientation and International Constitutional Protection." *Boston College Third World Law Journal* 17 (1997): 365-94.

Section 11:

HUMAN RIGHTS AND THE ENVIRONMENT

46. JAMES W. NICKEL

A biographical sketch of James Nickel appears in section 8. It seems clear that, in a very fundamental sense, the purpose of promoting human rights is to improve the quality of life of all people. It seems equally clear that protecting and enhancing human dignity depends greatly upon the condition of the biosphere that we inhabit. Starting from this realization, Nickel examines how discussions of human rights and the environment have come to be seen by many as interlinked. In particular, he analyzes the claim that humans have a right to a safe environment. Nickel concludes that such a claim is justifiable, given the threats to human security and well-being posed by destruction of the environment.

Text—The Human Right to a Safe Environment: Philosophical Perspectives on Its Scope and Justification

James W. Nickel, "The Human Right to a Safe Environment: Philosophical Perspectives on Its Scope and Justification," Yale Journal of International Law *18 (1993): 281–95. Reprinted by permission of the* Yale Journal of International Law.

In the last twenty-five years, environmentalists have sought recognition for the right to a safe environment (RSE) in national and international fora. As a result, some countries have recognized RSE in their constitutions. Nevertheless, much skepticism exists about whether RSE is a genuine human right, and advocates of RSE still need to persuade critics that this right merits national and international recognition.[1] This paper presents a normative defense of RSE. It argues that a right to a safe environment—defined narrowly—is a genuine human right because it passes appropriate justificatory tests. Part I defends the modest use of the language of rights in expressing environmental norms. Part II offers a narrow account of the scope of RSE. Part III provides a justification for RSE as conceived in part II.

I. SHOULD ENVIRONMENTALISTS USE RIGHTS LANGUAGE?

Considerable controversy exists at present about how widely the language of rights should be used in expressing environmental values and norms. Enthusiasts are willing to use rights language in virtually all areas of environmentalism, including biotic rights, rights of species, and animal rights. By contrast, deep ecologists and non-anthropocentrists often hold that discussion in the environmental area should totally avoid the language of rights and the legalisms that allegedly accompany it.[2]

This paper supports neither of these extreme positions. Rights should not be the dominant normative concept of environmentalism. It is better to phrase most environmental discourse in terms of environmental *goods*, of *respect* for and *responsibilities* towards nature, and of *obligations* to future generations. However, speaking of rights is plausible and useful for dealing with some of the most serious human consequences of environmental degradation. In particular, the right to a safe environment can play a useful and justifiable role in protecting human interests in a safe environment and in providing a link between the environmental and human rights movements.

If the language of rights is used loosely in environmental discourse, people may begin to claim rights that are excessively metaphorical and rhetorical. Conversely, if the language of rights is used strictly, people may develop environmental prescriptions that are excessively rigid and that preclude tradeoffs necessary for providing for human needs while trying to work out today's environmental and population crises. Rights claims are not completely immune to tradeoffs, but the language of rights does imply the restriction of tradeoffs; thus, rights language should be used sparingly in a field in which tradeoffs are a necessary part of progress.

On the other hand, entirely avoiding the language of rights in the environmental area would needlessly abandon a valuable normative asset. When used to claim a safe environment for humans, the language of rights can be used without being either too metaphorical or engendering worries of excessive rigidity.

RSE is human oriented. It does not speak directly to issues

such as biodiversity, the claims of animals, conservation, or sustainable development. However, the fact that a norm does not apply to all subfields is not a significant objection if it can be supplemented by other norms that will address other issues. Nor does the premise that humanity should protect valuable things other than humans imply that human ethics should neglect to protect humans. The approach in this paper is accommodationist: RSE is presented as one useful part of the normative repertory of environmentalism. It can play a central role in justifying and guiding a wide range of environmental programs and regulations, but it should do this in concert with other environmental norms.

RSE is particularly useful because it links the environmental movement to the international human rights movement; thus, RSE allows environmentalists to appeal to traditional human rights norms and to use the institutions and mechanisms developed to promote and implement human rights at the international level.[3] The human rights movement has strong international recognition, support, and institutions and thus has valuable resources to offer environmentalism. Therefore, it is worthwhile to associate at least one norm pertaining to environmental protection with internationally recognized human rights standards. This is not to say, however, that RSE is justified solely on the instrumental grounds that it will be useful to environmentalists. In fact RSE will only prove useful to environmentalists if people find plausible the claim that it is a genuine human right. As a norm that satisfies the tests appropriate to human rights, RSE should be recognized both as a general human right and as an important footing for environmental claims.

II. THE SCOPE OF THE RIGHT TO A SAFE ENVIRONMENT

There are many possible formulations of environmental rights. For example, Melissa Thorme writes of "environment as a human right," but makes clear that she means a right to "a safe, healthy, and ecologically balanced environment."[4] Many national constitutions use similar language. The Constitution of Honduras speaks of maintaining "a satisfactory environment for the protection of everyone's health." The Constitution of South Korea declares a right "to a healthy and pleasant environment." The Constitution of Portugal speaks of a "healthy and ecologically balanced environment." The current buzzword, "sustainable," might also be added to these formulations. If one puts all these phrases together one would end up with a right to a safe, healthy, pleasant, ecologically balanced, and sustainable environment.

Although such a broad formulation of RSE sets out an attractive goal, a narrow formulation focusing exclusively on human health and safety has the best chance of gaining acceptance as a genuine human right. This paper therefore concentrates exclusively on just such a narrow formulation. This paper will speak of a right to a *safe* environment, meaning an environment that is not destructive of human health. Defining the scope of this right is best done in two steps. The first step describes the state of affairs that would exist if RSE were fully realized. The second step describes the duties that individuals, governments, corporations and international organizations must bear in order to realize this state of affairs.

A. The State of Affairs that the Right to a Safe Environment Prescribes

The meaning of "safe environment" is ambiguous, since this term may refer to freedom from threats of crime or from threats of pollution. For example, children have a right to a safe environment in school, meaning that schools should be free from crime and violence. Because RSE does not address crime or violence, it is important to realize that RSE is concerned only with a particular set of threats to human safety, namely those which stem from technological and industrial processes and the disposal of sewage and wastes. Broadly speaking, RSE is concerned with safety from contamination and pollution.

Threats to health are the primary focus of RSE because the most severe effects of pollution, toxic wastes, and inadequately processed sewage are sickness and death. Threats to health include ones that kill, shorten a person's life, make a person permanently incapable of normal functioning, and make a person temporarily (and perhaps recurrently) sick. Threats to some non-health aspects of well-being should also be included in RSE as a secondary focus. For present purposes, this paper will include only very basic aspects of well-being in RSE, those that pertain to avoiding extreme misery and to preserving the possibility of a minimally good life. For example, having to live with constant loud, screeching noise from a nearby factory might not destroy one's health, but it would make most people quite miserable. In sum, RSE should address forms of contamination and pollution that create significant risks of killing people, making them sick or seriously miserable, or depriving them of the possibility of a minimally good life.

To define the scope of RSE we must define acceptable levels of risk. This is a difficult matter. How safe must the environment be? The total elimination of risks is impossible, and using all available means to diminish risk is not affordable, given other important claims on resources, such as education, medical care, employment opportunities, and security against crime. A better approach is to specify that the environment, or the level of safety from environmental risks, should be satisfactory or adequate for health. These phrases, although vague, clearly set the level of acceptable risk at an intermediate level, and thus make it more likely that RSE can pass the feasibility test discussed below. On the other hand, they do not set the risk standard so low as to make RSE meaningless.

The fact that terms such as "satisfactory" and "adequate" are vague is not a significant problem in this context. Even if it were possible to give a more precise description of the level of acceptable risk, it probably would be inappropriate for international institutions to prescribe a single, precise standard worldwide. International human rights typically set broad normative standards that can be interpreted and applied by appropriate legislative, judicial, or administrative bodies at the national level. Consider, for example the broad normative standards set forth by the rights regarding *inhumane or degrading punishment*, *effective* remedy and *arbitrary* arrest or detention. The proposed standard of "*adequate* for health and well-being" fits this pattern. It provides a general, imprecise description of the level of protections against environmental risks that States should guarantee. Risk standards should be specified further at the national level through democratic legislative and regulatory processes, in light of current scientific knowledge and fiscal realities.

B. Duties Generated by the Right to a Safe Environment

A right is not merely a claim to some freedom or benefit; it is also a claim against certain parties to act so as to make that freedom or benefit available. The following sections consider the duties generated by RSE.

1. Duties of Individuals and Corporations

Persons, organizations, and corporations have a duty to refrain from activities that generate unacceptable levels of environmental risk. For example, individuals have a duty to refrain from pouring dangerous chemicals into sewers or waterways, to refrain from deactivating pollution control devices on their cars, and to refrain from avoidable car use on days when pollution alerts are in effect. Hospitals have a duty to dispose of medical wastes in ways that avoid risks of contamination and other injuries. Companies that transport oil and other hazardous material have a duty to take strong precautions against spills and other accidents. When environmental damage occurs, individuals, organizations, and corporations have a duty to restore the environment and compensate victims.

2. Duties of Governments

Like individuals and corporations, governments have negative duties to refrain from actions that generate large risks of damage to human life and health. For example, governments have a duty not to operate nuclear power plants without taking adequate measures to ensure safe design, construction, maintenance, operations, and waste disposal. Beyond these negative duties, governments also have a duty to protect the inhabitants of their territories against environmental risks generated by either governmental or private agencies. In our technologically advanced civilization, an effective system of environmental protection requires a governmentally enacted system of environmental regulation that sets safety standards for thousands of processes and substances. This system must encourage or pressure those using these processes and substances to comply with its regulations, and impose significant penalties on those who fail to comply. An adequate system of environmental regulation also requires that citizens, environmental organizations, and government agencies have the power to sue polluters, whether public or private, for compensatory damages.

Contemporary human rights documents require that governments be elected in periodic, free elections, and that all citizens be free to participate in politics by expressing their opinions, by voting, by campaigning, and by running for office. These rights to political participation reinforce the scope of RSE by requiring democratic participation in decisions about environmental risks. For such participation to be meaningful, the public must have access to information about the risks posed by the actions of governmental and private enterprises.

3. Duties of International Organizations

International agencies such as the United Nations and the Organization of American States have negative duties to refrain from generating large environmental risks. For example, the United Nations has a duty to ensure environmental safety when using military forces to conduct peacekeeping operations. The World Bank has a negative duty to refrain from loaning money to development projects that will generate major risks to human health and safety. These international organizations also have positive duties to promote and protect RSE through declarations, regulations, and enforcement measures. RSE should be added to international human rights conventions such as the European Convention on Human Rights and the International Covenant on Economic, Social and Cultural Rights. RSE is already included in the African Charter on Human and Peoples' Rights, and will be included in the American Convention on Human Rights when the Protocol of San Salvador comes into force. These conventions are implemented at the international level through periodic government reports on their progress to human rights agencies; complaints brought by individuals and States against violating States in human rights tribunals; mediation of complaints by standing human rights commissions; adjudication of disputes over the interpretation of key clauses by international judicial bodies; the publication of reports of violations; and the use of diplomatic, political, and economic pressure to coerce violators to comply.

III. THE JUSTIFICATION OF THE RIGHT TO A SAFE ENVIRONMENT

Human rights are fundamental international moral and legal norms which protect people—simply as people, and not in virtue of citizenship or allegiance—from severe but common social, political, and legal abuses. These rights may not effectively prevent these abuses until the rights are both widely accepted and legally implemented at the international and national levels. Nevertheless, rights exist independently of such acceptance.

To qualify as a human right, RSE must satisfy at least four criteria. First, proponents must demonstrate that the proposed rightholders have a strong claim to the liberty, protection, or benefit in question by showing that this liberty, protection, or benefit is of great value to individuals and society, and by showing that these values are frequently threatened by social and political abuses. Second, they must show that this claim cannot be adequately satisfied unless we grant people rights rather than weaker forms of protection. Rights are powerful and demanding norms that should only be used to formulate moral claims when weaker norms are inadequate. Third, proponents must demonstrate that the proposed addressees, the parties that bear duties under the right, can legitimately be subjected to the negative and positive duties required for compliance with and implementation of the right. Finally, the proposed right must be feasible given current institutional and economic resources. RSE satisfies each of these four criteria.

A. Are Fundamental Interests Threatened?

The specific rights included in the historic bills of rights were chosen in response to perceived abuses by governments. Indeed, the texts of some bills of rights actually begin with a list of complaints against the previous government. The right to a fair trial, for example, is a response to the fact that governments have often used the legal system to disadvantage, imprison, and kill political opponents. This linkage between abuses and specific rights suggests that rights can be selected partially on the basis of the specific kinds of abuses occurring at a particular time and place. This general idea can be applied to environmental issues by asking which environmental abuses frequently lead to substantial human harm.

Technological development and population growth have both contributed to the creation of major environmental threats to human health and well-being. Imagine a town and surrounding region that have become the location of a large, dirty, toxic industry governed by no significant pollution controls. Imagine that air, water, and noise pollution are severe, that few measures are taken to insulate residents of the town from pollutants, and that these pollutants have significant toxicity.

The costs to the health and welfare of people in this town will be large. Rates of miscarriage and birth defects will be substantially higher than normal; children's growth and intelligence will be stunted. People will suffer from higher than normal rates of allergies, respiratory problems, skin diseases, cancer, and premature death. Contamination of foodstuffs and reduced plant growth will hinder food production. Fishing and animal husbandry production will decrease as animals suffer the same health problems as humans. Nearby areas of natural beauty will be destroyed and made useless for recreation. Cases of this sort are likely to have an equity dimension as well because the poorest members of the population will live closest to the pollution source and will have the least ability to escape its effects.

When environmental problems reach this level of severity—as they have in many parts of the world—the health and welfare of many people clearly are suffering substantial damage. Few human rights violations other than programs of mass extermination cause such widespread and large scale damage to the health and welfare of a community.

Consider next a milder case with less severe air and water pollution. Air pollution of the sort one finds in cities such as Sao Paulo, Mexico City, and Los Angeles causes substantial damage to people's health. This is not to say, of course, that every person living in these cities is injured, or suffers a shortened lifespan. Nevertheless, elevated rates of cancer seem to be present in cities such as Los Angeles, and greater than normal numbers of people in such cities suffer from asthma and allergies. Estimates of the consequences of air pollution on life and health in the Los Angeles basin have produced astoundingly high figures. A recent study suggested that attaining the national clean air standard for particulate matter in the Los Angeles Basin would prevent approximately 1600 premature deaths each year.[5] The risk of premature death due to elevated particulate matter levels is 1 in 10,000 per year greater than if the federal standard were reached, and is equivalent to half the annual risk of death in a car accident. This study also estimated the annual mortality and morbidity costs of exceeding the federal standards for ozone and particulate matter as nearly $10 billion. These significant health risks and costs, imposed on those who are not profiting from the generation of pollution, justify imposing RSE in order to help achieve a safer environment.

The justification of a human right not only needs to identify abuses, but also needs to show that these abuses frustrate fundamental human interests. As Maurice Cranston observed, a human right protects an interest or value that is of "paramount importance."[6] Thus, the critical question about severe pollution is whether it threatens interests of paramount importance. If the only effect of severe air pollution were a slight dullness in the color of some people's hair, the interest at stake—having glossy hair—would be too slight to provide the foundation for a human right. Obviously, however, the effects of severe pollution are not trivial. Severe air pollution kills some people, shortens the lives of others, and makes still others recurrently sick. These interests in life, health, and a minimal level of welfare are already protected by a number of human rights, such as rights against murder, torture, or physical injury. Severe pollution is a significant and frequent threat to the fundamental interests that human rights protect; the right to a safe environment aims to protect people against severe pollution and its consequences, and should therefore be accorded a position equal to other human rights that seek to prevent these consequences.

B. Does Environmental Safety Require Environmental Rights?

After a proposed right passes the test described above, there is clearly a claim to some sort of social action. However, the interests in question might be adequately protected by norms weaker than rights. For example, charitable assistance or structural changes might eliminate the threats. In order to justify a right such as the right to a fair trial, proponents must articulate why the danger of unfairness in criminal trials cannot be eliminated by general improvements in legal processes, by self-help on the part of the accused, or by charitable assistance from the community. Proponents must demonstrate that only high-priority, effectively enforced and administered legal rights to a fair trial can provide adequate protection. Analogously, RSE can only be justified as a human right if measures weaker than declaring a right to a safe environment will not provide adequate protection against pollution and contamination.

If large parts of the population could be drawn into a "deep" rather than "shallow" environmental movement, a major re-evaluation of industrial, consumer society might occur. A successful reevaluation might make it unnecessary to formulate and seek enactment of environmental rights. Giagnocavo and Goldstein argue against articulating environmental rights because such rights are "predicated on violence and separation" from the environment and "shatter" the appropriate relation to it. They advocate "developing an ecological consciousness" rather than perpetuating the status quo "in the guise of environmental rights and environmental 'legal' reform."[7]

Although this author strongly endorses the development of

widespread ecological consciousness, he doubts that this development—if it occurred would make environmental rights unnecessary. The hope that ecological consciousness can make environmental rights and law unnecessary is an example of the threat-elimination strategy. This suggests that if people had the right sort of ecological consciousness, they would not willingly pollute and contaminate the environment, and that if threats of pollution were eliminated or greatly reduced, there would be no need for environmental rights.

The human population, or even a significant part of it, will not soon develop a worldwide environmental consciousness. Even if a worldwide revolution in environmental attitudes did occur and people were reasonably well motivated to act on those new attitudes, many environmental problems would remain because of the need to use dangerous industrial and agricultural processes to support the large populations that now exist. The approach represented by Giagnocavo and Goldstein overemphasizes the importance of good motivation and underestimates the importance of population size and the extent of the world's dependence on hazardous technological processes.

Many people who have tried to live a more environmentally sound lifestyle have found that they cannot avoid engaging in activities that cause significant pollution. They need an automobile to get to work in a reasonable amount of time. They rely on advanced technologies that create numerous environmental risks. They are part of a large, concentrated human population that requires large amounts of water and energy and generates large amounts of sewage and wastes. Furthermore, powerful economic interests, including people's interests in having jobs for themselves and their children, often work against requiring polluters to reform their practices. Consequently, although policy-makers should support strategies to promote environmental threat-elimination or reduction, society will continue to benefit from RSE until such threat elimination strategies have been totally successful.

C. The Duties of Addressees

Effective rights protect or empower rightholders by imposing moral or legal burdens on other parties, the addressees. Proponents of RSE must show not only that the rightholders have a strong case for desiring some freedom, protection, or benefit, but also that the burden of providing this freedom, protection, or benefit can be legitimately imposed on the addressees.[8]

As noted above, individuals, organizations, and corporations have negative duties to refrain from activities that create substantial threats to a safe environment. Governments and international organizations may also have positive duties to promote and protect a safe environment. Those who engage in and profit from activities which damage the environment should bear the burden of regulations which demand restraint and compensation.

One interesting aspect of environmental risks and harms is that they often result from activities engaged in by many people, such as driving on Los Angeles freeways. These activities produce risks or harms as a result of the cumulative effect of individual decisions made by thousands or millions of people, but would not produce risks or harms if done by only a few people. Most human rights violations do not result from the combined actions of thousands or millions of persons, but violations of RSE sometimes take this form. Because putting a small amount of automobile exhaust into the air would be permissible if nobody else did so, and because no malice is involved, it may seem strange to regard driving a car as a human rights violation. Consider, however, that collective action may inadvertently bring on a variety of human deprivations (rights violations without a direct actor), including starvation and malnutrition. Moreover, not all violations of traditional human rights are intentional and malicious; for example, a person's right to a fair trial can be violated by a judge's negligence or incompetence rather than his malice.

In order to prevent the widespread violation of RSE, each individual must change his behavior. In regard to automobile pollution, each person has a duty not to deactivate pollution control devices on her car and to comply with collective measures to diminish pollution, such as abiding by no drive days and using alternative transportation systems. Beyond this, each citizen has a duty to promote and support measures to improve pollution controls on automobiles, to create effective schemes to diminish automobile use, and to limit her own driving, particularly during periods of high pollution.

D. Feasibility

Although RSE is supported by important moral considerations, RSE could fail to be a fully-justified human right if its costs were excessively burdensome. Costs play this powerful normative role in the justification of RSE and other rights for two reasons. First, there are limits to the moral and legal duties that we can legitimately impose on each other, and costs help us decide whether these limits are being exceeded. Second, given limited resources, the cost of complying with and implementing one right may make it impossible to comply with and implement other important rights. Rights are not magical sources of supply. Their normative power is insufficient to automatically call into being the human, institutional, and financial resources needed for implementation. The obligations flowing from rights will be without effect if addressees are genuinely unable to comply with them, or if they are unable to comply while meeting other obligations.

This is not to say that human rights stand or fall with their cost-benefit ratios. The underlying moral claim does not stand or fall with its affordability, but the policy choice of recognizing this claim as one that must be fully satisfied here and now does depend on whether doing so is affordable. To illustrate this test, consider once more the right to a fair trial. Trials, and particularly fair ones, are an expensive way to administer the criminal law. They require a standing system of courts, judges, prosecutors, defense attorneys, and other legal officials. Nevertheless, the costs of creating, using, and maintaining this system are not so high as to make it unfeasible for countries to comply with this right. Countries around the globe at varying levels of economic development manage to run criminal justice systems that mostly comply with the right to a fair trial. Consider another example. One important, if not conclusive, objection to a right to medical care is that meeting all legitimate medical needs with an adequate quality of care is unaffordable, even for rich countries. Medical needs, this objection alleges, are a bottomless pit. The question therefore arises of whether RSE more closely resembles the attainable right to a fair trial or an unqualified right to the satisfaction of medical needs.

Effectively regulating pollution and contamination, like meeting all medical needs, may seem like a bottomless pit. Regulation requires standard setting, promulgation, and enforcement. These activities require expensive, highly educated personnel, such as scientists and lawyers. Pollution control often requires complicated technological systems and elaborate disposal processes. Nevertheless, numerous countries already have extensive experience with implementing constitutional or legislatively enacted RSEs; thus far, these programs have not proven so costly as to undermine economies or bankrupt governments because the standards they are designed to enforce were chosen with an eye toward costs. As these experiences suggest, one reason for setting the standard of protection prescribed by RSE at an adequate rather than optimal level is to keep pollution control affordable. Furthermore, the resources saved by preventing losses to health, life, property, and agricultural production can help finance RSE.

Some third world countries may find it difficult to marshal the human, institutional, and financial resources needed to create a meaningful system of environmental protection. However, three factors lessen the burden which RSE imposes on less-developed countries. First, poor countries have considerable discretion to give less demanding definitions to the notion of an adequate level of environmental safety through their own legislative and judicial processes. Less demanding definitions of adequacy will make RSE less expensive to implement. This discretion is not unique to RSE; most human rights contain vague key phrases that give countries discretion to interpret the right in ways that make it less costly to enforce. Discretion therefore provides a way of indexing the cost of human rights to a country's level of development. Scrutiny by international organizations makes this discretion less dangerous. Second, the amount of technology and industry in a society and the size of its pollution problems are roughly proportional. The countries with the greatest potential for pollution and contamination are also the most highly industrialized, and hence are better able to pay the costs of regulation and control. Brazil, for example, is generally much more polluted than Bolivia, but it also has an immensely greater ability to pay for pollution control. Finally, rich countries have a responsibility to assist poor countries in controlling serious pollution problems through measures such as technology transfer, technical assistance, loans, and grants.

IV. CONCLUSION

A strong case exists for RSE. When defined narrowly, it has an intelligible scope. If a right with this scope were effectively implemented at the international and national levels, it would protect human beings against substantial and recurrent threats. Weaker forms of promoting pollution control are inadequate. Therefore, a strong, enforceable right is needed. RSE has identifiable addressees who can legitimately bear the normative burdens associated with this right. Finally, RSE is feasible to implement in most parts of the world. The costs of effectively regulating pollution are substantial, and many countries will face difficulties in marshaling the resources needed for this task. In this respect, however, RSE is no different from other human rights.

Notes

1. The right to a safe environment has not been subjected to extended philosophical examination and debate in the way that economic and social rights have. W. Paul Gormley provided an early case for environmental rights in *Human Rights and the Environment* (1976). More recently, Joseph L. Sax offered a cogent defense of RSE in "The Search for Environmental Rights," 6 *Land Use & Envtl. L.* 93 (1990). Melissa Thorme surveyed a variety of possible grounds for environmental rights in "Establishing Environment as a Human Right," 19 *Denv. J. Int'l L. & Pol'y* 301 (1991). Edith Brown Weiss briefly reviewed views on RSE in *In Fairness to Future Generations* 114 (1989). I know of no systematic criticism of RSE as a human right, although Philip Alston cautions against creating new rights in "Conjuring up New Human Rights: A Proposal for Quality Control," 78 *Am. J. Int'l L.* 607 (1984).

2. For non-anthropocentric approaches to environmental ethics, see, e.g., J.

Baird Callicott, *In Defense of the Land Ethics: Essays in Environmental Philosophy* (1989); Holmes Rolston, III, *Philosophy Gone Wild* (1986); Christopher D. Stone, *Earth and Other Ethics: The Case for Moral Pluralism* (1987); and Paul W. Taylor, *Respect for Nature* (1986).

3. This is not meant to suggest that traditional human rights have no relevance to environmental concerns. They obviously do. Rights to life and property clearly protect people against some kinds of environmental abuses. Rights of political participation empower people who would take political action on behalf of the environment. Rights against murder, torture, and arbitrary arrest protect environmental activists.

4. Thorme, *supra* note 1, at 310.

5. Jane V. Hall, et al., "Valuing the Health Benefits of Clean Air," 255 *Science* 812, 812 (1992); see also Robert Read and Cathy Read, "Breathing Can Be Hazardous to Your Health," *New Scientist*, Feb. 1991, at 34.

6. Maurice Cranston, *What Are Human Rights?* 67 (1973). For example, justification of the right against torture emphasizes that torture imposes severe pain and suffering, threatens physical and mental health, and is an extreme form of coercion.

7. Cynthia Giagnocavo and Howard Goldstein, "Law Reform or World Reform: The Problem of Environmental Rights," 35 *McGill L.J.* 345, 373-74 (1990).

8. For a fuller discussion of the topics in this section and the next, see James W. Nickel, "How Human Rights Generate Duties to Protect and Provide," 15 *Hum. Rts. Q.* 77 (1993).

Questions for Reflection

1. Nickel describes a new willingness to link human rights and environmental concerns. How would you account for past (and continued) resistance to this linkage? Are the barriers theoretical, political, or economic? How do you interpret the significance of the growing willingness to make this linkage?

2. Nickel claims that the right to a safe environment must satisfy four criteria if it is to qualify as a legitimate human right. What are those four criteria, and how does Nickel explain that they are satisfied with respect to the right to a safe environment?

3. Many human rights theorists and activists now consider the right to a safe environment to be the "paramount" human right. Do you agree that this is so? Why or why not?

47. EDITH BROWN WEISS

Edith Brown Weiss (1942-) is Francis Cabell Brown Professor of International Law at the Georgetown University Law Center. A specialist in international and environmental law, Weiss has been active in these areas in both academia and government. Her many publications include *In Fairness to Future Generations: International Law, Common Patrimony, and the Intergenerational Equity* (1989) and *International Environmental Law and Policy* (1998). Advancing Nickel's argument the there exists a right to a safe environment, Weiss proposes that we think of such a right not in terms of individual rights but in terms of collective rights, that is, as a right that belongs to entire groups of people. In her analysis, Weiss notes that the condition of the global environment affects the collective security of all. Therefore, the right to a safe environment is properly understood as a "planetary" right, which creates obligations on the part of citizens and governments alike to leave a healthful environment for future generations. Only by doing so will we provide the necessary conditions for enjoying the rest of the rights that humans possess.

Text—Planetary Rights

Principles of equity between generations lead to a set of planetary, or intergenerational, rights and obligations, with associated international duties of use. These planetary rights are the obverse of planetary obligations. They are the rights which each generation has to receive the planet in no worse condition than that of the previous generation, to inherit comparable diversity in the natural and cultural resource bases, and to have equitable access to the use and benefits of the legacy.

NATURE OF PLANETARY RIGHTS

Planetary rights are derived from the temporal relationship among generations in using the natural environment and cultural resources. They are intergenerational rights. They may be regarded as group rights in the sense that generations hold these rights as groups in relation to other generations—past, present, and future. They exist regardless of the number and identity of the individuals making up each generation. As the threats to the integrity of our planet and our natural and cultural resources have become increasingly severe and long-term, it has become necessary to look at the human species as part of an ongoing global system and to look at the rights which generations have in relation to each other for the use of this planet.

Now it may be asked how future generations can have rights. According to this argument, rights can only exist when there are identifiable interests, which in turn can only happen if we can identify the individuals who have interests to protect. Since we cannot know whom the individuals in future generations will be nor how many of them there will be, it is not possible for future generations to have rights.

The planetary rights proposed here for future generations are not rights possessed by individuals. Rather they are generational rights, which can only be usefully conceived at a group level. They involve rights to planetary conditions of diversity and quality comparable to those enjoyed by previous generations, which can be evaluated by objective criteria and indices applied to the planet from one generation to the next. Thus, the question of whether the interests protected by planetary rights are in fact being protected for future generations does not depend on knowing the number or kinds of individuals that may ultimately exist in any given future generation.

Enforcement of planetary rights is appropriately done by a guardian or representative of future generations as a *group*, not of future *individuals*, who are of necessity indeterminate. The fact that the holder of the right lacks the standing to bring grievances forward and hence must depend upon the decision of the representative to do so does not affect the existence of the right or the obligation associated with it.

Now it may be asked, if future generations have rights, how far into the future do these rights extend? Do they apply only to immediately successive generations or to all generations? Planetary rights of necessity inhere to all generations. There is no theoretical basis for limiting such rights to immediately successive generations; indeed to do so would in some cases offer little or no protection to more distant future generations. Nuclear and hazardous waste disposal, the loss of biological diversity, and ozone depletion, for example, have significant effects on the natural heritage of the more distant generations.

Members of the present generation also possess planetary rights, which are rights derived from membership in the present generation to enjoy the natural resources of earth and our cultural heritage. They derive from intergenerational rights but are enforced on an intragenerational basis. These rights are associated with corresponding duties, which members of the present generation have toward other members of the same generation. At this stage, they could be viewed as individual rights in the sense that there are identifiable interests of individuals that the rights protect. However, the remedies for violations of these rights will often benefit the rest of the generation, not only the individual, and in this sense they may be said to retain their character as group rights.

Planetary rights focus on rights to common patrimony, which each generation may use and develop but must pass on in at least comparable condition to future generations. The common patrimony includes the natural environment and our natural and cultural resources. It is perhaps useful to distinguish different elements of this common patrimony in analyzing planetary rights. Some common patrimony elements of the natural environment are appropriately viewed as a public good in the economist's term in the sense that it is not possible to exclude people from them. These include the air or atmosphere, the ozone layer, and indeed the functioning of the geosphere-biosphere system. Other aspects of the natural environment could be enjoyed by individuals separately, such as forests, but the element that makes them common patrimony, namely the ecosystem of which they are a part, cannot effectively be enjoyed by individuals separately. It is too intricately linked with forces that no individual can control. In this sense they are at least impressed with elements of a common good. Cultural resources, by contrast, are collective goods in the sense that they are jointly produced by members of the culture and can only be enjoyed in relation to other members of the collectivity.

Thus, rights to the natural patrimony are generational rights that may be viewed as group rights in the intergenerational context and as having elements of individual rights when they exist intragenerationally in the present generation. Rights to cultural patrimony may be group or community rights both in the intergenerational and intragenerational setting, since they normally depend on others for their enjoyment.

Some theorists of rights...have argued that public goods cannot be made the subject of individual rights.[1] Primarily this is because rights "concern the enjoyment of goods by individuals separately, not simply as members of a collectivity enjoying a diffuse common benefit in whom all participate in indistinguishable and unassignable shares."[2] But in individual rights you also cannot exclude others from enjoying the protection of the right, because once protection is upheld for one holder of the right, the benefits accrue to all. When a case is before a human rights court, for example, the judgment goes to the individual, but it affects the way many other people in similar circumstances are treated. In this sense it is like a right to a public good, where protection of the right, for example, to uncontaminated air benefits not only the individual but all.

These arguments assume that rights can only be individual rights. They may have important implications for the contemporary claim in human rights law of a right to environment, to the extent that advocates claim the right as an individual right. But they are less cogent for planetary rights, which are intergenerational and exist for each generation as a group. Intergenerational rights are rights to diversity and quality of the planet, the satisfaction of which can be judged by objective, independent criteria. Of necessity these rights involve common patrimony, such as air, which cannot be parceled out to individuals, but they are defined interests of each generation which must be protected.

In the theory of intergenerational equity presented here, planetary rights and planetary obligations exist together. A right is an interest that is juridically protected. It is always associated with a duty or obligation. If a person has a right, he or she has an interest that is sufficient ground for holding another subject to a duty.

There is substantial philosophical disagreement as to whether duties must derive from rights, which implies that rights are prior to duties, whether rights derive from duties, or whether they are logically equivalent.... If one party's right logically entails another party having an obligation, then it is arguably confusing to treat the right as a reason for the obligation. Planetary rights entail planetary obligations and vice versa.

While rights always entail obligations, the converse is not always true. Theoretically,...an obligation need not always entail a right. For example, a moral obligation of charity does not give those who benefit a right to such charity. Positivists such as Kelsen hesitate in finding a legal right connected to certain legal obligations.

> If the obligated behavior of one individual does not refer to a specifically designated other individual...but refers only to the legal community as such, then...one is satisfied...to assume a legal obligation without a corresponding reflex right: for example in case of the legal norms that prescribe a certain human behavior toward some animals, plants, or inanimate objects by pain of punishment. It is forbidden to kill certain animals at certain times (or altogether), to pick certain flowers, to cut certain trees or to destroy certain historical monuments. These are obligations which—indirectly—exist toward the legal community interested in these objects.[3]

For Austin, these obligations are viewed as absolute duties, which exist independently of any correlative right. Austin defines absolute duties as those which prescribe actions toward parties other than the one obliged, who are not determinate persons, such as members generally of an independent society and mankind at large.[4]

The question is whether it is necessary to have planetary, or intergenerational, rights, or whether planetary obligations could alone suffice. If we were to follow Kelsen and Austin, we would contend that the obligations of the present generation to future generations constituted obligations or duties for which there were no correlative rights, because there are not determinate persons to whom the right attaches. Similarly, in the intragenerational context, obligations to conserve diversity, quality, and access would be viewed as absolute duties for which there is no correlative right.

While this approach may be attractive to some, it ignores the fundamental temporal relationship which each generation has to all other generations and which gives rise to the rights of each generation to share equitably in the use of the planet and its natural and cultural resources. Planetary rights represent valued interests of present and future generations, which must be protected to achieve intergenerational equity. They focus discussion on the welfare of generations, what each generation is able to have and to enjoy, in a way that obligations do not. They carry much greater moral force than do obligations and encourage parties to protest when they are not being respected.

If we have planetary rights, it is inevitable that they will at times conflict with other rights. Justice Holmes of the United States Supreme Court once commented that every legal right tends to become absolute over time.[5] Indeed this tendency to become absolute is part of what differentiates rights from other claims. No one right is more a right than another. Theorists of human rights object to the nomenclature of first, second, and third generations of human rights on the ground that such classification implies that one fundamental human right may substantially annihilate another right or whole groups of rights.

If rights were absolute, however, there would be no means for resolving disputes in which the rights of opposing parties conflicted, or in which one party's rights contravened public policy. Thus, all rights may be only *prima facie* in that they may be overridden either by other rights in cases of conflict or by policy considerations. Moreover, the designation of the protection of an interest as a right depends on the economic and social structure of the society, which means that rights may vary from one country to another.

The more rights that exist, the more likely it is that conflicts between them will arise. This means that as planetary rights are recognized, we need to establish criteria for resolving conflicts between them and other existing rights. Since planetary rights are intertemporal and fundamental to the continued well-being of the human species and of our planet, one can argue that they should have priority in those instances where they conflict with other rights. But the relative degree of infringement of the competing rights may be important in defining the protection to be given them.

If we have planetary obligations and planetary rights, what is their status? Are we still in the stage where these are only moral values, or can we speak of them as legal obligations and rights?

The status of legal rights is firmly institutionalized and recognized, but there is disagreement between the civil and common law traditions as to whether moral rights can exist. The English philosopher Bentham referred to the notion of moral rights as "nonsense on stilts," but most commentators in the common law system, though not the civil law system, recognize moral rights. They arise only if they are inalienable or if people are strongly motivated to protect an interest. Since they are not institutionalized, they are much more difficult to define and characterize. Brandt has commented, "We speak of a moral right when it is not thought that there should be a legal right, for instance when we speak of the moral right of a child to equal treatment in a family."[6] Moral pressure can encourage protection of such an interest. In the common law system, moral rights can be protected by legal means, as well as moral pressure, but there is disagreement as to whether the use of legal means to protect a moral right can transform it into a legal right.

At the present time, our concern for future generations can be considered as a moral protection of interests. The concern reflects a value that society—of necessity, the international community—wants to protect. But recognition of a moral obligation does not in itself create legal obligations and rights. Rather it is a stage in the evolution of the public conscience. When this evolution has achieved a certain degree of maturity—the definition of which is impossible *in abstracto*—legal obligations and rights are formulated. This is the first condition for the legal protection by society.

In international law, we must regard planetary obligations and planetary rights as in the formative stage. Concern for future generations exists, although there is limited awareness of the issues. The first step is for society to formulate planetary obligations and planetary rights, as by a solemn declaration of principles. Such declarations have been frequent since 1945 for other principles, and have assumed the crucial role of formulating social values. These declarations constitute only "soft law" instruments, which are not mandatory and may not be applied. But we can speak of prelegal rules or emerging principles which can either prepare "hard law" rules (conclusion of treaties) or contribute to the creation of rules of customary international law.

CONTENT OF PLANETARY RIGHTS

Planetary rights extend to both natural and cultural resources. In the natural system, they include the condition of the biosphere and those resources essential to the continued health of our planet and to the sustainability of our ecosystem. For cultural resources, they cover those resources that contribute significantly to the health and well-being of the human species and of the planet.

The specific content of the planetary rights is logically linked to the obligations that the present generation owes to future generations and the obligations that members of the present generation owe to other members as beneficiaries of the planetary legacy. Each generation has the responsibility to set the criteria for defining the actions that infringe on these rights. Appropriate criteria would be whether the actions have an important impact either over a large area or over an extended period of time, whether the effects are irreversible or reversible only with unacceptable costs, and whether they are viewed as significant by a substantial number of people.

To give specificity to planetary rights, we can tentatively identify categories of actions that are likely to be viewed as infringing on the basic right to live on a planet with as good environmental quality and natural and cultural resource diversity as previous generations had and the right to have equitable access to the benefits and use of these resources. These actions include the following:

- wastes that cannot with acceptable confidence be contained in impact either spatially or over time;
- damage to soils so extensive as to render them incapable of supporting plant or animal life;
- destruction of tropical forests sufficient to affect significantly the overall diversity of species in the region;
- pollution of air or transformation of land sufficient to induce significant and widespread climate change;
- destruction of knowledge essential to understanding social and natural systems, such as residence and decay times of nuclear wastes;
- destruction of cultural monuments acknowledged by countries to be part of the common heritage of mankind;
- destruction of specific endowments established by the present generation for the benefit of future generations, such as gene banks and libraries of international importance.

Some international agreements already impose duties on countries to guard against such actions. They include the London Ocean Dumping Convention, which controls dumping of nuclear and other hazardous wastes; the Treaty on Antarctica, which prohibits the disposal of nuclear wastes in Antarctica; the World Soil Charter, which protects the quality of soils; the draft IUCN Convention on preservation of wild genetic resources; to the Vienna Convention on the Ozone Layer together with the Montreal Protocol controlling chlorofluorocarbon emissions; and the World Heritage Convention, which protects designated international natural and cultural heritages.

As an initial step in formulating planetary rights, we need to consider drafting a Declaration of Planetary Obligations and Rights. As indicated previously, this would be a first step in formulating "soft law" and could lead to the conclusion of formal agreements or eventual transformation into customary international law. It would be an important symbol for the planetary citizenship which we all share.[7]

The Declaration must reaffirm several general assertions: that we have responsibilities to future generations and therefore must conserve the planet for them, that we are also entitled to enjoy the fruits of our planetary heritage in a manner consistent with this responsibility, that we face many threats to the integrity of our natural and cultural resources, and that only by working together can we alleviate the poverty of some communities in the present generation and conserve the planet and our cultural resources for future generations. It should set forth guiding principles for achieving justice between generations and detail the planetary rights and obligations. The World Charter for Nature, the Stockholm Declaration on the Human Environment, and the World Conservation Strategy contain points which could be useful in this endeavor.

A Declaration of Planetary Obligations and Rights would build upon the concern for future generations and the human environment which is already implicitly reflected in many of the human rights covenants and declarations. These refer to common heritage, to cultural heritage, to education and training, to social and medical assistance, to rights in old age, and to rights of children to protection.[8] The African Charter on Human and Peoples' Rights, for example, provides in Article 22 that "All peoples shall have the right to their economic, social and cultural development with due regard to their freedom and identity and in the equal enjoyment of the common heritage of mankind." The provisions in other human rights agreements which refer to rights of children, to rights of elderly, to education and training, and similar rights are inherently temporally oriented and concerned with future conditions of life.

A Declaration of Planetary Rights and Obligations concerned

with natural and cultural patrimony would be consistent with many of the provisions found in national constitutions. The constitutions of Yugoslavia, Guyana, Iran, Papua New Guinea, and Vanuatu explicitly impose duties to conserve the environment for future generations, as do the constitutions of Hawaii, Illinois, and Montana in the United States. Japan confers on its citizens the right to wholesome and cultured living and explicitly indicates that the fundamental human rights guaranteed by the Constitution are conferred on present and future generations in trust.

While relatively few constitutions explicitly address future generations, many contain provisions imposing duties on state authorities and on citizens to conserve the natural environment.... Some...constitutions...also impose a duty on the country's citizens to conserve the natural environment. These include Albania, Bulgaria, Ethiopia, German Democratic Republic, Guyana, Haiti, Honduras, Hungary, India, Republic of Korea, Panama, Peru, Poland, Portugal, Spain, Sri Lanka, Vanuatu, and Yugoslavia. India's provision is a particularly useful precedent. Part IV A, Art. 51A provides that it shall be the duty of every citizen of India "...to protect and improve the natural environment including forests, lakes, rivers and wild life, and to have compassion for living creatures."

Several of the constitutions combine rights to use the environment with duties to conserve it.... The new constitution of Brazil provides that everyone has a right to the ecological balance of the environment essential to the quality of life and that the public authorities and the community have a duty to preserve and defend it. These are especially useful precedents, since planetary rights and obligations link duties with rights.

At the same time that national constitutions call for conservation of natural resources, they contain multiple provisions aimed at enhancing the economic development of the country and its citizens.... This link is useful as support for the planetary principle of conserving access to the natural and cultural resources. There is also support in many of the constitutions for the conservation of cultural resources and for the rights of access and use.... These may include archaeological sites, art objects, monuments, buildings, and other objects of cultural or historical value....

ENFORCEMENT OF PLANETARY RIGHTS

Once planetary rights have been formulated and this formulation accepted by countries, they can be implemented. Enforcement undoubtedly raises the most difficult issues. Theoretically, the state has the primary duty to implement planetary rights and to enforce them. It serves both as a guarantor for the present generation's access to the planetary legacy and as a guardian *ad litem* for future generations. Since the interests of future generations may sometimes conflict with those of some members of the present generation, it is important to designate a representative of future generations, or a guardian *ad litem*. This could take the form of an ombudsman for future generations.... States will need to report on how they are implementing and enforcing planetary rights.

Communities and even individuals theoretically also have a duty to enforce planetary rights and obligations in their capacities as trustees and beneficiaries of the legacy. Nongovernmental organizations can serve an important role in enforcing planetary rights, much as they now do in the human rights field.

If a violation of planetary rights occurs, States, as continuing entities, should have standing to raise claims on behalf of both present and future generations. This is elaborated on in the chapter on implementation. States can enforce planetary rights and obligations directly to the extent that they are parties to agreements which set them forth or to the extent that the rights and obligations represent customary international law. They should be able to raise claims for planetary rights violations whether or not their own nationals have been directly affected yet.

Experience with enforcing international human rights law is relevant. Since the obligations of the customary law of human rights are generally regarded now as obligations *erga omnes*, any State may enforce them, whether or not their nationals were involved in the violation. The *Restatement (Third) of the Foreign*

Relations Law of the United States expressly notes that in these cases any State may make a claim against the State violating the norm. Support for this can be found in the *Barcelona Traction* case (second phase), in which the International Court of Justice distinguished between obligations of States toward the international community as a whole, obligations *erga omnes*, and obligations arising from diplomatic protection.[9] According to the Court, the former includes such obligations as those deriving from the prohibition of genocide, and "the principles and rules concerning the basic rights of the human person, including protection from slavery and racial discrimination," in the protection of which all States have a legal interest. While the Court, nevertheless, denied standing to Ethiopia and Liberia to complain about apartheid practices in the 1966 *South West Africa* cases, many believe that, today, States have the right to make claims for violation of basic human rights without regard to the nationality of the victim. There is also support for this in practices under existing agreements. Under Article 26 of the International Labour Organization constitution, for example, states may lodge a complaint for a violation against any other state party, whether or not the state or any of its nationals has suffered any direct injury. States have done so in at least five cases.

State enforcement can take place through international tribunals, regional tribunals, or, in appropriate circumstances, national judicial or administrative proceedings. Under certain conditions, foreign nationals may be able to obtain redress in another country's courts for violations of human rights by former foreign officials, if there is personal jurisdiction. The *Filártiga v. Peña-Irala* case in the United States courts, which involved torture in Paraguay in violation of "the law of nations," illustrates this.[10]

It would be appropriate to develop mechanisms to enforce planetary rights at the regional or international level, in patterns reflective of regional enforcement of international human rights law. Both the European Convention for the Protection of Human Rights and Fundamental Freedoms and the American Convention on Human Rights permit States to bring petitions against governments before regional human rights commissions for violations of human rights. Possible approaches include establishment of a Planetary Rights Commission analogous to a Human Rights Commission or of a nongovernmental organization such as Amnesty International. Planetary Rights Commissions, if modeled after Human Rights Commissions, might be established at the regional level, in those areas suited to regional institutions. The jurisdiction of any organization established must extend both to public bodies and to private multinational entities.

Members of the present generation theoretically would also be entitled to enforce planetary rights against other individuals, corporations, and governments. This reflects the ancient Roman concept of *actio popularis*, which allowed any member of the public to bring an action to vindicate legal rights in the public interest. At a minimum this would impose a duty on individuals or communities to report grievances to designated bodies. But it could also support a right in case of violations of planetary rights to bring proceedings before the relevant bodies.[11]

In a world based on nation-states, the right of individuals to make claims will not be universally acceptable. Examples exist at local levels, however, of individuals having the capacity to file claims against local governments, individuals, or corporations for having violated the public interest in the conservation of the environment. The World Charter for Nature anticipates the possibility of individual enforcement in Article 23, which provides that "all persons, in accordance with national legislation...shall have access to means of redress when their environment has suffered damage or degradation."

Moreover, there are many important examples in international human rights of individuals having the authority to enforce these rights. The European Convention for the Protection of Human Rights and Fundamental Freedoms, the American Convention on Human Rights, the Constitution of the International Labour Organization, and the resolution governing the United Nations Sub-Commission on the Prevention of Discrimination and Protection of Minorities, for example, permit individuals to bring petitions against human rights violations. These provisions have been frequently used.

A difficult issue arises when States fail to perform their duty to enforce planetary rights, either against other States or against entities within their own borders. In some domestic legal systems citizens have the right to sue their government to force it to perform the duties set forth in specific statutes, such as for the control of air or water pollution. While this approach to enforcement is important, it is not universally shared among countries and will be adopted only to the extent that it is consistent with national legislation.

One of the most effective ways to enforce planetary rights may be to create one or more Planetary Rights Commissioners who could receive complaints from individuals and nongovernmental bodies and investigate them. These Commissioners could be established at an international level, or as a component of regional institutions with jurisdiction over planetary rights and obligations. Alternatively, they could serve as an international nongovernmental organization dedicated to enforcing these rights and obligations. In the international human rights field, the many nongovernmental organizations, such as Amnesty International, have played a critical role in receiving complaints, investigating them, and trying to curb abuses.

An important component in enforcing planetary rights must be education. Nongovernmental organizations and individuals, as well as governments, have important roles in informing people about their planetary rights to natural and cultural patrimony and their duty to conserve it for future generations. The education must take place at the local as well as national level, and must involve all age groups, particularly the young. Only by raising public consciousness can we protect the rights of both present and future generations to our planet and its resources.

RELATIONSHIP TO INTERNATIONAL HUMAN RIGHTS LAW

Planetary rights and obligations represent an intertemporal doctrine which derives from relationships between generations. As such they extend traditional human rights, which focus primarily on relationships today. Planetary rights are held collectively, by each generation, in contrast to traditional human rights, which focus primarily on relationships between the individual and the State. For example, rights to be free of torture, genocide, and racial discrimination are rights that the individual has in relation to the government. The government has a duty to the individual not to torture, commit genocide, discriminate on racial grounds, and so forth. But while planetary rights are intertemporal and collectively held, they share the focus of traditional human rights: the welfare and dignity of human beings.

The temporal dimension of planetary rights may offer a theoretical basis for those human rights that we now consider to be group rights or social rights, and for the so-called new human rights, such as the right to development. There has been no unifying concept to link these rights together or to explain the basis for the rights. Theoretically, rights to development, to health, to food, to cultural integrity, and to a decent environment could be viewed as temporal or intergenerational rights of access of each generation to use and benefit from our natural and cultural heritage. By introducing the element of time, we may be able to provide a unifying basis for them. Moreover, those rights which are now defined by given groups or communities, such as cultural rights or economic rights, have a temporal dimension since the community inherently extends over time. As such they involve rights of access by generations.

There is considerable discussion in contemporary human rights literature about whether a right to a decent human environment exists. If it does, it would cover some of the concerns addressed by planetary rights.

Some scholars have urged that human rights doctrine includes the right to a clean, healthy, and decent environment. A few have contended that the right to environment is already part of customary international law, because it can be derived from the United Nations Charter, UN declarations, and covenants. The World Commission on Environment and Development proposed that, as a fundamental legal principle, "All human beings have the fundamental right to an environment adequate for their health and well-being."[12] The African Charter on Human and Peoples' Rights is the only covenant to refer to such a right, which it links to development. Article 24 of the African Charter provides "All peoples shall have the right to a general satisfactory environment favorable to their development."

A human right to a decent environment has evoked controversy. A primary reason is the perceived tension between economic development and environmental protection. While this conflict was prominent at the UN Conference on the Human Environment in 1972, it has much less force today. Increasingly, all countries have come to realize that sound economic development requires development on the basis of sustainable use of the planet.

Controversy also arises over the potential convergence of protecting the environment and protecting minority rights. For example, clear-cutting forests and/or converting them to other uses can cause environmental degradation and destroy tribal peoples and their habitats. A right to a decent environment, if enforced, could at the same time protect these ethnic groups. Governments could view this as interfering with matters that are considered to be internal affairs.

If there is to be a human right to a decent environment, there is disagreement over how to treat it: as encompassed within fundamental human rights, within a basic human needs doctrine, or within a third generation of human rights (for those accepting the position that generations of rights can exist).

The fundamental rights approach strives to identify a core group of universal rights that reflect the value of competing ideologies. Recent compilations of fundamental rights by a number of scholars either implicitly or explicitly mention the right to a decent environment.

The right to a decent environment is sometimes treated as a basic human need. This approach demands positive State action to guarantee the minimum requirements for human existence. Several covenants reflect this approach....

Finally, the right to a decent environment has been put forward by some as a so-called third-generation right. These rights belong neither to the individualistic tradition of first-generation rights (civil and political) nor to the tradition of the second-generation (economic and social). They are collective rights which are intended to acknowledge a continuing evolution of human rights doctrine. The existence of generations of rights, however, is strongly contested.[26] The reasons range from a concern that they will trivialize human rights doctrine or imply that the concerns of earlier human rights are passé, to fears that they would serve as convenient ruses for leaders who may pay only lip service to existing rights. It is unlikely that the striking disagreements over how to treat a right to a decent environment in human rights doctrine will be resolved quickly.

Planetary rights offer a resolution of the controversy. They represent minimum interests, shared by all generations, which include many aspects of what people have tried to define as rights to a decent environment or the related right to health. While planetary rights are intergenerational rights, they apply also in the intragenerational context. In this context, much of what is loosely included in a right to environment could be considered as the intragenerational manifestation of planetary rights. These planetary rights have their own doctrinal base in the temporal relationship between generations. It complements existing human rights doctrine and may extend it. Planetary rights and obligations are part of our planetary citizenship.

Notes

1. Neil MacCormick, *Legal Right and Social Democracy: Essays in Legal and Political Philosophy* (Oxford: Oxford University Press, 1982), 143; MacCormick, "Rights in Legislation," in *Law, Morality and Society: Essays in Honour of H. L. A. Hart*, P. M. S. Hacker and Joseph Raz, eds. (Oxford: Clarendon Press, 1977), 204-06; Joseph Raz, *The Morality of Freedom* (Oxford: Clarendon Press, 1986), 198-202.

2. MacCormick, "Rights in Legislation," 284.

3. Hans Kelsen, *Pure Theory of Law*, trans. Max Knight (Berkeley: University of California Press, 1967), 62.

4. John Austin, *Austin's Jurisprudence, Lectures on Jurisprudence* (London: J. Murray, 1873), 413-15.

5. *Hudson County Water Co. v. McCarter*, 209 US 3249, 355 (1908). Cited in Lon L. Fuller, *The Morality of Law* (New Haven, CT: Yale University Press, 1964), 29.

6. Richard Brandt, "The Concept of a Moral Right and Its Function," *Journal of Philosophy* 80 (1983): 29.

7. The World Commission on Environment and Development has proposed a universal declaration, to be followed by a Convention, on environmental protection and sustainable development. The World Commission on Environment and Development, *Our Common Future* (Oxford and New York: Oxford University Press, 1987), 332-33. This could be linked with the proposed Declaration on Planetary Rights and Obligations.

8. See, e.g., African Charter on Human and Peoples' Rights, which provides that "all peoples shall have the right to their economic, social and cultural development with due regard to their freedom and identity and in the equal enjoyment of the common heritage of mankind"; and the American Convention on Human Rights, Art. 19 (Rights of the Child), Nov. 22, 1969, O.A.S.T.S. No 36, O.A.S. Off. Rec. OEA/Ser. L/V/II.23, Doc. 21, Rev. 2., which provides that "every minor child has the right to the measures of protection required by his condition as a minor on the part of his family, society and the state."

9. *Barcelona Traction, Light and Power Company, Limited* (New Application 1962) (*Belgium v. Spain*, Second Phase) 1970 I.C.J. 4.

10. *Filártiga v. Peña-Irala*, 630 F.2d 876 (2d Cir., 1980).

11. Individuals and groups now have the right to lodge petitions for human rights violations before certain human rights commissions. For example, the American Convention on Human Rights, Art. 44, Nov. 22. 1969, gives standing to individuals and organizations to bring violations of rights under the treaty to the Inter-American Commission on Human Rights, even if they were not directly affected by the violation.

23. World Charter for Nature adopted by the United Nations General Assembly, Nov. 9, 1982. G.A. Res. 37/7, 37 UN GAOR Supp. (No. 51), 17, UN Doc. A/37/51 (1982).

12. World Commission on Environment and Development, *Our Common Future*, 348.

QUESTIONS FOR REFLECTION

1. Why does Weiss make the claim that planetary rights are collective or group rights rather than individual rights? Why are planetary rights also called intergenerational rights?

2. What theoretical, ethical, and legal justifications are made

by Weiss in support of the claim to a clean, healthy environment? Do you agree or not that planetary rights are justifiable human rights? Do you think that planetary rights are enforceable?

3. In what ways might the right to a clean, healthy environment conflict with the right to economic development? With state sovereignty? What kinds of changes do you think must be made to the international system if it is to accommodate both traditional human rights and the right to a clean environment?

FURTHER READINGS FOR SECTION 11

Aiken, William. "Human Rights in an Ecological Era." *Environmental Values* 1 (1992): 191-203.

Cooper, David E. and Joy A. Palmer, eds. *Just Environments: Intergenerational, International, and Interspecies Issues*. London and New York: Routledge, 1995.

Goodin, Robert E. "International Ethics and the Environmental Crisis." In *Ethics & International Affairs: A Reader*, Joel H. Rosenthal, ed. Washington, DC: Georgetown University Press, 1999.

Human Rights Watch and Natural Resources Defense Council. *Defending the Earth: Abuses of Human Rights and the Environment*. Washington, DC: Human Rights Watch and Natural Resources Defense Council, 1992.

Merrills, J.G. "Environmental Protection and Human Rights: Conceptual Aspects." In *Human Rights Approaches to Environmental Protection*, Alan E. Boyle and Michael R. Anderson, eds. Oxford: Clarendon Press, 1996.

Nickel, James W. and Eduardo Viola. "Integrating Environmentalism and Human Rights." *Environmental Ethics* 16 (1994): 265-73.

Shelton, Dinah. "Human Rights, Environmental Rights and the Right to the Environment." *Stanford Journal of International Law* 28 (1992): 103-38.

Thorme, Melissa. "Establishing Environment as a Human Right." *Denver Journal of International Law and Policy* 19 (1991): 301-31.

Section 12:

DOCUMENTS FOR PART TWO

48. VIENNA DECLARATION AND PROGRAMME OF ACTION (1993)

The World Conference on Human Rights,

Considering that the promotion and protection of human rights is a matter of priority for the international community, and that the Conference affords a unique opportunity to carry out a comprehensive analysis of the international human rights system and of the machinery for the protection of human rights, in order to enhance and thus promote a fuller observance of those rights, in a just and balanced manner,

Recognizing and affirming that all human rights derive from the dignity and worth inherent in the human person, and that the human person is the central subject of human rights and fundamental freedoms, and consequently should be the principal beneficiary and should participate actively in the realization of these rights and freedoms,

Reaffirming their commitment to the purposes and principles contained in the Charter of the United Nations and the Universal Declaration of Human Rights,

Reaffirming the commitment contained in Article 56 of the Charter of the United Nations to take joint and separate action, placing proper emphasis on developing effective international cooperation for the realization of the purposes set out in Article 55, including universal respect for, and observance of, human rights and fundamental freedoms for all,

Emphasizing the responsibilities of all States, in conformity with the Charter of the United Nations, to develop and encourage respect for human rights and fundamental freedoms for all, without distinction as to race, sex, language or religion,

Recalling the Preamble to the Charter of the United Nations, in particular the determination to reaffirm faith in fundamental human rights, in the dignity and worth of the human person, and in the equal rights of men and women and of nations large and small,

Recalling also the determination expressed in the Preamble of the Charter of the United Nations to save succeeding generations from the scourge of war, to establish conditions under which justice and respect for obligations arising from treaties and other sources of international law can be maintained, to promote social progress and better standards of life in larger freedom, to practice tolerance and good neighbourliness, and to employ international machinery for the promotion of the economic and social advancement of all peoples,

Emphasizing that the Universal Declaration of Human Rights, which constitutes a common standard of achievement for all peoples and all nations, is the source of inspiration and has been the basis for the United Nations in making advances in standard setting as contained in the existing international human rights instruments, in particular the International Covenant on Civil and Political Rights and the International Covenant on Economic, Social and Cultural Rights.

Considering the major changes taking place on the international scene and the aspirations of all the peoples for an international order based on the principles enshrined in the Charter of the United Nations, including promoting and encouraging respect for human rights and fundamental freedoms for all and respect for the principle of equal rights and self-determination of peoples, peace, democracy, justice, equality, rule of law, pluralism, development, better standards of living and solidarity,

Deeply concerned by various forms of discrimination and violence, to which women continue to be exposed all over the world,

Recognizing that the activities of the United Nations in the field of human rights should be rationalized and enhanced in order to strengthen the United Nations machinery in this field and to further the objectives of universal respect for observance of international human rights standards,

Having taken into account the Declarations adopted by the

three regional meetings at Tunis, San José and Bangkok and the contributions made by Governments, and bearing in mind the suggestions made by intergovernmental and non-governmental organizations, as well as the studies prepared by independent experts during the preparatory process leading to the World Conference on Human Rights,

Welcoming the International Year of the World's Indigenous People 1993 as a reaffirmation of the commitment of the international community to ensure their enjoyment of all human rights and fundamental freedoms and to respect the value and diversity of their cultures and identities,

Recognizing also that the international community should devise ways and means to remove the current obstacles and meet challenges to the full realization of all human rights and to prevent the continuation of human rights violations resulting thereof throughout the world,

Invoking the spirit of our age and the realities of our time which call upon the peoples of the world and all States Members of the United Nations to rededicate themselves to the global task of promoting and protecting all human rights and fundamental freedoms so as to secure full and universal enjoyment of these rights,

Determined to take new steps forward in the commitment of the international community with a view to achieving substantial progress in human rights endeavours by an increased and sustained effort of international cooperation and solidarity,

Solemnly adopts the Vienna Declaration and Programme of Action.

1. The World Conference on Human Rights reaffirms the solemn commitment of all States to fulfill their obligations to promote universal respect for, and observance and protection of, all human rights and fundamental freedoms for all in accordance with the Charter of the United Nations, other instruments relating to human rights, and international law. The universal nature of these rights and freedoms is beyond question. In this framework, enhancement of international cooperation in the field of

human rights is essential for the full achievement of the purposes of the United Nations. Human rights and fundamental freedoms are the birthright of all human beings; their protection and promotion is the first responsibility of Governments.

2. All peoples have the right of self-determination. By virtue of that right they freely determine their political status, and freely pursue their economic, social and cultural development. Taking into account the particular situation of peoples under colonial or other forms of alien domination or foreign occupation, the World Conference on Human Rights recognizes the right of peoples to take any legitimate action, in accordance with the Charter of the United Nations, to realize their inalienable right of self-determination. The World Conference on Human Rights considers the denial of the right of self-determination as a violation of human rights and underlines the importance of the effective realization of this right....

4. The promotion and protection of all human rights and fundamental freedoms must be considered as a priority objective of the United Nations in accordance with its purposes and principles, in particular the purpose of international cooperation. In the framework of these purposes and principles, the promotion and protection of all human rights is a legitimate concern of the international community. The organs and specialized agencies related to human rights should therefore further enhance the coordination of their activities based on the consistent and objective application of international human rights instruments.

5. All human rights are universal, indivisible and interdependent and interrelated. The international community must treat human rights globally in a fair and equal manner, on the same footing, and with the same emphasis. While the significance of national and regional particularities and various historical, cultural and religious backgrounds must be borne in mind, it is the duty of States, regardless of their political, economic and cultural systems, to promote and protect all human rights and fundamental freedoms.

6. The efforts of the United Nations system towards the universal respect for, and observance of, human rights and fun-

damental freedoms for all, contribute to the stability and well-being necessary for peaceful and friendly relations among nations, and to improved conditions for peace and security as well as social and economic development, in conformity with the Charter of the United Nations....

8. Democracy, development and respect for human rights and fundamental freedoms are interdependent and mutually reinforcing. Democracy is based on the freely expressed will of the people to determine their own political, economic, social and cultural systems and their full participation in all aspects of their lives. In the context of the above, the promotion and protection of human rights and fundamental freedoms at the national and international levels should be universal and conducted without conditions attached. The international community should support the strengthening and promoting of democracy, development and respect for human rights and fundamental freedoms in the entire world.

9. The World Conference on Human Rights reaffirms that least developed countries committed to the process of democratization and economic reforms, many of which are in Africa, should be supported by the international community in order to succeed in their transition to democracy and economic development.

10. The World Conference on Human Rights reaffirms the right to development, as established in the Declaration on the Right to Development, as a universal and inalienable right and an integral part of fundamental human rights. As stated in the Declaration on the Right to Development, the human person is the central subject of development.

While development facilitates the enjoyment of all human rights, the lack of development may not be invoked to justify the abridgement of internationally recognized human rights.

States should cooperate with each other in ensuring development and eliminating obstacles to development. The international community should promote an effective international cooperation for the realization of the right to development and the elimination of obstacles to development. Lasting progress towards the implementation of the right to development requires effective development policies at the national level, as well as equitable economic relations and a favourable economic environment at the international level.

11. The right to development should be fulfilled so as to meet equitably the developmental and environmental needs of present and future generations. The World Conference on Human Rights recognizes that illicit dumping of toxic and dangerous substances and waste potentially constitutes a serious threat to the human rights to life and health of everyone. Consequently, the World Conference on Human Rights calls on all States to adopt and vigorously implement existing conventions relating to the dumping of toxic and dangerous products and waste and to cooperate in the prevention of illicit dumping. Everyone has the right to enjoy the benefits of scientific progress and its applications. The World Conference on Human Rights notes that certain advances, notably in the biomedical and life sciences as well as in information technology, may have potentially adverse consequences for the integrity, dignity and human rights of the individual, and calls for international cooperation to ensure that human rights and dignity are fully respected in this area of universal concern.

12. The World Conference on Human Rights calls upon the international community to make all efforts to help alleviate the external debt burden of developing countries, in order to supplement the efforts of the Governments of such countries to attain the full realization of the economic, social and cultural rights of their people.

13. There is a need for States and international organizations, in cooperation with non-governmental organizations, to create favourable conditions at the national, regional and international levels to ensure the full and effective enjoyment of human rights. States should eliminate all violations of human rights and their causes, as well as obstacles to the enjoyment of these rights.

14. The existence of widespread extreme poverty inhibits the full and effective enjoyment of human rights; its immediate alleviation and eventual elimination must remain a high priority for the international community.

15. Respect for human rights and for fundamental freedoms

without distinction of any kind is a fundamental rule of international human rights law. The speedy and comprehensive elimination of all forms of racism and racial discrimination, xenophobia and related intolerance is a priority task for the international community. Governments should take effective measures to prevent and combat them. Groups, institutions, intergovernmental and non-governmental organizations and individuals are urged to intensify their efforts in cooperating and coordinating their activities against these evils....

17. The acts, methods and practices of terrorism in all its forms and manifestations as well as linkage in some countries to drug trafficking are activities aimed at the destruction of human rights, fundamental freedoms and democracy, threatening territorial integrity, security of States and destabilizing legitimately constituted Governments. The international community should take the necessary steps to enhance cooperation to prevent and combat terrorism.

18. The human rights of women and of the girl-child are an inalienable, integral and indivisible part of universal human rights. The full and equal participation of women in political, civil, economic, social and cultural life, at the national, regional and international levels, and the eradication of all forms of discrimination on grounds of sex are priority objectives of the international community. Gender-based violence and all forms of sexual harassment and exploitation, including those resulting from cultural prejudice and international trafficking, are incompatible with the dignity and worth of the human person, and must be eliminated. This can be achieved by legal measures and through national action and international cooperation in such fields as economic and social development, education, safe maternity and health care, and social support. The human rights of women should form an integral part of the United Nations human rights activities, including the promotion of all human rights instruments relating to women.

The World Conference on Human Rights urges Governments, institutions, intergovernmental and non-governmental organizations to intensify their efforts for the protection and promotion of human rights of women and the girl-child.

19. Considering the importance of the promotion and protection of the rights of persons belonging to minorities and the contribution of such promotion and protection to the political and social stability of the States in which such persons live, The World Conference on Human Rights reaffirms the obligation of States to ensure that persons belonging to minorities may exercise fully and effectively all human rights and fundamental freedoms without any discrimination and in full equality before the law in accordance with the Declaration on the Rights of Persons Belonging to National or Ethnic, Religious and Linguistic Minorities. The persons belonging to minorities have the right to enjoy their own culture, to profess and practice their own religion and to use their own language in private and in public, freely and without interference or any form of discrimination.

20. The World Conference on Human Rights recognizes the inherent dignity and the unique contribution of indigenous people to the development and plurality of society and strongly reaffirms the commitment of the international community to their economic, social and cultural well-being and their enjoyment of the fruits of sustainable development. States should ensure the full and free participation of indigenous people in all aspects of society, in particular in matters of concern to them. Considering the importance of the promotion and protection of the rights of indigenous people, and the contribution of such promotion and protection to the political and social stability of the States in which such people live, States should, in accordance with international law, take concerted positive steps to ensure respect for all human rights and fundamental freedoms of indigenous people, on the basis of equality and non-discrimination, and recognize the value and diversity of their distinct identities, cultures and social organization.

21. The World Conference on Human Rights, welcoming the early ratification of the Convention on the Rights of the Child by a large number of States and noting the recognition of the human rights of children in the World Declaration on the Survival, Protection and Development of Children and Plan of Action adopted by the World Summit for Children, urges uni-

versal ratification of the Convention by 1995 and its effective implementation by States parties through the adoption of all the necessary legislative, administrative and other measures and the allocation to the maximum extent of the available resources. In all actions concerning children, non-discrimination and the best interest of the child should be primary considerations and the views of the child given due weight. National and international mechanisms and programmes should be strengthened for the defense and protection of children, in particular, the girl-child, abandoned children, street children, economically and sexually exploited children, including through child pornography, child prostitution or sale of organs, children victims of diseases including acquired immunodeficiency syndrome, refugee and displaced children, children in detention, children in armed conflict, as well as children victims of famine and drought and other emergencies. International cooperation and solidarity should be promoted to support the implementation of the Convention and the rights of the child should be a priority in the United Nations system-wide action on human rights. The World Conference on Human Rights also stresses that the child for the full and harmonious development of his or her personality should grow up in a family environment which accordingly merits broader protection.

22. Special attention needs to be paid to ensuring non-discrimination, and the equal enjoyment of all human rights and fundamental freedoms by disabled persons, including their active participation in all aspects of society....

28. The World Conference on Human Rights expresses its dismay at massive violations of human rights especially in the form of genocide, "ethnic cleansing" and systematic rape of women in war situations, creating mass exodus of refugees and displaced persons. While strongly condemning such abhorrent practices it reiterates the call that perpetrators of such crimes be punished and such practices immediately stopped....

32. The World Conference on Human Rights reaffirms the importance of ensuring the universality, objectivity and non-selectivity of the consideration of human rights issues.

49. DECLARATION ON THE RIGHTS OF PERSONS BELONGING TO NATIONAL, ETHNIC, RELIGIOUS OR LINGUISTIC MINORITIES (1993)

The General Assembly....

1. *Takes note* of the report of the Secretary-General on the effective promotion of the Declaration on the Rights of Persons belonging to National or Ethnic, Religious and Linguistic Minorities;

2. *Urges* States and the international community to promote and protect the rights of persons belonging to national or ethnic, religious and linguistic minorities, as set out in the Declaration, including through the facilitation of their full participation in all aspects of the political, economic, social, religious and cultural life of society and in the economic progress and development of their country;

3. *Calls upon* the Commission on Human Rights to examine ways and means to promote and protect effectively the rights of persons belonging to minorities, as set out in the Declaration;

4. *Calls upon* the Secretary-General to provide through the Centre for Human Rights of the Secretariat, at the request of Governments concerned and as part of the programme of advisory services and technical assistance of the Centre, qualified

expertise on minority issues and human rights, as well as on the prevention and resolution of disputes, to assist in existing or potential situations involving minorities;

5. *Appeals* to States to take all the necessary legislative and other measures to promote and give effect, as appropriate, to the principles of the Declaration;

6. *Also appeals* to States to make bilateral and multilateral efforts, as appropriate, to protect the rights of persons belonging to national or ethnic, religious and linguistic minorities in their countries, in accordance with the Declaration;

7. *Urges* all treaty bodies and special representatives, special rapporteurs and working groups of the Commission on Human Rights and the Subcommission on Prevention of Discrimination and Protection of Minorities to give due regard to the promotion and protection of the rights of persons belonging to minorities, as set forth in the Declaration, as appropriate, within their mandates;

8. *Encourages* intergovernmental and non-governmental organizations to continue to contribute to the promotion and protection of the rights of persons belonging to national or ethnic, religious and linguistic minorities....

50. DRAFT DECLARATION ON THE RIGHTS OF INDIGENOUS PEOPLES (1994)

Affirming that indigenous peoples are equal in dignity and rights to all other peoples, while recognizing the right of all peoples to be different, to consider themselves different, and to be respected as such,

Affirming also that all peoples contribute to the diversity and richness of civilizations and cultures, which constitute the common heritage of humankind,

Affirming further that all doctrines, policies and practices based on or advocating superiority of peoples or individuals on the basis of national origin, racial, religious, ethnic or cultural differences are racist, scientifically false, legally invalid, morally condemnable and socially unjust,

Reaffirming also that indigenous peoples, in the exercise of their rights, should be free from discrimination of any kind,

Concerned that indigenous peoples have been deprived of their human rights and fundamental freedoms, resulting, *inter alia*, in their colonization and dispossession of their lands, territories and resources, thus preventing them from exercising, in particular, their right to development in accordance with their own needs and interests,

Recognizing the urgent need to respect and promote the inherent rights and characteristics of indigenous peoples, especially their rights to their lands, territories and resources, which derive from their political, economic and social structures and from their cultures, spiritual traditions, histories and philosophies,

Welcoming the fact that indigenous peoples are organizing themselves for political, economic, social and cultural enhancement and in order to bring an end to all forms of discrimination and oppression wherever they occur,

Convinced that control by indigenous peoples over developments affecting them and their lands, territories and resources will enable them to maintain and strengthen their institutions, cultures and traditions, and to promote their development in accordance with their aspirations and needs,

Recognizing also that respect for indigenous knowledge, cultures and traditional practices contributes to sustainable and equitable development and proper management of the environment,

Emphasizing the need for demilitarization of the lands and territories of indigenous peoples, which will contribute to peace, economic and social progress and development, understanding and friendly relations among nations and peoples of the world,

Recognizing in particular the right of indigenous families and communities to retain shared responsibility for the upbringing, training, education and well-being of their children,

Recognizing also that indigenous peoples have the right freely to determine their relationships with States in a spirit of coexistence, mutual benefit and full respect,

Considering that treaties, agreements and other arrangements between States and indigenous peoples are properly matters of international concern and responsibility,

Acknowledging that the Charter of the United Nations, the International Covenant on Economic, Social and Cultural Rights and the International Covenant on Civil and Political Rights affirm the fundamental importance of the right of self-determination of all peoples, by virtue of which they freely determine their political status and freely pursue their economic, social and cultural development,

Bearing in mind that nothing in this Declaration may be used to deny any peoples their right of self-determination,

Encouraging States to comply with and effectively implement all international instruments, in particular those related to human rights, as they apply to indigenous peoples, in consultation and cooperation with the peoples concerned,

Emphasizing that the United Nations has an important and continuing role to play in promoting and protecting the rights of indigenous peoples,

Believing that this Declaration is a further important step forward for the recognition, promotion and protection of the rights and freedoms of indigenous peoples and in the development of relevant activities of the United Nations system in this field,

Solemnly proclaims the following United Nations Declaration on the Rights of Indigenous Peoples:

PART I

Article 2. Indigenous individuals and peoples are free and equal to all other individuals and peoples in dignity and rights, and have the right to be free from any kind of adverse discrimination, in particular that based on their indigenous origin or identity.

Article 3. Indigenous peoples have the right of self-determination. By virtue of that right they freely determine their political status and freely pursue their economic, social and cultural development.

Article 4. Indigenous peoples have the right to maintain and strengthen their distinct political, economic, social and cultural characteristics, as well as their legal systems, while retaining their rights to participate fully, if they so choose, in the political, economic, social and cultural life of the State.

Article 6. Indigenous peoples have the collective right to live in freedom, peace and security as distinct peoples and to full guarantees against genocide or any other act of violence, including the removal of indigenous children from their families and communities under any pretext. In addition, they have the individual rights to life, physical and mental integrity, liberty and security of person.

Article 7. Indigenous peoples have the collective and individual right not to be subjected to ethnocide and cultural genocide, including prevention of and redress for:

(a) Any action which has the aim or effect of depriving them of their integrity as distinct peoples, or of their cultural values or ethnic identities,

(b) Any action which has the aim or effect of dispossessing them of their lands, territories or resources;

(c) Any form of population transfer which has the aim or effect of violating or undermining any of their rights;

(d) Any form of assimilation or integration by other cultures or ways of life imposed on them by legislative, administrative or other measures;

(e) Any form of propaganda directed against them.

Article 9. Indigenous peoples and individuals have the right to belong to an indigenous community or nation, in accordance with the traditions and customs of the community or nation concerned. No disadvantage of any kind may arise from the exercise of such a right....

Article 12. Indigenous peoples have the right to practise and revitalize their cultural traditions and customs. This includes the right to maintain, protect and develop the past, present and future manifestations of their cultures, such as archaeological and historical sites, artifacts, designs, ceremonies, technologies and visual and performing arts and literature, as well as the right to the restitution of cultural, intellectual, religious and spiritual property taken without their free and informed consent or in violation of their laws, traditions and customs.

Article 13. Indigenous peoples have the right to manifest, practise, develop and teach their spiritual and religious traditions, customs and ceremonies; the right to maintain, protect, and have access in privacy to their religious and cultural sites; the right to the use and control of ceremonial objects; and the right to the repatriation of human remains. States shall take effective measures, in conjunction with the indigenous peoples concerned, to ensure that indigenous sacred places, including burial sites, be preserved, respected and protected.

Article 15. Indigenous children have the right to all levels and forms of education of the State. All indigenous peoples also have this right and the right to establish and control their educational systems and institutions providing education in their own languages, in a manner appropriate to their cultural methods of teaching and learning. Indigenous children living outside their communities have the right to be provided access to education in their own culture and language. States shall take effective measures to provide appropriate resources for these purposes.

Article 16. Indigenous peoples have the right to have the dignity and diversity of their cultures, traditions, histories and aspirations appropriately reflected in all forms of education and public information. States shall take effective measures, in consultation with the indigenous peoples concerned, to eliminate prejudice and discrimination and to promote tolerance, understanding and good relations among indigenous peoples and all segments of society.

Article 19. Indigenous peoples have the right to participate fully, if they so choose, at all levels of decision-making in matters which may affect their rights, lives and destinies through representatives chosen by themselves in accordance with their own procedures, as well as to maintain and develop their own indigenous decision-making institutions.

Article 25. Indigenous peoples have the right to maintain and strengthen their distinctive spiritual and material relationship with the lands, territories, waters and coastal seas and other resources which they have traditionally owned or otherwise occupied or used, and to uphold their responsibilities to future generations in this regard.

Article 26. Indigenous peoples have the right to own, develop, control and use the lands and territories, including the total environment of the lands, air, waters, coastal seas, sea-ice, flora and fauna and other resources which they have traditionally owned or otherwise occupied or used. This includes the right to the full recognition of their laws, traditions and customs, land-tenure systems and institutions for the development and management of resources, and the right to effective measures by States to prevent any interference with, alienation of or encroachment upon these rights.

Article 27. Indigenous peoples have the right to the restitution of the lands, territories and resources which they have traditionally owned or otherwise occupied or used, and which have been confiscated, occupied, used or damaged without their free and informed consent. Where this is not possible, they have the right to just and fair compensation. Unless otherwise freely agreed upon by the peoples concerned, compensation shall take the form of lands, territories and resources equal in quality, size and legal status.

Article 28. Indigenous peoples have the right to the conservation, restoration and protection of the total environment and the productive capacity of their lands, territories and resources, as well as to assistance for this purpose from States and through international cooperation....

Article 31. Indigenous peoples, as a specific form of exercising their right to self-determination, have the right to autonomy or self-government in matters relating to their internal and local affairs, including culture, religion, education, information, media, health, housing, employment, social welfare, economic activities, land and resources management, environment and entry by non-members, as well as ways and means for financing these autonomous functions.

Article 33. Indigenous peoples have the right to promote, develop and maintain their institutional structures and their distinctive juridical customs, traditions, procedures and practices, in accordance with internationally recognized human rights standards.

Article 34. Indigenous peoples have the collective right to determine the responsibilities of individuals to their communities....

Article 42. The rights recognized herein constitute the minimum standards for the survival, dignity and well-being of the indigenous peoples of the world.

51. CONVENTION ON THE PREVENTION AND PUNISHMENT OF THE CRIME OF GENOCIDE (1948)

The Contracting Parties,

Having considered the declaration made by the General Assembly of the United Nations in its resolution 96 (I) dated 11 December 1946 that genocide is a crime under international law, contrary to the spirit and aims of the United Nations and condemned by the civilized world,

Recognizing that at all periods of history genocide has inflicted great losses on humanity, and

Being convinced that, in order to liberate mankind from such an odious scourge, international co-operation is required,

Hereby agree as hereinafter provided:

Article 1. The Contracting Parties confirm that genocide, whether committed in time of peace or in time of war, is a crime under international law which they undertake to prevent and to punish.

Article 2. In the present Convention, genocide means any of the following acts committed with intent to destroy, in whole or in part, a national, ethnical, racial or religious group, as such:

(a) Killing members of the group;

(b) Causing serious bodily or mental harm to members of the group;

(c) Deliberately inflicting on the group conditions of life calculated to bring about its physical destruction in whole or in part;

(d) Imposing measures intended to prevent births within the group;

(e) Forcibly transferring children of the group to another group.

Article 3. The following acts shall be punishable:

(a) Genocide;

(b) Conspiracy to commit genocide;

(c) Direct and public incitement to commit genocide;

(d) Attempt to commit genocide;

(e) Complicity in genocide.

Article 4. Persons committing genocide or any of the other acts enumerated in article III shall be punished, whether they are constitutionally responsible rulers, public officials or private individuals.

Article 5. The Contracting Parties undertake to enact, in accordance with their respective Constitutions, the necessary legislation to give effect to the provisions of the present Convention, and, in particular, to provide effective penalties for persons guilty of genocide or any of the other acts enumerated in article III.

Article 6. Persons charged with genocide or any of the other acts enumerated in article III shall be tried by a competent tribunal of the State in the territory of which the act was committed, or by such international penal tribunal as may have jurisdiction with respect to those Contracting Parties which shall have accepted its jurisdiction.

Article 7. Genocide and the other acts enumerated in article III shall not be considered as political crimes for the purpose of extradition. The Contracting Parties pledge themselves in such cases to grant extradition in accordance with their laws and treaties in force.

Article 8. Any Contracting Party may call upon the competent organs of the United Nations to take such action under the Charter of the United Nations as they consider appropriate for the prevention and suppression of acts of genocide or any of the other acts enumerated in article III.

52. CONVENTION ON THE ELIMINATION OF ALL FORMS OF DISCRIMINATION AGAINST WOMEN (1979)

The States Parties to the present Convention,

Noting that the Charter of the United Nations reaffirms faith in fundamental human rights, in the dignity and worth of the human person and in the equal rights of men and women,

Noting that the Universal Declaration of Human Rights affirms the principle of the inadmissibility of discrimination and proclaims that all human beings are born free and equal in dignity and rights and that everyone is entitled to all the rights and freedoms set forth therein, without distinction of any kind, including distinction based on sex,

Noting that the States Parties to the International Covenants on Human Rights have the obligation to ensure the equal rights of men and women to enjoy all economic, social, cultural, civil and political rights,

Considering the international conventions concluded under the auspices of the United Nations and the specialized agencies promoting equality of rights of men and women,

Noting also the resolutions, declarations and recommendations adopted by the United Nations and the specialized agencies promoting equality of rights of men and women,

Concerned, however, that despite these various instruments extensive discrimination against women continues to exist,

Recalling that discrimination against women violates the principles of equality of rights and respect for human dignity, is an obstacle to the participation of women, on equal terms with men, in the political, social, economic and cultural life of their countries, hampers the growth of the prosperity of society and the family and makes more difficult the full development of the potentialities of women in the service of their countries and of humanity,

Concerned that in situations of poverty women have the least access to food, health, education, training and opportunities for employment and other needs,

Convinced that the establishment of the new international economic order based on equity and justice will contribute significantly towards the promotion of equality between men and women,

Emphasizing that the eradication of apartheid, all forms of racism, racial discrimination, colonialism, neo-colonialism, aggression, foreign occupation and domination and interference in the internal affairs of States is essential to the full enjoyment of the rights of men and women,

Affirming that the strengthening of international peace and security, the relaxation of international tension, mutual co-operation among all States irrespective of their social and economic systems, general and complete disarmament, in particular nuclear disarmament under strict and effective international control, the affirmation of the principles of justice, equality and mutual benefit in relations among countries and the realization of the right of peoples under alien and colonial domination and foreign occupation to self-determination and independence, as well as respect for national sovereignty and territorial integrity, will promote social progress and development and as a consequence will contribute to the attainment of full equality between men and women,

Convinced that the full and complete development of a country, the welfare of the world and the cause of peace require the maximum participation of women on equal terms with men in all fields,

Bearing in mind the great contribution of women to the welfare of the family and to the development of society, so far not fully recognized, the social significance of maternity and the role of both parents in the family and in the upbringing of children, and aware that the role of women in procreation should not be a basis for discrimination but that the upbringing of children requires a sharing of responsibility between men and women and society as a whole,

Aware that a change in the traditional role of men as well as the role of women in society and in the family is needed to achieve full equality between men and women,

Determined to implement the principles set forth in the Declaration on the Elimination of Discrimination against Women and, for that purpose, to adopt the measures required for the elimination of such discrimination in all its forms and manifestations,

Have agreed on the following:

PART I

Article 1. For the purposes of the present Convention, the term "discrimination against women" shall mean any distinction, exclusion or restriction made on the basis of sex which has the effect or purpose of impairing or nullifying the recognition, enjoyment or exercise by women, irrespective of their marital status, on a basis of equality of men and women, of human rights and fundamental freedoms in the political, economic, social, cultural, civil or any other field.

Article 2. States Parties condemn discrimination against women in all its forms, agree to pursue by all appropriate means and without delay a policy of eliminating discrimination against women and, to this end, undertake:

(a) To embody the principle of the equality of men and women in their national constitutions or other appropriate legislation if not yet incorporated therein and to ensure, through law and other appropriate means, the practical realization of this principle;

(b) To adopt appropriate legislative and other measures, including sanctions where appropriate, prohibiting all discrimination against women;

(c) To establish legal protection of the rights of women on an equal basis with men and to ensure through competent national tribunals and other public institutions the effective protection of women against any act of discrimination;

(d) To refrain from engaging in any act or practice of discrimination against women and to ensure that public authorities and institutions shall act in conformity with this obligation;

(e) To take all appropriate measures to eliminate discrimination against women by any person, organization or enterprise;

(f) To take all appropriate measures, including legislation, to modify or abolish existing laws, regulations, customs and practices which constitute discrimination against women;

(g) To repeal all national penal provisions which constitute discrimination against women.

Article 3. States Parties shall take in all fields, in particular in the political, social, economic and cultural fields, all appropriate measures, including legislation, to ensure the full development and advancement of women, for the purpose of guaranteeing them the exercise and enjoyment of human rights and fundamental freedoms on a basis of equality with men....

Article 5. States Parties shall take all appropriate measures:

(a) To modify the social and cultural patterns of conduct of men and women, with a view to achieving the elimination of prejudices and customary and all other practices which are based on the idea of the inferiority or the superiority of either of the sexes or on stereotyped roles for men and women;

(b) To ensure that family education includes a proper understanding of maternity as a social function and the recognition of the common responsibility of men and women in the upbringing and development of their children, it being understood that the interest of the children is the primordial consideration in all cases.

Article 6. States Parties shall take all appropriate measures, including legislation, to suppress all forms of traffic in women and exploitation or prostitution of women.

PART II

Article 7. States Parties shall take all appropriate measures to eliminate discrimination against women in the political and public life of the country and, in particular, shall ensure to women, on equal terms with men, the right:

(a) To vote in all elections and public referenda and to be eligible for election to all publicly elected bodies;

(b) To participate in the formulation of government policy and the implementation thereof and to hold public office and perform all public functions at all levels of government;

(c) To participate in non-governmental organizations and associations concerned with the public and political life of the country.

Article 8. States Parties shall take all appropriate measures to ensure to women, on equal terms with men and without any discrimination, the opportunity to represent their Governments at the international level and to participate in the work of international organizations.

Article 9. 1. States Parties shall grant women equal rights with men to acquire, change or retain their nationality. They shall ensure in particular that neither marriage to an alien nor change of nationality by the husband during marriage shall automatically change the nationality of the wife, render her stateless or force upon her the nationality of the husband. 2. States Parties shall grant women equal rights with men with respect to the nationality of their children.

PART III

Article 10. States Parties shall take all appropriate measures to eliminate discrimination against women in order to ensure to them equal rights with men in the field of education and in particular to ensure, on a basis of equality of men and women:

(a) The same conditions for career and vocational guidance, for access to studies and for the achievement of diplomas in educational establishments of all categories in rural as well as in urban areas; this equality shall be ensured in pre-school, general, technical, professional and higher technical education, as well as in all types of vocational training;

(b) Access to the same curricula, the same examinations, teaching staff with qualifications of the same standard and school premises and equipment of the same quality;

(c) The elimination of any stereotyped concept of the roles of men and women at all levels and in all forms of education by encouraging coeducation and other types of education which will help to achieve this aim and, in particular, by the revision of textbooks and school programmes and the adaptation of teaching methods;

(d) The same opportunities to benefit from scholarships and other study grants;

(e) The same opportunities for access to programmes of continuing education, including adult and functional literacy programmes, particulary those aimed at reducing, at the earliest possible time, any gap in education existing between men and women;

(f) The reduction of female student drop-out rates and the organization of programmes for girls and women who have left school prematurely;

(g) The same opportunities to participate actively in sports and physical education;

(h) Access to specific educational information to help to ensure the health and well-being of families, including information and advice on family planning.

Article 11.-1. States Parties shall take all appropriate measures to eliminate discrimination against women in the field of employment in order to ensure, on a basis of equality of men and women, the same rights, in particular:

(a) The right to work as an inalienable right of all human beings;

(b) The right to the same employment opportunities, including the application of the same criteria for selection in matters of employment;

(c) The right to free choice of profession and employment, the right to promotion, job security and all benefits and conditions of service and the right to receive vocational training and retraining, including apprenticeships, advanced vocational training and recurrent training;

(d) The right to equal remuneration, including benefits, and to equal treatment in respect of work of equal value, as well as equality of treatment in the evaluation of the quality of work;

(e) The right to social security, particularly in cases of retirement, unemployment, sickness, invalidity and old age and other incapacity to work, as well as the right to paid leave;

(f) The right to protection of health and to safety in working conditions, including the safeguarding of the function of reproduction.

Article 12.-1. States Parties shall take all appropriate measures to eliminate discrimination against women in the field of health care in order to ensure, on a basis of equality of men and women, access to health care services, including those related to family planning.

2. Notwithstanding the provisions of paragraph I of this article, States Parties shall ensure to women appropriate services in connection with pregnancy, confinement and the post-natal period, granting free services where necessary, as well as adequate nutrition during pregnancy and lactation.

Article 13. States Parties shall take all appropriate measures to eliminate discrimination against women in other areas of economic and social life in order to ensure, on a basis of equality of men and women, the same rights, in particular:

(a) The right to family benefits;

(b) The right to bank loans, mortgages and other forms of financial credit;

(c) The right to participate in recreational activities, sports and all aspects of cultural life.

Article 14.-1. States Parties shall take into account the particular problems faced by rural women and the significant roles which rural women play in the economic survival of their families, including their work in the non-monetized sectors of the economy, and shall take all appropriate measures to ensure the application of the provisions of the present Convention to women in rural areas.

2. States Parties shall take all appropriate measures to eliminate discrimination against women in rural areas in order to ensure, on a basis of equality of men and women, that they participate in

and benefit from rural development and, in particular, shall ensure to such women the right:

(a) To participate in the elaboration and implementation of development planning at all levels;

(b) To have access to adequate health care facilities, including information, counselling and services in family planning;

(c) To benefit directly from social security programmes;

(d) To obtain all types of training and education, formal and non-formal, including that relating to functional literacy, as well as, *inter alia*, the benefit of all community and extension services, in order to increase their technical proficiency;

(e) To organize self-help groups and co-operatives in order to obtain equal access to economic opportunities through employment or self employment;

(f) To participate in all community activities;

(g) To have access to agricultural credit and loans, marketing facilities, appropriate technology and equal treatment in land and agrarian reform as well as in land resettlement schemes;

(h) To enjoy adequate living conditions, particularly in relation to housing, sanitation, electricity and water supply, transport and communications.

PART IV

Article 15.-1. States Parties shall accord to women equality with men before the law.

2. States Parties shall accord to women, in civil matters, a legal capacity identical to that of men and the same opportunities to exercise that capacity. In particular, they shall give women equal rights to conclude contracts and to administer property and shall treat them equally in all stages of procedure in courts and tribunals.

3. States Parties agree that all contracts and all other private instruments of any kind with a legal effect which is directed at restricting the legal capacity of women shall be deemed null and void.

4. States Parties shall accord to men and women the same rights with regard to the law relating to the movement of per-

sons and the freedom to choose their residence and domicile.

Article 16.-1. States Parties shall take all appropriate measures to eliminate discrimination against women in all matters relating to marriage and family relations and in particular shall ensure, on a basis of equality of men and women:

(a) The same right to enter into marriage;

(b) The same right freely to choose a spouse and to enter into marriage only with their free and full consent;

(c) The same rights and responsibilities during marriage and at its dissolution;

(d) The same rights and responsibilities as parents, irrespective of their marital status, in matters relating to their children; in all cases the interests of the children shall be paramount;

(e) The same rights to decide freely and responsibly on the number and spacing of their children and to have access to the information, education and means to enable them to exercise these rights;

(f) The same rights and responsibilities with regard to guardianship, wardship, trusteeship and adoption of children, or similar institutions where these concepts exist in national legislation; in all cases the interests of the children shall be paramount;

(g) The same personal rights as husband and wife, including the right to choose a family name, a profession and an occupation;

(h) The same rights for both spouses in respect of the ownership, acquisition, management, administration, enjoyment and disposition of property, whether free of charge or for a valuable consideration.

2. The betrothal and the marriage of a child shall have no legal effect, and all necessary action, including legislation, shall be taken to specify a minimum age for marriage and to make the registration of marriages in an official registry compulsory.

53. DRAFT DECLARATION OF PRINCIPLES ON HUMAN RIGHTS AND THE ENVIRONMENT (1994)

Preamble

Guided by the United Nations Charter, the Universal Declaration of Human Rights, the International Covenant on Economic, Social and Cultural Rights, the International Covenant on Civil and Political Rights, the Vienna Declaration and Program of Action of the World Conference of Human Rights, and other relevant international human rights instruments,

Guided also by the Stockholm Declaration of the United Nations Conference on the Human Environment, the World Charter for Nature, the Rio Declaration on Environment and Development, Agenda 21: Programme of Action for Sustainable Development, and other relevant instruments of international environmental law,

Guided also by the Declaration on the Right to Development, which recognizes that the right to development is an essential human right and that the human person is the central subject of development,

Guided further by fundamental principles of international humanitarian law,

Reaffirming the universality, indivisibility and interdependence of all human rights,

Recognizing that sustainable development links the right to development and the right to a secure, healthy and ecologically sound environment,

Recalling the right of peoples to self-determination by virtue of which they have the right freely to determine their political status and to pursue their economic, social and cultural development,

Deeply concerned by the severe human rights consequences of environmental harm caused by poverty, structural adjustment and debt programmes and by international trade and intellectual property regimes,

Convinced that the potential irreversibility of environmental harm gives rise to special responsibility to prevent such harm,

Concerned that human rights violations lead to environmental degradation and that environmental degradation leads to human rights violations,

THE FOLLOWING PRINCIPLES ARE DECLARED:

Part I

1. Human rights, an ecologically sound environment, sustainable development and peace are interdependent and indivisible.

2. All persons have the right to a secure, healthy and ecologically sound environment. This right and other human rights, including civil, cultural, economic, political and social rights, are universal, interdependent and indivisible.

3. All persons shall be free from any form of discrimination in regard to actions and decisions that affect the environment.

4. All persons have the right to an environment adequate to meet equitably the needs of present generations and that does not impair the rights of future generations to meet equitably their needs.

Part II

5. All persons have the right to freedom from pollution, environmental degradation and activities that adversely affect the environment, threaten life, health, livelihood, well-being or sustainable development within, across or outside national boundaries.

6. All persons have the right to protection and preservation

of the air, soil, water, sea-ice, flora and fauna, and the essential processes and areas necessary to maintain biological diversity and ecosystems.

7. All persons have the right to the highest attainable standard of health free from environmental degradation.

8. All persons have the right to safe and healthy food and water adequate to their well-being.

9. All persons have the right to a safe and healthy working environment.

10. All persons have the right to adequate housing, land tenure and living conditions in a secure, healthy and ecologically sound environment.

11. All persons have the right not to be evicted from their homes or land for the purpose of, or as a consequence of, decisions or actions affecting the environment, except in emergencies or due to a compelling purpose benefiting society as a whole and not attainable by other means. All persons have the right to participate effectively in decisions and to negotiate concerning their eviction and the right, if evicted, to timely and adequate restitution, compensation and/or appropriate and sufficient accommodation or land.

12. All persons have the right to timely assistance in the event of natural or technological or other human-caused catastrophes.

13. Everyone has the right to benefit equitably from the conservation and sustainable use of nature and natural resources for cultural, ecological, educational, health, livelihood, recreational, spiritual or other purposes. This includes ecologically sound access to nature. Everyone has the right to preservation of unique sites, consistent with the fundamental rights of persons or groups living in the area.

14. Indigenous peoples have the right to control their lands, territories and natural resources and to maintain their traditional way of life. This includes the right to security in the enjoyment of their means of subsistence. Indigenous peoples have the right to protection against any action or course of conduct that may result in the destruction or degradation of their territories, including land, air, water, sea-ice, wildlife or other resources.

Part III

15. All persons have the right to information concerning the environment. This includes information, howsoever compiled, on actions and courses of conduct that may affect the environment and information necessary to enable effective public participation in environmental decision-making. The information shall be timely, clear, understandable and available without undue financial burden to the applicant.

16. All persons have the right to hold and express opinions and to disseminate ideas and information regarding the environment.

17. All persons have the right to environmental and human rights education.

18. All persons have the right to active, free, and meaningful participation in planning and decision-making activities and processes that may have an impact on the environment and development. This includes the right to a prior assessment of the environmental, developmental and human rights consequences of proposed actions.

19. All persons have the right to associate freely and peacefully with others for purposes of protecting the environment or the rights of persons affected by environmental harm.

20. All persons have the right to effective remedies and redress in administrative or judicial proceedings for environmental harm or the threat of such harm.

Part IV

21. All persons, individually and in association with others, have a duty to protect and preserve the environment.

22. All States shall respect and ensure the right to a secure, healthy and ecologically sound environment. Accordingly, they shall adopt the administrative, legislative and other measures necessary to effectively implement the rights in this Declaration. These measures shall aim at the prevention of environmental harm, at the provision of adequate remedies, and at the sustainable use of natural resources and shall include, *inter alia*, collection and dissemination of information concerning the environment prior assessment and control, licensing, regulation or pro-

hibition of activities and substances potentially harmful to the environment; public participation in environmental decision-making; effective administrative and judicial remedies and redress for environmental harm and the threat of such harm; monitoring, management and equitable sharing of natural resources; measures to reduce wasteful processes of production and patterns of consumption; measures aimed at ensuring that transnational corporations, wherever they operate, carry out their duties of environmental protection, sustainable development and respect for human rights; and measures aimed at ensuring that the international organizations and agencies to which they belong observe the rights and duties in this Declaration.

23. States and all other parties shall avoid using the environment as a means of war or inflicting significant, long-term or widespread harm on the environment, and shall respect international law providing protection for the environment in times of armed conflict and cooperate in its further development.

24. All international organizations and agencies shall observe the rights and duties in this Declaration.

Part V

25. In implementing the rights and duties in this Declaration, special attention shall be given to vulnerable persons and groups.

26. The rights in this Declaration may be subject only to restrictions provided by law and which are necessary to protect public order, health and the fundamental rights and freedoms of others.

27. All persons are entitled to a social and international order in which the rights in this Declaration can be fully realized.

BIBLIOGRAPHY

Aiken, William. "Human Rights in an Ecological Era." *Environmental Values* 1 (1992): 191-203.

An-Na'im, Abdullahi Ahmed, ed. *Human Rights in Cross-Cultural Perspectives: A Quest for Consensus*. Philadelphia: University of Pennsylvania Press, 1992.

An-Na'im, Abdullahi Ahmed, and Francis M. Deng, eds. *Human Rights in Africa: Cross-Cultural Perspectives*. Washington, DC: Brookings Institution Press, 1990.

Ashworth, Georgina. "The Silencing of Women." In *Human Rights in Global Politics*, Tim Dunne and Nicholas J. Wheeler, eds. Cambridge: Cambridge University Press, 1999.

Avineri, Shlomo. *The Social and Political Thought of Karl Marx*. Cambridge: Cambridge University Press, 1968.

Baker, Judith, ed. *Group Rights*. Toronto: University of Toronto Press, 1994.

Beiner, Ronald. *Kant and Political Philosophy*. New Haven: Yale University Press, 1993.

Berlin, Isaiah. *Four Essays on Liberty*. Oxford: Oxford University Press, 1969.

Best, Steven and Douglas Kellner. *Postmodern Theory*. New York: The Guilford Press, 1991.

Bielefeldt, Heiner. "Human Rights in a Multicultural World." *Jahrbuch für Recht und Ethik* 3 (1995): 283-294.

Binion, Gayle. "Human Rights: A Feminist Perspective." *Human Rights Quarterly* 17 (1995): 509-526.

Bobbio, Norberto. *The Age of Rights*. Translated by Allan Cameron. Cambridge: Polity Press, 1996.

Boulware-Miller, Kay. "Female Circumcision: Challenges to the Practice as a Human Rights Violation." *Harvard Women's Law Journal* 8 (1985): 155-77.

Brandt, Richard B. "The Concept of a Moral Right and Its Function." *Journal of Philosophy* 80 (1983): 29-45.

Brown, Chris. "Universal Human Rights: A Critique." *International Journal of Human Rights* 1 (1997): 41-65.

Brown, Michael. *The International Dimensions of Internal Conflict*. Cambridge, MA: MIT Press, 1996.

Bull, Hedley, Benedict Kingsbury, and Adam Roberts, eds. *Hugo Grotius and International Relations*. Oxford: Clarendon Press, 1990.

Bunch, Charlotte. "Women's Rights as Human Rights: Toward a Re-Vision of Human Rights." *Human Rights Quarterly* 12 (1990): 486-98.

Cobbah, Josiah A.M. "African Values and the Human Rights Debate: An African Perspective." *Human Rights Quarterly* 9 (1987): 309-31.

Comstock, G.D. *Violence Against Lesbians and Gay Men*. New York: Columbia University Press, 1991.

Cooper, David E. and Joy A. Palmer, eds. *Just Environments: Intergenerational, International, and Interspecies Issues*. London and New York: Routledge, 1995.

Cornell, Drucilla, Michael Rosenfield, and David G. Carlson, eds. *Deconstruction and the Possibility of Justice*. New York: Routledge, 1993.

Crawford, James, ed. *The Rights of Peoples*. Oxford: Clarendon Press, 1992.

Davis, Michael C., ed. *Human Rights and Chinese Values*. Hong Kong: Oxford University Press, 1995.

Dinstein, Yoram. "Collective Human Rights of Peoples and Minorities." *International and Comparative Law Quarterly* 25 (1976): 102-120.

Donnelly, Jack. "Natural Law and Right in Aquinas' Political Thought." *Western Political Quarterly* 33 (1980): 520-35.

——. "Cultural Relativism and Universal Human Rights." *Human Rights Quarterly* 6 (1984): 400-418.

——. "Human Rights, Humanitarian Intervention, and American Foreign Policy: Law, Morality and Politics." *Journal of International Affairs* 37 (1984): 311-28.

Douzinas, Costas and Ronnie Warrington. *Postmodern Jurisprudence*. New York: Routledge, 1991.

Dunn, John. *The Political Thought of John Locke*. Cambridge: Cambridge University Press, 1969.

Dworkin, Ronald. *Taking Rights Seriously*. Cambridge, Mass.: Harvard University Press, 1977.

Eisler, Riane. "Human Rights: Toward an Integrated Theory for Action." *Human Rights Quarterly* 9 (1987): 287-308.

Engle, Karen. "International Human Rights and Feminism: When Discourses Meet." *Michigan Journal of International Law* 13 (1992): 517-610.

Falk, Richard. "The Challenge of Genocide and Genocidal Politics in an Era of Globalization." In *Human Rights in Global Politics*, Tim Dunne and Nicholas J. Wheeler, eds. Cambridge: Cambridge University Press, 1999.

Finnis, John. *Natural Law and Natural Rights*. Oxford: Oxford University Press, 1982.

Forst, Rainer. "The Basic Right to Justification: Toward a Constructivist Conception of Human Rights." *Constellations* 6 (1999): 35-60.

Foucault, Michel. *Power/Knowledge: Selected Interviews and Other Writings, 1972-77*, Colin Gordon, ed. New York: Pantheon, 1980.

Gaete, Rolando. "Postmodernism and Human Rights: Some Insidious Questions." *Law and Critique* 2 (1991): 140-70.

Gauthier, David. *The Logic of Leviathan: The Moral and Political Theory of Thomas Hobbes*. Oxford: Blackwell, 1978.

Gewirth, Alan. "The Basis and Content of Human Rights." In J. Roland Pennock and John W. Chapman, eds. *Human Rights: NOMOS XXIII*. New York: New York University Press, 1981.

——. *Human Rights: Essays on Justification and Applications*. Chicago: University of Chicago Press, 1982.

Goodin, Robert E. "International Ethics and the Environmental Crisis." In *Ethics & International Affairs: A Reader*, Joel H. Rosenthal, ed. Washington, DC: Georgetown University Press, 1999.

Gray, John. *Mill on Liberty: A Defence*. London: Routledge, 1983.

Haakonssen, Knud and Michael J. Lacey, eds. *A Culture of Rights: The Bill of Rights in Philosophy, Politics and Law*. Cambridge: Cambridge University Press, 1991.

Halperin, Morton H., and David J. Scheffer with Patricia L. Small. *Self-Determination in the New World Order*. Washington, DC: Carnegie Endowment for International Peace, 1992.

Hamilton, Alexander, John Jay, and James Madison. *The Federalist Papers*. New York: Modern Library, 1937.

Hampton, Jean. *Hobbes and the Social Contract Tradition*. Cambridge: Cambridge University Press, 1986.

Harff, Barbara. *Genocide and Human Rights: International Legal and Political Issues*. Denver, CO: University of Denver Press, 1984.

Hayden, Patrick. "Rawls, Human Rights, and Cultural Pluralism: A Critique." *Theoria: A Journal of Social and Political Theory* 92 (1998): 46-56.

——. "Sentimentality and Human Rights: Critical Remarks on Rorty." *Philosophy in the Contemporary World* 6 (1999): 59-66.

Howard, Rhoda. "Is There an African Concept of Human Rights?" In *Foreign Policy and Human Rights*, R.J. Vincent, ed. Cambridge: Cambridge University Press, 1986.

——. "Human Rights and Culture Wars: Globalization and the Universality of Human Rights." *International Journal* 53 (1997-98): 94-112.

Hsiung, James C., ed. *Human Rights in East Asia: A Cultural Perspective*. New York: Paragon House, 1985.

Hughes, Cheryl L. "Reconstructing the Subject of Human Rights." *Philosophy and Social Criticism* 25 (1999): 47-60.

Human Rights Watch. *Slaughter Among Neighbors: The Political Origins of Communal Violence*. New Haven: Yale University Press, 1995.

Human Rights Watch and Natural Resources Defense Council. *Defending the Earth: Abuses of Human Rights and the Environment*. Washington, DC: Human Rights Watch and Natural Resources Defense Council, 1992.

Hunt, H.A.K. *The Humanism of Cicero*. Melbourne: Melbourne University Press, 1954.

Inada, Kenneth K. "The Buddhist Perspective on Human Rights." In *Human Rights in Religious Traditions*, Arlene Swidler, ed. New York: Pilgrims Press, 1982.

Irwin, T. H. *Plato's Ethics*. Oxford: Oxford University Press, 1995.

Kavka, Gregory. *Hobbesian Moral and Political Theory*. Princeton: Princeton University Press, 1986.

Keown, Damien. "Are There 'Human Rights' in Buddhism?" *Journal of Buddhist Ethics* 2 (1995): 3-27.
Korsgaard, Christine. *Creating the Kingdom of Ends*. Cambridge: Harvard University Press, 1996.
Kraut, Richard. *Socrates and the State*. Princeton: Princeton University Press, 1984.
Kukathas, Chandran. "Are There Any Cultural Rights?" *Political Theory* 20 (1992): 105-139.
Kuper, Leo. *The Prevention of Genocide*. Hew Haven: Yale University Press, 1985.
Kymlicka, Will. *Multicultural Citizenship: A Liberal Theory of Minority Rights*. Oxford: Clarendon Press, 1995.
——, ed. *The Rights of Minority Cultures*. Oxford: Oxford University Press, 1995.
Levinas, Emmanuel. *Outside the Subject*, Michael B. Smith, trans. Stanford: Stanford University Press, 1994.
Li, Xiaorong. "Postmodernism and Universal Human Rights: Why Theory and Reality Don't Mix." *Free Inquiry*, Fall 1998: 28-31.
Lisska, Anthony. *Aquinas's Theory of Natural Law*. Oxford: Oxford University Press, 1996.
Lomasky, Loren. *Persons, Rights, and the Moral Community*. Oxford: Oxford University Press, 1987.
Lukes, Steven. *Marxism and Morality*. Oxford: Clarendon Press, 1985.
Lyons, David. "The Correlativity of Rights and Duties." *Nous* 4 (1970): 45-55.
——. *In the Interest of the Governed*. Oxford: Oxford University Press, 1991.
Lyotard, Jean-François. *The Postmodern Condition*, trans. Geoff Bennington and Brian Massumi. Minneapolis: University of Minnesota Press, 1984.
Macpherson, C. B. *The Political Theory of Possessive Individualism*. Oxford: Clarendon Press, 1962.
Margalit, Avishai and Joseph Raz. "National Self-Determination." *Journal of Philosophy* 87 (1990): 439-61.
Martin, Rex. "Human Rights and Civil Rights." *Philosophical Studies* 37 (1980): 391-403.
McMahan, Jeff. "Intervention and Collective Self-Determination." *Ethics & International Affairs* 10 (1996): 4-11.
Merrills, J.G. "Environmental Protection and Human Rights: Conceptual Aspects." In *Human Rights Approaches to Environmental Protection*, Alan E. Boyle and Michael R. Anderson, eds. Oxford: Clarendon Press, 1996.
Miller, Fred. *Nature, Justice, and Rights in Aristotle's Politics*. Oxford: Oxford University Press.
Miller, Seumas. "Collective Responsibility, Armed Intervention and the Rwandan Genocide." *International Journal of Applied Philosophy* 12 (1998): 223-38.
Mineau, Andre. "Human Rights and Nietzsche." *History of European Ideas* 11 (1989): 877-82.
Moosa, Najma. "Human Rights in Islam." *South African Journal on Human Rights*

14 (1998): 508-524.

Morsink, Johannes. "Cultural Genocide, the Universal Declaration, and Minority Rights." *Human Rights Quarterly* 21 (1999): 1009-1060.

Nardin, Terry and Jerome Slater. "Non-Intervention and Human Rights." *Journal of Politics* 48 (1986): 86-96.

Nickel, James W. *Making Sense of Human Rights*. Berkeley and Los Angeles: University of California Press, 1987.

Nickel, James W. and Eduardo Viola. "Integrating Environmentalism and Human Rights." *Environmental Ethics* 16 (1994): 265-73.

Nino, Carlos Santiago. *The Ethics of Human Rights*. Oxford: Clarendon Press, 1991.

Nussbaum, Martha C. *Sex and Social Justice*. New York and Oxford: Oxford University Press, 1999.

Nussbaum, Martha C. and J. Glover, eds. *Women, Culture, and Development*. Oxford: Clarendon Press, 1995.

Okin, Susan Moller. "Feminism, Women's Human Rights, and Cultural Differences." *Hypatia* 13 (1998): 32-52.

Olayiwola, Abdur Rahman. "Human Rights in Islam." *The Islamic Quarterly* 36 (1992): 262-79.

Panikkar, Raimundo. "Is the Notion of Human Rights a Western Concept?" *Diogenes* 120 (1982): 75-102.

Pease, Kelly Kate and David P. Forsythe. "Human Rights, Humanitarian Intervention, and World Politics." *Human Rights Quarterly* 15 (1993): 290-314.

Peters, Julie and Andrea Wolper, eds. *Women's Rights, Human Rights*. New York and London: Routledge, 1995.

Philipose, Liz. "The Laws of War and Women's Human Rights." *Hypatia* 11 (1996): 46-62.

Phillips, Allan and Allan Rosas, eds. *Universal Minority Rights*. Turku, Finland: University Institute for Human Rights, 1995.

Phillips, Robert L. and Duane L. Cade. *Humanitarian Intervention: Just War vs. Pacifism*. Lanham, MD: Rowman & Littlefield, 1996.

Ramsbotham, Oliver and Tom Woodhouse. *Humanitarian Intervention in Contemporary Conflict*. Cambridge: Polity Press, 1996.

Raphael, D. D., ed. *Political Theory and the Rights of Man*. Bloomington and London: Indiana University Press, 1967.

Rawls, John. *A Theory of Justice*. Revised Edition. Cambridge, MA.: Harvard University Press, 1971, 1999.

Raz, Joseph. "On the Nature of Rights." *Mind* XCIII (1984): 194-214.

Renteln, Allison D. *International Human Rights: Universalism Versus Relativism*. Newbury Park, CA: Sage Publications, 1990.

Ryan, Alan. *J. S. Mill*. London: Routledge, 1974.

Schofield, Malcolm. *The Stoic Idea of the City*. Cambridge: Cambridge University Press, 1991.

Schuler, Margaret, ed. *Freedom from Violence: Women's Strategies from around the*

World. New York: UNIFEM, 1992.

Sen, Amartya. "Human Rights and Asian Values." In *Ethics & International Affairs*, Joel H. Rosenthal, ed. Second Edition. Washington, DC: Georgetown University Press, 1999.

Shapiro, Ian and Will Kymlicka, eds. *Ethnicity and Group Rights*. New York and London: New York University Press, 1997.

Shell, Susan Meld. *The Rights of Reason: A Study of Kant's Philosophy and Politics*. Toronto: University of Toronto Press, 1980.

Shelton, Dinah. "Human Rights, Environmental Rights and the Right to the Environment." *Stanford Journal of International Law* 28 (1992): 103-38.

Shklar, Judith. *Men and Citizens: A Study of Rousseau's Social Theory*, 2nd ed. Cambridge: Cambridge University Press, 1985.

Shue, Henry. *Basic Rights*. Second Edition. Princeton, NJ: Princeton University Press, 1996.

Simmons, John. *The Lockean Theory of Rights*. Princeton: Princeton University Press, 1992.

——. *Moral Principles and Political Obligations*. Princeton: Princeton University Press, 1979.

Stephen, J. F. *Liberty, Equality, Fraternity*. Cambridge: Cambridge University Press, 1967.

Strauss, Leo. *Natural Right and History*. Chicago: University of Chicago Press, 1953.

Sumner, L.W. *The Moral Foundation of Rights*. Oxford: Clarendon Press, 1987.

Sweet, William. "Human Rights and Cultural Diversity." *International Journal of Applied Philosophy* 12 (198): 117-32.

Thorme, Melissa. "Establishing Environment as a Human Right." *Denver Journal of International Law and Policy* 19 (1991): 301-31.

Tomasevski, Katarina. *Women and Human Rights*. London: Zed Books, 1993.

Tuck, Richard. *Natural Rights Theories: Their Origin and Development*. Cambridge: Cambridge University Press, 1979.

Walzer, Michael. *Just and Unjust Wars*. New York: Basic Books, 1977.

Welch, Claude E., Jr., and Virginia A. Leary, eds. *Asian Perspectives on Human Rights*. Boulder: Westview Press, 1990.

INDEX